Logic® Pro 7 POWER!

By Orren Merton

THOMSON
COURSE TECHNOLOGY™
Professional ■ Trade ■ Reference

LOGIC® PRO 7
POWER!

SVP, Thomson Course Technology PTR: Andy Shafran
Publisher: Stacy L. Hiquet
Senior Marketing Manager: Sarah O'Donnell
Marketing Manager: Heather Hurley
Manager of Editorial Services: Heather Talbot
Senior Acquisitions Editor: Todd Jensen
Senior Editor: Mark Garvey
Associate Marketing Manager: Kristin Eisenzopf
Marketing Coordinator: Jordan Casey
Project Editor: Kim V. Benbow
Technical Reviewer: Len Sasso
PTR Editorial Services Coordinator: Elizabeth Furbish
Copy Editor: Libby Larson
Interior Layout Tech: Marian Hartsough
Cover Designer: Mike Tanamachi
CD-ROM Producer: Steve Albanese
CD-ROM Author: Lars von Sneidern
Indexer: Katherine Stimson
Proofreaders: Tonya Cupp and Gene Redding

ISBN: 1-59200-541-1
Library of Congress Catalog Card Number: 2004114489
Printed in the United States of America

05 06 07 08 BH 10 9 8 7 6 5 4 3 2 1

THOMSON
COURSE TECHNOLOGY
Professional ■ Trade ■ Reference

Thomson Course Technology PTR,
a division of
Thomson Course Technology
25 Thomson Place
Boston, MA 02210

http://www.courseptr.com

Dedication

This book is dedicated to everyone who uses Logic to express their creativity; to my mom and dad, to Michelle, to Shadow and Luna, and to my grandfather, who I know would be joyful beyond words if he could have seen this book.

Acknowledgments

I had thought that *Logic Pro 7 Power!* would be a walk in the park after writing *Logic 6 Power!* but I could not have been more wrong! Thank God I have been blessed to have the assistance, input, and support of fantastic people. Certainly, this book stands as a testament to the unwavering support of my Michelle and my mother, and in the recent past, my late father, grandfather, and grandmother.

I would also like to thank Dr. Gerhard Lengeling, Jan-Hennerk Helms, Thorsten Adam, Sascha Kujawa, Manfred Maraun, and everyone at Emagic GmbH, both for their part in creating and developing software that assists so many of us to realize our musical creativity, and for their part in including me in the processes! Further, I would like to thank the entire Emagic Beta-test Community, present and past, for their insight and assistance on my own journey into this program.

Some of those testers and Logic User Group power users offered more than moral support—they contributed their thoughts, tips, and time to help make this book everything it could be. I am exceedingly grateful for the friendship and efforts of Graham Hunter, Don Gunn, Jeremy Martin, Jay Asher, and perhaps most of all to Len Sasso, a friend and longtime contributor to the Emagic and Logic communities, and excellent writer of many books on Logic and other subjects. Len served not only as a sounding board for me, but as the technical editor for this book as well. Thanks, Len!

Finally, the Muska & Lipman team has been exceptional, supporting me in every way I could have hoped all the way through this process. I would especially like to tip my hat to Todd Jensen, Mark Garvey, Jenny Davidson, and Kim Benbow, who figuratively held my hand through this entire process.

About the Author

Orren Merton, author of *Logic 6 Power!* (Muska & Lipman, 2003) and *GarageBand Ignite!* (Muska & Lipman, 2004) has been a computer musician since his days at UC Berkeley in 1988. He has been consulting and writing in the professional audio field for over six years. He has done technical writing for Emagic Soft- und Hardware GmbH and writes for numerous American and British professional audio magazines such as *Electronic Musician, Computer Music,* and *MIX*. He has a master's degree in English from California State University, Long Beach. He also helps moderate the Logic User Group, an online community of over 15,000 Logic users, and he beta tests for a number of audio software companies. Orren lives in Costa Mesa, California, and he can be reached at orren@mertonfolio.com.

TABLE OF Contents

Introduction

If you've gotten this far into the book, you've already figured out that this book deals with Emagic's Logic Pro 7 digital audio sequencer. There have been a number of other books written about Logic in the past, but this is one of the first about Logic Pro 7. Moreover, this book takes a different angle than most of the others. In general, the books written about Logic tend to be geared toward beginners and consist of a few hundred pages of incredibly basic information. If not, they are geared toward specific features of Logic and not the whole application. This book takes on a fairly ambitious task—to be a complete introduction and reference for Logic in less than one-third the size of the Logic Pro 7 manual! It's a goal that no other Logic book really attempts, and while I make no claims of objectivity, I think this book achieves it nicely. I don't attempt to write everything about everything, but I make sure I cover those things that you are likely to run into while using Logic to make music and to explain them simply, thoroughly, and completely. Moreover, I attempt to go into the philosophy behind why Logic works the way it works, so hopefully you will not simply learn the mechanics of how to do something, but you'll really understand what you are doing. So when you want to explore on your own, you'll be fully prepared—and successful!

This book, while authored completely by me, doesn't contain only my efforts—some other great Logic beta testers and users contributed ideas and great tips and tricks. In addition to writing *Logic Pro 7 Power!* I have been writing and teaching for years; and I've been using Logic and been involved with Emagic for quite a while also. I have worked with Emagic as a technical writer for the documentation of Logic 6, and a portion of the Logic manual itself bears my imprint. Perhaps most importantly, as a musician, I use Logic daily to compose and record. I'm not some pro audio mercenary with a resumé and a computer. I'm in the trenches, just like you, using the software to help me create. And that, in the end, is my goal with this book. Logic helps me to create, and hopefully this book will help you learn how to use Logic to help you create and continue to serve as a reference as you continue to create.

Who This Book Is For

Well, the glib answer is, "Anyone who owns Logic!" To give you a more complete answer, I'm sure some of you with older versions of Logic, Windows versions of Logic, different levels of Logic (Logic, Logic Silver, Logic Audio, Logic Gold, or Logic Platinum), and so on, are wondering how much use you can get out of a book focused on the Macintosh OS X–only Logic Pro 7. This is covered in more detail in Chapter 1, but let me quickly say this. Logic Pro 7 is one of the most comprehensive updates Logic has seen in a very long time. It not only looks updated from versions past, but it offers many new and updated features. Nonetheless, the fundamentals of how Logic works have not really changed since the earliest days of Notator Logic for the Atari. Features get added and the look changes a bit, so the older your version, the fewer features your Logic version may have compared to this one. But the basic operating procedures and features in your Logic version should be covered here in a way that will help you; so if you're looking for help with Logic, this book will help you.

As for what level of user this book is aimed at, really, I took pains to include everyone. The book opens with very basic information aimed at novices and beginners, then the bulk of this book continues with more intermediate reference information and is sprinkled with expert tips and tricks throughout. The final chapters discuss more esoteric, "expert" functions, but hopefully in a way that is accessible to intermediate users. If you are a beginner, don't feel that only the beginning will be appropriate for you; the chapters are written to bring you up to speed in no time! Intermediate and advanced users, don't feel the beginning of the book is wasted on you, although you're welcome to skip it. It's good stuff, with lots of historical and architectural information you may not be familiar with, even if you're already fast and efficient with Logic and are just looking for a good reference book. My goals were to start simple, get more advanced, and hopefully leave nobody behind. This book really does try to include something for everyone.

How This Book Is Organized

Every book on computer software starts with a number of assumptions, and organizes the chapters accordingly. For this book, I am starting from the assumption that the reader has a very basic knowledge of sequencing and recording, but little else. The beginning chapters are introductions—introductions to digital audio, MIDI, sequencing, and Logic. From about Chapter 5 onward, the book becomes far less basic. At that point, as you start getting into the meat of Logic Pro 7, the thought is that you have a working knowledge of the basics and general layout discussed in the previous four chapters, that you have set up your Autoload (don't worry, you'll know what that is soon!), and that you want to start composing, recording, and editing music. The general flow of the chapters follows a Logic project: After setting up Logic, you'll need to learn about Transport and Arrange, then you'll want to record and edit audio and MIDI, mixdown your song, and finally save your song and organize your files. The final chapters are about more advanced, esoteric features of Logic that, as you create more complex compositions and build a more involved project studio, will become more important.

As for each chapter, there is no single model that I adhere to regarding the subdivisions of sections. It is the content that determines the organization of each individual chapter. One thing I do cover, however, is that every time a new Logic window is introduced, I am sure to cover each local menu in that window. In fact, you'll find Appendix C offers a cross-reference index of every single local menu in every single Logic window because I feel that covering all these commands is vital for making this book a complete reference. No other book available for Logic does this, by the way—this is the only game in town as far as owning a complete local menu reference!

1 Introducing Logic Pro 7

Logic has a reputation for being complex. It isn't, really, but it's not the sort of application that you can simply launch and immediately feel comfortable using without understanding its internal, well, logic! In this chapter, you'll learn what Logic is, where it's from, and its basic working premises.

What Is Logic Pro?

If you hear people discussing Logic, you're likely to hear words like "professional," "powerful," "flexible," and "steep learning curve" thrown around. So what is Logic Pro really?

Put simply, Logic Pro is the most flexible, powerful, professional, and elegant application for producing music on a computer. Although you might consider that a rather contentious statement, after reading through this book you will probably at least concede that this claim is not outrageous. A number of other powerful, professional, and worthy music production programs are on the market today. I don't mean to downplay their functionality. Some applications have a feature or two that Logic lacks, or they implement one of the features that Logic also includes in a way that some prefer. Logic does, however, offer the best combination of features, flexibility, and power of all available music production applications. Logic offers you

- **MIDI recording**. Record and play back MIDI information.
- **MIDI editing**. Edit MIDI information in one of several MIDI editors.
- **MIDI notation editing**. Edit and print out professional scores and music charts.
- **Environment**. Build an entire virtual studio and processing environment inside Logic.

- **Global Tracks**. Easily set up and edit song marker, tempo, key, chord, and video frame information.
- **Audio Instruments.** Use software synthesizers from within Logic.
- **Audio Recording**. Record audio directly into Logic.
- **Audio Editing**. Edit audio files using Logic's many editing tools.
- **Arranging**. View all your song elements as graphic regions and arrange them visually.
- **Mixing**. Mix your audio tracks and your MIDI tracks within the same song using Logic's completely customizable mixer.
- **Processing**. Use Logic's professional offline and realtime processors and functions.
- **Control Surface Support**. Configure any hardware MIDI controller to be a hardware controller of any Logic function.
- **Nodes**. Network as many Macintosh computers as you want for unlimited processing power for Logic's effects and instruments.
- **Project Manager**. Manage all the multimedia files on your hard disks with Logic's powerful new database.

For these features and more, Logic earned its well-deserved reputation as the most professional music production application, and it continues to break new ground. But what about that talk of Logic's "steep learning curve"? As with most applications that are as deep as this one, it helps to know the application's internal workings in order to more readily understand how to use it. To give you a solid grounding in the fundamental concepts of Logic, I'll start at the very beginning with where Logic came from, and see how the functionality of those previous applications relates to the current version of Logic.

A Brief History of Logic

Once upon a time, in the mid-1980s, during what now would be considered the "prehistoric" era of computer music, a small German software company named C-LAB created a Commodore 64 program called Supertrack. Supertrack, like all early sequencers, was designed to allow users to store, edit, and play back the notes and performance information generated on MIDI synthesizers (see "A Brief Overview of MIDI" below for an explanation of MIDI). By 1987, this basic program evolved into Creator, and finally into Notator. Notator, which ran on the Atari ST, added a musical notation (or musical score) editor to Creator and became an instant power player in the burgeoning field of computer-based MIDI sequencers. Notator offered a clean, simple interface for four powerful MIDI editors: a realtime musical notation editor, an event editor for displaying MIDI information in a scrolling list, a matrix editor for displaying notes graphically, and a hypereditor for editing non-note MIDI data (such as pitch bend). With these editors, you could play a song on your synthesizer or program it on your computer from scratch, then rearrange, edit, and manipulate your data as sheet music in the notation editor, in a text list, a graphic "piano roll," or a bar graph–style display. As you can see in Figure 1.1, which shows an edit screen from the final version of Notator for the Atari, the program used the very same concepts and offered many of the same tools for manipulating MIDI information that are still used today. Notator's extensive editing options gave musicians powerful tools for creating and arranging music in an easy-to-use package. Notator won rave reviews from power users and hobbyists alike, and garnered a huge following among early MIDI musicians, and even 10 years after its final version, Notator still has a very lively following. In fact, there are Web sites and mailing lists on the Internet for people who still use Notator today.

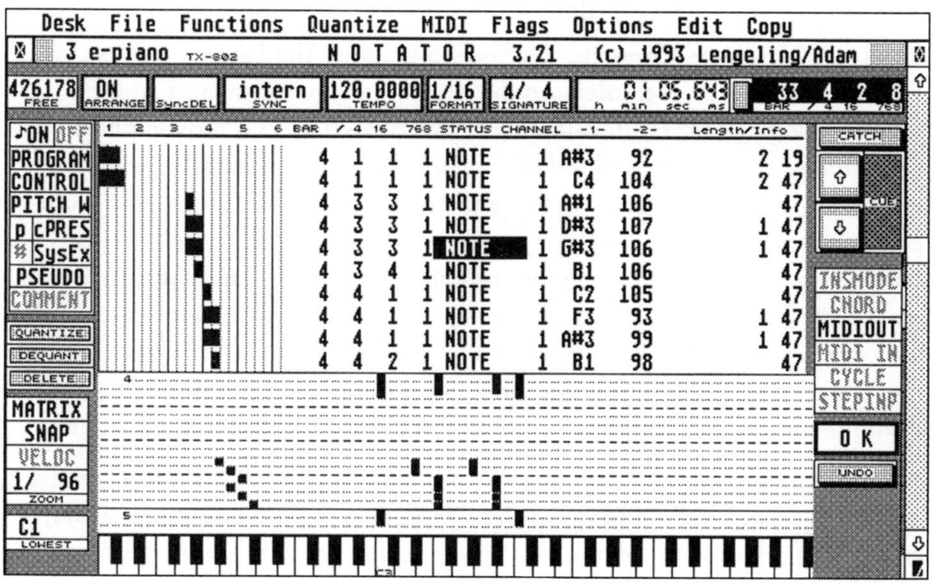

Figure 1.1

This screenshot from Notator Version 3.2.1 shows the matrix and event editors. Users of Notator would feel right at home with the evolved matrix and event editors of Logic, which are fundamentally the same a decade later. (Screen image used by permission from the Notator Users Group at http://www.notator.org.)

By 1993, the principals who developed Notator left to form their own company, Emagic, and built upon their previous efforts by adding a graphical arrangement page and object-oriented editing, among other innovations; this product was named Notator Logic, and later simply Logic. Logic was soon ported to run on the Macintosh computer, which was quickly overtaking the Atari as the music computer of choice for professionals. This early version of Logic introduced the basic architecture and concepts that would form the basis for future iterations of Logic.

By the late 1990s, Logic's developers had ported Logic to run on Windows computers as well as the Macintosh, quietly discontinued the Atari version, and added to the program the ability to record and edit audio in addition to MIDI. To signify this, the developers modified the name of the application to Logic Audio. By the end of the 1990s, there were three versions of the application, each with an expanded feature set. Logic Audio Platinum had the most professional recording options, offering the most hardware options including unsurpassed support for Digidesign's industry standard hardware, ProTools TDM. Logic Audio Platinum became nearly ubiquitous in the software lists of professional studios worldwide. Logic Audio Gold and Logic Audio Silver offered consumers more affordable versions of Logic with the same depth and power but fewer features. In addition, Emagic developed a separate application, MicroLogic, which was a basic and inexpensive derivative of Logic that offered beginners a way to get their feet wet in music production.

In July 2002, Apple Computer purchased Emagic. The Logic 6 release in February 2003 focused solely on the Macintosh, representing Emagic's return to single-platform development after a decade as a cross-platform application. The names of the three versions of Logic changed again, this time to Logic Platinum, Logic Gold, and Logic Audio. In 2004, Apple Computer streamlined Emagic's Logic line to only Logic Pro and Logic Express, and in late 2004, Apple Computer released Logic Pro 7 and Express 7, the most profound update to Logic in nearly a decade. Logic continues to lead the way in professional music production on the Macintosh platform, garnering awards and rave reviews in addition to an honored place in more professional recording studios in the world than any other sequencer package.

As you can see, Emagic and Logic have a long and illustrious history in the computer music field. To this day, the hypereditor and the notation, event, and matrix editors of even the most recent Logic Pro 7 release would be instantly recognizable to an early Notator user, which speaks volumes about Emagic's commitment to supporting its user community.

Will This Book Help You with Your Version of Logic?

The short answer is, Yes.

The long answer is that this book will offer you something no matter which version of Logic you are using. Exactly how much of the material is applicable depends on the specific platform and version number you are using. This book covers the features of the most current, feature-rich version of Logic, the Mac OS X-only Logic Pro 7. This means that this book will cover features that are not found in any other version of Logic on any other platform. Depending on how early your version of Logic, the number of extra features explained in this book might be considerable—and the difference in appearance will be considerable as well.

Clearly, if you just purchased Logic 7, this book applies to your version. If you currently do not own Logic at all and want to learn about it before purchasing it, this book will give you the ins and outs of the most current version of Logic. However, current users of different versions of Logic will find this book eminently useful as well.

The concepts and basic MIDI editing functionality in Logic haven't changed since the program's creation. In other words, users who have held on to Notator Logic 1.5 on their Atari ST could read this book and recognize many of the editors, the nomenclature, the architecture, and so on, even though the developers have seriously updated the look and added many features in the last decade. For users of more recent versions, the differences become even less pronounced. Through Logic 5.5, the features, look and feel, and operation of Logic were nearly identical whether it was running under Windows XP, Mac OS 9, or Mac OS X. Logic 7 is really the first version in nearly half a decade with a significantly redesigned application, but most operations themselves have not been fundamentally changed. As you can see by comparing Figure 1.2a and Figure 1.2b, 2001's Logic Pro 5.5 running under Windows XP and 2004's Logic Pro 7 look different, yet clearly maintain a profound similarity.

In other words, users of previous versions of Logic looking for assistance with basic concepts and operation procedures will find it here. This book will of course address the newer features in Logic Pro 7 but users of different versions can easily skip those discussions. In fact, users with earlier or less feature-rich versions of Logic can consider the coverage of the latest features a sneak peak at what the new version has to offer when making the decision about whether to upgrade!

Figure 1.2a

Figure 1.2a shows Logic Pro 7, the most recent version of Logic, running on Mac OS X.

Figure 1.2b

Figure 1.2b shows Logic Pro 5.5, the final version of Logic developed for Windows XP in 2001. As you can see, while Logic 7 definitely has the modern look and feel of Apple Computer's Pro application suite, the two versions of Logic still resemble each other.

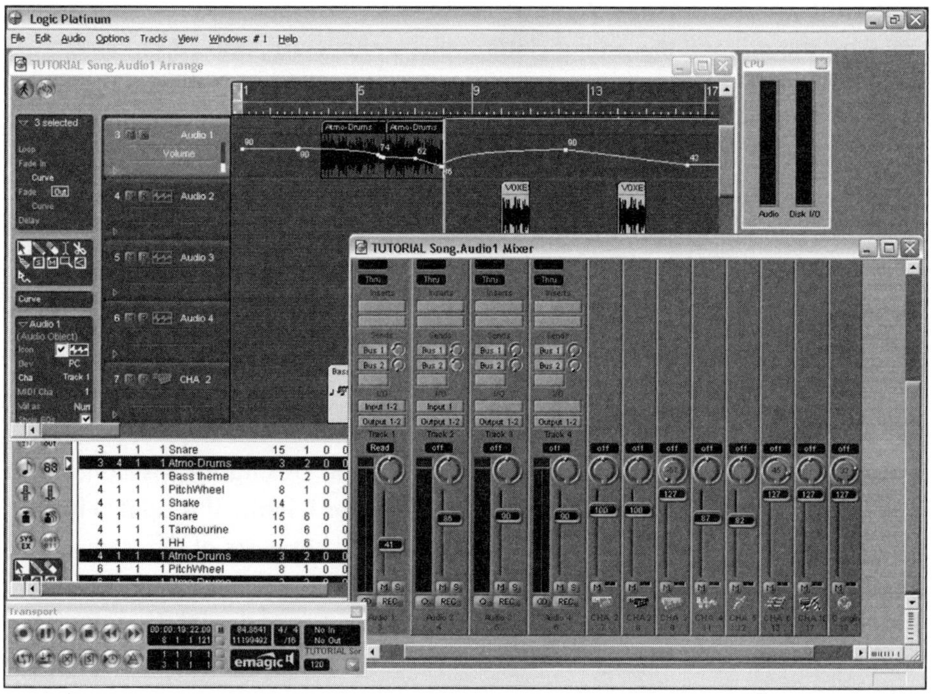

A Brief Overview of MIDI

MIDI (Musical Instrument Digital Interface) was formally introduced in August 1983. The MIDI 1.0 protocol was absolutely revolutionary—it allowed MIDI instruments (such as synthesizers, drum machines, and sequencers) to communicate with, control, and be controlled by other MIDI instruments and MIDI controllers. The development of MIDI enabled the rise of electronic music and computer sequencers. MIDI makes possible much of what we use computers for in music production. If you are interested in a complete technical discussion of every aspect of the MIDI protocol, you should read *MIDI Power!* by Roland Guerin (Muska & Lipman; 2002), a very thorough and readable exploration of MIDI in depth. Using Logic doesn't require that sort of deep understanding of MIDI, but a basic knowledge of what MIDI is and how it works is invaluable.

The MIDI protocol specified that every MIDI-compliant device that can both send and receive MIDI information must have a MIDI IN port to accept MIDI data, a MIDI OUT port to transmit MIDI data, and optionally a MIDI THRU port for transferring data between other MIDI devices. When you connect the MIDI OUT port of one device to the MIDI IN port of another device, the first device enables you to press a key, turn a dial, engage a control message, and so on, and the second device will receive the data.

In addition to providing hardware specifications that allow devices to send and receive MIDI, the MIDI protocol also defined how to pass data from one device to another. MIDI is a *serial protocol,* meaning that MIDI information is sent one *event* (or MIDI message) at a time. That may sound inefficient, but the speed of MIDI transfer is 31,250 bps (bits per second, where *bit* stands for *b*inary dig*it*), and since each MIDI message uses 10 bits (eight for the information, two for error correction), the MIDI protocol can send 3,906 bytes of data every second (31,250 divided by 8 bits to convert bits to bytes). Since one MIDI note can take up to six bytes, the protocol enables a device to play approximately 500 MIDI notes per second. This may seem like a lot of notes, but as soon as you add a couple 5-note chords in a single 10-millisecond span of time, with multiple, MIDI control messages, you might very well start seeing some compromised timing. That's why for the most demanding MIDI productions, there are MIDI Time Stamping features on many MIDI interfaces to improve MIDI timing even further.

Even if you have no external MIDI hardware, MIDI is still the protocol that Logic uses for internal playback and automation of virtual instruments, so it's still useful to understand some basics about MIDI.

What MIDI Really Transmits

The most important thing to understand is that MIDI doesn't transmit any sound at all. It only transmits data. In other words, when you record digital audio, you're recording an actual file of digital information that will play back as sound. When you record MIDI data, you'll then need some sort of device—a synthesizer, drum machine, sampler, or software synthesizer—to actually hear that MIDI information. MIDI data can transmit the following:

- Performance events, such as when you play and release notes.
- The pressure with which you press the keys as you play (known as *aftertouch*).
- Information from MIDI controller wheels, knobs, pedal controls, ribbon controllers, pitchbend controllers, and so on, that send parameters that affect performance.
- Channel settings. Each MIDI cable can support up to 16 channels, so each device can operate as 16 devices in one. Those devices that can support multiple MIDI channels are called *multitimbral* devices.
- Synchronization information, so that all time-sensitive instruments or functions on various devices can all operate from the same master clock and play in sync with each other.
- Program changes and sound bank selections.
- MIDI Time Code (MTC), which allows MIDI devices to lock to devices that use SMPTE (Society of Motion Picture and Television Engineers) format time code by translating SMPTE into something that the MIDI device can understand.
- System Exclusive messages, which are unique messages that can alter parameters and control of one specific MIDI device. Most MIDI synthesizers and some multitrack recorders offer unique System Exclusive commands.

MIDI Connections and Signal Flow

As described previously, connecting MIDI devices couldn't be simpler. The most basic type of MIDI connection, in which the MIDI OUT jack of one MIDI device is connected to the MIDI IN jack of another MIDI device, allows the first unit to send MIDI to the second unit, as shown here:

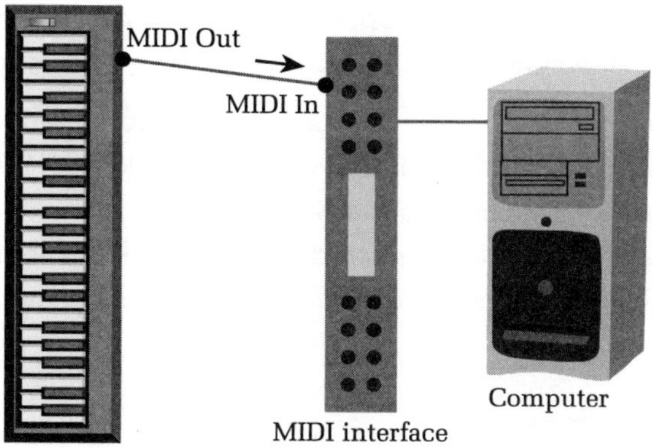

Note that this type of connection does not allow for two-way communication, only one-way communication. This type of a connection is most common when connecting a MIDI controller, which is a MIDI device that does not itself produce sounds (and doesn't *receive* MIDI), but can send MIDI to other devices, such as to a computer MIDI interface or another MIDI device.

An example of another simple but more dynamic MIDI connection is to connect both the MIDI IN and the MIDI OUT of one device to the MIDI OUT and MIDI IN of another device, as shown in the following illustration:

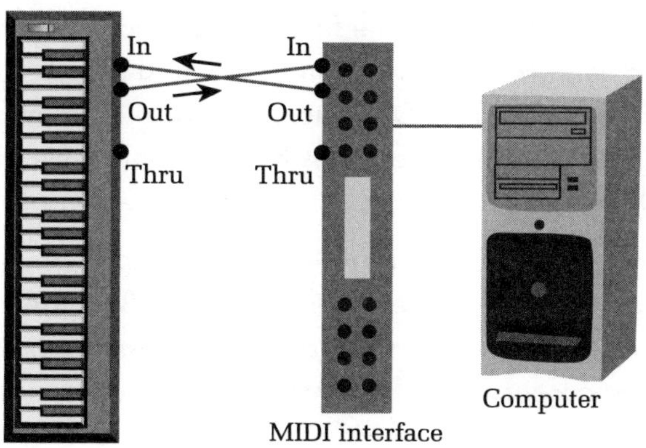

This enables two-way communication between MIDI devices, so each is capable of both sending and receiving data from the other. This is the most common form of routing between two devices capable of sending and receiving MIDI information, such as two synthesizers, or a computer and a synthesizer. When making connections like this, be sure both units have MIDI THRU and/or Local control turned off or else you might end up with a MIDI feedback loop. In a MIDI feedback loop, one unit sends a command to the other, which then sends the command back to the first unit, and on and on endlessly.

A final example of a basic MIDI connection illustrates how three MIDI devices might be connected together via a MIDI THRU port. The MIDI OUT of the first device is connected to the MIDI IN of the second device, the MIDI OUT of the second device is connected to the MIDI IN of the first device, and the MIDI THRU of the second device is connected to the MIDI IN of the third device:

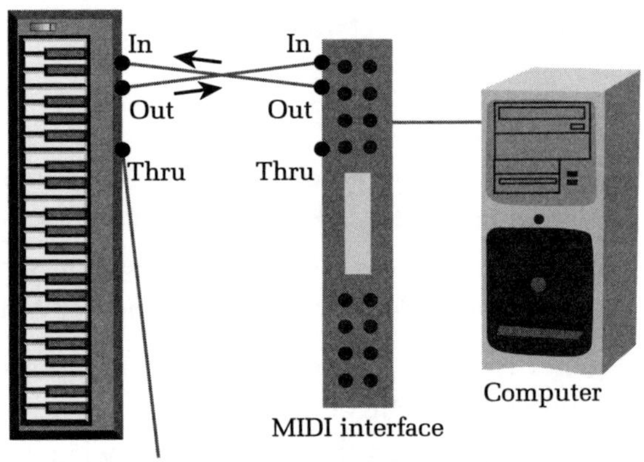

In the preceding diagram, complete two-way communication between the first two devices is possible, and the first device (and often the second device) can also send MIDI information to the third device. Such connections are often used when a third MIDI device, such as a drum machine, is not being used to issue any MIDI messages but only to receive them from the rest of the MIDI setup.

At this point, you should have a good understanding of what MIDI is and the importance of getting MIDI information into Logic. Because Logic can both send and receive MIDI, you will want a *MIDI interface*—Universal Serial Bus (USB) device that accepts MIDI from MIDI devices and sends it into Logic—

that has as many MIDI IN and MIDI OUT ports as you have MIDI devices. This will be discussed later in this chapter in the section "A Brief Primer on Hardware."

A Brief Overview of Digital Audio

These days, recording digital audio is perhaps the most popular use of sequencers such as Logic Audio. In fact, the popular term used to describe a computer used as the hub of a music production system is a Digital Audio Workstation (DAW). So what is digital audio? How does it differ from analog audio? Why is it important?

While a complete technical reference on the details of digital audio would result in a book almost as large as this one, it is important to know at least enough about the fundamentals of digital audio to be able to make a good recording. The following subsections should give you just enough of a background to get the most out of your audio recordings.

The Differences Between Analog and Digital Sound

We hear sound when our eardrums vibrate. Please read that carefully, and realize that I did not say that we hear sound whenever *some object* vibrates. Many objects vibrate outside our ability to hear them (think of dog whistles or ultralow subfrequencies). Our ears are theoretically capable of registering vibrations (also called *cycles*) that are oscillating between 20 and 20,000 times a second. This is called the *frequency*—pretty logical when you think about it, since the term refers to the frequency of vibrations per second. Theoretically, then, humans can hear frequencies from 20Hz to 20kHz. (The measurement Hertz, or Hz, is named after Henry Hertz, who in 1888 developed the theory of the relationship between frequency and cycles.) In practice, hardly any adult's hearing reaches that theoretical maximum, because people lose the ability to hear certain frequencies (high-pitched ones in particular) as they age, are subjected to loud noises, and so on.

If the frequency of vibration is slow (say 60 vibrations per second, or 60Hz), we perceive a low note. If the frequency of the vibration is fast (say 6,000 vibrations per second, or 6kHz), we would perceive a high note. If the vibrations are gentle, barely moving our eardrums, we perceive the sound as soft. The loudness and softness of the sound is called the *amplitude*, because the term refers to the volume, or amplification, of the sound. Thus we can graph sound like this:

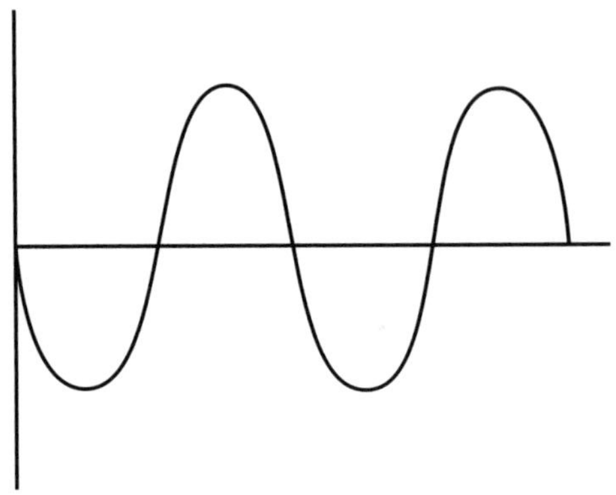

In this graph, the frequency is the distance between the oscillations of the waveform, and the amplitude is the height of the waveform. Most sounds we hear in the real world are complex ones that have more than a single frequency in them, as in the following graph:

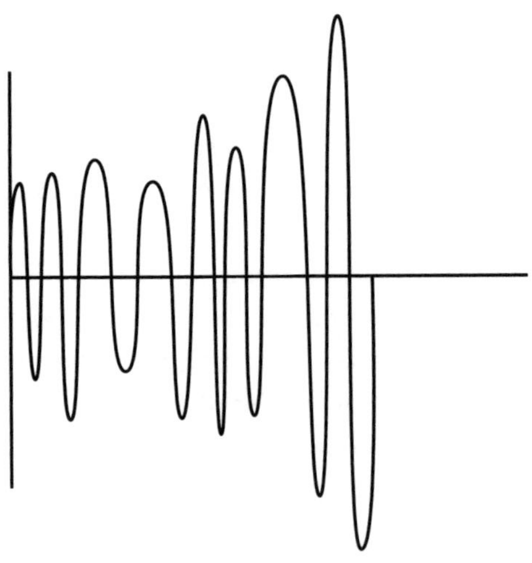

This example has more than a single tone in it, and not every frequency is being heard at the same volume (amplitude).

Now that you understand a little about sound waves, let's tie it in to recording. One way to record sound is to make an exact replica of the original waveform on some other media. For example, you might carve an image of the waveform onto a vinyl surface, or imprint the waveform on magnetic tape. In these cases, you have recorded an actual copy of the original sound wave. Now you just need a machine to amplify the sound so it's loud enough to listen to (or to rattle the windows, if that's your style). Because this type of recording results in a continuous waveform, it's called analog recording. *Analog* refers to any signal represented by a continuous, unbroken waveform.

Because a computer works using mathematical codes instead of actual pictures of objects, to use a computer for recording audio, we need to translate the actual analog signal into math. Luckily, sound can also be represented *digitally*—meaning by use of digits, or numbers. Basically, complex mathematical analysis has proven if we sample a waveform twice in each cycle, or *period,* and record its variation in sound, we can reproduce the waveform. Now, each period is a full cycle, or vibration. This means that if we wanted to reproduce a 60Hz sound, which is 60 cycles, we'd need to take at least 120 samples. From this, you can see that if you want to be sure to capture the full range of human hearing—20kHz, or 20,000 cycles—you have to take at least 40,000 samples.

What's Meant by Sampling Frequency and Bit Depth

From the preceding, we understand that we have to represent the sound wave as numbers to store it in the computer, and that by storing two samples per cycle we can represent that cycle. You've probably noticed that every recording interface and program that handles digital audio refers to sample rate and bit depth. Let me explain what they mean, and how they affect your recording.

As explained previously, it takes two samples per cycle to represent each cycle accurately. It follows that the total number of samples taken of a waveform determines the maximum frequency that will be recorded. This is called the *sampling frequency* or *sampling rate*. For example, the sampling rate of the compact disc is fixed at 44.1kHz, or 44,100 samples; it's a few thousand samples more than the minimum needed to represent the highest-frequency sound wave that humans can hear.

You've probably noticed that many audio interfaces today boast sampling rates of 96kHz or even 192kHz (kHz is short for kilohertz, or 1,000Hz). That means that these devices can represent sounds up to 48kHz and 96kHz. The obvious question is, why bother? We can only hear up to a theoretical 20kHz anyway, right? Of course, it's not quite that simple. While we may not be able to distinguish sounds accurately above a certain frequency, every sound also contains additional overtones, harmonics, spatial cues, and so on. These features enrich the sound to our ears and help us place it in space and so on. When our sampling rate is too low to represent such features, they are simply discarded and lost forever. We may not consciously notice these "ultrasonic" frequencies when we listen to recordings, but many audiophiles and sound engineers believe that they contribute to a far more realistic listening experience.

That explains sampling rates, but what about bit depth? Remember, the sound wave has two components: the frequency and the amplitude. The mathematical representation of the amplitude at a particular instant in a particular cycle is stored in *bits*. A computer cannot interpolate information in between the amplitudes you have stored—it only knows what the amplitude at a given instant in the cycle is if the amplitude is stored in a bit. The more bits used to store the amplitude per cycle, the more accurate the representation.

Finally, here is a loose analogy, but a good one, to give you a basic understanding of analog versus digital audio, sampling rate, and bit depth. If you make an analog recording, you are left with an actual copy of the audio waveform imprinted onto your media. If you make a digital recording, you are instead taking "snapshots" of the waveform and then attempting to re-create the waveform from those snapshots. Your sampling rate would be the number of cameras you have set up to take snapshots every second, and your bit depth would represent the number of times each second those cameras are taking snapshots. As you can see, the higher the sampling rate and bit depth, the closer your snapshots will get to the actual sound wave, as follows:

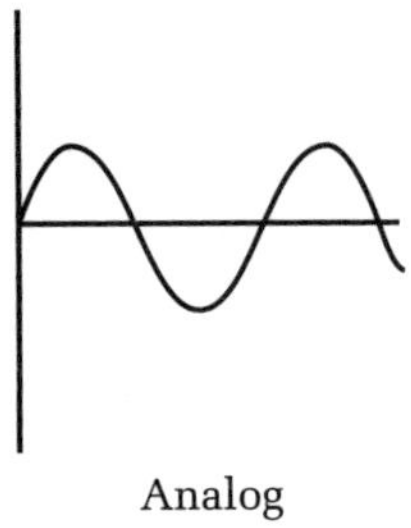
Analog

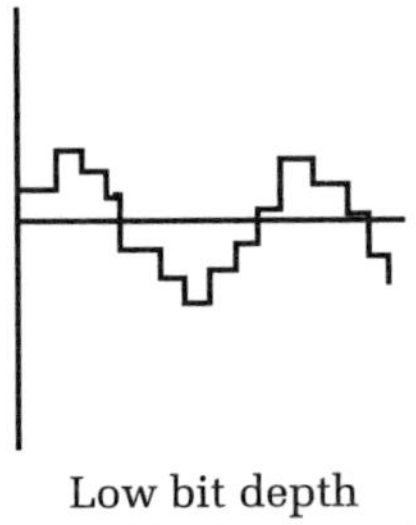
Low bit depth sampling frequency

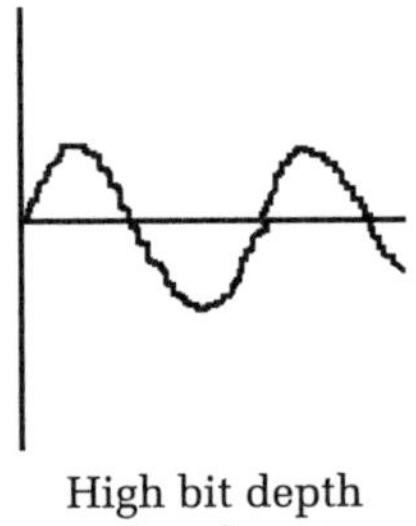
High bit depth sampling frequency

You should also keep in mind that as your bit depths and sampling rates increase, so do the processor, memory, and hard drive requirements. The larger the bit depth and sample rate, the more CPU is required to process it, the more memory the audio requires during processing, and the more space on your hard disk the audio will require.

It is beyond the scope of this book to give comprehensive position papers on the merits of analog versus digital audio, but the important things to remember are that any audio waveform that gets into your computer will be digital audio, and that you need to be aware of sampling frequency and bit depth to get the most out of your hardware, and out of Logic.

Audio and MIDI in Logic Pro

It's time to relate all of this to what it means for Logic. In its simplest description, Logic can be viewed as a software equivalent of a MIDI and digital audio tape recorder. In other words, if you connect your MIDI devices to your computer, connect your audio devices to your computer, and then activate Record in Logic, you will record your audio and MIDI into Logic. If you then activate Play, you will hear the MIDI and audio you've just recorded. So far, this should be familiar to pretty much anyone who has ever used a tape recorder or VCR.

For Logic to be able to record MIDI and digital audio information, you need a way to capture that information into the computer, and then a way to transfer that information out of the computer when you activate playback. In the case of audio, you capture and transfer this information through your *audio interface*. In the case of MIDI, you handle all of this with your *MIDI interface*. Both of these devices will be explained in more detail in the section "A Brief Primer on Hardware," later in this chapter; for now, what is important to know is that if you have an audio interface and a MIDI interface attached to Logic, you can then use Logic as described previously for software MIDI and audio recording and playback.

Unlike a tape recorder, which requires little more setting up other than putting in a cassette tape, Logic is famous (and perhaps infamous) for the depth and breadth of setup and configuration options it offers. To deliver these setup options, Logic organizes its components into virtual structures called *objects*. This is the first and perhaps most fundamental concept of how Logic works that you'll need to understand.

Objects in Logic Pro

As described previously, Logic organizes its basic structures into objects. When you hear Logic referred to as an object-oriented program, it basically means that the program is designed so that you will interact with the program by manipulating onscreen graphical objects.

That sounds pretty broad, doesn't it? It is, which is unfortunately why it can be a source of confusion if you are not yet familiar with Logic's terminology. In one sense, anything can be an object—a region (graphical representation) of audio in the Arrange screen could be considered an object, a MIDI instrument in the Environment could be considered an object, and a fader in the Track Mixer could be considered an object. Logic clears up some of this confusion by referring to structures that are represented as music studio building blocks in the Environment as objects, as shown in Figure 1.3, and assigning different terms to the other onscreen graphic elements of Logic.

In other words, while most graphic items in Logic may be referred to as objects in the general context of the program, only Environment building blocks are actually referred to as objects in Logic. This seems confusing, but

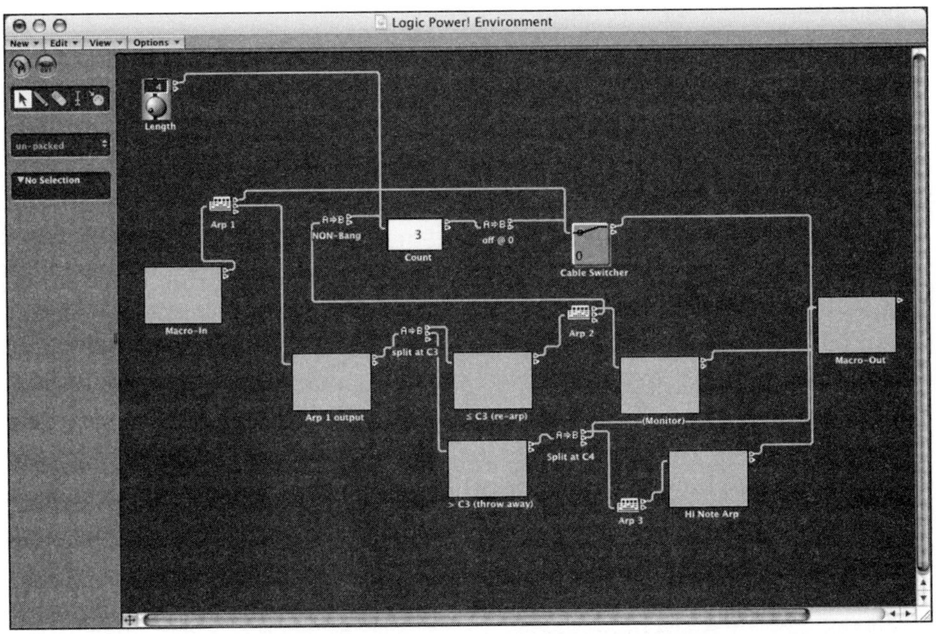

Figure 1.3

This is the Environment window of Logic, with a number of objects showing. The Environment is a virtual representation of your studio, and the objects are the devices within it. Some of the visible objects represent physical inputs and instruments, while others represent "virtual devices" such as arpeggiator devices and delay devices.

it's similar to the way people refer to "doing the dishes" when they describe washing all the dirty bowls, glasses, silverware, and plates in the sink. While all of those items may be referred to as dishes in the context of washing all the eating utensils, only serving vessels are actually named dishes.

So what is this Environment that I have mentioned a few times now? It's perhaps the most flexible, powerful, and (for some) daunting aspect of Logic. For now, think of the Environment as a graphical window that allows you to set up a "virtual studio" inside Logic, including all your studio objects and hardware routings. In other words, unlike less powerful applications that simply give you a dialog box in which to select your instruments, a dialog box in which to specify where you want to route those instruments, and so on, Logic offers you a library of graphical, on-screen objects representing all the devices you can choose from, and you can then "cable" them together (using virtual representations of cables) in unique and creative ways. Objects can be cabled together, then clicked and dragged all over the window the same way you can drag icons around your computer's desktop. (This functionality is available only in Logic, by the way!) As you can already imagine, the Environment is very deep, and you'll explore it in depth in Chapter 14, "The Environment." For now, this short introduction to the Environment should suffice to understand the "MIDI Objects" and "Audio Objects" sections that follow.

MIDI Objects

Most of the available objects to choose from in the Environment are *MIDI Objects*. MIDI Objects are virtual devices that represent external MIDI devices—such as an *instrument* object, which is an object that represents one channel of an external MIDI instrument, or a *Multi-Instrument* Object, which is an object that represents the full 16 channels of a multitimbral external MIDI instrument. MIDI Objects can also represent MIDI processes that can affect or transform the MIDI notes, values, or messages sent by MIDI devices. The objects appear as iconlike images in the Environment window, with a connector that looks like a small instrument jack on the top-right of the icon. You can drag a "virtual cable" from those jacks to cable objects together in order to create powerful processing and routing configurations—but you'll learn more about that when you are further along in using Logic. Figure 1.4 shows a number of MIDI Objects.

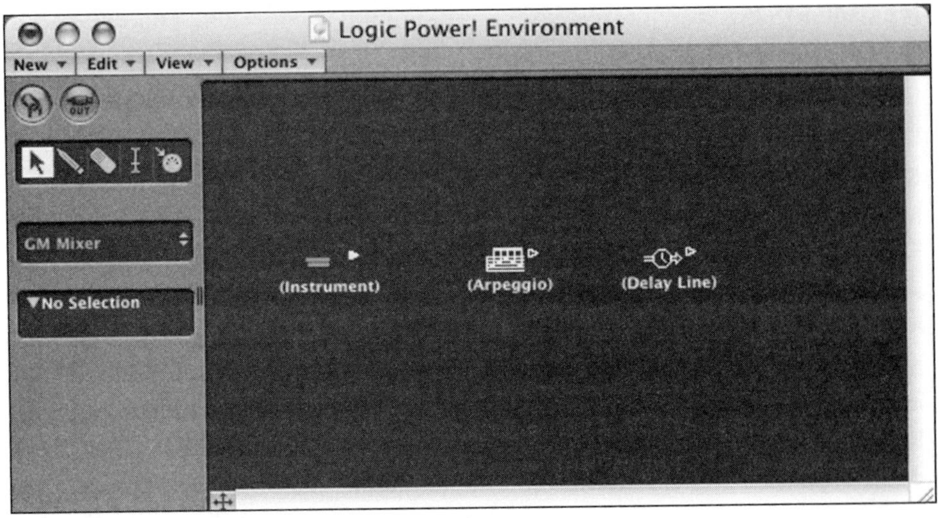

Figure 1.4

Here are some examples of MIDI Objects—a MIDI Instrument Object, an Arpeggiator Object, and a MIDI Delay Object. There are far more complex objects than these, but you'll learn about those as you get deeper into Logic.

An important feature of MIDI Objects is their parameter box, in which you can configure important settings, such as the hardware port in which the instrument is located, the internal program that it should use, its note range, and so on. Or if you are looking at the parameter box of a virtual processing device, such as the delay or arpeggiator, this is where you would determine how you want it to affect the notes from the MIDI instrument. Figure 1.5 shows the parameter box of the selected MIDI Object.

You should now have a solid idea of what MIDI Objects are; you don't need to worry about cabling just yet, but you do need to understand that your external MIDI devices are reflected by MIDI Objects in the Environment. You will need that information to set up Logic in the next couple of chapters.

Audio Objects

Audio objects are not quite like MIDI Objects, although when they are first added to a blank Environment window, they do look much the same. They consist of an iconlike graphic and a parameter box, as Figure 1.6 illustrates.

However, if you double-click on an Audio Object, it expands into a channel strip, as you can see in Figure 1.7.

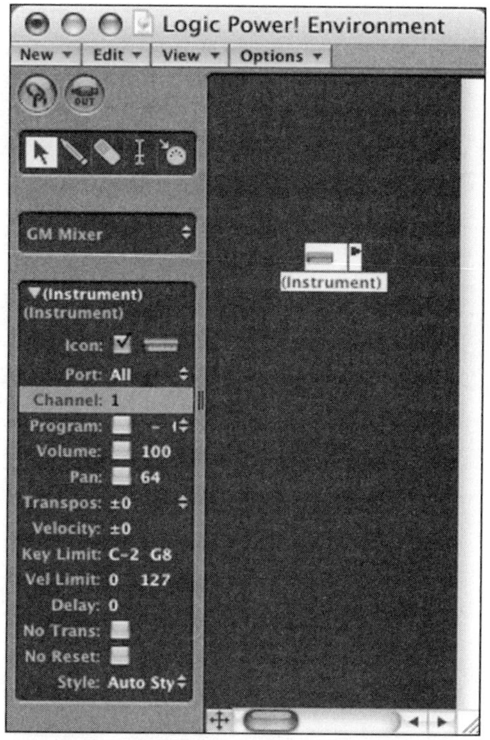

Figure 1.5
A MIDI Instrument Object with its parameter box showing.

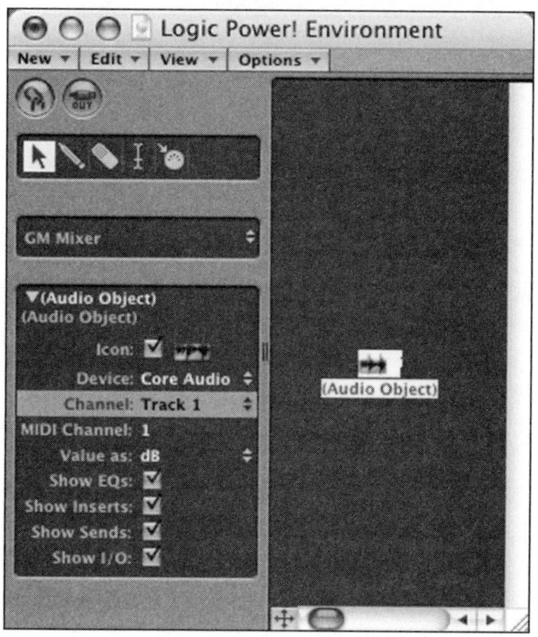

Figure 1.6
A newly created Audio Object and its parameter box.

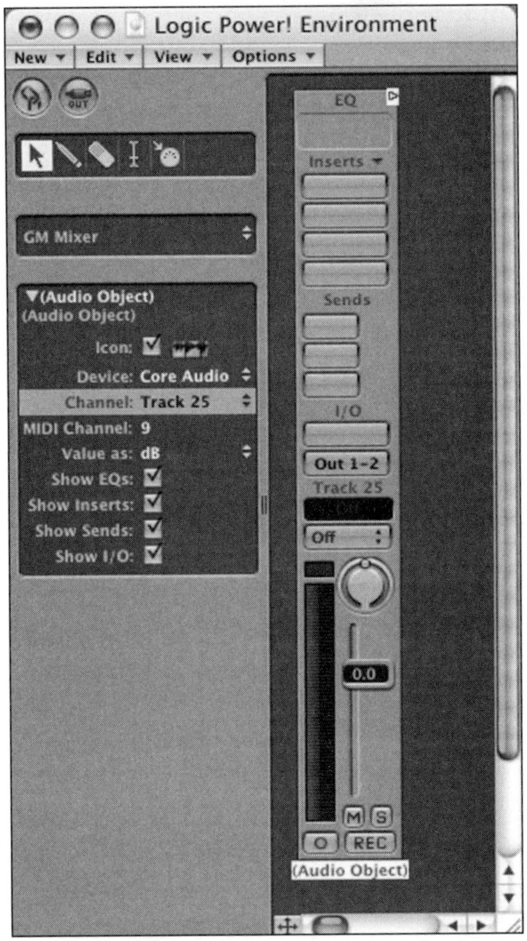

Figure 1.7

An Audio Object that has been expanded to show its channel strip.

These channel strips look like the channel strips in other areas of the program (the Track Mixer and the Arrange window, which we will explore in future chapters), with two major differences:

- Only in the Environment do they have the instrument jack at the top right. You can use this instrument jack to cable an Audio Object to MIDI Objects (since only MIDI flows through Environment cables, never audio data).
- You can move Audio Objects all around the Environment window (channel strips in the Track Mixer or in Arrange are static).

This might seem a little confusing at first, so let me explain this a bit more.

Just as some MIDI Objects can be "virtual representations" of external MIDI hardware, Audio Objects also can be considered virtual representations of a hardware audio mixer. Each Audio Object represents a single channel on a multichannel audio mixer. The following illustration should make this clearer.

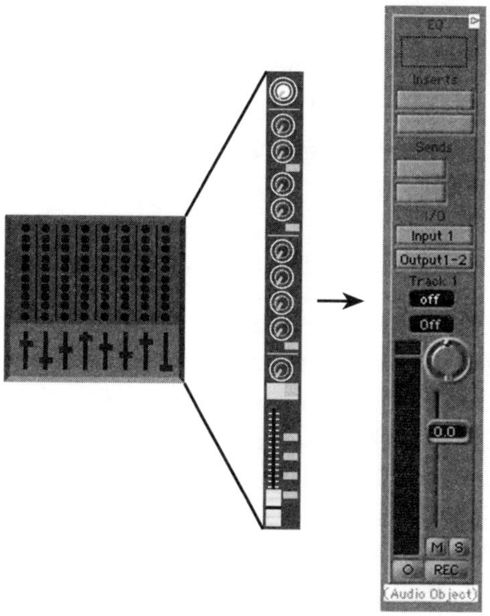

Just as channels on a hardware mixer can have different purposes—for example, some might be for tracking audio, others for busses or auxiliary tracks, while others provide a master fader for the mixer, and so on—you can specify the purpose or the type of channel that an Audio Object will represent in its parameter box. As you have most likely surmised, since Logic allows you to determine what type of channel an Audio Object will represent, you can use Audio Objects to set up your virtual audio studio in nearly unlimited ways.

So remember that an Audio Object in the Environment directly refers to what other areas of the program may call channel strips. We call them Audio Objects when setting them up in the Environment because they can be manipulated and cabled together like any other object in the Environment, whereas in the other areas of the program, no cabling and repositioning of channel strips is possible. Don't worry if the distinction seems confusing at first; it will make sense after a while.

A Brief Primer on Hardware

It is beyond the scope of this book to give you a complete buyer's guide on computer hardware. It is also relatively pointless, since new products are being introduced almost daily. But it is important to touch a little bit on the basic kinds of hardware you'll need to get the most out of Logic.

I assume that you already have any musical instruments or MIDI controller devices you will be using. If you already have your computer hardware as well and are ready to set it up, feel free to skip to Chapter 2, "Initial Setup."

How Fast Does Your Computer Need to Be?

The simple answer to this question is, "As fast as possible"! The more detailed answer is that it depends on what sort of music production you expect to be doing, and what your expectations are.

Emagic's stated minimum requirements are for a G4/400MHz or faster Macintosh computer with 256MB of random access memory (RAM), running the Mac OS X 10.3 (Panther) or later operating system. If you intend to run a sizable number of effects and software synthesizers, your processor and RAM requirements increase even more. Logic 7 has a freeze function that helps conserve CPU power, but you should still use at least a G4/800MHz with 512MB or more of RAM. And if you plan on networking computers together as Logic Nodes, those other computers should be G5s.

If your computer is very old and you are thinking of pushing the minimum, be warned: Slow computers not only have slower CPUs, but also usually have slower motherboards, hard drives, RAM, and so on. When you ask your computer basically to replace an entire building full of mixing desks, tape machines, effects units, and MIDI synthesizers, you're asking a lot. Keep that in mind.

My recommendation is that you get the fastest laptop or desktop Macintosh you can afford and load it with as much RAM as you can. You won't be sorry!

MIDI Interfaces

The section "A Brief Overview of MIDI" above concluded by mentioning the MIDI interface. This device has the same MIDI IN and MIDI THRU ports that your MIDI hardware does and connects to your computer via USB to send that MIDI information from your external units into Logic. If you want Logic to be able to communicate with MIDI devices outside the computer, you need a MIDI interface.

So what size of interface do you need? That depends completely on how many MIDI devices you have. Do you have only one controller keyboard? Then you just need a simple MIDI interface with one MIDI IN and one MIDI OUT port. If your needs are modest enough, your audio interface may already have all the MIDI ports you need (see the following section, "Audio Interfaces"). Do you have a full MIDI studio and need 12 MIDI ports? In that case, you need to buy multiple MIDI interfaces of the largest size you can find (usually eight MIDI IN and eight MIDI OUT ports). Also think about whether you plan to expand your MIDI hardware over time or not; if you do, you might want to get a MIDI interface with more ports than you currently need.

Another thing to consider is whether your MIDI interface needs any professional synchronization features. Some of the more professional interfaces include a lot of video and hardware synchronization options that you might need if you do a lot of sound-to-picture work. Also, many of the larger interfaces include time stamping functionality, which allows them to stamp the exact time that a MIDI event should occur as part of the MIDI message. Time stamping doesn't have a noticeable effect for small numbers of MIDI devices, but it can make a world of difference with MIDI studios containing large amounts of external hardware.

Finally, keep in mind that many different manufacturers make MIDI interfaces, and these interfaces are all equally compatible with Logic. As long as your interface has a USB connector and drivers for your operating system, it should do the job.

Audio Interfaces

Because there are so many audio interfaces on the market, choosing one might seem daunting. But here are a few tips to help you with your selection.

First, consider how many audio channels you intend to record at one time. Do you see yourself recording a rock band or an entire symphony at once? If so, you will want to investigate those audio interfaces that enable users to daisy chain more than one interface, so you can expand your system as your recording needs grow. Some systems today not only enable users to record 24 channels at once, but to connect two or three such boxes, for a truly impressive audio recording system. On the other hand, do you see yourself recording only yourself, or a single stereo instrument at a time? If so, then a small interface will do.

Next, consider how you would prefer or need your audio interface to connect to your computer. Are you using a laptop? If so, you want an interface that connects to the computer via USB or FireWire, which all modern Macintosh laptops have. If you have a PowerBook, you can also select a PCMCIA (Personal Computer Memory Card International) format interface. If you have a desktop machine, you might also prefer a USB or FireWire interface because those interfaces don't require opening up your machine and installing anything. If you own a desktop machine and don't mind installing hardware, you can choose an audio interface that is a Peripheral Component Interface (PCI) card. PCI options are usually more expandable and less expensive than USB, FireWire, or PCMCIA interfaces, but are more difficult to install.

You need to consider the sampling frequency and bit depth at which you want to record. Compact discs are standardized at 16 bits, with a sampling frequency of 44.1kHz. Every audio interface available today can record at least at this level of fidelity. Do you want to be able to record at 24 bits, which is the industry standard for producing music? Do you want to be able to record at higher sampling frequencies, such as the 96kHz that DVDs can use? All these decisions influence what kind of audio interface will fit your needs. Because the higher bit depths and sample rates capture a more accurate "picture" of the sound, as explained previously, you might want to record and process your audio at higher bit rates than your final format, if you have the computer power to do so.

Finally, you should consider whether you want your audio interface to have additional features. For example, some audio interfaces have MIDI control surfaces, or MIDI interfaces, as part of a package. Does that appeal to you, or would you prefer to fill those areas with other devices?

Now that I've introduced Logic, some of its basic concepts, and the hardware you'll need, it's time to set up your hardware for use in Logic in the next chapter, "Initial Setup."

2 Initial Setup

As Chapter 1 explained, you need three vital hardware components in order to use Logic Pro 7: a Macintosh, an audio interface, and a MIDI interface. While modern audio and MIDI devices are more plug-and-play than ever, some basic configuration is required before you start.

Note that the information that follows is in no way intended to substitute for the documentation that came with your hardware!

Setting Up Your Hardware

Chapter 1's information on various types of audio interfaces should help you select an audio and MIDI interface that will fit your requirements. Before using Logic, you'll need to connect the device or devices physically to your computer and install the drivers. This section will help you configure your hardware's software.

Interfaces and Drivers

Sometimes, simply plugging your audio interface into your computer is enough to enable your computer to recognize the interface so that you can start using it. Other times, the audio interface comes with *drivers*—files that explain to your computer how to communicate with your interface. For example, if you are using Mac OS X, audio interfaces that use the support for standard USB audio or mLAN (a FireWire audio/MIDI format developed by Yamaha) that is built into Core Audio (explained later in this chapter) do not require additional drivers, whereas all other audio and MIDI devices require installation of manufacturer-supplied drivers.

In general, most of the configuration of audio and MIDI devices is done inside Logic, so the driver installation is usually a very straightforward process of inserting the CD that came with your hardware or perhaps downloading drivers from the Internet, and then launching an installation application. Most device driver installations require you to restart your computer at the end of the process, as most operating systems scan for new drivers only when the system starts up.

Once your new devices are installed, you are ready to tell Logic about them. Logic 7 comes with a new *wizard*, or walk-through assistant, to help tell Logic about your studio.

Using the Logic Setup Assistant

To walk you through the process of configuring Logic to default to an audio and MIDI configuration, Logic 7 comes with the Logic Setup Assistant (LSA). It automatically launches the first time you run Logic, or you can manually run it at any time by choosing Launch Logic Setup Assistant from the Preferences menu, as shown in Figure 2.1. You can find the Preferences menu by selecting **Logic Pro > Preferences > Start Logic Setup Assistant**. If you launch the LSA from within Logic, the LSA will first quit Logic, then launch the LSA.

Figure 2.1

Any time you want to redo your default studio setup without going through the Audio Hardware and Driver dialog boxes or the Environment window, you can select the Start Logic Setup Assistant menu option.

SAVE YOUR CUSTOMIZATIONS

Keep in mind that if you do decide to run the LSA after you have made some customizations to the default song, those customizations will be lost. Therefore, be sure to use **File > Save As Template** to save your current Logic song first, so you can come back to it.

The Welcome Page

When the LSA first launches, it presents a welcome page with a Next button in the bottom right of the window, as shown in Figure 2.2.

Click **Next**, and as Figure 2.3 illustrates, the LSA prompts you to connect all your audio and MIDI interfaces so that it can scan them automatically.

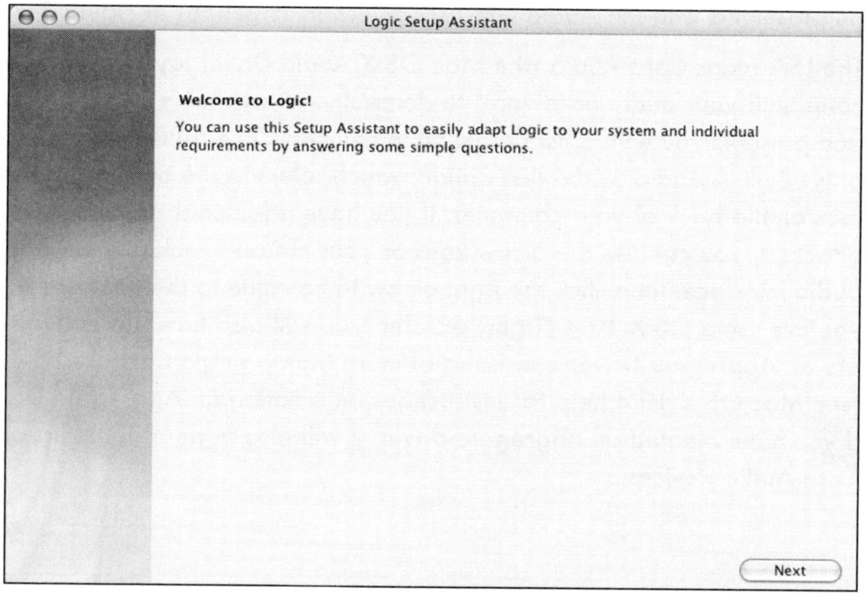

Figure 2.2
The Logic Setup Assistant welcome screen.

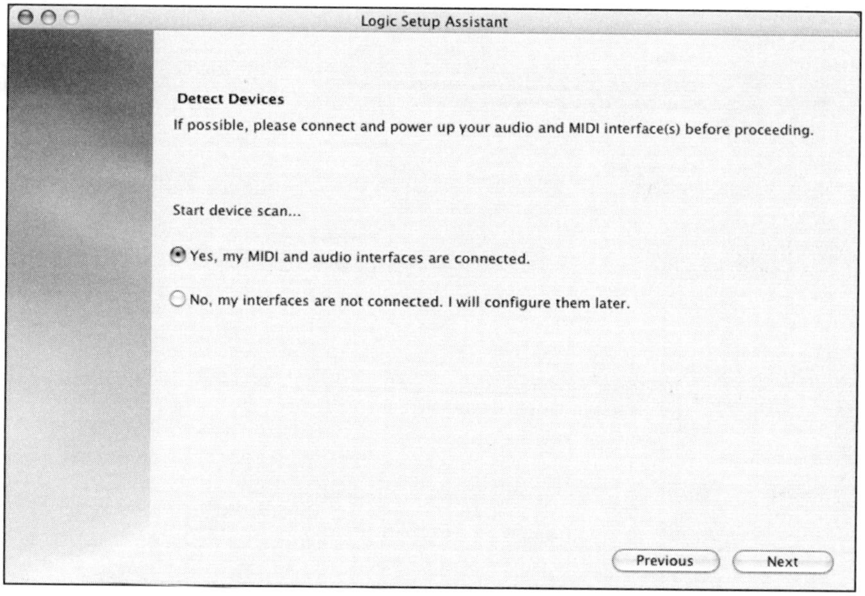

Figure 2.3
The first thing the LSA asks you to do is to attach your audio and MIDI interfaces to your computer.

You definitely should follow the LSA's advice and let it scan for your attached interfaces. It makes things much easier for you and allows the LSA to be more thorough in its configuration of Logic's default settings. Click the **Next** button when you are done with this page.

The Audio Page

After the LSA scans your devices and you move to the next screen, you will be presented with the Audio interface selection screen, as in Figure 2.4.

The LSA scans Core Audio (the Mac OS X Audio Driver layer that communicates with your audio hardware) to determine all available audio devices and presents you with a list of available devices. Core Audio always displays Built-In Audio as the first option, which refers to the built-in speaker-out jack on the back of your computer. If you have additional interfaces attached, you can use the arrow keys or your mouse to select a different audio interface, then click the right arrow to continue to the next screen. If you are using OS X 10.4 (Tiger) or later, you will also have an option to create an Aggregate Driver consisting of more than a single Core Audio device (see Mac OS X 10.4 help for instructions on creating an Aggregate Driver). If you have created an aggregate driver, it will also appear in the list of Core Audio devices.

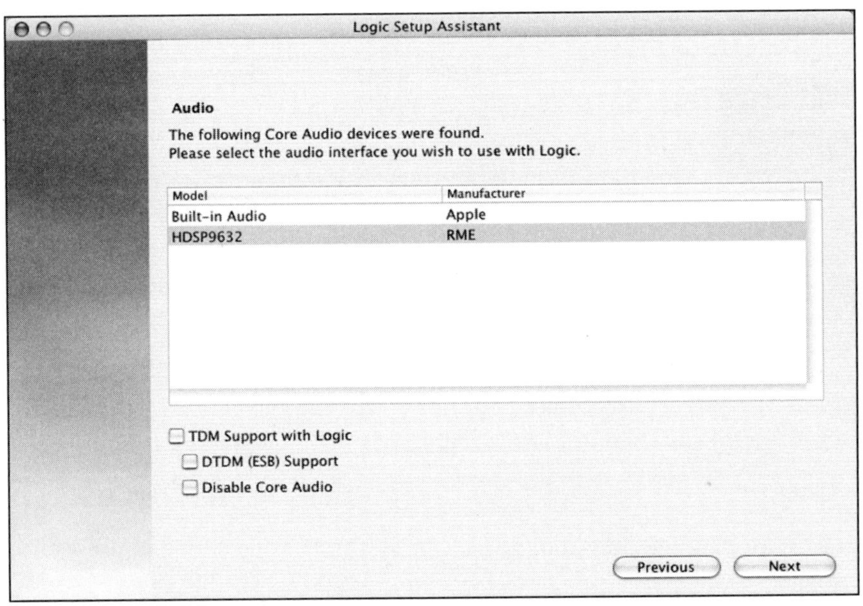

Figure 2.4
In the LSA Audio interface selection window, choose the audio interface or Digidesign TDM hardware driver you want Logic to use.

If you use Digidesign's TDM hardware driver, the Logic Setup Assistant offers you a number of driver combinations. If you wish to use the Digidesign Audio Engine (DAE) instead of Core Audio, you can select TDM Support with Logic. With this configuration, you will have access to all your TDM-based audio processing and plug-ins, but you will have no access to CPU-based processing and plug-in software (often called "native" software, because it runs on your computer's "native" CPU rather than an external chip). If you do want the advantage of both TDM and native processing, you can check DTDM (ESB) Support, which will give you both.

If you would rather run Logic with no audio engine at all (just for MIDI), you can select Disable Core Audio. (You can temporarily disable all audio drivers by pressing the **CONTROL** key while launching Logic Pro.) Click the **Next** button when you are done with this page.

Core Audio Mixer Setup Page

The next two screens determine how Logic will set up your Audio Objects. Figure 2.5 shows the first screen, Mixer Setup.

This screen allows you to choose how many channel strips Logic will automatically create for you in the Environment of your default song. You can adjust the sliders to raise or lower the numeric value in the boxes, or you can

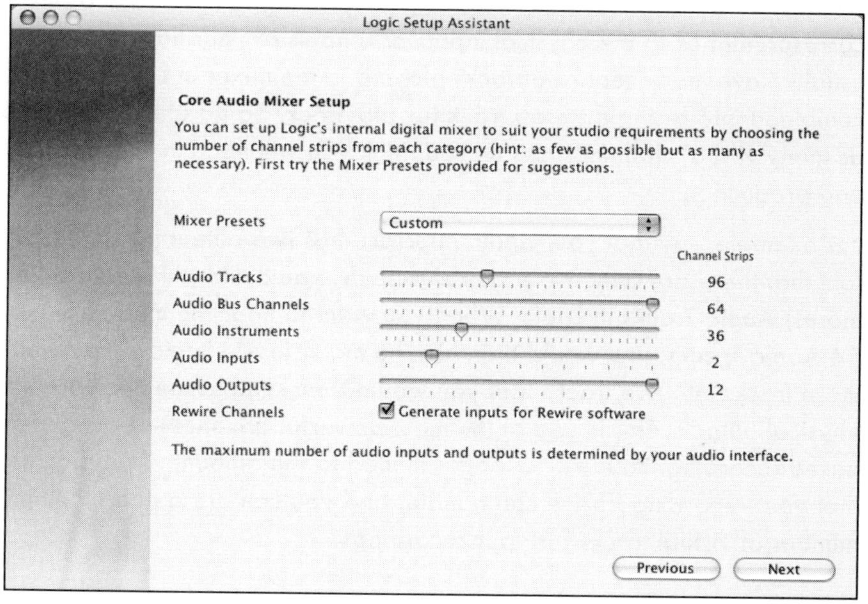

Figure 2.5
In the Core Audio Mixer Setup page, you can determine how many channel strips Logic will create in your default song.

type a number directly into the boxes. The maximum number of objects you can select for each option depends on both the version of Logic 7 you are using (Pro or Express) and the capabilities of your audio hardware.

WAIT—ARE WE SETTING UP CHANNEL STRIPS OR AUDIO OBJECTS?

You might be wondering why the LSA refers to "channel strips" whereas the last chapter noted that the channel strip is really just one view of an Audio Object. Good question! As stated earlier, the distinction between Audio Objects and channel strips can sometimes be confusing.

As previously explained, all graphical representations that appear in the environment are called objects, and those used for processing audio are called Audio Objects. When an Audio Object is expanded, as shown in Figure 1.7, this expanded view is called the channel strip view of the Audio Object, as it looks exactly like the channel strip of a hardware mixer. The Mixer Setup page of the LSA controls the number of audio processing objects that will be created inside the Environment. When the LSA creates these objects, each one is expanded into its channel strip mode, as shown in Figure 1.7.

Don't worry if the concept of objects seems convoluted—it will get easier to understand with each passing chapter!

Keep in mind that the number of Audio Objects (including Audio Tracks, Instruments, and Busses) does not have to correlate exactly with the number of hardware inputs and outputs you have available—they are *virtual tracks,* meaning that they exist inside Logic but they don't need to have a one-to-one correspondence to the physical inputs or outputs of your hardware. You will usually have many separate tracks playing in the mixer in Logic that will be combined into a single stereo track for playback. So go ahead and create as many virtual channel strips as you think you will need in your songwriting and production.

For example, say that your audio interface has two output jacks. Despite the fact that there are only two physical outputs, you could still create 64 (or more!) Audio Tracks in Logic. When you want to hear the music from those 64 Audio Tracks, you would then use the mixer inside Logic to combine all of these tracks into two tracks that you would then send to the interface's two physical outputs. This is one of the most powerful advances of computer-based recording: You are no longer limited to the amount of physical tracks that your recording device can handle, and you can use a nearly unlimited number of virtual tracks for your recordings.

Don't feel like you have to know what all of the track varieties listed to the left of the sliders are; you'll learn about all these later in this book. If you don't have a clue as to how many tracks of various types you might want, you can open the Mixer Presets pull-down menu as shown in Figure 2.6 and select from one of the mixer configurations that Emagic offers.

If you are using any additional software applications that connect to Logic via Propellerhead's Rewire protocol (such as Reason, Live, Storm, and so on), be sure to check the Generate Inputs for Rewire Software box in the Rewire Channels column. If you have no idea what Rewire or any of these programs are, chances are you don't have any Rewire software and you can leave the box unchecked. Click the **Next** button when you are done with this page.

The Audio Input Page

The next screen offers three options for determining how many inputs to activate for recording, as Figure 2.7 shows.

The first option activates inputs one and two for all your Audio Track Objects, and if you have more than two inputs, Logic will ignore the remainder. The second option does not activate any inputs on your Audio Objects.

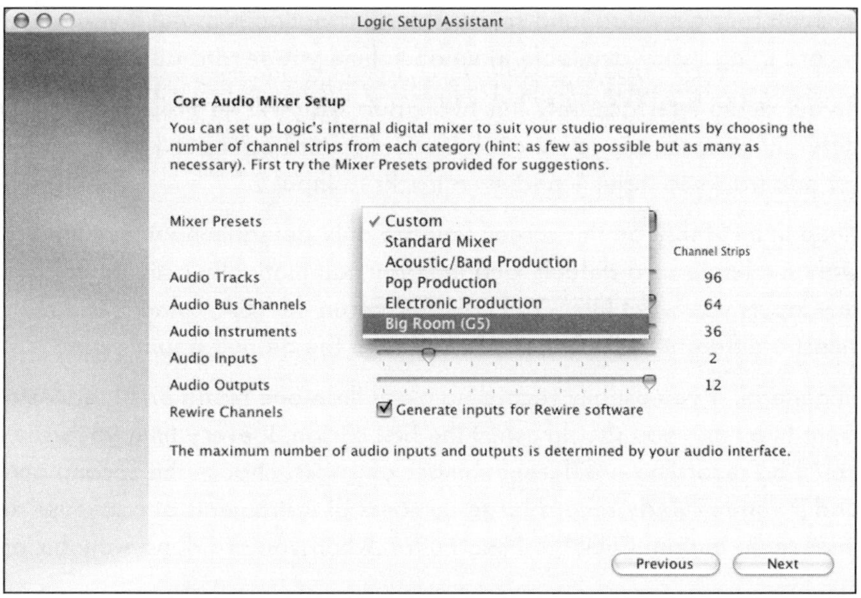

Figure 2.6

The LSA Core Audio Mixer Setup screen offers a number of preset mixer configurations that you can access via the pull-down Mixer Presets menu.

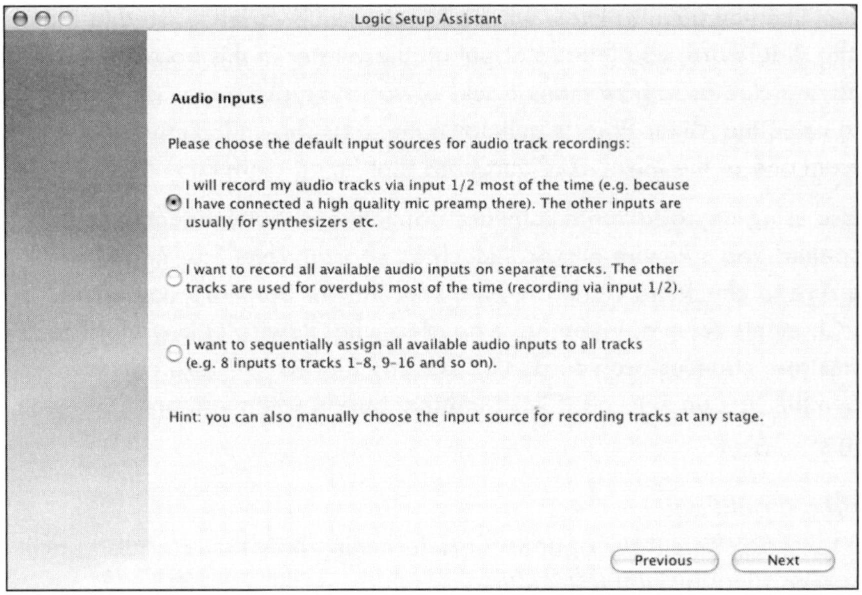

Figure 2.7

The LSA allows you to select how many inputs will be active for Audio Track recordings.

The third option sequentially activates all available inputs on all Audio Track Objects—in other words, if your audio interface has four inputs, tracks one through four will have inputs one through four activated, at which point the count starts over so that tracks five through eight will also have inputs one through four activated, and so on. This third option is useful if you always record using every available input each time you record audio.

If your audio interface only has two inputs, you will be presented with two different options: one to set each track to record on Input 1, and another to set odd tracks to Input 1 and even tracks to Input 2.

Keep in mind that on this screen you are only determining which inputs you want available as a default, and that you can manually activate or change any inputs you want later. You can then rerun the LSA, select this screen, select a different radio button, and change the default again.

In general, if you usually record no more than one mono or stereo instrument at a time, you should select the first option; if every time you use Logic you'll be recording a different number of tracks, choose the second option; and if you regularly record large numbers of instruments at once, use the third radio button. Click the **Next** button when you are done with this page.

The Key Command Page

Key commands are extremely important in Logic. In fact, many functions can be accessed only via key commands, as you'll learn later in this book. The LSA allows you to assign several default key command sets, as shown in Figure 2.8.

As you get more comfortable with Logic, you will assign your own key commands to the majority of the functions you wish to access via your computer keyboard, so you might as well start off either by not changing the default key commands or by using the default set for your country or language. If you are a ProTools user, you might feel more comfortable starting with the ProTools Set U.S. option, which assigns Logic commands to a familiar set of keyboard shortcuts.

If you are running the LSA after you have already been using Logic for some time and have added your own key commands, this screen gives you a window in which to import your previous key commands, or any saved key command sets created by others. Simply click the **Import other key commands** button and the LSA presents the standard Mac OS X Open File dialog box. Navigate to your key command file, then click the **Open** button. You can also choose to import or export Key Command sets from the Key Commands window in Logic. Click the **Next** button when you are done with this page.

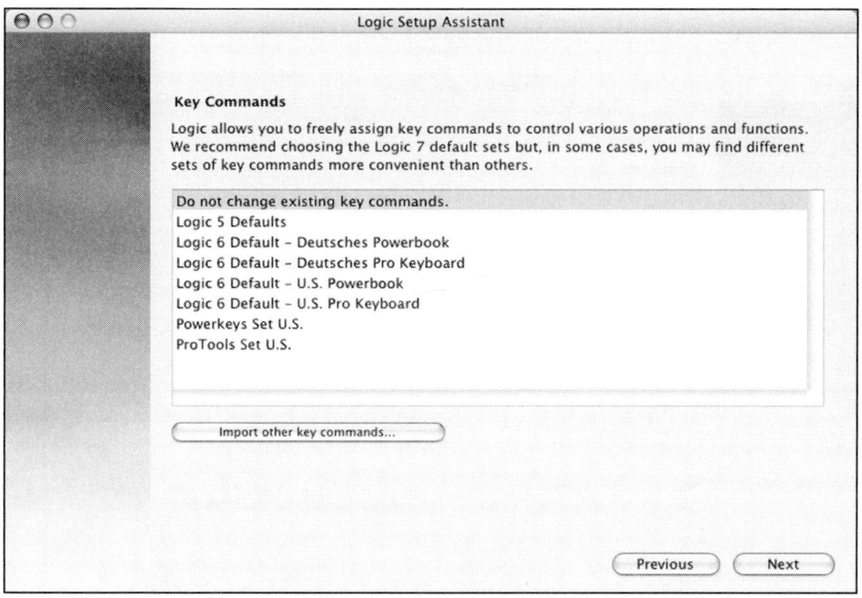

Figure 2.8
The LSA offers different options for Logic's default key command sets.

The Screensets Page

One of Logic's most powerful features is the ease of setting up unique screensets, or different arrangements of editors, mixers, and windows that you can instantly recall by pressing a single key on your keyboard. As you can see in Figure 2.9, Logic's screensets can use any and all available video displays you have connected to your computer.

As a general rule, you will want to have all available video monitors activated for use by Logic—indeed, few applications benefit as much from the added screen real estate of a second or third monitor as Logic. Click the **Next** button when you are done with this page.

The MIDI Devices Page

Just as the Audio screen had a list of your available audio interfaces, the MIDI Devices screen of the LSA contains a list of the MIDI devices it detected, as shown in Figure 2.10.

All the MIDI devices shown in this page are reflected in Logic's Environment by MIDI Instrument Objects, just as the Audio Objects that you set up are represented by their channel strips in Logic's Environment.

Even though Logic attempts to scan for all MIDI devices connected to your MIDI interface, it may not detect them all, or you may want to add or remove devices to this list manually. You can accomplish this easily by pressing the Remove or Add button above the list of MIDI devices.

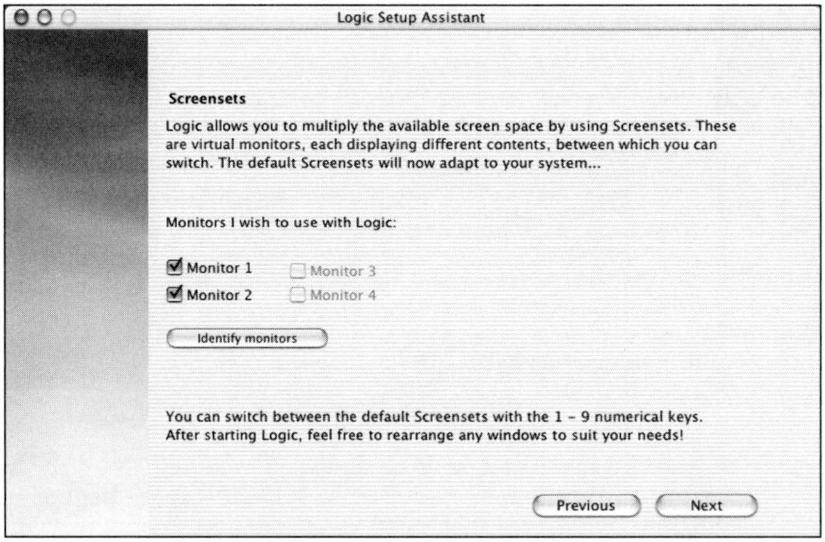

Figure 2.9

Activate as many connected video monitors as you wish in the LSA's Screensets page.

Figure 2.10
The MIDI Devices screen lets you add and remove MIDI devices from your Logic Environment.

When you highlight a device and press **Remove**, that device disappears from your list. When you press **Add**, the dialog box shown in Figure 2.11 appears.

The first thing you'll want to do is check the pull-down menus to see whether the pull-down lists of manufacturers and models include the names for your equipment. If not, you can type the names in yourself. Finally, for the Connected to MIDI Out Port and Connected to MIDI In Port entries, pull down the menus and select the ports to which your device is attached, as shown in Figure 2.12.

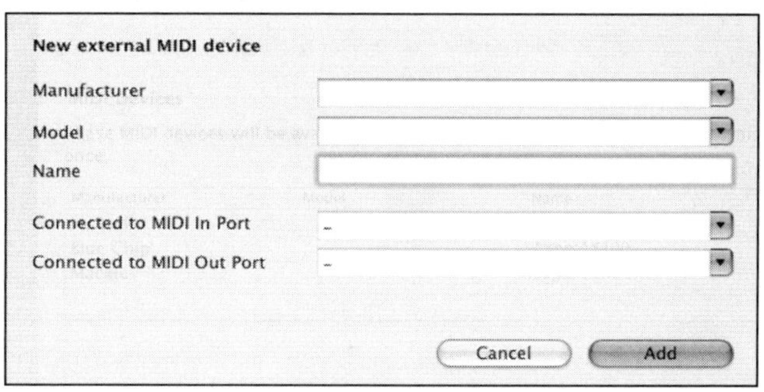

Figure 2.11
In the Add MIDI Device dialog box, fill in each field, then press **Add**.

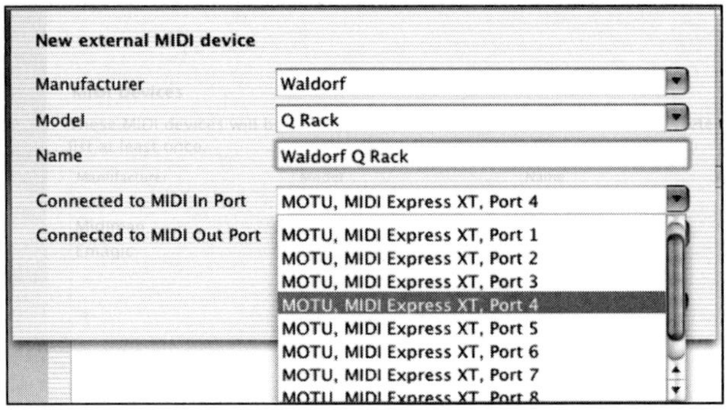

Figure 2.12
Selecting the MIDI port in the Add MIDI Device dialog box.

When you have configured all of your MIDI devices, click **Next** to move to the next page.

The Summary Page

Finally, the LSA presents you with the Summary page shown in Figure 2.13. This page lists everything that the wizard has created.

At this point, simply click **Finish**, and Logic will have configured its default setup based on both your audio and MIDI devices and your personal preferences.

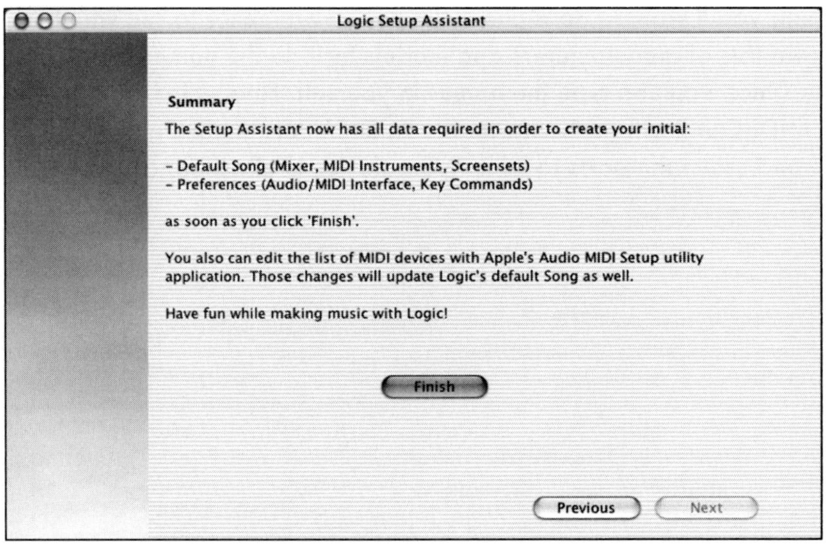

Figure 2.13
The Summary page details all the data collected by the Logic Setup Assistant.

Configuring Your Audio Driver

Installing your audio driver and using the Logic Setup Assistant to select your device in Logic is only the first step. At this point, you want to tell Logic exactly how you want to use your hardware. You can tell Logic how you want to use your audio interface in the Drivers tab of the Audio Preferences window, which you can access at **Logic Pro > Preferences > Audio**, and then clicking on the Drivers tab. The Drivers tab of Audio Preferences is shown in Figure 2.14.

Notice that the dialog box contains the default settings for some items, such as the Max. Number of Audio Tracks and the 64 Busses settings. Your defaults may have already been set up in the Logic Setup Assistant, but you can always change them here if you wish. I'll briefly go over all of the options here. As the Process Buffer Range and Software Monitoring options are more complex and require detailed explanation, each will get its own section later in this chapter.

The first thing you'll notice is a tab for each of the audio engines that Logic can use. In Figure 2.14, the Core Audio driver is selected, but you can also choose to use any of the other available drivers if you have compatible hardware. Unlike many other audio applications, Logic allows you to use

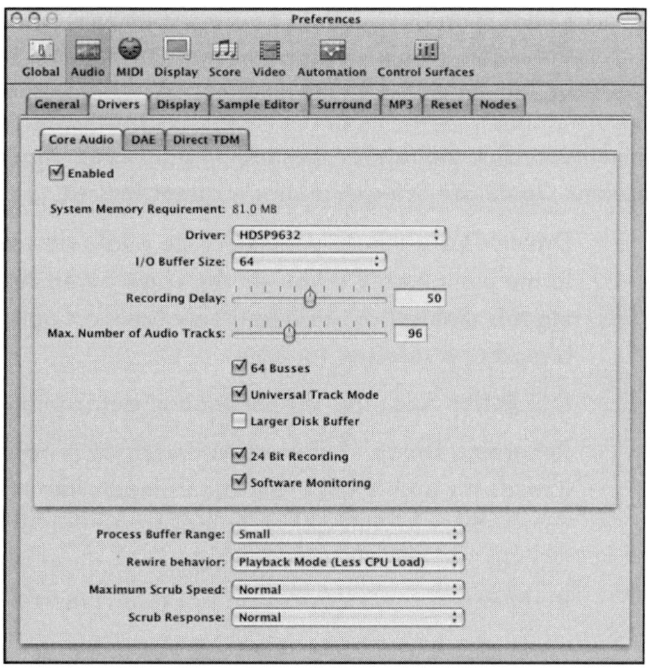

Figure 2.14

The Drivers tab of the Audio Preferences dialog. Here you can configure how you wish Logic to use your audio device.

multiple audio engines simultaneously. Here is a brief explanation of each audio engine:

- **Core Audio.** This is the built-in audio engine of the Mac OS X operating system. Almost every new audio device comes with Core Audio drivers, and this is the audio engine that you will most likely keep checked. In fact, since the built-in audio jack of your Macintosh uses Core Audio, even if you have one of the other audio engines checked, you can still run Core Audio alongside it. Core Audio is a *native* audio engine, which means that when you use Core Audio, all of your Audio Tracks, effects, and so on will run from the central processing unit (CPU) of your computer, instead of running on external hardware. Core Audio gives you full access to all of Logic's effects and synthesizers, and to all third-party native Audio Unit (AU) plug-ins.
- **DAE.** This is the Digidesign Audio Engine. Select this engine if you wish to use the DSP (Digital Signal Processing) engine of Digidesign TDM (Time Division Multiplexing) or TDM II hardware. You will not have access to native audio and effects (such as VST [Virtual Studio Technology] or AU) unless you are also running a native audio engine in addition to DAE. Using Digidesign TDM/TDM II with Logic is covered briefly in Appendix D, "Logic Resources on the Internet."
- **Direct TDM.** If you want to use Digidesign TDM audio hardware with the native plug-ins instead of the TDM/TDM II DSP, Direct TDM allows you to do so.

When you click the tab for the audio engine you chose, you see a number of options. Some are self-explanatory, others less so.

- **Driver.** This is where you select the audio device you have connected to the computer. If you used the Logic Setup Assistant prior to opening this dialog box, or if you only have a single device, it should already be selected for you.
- **I/O Buffer Size.** This is explained in detail later.
- **Recording Delay.** If your audio interface properly discloses how long it takes for audio to travel from its inputs into the computer, Logic can compensate for this delay, to make sure that everything you record appears on Logic's Arrange page exactly at the instant you recorded it. However, some devices do not report their delay, and so Logic

would have no way of knowing exactly how to compensate for this "record offset" caused by your hardware. The Record Delay parameter allows you to manually adjust Logic's recording offset compensation, so that you can even compensate for devices that do not report their delay. If this sounds complicated, or if your tracks sound like they are not out of time, you don't need to worry about this parameter. For most modern interfaces, you won't need to adjust this.

- **64 Busses.** Logic gives you the option to use 64 busses to route your Audio Tracks and Audio Instruments. Otherwise, you are limited to 16 busses. Since having a large mixer takes up more CPU power and RAM, having the option to limit your mixer to 16 busses conserves resources on slower machines. Remember, you can always return to this page and turn on the 64 Busses option if you need it.
- **Universal Track Mode.** When this is turned on, all stereo tracks take up a single mixer channel. Without Universal Track Mode selected, a stereo track takes up two mixer channels (one for the right channel and one for the left channel). With Universal Track Mode off, you have some extra routing options (such as routing one side of a stereo track to a different destination than the other side), but you will not be able to save a stereo track into a single file. Most users will want to keep Universal Track Mode active just for the simpler option of having a single mixer strip for stereo objects and saving them as a single file.

UNIVERSAL TRACK MODE AND THE DAE AUDIO ENGINE

The DAE engine cannot use Universal Track Mode, so this option does not appear at all in the DAE parameters.

- **Larger Disk Buffer.** This is explained in detail below.
- **20/24 Bit Recording.** If you want to record into 20-bit or 24-bit audio files, keep this option checked. Using 24-bit files takes up more processing power and hard disk space, so some users prefer to record at 16-bit to conserve their CPU and hard disk. In addition, some older or inexpensive audio interfaces do not have 24-bit recording capability. These days, almost every device is capable of 24-bit recording. As Chapter 1's sections about digital audio explained, it is advantageous to use the highest bit rate you can, so you should keep this option selected.

- **Software Monitoring.** This button selects or deselects software monitoring. Software monitoring is explained in detail later.
- **Process Buffer Range.** Process buffer range is explained later in detail.
- **Rewire Behavior.** Rewire is a technology developed by Propellerhead Software (the Swedish audio software company famous for ReCycle, ReBirth, and Reason) to allow separate stand-alone audio applications to interoperate. Setting up Logic as a Rewire host is addressed in detail in the "Using Rewire 2 Instruments" section of Chapter 10. This preference determines whether Logic utilizes Rewire in Playback mode, which takes up less CPU processing, or in Live mode, which allows you to send MIDI from Logic to your Rewire applications with lower latency, at the expense of a high CPU load.
- **Max Scrub Speed.** *Scrubbing* refers to moving the playback cursor over an audio file to play it back, as opposed to simply pressing Play. This option is particularly useful if you are doing some very fine editing and are listening for a very specific point in the song. This option determines the maximum possible playback speed when you scrub: normal or double speed. When you select normal, even if you scrub your mouse as fast as you can across a section of audio, you'll never hear it faster than realtime. If you select double, you will hear the section play back at double the normal speed. You might want to change the scrub speed if you want to be able to quickly scrub through your song.
- **Scrub Response.** This preference determines how quickly the scrub function will react to changes in your mouse speed. Your options are Slow, Normal, Fast, and Faster. The faster the response, the more the playback reflects your actual speeding up and slowing down, but the more jerky the sound will be unless you keep your speed extremely steady. I keep both scrub options set to Normal.

Adjusting the Audio Hardware Buffers

One of the most important reasons for opening the Audio Drivers tab of the Preferences dialog box is to adjust the various input and output buffers. Adjusting buffers is how you fine-tune Logic's performance to get the most out of your system. To do this properly, it is important to know what each of the buffers does, so that you can tailor the settings to meet your requirements exactly.

The fundamental concept is that it takes a set amount of time for the CPU to do a given amount of work. Because timing is so integral to making music, having control over the exact amount of time it takes the CPU to complete a given task is crucial. Logic allows users to have independent control over three separate but related audio buffers: the input/output (I/O) buffer, the process buffer, and the disk buffer.

I/O Buffer Size

When you record audio into Logic, it naturally takes a certain amount of time before you hear it played back through the audio interface's outputs. First, the audio has to travel from your audio interface into the audio driver of your audio interface. The driver then passes the signal information to Logic. After Logic records the audio onto your hard drive, Logic then returns the audio to your audio driver for output, and finally the driver sends the audio to your interface. This is shown in the following diagram:

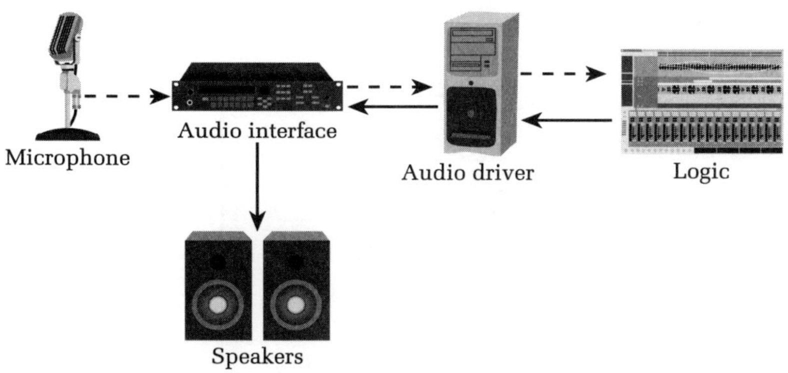

As this diagram shows, the audio driver is in charge of regulating the input and output of audio to and from the application. To do this effectively and in perfect synchronization, the audio driver passes to Logic a chunk of audio that consists of a variable number of samples, and Logic then sends to the driver chunks of audio with that same number of samples. The amount of time that elapses in this process is called *latency*.

If the number of samples in each chunk of audio is very small, the latency will be very low. The drawback is that the audio driver has to work very quickly to keep those small chunks of audio moving. This requires more CPU power and, if the audio drivers are not well written, can cause audible crackles and pops as the audio driver struggles to keep up with the demands placed on it. If the number of samples in each chunk is very large, the driver does not need to work nearly as hard, resulting in a far lower CPU drain and better performance from audio drivers. However, large buffers result in a higher latency.

Most audio interfaces give you a number of options for buffer sizes, as you can see in Figure 2.15. Note that the specific options and sample sizes differ between audio interfaces, so don't be surprised if your interface has different sizes than in the figure.

There are a number of situations in which you need your latency to be as low as possible:

- To get the most out of Software Monitoring (See the "Using Software Monitoring" section later in this chapter.)
- To play virtual instruments in realtime
- To use external hardware alongside playback from Logic

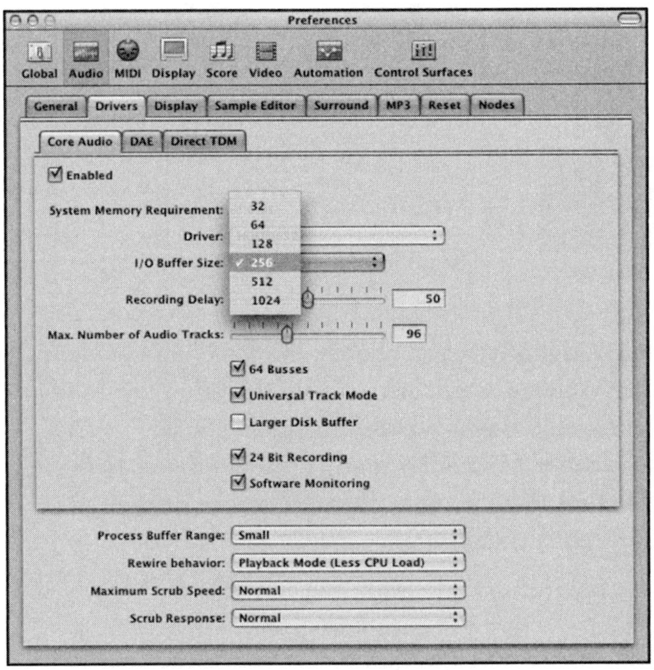

Figure 2.15

You can select any of these different buffer sizes in the I/O Buffer Size pull-down menu.

In these cases you should set your buffer as low as your system can handle without glitches (audible pops and crackles during playback), which usually ranges between 64 and 256 samples. Otherwise you can set your buffer to a high setting, as higher settings usually offer the best CPU performance—try between 512 and 2,048 samples. As a rule, you should start with as low a setting as you can, and if you notice audio glitches or sluggish computer performance due to the CPU strain, slowly raise the I/O buffer until you reach the lowest comfortable setting.

Process Buffer Range

As described in the explanation of the audio engines, when you use a native audio engine, your computer's CPU handles all the audio processing. Just as the audio drivers handle audio in chunks to increase efficiency, the CPU also handles audio processing in chunks. The size of these chunks is set with the Process Buffer Range pull-down menu. The process buffer size may be Small, Medium, or Large. The smaller the buffer, the faster audio is processed, but the more CPU is required, leaving less total CPU power available for other processing. The larger the buffer, the slower the CPU processes audio, which leaves more power available for everything else (such as playing tracks, screen redraws, and so on).

If your process buffer is too small for your system, your system will quickly run out of power, presenting you with cryptic messages informing you "Error: Core Audio too slow," and the like. Regardless of the exact text, the reason is the same: Logic can't keep up with everything you're asking it to do. If your buffer is too large, you may find that some operations that rely on fast response—such as external storage devices, recording, or realtime processing—will become out of sync because each chunk is too large to keep up with the rest of the song. You have to adjust this setting to find the ideal buffer size for your particular system, but in general you should keep the process buffer as small as possible. Most modern computers should be able to handle a process buffer of small or medium without a problem. As with the I/O buffer, start with a setting of Small, and then increase it as necessary to find the ideal setting.

Larger Disk Buffer Option

When you are playing back large numbers of Audio Tracks, a slower hard drive may not be fast enough to handle the demands that Logic places on it.

If you have one of these slower hard drives, you can activate the Larger Disk Buffer option. Logic will then retrieve larger chunks of audio from your hard drive with each access, resulting in fewer requests from the hard drive at the expense of more RAM and CPU usage. If you have a newer computer or have purchased hard drives that can run at 7,200 revolutions per minute (RPM) or faster, you shouldn't need to use the Larger Disk Buffer option. But if you have an older computer or a laptop with a slower drive, this option can help you get the most out of your hard drive. You'll learn more about this in Chapter 5's discussion of the System Performance window.

Using Software Monitoring

When you select Software Monitoring, you can listen to any audio that you are sending into Logic right after it goes through the Logic software. The signal path follows the illustration shown previously in the "I/O Buffer Size" subsection, and the latency, or delay between when you record a signal and when you hear it back, will depend on the I/O Buffer Size settings.

Latency is the most serious drawback to recording audio on a computer versus recording onto tape machines. When you perform live, you hear what you play almost instantly and rarely will the delay exceed one or two milliseconds (most people can't detect differences smaller than 10 milliseconds). However, depending on your audio interface and your buffer setting, you may not hear what you record onto a computer more than 50 milliseconds later. This is long enough that everyone can hear it, and it makes listening as you're singing or playing next to impossible, as you'd hear an echo of your performance that would be too confusing.

Audio interface designers have been trying to combat latency in two ways: first, by writing drivers that allow for the lowest possible latency and, second, by designing hardware monitoring options directly into their audio interfaces.

With low-latency drivers, at the lowest I/O Buffer Size settings it's often possible to bring the latency of hard disk recording below 7 milliseconds even when using software monitoring. This is a very reasonable value. However, as you've already learned, reducing latency can take a heavy toll on the host CPU, reducing performance significantly.

Hardware monitoring means that when you record, instead of listening back to your audio after it is recorded by Logic, the signal is routed in the hardware itself directly from its input to its output in addition to going into the computer, as illustrated here:

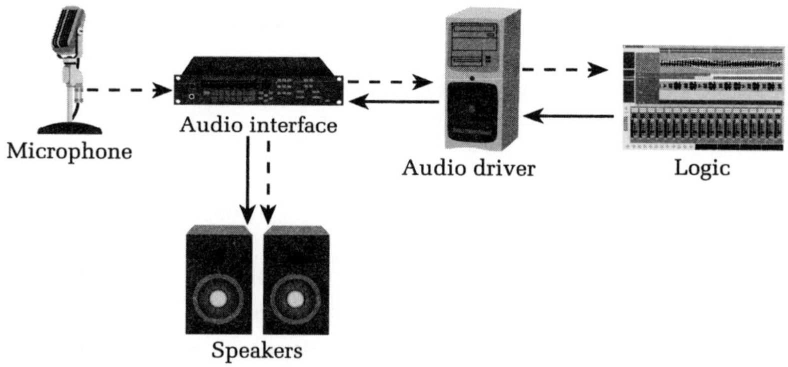

The advantage of hardware monitoring is that there is barely any perceivable latency, since the audio isn't processed at all but simply redirected back out. That is also one of the disadvantages, as you will not hear any processing of the signal as you record it. Additionally, since what you are hearing is not the actual signal being recorded, you won't be able to detect whether you need to adjust the tone or volume of your signal to get the best recording.

So do you need to use software monitoring? The answer is no if you are comfortable with using only hardware monitoring or if you are mostly creating instrumental music with software synthesizers. If you want to hear exactly what Logic is going to be recording, or if you are using external hardware units to perform or process your audio in realtime within the Logic mixer, then you need to select the Software Monitoring check box. If you want to hear Logic's effects while recording, you'll need to turn on Software Monitoring. Also keep in mind that you can turn this option on or off at any time. Therefore, you could, for example, record an entire group of musicians without Software Monitoring, then turn on Software Monitoring to record a singer so you can fine-tune the signal that Logic will record precisely. You could then perhaps send the singer a mix with some of Logic's realtime effects processing the signal.

> **THE DIGIDESIGN TDM LATENCY ADVANTAGE**
>
> Digidesign's TDM system relies on its Time Division Multiplexing (TDM) hardware PCI cards to do all the processing. This means that the audio you record using TDM never goes through the computer—in other words, any recording done with TDM utilizes hardware monitoring as explained above. This is why TDM systems offer such amazingly low recording latency (just a few milliseconds) even when recording huge numbers of tracks simultaneously, and with absolutely no CPU hit at all. This is a major advantage when recording—not even the fastest native recording systems can do this. If this advantage is worth the exorbitant price of TDM hardware, however, depends on the budget and needs of the individual user.

Setting Up Your MIDI Hardware

Because most MIDI devices don't have many configurable options, setting them up is far more straightforward than with audio devices. When connecting your MIDI hardware to your MIDI interface, however, you need to be conscious of MIDI ports.

Selecting MIDI Ports

The smallest MIDI interfaces have a single MIDI IN and a single MIDI OUT jack. However, most MIDI interfaces will have multiple jacks (usually two to eight of each). Each pair of IN and OUT jacks is referred to as a *MIDI port*. You'll need to keep track of which device you have plugged into which port, because while Logic can detect that something is connected to any MIDI port, it's up to you to tell Logic what that device is and what it can do. This becomes especially important when you add devices or change the port to which they are connected. You can run into problems such as devices not being detected, or, if you select the wrong MIDI port, MIDI data being sent to the wrong devices.

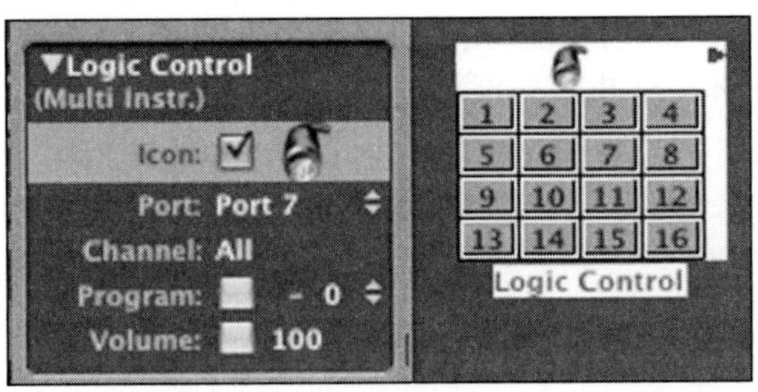

Figure 2.16

By looking at the Port setting in the parameter box of this MIDI Object, you can quickly determine that the device is connected to port 7 of the MIDI interface.

Every MIDI object in Logic has a parameter box; the second parameter (right under the Icon check box) is the Port setting. Figure 2.16 shows a MIDI Object in the Environment for a Logic control, with its port set to port 7.

If you change the MIDI ports to which your MIDI devices are connected, make sure that the Port settings of your MIDI objects are still accurate. While audio settings are global for all Logic songs, MIDI settings are song-specific, and may need to be updated. If you remove devices that are being sent MIDI data from Logic, be sure to set the MIDI port on those objects to the new device to which you'd like the signals sent. Keeping Logic properly up to date with what MIDI device is connected to which MIDI port is an essential part of setting up and maintaining your system.

Computer Setup

There are wonderful mailing lists on the Internet, as well as entire books dedicated to theories and advice regarding different methods of optimizing a computer system to be a digital media workstation. Far too much information is available to include here, but it is important to know a few basics about hard drives (and the role they play in recording audio) and about operating systems.

JOIN THE LUG!

I highly recommend joining the Logic Users Group (LUG), which is an international mailing list of Logic users. You can find its home page at http://groups.yahoo.com/groups/logic-users. The LUG is one of the largest mailing lists in existence, boasting a membership of over tens of thousands of users, and its members are very generous about helping fellow Logic users optimize their specific systems, as well as helping out with troubleshooting, usage tips, and advice.

Different Types of Hard Disks

All hard drives operate on the same principle: A set of needles read and write data on magnetic platters that spin around incredibly fast. The differences among the various types of hard drives are mainly in how fast these platters spin and what mechanism they use to connect to the rest of the computer.

Hard disks use two mainstream transfer mechanisms to communicate with the host computer: ATA (Advanced Technology Attachment) and SCSI (Small Computer Systems Interface). Both formats have different performance subcategories, such as SATA, ATA/66 or ATA/100, and SCSI-2 or SCSI-3. SCSI drives have higher top speeds, usually require an additional PCI or PCMCIA card that supports the SCSI protocol, and generally cost double or more the price of a similar-sized ATA drive. ATA is inexpensive, ubiquitous, and is supported internally by every desktop and notebook system designed since 1998.

Recording audio files to a hard drive can be a very disk-intensive task, and a faster hard drive can record and play back more simultaneous tracks. Most desktop and external hard drives these days spin at 7,200 RPM, which is fast enough to reliably handle songs with around 64 to 72 Audio Tracks, which should be more than enough for most people. Some older internal desktop hard drives run at only 5,400 RPM, and are capable of maybe half the track count of the faster drives, even though they spin at 75 percent of the speed. If you are using a desktop machine with a 5,400 RPM hard drive, you should consider replacing it with a faster drive. If you have a 7,200 RPM hard drive and still need more tracks, you can either record audio to two different hard drives or you can get a faster drive. These days, hard drives running up to 10,000 RPM are available, although they are expensive, and almost always require SCSI.

If you are using a laptop, your internal hard drive spins at either 4,200 RPM or 5,400 RPM, and you'll be lucky to see consistent performance above 24 tracks with your internal hard drive. For high-performance mobile use, you should consider using an external hard drive that runs at 7,200 RPM as your audio drive. Several external hard drives are available in USB or FireWire enclosures that offer plug-and-play connectivity to all notebook computers with those ports. If your notebook doesn't have USB or FireWire, you can also buy a PCMCIA card that will allow you to connect USB or FireWire devices.

Do You Need a Separate Hard Disk for Audio Files?

In general, the more that a hard drive has to do, the less performance it has left over for audio. In other words, if your hard drive needs to read system files as well as audio files, it needs to divide its attention and not focus on audio file performance. If you have a hard drive devoted to nothing but recording audio files, that hard drive could dedicate 100 percent of its performance to audio-related tasks.

Clearly, having a separate hard drive for audio seems advantageous, but is it absolutely necessary? The answer to this depends on how audio-intensive your projects are. Even a slower hard disk should be able to run both system software and approximately 16–24 tracks of audio. If your needs are modest, you really shouldn't need a separate hard drive for your Audio Tracks. On the other hand, professional studios that need to record anything from solo singers all the way to full orchestras often have entire banks of hard drives. If you regularly work with songs in excess of 24 tracks, or you can easily afford it, you should go ahead and buy a separate hard drive for audio files.

Once you have your hardware configured, you're ready to advance to a complete overview of Logic in the following chapter, "A Quick Tour of Logic Pro."

3 A Quick Tour of Logic Pro

Now that you have a basic understanding of what Logic can do and your hardware is installed and ready to go, it's time to start exploring. This chapter gives you a broad overview of the application, and the following chapters will delve into the details of the individual areas. At this point, don't worry if you look at the various windows in Logic Pro 7 and are left with all sorts of questions. As you proceed, I promise that it will become clear!

Terminology: Understanding Things Logic-ally

As you begin your examination of Logic, you should already be comfortable with some of the terms that are used in Logic to describe the most common functions and concepts. Of course, every sequencer uses its own terminology, and if you understand this, you'll find it far easier to comprehend the "logic" of the application, both figuratively and literally. Here are the key terms that you'll need to know to work with Logic effectively:

- **Object.** Chapter 1 defined objects, so refer to that discussion if you have questions. The term *object* can broadly apply to nearly anything graphically represented on your display, but in Logic, *object* specifically refers to a virtual studio building block in the Environment.
- **Audio File.** Audio files are just files on your computer that contain digital audio information. When you record digital audio into Logic, it saves an audio file on your hard drive. When you use Logic to manipulate audio data, that data will always originate from an audio file, whether it was initially recorded in Logic or not.

- **Apple Loop.** An Apple Loop is a special type of audio file. I will discuss Apple Loops in depth in Chapter 5, "Global Elements of Logic." But for now, Apple Loops have digital audio information that has been specifically "tagged" so that it will automatically play back at the correct time, and in the correct musical key, as your Logic song, regardless of the tempo or key the original audio was recorded in. Apple Loops may also contain MIDI and channel strip information, in addition to audio information.
- **Audio Region.** An Audio region is a graphical representation of a slice of audio from an audio file in the Audio window, Sample Editor, or Arrange window. An Audio region can be as long as the entire audio file in which it is located, or it may be only a few microseconds long. A single audio file can contain a virtually limitless number of Audio regions that can be contained in a single audio file, and any audio that is recorded or loaded into Logic always contains at least one Audio region that is, by default, the length of the entire audio file.
- **MIDI Region.** Similar to Audio regions, a MIDI region is a graphical representation of some MIDI data. Unlike Audio regions, however, MIDI regions are not necessarily related to any external information stored in a file on your hard disk. MIDI regions representing sections of MIDI data can be saved to files if you so choose, but they do not need to be stored anywhere but inside the Logic song file. If you do save a MIDI file to your hard disk, the MIDI data will still remain in the Logic song as well.
- **Event.** An *event* is a single occurrence of any MIDI message. This can be as simple as a single MIDI message such as a program change, or it can be a note message, which is actually a compound MIDI message consisting of multiple MIDI messages that are represented as a single MIDI event in Logic.
- **Track.** Audio and MIDI data are recorded into horizontal lanes in the Arrange window known as *tracks*. The term *tracks* is a holdover from the days of recording onto tape, where each separate strip of a tape recording was known as a track (so a stereo cassette would have two tracks, left and right, and an old eight-track tape had—you guessed it—eight tracks).

- **MIDI Channel.** This refers to one of the 16 channels that each MIDI port can transmit, or the All option. Every MIDI track is assigned to a MIDI channel, except in the case of the All option in which case the track itself is not assigned to a MIDI channel, but the individual messages are. You can have more than one MIDI track assigned to the same MIDI port and channel.
- **Audio Channel.** Every channel strip in the mixer is assigned to an Audio channel, and every Audio Track in the Arrange window has an Audio channel assigned to it. You can have more than one Audio Track assigned to the same Audio channel, but only one at a time can be playing sound.
- **Song.** A Logic song file contains information about all your editing, MIDI performances, mixing, and recording. It contains pretty much everything but the audio information, which is stored in separate files on disk, and the global preferences, which are stored in the Logic preference file in the System directory.
- **Project.** A project consists of the complete collection of Logic song files, as well as those related files, such as Audio Tracks, sampler instruments, effects presets, and so on, that are required by the song or songs that make up the project. Saving Logic songs as projects (you'll learn how to do that in Chapter 13, "Working with Files") is a great way to keep every necessary piece of data used in one place.

The Arrange Window

The Arrange page, as shown in Figure 3.1, is the first window you are presented with when you launch Logic. This is the main view in Logic, and in it you can create tracks, record audio and MIDI, slice up MIDI and Audio regions and rearrange them however your creativity dictates, and even edit most parts of a song.

The left side of the Arrange page contains a list of all your tracks, and then a parameter box and channel strip for the currently selected track. To the right of the track names are horizontal strips for each track that contains regions of audio or MIDI that are on that track. If you have Automation View on you will also see Track Automation data in a track lane, meaning that track contains some automation data.

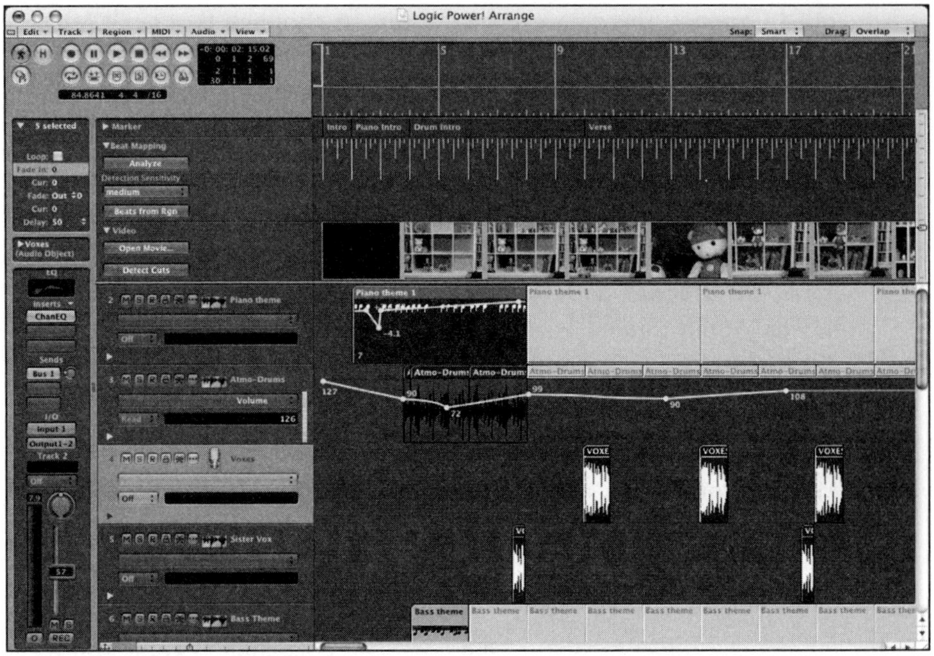

Figure 3.1

The Arrange page in Logic contains most of the commonly used arrangement and recording functions. (Video thumbnails ©Bar Ben-Yossef)

The transport buttons to activate recording can be in a floating window or at the top left, as in Figure 3.1, or both. The bar rule above the track strip displays the measures of the song, and the Song Position Line (SPL) is the vertical line you see at measure 1, bar 1; it shows your exact location. Also, any Global Tracks that you have activated will be above the track strip (Global Tracks are covered in Chapter 5). In Chapter 7, "The Arrange Window," you'll explore in depth all the possibilities that the Arrange window offers.

The Track Mixer

The Track Mixer contains a new channel strip for every Audio and MIDI track in the Arrange window. It instantly adapts to your current Arrange page, adding, deleting, and rearranging channel strips based on the state of the Arrange window. As you can see in Figure 3.2, the Track Mixer resembles a standard mixing desk, with a channel strip for each channel.

You can use the Track Mixer to mix the volume, panorama, routings, effects, and so on of the Audio and MIDI tracks in your song. You can move effects from one slot to another either within or between channel strips in the Track Mixer. You can choose to view only certain types of channels, all your

Figure 3.2

The Track Mixer automatically adjusts itself to reflect the audio and MIDI channels currently in your Arrange window.

Arrange channels, or every channel strip in your entire Environment. You can adjust single or multiple channel strips at the same time. Finally, you can print a final stereo or surround audio file of your entire song from the Track Mixer.

Using the Track Mixer to mix your song is explained further in Chapter 12, "Mixing in Logic."

The Environment

I've already defined the Environment (see Figure 3.3) briefly in Chapter 1. In this window, you can build a virtual representation of your studio. The Environment window also allows you to route external hardware with virtual processes and transformers. No other sequencer allows you to get under the hood to create unique devices and routings like Logic's Environment, but it will take time until you feel comfortable using this power.

Notice that the Environment window itself is just an expansive workspace, and that's exactly what the Environment offers you: an open surface on which to create your ideal studio. You'll learn about the Environment window in depth in Chapter 14, "The Environment." For now, let's just look at one more aspect of the Environment: layers.

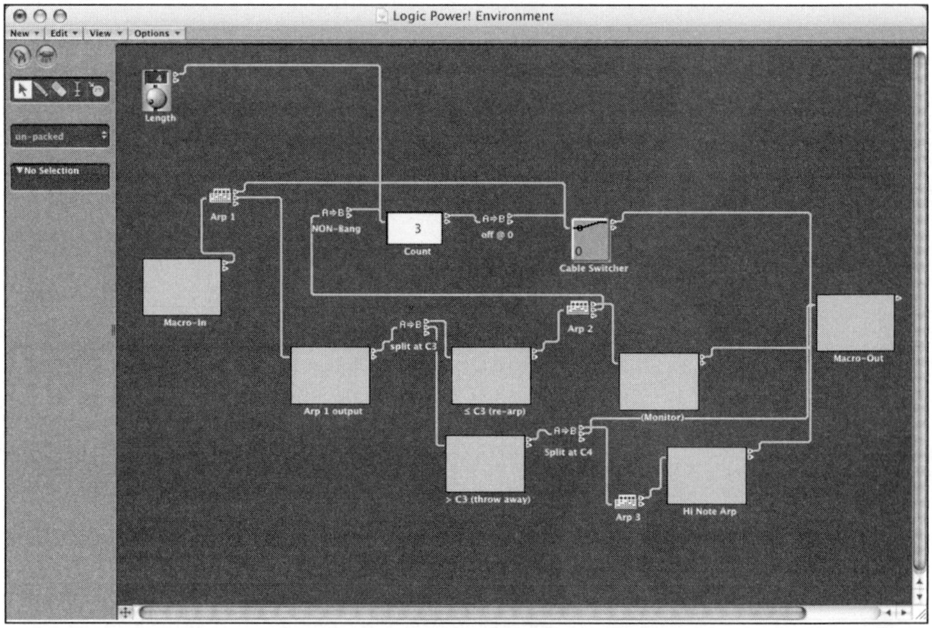

Figure 3.3

The Environment offers you nearly unlimited options for the construction of your own devices and routings inside Logic.

Environment Layers

Because the Environment offers nearly infinite routing possibilities, without some sort of organization the Environment window would quickly become an unmanageably large space in which you would find yourself scrolling constantly to get to any structure that you have created. To simplify and organize the Environment, Logic introduces the concept of Environment layers. Notice that the left frame of the Environment window in Figure 3.3 includes a box that features a layer name and a downward arrow—in the case of Figure 3.3, the layer is named "unpacked." That is the Environment layer pop-up menu, and, if you click it, Logic displays a menu that contains all the available layers in that song's Environment, as shown in Figure 3.4.

Layers allow you to organize your Environment into different levels, into which you can put as much or as little as you like, to keep each Environment construction easily accessible. Putting different objects on different layers doesn't affect the way Logic processes the signals, but it does allow you to organize the Environment into more manageable sections.

You'll notice that Logic includes a few Environment layers out of the box. There is a special one worth looking at here: the Audio Layer.

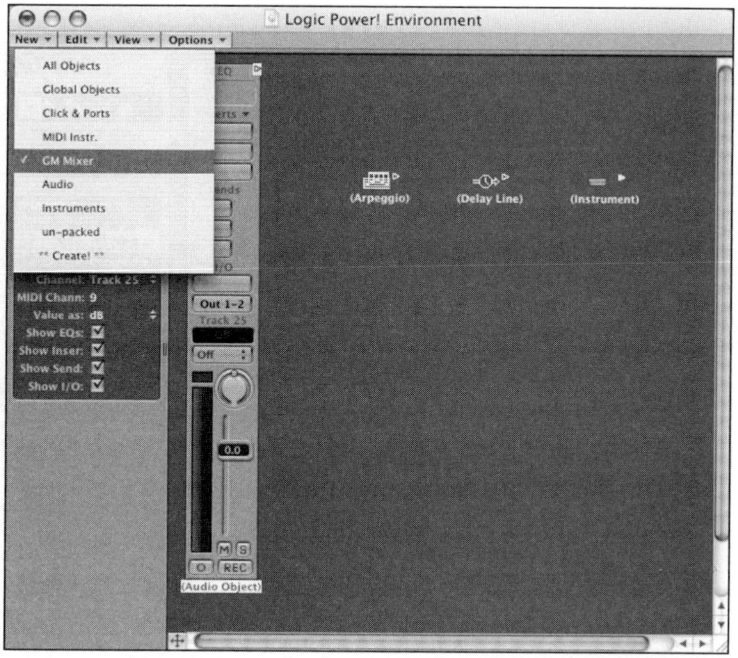

Figure 3.4

This pop-up menu shows all the different layers available in the Environment of this song and enables you to create new layers on the fly.

The Audio Layer

As the first two chapters explained, every Audio Object can expand to a channel strip. For your convenience, Logic automatically creates an Environment layer, called the Audio layer, that consists of every Audio Object that you have configured for your system (either manually or by using the Logic Setup Assistant). By placing all these objects in the Audio layer of the Environment, you keep the layer's contents separate from all the other layers in the Environment. You can access this layer from the Layer pop-up menu, or directly from the Audio menu in Logic by selecting **Audio > Audio Mixer**. Figure 3.5 shows an Audio Mixer for a newly created Logic song.

At first blush, this screen looks a lot like the Track Mixer shown in Figure 3.2, but the Audio Mixer in the Audio layer of the Environment only has Audio Objects and doesn't contain any MIDI channel strips. It also doesn't "adapt" to your Arrange window—it includes what you told it to include, nothing more, nothing less. You'll learn more about both mixers later; for now, you should just know you have a choice.

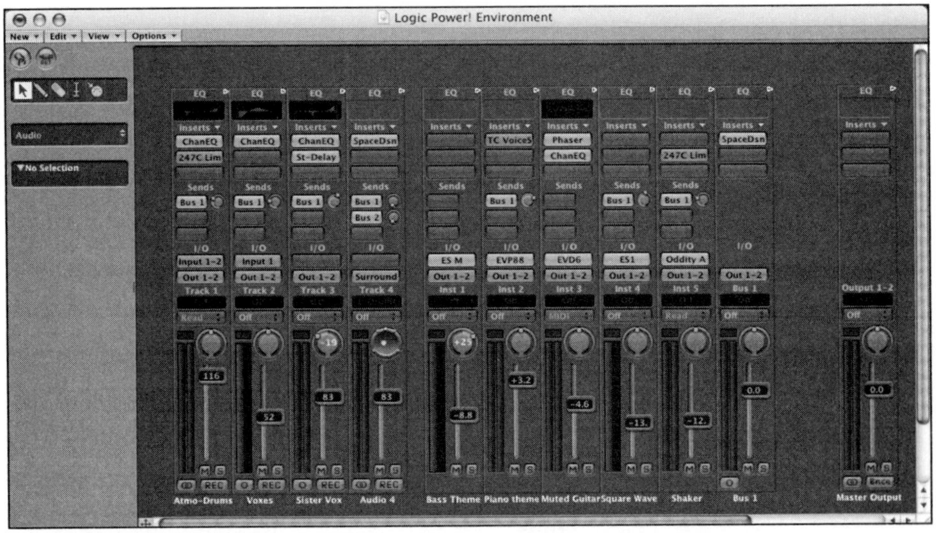

Figure 3.5
The Audio layer of the Environment contains the Audio Mixer, a complete mixer representing every audio channel and routing that you created for your default song.

The Audio Window

The Audio window is a catalog of all the Audio files and Audio regions used in a given Logic song. This window may look unassuming compared to some of the others, but don't be fooled—as you can see in Figure 3.6, the Audio window is far more than a simple list of Audio regions.

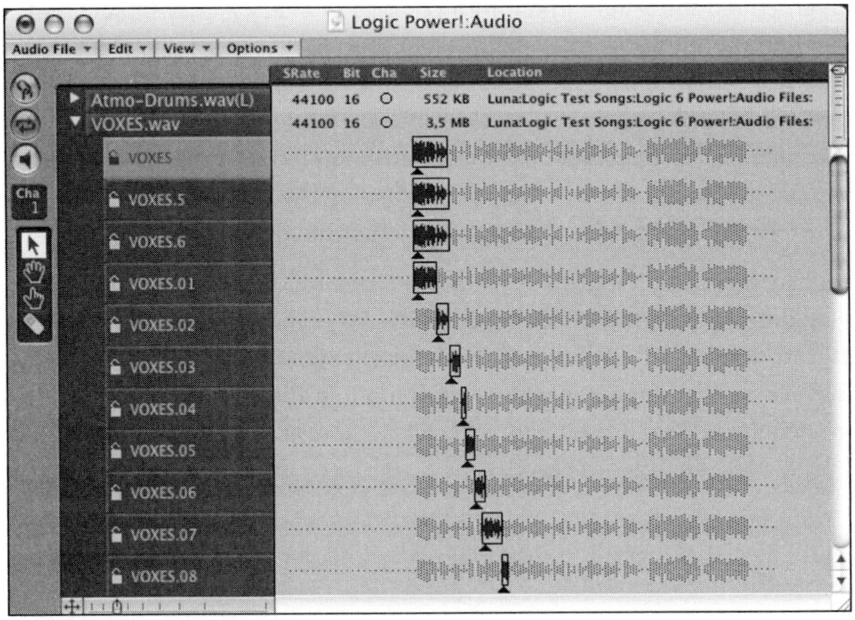

Figure 3.6
In the Audio window, you can add, subtract, loop, convert, and otherwise manipulate the audio files and regions in your Logic song.

Using the various tools and menu options in the Audio window, you can audition, group, adjust, and loop regions, as well as perform all sorts of file processes and conversions. You can also easily add Audio regions to your Arrange window by simply dragging regions from the Audio window. The Audio window is easily one of the most important areas in Logic when you are using audio in your songs, as you'll see in Chapter 8, "Working with Audio and Apple Loops."

The Matrix Editor

The Matrix Editor is a MIDI note editor that displays MIDI note events as horizontal bars across the screen. The Matrix Editor resembles a "piano roll" style of editor (so named because of its similarity to an old-time player piano song roll), with notes scrolling to the right of a graphic keyboard, as in Figure 3.7.

If you want to program and edit your MIDI notes graphically, the Matrix Editor is the place to do it. You not only can create and manipulate notes and control messages using the Matrix Editor, but you can also use its more advanced features, which are detailed in Chapter 9, "Working with MIDI."

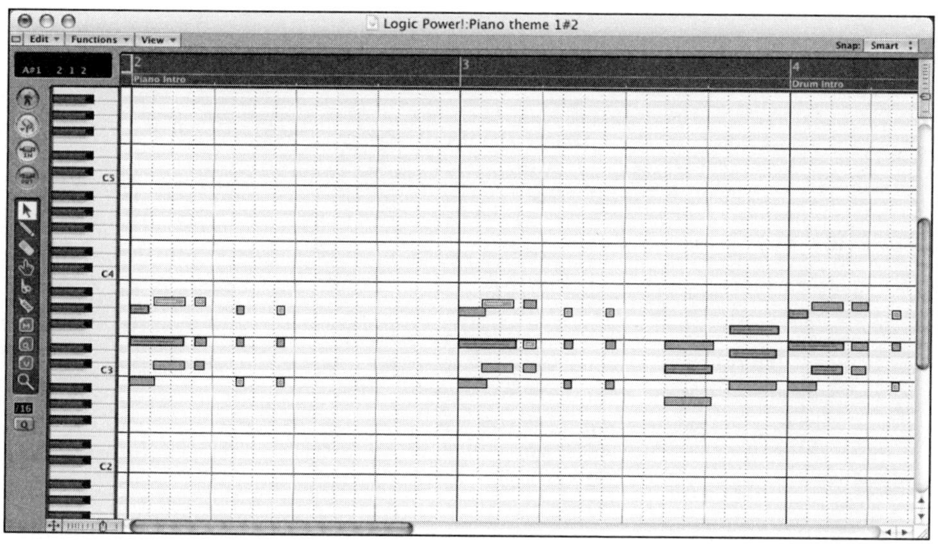

Figure 3.7
The Matrix Editor is just one of the powerful MIDI editors in Logic. It allows you to edit MIDI notes and controller values graphically.

The Event List

As you would imagine, the Event List gives you a detailed list of all the events for the selected window or region. If you are looking at the entire Arrange window, the Event List shows you what region is coming up next; if you're on a MIDI track, the Event List displays a detailed list of all the MIDI events in the track; and so on. Figure 3.8 shows an Event List of a MIDI track.

The Event List is not simply a textual view of information. It is a very powerful editor, offering you precise access to more parameters than any other editor. The Event List is also an excellent tool to use in tandem with the other editors. For example, you can use the Event List to give yourself a precise view of your data, while using another editor to operate on your song. You'll learn more about methods of using the Event List in Chapter 9.

The Hyper Editor

The Hyper Editor is one of the least understood editors in Logic. It is a controller editor, a drum editor, and a grid editor all in one. It allows you to save event definitions as hyper sets—or MIDI view filter templates if you will—and complements the other Logic editors very well. Figure 3.9 shows a Hyper Editor used to edit the MIDI controllers of a piano track.

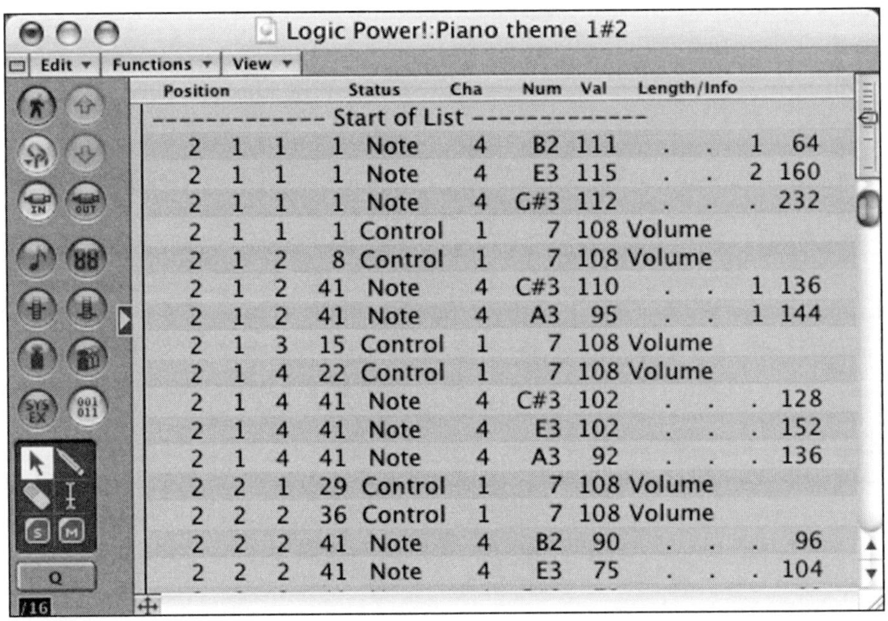

Figure 3.8

The Event List allows users to view and edit data in a text list.

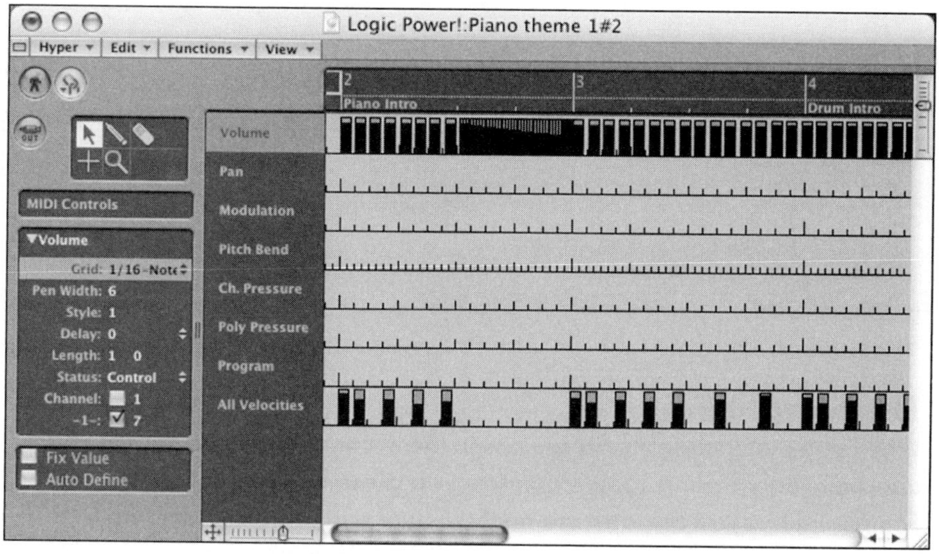

Figure 3.9

The Hyper Editor can be a grid editor, a drum editor, or a controller editor. Here, it's being used to edit the MIDI controller messages on a piano track.

Don't worry if the definition above seems a bit confusing right now. Chapter 9 will describe the many different uses for this powerful and often overlooked MIDI editor. The Hyper Editor may seem unusual at first, but its uniqueness and functionality are two of the advantages that set Logic apart from the pack.

The Score Editor

If you are comfortable working with musical notation, you will be comfortable with the Score Editor. Logic's Score Editor not only allows you to view, create, and edit MIDI as if you were writing on sheet music instead of a computer, but it allows you to print out professional-quality score charts as well. Figure 3.10 shows a piano part of a song displayed as musical notation in the Score Editor.

The Score Editor offers traditional musicians and composers complete access to the world of sequencing in a familiar format while being as customizable and powerful as the rest of Logic. The Score Editor of Logic is considered to be one of the best, if not the best, in the entire sequencing world, and when you learn about it in detail in Chapter 9, you'll be sure to agree!

Figure 3.10
The Score Editor allows you to create, view, edit, and print your MIDI tracks in musical notation.

The Sample Editor

When you manipulate Audio regions in the Arrange or Audio window, you are really only editing Logic's pointers to a given audio file. However, in the Sample Editor, you can operate on the actual audio file itself. Figure 3.11 shows a stereo audio file in the Sample Editor window.

To enable you to make the most accurate edits possible, the Sample Editor allows you to view and manipulate your audio with single-sample precision. The Sample Editor is also the location for many of the "destructive" (in other words, permanent) audio processing options. Chapter 8, "Working with Audio and Apple Loops," will give you more explanation on how to use this editor.

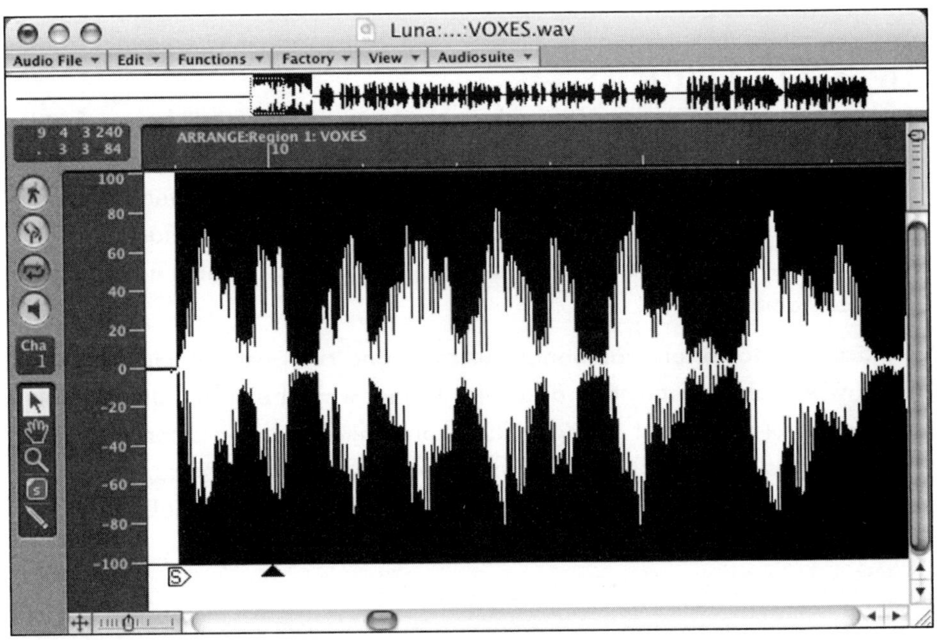

Figure 3.11
The Sample Editor allows you to process and edit an audio file and offers amazingly precise resolution and editing tools.

The Transform Window

The Transform window allows you to alter events according to definable parameters. If that sounds confusing to you, you're not alone—the Transform window is definitely complicated. To give you a quick example of a use for the Transform window, if you wanted to change all the D# notes in a given track to F# without manually editing the notes, you could quickly perform that action in the Transform window, as shown in Figure 3.12.

You can design your own transformations, using amazingly complex data manipulations involving multiple criteria and data mapping, or use the transformations that Emagic includes for you with Logic. If all that sounds difficult, don't worry; Chapter 9 explains this feature in detail.

The Key Commands Window

Every program allows you to access its features through keyboard shortcuts in addition to selecting commands with the mouse—this is nothing new. But Logic makes more extensive use of key commands than most applications. In fact, the Key Commands window by itself offers many more options than most applications, as you can see in Figure 3.13.

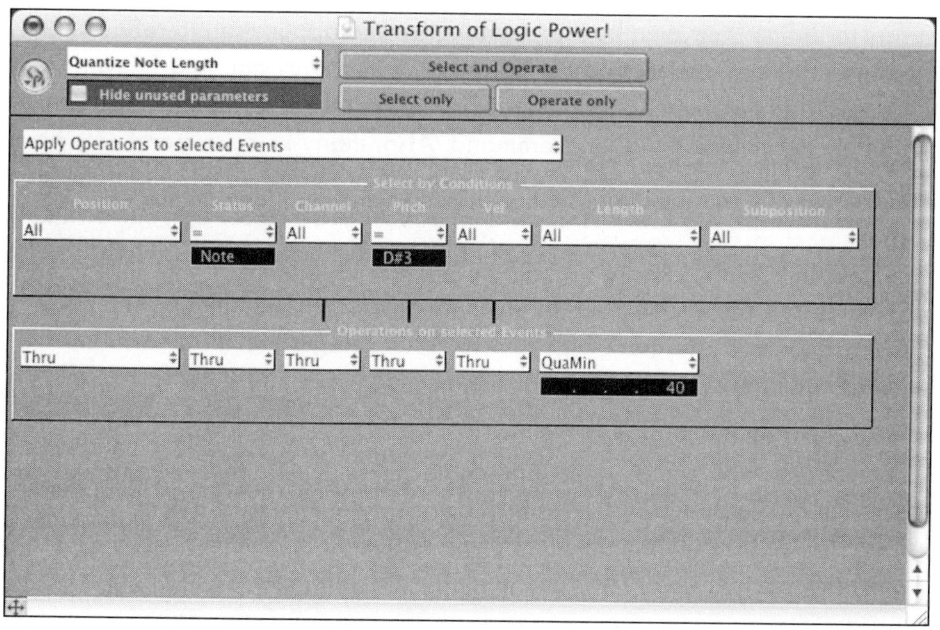

Figure 3.12

The Transform window is powerful enough to make complex global data transformations based on a custom set of criteria. You can also use it to make relatively uncomplicated changes, such as the simple note transposition here.

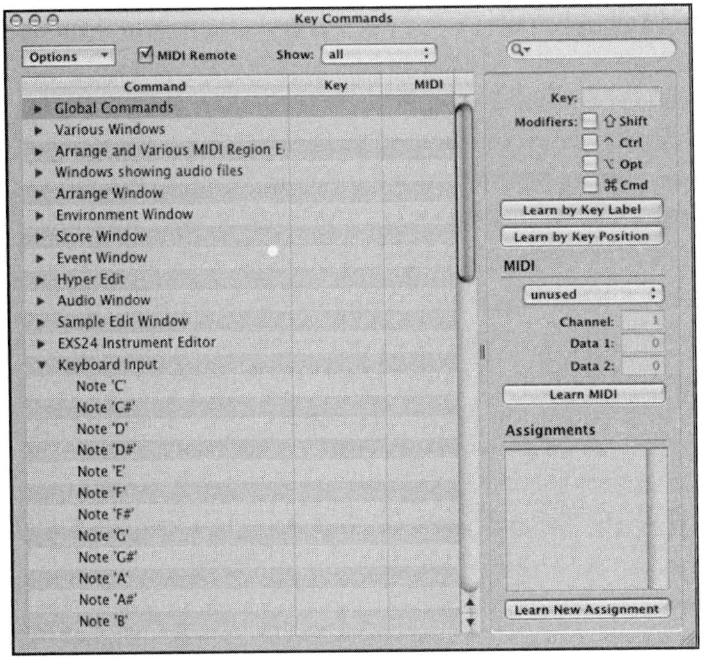

Figure 3.13

Key commands are an integral part of Logic, as you can see by the features of the Key Commands window and the number of commands that are available only as key commands.

For most users, accessing functions via key commands is much quicker than using the mouse, so most professional applications offer a vast selection of their functions via key commands. The more flexible applications often allow users to define their own keys to personalize the application to reflect their preferences. Logic takes this a step further, as not only can nearly every feature be accessed via a key command, but in fact many commands in Logic can *only* be accessed via key command. Also, many key-command-only functions do not come with those commands preassigned to keys, so to access such commands, the user first must define them. How to set up your own key commands in Logic is discussed in the following chapter.

It might seem counterintuitive for some commands to only be available via key commands, fueling Logic's reputation for being difficult to learn. In truth, it is for ease of use that some of the advanced, expert features are available only via key commands. Rather than crowd each menu with commands that most people would never use, Logic makes the least accessed and most obscure functions available for those who need them, but keeps them out of the way of everyone else.

The Loop Browser

As discussed earlier in this chapter, Apple Loops are a special kind of audio file. To help distinguish them from the normal audio files in your Audio window, Apple Loops get their own special browser, as shown in Figure 3.14.

The Loop Browser allows you to quickly search, audition, and drag loops into your song. Apple Loops that you buy and drag onto the Loop Browser window will automatically be indexed with the rest of your Apple Loops. You can index Apple Loops that you create however you choose to. Other types of loops, such as ACID loops, may be accessible through the Loop Browser, but will not be indexed as well as Apple Loops.

Screensets

Most sequencers allow you to arrange the various windows and editors on screen and save these screen formats. As with key commands, however, Logic takes the concept and runs with it, in its own uniquely powerful ways. Screensets are not simply an available option in Logic; they are an integral part of how you use the application. Notice that a number appears in the

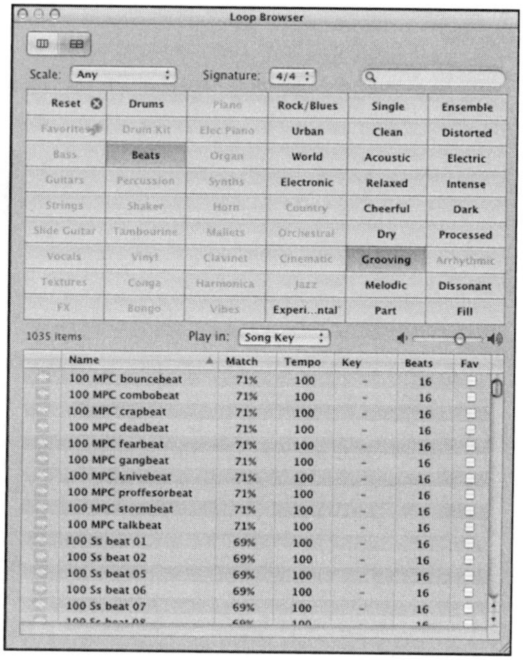

Figure 3.14

The Loop Browser lets you quickly locate and audition Apple Loops, as well as certain other types of loops such as ACID loops.

menu bar of Logic, as shown in Figure 3.15. This number (4 in Figure 3.15) indicates the designated number of the screenset that you are currently accessing. You can access up to 99 screensets directly from the numeric keypad, and access additional screensets from the Next Screenset and Previous Screenset key commands. As you open, close, and move windows around, Logic automatically remembers them, and the next time you launch your Logic song, it will automatically have the same windows, open in the same location, in each screenset.

Setting up your screensets helps you create your own ideal workspace and is one of the ways in which Logic is unique—allowing every user to customize Logic to suit that individual user. In fact, setting up screensets is one of the first things you'll want to do as you customize Logic for yourself, as you will see in the next chapter.

And speaking of customizing Logic to suit your needs, now that you have an idea of the possibilities of Logic, it's time to set up your Autoload (or default) song template. The next chapter, "Creating Your Autoload Song," will explain how.

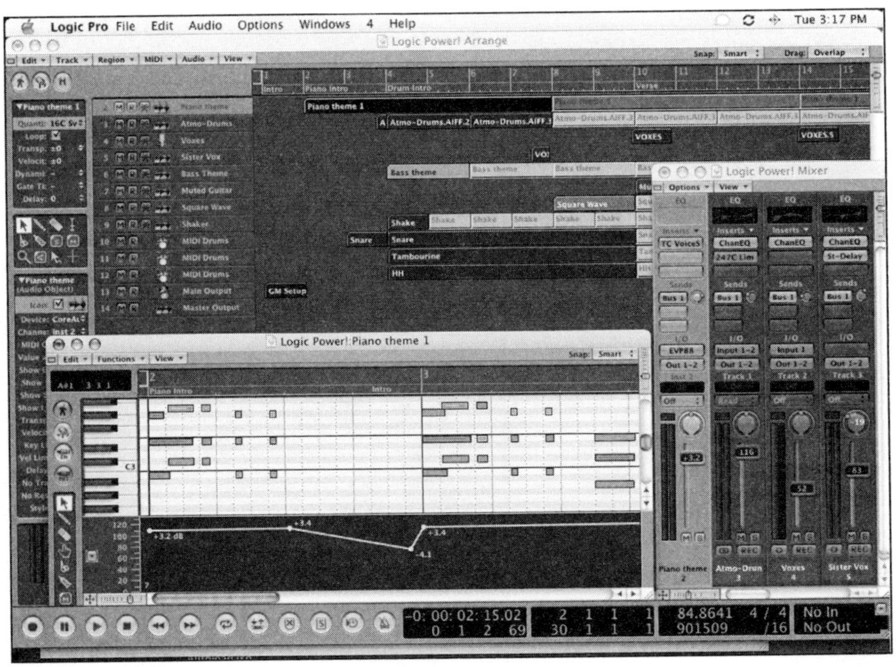

Figure 3.15
Screensets are not an afterthought or a hidden option in Logic. The active screenset is prominently displayed in Logic's menu bar. Here the menu bar shows that screenset 4 is active.

4 Creating Your Autoload Song

An important distinction between Logic and other music workstation applications is just how much information is stored in each document file (which is called a *song* in Logic). In most applications, you set up the *application* the way you want to by arranging windows, toolbars, and so on. When you load a document, that document uses the *application* configuration. In Logic, the *song* contains everything about your studio—the setup of all your instruments, editors, windows, screensets, and everything else that is configurable in Logic. In fact, each song in Logic is a self-contained virtual studio. This means that if you create a song on your copy of Logic, then open it on someone else's copy of Logic, you will still find your own familiar virtual studio waiting for you; you won't need to acclimate to any changes in visual arrangement at all!

When you launch Logic for the first time, it automatically presents you with an empty song that reflects Logic's default settings. These default settings represent Emagic's effort to provide a ready-made song setup that most people will find generally useful. This song is called (not surprisingly) the *default song*. It is not saved on your hard drive anywhere; it is simply generated automatically based on how you directed the Logic Setup Assistant to set it up (if you never ran the LSA, a default song is still provided).

The default song is a perfectly reasonable place to start—it will give you a usable configuration of Audio Objects, and as many MIDI Objects as you have configured in the LSA. You'll instantly be able to switch between screensets to access the various editors and windows. The default song is designed to enable you to start making music immediately.

While acceptable, the default song isn't ideal. It doesn't represent exactly how you want to work, the editors that you want to use, or the precise instrument routings that you want in your virtual studio. Logic Pro 7 introduces another feature that will help you create songs that more specifically meet your needs, called *templates*. Templates are blank songs with a specific configuration that you might want to start from. Templates are stored in the Application Support folder for Logic, which you can find at the following path: ~/Library/Application Support/Logic/Song Templates. I'll go over templates in depth in Chapter 13, "Working with Files." This chapter is going to deal with one special template, called the *Autoload*.

For all but one template, you need to select **File > New** in Logic to open that template. Logic, however, allows you to create one custom template that will automatically open every time you launch Logic. This song is named the *Autoload*, since it *auto*matically *load*s every time you launch Logic. With this song, you can have Logic immediately open into your personal virtual studio instead of a general default song. Trust me on this: *Creating your Autoload song is one of the most important things that you will do in Logic!*

The actual mechanics involved in creating an Autoload song couldn't be simpler: You set up a Logic song, name it Autoload, and save it into ~/Library/Application Support/Logic/Song Templates. Exactly how you set up the Autoload song, however, takes some serious thought and preparation. Creating your Autoload song is a continuous process. As you learn more about Logic and your working preferences, you can always go back and change your Autoload song accordingly. To get you started, here are a few points that you need to consider.

Visualizing Your Workspace

The first and most important aspect of creating your Autoload song is to have a general idea of what aspects of the program you'll want to access. Chapter 3 gave you an overview of some of the windows and editors in Logic. Did you already get a sense of which ones you expect to use the most? Do you imagine yourself needing the Arrange window and Audio window all the time, the Matrix Editor a little, and the Score Editor not at all? Or do you imagine that your most important windows will be the Score Editor and Event List, and then Arrange and Track Mixer? Do you need to access Environment Objects creatively for each composition? You don't need to know how to use all the windows and editors yet—that's what the rest of the book is for. For now, consider how you might want to work, and which windows you'll want to have readily available.

Next, consider how much screen real estate you have. Do you have dual 23-inch screens, so that you can spread out nearly everything you'll need at once? Or are you making do with a 12-inch laptop screen? Do you like to squeeze in multiple program windows on the screen at one time, or do you like to give each program window as much room as you can? Luckily, Logic's screensets allow you to build your Autoload to fit any of these configurations; all you need to have is a general idea of where you'd like to start.

Remember, the core idea behind Logic is to be as configurable as possible to allow you the flexibility to create your own ideal workspace. If you have an image of what the makeup of that ideal space will be, then it will be that much easier to create it. The name of the game here is experimentation—if you're not sure you'll have enough room, open the editor or window you have in mind, resize it as much as possible, move it around, and see how it feels to use it in that size and position. When you're comfortable with Logic, rearranging your Autoload will be as simple as opening the application, placing the window you need in the screenset you desire, perhaps locking the screenset (explained later in this chapter in the section "Setting Up Screensets"), and resaving the song. For now, with just what has already been discussed and a bit of careful planning, you can already set up an almost optimal Autoload song.

Creating Your Initial Environment

If your Autoload is your virtual studio, then your Autoload's Environment window is where the objects that represent that studio reside. In other words, if you want to create a track in the Arrange window that uses a given MIDI Instrument, that MIDI Instrument will be available in the Arrange window only if it has already been created in the Environment. The Logic Setup Assistant might have created objects in the Environment for you, but if you didn't use the LSA, or you have added some MIDI devices afterward, you may need to create objects in the Environment for all the MIDI, audio, and internal routings that you'll need. Personally, I like my Autoload Environment to include every object possible, so that I don't have to go back and create any later. Creating objects in the Environment is easy, once you know how.

You create all types of objects by opening up your Environment window and pulling down the **New** local menu, as shown in Figure 4.1. As you can see, this menu offers all the various types of Environment Objects that you can create. The following sections describe the most common Environment Objects for your Autoload song.

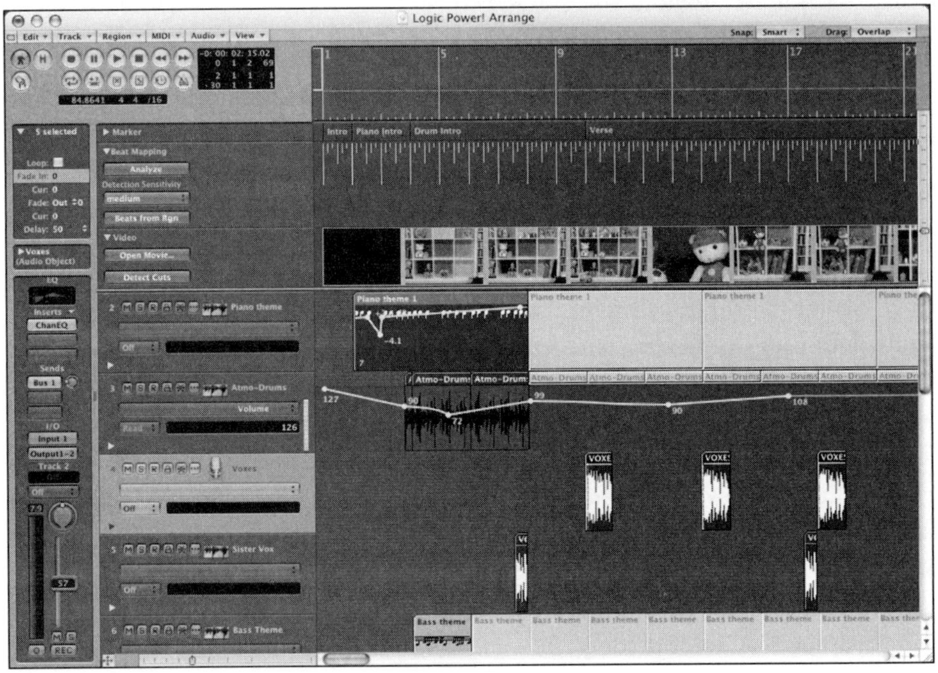

Figure 4.1

Here you see the New local menu of the Environment window pulled down, and all the different Environment Objects that you can create.

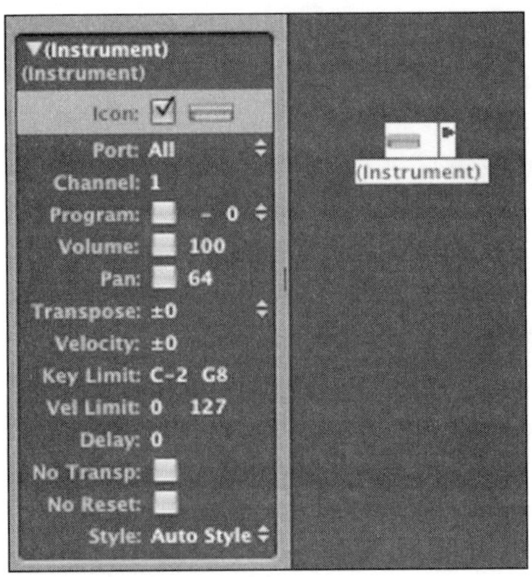

Figure 4.2

An Instrument Object with its parameter box.

Setting Up Instrument Objects

The Instrument Object represents a simple MIDI device that plays on only one MIDI channel. You create this object by selecting **New > Instrument**, and you'll see the icon for an instrument in your current Environment layer. Figure 4.2 shows a newly created Instrument Object and its parameter box.

You might notice that some objects in the Environment are cabled to other objects. Don't worry about cabling the new instrument to anything for now. Cabling isn't required for the instrument to automatically appear in the hierarchal menu of MIDI Instruments in your Arrange window. However, you should set a few of its parameters immediately:

- **Instrument name.** First, you should give your new instrument a name. Simply click on *(Instrument)* to the right of the triangle, and Logic displays a text entry box in which you can type the new name.
- **Icon.** Selecting an appropriate icon isn't really important, but the added visual cue of an icon can help you visualize your device, and you might as well take care of this while creating the object. If you click and hold down the mouse button on the small picture next to Icon, a large pop-up menu appears with small picture options. Find one that represents your device in some way (for example, if it's a keyboard, you can use a synth image; if it's a drum machine, a module image, and so on). The check box to the right of the image determines whether the instrument will appear in the Arrange window hierarchal list or not. *Always make sure this box is checked*, since you'll want your instruments to be available to you in the Arrange window.
- **Port.** You'll also want to make sure your instrument is set to the correct port. Click the number (or it might be the word All, as in Figure 4.2) next to the Port parameter, and you'll see a list of all your available MIDI ports. Choose the one to which your device is connected, as in Figure 4.2.
- **Channel.** If your device is only capable of operating on a single MIDI channel, or if your instrument represents only a single patch on a synth, you want to be sure to select that channel in the Cha parameter. Click the number next to Channel and select the proper MIDI Channel, from 1 to 16. If you want the notes in your MIDI regions to determine the MIDI Channel, set the channel parameter to All.

The rest of the options in the Instrument parameter box are performance parameters. If you already know how you want to set them, feel free to do so now. If you plan to change these parameters only after you actually create a track and use the instrument in a song, then you're finished and ready to move on. But to be thorough, take a brief look at the rest of the parameters:

- **Program.** Check this box and select a program number between 0 and 127 if you want this instrument to always select a specific patch in your MIDI device.
- **Volume.** Check this box and select a MIDI volume level between 0 and 127 if you want this instrument to always set your MIDI device to a specific volume.
- **Pan.** Check this box and select a MIDI pan value between 0 and 127 if you want this instrument to always pan your MIDI device to a specific point in the stereo field. A value of 64 is centered, values 63 and below will pan the instrument left, values 65 and above will pan the instrument right.
- **Transpose.** If you enter a value here, every time you play this MIDI device, Logic will automatically transpose the note it sends the device up or down by the amount you specified. You can either double-click in the space to the right of Transpose to display a text box, or drag the mouse up or down to add or subtract up to 96 steps (a full eight octaves!) from the original value in single-step (half-note) increments.
- **Velocity.** If you enter a value here, every time you play this MIDI device, Logic will automatically increase or reduce the velocity of the MIDI note it sends to the device by this value. You can click to the right of Velocity to display a text box, or drag the mouse up or down to increase or reduce the velocity of the MIDI note by up to 99 steps. (MIDI values are represented from 0 to 127, which is nearly the entire velocity range.)
- **Key Limit.** This parameter sets the upper- and lower-note boundaries of the instrument. You can use this parameter to make certain that you do not send a given device a note outside of its range, or to reduce artificially the range of the notes you choose to send a device. (So, for example, even if a piano module device were physically capable of reproducing notes outside the range of a piano, you might want to limit the notes to a piano's physical range to ensure a realistic piano sound.) As with the previous two parameters, you can either double-click on each value to display a text box or click and hold on the value to use the mouse to raise or lower the values.

- **Vel Limit.** This parameter sets up the upper and lower velocity boundaries of the instrument. As with the previously discussed parameters, you can double-click on each value to display a text box, or click and hold on the value to use the mouse to raise or lower the values.
- **Delay.** The term *delay* has many meanings in a musical (and even in a MIDI-related) context. In this context, it warrants further explanation. Basically, this delay parameter allows you to send MIDI information to this device either early or late, depending on the setting. This parameter is not a "MIDI echo" that allows you to create doubling or echo effects that are also often called *delay*. This parameter only adjusts the point at which Logic will commence sending data to your instrument. Why would you want the ability to send data early or late? Some devices process information more slowly than others, or you might need to account for other delays in your system, for example. You can double-click in the space to the right of Delay, or click and hold the mouse to raise or lower the value between –99 and +99 ticks (a *tick* is the smallest amount of distance possible on the Arrange window's time ruler).
- **No Transp.** If you check this box, the instrument is set to No Transpose. This means that even if you are transposing all MIDI tracks globally or with the Transpose setting in the region parameter box (which is discussed in Chapter 7, "The Arrange Window"), the process will not affect this instrument. This check box is especially valuable for percussion tracks, where transposing notes often results in selecting completely different sounds.
- **No Reset.** If you check this box, this instrument will not respond to MIDI Reset messages, such as Mod Wheel and Pitchbend resets, even if they are sent to all devices.
- **Style.** This parameter is set to Auto Style by default. If you click and hold the up/down arrows to the right of the parameter name, Logic displays a pop-up list of all the available default Score Editor styles. In the Auto Style, Logic picks an appropriate style based on the pitch range of the notes on the track. If you do not use the Score Editor, you can ignore this parameter.

Setting Up Multi-Instruments

A *multi-instrument*, or multitimbral instrument, is an instrument that can play sounds on up to 16 MIDI Channels simultaneously. You create a Multi-Instrument Object by choosing **New > Multi-Instrument**. When you first create a Multi-Instrument Object, you'll see the object and parameter box shown in Figure 4.3. The first thing you'll notice is that the parameters available are identical to the first six parameters in the Instrument Object as shown in Figure 4.2. These parameters have the same definition and function in a multi-instrument as they do an instrument. Typically, you will leave the global Channel parameter set to All so that the multi-instrument can send and receive MIDI on all channels.

After you have set parameters for the Multi-Instrument Object as a whole, it's time to activate its individual subchannels. All 16 boxes in the multi-instrument parameter box have lines through them because every subchannel is turned off by default. You'll want to activate as many subchannels as your instrument supports; for example, if your synth is eight-part multitimbral, you'll activate eight subchannels in the multi-instrument by clicking on them. Figure 4.4 shows the Multi-Instrument Object after you have activated some subchannels.

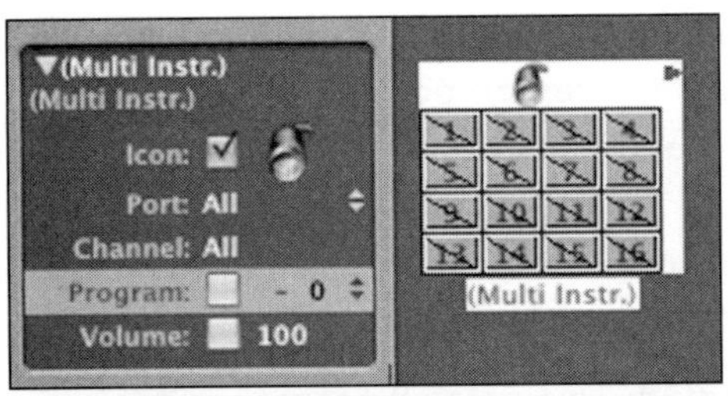

Figure 4.3
A Multi-Instrument Object and its parameter box.

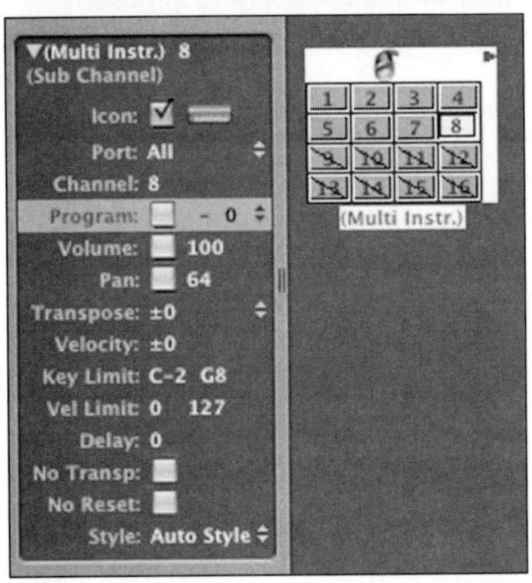

Figure 4.4
A Multi-Instrument Object once eight subchannels have been activated. The parameter box shown is the unique parameter box for subchannel 8.

Notice that each subchannel has its own on/off toggle and associated parameter box, and that each parameter box is identical to that of the Instrument Object parameter box previously discussed. This is because each subchannel of a multi-instrument is basically a unique single-channel MIDI Instrument. So while you get a set of six "general" parameters for the entire MIDI Instrument, you might want each subchannel to be completely unique. If you already know how you want to set up your subchannels, go ahead and set the parameter boxes as you activate the channels. Be careful about setting a global port value, however, as it applies to the entire multi-instrument.

The Multi-Instrument Window

The other window that you can access from a Multi-Instrument Object is called the Multi-Instrument window. If you double-click any Multi-Instrument Object, Logic displays the window shown in Figure 4.5. Here you can set up the banks and patch names of your multi-instrument.

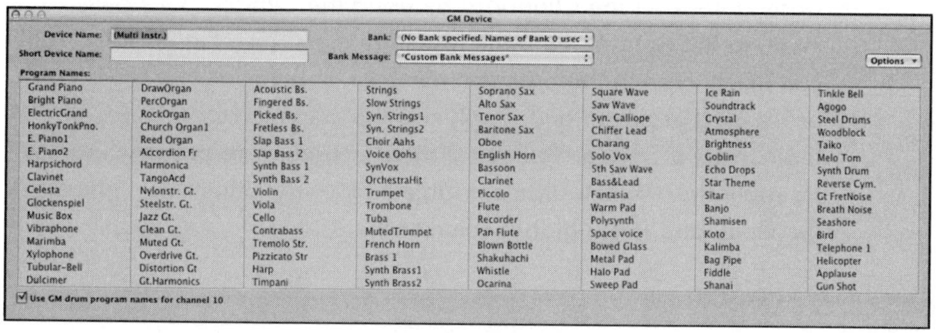

Figure 4.5

A Multi-Instrument window of a Multi-Instrument Object.

You can set several parameters in this window:

- **Device Name and Short Device Name.** The device name is simply the name of your Multi-Instrument Object. You should have already named your multi-instrument, and that name should already appear in the Device Name box. In the Short Device Name box, you can type in a short abbreviation of the instrument name that will appear in the Arrange window track list when a multi-instrument's program name is also being displayed.
- **Bank Select Menu.** This pull-down menu allows you to select among banks of patches on your MIDI device. Each Multi-Instrument Object allows up to 15 banks, numbered 0–14. If you choose bank 1–14, Logic asks whether you want to initialize the bank. If you want to enter your own bank names, then press Enter. If you want to use the

generic General MIDI names from bank 0, click Cancel. In general, unless your instrument is specifically a General MIDI device, you'll want to input your own names.

- **Bank Message Menu.** This pull-down menu allows you to select among different MIDI messages that will be sent to your MIDI device when you switch banks. Different manufacturers and devices use different messages to switch banks, so you need to consult your MIDI device's documentation to see which selection is appropriate for each device.
- **Program Names.** You'll notice that 128 program names are visible in the Multi-Instrument window for each bank. You can enter the specific names for the various programs of your device here. You can do this a number of ways:
  - Double-click on each program name one by one, and manually type in the new program name in the text boxes that appear.
  - Copy data from the Clipboard by using the Options pull-down menu to the right of the Bank Message menu (see Figure 4.6). You can easily type in the program numbers and names into a word processing program and simply use the menu to copy them all to the correct program. You can also copy and paste program names from another Multi-Instrument Object by using either this menu or the Copy and Paste global commands.

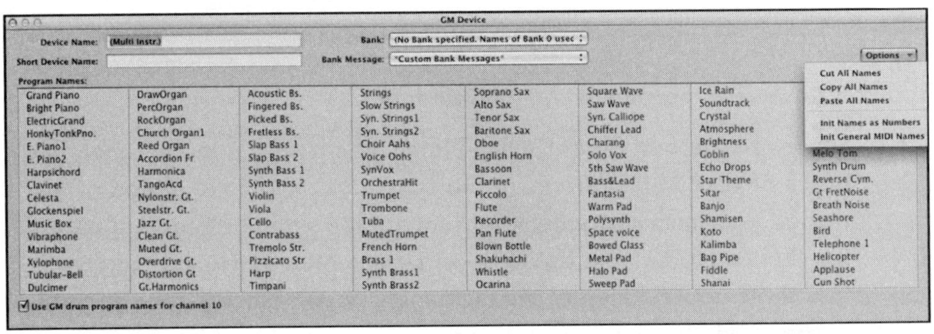

Figure 4.6

The Text Import menu of the Multi-Instrument window.

  - If you just want program numbers instead of names, select **Options > Init Names as Numbers**.
  - If you wish to use General MIDI program names, select **Options > Init General MIDI Names**.

- **Use GM Drum Names for Channel 10.** In General MIDI devices, channel 10 is reserved for drums. The General MIDI drum kit also contains a standard set of drum kits. If you check this box, Logic automatically uses the standard drum set names for subchannel 10.

> **EXPERT TIP: CREATE MULTI-INSTRUMENT OBJECTS FOR ALL YOUR MIDI SYNTHS**
>
> The best part about customizing the program names for your Multi-Instrument Object is that if you select it in a track in the Arrange window and your track lane has enough room, it will display the actual track name. Also, if you have the Prg button (one of the performance parameters in the instrument parameter box mentioned but not detailed above) checked for that subchannel, you can send your device program changes from the Arrange window by clicking on program names (and scroll through your synth's programs by scrolling through the program names on the Arrange window). Because you have all the names typed in, you can send changes by name rather than number. For this reason, even for mono synths that are not multitimbral, you should seriously consider using a Multi-Instrument Object for the device and only activating one subchannel. This might seem like overkill, but it conveniently enables you to customize patch names, which is worth the minimal additional effort.
>
> So does this mean that the Instrument Object is practically useless? Not at all.

Setting Up Mapped Instruments

Mapped instruments are a different sort of object than either Instrument or Multi-Instrument Objects. Mapped instruments allow settings to be specifically defined, or *mapped*, for every note in the instrument; this means that with a mapped instrument, you may

- Name the notes.
- Map notes to sounds in MIDI sound sources. (You can even map multiple sound sources to the same note, or different notes to the same sound source.)
- Assign each note its own MIDI channel.
- Send each note to its own output cable.
- Give each note its own musical notation parameters such as note head shape, relative vertical position in the staff, and drum group assignment.

As you've probably guessed, Mapped Instrument Objects are most often used with drum kits, where each MIDI note represents a different drum sound, and you might even play a complete kit across different MIDI devices (if you are constructing a single drum kit from drum sounds scattered among several synthesizers, for example). You can create a mapped instrument by selecting **New > Mapped Instrument** in the Environment window. Logic then displays the icon and parameter box shown in Figure 4.7. Logic also automatically opens the Mapped Instrument window, which is discussed further on.

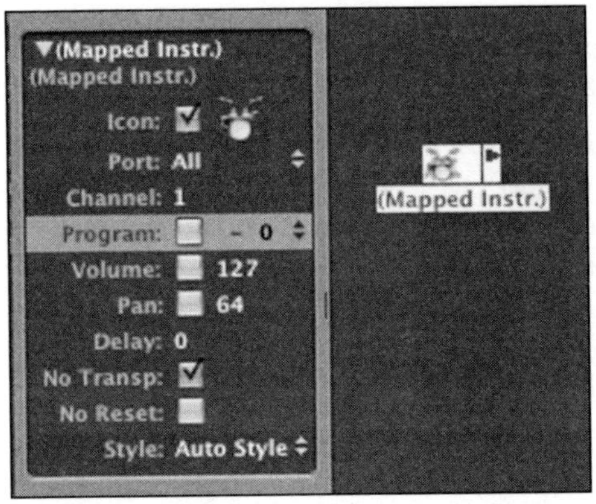

Figure 4.7
A Mapped Instrument Object and its parameter box.

Notice that a mapped instrument has the exact same parameters as a subchannel of a Multi-Instrument Object, except for those parameters relating to the notes themselves: Transpose, Velocity, Key Limit, and Vel Limit. That's because these missing parameters are set for each note of the mapped instrument, and not the object as a whole. When you are ready to continue with your setup, click into the Mapped Instrument window shown in Figure 4.8. This is where you do the main work of defining the Mapped Instrument Object.

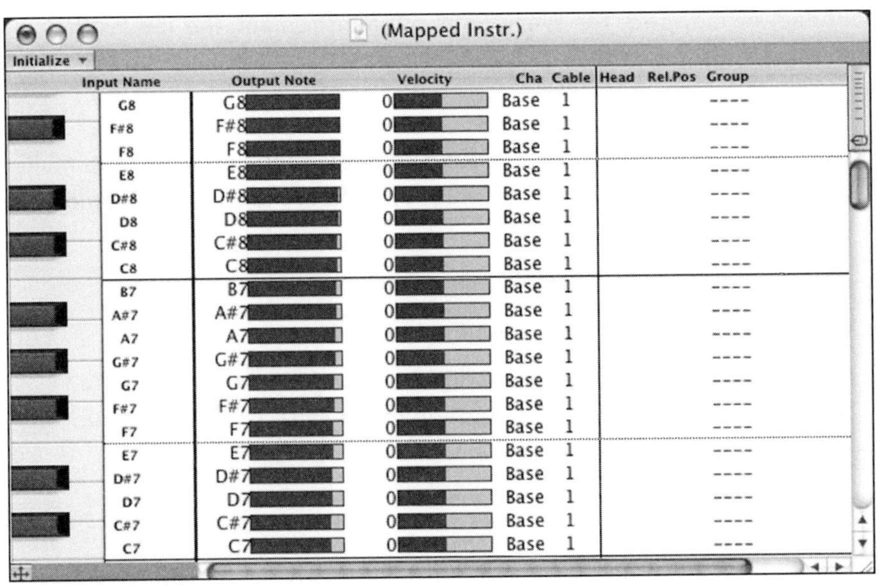

Figure 4.8
The Mapped Instrument window presents the majority of the settings for Mapped Instrument Objects.

The first thing you'll notice is the graphic keyboard at the left of the Mapped Instrument window. The notes on these keys represent the input notes, meaning the notes that you play from a controller that are received by the mapped instrument. You can play this keyboard by clicking on a note, or you can select a range of notes by dragging the mouse across the desired notes. To add notes to an existing range, hold the Shift key down while clicking on the desired notes. When you select multiple notes, any value changes you make (for example, adding a step to the first note) will be made to the entire range (so all the notes you selected will then increase by one step). Directly above the keyboard, you'll notice that the Mapped Instrument window has its own local menu, the Initialize menu, as shown in Figure 4.9.

The explanations of the various columns in the Mapped Instrument window also detail the functions of the various menu items in the Initialize local menu:

- **Input Name.** This is where you can name your note. For example, you could name the note G8 Piccolo Snare to represent the drum sound that G8 triggers, and so on. You can also reset all the names back to the default note pitch by selecting **Initialize > Names as Note**. If you want to assign the General MIDI drum names to notes, you can select **Initialize > Names as General MIDI**.

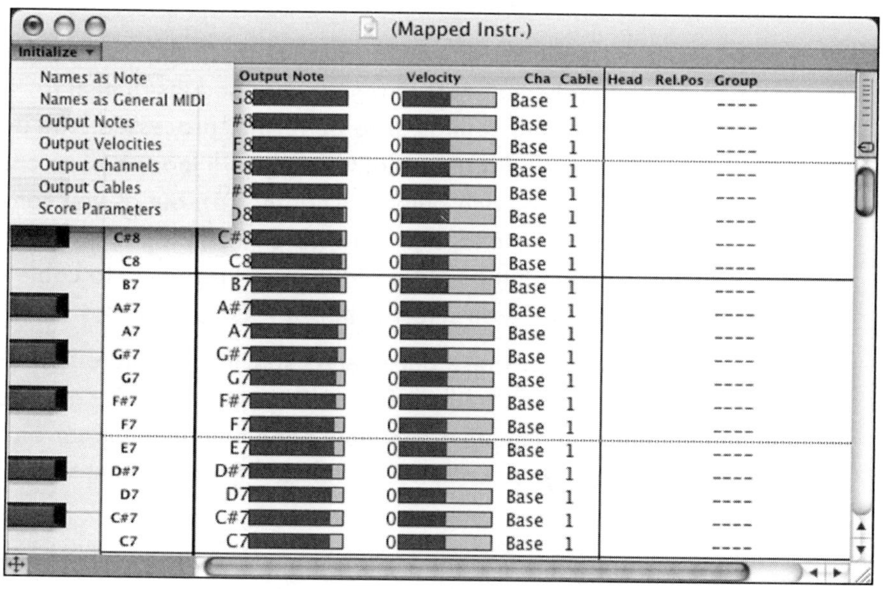

Figure 4.9

The Initialize local menu of the Mapped Instrument window.

- **Output Note.** Here you can set the output note independently, so it can actually be different from the input note. For example, if you are playing a drum controller that sends out a C#3 when you hit a particular pad, but you want that pad to trigger the drum sound located in your sound module at G#5, you could set the output note of C#3 in your mapped instrument to G#5. You can quickly return all the output note assignments to the same as the input notes by selecting **Initialize > Output Notes**.
- **Velocity.** This is the same as the velocity adjustment for Instrument Objects. You can grab the beam with the mouse by clicking on it and dragging it, add or subtract from the offset value by dragging, or you can simply click inside the beam at the desired point. You can quickly reset all offsets to zero by selecting **Initialize > Output Velocities**.
- **Cha.** In this column, you can set the MIDI Channel for each note. This allows you to trigger drum sounds from different modules on different MIDI Channels. The default setting for the parameter is Base, which specifies that each note uses the MIDI Channel that has been set globally for the mapped instrument in its parameter box. You can change any note's MIDI Channel to any of the available 16 MIDI Channels, or to All if you wish to send a note on all available channels. If you want to reset all selected notes to the Base value, you can select **Initialize > Output Channels**.
- **Cable.** This parameter allows you to have up to 16 different cables, so you can send individual notes from the mapped instrument to unique objects to trigger sounds or to be further processed. You don't need to worry about this feature right now (you'll learn how to cable Environment Objects to each other in Chapter 14), but as you can already begin to understand, this is a very powerful option. If you ever wanted to reset all the cables of the multi-instrument to cable #1 (the default cable), you can select **Initialize > Output Cables**.
- **Head, Rel. Pos, Group.** These parameters specifically relate to the score notation and don't really affect MIDI performance at all. You can use these parameters to adjust how each note will appear on the staff. To reset them, you can select **Initialize > Score Parameters**.

METHOD TIP: MAKING MIDI AND AUDIO CONNECTIONS FOR MIDI SYNTHS

When Logic sends MIDI data to your external MIDI hardware sound modules or synthesizers, your hardware will produce audio. You have two ways of dealing with the audio output. One method is to plug all the outputs from your synthesizer or sound module into a hardware mixer, then plug the outputs from your audio interface into the same mixer. Another method, especially if you ultimately want to mix all your tracks in Logic, is to take the audio outputs of your MIDI sound modules and plug them into the inputs of your audio inputs.

If you intend to bring your synth's audio back into Logic, then in addition to creating all these MIDI Objects to send MIDI data to your MIDI device, you will also want to create Audio Track Objects with their inputs set to the audio interface inputs your MIDI devices are connected to. Keep that in mind as you read the "Setting Up Audio Objects" section below.

If you are only using stereo outputs from your MIDI device, you may want to create Audio Instrument Objects and use Logic's external instrument for your hardware. You'll learn about using Audio Instruments in Chapter 10.

Setting Up Internal Instruments

Internal instruments are a type of software synthesizer. They are not as tightly integrated into Logic as Logic's own Audio Instruments or third-party plug-ins that integrate directly with Logic. But they are still internal to your computer as they are software applications running on your computer connecting to Logic via Rewire or QuickTime, and do not require external wires to access their sounds—hence the need for an Internal Object to represent them. The differences between plug-ins and internal instruments will be explained in more detail in Chapter 10, "Working with Audio Instruments in Logic." There are two different types of Internal Objects: the Rewire Object and the QuickTime Object. Figure 4.10 shows you a pair of internal instruments, with the Rewire Object's parameter box on display.

These objects have very few parameters, so there is very little for you to do after you create the objects. In fact, until you've read Chapter 10, "Working with Audio Instruments in Logic," you should not experiment with any of these parameters. When using the QuickTime musical instruments that came with your Macintosh, you can simply create a QuickTime Object by selecting **New > Internal > QuickTime** in the Environment window. When using a Rewire application such as Reason, select **New > Internal > Rewire** to create the object. This will get you up and running, and should suffice until you've read Chapter 10.

Figure 4.10
Two Internal Instrument Objects, a Rewire Object, and a QuickTime Synth Object. Note either type of internal instrument features identical parameters.

METHOD TIP: AN OBJECT FOR EVERY WHIM

The preceding sections have mostly discussed creating objects in Logic's Environment to represent physical devices. But remember, Logic's Environment is a virtual studio—you aren't limited to creating only one object to represent each physical object. Imagine walking into a recording studio and having an entire wall of synthesizers at your disposal, each already turned on and set to your favorite patch. In Logic, you can do just that. Use Instrument Objects, mapped instruments, Internal Objects, and so on to create separate objects for all your favorite patches on all your favorite synths. You can gather them all on one Environment layer, such as the Instruments layer. That way, you'll always have a place to store objects representing your favorite programs and patches. Figure 4.11 gives you an example of an Environment layer with Instrument Objects for often-used patches, instruments, and drum kits.

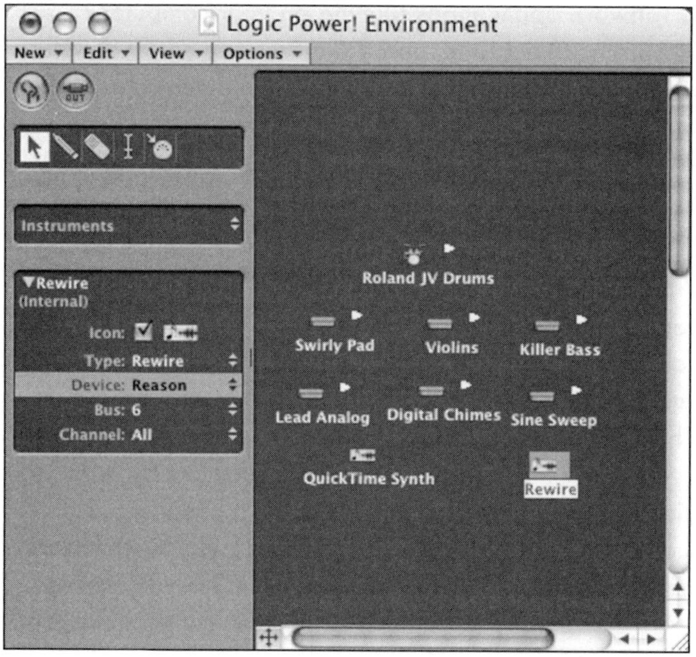

Figure 4.11
You can use the Environment to create separate objects for your favorite patches. This will give you instant access to your favorite sounds in the Arrange window.

The main advantage to creating Environment Objects for your favorite patches is that they will be instantly available for you to assign to tracks in the Arrange window without any additional setup required at all. Simply select the instrument you want from the hierarchal menu and you'll be ready to perform, as you'll see later in the section "Setting Up Tracks." Remember, the Autoload song is your chance to set up your workspace to make using Logic as easy and convenient as possible. The more comfortable you are customizing your Autoload song, the easier Logic will be to use.

Setting Up Audio Objects

Luckily, the default song that Logic launches with should already have a fairly complete mixer in the Audio layer of the Environment. This mixer will be determined by your audio device's capabilities, your Logic Setup Assistant selections, and your settings from the Audio Preferences Drivers tab. If you find yourself needing to create additional Audio Objects, simply select **New > Audio Object**, and Logic will display a new, unexpanded Audio Object such as the one in Figure 4.12.

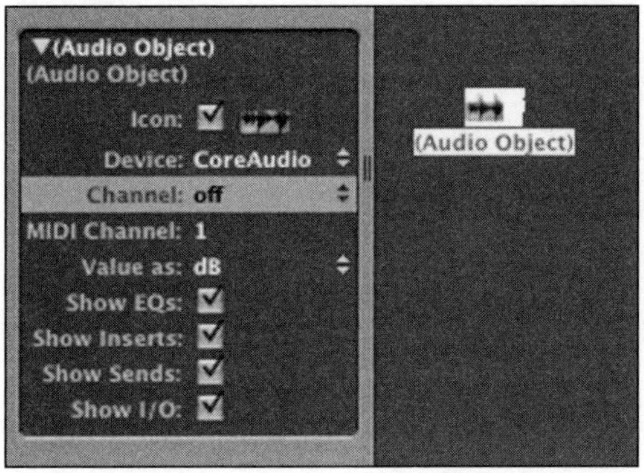

Figure 4.12
An Audio Object and its parameter box.

The various Audio Object parameters are as follows:

- **Icon.** Use this setting to select the icon you want to represent the Audio Track. If you click and hold the mouse on the image, Logic displays a pop-up menu of available icons. If you have the check box checked, then the Audio Object will be available for selection in the Arrange window, and if you do not check the box you will not be able to assign a track to the Audio Object in the Arrange window.
- **Device.** This setting specifies the device driver that your audio hardware is using. You won't need to adjust this setting unless you are using more than a single hardware device. If you are, you can use this to select which device to use.
- **Channel.** The newly created Audio Object initially will not be assigned to an Audio channel. Click on the up/down arrows next to

the Channel parameter and you will see a hierarchal menu like the one shown in Figure 4.13. Simply navigate to the channel type you desire and select an available track. If the variety of Audio channel types seems overwhelming, don't worry; you will learn about the various Audio channels and their uses in later chapters, specifically Chapters 8 and 10.

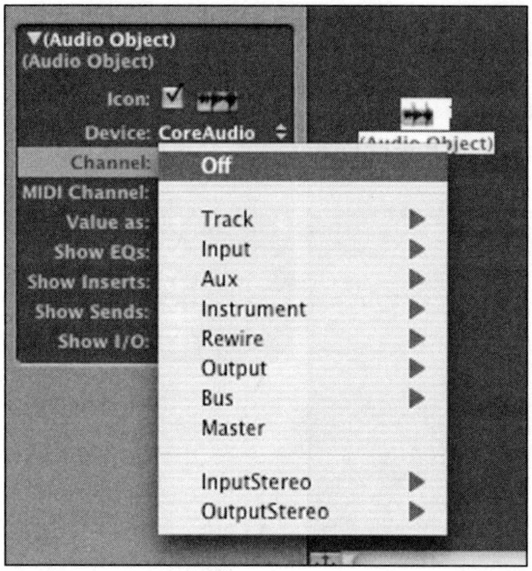

Figure 4.13
After you click and hold the mouse over the Channel assignment in an Audio Object, Logic displays a pop-up menu in which you can navigate through the hierarchal options to select what channel type you want for the Audio Object.

- **MIDI Channel.** In old-style automation in Logic, this parameter determined what channel the automation for the track would need to be on. Since Logic 5, this parameter hasn't been of much use, although it still appears if you are using some of the region-based automation (which you'll explore in Chapters 7 and 9), which is steeped in MIDI. This value automatically changes when you change the Channel setting above. Just leave this value at its default setting, unless you specifically need to override the default.
- **Value As.** This setting determines whether Logic displays volume meter readings as decibels (dB) or numeric values.
- **Show EQ, Show Inserts, Show Sends, Show I/O.** These check boxes allow you to turn off various sections of the Audio Object's channel strip if you are not using them. By turning these sections off, you conserve space. Figure 4.14 shows two Audio Objects displaying their channel strip at different sizes.

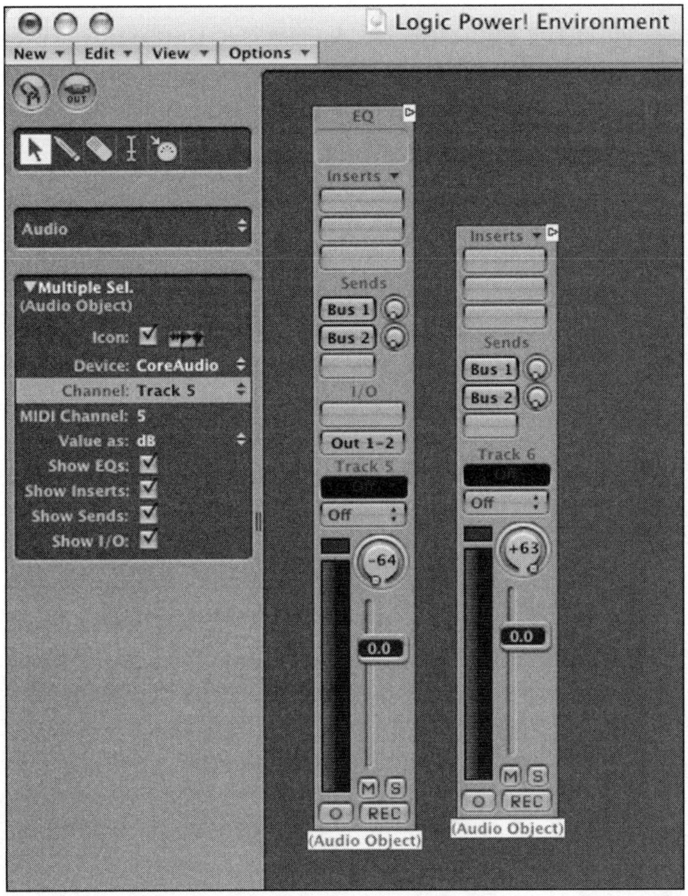

Figure 4.14

One Audio Object showing all its components, and an Audio Object next to it that has its Show EQ and Show I/O sections unchecked. Notice the height difference of the channel strips.

REMEMBER: ALL AUDIO OBJECTS BEGIN LIFE THE SAME

Let's go over the idea of Audio Objects versus channel strips one more time. As you see in the preceding example, when you create an Audio Object, it looks just like the other Environment Objects you've created, with a similar parameter box and icon. However, when you double-click your Audio Object, instead of bringing up a Multi-Instrument window or a Mapped Instrument window as with those two types of objects, Logic displays a channel strip. That channel strip then becomes the graphic for your Audio Object. I hope that this concept is beginning to make more sense as you advance through the book!

METHOD TIP: MAKING A COMPLETE REWIRE CONNECTION

Chapter 10, "Working with Audio Instruments in Logic," explains in detail how Logic and Rewire applications interact. Logic Pro 7 should also ship with Song Templates that have complete Rewire connections pre-created for you. However, just in case you want to build your own for your Autoload, here's a quick explanation.

In Logic, you'll need to create a MIDI Rewire Instrument to send MIDI to your Rewire application, and you'll need to create two or more Audio Objects to accept the audio streams from your Rewire application. So follow the directions above to create an Internal Rewire Instrument, and set it to your Rewire application (Reason, Abelton Live, Storm, and so on). Then create two (or more) Audio Objects, and set their channels to Rewire: Mix L and Rewire: Mix R. (Note that since Rewire channels are mono only in Logic, you'll need two of them for each stereo stream.) You should end up with one Rewire Instrument and two Rewire channel strips as shown in Figure 4.15.

You can of course have more Audio channels coming from your Rewire applications, and you can send MIDI directly to specific MIDI devices within your Rewire application. But for more advanced routing, please see Chapter 10.

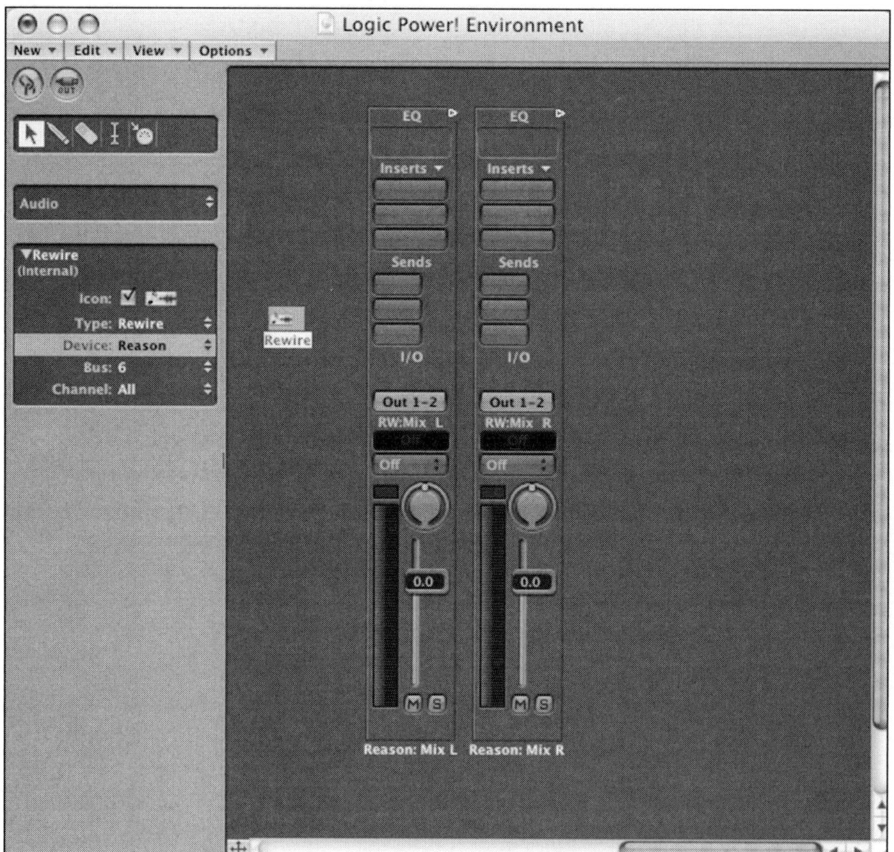

Figure 4.15

The figure shows a basic connection to Propellerhead's Reason application; there is a Rewire Instrument to send MIDI from Logic to Reason, and a pair of channel strips that receive the stereo audio output from Reason.

Just as in the preceding expert tip for MIDI Objects, if you already know what sort of routing you need for your Audio Mixer or what Audio Instruments you want preloaded and are ready to use in your Autoload song, go ahead and set them up now.

Setting Up Your Arrange Window

I've spent quite a few pages discussing basic setup of your Autoload song's Environment, but no less important is setting up the Arrange window. For example, Figure 4.16 contains the Arrange window generated by the default song.

Does this look like your ideal workspace? Or do you imagine yourself using a different combination of tracks? Perhaps with different instrument names? Do you want your track lanes to have more room? The Arrange window in the default song is designed to offer users a sampling of available track types, in the hopes that some of what they need might be included. For your Autoload song, you want your Arrange window to represent *your* personal working needs.

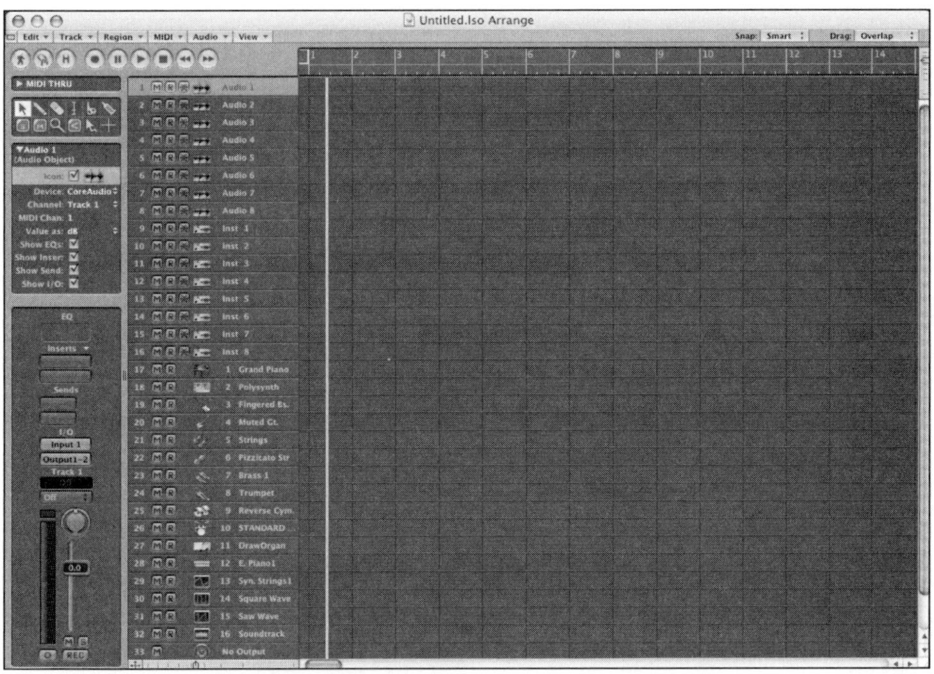

Figure 4.16
An example of an Arrange window generated by Logic for the default song. Most likely, you will prefer a different configuration for your own personalized Autoload song.

Setting Up Tracks

If you created 48–64 Audio Tracks in the LSA or in the Audio Drivers Preferences dialog box, you might initially be disappointed to see only eight Audio Tracks in the Arrange window. Don't worry; all of those Audio Tracks (and indeed all your different Audio Objects) are available to be added to your Arrange window, but you have to add them yourself.

Adding Tracks

Let's start by adding more tracks of each type you'll need. There are two ways to do this.

If you just want to add a single track or two, use the arrow keys to select the track with the highest number of that track type. For example, if you are starting with Audio Tracks, you would press the arrow key seven times to navigate down to Audio 8, which is the last audio track that Logic created for you in the default song. Now either use your mouse to select **Track > Create with Next Instrument** as shown in Figure 4.17 or, even better, press the key command **CONTROL + SHIFT + RETURN**. Logic then adds the next track in the sequence to the Arrange window. Because this track will automatically be selected, you can continue using the key command (or selecting the menu option) to create as many tracks as you want.

If you want to add a number of tracks of the same type to the Arrange window, even faster than Create with Next Instrument is the Create Multiple command. New to Logic 7, this command can be found in **Track > Create Multiple** as shown in Figure 4.18. You can also set your own key command for this function; defining key commands is explored later in the chapter.

Figure 4.17

You can easily create a track following the selected one using the Create with Next Instrument command.

Figure 4.18

You can very quickly add multiple tracks to the Arrange window with the Create Multiple command.

Once you activate this command, you will be presented with the Create Multiple Tracks window shown in Figure 4.19.

In this window, you have a number of pull-down menus and options for exactly the kind of track you wish to create. Your options are the following:

- **Driver.** If you are creating Audio Tracks, you can select which of your enabled audio drivers you wish these tracks to be attached to. If you only have a single audio driver enabled (as most of us just have Core Audio enabled) leave this as is.
- **Track Type.** You can choose to create Audio, Audio Instrument, or Auxiliary (TDM only) tracks.
- **Number of Tracks.** Type in how many tracks you wish to create here.
- **Mode.** If you are creating Audio, Audio Instrument, or Auxiliary tracks, you will be able to create either mono or stereo tracks. Keep in mind that this will change the mono/stereo setting of existing Objects.

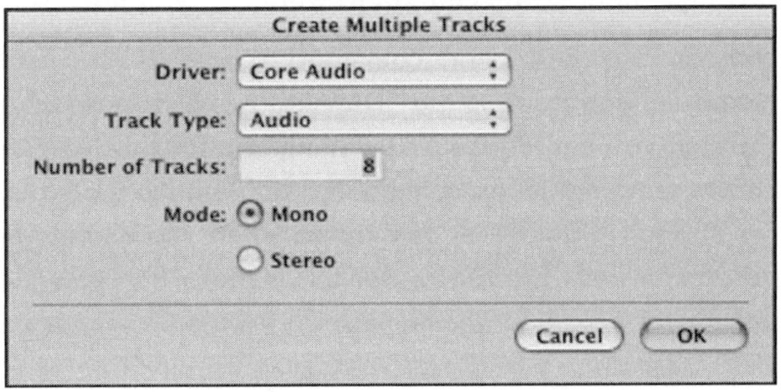

Figure 4.19

The Create Multiple Tracks window.

EXPERT TIP: USE KEY COMMANDS!

As you can already see, using key commands in Logic is a major time saver. Creating tracks isn't fun, creative work—it's an administrative task that most people just want to finish as soon as they can. If you are creating 50 or more tracks of different types, that means you have to navigate to the menu option, then renavigate to the menu option, then renavigate to the menu option—if you're using menu commands (are you getting the idea?). However, if you use the key command, creating each new track is as rapid as click, click, click, and click. I'll continue to show you the menu options as well as the default key commands throughout this book, but you should commit some time to learning to use Logic via the key commands. Now is an excellent time to start!

After pressing OK, Logic will add your selected tracks to the Arrange window.

Naming Tracks

Now that you've created as many tracks as you think you'll need, you might want to think about giving them slightly more descriptive names than simply Audio 1, Audio 2, and so on. Of course, you don't know what your final track names will be, but do you expect you will need 12 separate Audio Tracks for your drums? If so, you might name Audio 24–36 (or whichever tracks you choose) as Drums 1 to Drums 12 instead of Audio 24 to Audio 36. Did you only need eight MIDI tracks that you divide between two separate MIDI synths, such as a Roland and a Korg synth? Why not name the MIDI tracks Korg 1 to Korg 4 and Roland 1 to Roland 4 to be more descriptive. Remember, customizing your Arrange window to be your personal workspace is the name of the game!

The easiest way to name tracks is to click the instrument name in the parameter box to the left of the track list. As soon as you do, a text box appears with the current name of the track highlighted, as shown in Figure 4.20. Type any name you want, then press Return. The name of the instrument in the Arrange window will change to whatever you have selected.

You can also use a menu command to name tracks: **Tracks > Create Track Name**. As you'll see in the "Defining Key Commands" section later in this chapter, you can define a key command for this function. If you change track names using the menu command, you'll notice that your track names will not appear in boldface, as they do when you change the names from the parameter box. The reason for this is that when you click in the Instrument parameter box, you are naming the Audio Object or instrument; when you

Figure 4.20

To rename an Audio Object or instrument in your track list, click the Audio Object or instrument name next to the triangle in that track's parameter box. When the text box appears, type the new name.

use this command, you are actually naming the *track itself*. By default, this distinction makes no difference; however, if you select **View > Instrument Names** in the Arrange window, you will turn on a view that displays two names per track. This view displays both the instrument (parameter box) name, and the track name created with the Create Track Name command. Thus you could have an instrument named Korg Triton on a track named Analog Lead, for example, or an instrument named Guitar 1 on a track named Funky Rhythm. Figure 4.21 shows a track with this view enabled.

The primary disadvantage to displaying both the instrument name and the track name is screen clutter. You might prefer to leave **View > Instrument**

Figure 4.21

When you use the Create Track Name command, if you have Instrument Names turned on by selecting **View > Instrument Names**, you'll see the bold instrument name from the parameter box as well as the track name in the track list.

Names turned off, in which case the instrument name and track name are interchangeable, and each track will display only one or the other, whichever exists for a given track. On the other hand, if you use MIDI devices heavily, displaying both the instrument and the track name could be a lifesaver. That's the glory of Logic: What one user finds useless, another might find indispensable, and vice versa.

Either way, using the Functions local menu every time you want to rename a track tends to become far too tedious. There's little reason to use this method to rename your tracks when the key command is so simple to use.

Coloring Tracks

As a final method of customizing your Autoload tracks, you might want to think about coloring them. Certainly it won't affect your music or creativity in any way if you do or do not use a unique color for each track, but it does help to keep tracks separate, and to help visually group tracks that you want to keep together, such as tracks for the same MIDI Instrument, or for similar types of audio recordings. (For example, you might color all your drum tracks the same color.)

First, to see the colors you are choosing before each track lane has any regions on it, make sure **View > Track Instrument Color** is checked. You will then be presented with a small line at the right of each track name that shows you the color for that track. To change the color, display the color palette by selecting **View > Colors**, or (better yet) by pressing the key command **OPTION + C**. Logic then presents its color palette, as shown in Figure 4.22. When you click on any of the palette's colors, you will see the line of color change to the selected color.

If you want a color that is not represented in Logic's color palette, you can double-click any color to bring up the standard Mac OS X Pro Application color wheel. You can then adjust that color to taste and apply it to your track. Changing a color this way will also change the color of any region, object, or track already using that color.

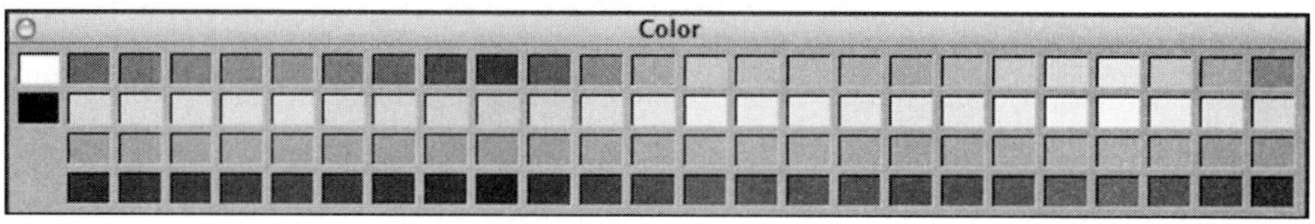

Figure 4.22
Logic's color palette. Click on a color to choose it for the selected track in the Arrange window.

Configuring the Initial Zoom and Automation Settings

You may want all of your track lanes to be wider or thinner than the default "skinny" tracks that Logic creates in the Arrange window. Basically, the skinnier the track lane, the more tracks will fit in the track list, but the less detail you will see for each track. You may also want the horizontal zoom in Arrange to be more zoomed in (for more precise detail) or more zoomed out (for an overview of an entire song). Many Logic users choose to set up an initial screenset with an Arrange window with wider track lanes, and a tight horizontal zoom, to focus on a specific group of tracks, and then another screenset with an Arrange window with very skinny track lanes horizontally zoomed out for viewing the whole song at once.

To accomplish this, you can use the zoom sliders at the top-right and bottom-left of the Arrange window. These sliders are pointed out in Figure 4.23. The top-right slider controls vertical zoom. Dragging the slider down decreases the track lane height, and dragging the slider up increases the track lane height. The bottom-left slider controls horizontal zoom. Dragging the slider left decreases how much horizontal space is shown between each bar/SMPTE location, and dragging the slider right increases how much horizontal space is

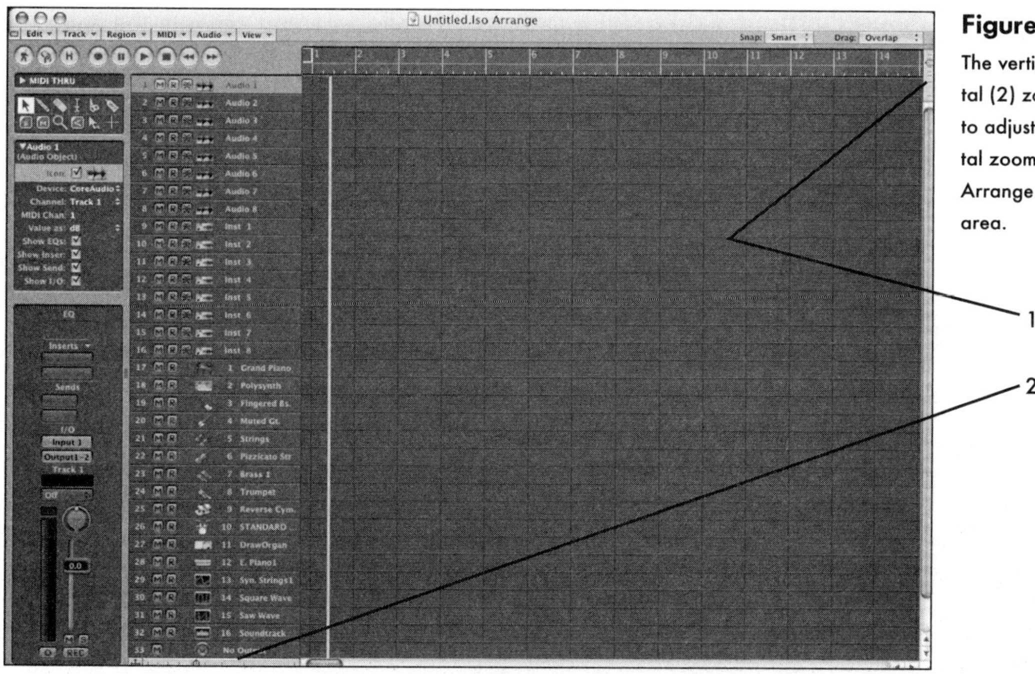

Figure 4.23

The vertical (1) and horizontal (2) zoom sliders allow you to adjust vertical and horizontal zoom for the entire Arrange window track lane area.

shown between each bar/SMPTE location. You can also use the zoom key command, which is **CONTROL + ARROW** (press the appropriate arrow key, depending on whether you are increasing [up] or decreasing [down] zoom).

EXPERT TIP: ZOOMING HORIZONTALLY AND VERTICALLY FROM A SINGLE ZOOM SLIDER

If you want to zoom both horizontally and vertically, it isn't very convenient to have to drag one slider at one corner of your Arrange window, and then move the mouse all the way diagonally across Arrange to drag the other slider. That's why Logic allows you to zoom horizontally and vertically from the same slider if you drag the zoom slider while holding down the **OPTION** key. If you **OPTION + DRAG** the vertical slider, you will zoom horizontally, and if you **OPTION + DRAG** the horizontal slider, you will zoom horizontally.

Logic also gives you a number of ways to vertically resize individual tracks without resizing the other tracks on the Arrange window. First of all, if you move the mouse to the left top or bottom edge of a track, the cursor will turn into a finger, as shown in Figure 4.24. When the cursor is a finger, you can click and drag the mouse to increase or decrease the height of that individual track. You can also select a track and use the key commands for Individual Track Zoom In (**CONTROL + OPTION + UP**) and Individual Track Zoom Out (**CONTROL + OPTION + DOWN**). Finally, you can activate the Auto Track Zoom feature in the View menu. Auto Track Zoom will increase the size of whichever track in the Arrange window you have currently selected, leaving all unselected tracks at their normal height.

Another function that increases the height of all your tracks is automation. I'll discuss automation a bit more in the next chapter, and in depth in Chapter 11, "Using Automation in Logic." For now, you just need to know that Logic has a very powerful automation system that allows you to set up mixing

Figure 4.24
If you move the cursor to the top- or bottom-left side of an Arrange track, the cursor turns into a finger, indicating that you can adjust the height of the track by dragging up or down with your mouse.

moves that will happen automatically, without you having to control them every time you play the song. When you turn on automation, all your track lanes will zoom out so that each track has enough room to display the automation information. If automation seems like something you'll definitely be using, you can turn automation on by selecting **View > Track Automation**. You will see every track instantly widen, and Logic will display the dialog box shown in Figure 4.25.

Figure 4.25
When you turn on Track Automation, this dialog box asks you which displays you want to turn on. For your Autoload song, it's best to start with automation turned off for all of them.

This dialog box asks whether you want to enable the automation lane inside the track lane for your currently selected track, all your tracks, or none of your tracks. It's valuable to turn the Track Automation view on in your Autoload song if you know you'll be using automation, but if you enable the automation lane in every track at this point, it will only clutter your track lanes until you actually do use the automation. You should click Cancel in this dialog box, which will leave you with Track Automation turned on, but not display any automation parameters yet. You can turn those on later in individual tracks as they become necessary.

Setting Up Screensets

I've already discussed screensets, which are one of Logic's powerful customization tools. Using screensets, you can set up each view in Logic to have exactly the editors and windows you want, and switch between the views conveniently by using the numeric keys. Setting them up couldn't be simpler: You simply press a number key to go to a screenset, organize the various windows and editors as you like, and when you save your Autoload song, all your screensets are automatically saved as well. No muss, no fuss! There are only a couple of special options for creating screensets that you might want to consider using, and they are discussed in this section.

First, if you select **Windows > Screensets**, you'll notice a small hierarchal menu of screenset options as shown in Figure 4.26.

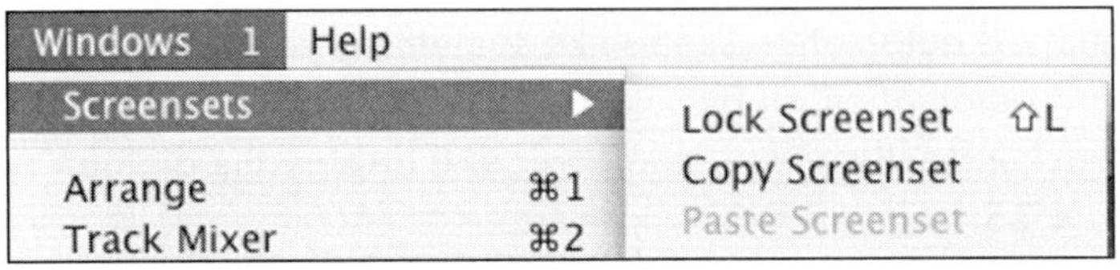

Figure 4.26
Selecting **Windows > Screensets** brings up a menu of screenset options.

If you know that even if you open and close windows while using Logic you'll want the windows of a particular screenset never to change from Logic session to Logic session, you can choose to lock the screenset using the **Lock Screenset** menu command (or pressing **SHIFT + L**). If you want to create a new screenset using the current screenset as a base, you can select **Copy Screenset**, then press a numeric key to move to a different screenset, and select **Paste Screenset** to paste the contents of the first screenset into this new screenset.

The only other options you might want to consider involve window placement. You may want some windows to always be in front of other windows independent of which window is currently selected. For example, you may want to open a single channel-wide Track Mixer that is only showing your Output channel, so you can always monitor your song's main output level. You can do this by opening any window as a floating window (meaning, floating above the other windows) by opening the window while pressing the **OPTION** key. Further, if it's just a window designed to show you one specific item, such as a one channel-wide Track Mixer, you can **COMMAND + OPTION + CLICK** on the local menu bar at the top of the window, and the bar will disappear. This way, you can truly open any window to display exactly what it is you want to see—no more, no less.

Setting up your screensets in your Autoload song is really this easy! Trust me: Using screensets is one of the best ways to configure Logic to reflect how you want to work.

Defining Key Commands

Don't worry; you're not going to give every command in Logic a key command at this point. But as you work on your Autoload song, you should begin to get a feel for which commands you might like to access from the keyboard instead of the menus, so you can begin defining your own key commands. Logic makes this process simple with its extremely powerful and intuitive Key Commands window.

First, you need to access the Key Commands window by selecting **Logic Pro > Preferences > Key Commands**, or simply pressing **OPTION + K**. Figure 4.27 shows Logic's Key Commands window.

You will notice that the key commands are grouped into commands relating to specific windows and editors in the command list. You can click open any of the triangles from any or all of the groups to see what key commands are available for that window or editor.

The easiest way to define a key command is simply to search for it, then have Logic learn the key you wish to be the key command. For example, suppose that you want to assign a key command to the Copy Screenset command. Type the word **screenset** into the Find field of the Key Commands window as shown in Figure 4.28. Logic then displays a list of all key commands with the word screenset in their name. Select the Copy Screenset command from the list.

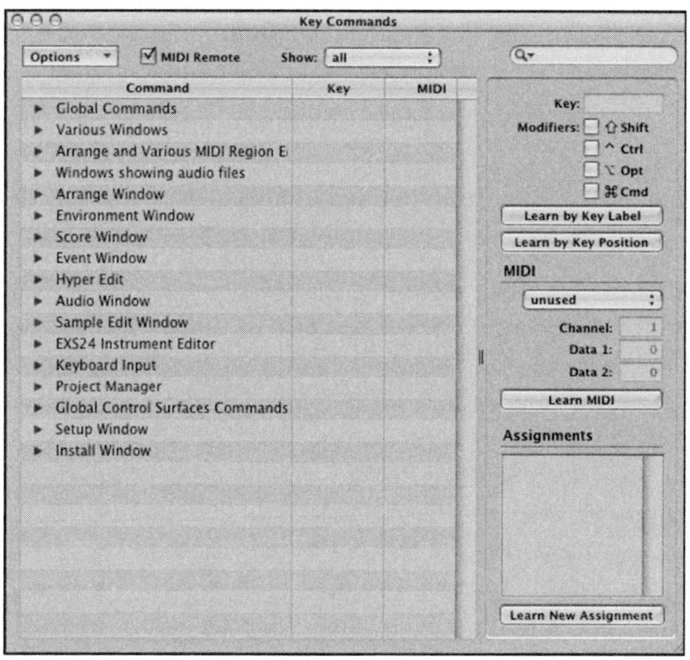

Figure 4.27

Logic Pro 7's Key Commands window offers many different methods to search for and assign key commands.

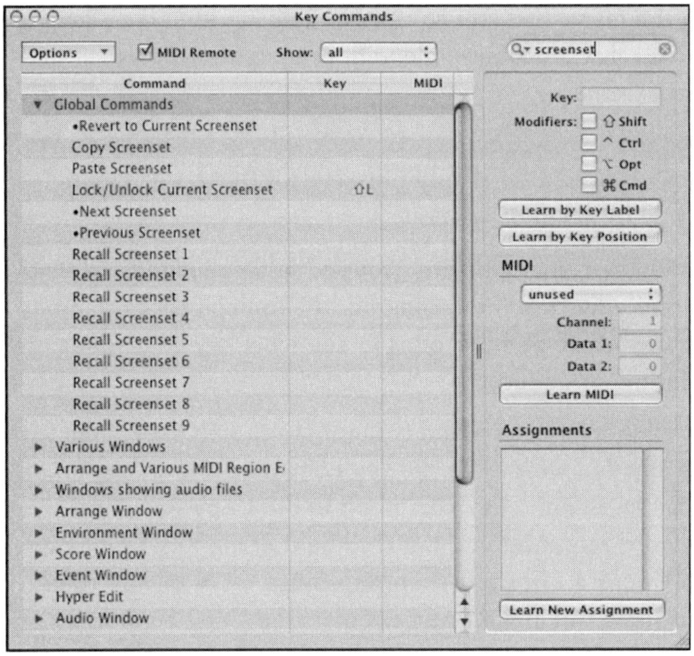

Figure 4.28

To search for key commands, type a search word into the Find field of the Key Commands window.

First, you need to select the command you wish to assign a key command to. From here, assigning keys (and more) to a command couldn't be easier. There are four ways to assign keys to a command, depending on your preference.

- **Learn by Key Label.** This learns key sequences based on the label of the key you press. In other words, if you press a key labeled "3," then 3 will be assigned to that command. In this example, press the **Learn by Key Label** button, then press the **CONTROL**, **SHIFT**, and **2** keys. You will see the Assignments window and boxes reflect your choice, as shown in Figure 4.29. You can now press **CONTROL + SHIFT + 2** (either the two on the keyboard or on the numeric keypad) to copy a screenset. Your new key command is listed in the Key column of the command list.
- **Learn by Key Position.** This key command option allows you to assign a key command not based on the label on the key, but the position of the key on the keyboard. The advantage of this is that you can assign different key commands to the number 2 above the keyboard and the number 2 in the numeric keypad. It also means that if you switch between different languages, your key assignments will remain the

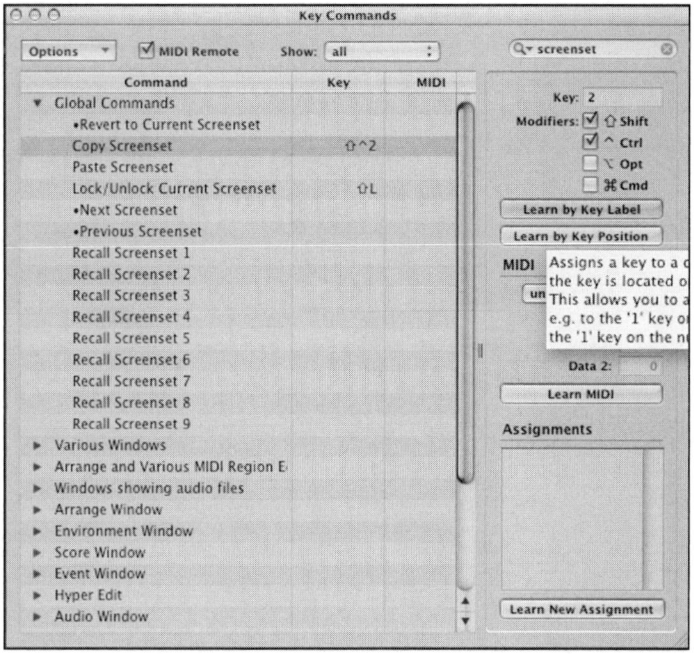

Figure 4.29

Pressing **Learn by Key Label** then pressing **CONTROL, SHIFT**, and **2** assigns the key sequence **CONTROL + SHIFT + 2** to the Copy Screenset command.

same. Using the same example, if you press the **Learn by Key Position** button and your **CONTROL, SHIFT**, and **2** keys, the Assignments window will reflect the location code (or scan code) of the key pressed (in this case, the number 2 above the keyboard, not the numeric keypad) and only those exact keys will be assigned to the command, as Figure 4.30 illustrates. Your new key command is listed in the Key column of the command list.

- **Learn MIDI.** Logic lets you not only assign a keyboard key to a command, but a MIDI controller to a command. Simply click on the **Learn MIDI** button and press a MIDI key on your MIDI device or any MIDI controller you wish to be assigned to the key. Your chosen controller will be reflected in the Key Assignment column and in the MIDI column of the command list, as shown in Figure 4.31. You can assign both a MIDI and key sequence to a command.
- **Learn New Assignment.** If you want to assign a command to a control surface, press this button, then move or press the control on the control surface you wish to assign to this command. The Assignments window will reflect what you pressed, as in Figure 4.32.

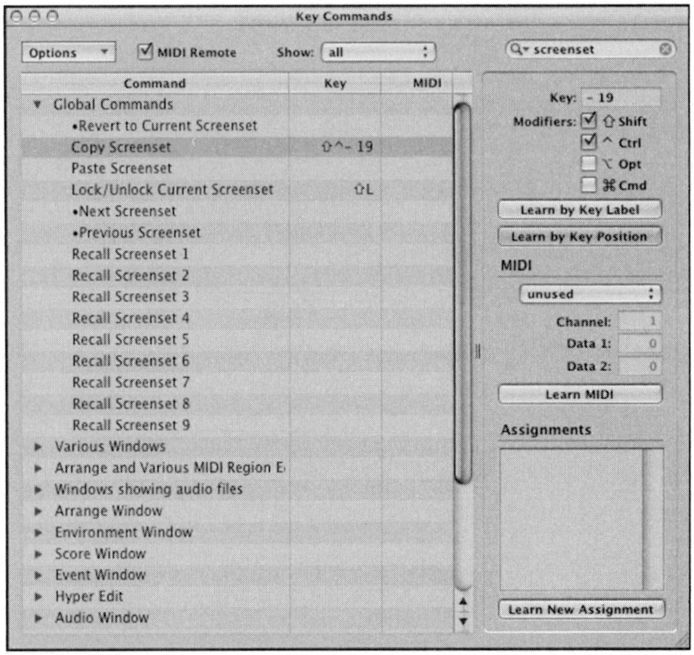

Figure 4.30

Using Learn by Key Position memorizes the specific keys you have pressed and assigns that sequence to your key command, in this case **CONTROL + SHIFT + 2** (above the keyboard, not the numeric keypad).

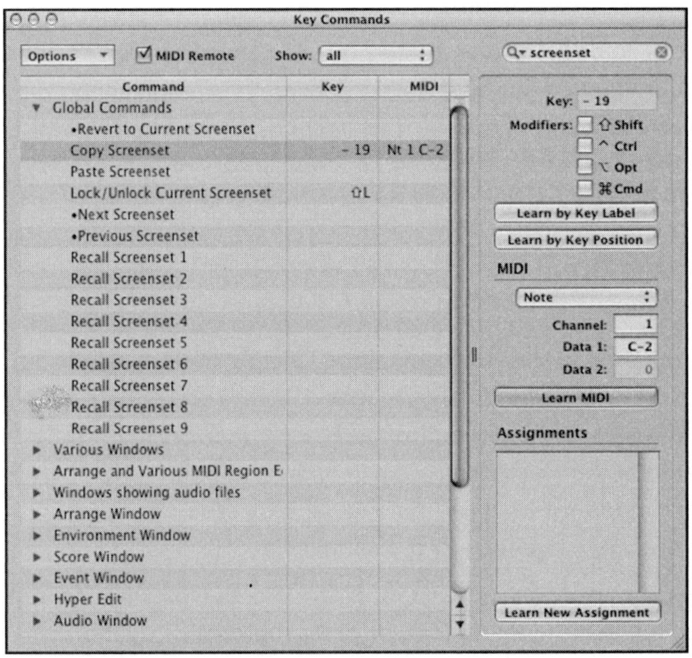

Figure 4.31

Using Learn MIDI, you can assign a MIDI controller to trigger a command in addition to a keyboard sequence.

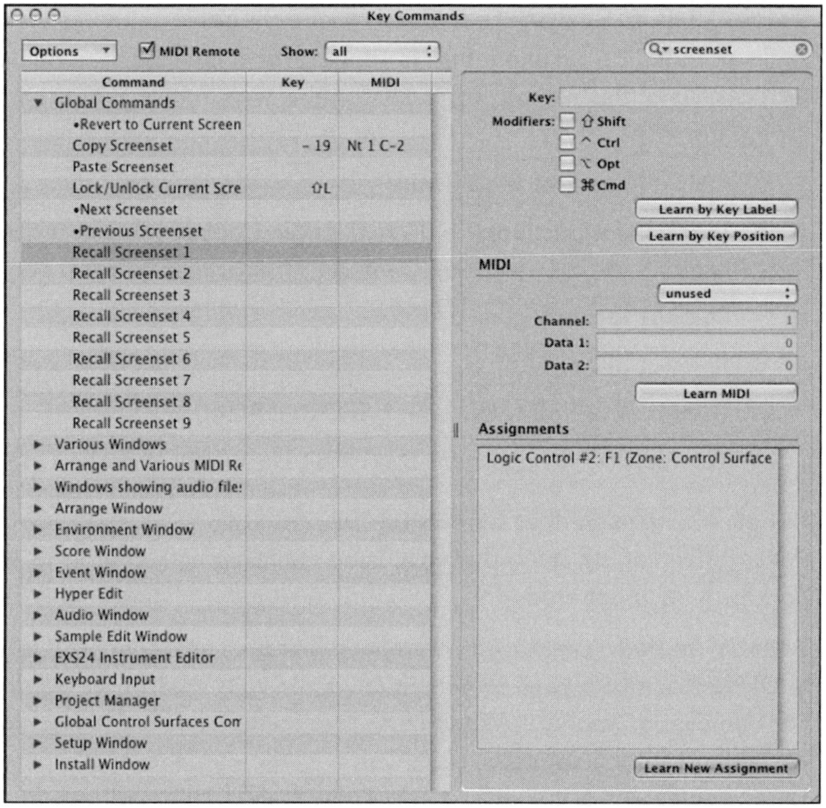

Figure 4.32

You can assign key commands to control surfaces as well as keyboards and MIDI devices by using the Learn New Assignment button. The figure shows the F1 key on Logic Control #2 assigned to Recall Screenset 1.

That's it! You've just activated a new key command! As you become more familiar with Logic, you will not only use these methods to activate key commands that do not have defaults, but to assign different key commands than the Logic default key sequences to better suit your own working methods.

Setting Up Your Control Surface

If you have a software controller, you are in for a special treat. A control surface can actually be any MIDI device capable of sending and receiving MIDI in order to control functions within Logic. The most common control surfaces, however, resemble hardware mixers, except instead of controlling audio, they control your Logic software. A full explanation of how to use your control surface is beyond the scope of this book; this section is going to just focus on how to set up your control surface to work with Logic.

Setting Up a Supported Control Surface

Logic already has complete built-in support for a number of popular control surfaces. As of this writing, Logic Pro 7 ships with built-in support for the following devices:

- **CM Automation:** Motor Mix
- **Mackie Designs:** Baby HUI, HUI, Logic Control (Mackie Control), Logic Control XT (Mackie Control XT), Mackie Control C4
- **Radikal Technologies:** SAC-2k
- **Roland:** SI-24
- **Tascam:** FW-1884, US-224, US-428, US-2400
- **Yamaha:** 01V96, 02R96, DM1000, DM2000, Yamaha O1X

Emagic is always adding support for new controllers, so if you have a control surface that is not listed above, keep checking with Emagic to see if support for it has been added.

With any of these supported controllers, first properly connect it to your MIDI interface (see your owner's manual for your control surface for instructions on proper hookup). When Logic first opens its default song, you will be presented with the control surface Setup window as shown in Figure 4.33. This indicates that Logic was able to sense immediately that you had a control surface plugged in, and that all is well.

If this window does not pop up immediately, don't worry, as all is not lost. In the Setup window select **New > Scan All Models** and Logic will rescan your MIDI interface to find any connected control surfaces. If your control surface is found, but does not seem to be responding, then from the global Logic Pro menu select **Logic Pro > Preferences > Control Surfaces > Rebuild Defaults**. That should do the trick. If this works, it means that Logic always knew where your control surface was among your devices, but it was simply not connecting. If that doesn't work, you'll need to start looking for loose cables and hardware connections, then try again. If nothing works, don't be afraid to call tech support and ask them to walk you through the connection process.

Once Logic senses your control surface, you're ready to go. Close the window and bask in the joy of your control surface!

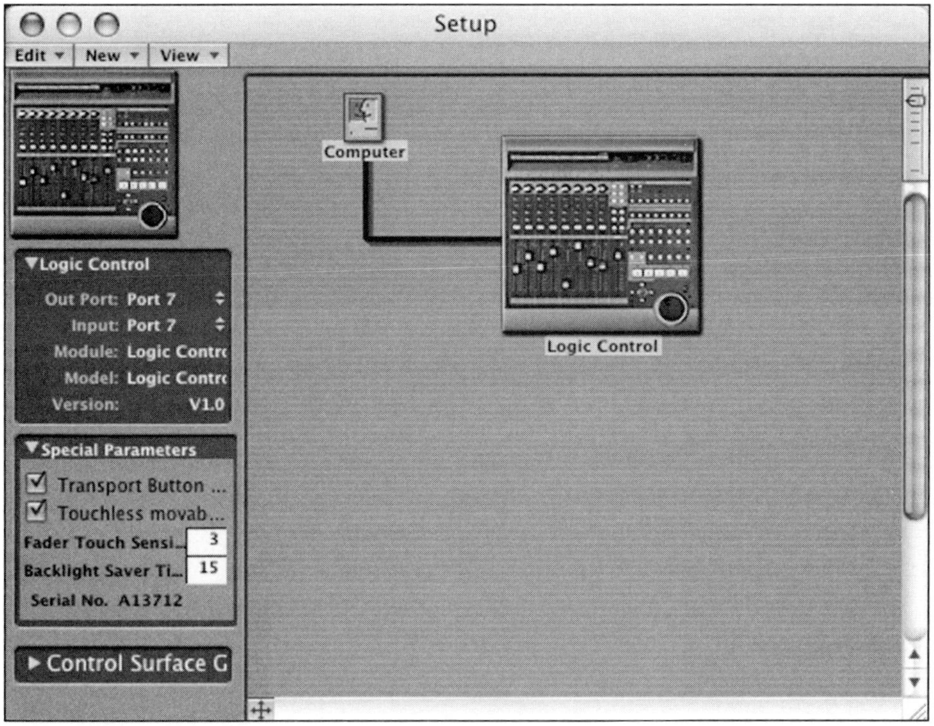

Figure 4.33
The control surface Setup window. If Logic automatically opened to this window, you're home free. Otherwise, you may need to connect to your Logic control manually.

Setting Up Any MIDI Device as a Control Surface

As mentioned above, if your control surface is not supported, you can still configure Logic to use it to control the application. If you want to use a non-supported control surface you will need to set up what each knob, fader, and button on your controller does. The basic procedure is to first click on an onscreen control or menu option. After you have done this, immediately select **Logic Pro > Preferences > Control Surfaces > Learn Assignment for.** You will immediately notice the word following "for" will be the control or command that you just selected. Figure 4.34 illustrates how this should work.

After you select the **Learn Assignment** command, you will be presented with the Controller Assignments window shown Figure 4.35. At this point, simply press the **Learn Mode** button and twist, press, slide, or otherwise manipulate a control on your MIDI controller, and it will be automatically assigned to the chosen control or command in Logic. You can use this to assign each button, knob, and fader on your MIDI controller to control a function in Logic.

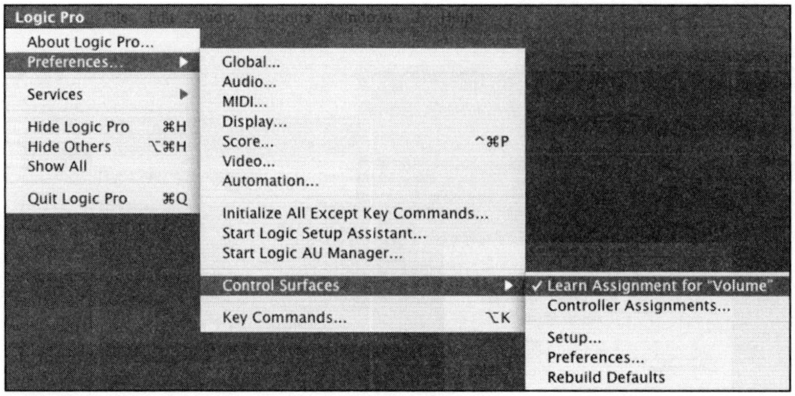

Figure 4.34
In the example, the volume slider of the first track in the Track Mixer was clicked. As you can see, the Learn Assignment parameter now says "Learn Assignment for 'Volume,'" reflecting that any controller assignment you make will be mapped to the volume of that track.

Figure 4.35
Once you have activated Learn Assignment, you will be presented with the Controller Assignments window. Press **Learn Mode** and move a control on your MIDI device, and it will be assigned to that control or command.

As you can see, this is an amazingly powerful feature in Logic, allowing virtually every aspect of the application to be remotely controlled! As you can also see, going into every detail of this extremely powerful feature would take a whole chapter by itself, and it's beyond the scope of this book. The previous description should be enough to get you started with a basic setup, and when you want to get into more complex and esoteric assignments the Logic Pro 7 manual offers a complete description of the Controller Assignments feature.

Saving Your Autoload Song

As I mentioned at the beginning of the chapter, the Autoload song is actually a Song Template. When you are ready to save your Autoload song, you'll want to select **File > Save As Template**. You will be presented with the Save As dialog box, already opened to the Song Template folder in the user directory. *Do not change directories!* If you do, Logic Pro may not open your Autoload automatically! Just type in **Autoload** and click **OK**.

A NOTE ON LOGIC'S USE OF MAC OS X DIRECTORIES

You may have already noticed that the Logic Pro 7 file in your Applications directory does not have a folder around it, as some other programs you may own do. This is because Logic Pro follows Apple Computer's guidelines for where the support files for applications should go. This may be confusing for upgrading Logic 6 users who are looking for the Logic folder, but in fact it's very intuitive. Logic Pro files are either in one of two places:

Factory presets and support files are in the local directory (meaning, at the level of your hard drive):

/Library/Application Support/Logic

User presets and support files are in your user directory, with ~ being the UNIX symbol for the Home directory for a given user:

~/Library/Application Support/Logic

So as you see, there's really only a single folder you'll be adding information to, and that's the user folder. It's also very convenient to back up just this one folder and know that all your presets, templates, sampler instruments, and so on have been backed up.

EXPERT TIP: PROTECTING YOUR AUTOLOAD SONG

Being that the Autoload song is so important and painstakingly constructed, you most likely will want to save it from being accidentally modified. Luckily, the Macintosh OS offers two easy methods to protect a file. For either, you'll need to select your Autoload song in the Mac OS Finder and choose **File > Get Info** (or press **COMMAND + I**). When the Get Info box appears, you'll notice two check boxes. If you check the Stationary Pad box, Logic opens a copy of your Autoload and names it "Untitled" instead of your actual Autoload file; this way, accidentally hitting Return creates a new file, and doesn't overwrite your previous Autoload. You may also want to check the second box in the Get Info window, labeled Locked. With this checked, you simply cannot make any changes to the Autoload file without unlocking the file in the Finder first. Either method will protect your Autoload from any accidental changes.

You should now understand the basics of what Logic is and what Logic can do, and should also have completed your basic configuration and Autoload song. From this point forward, the focus shifts from explaining to exploring, and as such, you will encounter many details very quickly. Don't feel intimidated if you need to slow down, or reread a section a few times before you are comfortable with the information. Logic is a very deep program, and it takes time to absorb. In the next chapter, you will start exploring some of the global functions, options, menus, and tracks Logic has to offer.

5 Global Elements of Logic

Most of Logic's commands and options only make sense within the specific window where the command or feature is used. For example, having a function to select notes wouldn't make sense in the Track Mixer, and having a way to adjust the stereo field of an Audio Track doesn't matter in the Score Editor. That's why most commands and tools in Logic reside in *local* menus—menus specific for the window you are using. This allows Logic to put many more commands at your fingertips than if Logic were limited to the few menus in the OS X menu bar.

Some functions, however, do apply to more than one window, affect the entire song, or affect the whole application. These elements of Logic can be considered *global*. Before covering the more specific elements of Logic Pro 7, I want to use this chapter to give you one more broad view of the kinds of options and features available to you in Logic.

WHAT DO YOU KNOW?

Believe it or not, trying to decide where to put this chapter in the book was actually one of my tougher decisions. For intermediate and advanced music software users, it's not a problem—you're familiar with the concepts of global menus, local menus, using tools from a Toolbox, and so on. Intermediate and advanced Logic users may already understand what most of the features, functions, and concepts are all about. But for a beginner, reading about these menus, and later learning how to create and manipulate data in Global Tracks, might seem overwhelming.

In the end, I decided that since the global menus and Global Tracks play a part in almost every section after this one, I really had no choice but to cover it here. If you feel that you need more details, I list the section that covers the issue more in depth, so you can fill in any questions you might be left with. Hopefully, for those of you who are a bit perplexed, after you've read a little further, you can come back to this chapter, and everything will be clearer.

The Global Menus

You've already looked at and used commands from both global and local menus. The following chapters will explore all of the local menus in depth. Detailed information on many functions of the global menus will be offered later on in the appropriate chapter, but below is a brief description of each global menu and its contents. When menu commands have default key commands, these will also be listed with the menu command.

The Logic Pro Menu

The Logic Pro menu, shown in Figure 5.1, contains commands and options that affect the entire application.

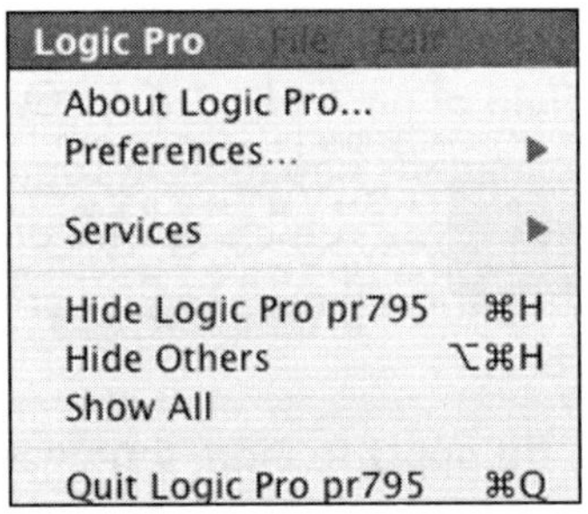

Figure 5.1
The Logic Pro menu.

It contains the following commands and submenus:

- **About Logic Pro.** You can get another look at the Logic Pro splash screen by selecting this command.
- **Preferences.** The Preferences submenu, detailed below, offers shortcuts to the main tabs in the Preference window. The preferences themselves are described in the following chapters where appropriate.
- **Services.** This is a standard Mac OS X submenu included by the system in every Mac OS X application. This submenu is of no use in Logic.
- **Hide Logic Pro.** This command will remove all the Logic Pro windows from your screen until you select the application in the Finder. **<COMMAND + H>**
- **Hide Others.** You can hide every application except Logic Pro with this command. **<COMMAND + OPTION + H>**
- **Show All.** You can reveal all applications, including those that are hidden, with this command.
- **Quit Logic Pro.** Use this command to quit Logic Pro. **<COMMAND + Q>**

The Preferences Submenu

The Preferences submenu, shown in Figure 5.2, gives you access to the individual tabs of the Preferences window and other global preference-related elements of Logic Pro.

Figure 5.2
The Preferences submenu. Selecting any of these will open the Preferences window to that preference tab.

The commands in the Preferences submenu are explained below:

- **Global, Audio, MIDI, Display, Score, Video, and Automation.** Each of these will open the Preferences window to the specific Preference tab you have selected. Each Preference tab has a number of sub-tabs that you'll have to navigate to from there. Each Preference tab is explained in the appropriate chapter for that preference.
- **Initialize All Except Key Commands.** You can reset every preference except your key commands by selecting this command.
- **Start Logic Setup Assistant.** This command allows you to launch the Logic Setup Assistant (LSA) to create a new default song. Using the LSA is described in Chapter 2.
- **Start Logic AU Manager.** You can launch the new Logic AU Manager with this command. The Logic AU Manager is new to Logic Pro 7 and allows you to turn on and off individual Audio Unit plug-ins within Logic. Chapters 10 and 12 detail the functions of Logic's AU Manager.
- **Control Surfaces.** This submenu, explained below, contains options for configuring and using MIDI control surfaces with Logic.
- **Key Commands.** This command opens the Key Commands window. Using the Key Commands window is described in Chapter 4.

The Control Surfaces Submenu

The Control Surfaces submenu, shown in Figure 5.3, offers the commands relating to the use and configuration of MIDI devices to be used as control surfaces for Logic.

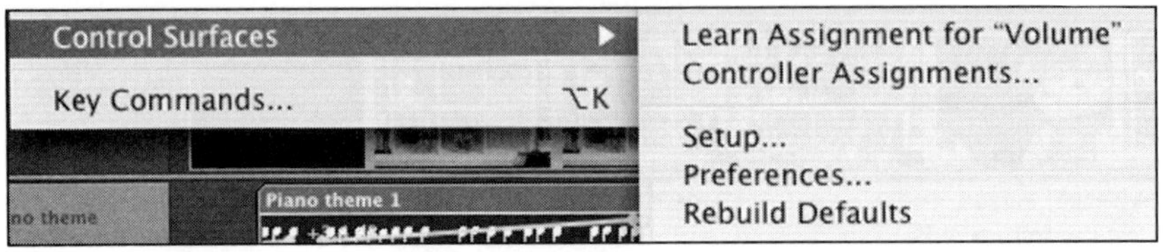

Figure 5.3
The Control Surfaces submenu of the Preferences submenu.

The commands in this submenu do the following:

- **Learn Assignment.** This command launches the Controller Assignments window for the selected option or command. This is discussed in Chapter 4.
- **Controller Assignments.** You can launch the Controller Assignments window without previously selecting an option or command directly here. The Controller Assignments window is discussed in Chapter 4.
- **Setup.** This launches the Control Surface Setup window. This window is briefly discussed in Chapter 4.
- **Preferences.** You can set a number of preferences for control surfaces here.
- **Rebuild Defaults.** This will reset the preferences for your control surface.

The File Menu

Not surprisingly, the File menu, as seen in Figure 5.4, contains options and commands that involve files. Most commands here will either get files into or out of Logic. If not otherwise noted, most of these commands will be explored in more detail in Chapter 13, "Working with Files."

The entries in the File menu are described below:

- **New.** This command opens a new song from the default song, your Autoload Song, or one of your Song Templates. **<COMMAND + N>**
- **Open.** The Open command opens a song created by Logic (any version or platform of Logic). **<COMMAND + O>**

Figure 5.4

The File menu.

- **Open Recent.** The Open Recent submenu contains a list of your recently opened songs. If the list gets too long, there is an option to Clear Menu and start over.
- **Project.** The Project submenu, described below, offers you a number of options relating to setting up Logic songs as projects:
  - **Settings.** You can choose how the project will handle various types of files.
  - **Clean up.** This command will revert projects to their original organization.
  - **Consolidate.** You can take a Logic song that does not have a Project structure and consolidate it into a project with this command.
  - **Rename.** This allows you to rename a project.
- **Close.** This will close the currently open song (or the currently selected song, if you have more than one song open). **<OPTION + COMMAND + W>**
- **Save.** Save will save the current song. **<COMMAND + S>**
- **Save As.** This command brings up a Save dialog box for you to save your song. **<OPTION + COMMAND + S>**
- **Save a Copy As.** This command brings up a Save dialog box for you to save a copy of your song.
- **Save as Template.** This command saves the current song as a template.
- **Save as Project.** This command brings up the Project Settings window for you to save your song as a project.
- **Revert to Saved.** If you aren't happy with the current state of your song, Revert to Saved will reload the last saved version of your song. Obviously, this only works if you'd previously saved your song!
- **Song Settings.** The Song Settings submenu, described below, allows you to open the Song Settings window to a specific settings tab.

- **Page Setup.** This command opens the Page Setup window of your printer driver.
- **Print.** This prints the contents of the selected window. This is useful if you wish to print musical notation from the Score Editor, for example. **<COMMAND + P>**
- **Import.** The Import command brings up the Open File window and it allows you to import any of the file types Logic supports. Currently, Logic Pro 7 can import MIDI, OMF, AAF, OpenTL, XML (FinalCut Pro), and SysEx files.
- **Export.** In the Export submenu, you can export your Logic song into any of the above formats that Logic supports. You can also export a single region, track, or all of your tracks into individual files. The various Export options are discussed in Chapter 7 (Export Track/Region) and Chapter 13.
- **Bounce.** This command allows you to create a stereo mixdown of all the tracks in your song. The Bounce command is discussed in Chapter 12, "Mixing in Logic." The File menu Bounce command can only bounce the audio routed to Output Objects 1–2.

The Song Settings Submenu

Song Settings are preferences for your individual song, unlike Logic's Preferences that apply to the entire application, regardless of the song. The Song Settings submenu is shown in Figure 5.5.

Figure 5.5
The Song Settings submenu.

The Song Settings submenu contains the following items:

- **Synchronization.** You can open the Song Settings Synchronization tab here. These settings are described in Chapter 15. **<OPTION + X>**

- **Metronome.** You can open the Song Settings Metronome tab here. These settings are described in Chapter 6.
- **Recording.** You can open the Song Settings Recording tab here. These settings are described in Chapter 6. **<OPTION + R>**
- **Tuning.** You can open the Song Settings Tuning tab here. These settings are described in Chapter 10.
- **Audio.** You can open the Song Settings Audio tab here. These settings are described in Chapter 7.
- **MIDI.** You can open the Song Settings MIDI tab here. These settings are described in Chapter 7. **<OPTION + M>**
- **Score.** You can open the Song Settings Score tab here. These settings are described in Chapter 9.
- **Video.** You can open the Song Settings Video tab here. These settings are described in Chapter 17.
- **Import Settings.** This command allows you to import the song settings of another Logic song. Selecting this command brings up a File dialog for you to choose the song you wish to import settings from. You may choose to import any or all of the following: Screensets, Transform Sets, Hyper Edit Sets, Score Instrument Sets, Score Styles, Score Settings.

The Edit Menu

The Edit menu, shown in Figure 5.6, includes a standard set of global editing, moving, selection, and undo commands.

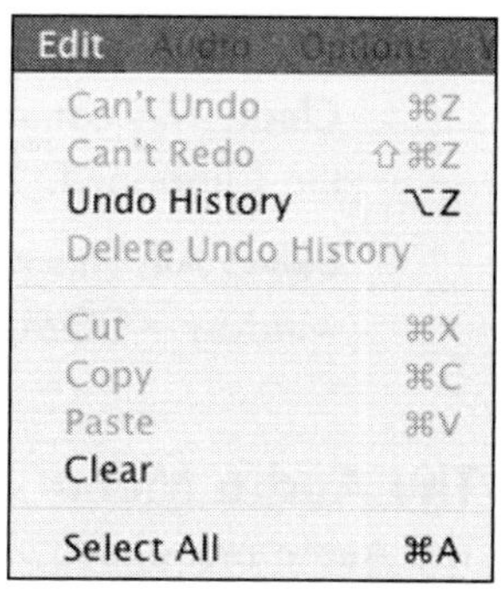

Figure 5.6
The Edit menu.

The commands in the Edit menu are explained below:

- **Undo.** If you are not happy with your most recent action, Undo will revert Logic to the condition before that action. Not all actions can be undone—if you try to undo an action that cannot be undone, the command will be grayed out, and read "Can't Undo."
  <COMMAND + Z>

* **Redo.** If you have undone an action and wish to bring it back, you can use the Redo command. Not all actions can be redone—if you try to redo an action that cannot be redone, the command will be grayed out, and read "Can't Redo." **<COMMAND + SHIFT + Z>**
* **Undo History.** Logic has multiple levels of undo. This means that each action gets stored in the Undo History window, and you can decide at any time to go back and undo as many actions as you'd like. The Undo History window is explored in more detail in Chapter 7. **<OPTION + Z>**
* **Delete Undo History.** Use this command to empty the Undo History window and start over with a brand new list of actions, starting from the action after selecting Delete Undo History.
* **Cut.** This command removes the selected data from its current location and adds it to the Clipboard. **<COMMAND + X>**
* **Copy.** This command adds the currently selected data to the Clipboard without removing it from its current location. **<COMMAND +C>**
* **Paste.** This command adds the data in the Clipboard to the current pointer location. Note that this only works for compatible data—for example, if an audio file is in the Clipboard, you can't paste it into the Score Editor, only into the Audio window, Sample Editor, or Arrange window, as these windows can contain audio data. **<COMMAND + V>**
* **Clear.** This command will clear the selected data without adding it to the Clipboard.
* **Select All.** This command will select all of the data in the current window. **<COMMAND + A>**

The Audio Menu

The Audio menu, shown in Figure 5.7, contains global options and functions relating to audio.

Many of these options are explained in more depth in Chapter 8, "Working with Audio and Apple Loops." Below is a brief list of Audio menu options:

* **Audio Window.** This command opens the Audio window. The Audio window is explored in Chapter 8. **<COMMAND + 9>**

- **Loop Browser.** This command opens the Loop Browser. The Loop Browser is explored in Chapter 8.
- **Sample Editor.** This command opens the Sample Editor window. The Sample Editor is explored in Chapter 8.
- **Audio Mixer.** You can open the Audio layer of the Environment with this command. The Audio layer of the Environment contains a complete Audio Mixer with all of your channel strips. This is different from the Track Mixer, however. The various Mixer windows are explored in more detail in Chapter 12, "Mixing in Logic."

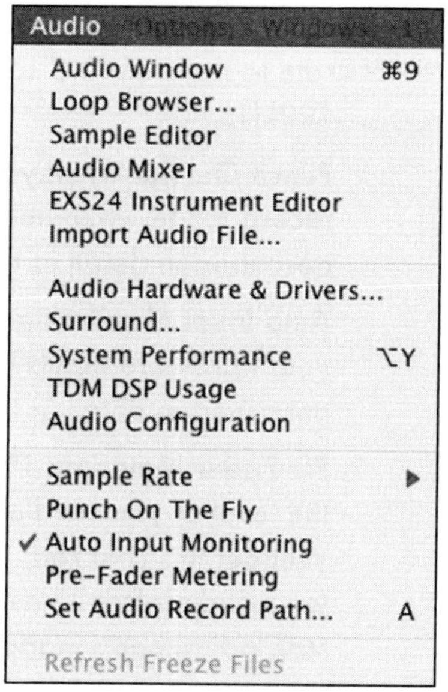

Figure 5.7
The Audio menu.

- **EXS24 Instrument Editor.** Use this command to open the EXS24mkII Sampler's Instrument Editor. Unfortunately, there's not enough space in this book to detail Emagic's included synthesizers, plug-ins, and samplers.
- **Import Audio File.** You can import an audio file into the Audio window using this command. Importing audio files into the Audio window is explored in more detail in Chapter 8.
- **Audio Hardware & Drivers.** This command will open the **Preferences > Audio > Drivers** tab.
- **Surround.** This command will open the **Preferences > Audio > Surround** tab.
- **System Performance.** This opens the system performance floating window that offers meters for your audio, disk, and node usage. **<OPTION + Y>**
- **TDM DSP Usage.** This opens the TDM DSP Usage window. Obviously, this window is only for users using Logic with Digidesign TDM systems.
- **Audio Configuration.** This opens the Audio Configuration window. Use this window to name inputs, outputs, busses, and to move plug-ins around the mixer. This window is explored in more detail in Chapter 8 and Chapter 12.

- **Sample Rate.** This submenu allows you to change your song's sample rate to the standard sample rate settings between 44.1kHz and 192kHz.
- **Punch On The Fly.** If you want to be able to immediately drop into record mode when needed, you can check this command. This is described in detail in the next chapter.
- **Auto Input Monitoring.** If you want to monitor what is coming through your hardware inputs into Logic, you can check this command. This is described in detail in the next chapter.
- **Pre-Fader Metering.** This sets up the channel strip meters to show you the level of your audio *before* it is processed by the channel strip. Without this checked, the channel strip meters will show the level of your audio after it has been processed by any effects and channel strip adjustments made on the channel strip.
- **Set Audio Record Path.** You can set the Audio Record Path with this command. Audio Record Paths are described in detail in the next chapter. **<A>**
- **Refresh Freeze Files.** If you have used Freeze on any Arrange tracks, then turned off Freeze to edit those tracks and turned it on again, this command will re-Freeze those tracks. The Freeze Tracks function is described in detail in Chapter 7.

The Options Menu

The Options menu, as seen in Figure 5.8, is a catchall menu for commands and options that impact the song as a whole, more than one window, Global Tracks, and so on. Most of these submenus are described further on in the book where appropriate.

The entries in the Options menu are described below:

- **Marker.** This submenu includes options relating to song Markers. Markers, including the options in this submenu, are explained below in "The Marker Track."
- **Tempo.** This submenu includes options relating to Logic's display and control of tempo. The options in this submenu are explored in Chapter 15.

- **Signature/Key Change List Editor.** This command launches the Signature/Key Change List Editor. This editor is used for entering new time signature and key change information. This window is explored below in "The Signature Track." **<COMMAND + 0>**

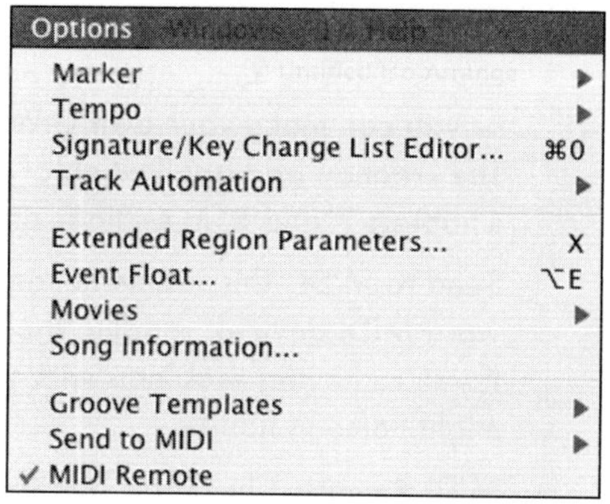

Figure 5.8

The Options menu.

- **Track Automation.** This submenu includes options relating to Logic's Track Automation feature, described in Chapter 7.
- **Extended Region Parameters.** This opens a floating window with more parameters that affect MIDI Regions than the standard Region parameter box. This is explored in Chapter 7. **<X>**
- **Event Float.** If you want a one-entry Event List in a floating window in order to always show you the currently selected data, you can launch one with this command. **<OPTION + E>**
- **Movies.** This submenu contains options that pertain to using QuickTime movies in Logic Pro. These options are discussed in Chapter 17.
- **Song Information.** You can open the Song Information window, shown below in Figure 5.9, with this command. It gives you a concise list of all the elements of your song, and how much memory they require.

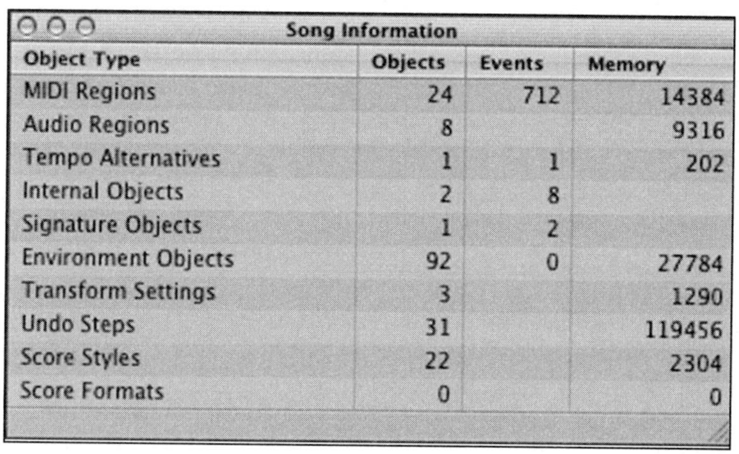

Song Information

Object Type	Objects	Events	Memory
MIDI Regions	24	712	14384
Audio Regions	8		9316
Tempo Alternatives	1	1	202
Internal Objects	2	8	
Signature Objects	1	2	
Environment Objects	92	0	27784
Transform Settings	3		1290
Undo Steps	31		119456
Score Styles	22		2304
Score Formats	0		0

Figure 5.9

The Song Information window.

- **Groove Templates.** This submenu contains options for Groove Templates. Groove Templates are either pre-made MIDI timing patterns, or you can make your own Groove Templates from Audio regions. The creation and application of Groove Templates is explained in Chapters 7 and 8, in sections on quantization.
- **Send to MIDI.** This submenu contains a few options for resetting hardware MIDI devices, sending them global volume increases, and so on. If you're having problems with your MIDI hardware, these options might come in handy.
- **MIDI Remote.** Check this box to allow MIDI devices to remote control Logic. Honestly, I can't imagine why you would ever uncheck it.

The Windows Menu

The Windows menu, as shown in Figure 5.10, contains commands relating to opening and manipulating windows.

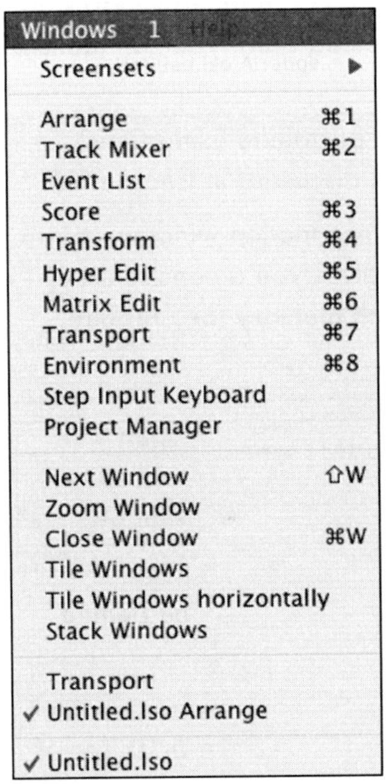

Figure 5.10

The Windows menu.

The Windows menu contains the following commands:

- **Screensets.** This submenu includes commands relating to screensets. This submenu was explored in Chapter 4.
- **Arrange.** This command will launch an Arrange window. The Arrange window is discussed in Chapter 7. **<COMMAND + 1>**
- **Track Mixer.** This command will launch a Track Mixer window. The Track Mixer is discussed in Chapter 12. **<COMMAND + 2>**
- **Event List.** This command will launch an Event List window. The Event List is discussed in Chapter 9.
- **Score.** This command will launch a Score Editor. The Score Editor is discussed in Chapter 9. **<COMMAND + 3>**

- **Transform.** This command will launch a Transform window. The Transform window is discussed in Chapter 9. **<COMMAND + 4>**
- **Hyper Edit.** This command will launch a Hyper Editor. The Hyper Editor is discussed in Chapter 9. **<COMMAND + 5>**
- **Matrix Edit.** This command will launch a Matrix Editor. The Matrix Editor is discussed in Chapter 9. **<COMMAND + 6>**
- **Transport.** This command will launch a Transport window. The Transport window is discussed in Chapter 6. **<COMMAND + 7>**
- **Environment.** This command will launch an Environment window. The Environment window has been discussed previously, but will be discussed in depth in Chapter 14. **<COMMAND + 8>**
- **Step Input Keyboard.** This command will launch the Step Input Keyboard. The Step Input Keyboard is discussed in Chapter 9.
- **Project Manager.** This command launches the Project Manager. The Project Manager is discussed in Chapter 13.
- **Next Window.** You can switch from the current window to the next unselected window with this command. **<SHIFT + W>**
- **Zoom Window.** You can instantly resize a window to fill the entire screen with this command.
- **Close Window.** You can close the selected window with this command. **<COMMAND + W>**
- **Tile Windows.** This command will resize any open windows into vertical columns extending from the top to the bottom of your screen. The width of the columns depends on how many windows are tiled.
- **Tile Windows Horizontally.** This command will resize any open windows into a horizontal column from the top to the bottom of your screen. The height of the columns depends on how many windows are tiled.
- **Stack Windows.** This command will stack your windows one behind the other.
- **List of Open Windows.** Under the Stack Windows command, a list of all the windows currently open in Logic follows. In Figure 5.10, for example, the only open windows are the Transport window and the Untitled.lso Arrange window.

- **List of Open songs.** Under the list of open windows above is a list of all currently open Logic songs. In Figure 5.10, for example, the only open song is Untitled.lso.

Help Menu

The Help menu is the standard Mac OS X Help menu. It contains an entry to launch Logic Pro Help. The online help allows you to open a number of PDF files of information on Logic Pro. If the help text reminds you of the Logic Pro 7 manual, there's a reason—they are the same. So Logic Help really is another way to access the manual while online.

Global Tracks

Global Tracks are a new addition to Logic Pro 7. These unique tracks contain information that pertains to the entire Logic song, such as song tempo, key signature, time signature, song markers, thumbnails of video you are writing audio for, and so on. Global Tracks can be displayed in the Arrange window, and the Matrix, Score, and Hyper Editors. There are seven types of Global Tracks:

- **Marker Track.** This track contains song Markers, or position holders, you can use to label and separate sections of your song.
- **Signature Track.** This track contains all your time signatures and key signatures for your song.
- **Chord Track.** This track contains chord symbols, and acts as a chord chart for your entire song.
- **Transposition Track.** This track shows any global transposition events—in other words, any chord changes or note transpositions that would result in all MIDI regions and Apple Loops being transposed from their original pitch.
- **Tempo Track.** This track contains the tempo and tempo changes for your song.
- **Beat Mapping Track.** This powerful addition to Logic allows you to use any Audio or MIDI region with strong rhythmic accents to create a "beat map" that Logic will use to adjust the musical timeline.
- **Video Track.** This track contains thumbnail frames of QuickTime video in sync with Logic.

Figure 5.11 shows all the Global Tracks expanded in an Arrange window.

Figure 5.11

An Arrange window with all seven Global Tracks displayed and expanded. (Video thumbnails ©Bar Ben-Yossef)

As you've seen from Figure 5.11, Global Tracks can eat up your screen real estate fast! Don't worry; you don't need to view them all at the same time. Each View local menu of all the windows that can show Global Tracks contains options to show only those Global Tracks that you wish to see (there are also key commands to toggle each Global Track on or off). You can, for example, choose only to view the Marker and Video tracks, or you might choose to show the Tempo track in Arrange, but not in the Score Editor. Each Global Track also has a disclosure triangle at its left edge, which you can use to expand or collapse the Global Track. If you want to rearrange your displayed Global Tracks, you can do this by grabbing a Global Track in the track list and dragging it to its new location. Finally, when you move the cursor to the border of a Global Track, it turns into a resize cursor, and you can drag that track to resize it. Figure 5.12 gives an example of these Global Track features.

Figure 5.12

In the figure, only four of the seven Global Tracks are showing. The Marker track has been resized to be larger via the resize cursor (shown). The Tempo and Beat Mapping tracks have been collapsed via their disclosure triangles. Finally, the Video track is expanded and normal size.

Common Features of Global Tracks

The Video and Beat Mapping tracks are quite unique in their function and features. But the other five Global Tracks share a number of common features. The data on these Global Tracks consist of *global events*. These global events are different types of data depending on the specific Global Track, but they can be created, moved, copied, and deleted similarly. The next sections will explain how.

Creating a Global Event

To create a global event on a Global Track, simply click with the Pencil tool in the desired position in the track. As the mouse button is down, a help tag with the exact position (and value, if applicable to that Global Track) will be displayed below the cursor. Figure 5.13 illustrates creating a global event in the Tempo track.

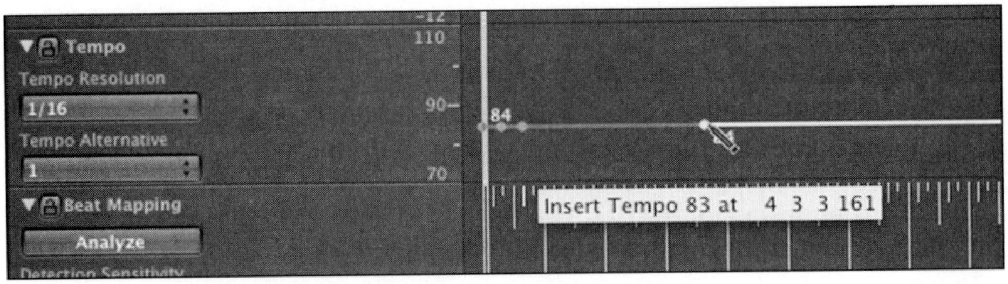

Figure 5.13
Inserting global events in the Tempo track. Just click in the track with the Pencil tool to create the event. The Help tag below your Pencil tool will give you the exact information and position regarding your action.

If you have not changed the default command-button tool, you can access the Pencil tool via the **COMMAND** key. If you have set your Right Mouse Button preference in **Logic Pro > Preferences > Global > Edit** tab to "Is assignable to a tool," and you have assigned it to the Pencil tool by right-clicking on the Pencil tool in the Toolbox, then you can access the Pencil tool via the right mouse button.

If not, you can still select the Pencil tool from the Toolbox of the current window. You can also access the Toolbox by pressing the ESC key. If you have set your Right Mouse Button preference in **Logic Pro > Preferences > Global > Edit** tab to Open Toolbox, you can use your right mouse button to open the Toolbox and select the Pencil tool.

If the concept of tools and Toolboxes isn't familiar to you, you might want to skip to Chapter 7 where, in the context of the Arrange page tools, I explain the Toolbox and the Pencil tool in detail.

Selecting and Moving Global Events

You can select global events using the common selection methods you are familiar with from other applications. Click on an event with the mouse pointer to select it. To select multiple global events, **SHIFT + CLICK** on the events you wish to select. If you wish to make a "rubber band" (sometimes called "lasso") group selection, you can drag over a group of events with the **CONTROL** key down. If you click the name of the Global Track in the track list, you will select all the events on that track.

Once selected, global events can be moved and or changed simply by dragging them. As the mouse button is down, a help tag with the exact position (and value, if applicable to that Global Track) of your global event will be displayed below the cursor. Figure 5.14 shows a global event on the Tempo track being moved.

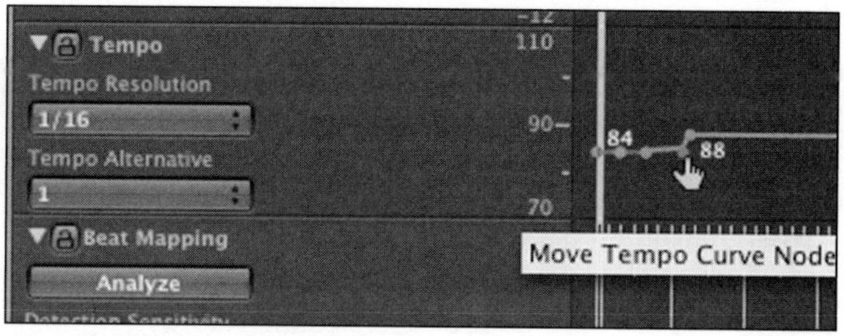

Figure 5.14

In this figure, a global event in the Tempo track has been selected and is being moved to the left.

Copying and Deleting Global Events

You can copy and delete global events using the standard Macintosh methods for copying and deleting information.

To copy data with the mouse, you can **OPTION + DRAG** any selected data. You can also use the Edit menu and keyboard commands for Cut and Paste, or Copy and Paste.

To delete data with the mouse, you can click on the data with the Eraser tool from that window's Toolbox. You can also use the **DELETE** or Backspace key on your keyboard. Finally, you can use the Edit menu command for Clear.

The Marker Track

The Marker track displays song Markers. Markers are very useful position holders for locations or sections of your song. They can appear as short place holders with a line or two of text in the Marker track, or as much longer messages in their own Marker Text window. The background and text of the Markers may be colored if you wish. Figure 5.15 shows Matrix Editor with the Marker track displayed.

Markers were tied to the Bar Ruler in previous versions of Logic, and still will be in windows that show the Bar Ruler if the Marker track is not displayed. If you do not have the Marker track displayed, the Markers themselves will still appear as they do in Figure 5.16 at the bottom of the Bar Ruler.

Markers are an invaluable aid in arranging your song and are very easy to create and use, as you will soon see.

Creating, Copying, Resizing, Moving, and Deleting Markers

As discussed above, Markers are global events, and can be created, copied, moved, resized, and deleted the same way as any global event on a Global Track.

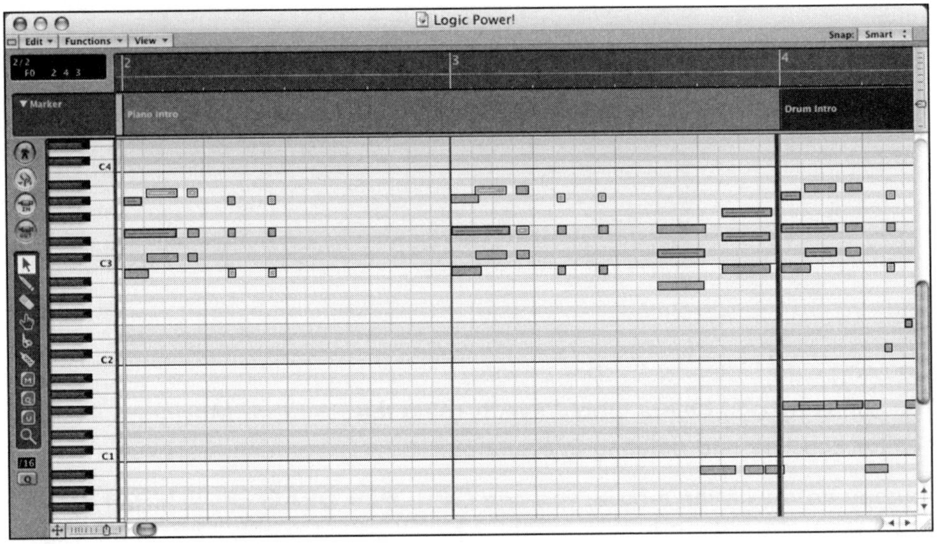

Figure 5.15
This Matrix Editor has a Marker track displaying song Markers at the top of the editor.

Figure 5.16
In this Matrix window, the Marker track is not displayed, but the Markers themselves are still visible on the Bar Ruler.

However, commands pertaining to the creation and use of Markers are also available in the global Options menu, as shown in Figure 5.17.

In addition to the standard global event methods, Logic offers a few additional ways to add Markers to your song.

- You can use the Create Marker command by selecting **Options > Markers > Create**.

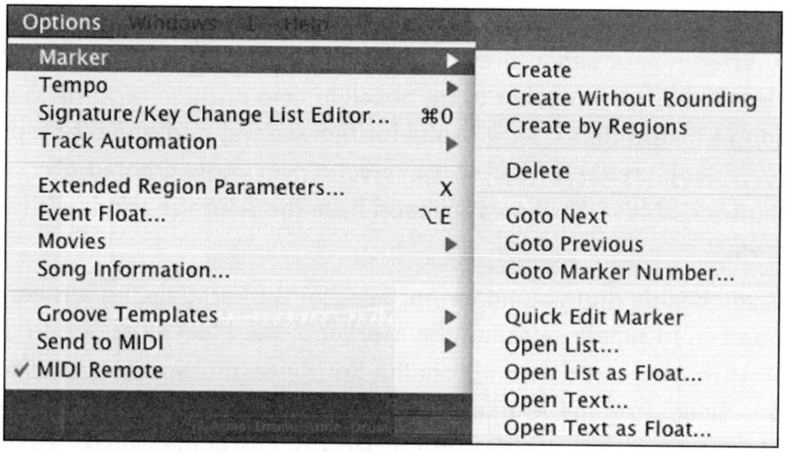

Figure 5.17
The **Options > Markers** submenu contains Marker commands.

- You can drag one or more regions from the Arrange window into the Marker track. A Marker will be created with the same length and position as the dragged region(s).
- If you click the From Regions button in the Marker track, Logic will automatically create a new Marker for each selected region. The Markers will have the same position, length, and name as the selected regions.
- You can use the command Create by Regions by selecting **Options > Markers > Create by Regions** to create a Marker for each selected region.
- Markers that you create using regions may be rounded to the closest bar line. If you wish your Marker to be at the exact position the regions are, even if they are not on a bar line, you can choose the Create Without Rounding command from **Options > Markers > Create Without Rounding**.
- If you click any point in the bottom third of the Bar Ruler while holding down the **OPTION + COMMAND** keys, Logic will create a Marker where you clicked. The Marker Text window appears in which you can customize your Marker (see the next subsection, "The Marker Text Window").
- You can create a Marker that corresponds to a Cycle area if Cycle mode is on (see Chapter 6, "The Transport Window") by dragging the Cycle area down into the Marker track or down into the bottom third of the Bar Ruler.
- If you are in the Marker List window, you can use the Pencil tool to create a new Marker (see "The Marker List Window" below).

If you attempt to create a Marker where a Marker already exists within a quarter note in either direction, Logic will not create the new Marker. If you want to assign a Marker to an absolute time position regardless of the song's tempo (this is very useful for film scoring and audio post-production for video), create a Marker (or select a previously created Marker) and use the Lock SMPTE Position command from the Arrange window's local Region menu.

If you decide that you no longer need a Marker, deleting it is very simple. In addition to simply selecting the Marker in the Marker track and pressing **DELETE**, you can delete it from the Bar Ruler and Marker List window. In the Bar Ruler, drag the Marker below the Bar Ruler and the Marker will vanish. Or you can use the Eraser tool or **DELETE** key in the Marker List window. Lastly, you can choose **Options > Markers > Delete**.

Adding or Changing Marker Color

You can easily add or change the color of a Marker on the Marker track. First, open the color palette from the local view menu of the selected window (**View > Colors**) or press **OPTION + C**. Select one or more Markers, and click the color in the palette you wish to add to the Marker(s). The Markers will now have the selected color. You can also change Marker color from the Text window, as explained below.

The Marker Text Window

The Marker Text window, shown in Figure 5.18, is where you customize the look and the text of the Marker you have created.

As you can see in Figure 5.18, there are five buttons to the left of the text-entry window. These buttons have the following functions:

- **Open Book.** When this button is not glowing, the window is the Marker List window. When this button is glowing, the window is the Marker Text window.
- **Walking Man (Catch).** When this button is glowing, it ensures that you will always see the text of the current Marker in the Marker Text window.
- **Up Arrow.** This button switches back to the previous Marker from the one currently displayed.
- **Down Arrow.** This button advances to the following Marker.

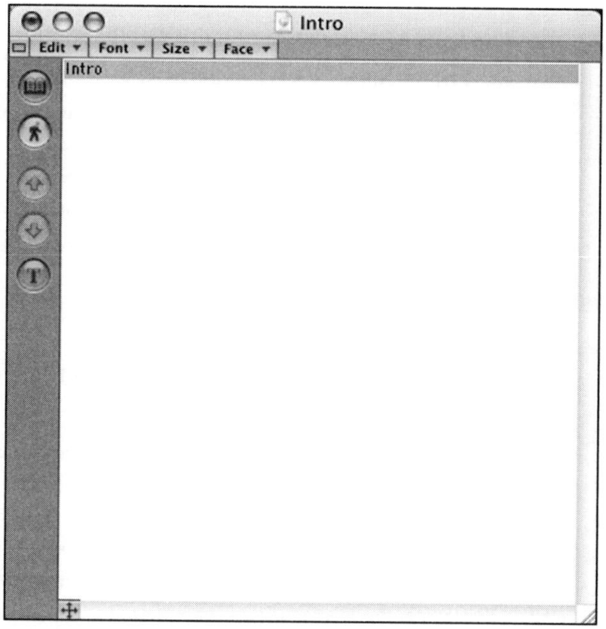

Figure 5.18

The Marker Text window contains all your options for customizing Markers.

- **T.** This is the Text Protection button. Make sure this button is glowing turquoise if you want to enter text. If you want to protect your text from changes, you can click this button again.

The local Edit menu contains all the standard text editing commands: Cut, Copy, Paste, Clear, and Select All. If you have text on the Clipboard, you can paste it into a Marker, or copy the text here onto the Clipboard to paste it elsewhere.

The Font, Size, and Face menus contain options for selecting a font, resizing the font, and choosing the font style and color. Keep in mind that in the Arrange window, the Marker space in the Bar Ruler is too small to display anything besides the name and color of your Marker. You'll need to keep the Marker Text window open in your screenset to view the customized Marker text—the Marker track itself uses only its default font.

If you choose **Face > Object Color** (or press **OPTION + C**), Logic's color palette appears; if you click on a color, the currently selected text assumes that color. If you press **COMMAND** and click a color, the Marker background assumes the clicked color, just as if you selected the Marker in the Marker track and chose a color.

MARKER BACKGROUND COLOR WITH MORE THAN ONE TEXT PARAGRAPH

If you create more than one paragraph of text in the Marker Text window by pressing the RETURN key, then change the background color, in the Marker Text window, the new background color will fill the entire text window. In the Marker track, however, it will not. A line will divide the first paragraph and second paragraph text through the Marker, and your color will only appear in the top half. There is currently no way to add color to the bottom half of a Marker on a Marker track.

EXPERT TIP: WHEN MARKER TEXT IS IMPORTANT, OPEN TEXT WINDOW AS FLOAT

Clearly, the Markers in the Global Track or the Bar Ruler are not designed for large amounts of text. They are perfect for a quick title and maybe a note or a lyric or two, but not much more than that. If you want your Markers to contain extensive notes and information for collaborators, future reference, and so on, you would be better off by keeping the Marker Text window open permanently. A great way to do this is by selecting **Options > Markers > Open Text Window as Float**. This creates the Marker window as a "floating" window, meaning it will not get lost behind other windows and will always be visible.

The Marker List Window

In addition to being visible on the Global Track or Bar Ruler, Logic stores the locations of all a song's Markers in a specialized Event List, called the Marker List window. The Marker List window displays all the Markers currently created in your song. It allows you to edit the positions of Markers, create Markers, and perform some additional functions as well. You can bring up the Marker List window either by selecting **Options > Markers > Open List** or by clicking the Open Book icon in the Marker Text window. The Marker List window is shown in Figure 5.19.

The Marker List window has two buttons and four tools on the left side of the list window. Brief explanations of their functions follow:

- **Open Book.** As explained previously, this button toggles the window between the Marker Text window and Marker List window.
- **Walking Man (Catch).** When lit, this button ensures the Marker List window follows along the song position Locator.

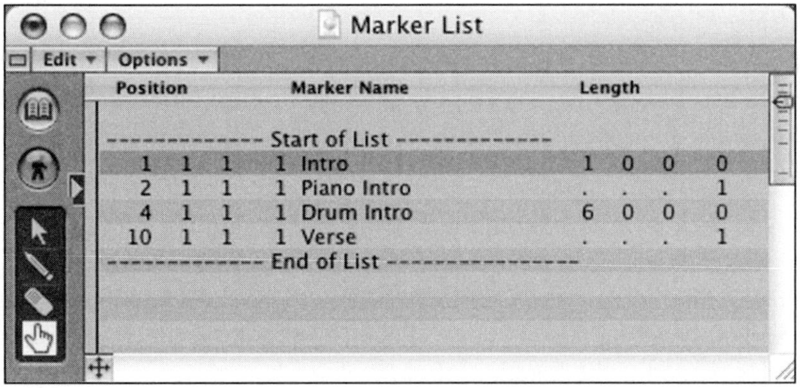

Figure 5.19
In the Marker List window, you can add Markers, edit their position and length, and more.

- **Pointer.** This is a normal selection tool. If you double-click on the position or length parameters of a Marker, you can use the mouse as a slider for adjusting values. Double-clicking on the name of a Marker switches the window to the Marker Text window, opened to the selected Marker.
- **Pencil.** If you double-click on a Marker, this tool creates a Marker identical to the selected Marker. You can then edit the Marker to suit your taste.
- **Eraser.** When you click on a Marker with this tool, this erases (deletes) the Marker.
- **Index Finger.** This tool not only selects a Marker when you click on it, but it moves the SPL to the beginning of that Marker, and sets the Locators to the Marker boundaries. If you hold the mouse button down, Logic begins playing your song from the beginning of this Marker as well. This is the default tool when you open the Marker List window.

The Marker List window serves as a single location in which to quickly view all your Markers. If you like to navigate or edit Markers from a list, the Marker List window serves that purpose. In fact, if you want to use the Marker List as a permanent navigation aid, you can select **Options > Markers > Open List as Float** to open a floating Marker List window that will always be visible.

Using Markers

I've already discussed using Markers as a visual cue to organize your song, or to create extensive text boxes filled with notes, lyrics, and such that will automatically follow your song. You can also use Markers to move the SPL (song position line) and set a Cycle area.

If you click on a Marker in the Marker track using the **OPTION** key, the SPL moves to the start of the Marker. You can also click on a Marker in the Bar Ruler while holding the **COMMAND** key to do the same thing. If you drag a Marker up to the top of the Bar Ruler, it will set the Locators and turn on Cycle mode for the length of that Marker.

The Signature Track

The Signature track shows any time and key signatures associated with the song. If you haven't set any, Logic will default to a time signature of 4/4 and a key of C. If you import a GarageBand song, your initial key and time signature settings from GarageBand will be carried over. If you are not familiar with music notation, or otherwise do not generally use time and key signatures in your music, you will most likely not use this Global Track very often. Figure 5.20 shows a Signature track open in a Score Editor window.

In general, the Signature track information is more for display purposes than anything else. Any key signature changes after the initial key signature affect the display of MIDI notes in the Score Editor but don't have any effect on playback. Similarly, even time signature changes don't affect the playback, but only the display of measures in the Score Editor.

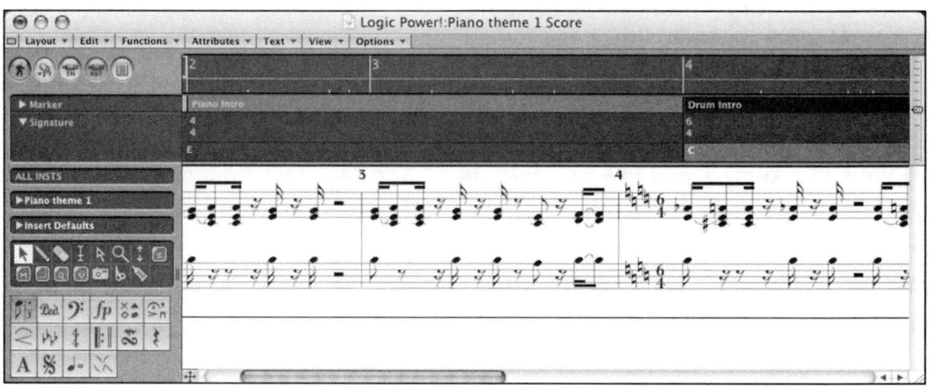

Figure 5.20

This figure shows the Signature track with some time and key signature changes displayed in a Score Editor.

The Signature track does interact in some ways with the Chord track. Apple Loops and transposable MIDI regions will be transposed based on the root note of chords in the Chord track. These root notes determine if there will be any transposition relative to the current key signature shown in the Signature track. If no chords are available in the Chord track, the global playback key for Apple Loops and MIDI regions is determined by the very first key signature.

Creating Time and Key Signature Global Events

You can create time and key signatures by creating global events in the Signature track as described in the "Creating a Global Event" section above. If you click with the Pencil tool in the top half of the Signature track, you will be shown the dialog box in Figure 5.21 to add a time signature event. If you click the Pencil tool in the bottom half of the Signature track, you will be shown the dialog box in Figure 5.22 to add a key signature event.

If you reduce the track height, you will only be able to create a time signature event. Only when the Signature track is at its normal height will both lines for time and key signatures be visible.

Figure 5.21
When you use the Pencil tool to create a time signature event, this dialog box lets you enter the time signature information. When you click OK, the time signature will be added to the Signature track.

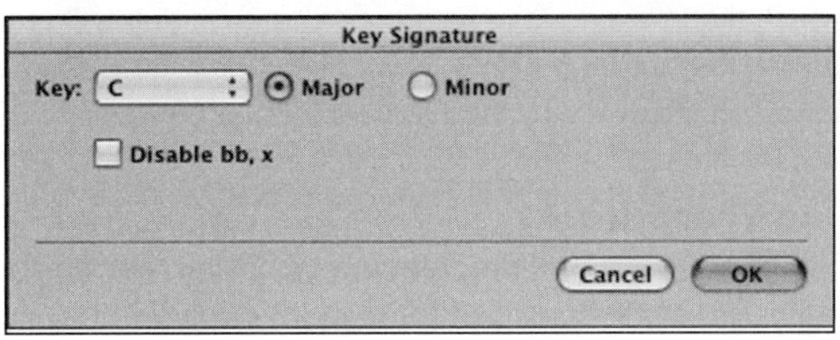

Figure 5.22
When you use the Pencil tool to create a key signature event, this dialog box lets you enter the key signature information. When you click OK, the key signature will be added to the Signature track.

Time and key signatures can also be added in the Score Editor. This is discussed in Chapter 9, "Working with MIDI."

Copying, Resizing, Moving and Deleting Signatures

Events on the Signature track can be selected, moved, deleted, and copied in the same way as other global events. If you wish to edit an existing signature, double-click a signature and the dialog boxes shown above will open. If you **SHIFT + DOUBLE CLICK** anywhere in the Signature track, you will open the Signature/Key Change List, shown in Figure 5.23. In this window, time and key signatures are shown in a list style editor, much like the Marker List above. Any other Score symbols such as repeat signs, double bar lines and so on, will also be shown in this list.

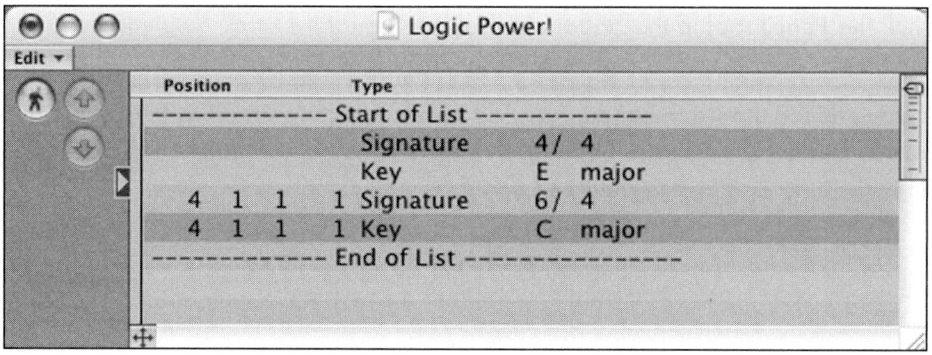

Figure 5.23
The Signature/Key Change List. This window shows all your time signatures and key changes in a list format.

Cutting Measures in the Signature Track

If you want to cut measures in the Signature track—for example, if you want to divide one 5/4 measure into a 3/4 measure and a 2/4 measure—you can select the Scissors tool from the Toolbox of the selected window and click at the desired location. If you make a cut in the middle of a bar in which there are no time signature changes, you will create two shorter measures with the original time. You can also merge two measures into one longer measure using the Glue tool in the Signature track.

The Chord Track

The Chord track contains letters symbolizing the chords in your song. The main uses of this track are for a visual display of the chord structure of your song and for determining the global transposition of MIDI regions and Apple Loops throughout your song. Figure 5.24 shows a Chord track being displayed in an Arrange window.

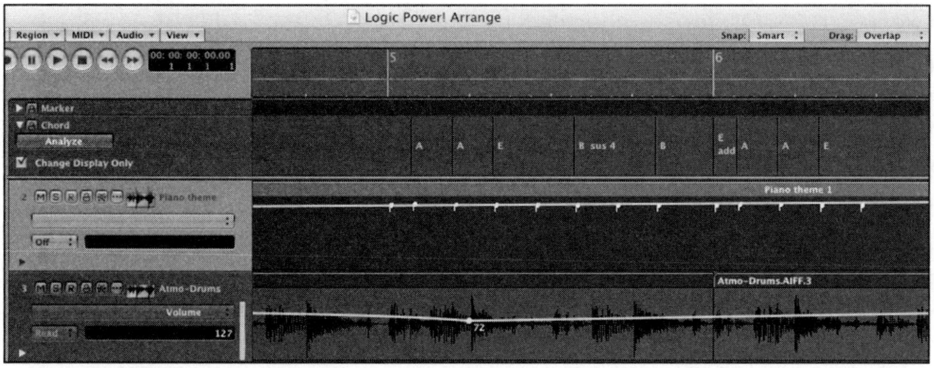

Figure 5.24

The Chord track displayed in this Arrange window reflects the current chord that will affect global transposition at each point of the song.

Creating Chord Track Global Events

There are a number of ways to create global events on the Chord track:

- As explained in the first section on creating global events, you can click the Pencil tool at the desired position in the Chord track. This will open the dialog window shown in Figure 5.25 for you to define your chord event.
- You can select one or more MIDI regions (preferably containing complete chords) and click the Analyze button in the Chord Track List. Logic analyzes the MIDI region and adds the resulting chords to the Chord track.

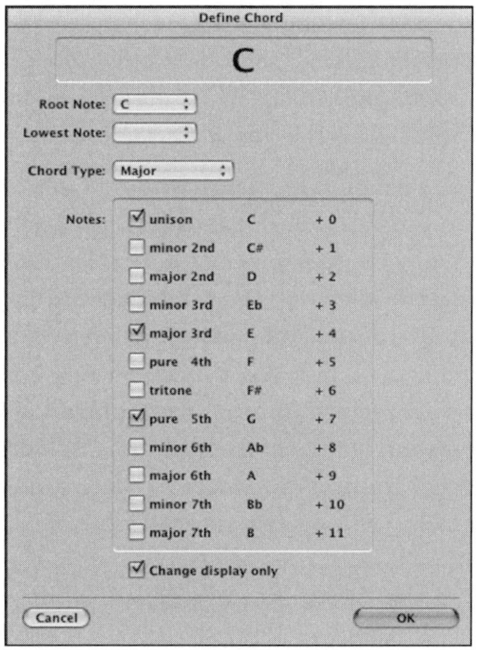

Figure 5.25

The Define Chord window opens when you use the Pencil tool to create a chord event.

- You can select one or more MIDI regions and drag them onto the Chord track. This has the same effect as selecting MIDI regions and clicking the Analyze button.
- When you create or alter a transposition event (see "The Transposition Track" section below), the root note of any affected chords on the Chord track will be shifted accordingly.

Global Transpositions Generated by the Chord Track

Any chord in the Chord track has the potential to affect global transposition, meaning it can affect the playback key of Apple Loops and MIDI regions. You can keep the MIDI regions on an Arrange track from being transposed by clicking the No Transpose check box in its Obect Parameter box (Object Parameter boxes are discussed in Chapter 7). Logic derives the transposition interval from the gap between the chord root and the first key signature root in the Signature track. If a chord is created, this will also be reflected in the Transposition track.

While Emagic's chord analyzation algorithm usually delivers accurate results, you still might find incorrect or missing chords in the Chord track occasionally. In these circumstances, you'll want to check the Chord track's Change Display Only button. With this mode active, you can adjust the chords manually, and the transposition events in the Transposition track adapt accordingly. Changes you make to chords while Change Display Only mode is active don't affect playback of the corresponding MIDI regions; your changes only adapt the chords displayed in the Chord track to the chords played in the MIDI region.

You cannot use Change Display Only mode to adjust the chords of a song to the chords in an audio-only Apple Loop. In general, this doesn't matter, since usually chord events are generally derived from MIDI regions. However, some Apple Loops do contain chord progressions. This means that your Apple Loop might end up getting transposed, even if you don't want it to. To get around this, you can cut an Apple Loop whenever chord changes happen and match the chords displayed in the Chord track with the chord progression in the cut Apple Loop. You can also use global transposition events in the Transposition track to make sure the Apple Loop matches its original parts. If you do not use the Chord track, this is obviously not an issue.

Moving, Copying, Resizing, Editing, and Deleting Chord Events

Chord events on the Chord track can be moved, copied, resized, and deleted as described in the first section on Global Tracks. If you want to edit a chord event, simply double-click it and the Define Chord window from Figure 5.25 will open, and you can change the event as you wish.

The Transposition Track

The Transposition track shows global transposition events that affect the transposition of Apple Loops and MIDI regions. In MIDI regions, the MIDI events themselves are changed, but nondestructively, meaning that the original data itself is not deleted—so if you remove the transposition, the original data will return. Apple Loops will be pitch-shifted based on the transposition events on the Transposition track. Regular Audio regions, and Apple Loops with no key information, will not be transposed. Figure 5.26 shows an Arrange window displaying the Transposition track.

The transposition events relate closely to the progression of the chord root notes in the Chord track. If you change a chord root in the Chord track, it will be reflected in the Transposition track, and vice versa. Creating or editing a transposition event will generate or alter the corresponding chord in the Chord track. All Apple Loops and MIDI regions will be pitch-shifted accordingly. If you do not want a MIDI region to transpose, click the No Transpose check box in its Region Parameter box. The current key signature in the Signature track determines the "zero position" of the Transposition track. If the key signature changes during a song, the zero position of the Transposition track also changes. The Transposition track always shows the difference between the Chord track and the Signature track at the position of the appropriate chord.

Editing Events in the Transposition Track

Transposition events on the Transposition track take the form of nodes (round dots). These transposition events are all connected by vertical and horizontal lines. The transposition event determines the global transposition value until the song position reaches the next transposition event (node) during playback.

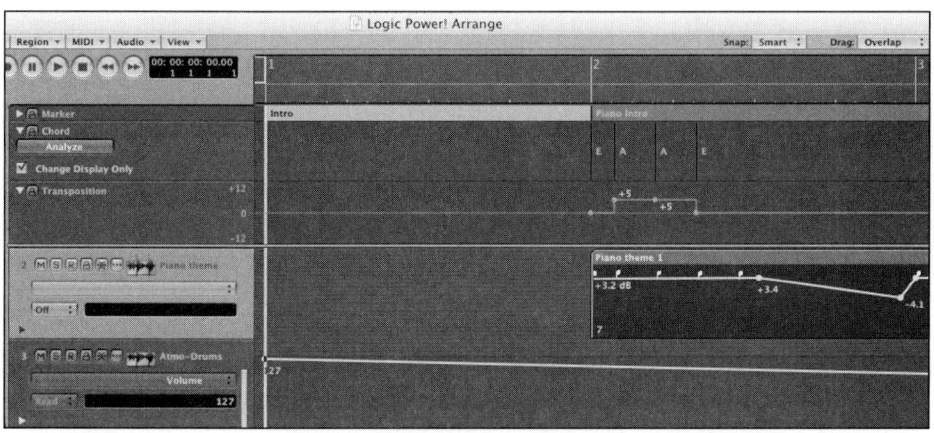

Figure 5.26

The Transposition track in an Arrange window. Notice the close relationship between the Chord track and the Transposition track.

You can create, copy, move, and delete transposition events as described in the "Common Features of Global Tracks" section above. Transposition events are limited to being moved horizontally (along the timeline) or vertically (the transposition value), not diagonally. The help tag will appear below the cursor when the mouse button is depressed with the exact transposition value and bar position of the current transposition event.

Pressing **CONTROL + OPTION + COMMAND** while clicking in the Transposition track opens a text window, as shown in Figure 5.27. You can directly enter a transposition value in the box, and, after pressing **RETURN**, you will create a transposition event of the typed value at the clicked position.

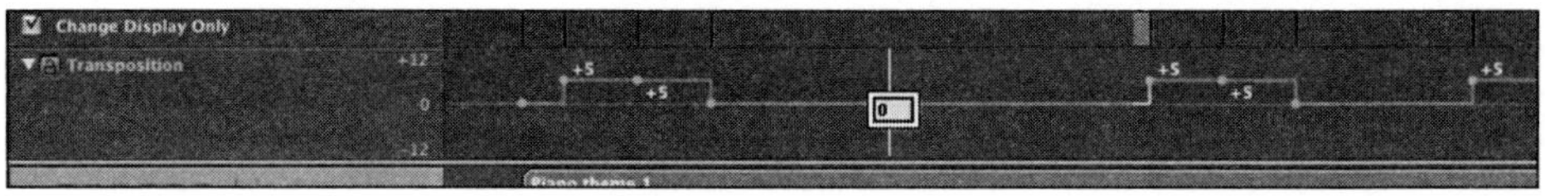

Figure 5.27
If you **CONTROL + OPTION + COMMAND + CLICK** on the Transposition track, a text window appears. When you type a value and press RETURN, a transposition event will be created at that location.

The scale range for the display of transposition events adjusts automatically: Dragging a transportation event beyond the current upper and lower boundaries of the Transposition track results in an automatic adjustment of the range. You can manually define the maximum and minimum of the transposition scale (up to a maximum of +12 semitones or -12 semitones) by grabbing the maximum and minimum values and dragging them vertically, or double-clicking on them and typing the desired value into the text window that appears. These user-defined values are displayed in yellow. To reset to the automatic adjustment mode, repeat the procedure and leave the text window blank.

The Tempo Track

Tempo, meaning speed and timing, is one of the most important elements in music. Tempo management can be as simple as agreeing on the timing of a song and asking all the musicians to play in time. Or it can be as complicated as keeping track of multiple tempo changes throughout a musical movement—or even continuous tempo changes. With digital audio sequencers being the nerve center for both electronic and acoustic, programmed and performed tracks, it becomes vital that the sequencer can keep everything synchronized, and that it gives the user the tools to fully implement whatever tempo requirements they have. The Tempo track gives you a visual track for displaying, setting, and editing tempo events for your song. Figure 5.28 shows the Tempo track in an Arrange window.

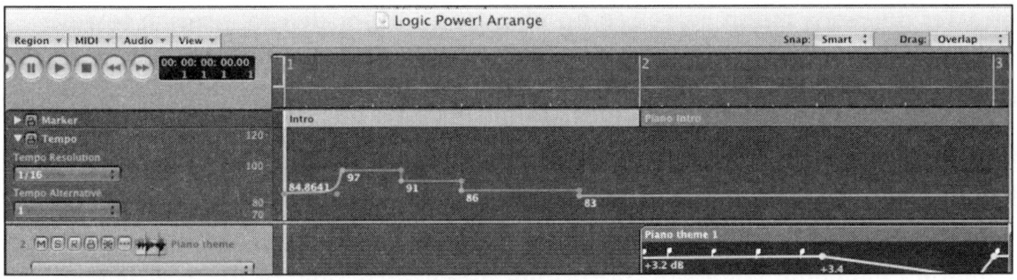

Figure 5.28

The Tempo track offers both a visual display and a convenient editing track for tempo changes in your song.

Like the Transposition track, the Tempo track is made up of nodes along a line. These nodes are tempo events, and the line is the current tempo.

Inserting, Deleting, Moving, and Copying Tempo Changes

You can insert tempo changes like any other global event—clicking in the Tempo track with a Pencil tool to create a tempo change at the current position. Pressing **CONTROL + OPTION + COMMAND** while clicking in the Tempo track opens a text window, as shown in Figure 5.29. You can directly enter a transposition value in the box, and after pressing **RETURN**, you will create a tempo change of the typed value at the clicked position.

You can also record tempo changes in realtime as explained in Chapter 15, and they will be reflected in the Tempo track.

Moving, copying, and deleting tempo changes is handled exactly the way other global events are handled. If you wish to create a continuous transition between two tempi, select the node at the tip of the right angle formed by the first and second node and drag it inside the angle. A curve or diagonal line will form. The pull-down Tempo Resolution menu, visible in Figure 5.28 above, defines how many tempo changes are performed between tempi.

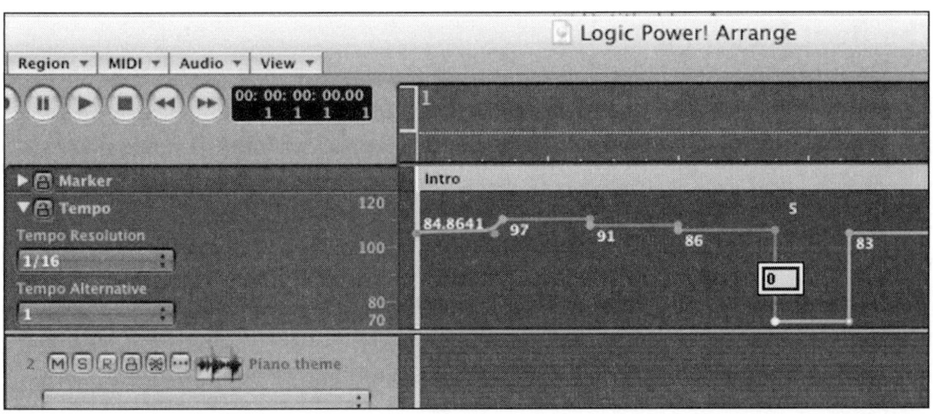

Figure 5.29

If you **CONTROL + OPTION + COMMAND + CLICK** on the Tempo track, a text window appears. When you type a value and press **RETURN**, a tempo change will be created at that location.

Shorter divisions mean more tempo changes; longer divisions mean fewer tempo changes. You can define this differently for each node.

The range for the display of tempo events adjusts automatically: Dragging a tempo event beyond the current upper and lower boundaries of the Tempo track results in an automatic adjustment of the range. You can manually define the maximum and minimum of the tempo scale by grabbing the maximum and minimum values and dragging them vertically, or double-clicking on them and typing the desired value into the text window that appears. These user-defined values are displayed in yellow. To reset to the automatic adjustment mode, repeat the procedure and leave the text window blank.

Accessing Logic Pro's Advanced Tempo Functions from the Tempo Track
Logic Pro 7 offers a number of more advanced tempo features, a few of which can be accessed directly from the Tempo track. These will be discussed in Chapter 15.

Logic's Tempo Alternative feature allows you to switch between nine completely unique tempo maps for each song. The Tempo Alternative pull-down menu in the Tempo track (see Figure 5.28) gives you instant access to all nine alternative tempo maps. You can hold **OPTION** while selecting the Tempo Alternative menu to copy all the tempo events from one tempo alternative to another.

You can press **SHIFT** while double-clicking in the Tempo track to open the Tempo List, a list view of your song's tempo changes.

The Tempo track has a close relationship with the Beat Mapping track, described below. After you use the Beat Mapping function in the Beat Mapping track, do not make any more changes in the Tempo track!

The Beat Mapping Track

The Beat Mapping track is perhaps one of the most unique and powerful Global Tracks in Logic, and perhaps in any sequencing application. It does exactly what the name implies—it maps Logic's tempo to a beat. In other words, let's say you recorded a fantastic audio or MIDI performance of an instrument, but the timing was a bit off the metronome click. Or maybe you recorded a live band without any metronome at all. The Beat Mapping track analyzes the performance and then creates a musically meaningful tempo map so that the bars and measures will fall in useful places. The performance is in no way moved or altered at all; it is only the tempo map and Bar Ruler of Logic that are adjusted to fit the performance. Beat Mapping allows you to then use a metronome that will follow the tempo of your recorded performance, you can quantize other regions to the performance, loops will play in tune, and so on. Figure 5.30 shows the Beat Mapping track.

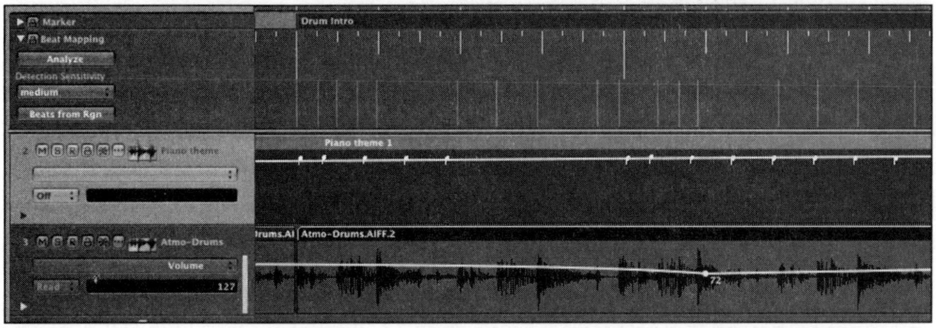

Figure 5.30
The Beat Mapping track shown in an Arrange window.

> **BEAT MAPPING TRACK VERSUS LOGIC'S RECLOCK FUNCTION**
> If you're already familiar with Logic, you may be thinking that the Beat Mapping track seems to do what the *Reclock* function in earlier versions did. Good guess! The Beat Mapping track supersedes the old Reclock function. It does the same thing, but far more accurately and intuitively.

Beat Mapping Process

The beat mapping process basically consists of two steps. First, you graphically link musical events (MIDI notes or audio transients, which correspond to the initial accent of rhythmically important notes) to the desired bar positions in the Beat Mapping track. Then, you tell the Beat Mapping track which measures to line up with which beat position lines. Logic will automatically insert tempo changes, causing the musical bars to correspond to the positions of the beat position lines.

As you can imagine, manually adding each and every beat position line for a song that is hundreds of bars long would require massive amounts of work! Luckily, Logic offers a number of automatic Beat Mapping functions to make this process as fast and intuitive as possible.

Beat Mapping from MIDI Regions

Beat mapping from MIDI regions is simple. First, you need to select a MIDI region for Logic to beat map. As soon as you select a MIDI region, beat position lines for each MIDI note will appear at the bottom of the Beat Mapping track, as shown in Figure 5.31.

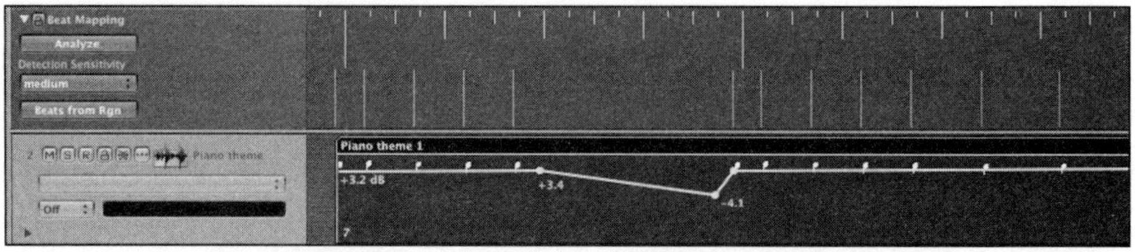

Figure 5.31

As you can see from the figure, the MIDI region Piano theme has been selected, and each note in the region has a corresponding beat position line in the Beat Mapping track.

Now you need to tell Logic exactly which position on the Bar Ruler you want to correspond to each note. At the first position you want to assign to a MIDI note, click-hold the mouse button. A yellow vertical line will appear in that location, as shown in Figure 5.32. The help tag will reflect your action and the pointer's exact location.

Now drag the vertical yellow line toward the beat position line you to which you want to assign the selected bar position. A darker yellow line will extend from the selected bar position location to the beat position line you have selected, as you see in Figure 5.33. The help tag will reflect your action and the pointer's exact location.

When you release the mouse button, Logic inserts a tempo change in order to shift the Bar Ruler so that the position you chose is linked to the note you chose, as shown in Figure 5.34.

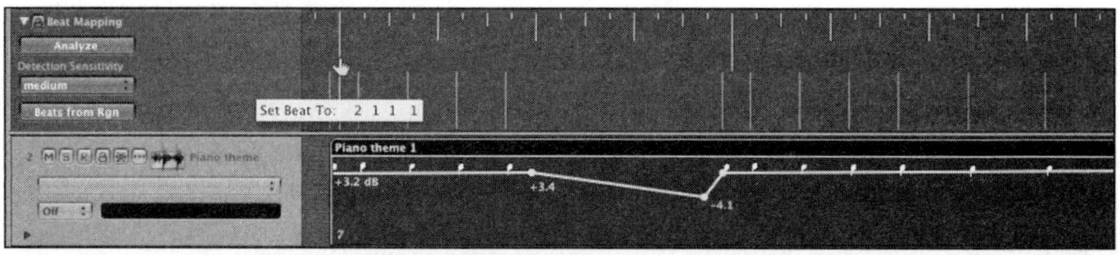

Figure 5.32

Click-hold the mouse at the first location at the first position on the Bar Ruler you want to assign a MIDI note.

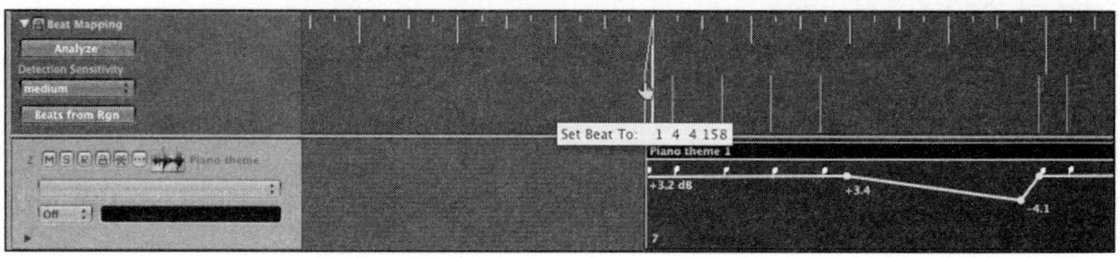

Figure 5.33

Drag the vertical yellow line to the beat position line you wish to assign to your selected bar position. A line will extend from the original vertical yellow line to the beat position line, as shown above.

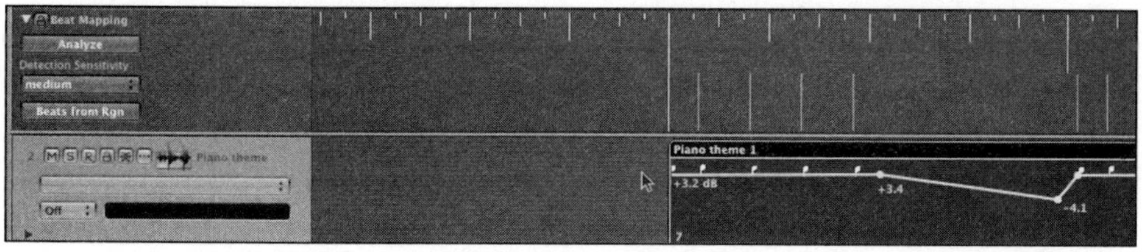

Figure 5.34

When you release the mouse, a tempo change will be created to shift the Bar Ruler to match the beat position. Notice between Figure 5.33 and 5.34, the entire Bar Ruler has moved over. No musical events have been affected at all, however, only the tempo map.

That's the whole procedure! Simply repeat the steps above for any additional Bar Ruler positions you wish to map to MIDI notes. If you to want connect a bar position line to a position in which there is no beat position line, you can do this by dragging the yellow vertical line while pressing the **CONTROL** key.

If you are not happy with a mapped beat, you can erase any beat allocation by either double-clicking on it, clicking on it with the Eraser tool from the selected window's Toolbox, or selecting it and pressing **DELETE**. You can erase all your beat mapping by clicking in the track list of the Beat Mapping track (except, obviously, the buttons or menus) and pressing **DELETE**.

EXPERT TIP: BEAT MAP MIDI REGIONS IN MIDI EDITORS

This example illustrated beat mapping a MIDI region on the Arrange window, but keep in mind that the Global Tracks all appear in the Matrix, Score, and Hyper Editors. You might find it more convenient to beat map MIDI regions in one of these MIDI editors, where you have a much better view of the actual MIDI notes.

Beat Mapping from Audio Regions

Beat mapping from Audio regions follows the same procedure as beat mapping from MIDI regions—you click on a Bar Ruler position to create the vertical yellow line, drag it to the beat position line you wish to allocate that bar position to, then release the mouse. Repeat this procedure until you have the completed beat map. There is one very significant difference, however, between beat mapping a MIDI and an Audio region: Whereas the notes of the selected MIDI region(s) will automatically generate beat position lines in the Beat Mapping track, Audio regions must be *analyzed* first. This means that Logic must search the Audio region for transients, or the initial attack of strong notes (in the waveform, these transients look like spikes in the signal). Generally, the more rhythmic the instrument (drums, percussion, and so on) the more distinct and accurate Logic's analysis of the transients will be.

To do this, simply select an **Audio** region (or regions) and click the **Analyze** button in the track list of the Beat Mapping track. Logic will analyze the region(s) for transients and generate corresponding beat position markers in the Beat Mapping track. You can also drag an Audio region (or regions) directly onto the Beat Mapping track to begin the analyzing process.

The Detection Sensitivity pull-down menu in the track list of the Beat Mapping track (see Figure 5.30) allows you to change the sensitivity to transients of the beat mapping algorithm. You have three choices: High, Medium, and Low. The default selection is Medium, which is generally the most useful. High sensitivity works well for regions with less distinct accents, but will detect too many peaks as transients in other files. If Medium sensitivity detects extraneous transients that are not musically useful, you can switch to Low sensitivity. If you change the Detection Sensitivity setting after you have analyzed an Audio region, you will retrigger the analysis procedure.

Beats from Regions

With this option, you create a Metronome region that you use to guide the Beat Mapping track as to where to generate beat position lines. For veteran Logic users, this is in fact almost identical to using a Guide region in the Reclock function. The advantage of using Beats from Regions is that the Metronome region you create will often be easier for the Beat Mapping track to detect beats from, resulting in more accurate beats. For example, you may want to beat map your song to an acoustic guitar part, but the accents may be too soft to accurately analyze. In that case, creating a Metronome region in the same timing as the acoustic guitar track and using Beats from Regions will result in the beat map you want.

To use this option, first create a MIDI track with an appropriately distinct rhythmic sound (hi-hat, cowbell, anvil hit, and so on) and tap out the exact beat to which you want Logic to beat map. If your Metronome region isn't exactly right, you can use the MIDI editors to shift notes, or keep trying until you get it right. When you are completely satisfied with the Metronome region, click the **Beats from Region** button. You will be presented with the Set Beats by Guide Region(s) window shown in Figure 5.35.

Select the note division you wish for your Metronome region, and click OK. The Bar Ruler of your song will be beat mapped to the Metronome region, as shown in Figure 5.36.

Figure 5.35
Choose the note division of your Metronome region in the Set Beats by Guide Region(s) window.

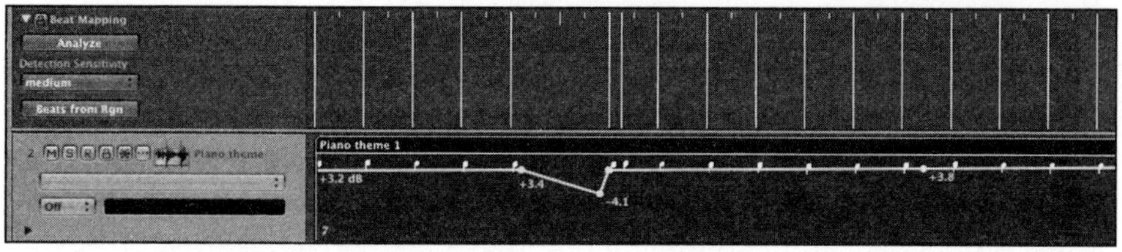

Figure 5.36
After the Beats from Regions process, your Bar Ruler will be mapped to the beats of your Metronome region.

Beat Mapping to Movie Cut Positions
This feature of the Beat Mapping track is especially useful for those scoring to picture. If you are using a Video track with a loaded QuickTime movie, and you have used the Detect Cuts function on the movie (see below), the detected scene cuts will generate beat position lines in the Beat Mapping track. If you want to define cut positions as the first downbeat of a bar, simply allocate the bar position to the beat position line as described in the "Beat Mapping from MIDI Regions" section.

Beat Mapping to Markers
You can even beat map to the Markers in the Marker track, if it is visible. Simply select one or more Markers and the beginning of the Marker(s) will appear as beat position lines in the Beat Marker track.

The Video Track

The Video track, unlike the other Global Tracks, does not contain any global events. Instead, it contains thumbnail images of single frames of a QuickTime movie loaded with your song. This track is especially for users who are doing sound for picture. Figure 5.37 shows an Arrange window with a Video track displayed.

You can open a QuickTime movie either by clicking the Open Movie button in the track list of the Video track, or clicking in the Video track with the Pencil tool of the window you are in to insert a movie into the Video track at the current mouse position.

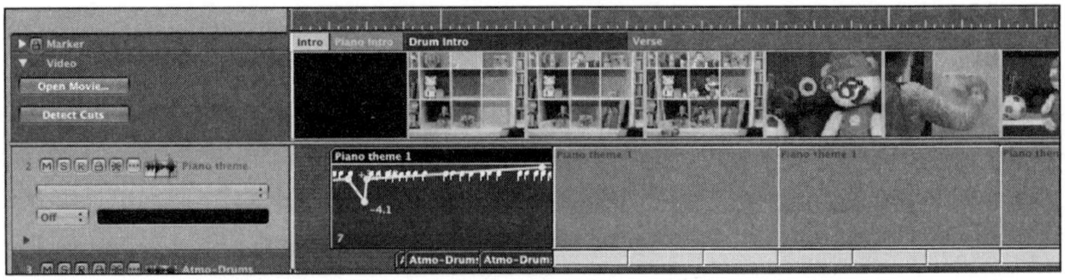

Figure 5.37
The Video track shows thumbnails of a QuickTime movie.

The number of thumbnails you see depends on the current zoom level. The frames are always left aligned, with the exception of the final movie frame, which is right aligned. In other words, the left border of every frame except the final frame represents the correct song position for that frame. The final frame is right aligned to insure that regardless of your zoom level, at least the first and last frames of a movie will be visible. No editing operations are possible on Video Thumbnail tracks.

Since the Video track contains no global events, you can't do any editing. You can, however, use the Detect Cuts feature, which searches for scene cuts in the movie. To do this, click the **Detect Cuts** button in the Video track track list. You can also select and drag thumbnails into the Marker track to create *Movie Markers*, which are special Markers locked to a specific SMPTE time and automatically deleted if the movie is removed from the song. Finally, as described in the Beat Mapping track subsection, you can use the detected cut scenes from a Video track to generate beat position lines in the Beat Mapping track.

THE VIDEO TRACK VERSUS THE VIDEO THUMBNAIL TRACK

The Video track replaces the Logic 6 Arrange window Video Thumbnail track. If you open an old Logic song that had a Video Thumbnail track, it will still be displayed in the old Video Thumbnail track, but you can no longer create them. I highly recommend that you simply delete the Video Thumbnail track of your old song, and open it in the more flexible Global Track, the Video track.

Now that you are familiar with some of the global options that you will be able to access from several areas of Logic Pro 7, it's time to start exploring the individual program areas, starting with the Transport window in the next chapter.

6 The Transport Window

The Transport window (usually simply referred to as "the Transport") contains perhaps the most fundamental functions in Logic—the controls for recording, playback, and song position. The Transport is modeled after the "transport" section of a tape machine, so named because pressing the buttons physically moves (transports) the magnetic tape. Of course, there's no tape in your computer, but because the metaphor of the tape machine transport for these controls is quite intuitive, it has found its way into Logic (and, in fact, almost all modern software-based audio applications). Figure 6.1 shows the Logic Pro Transport.

Notice that the Transport in Logic offers many more options other than a standard tape machine. This is because Logic offers far more functionality than simply recording and playback. All of the functions accessible on the Transport are directly related to playback or recording, as you'll explore in the next sections.

The Transport Buttons

The most immediately noticeable features of the Transport are the Transport buttons themselves. These are the buttons that directly correspond to those buttons on a tape machine that "transport" the tape. When you record on a computer, no actual tape is physically moved, so Logic uses a Song Position Line (SPL), a vertical line in the Arrange window from the Bar Ruler to the bottom of the Arrange window, to indicate the current playback location in the song. Figure 6.2 shows the Transport buttons.

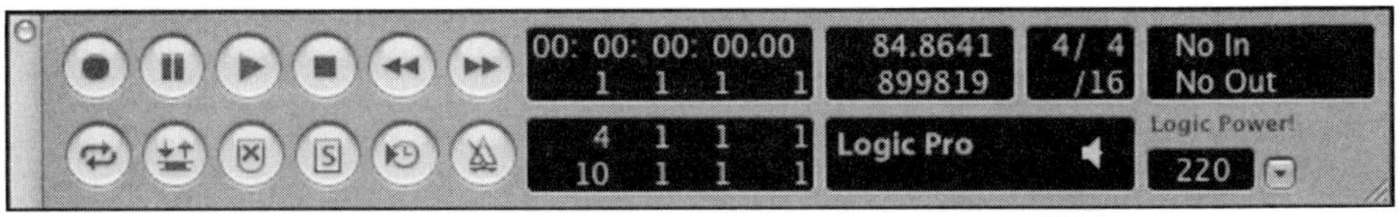

Figure 6.1
In the Transport window, you can control recording, playback, and related functions. The Transport also offers song display and other data viewing options.

Figure 6.2
The Transport buttons.

If you have help tags enabled, holding the mouse over these buttons will reveal the name of the button. While the functions of these buttons are self-evident if you've previously used a tape recorder, here is specific information about how these buttons function in Logic, starting from left to right in the Transport shown in Figure 6.2.

- **Record.** When you press this button, it turns red, along with the Bar Ruler, and Logic begins recording. Any data sent by connected MIDI controllers is recorded on the selected MIDI track in the Arrange window. Any audio sent into one or more channels of your audio interface is recorded as audio on record-enabled Audio tracks with one of those channels selected as inputs. Logic creates a region the length of your recording on the Arrange window for each track you record. If you click and hold down the Record button, you can access the Recording Options dialog box, which is explained later in this chapter.
- **Pause.** Pressing this button momentarily stops playback or recording. Pressing it again, or pressing Play, continues playback or recording.
- **Play.** Pressing this button begins playback at the current SPL, or, if you are in Cycle mode, playback begins at the start of the cycle.
- **Stop.** Pressing Stop halts playback or recording. If Logic is not currently playing or recording when you press Stop, the SPL will return to the first bar of the song or cycle.
- **Rewind.** Pressing this button moves the SPL backward. If you click-hold this button, the SPL moves backward faster. If you *short-click* the button (that is, click the button very quickly), the SPL jumps back one bar or one Marker (if you have Markers set up, as explained in Chapter 5).

- **Fast Forward.** This button moves the SPL forward. If you click-hold this button, the SPL moves forward faster. If you short-click the button, the SPL jumps forward one bar or one Marker (if you have Markers set up).

EXPERT TIP: TRANSPORT KEY COMMANDS

Remember, Logic is designed to allow users to really fly by using key commands everywhere possible. This means that not only are there key commands for all the Transport buttons, but there are key commands relating to Transport functions that offer even more functionality. For example, simply pressing Play will start playback at the current SPL position or the beginning of a cycle, but there are also key commands for Play from Beginning to begin playback from the start of the song, Play from Previous Bar to begin playback one bar behind the current SPL position, Play from Selection to begin playback from the start of a selected region, and so on. You can use a key command to Stop and Go to Left Locator or Stop and Go to Last Play Position, and there are key commands to increase or decrease Forward and Rewind speed. Assigning and using these and other Transport-related key commands will vastly speed up your workflow, so give them a try.

Mode Buttons

The mode buttons, which are located under the Transport buttons, toggle Logic's Playback and/or Record mode. Figure 6.3 shows three of the mode buttons.

Figure 6.3
The Cycle, Drop, and Erase mode buttons.

If you have help tags enabled, holding the mouse over these buttons will reveal their function. From left to right, here is a description of these buttons:

- **Cycle.** This button toggles Cycle mode on or off. Basically, in Cycle mode, playback and recording repeat within a given range defined by the left and right locator positions. You can numerically input the boundaries of the cycle in the locator display (see the "Locators" section later in this chapter), or you can graphically set the cycle boundaries in the Arrange window. Cycle mode is explained in more detail in Chapter 7.
- **Drop.** This button toggles Drop mode on or off. Drop mode automatically sends Logic into Record mode and Exit Record mode at predefined positions. You can set the Locators by typing in numeric values for them in the Locator Display or set them graphically in the Arrange window by dragging the green bar in the middle of the Bar Ruler. Note that if you have both Cycle and Drop mode on, Logic will have two Locator Displays, and two white bars in the Bar Ruler, to represent the Locator positions for each mode.

> **WHY CALL IT DROP MODE?**
> Back when recording required a needle or recording head to be physically lowered onto a recordable surface, entering into Record mode was referred to as "dropping" into Record mode; hence, the term Drop refers to dropping the record head automatically. This isn't very relevant in the world of digital recording, but the term has still stuck.

- **Erase.** This button toggles Erase mode for audio recording on and off. In Erase mode, any data you record onto a track will supersede previously recorded data on that track. In other words, if you record a region on a track, turn on Erase mode, and then record over that original region, the old data will be gone and the new data will be all that is left on that track. If Erase mode is off, recording over a region on a track leaves the original region intact—the old region is still present, but will not play back until you move it to an empty track.

There are three more mode buttons: Solo, Sync, and Metronome. Each of these buttons requires the additional explanation provided in the following subsections.

The Solo Button

Figure 6.4
The Solo button. A single-click turns on Solo mode, and a double-click turns on Solo Lock mode. Click again to turn Solo off.

Next to the first three mode buttons is the Solo mode button, which appears like an S in a box, as shown in Figure 6.4. When Solo mode is active, you may play back your song while only listening to those selected regions you wish to hear.

In Logic Pro, you have two ways to Solo tracks or regions in Arrange; you can select one or more regions and click the Solo button, or you can click the Solo button on a track to Solo the entire track. You can also press the key command **S** to toggle Solo on and off.

If Solo mode is active, and all selected regions are being soloed, what if you want to select a region for editing or moving but you don't want it to be soloed? Logic facilitates this by offering a Solo Lock feature. If you double-click the Solo button, you will activate Solo Lock, which locks the Solo function to those regions already selected. With Solo Lock active, you can go ahead and manipulate any other region without changing the Solo selection. If you want to return to selecting only the soloed regions, you can assign a key command for Reselect Solo-Locked Objects.

When Solo is activated, the button and the Bar Ruler glow yellow. When Solo Lock is activated, the button icon will have a small padlock image added to it.

The External Sync Button

The External Sync button, shown in Figure 6.5, is directly to the right of the Solo button. Turning on External Sync mode allows you to slave the sequencer in Logic Pro to external hardware such as tape machines, external hard disk recorders, hardware sequencers, and any other device that is capable of sending compatible time code, as well as internal software applications that receive MIDI clock via CoreMIDI. If Logic is the slave, that means Logic is taking its tempo cues from the external hardware. If you don't have any external hardware that generates its own tempo, or if all your external devices are slaves and Logic is the master, you will not need to use External Sync mode in Logic.

Figure 6.5
The External Sync button. Turn on Sync mode to slave Logic Pro to an external tempo.

If you click the External Sync button you will toggle the External Sync mode. If you hold the button down, you access a menu of synchronization options. These options allow you to select the type of sync that Logic will send, access to tempo editors, and so on. Chapter 16, "Synchronizing Hardware with Logic Pro," explains synchronization and Logic Pro's sync options in more detail.

The Metronome Button

The Metronome button, shown in Figure 6.6, turns the Metronome on and off in Logic. You can also press the key command **Y** to toggle the Metronome on and off. The Metronome emits a constant click at the current song tempo.

Figure 6.6
The Metronome button. This turns the Metronome on and off, and gives you access to the Metronome Settings dialog box.

If you hold the mouse button down over the Metronome button, Logic displays a pull-down menu that lets you open either the Recording Options dialog box (the same as with the Record button discussed previously) or the Metronome Settings dialog box.

Metronome Settings

The Metronome Settings dialog box, shown in Figure 6.7, consolidates all the various settings that affect Metronome. These settings can also be accessed from the Metronome Object's parameter box in the Environment and the Recording Options dialog box. You can also access the Metronome Settings dialog box by selecting **File > Song Settings > Metronome**.

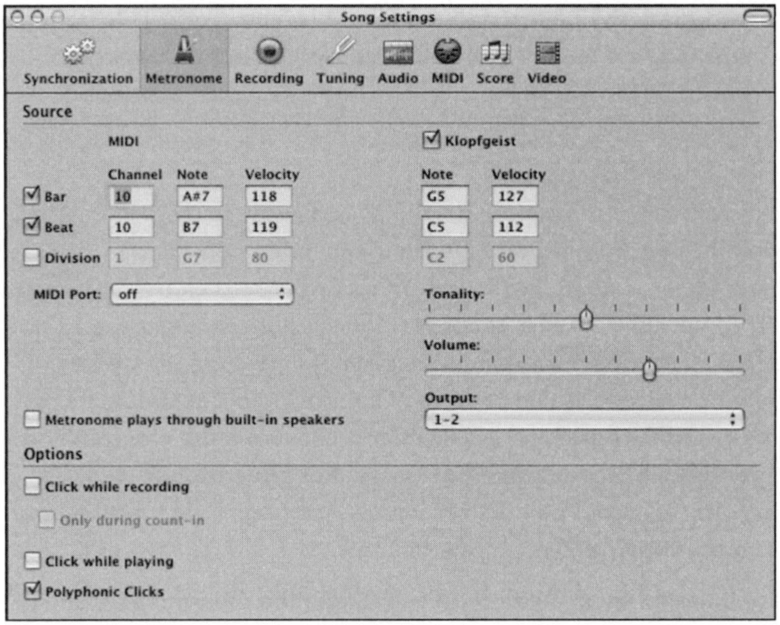

Figure 6.7

The Metronome Settings dialog box.

All the parameters in the top-left allow you to configure an external MIDI synthesizer to be your metronome. You can set the MIDI port of a hardware synth, determine whether you want different MIDI notes to be played on the bar, beat, or division, and set the channel, note, and velocity of each metronome note.

Most often, however, you will probably want to use Logic's internal click as a metronome. It's not only more convenient, but because an Audio Instrument generates the click, the timing is always sample-accurate, which means that the beat will always occur precisely when the master digital clock tells it to occur, not early or late. To use the internal Audio Instrument for your metronome, check the box named **Klopfgeist** in the top-right. Klopfgeist is the name of the metronome Audio Instrument in Logic. *Klopfgeist* translates literally to "knocking ghost"—so when you use it, you can honestly say there is a ghost in the machine!

As with the MIDI Metronome Object, you can have different notes for different time divisions and can set the note and velocity. You also have a control for Tonality, which allows you to tone shape the sound from Klopfgeist to a limited degree, and Volume, which sets the volume of the Audio Instrument. Finally, you can select the Output from which Klopfgeist will sound.

If you are using your computer's built-in sound, the Metronome Plays Through Built-In Speakers check box enables you to choose whether to have your computer's built-in speaker emit a metronome click. In general, if you use Klopfgeist, you do not need to select this option as well. In fact, if you check this box and then you check the Klopfgeist check box, Logic unchecks Metronome Plays Through Built-In Speakers for you, under the assumption that you won't need both clicks.

Below these settings are check boxes that determine when you will hear the Metronome. If you select Click While Recording, you'll hear the click when you are recording. Selecting Click While Playing ensures that you'll hear the click when you're recording. If you select Only During Count-In, the click will play only during the count-in, or measures before the recording begins.

You can set your click to be monophonic (one voice) or polyphonic (more than one voice) by checking or unchecking the Polyphonic Clicks check box. If you are using Klopfgeist, this setting will have no effect.

The Position Display

To the right of the Transport buttons is the Position Display, shown in Figure 6.8.

Figure 6.8
The Position Display, located to the immediate right of the Transport buttons.

The Position Display shows you a numeric representation of where the SPL currently is in your song. The top number is shown in SMPTE time format (hours: minutes: seconds: frames/subframes), and the bottom number is in bar position format (bar—beat—division—tick). SMPTE (Society of Motion Picture and Television Engineers) is the standard format used for synchronizing sound to pictures. The bar position format is so named because it follows the musical notation structure of bars and beats. This is the same format shown on the Arrange window on the Bar Ruler (unless you choose to show SMPTE time format in the Bar Ruler).

Position Display Format Preferences

You have some options in how you display the two formats. If you select **Logic Pro > Preferences > Display Preferences**, in the General tab are two pull-down menus that enable you to customize the display of the two formats. You can adjust the display of SMPTE time via the Display SMPTE pull-down menu shown in Figure 6.9.

Figure 6.9
The Display SMPTE pull-down menu in the Display Preferences General tab alters the way the SMPTE format appears in the position display.

These options change the way that SMPTE appears in the position display. You also can choose zeros to be displayed as spaces by checking the Zeros as Spaces box. Change the default SMPTE display only if you need a different format in order to synchronize your Logic song to a picture in that format.

If you pull down the Clock Format menu, Logic displays the various clock formats shown in Figure 6.10.

These options allow the clock to take on a slightly different look. It's worthwhile browsing through the different options here so you can find out which one you prefer working with. If you have a smaller screen, you might prefer the smaller numbers to save screen space, whereas if your screen is larger, you might prefer the larger numbers.

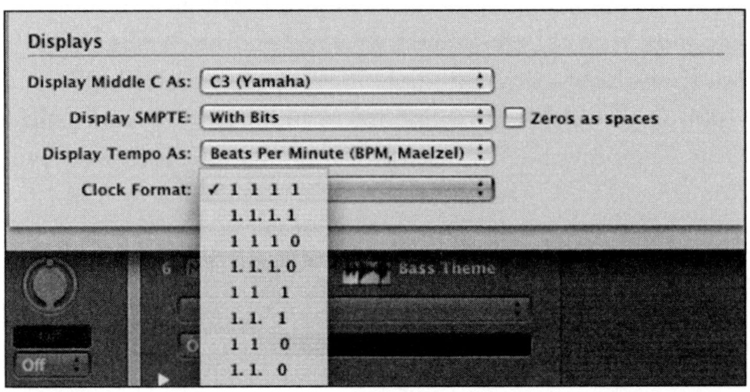

Figure 6.10
The Clock Format menu in the Display Preferences General tab. These parameters allow you to change the look of the clock in the Position Display to a different view.

Using the Position Display to Move the SPL

The Position Display has another function in addition to offering a numeric visual reference to the location of the SPL. If you double-click one of the numbers, the display presents a text box, as shown in Figure 6.11. Enter the desired numeric location here, and when you press Return, the value of both numeric displays will change and the SPL will jump to the specified location.

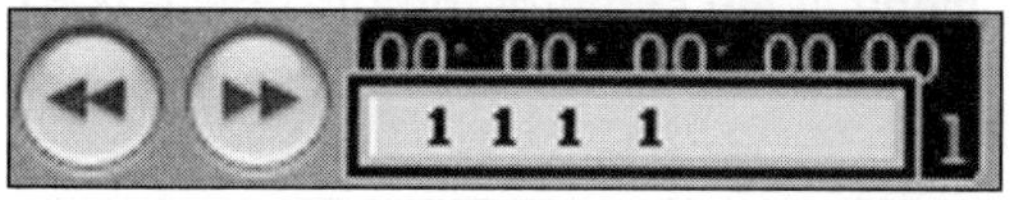

Figure 6.11
If you double-click on one of the numeric displays, the Position Display presents a text box in which you can enter a new SPL location.

Locators

Directly below the position display and to the immediate right of the mode buttons is a display window for the Locators. Figure 6.12 shows the Locator Display.

Figure 6.12
The Locators are displayed numerically to the right of the mode buttons.

These locators define the start and end for Cycle mode, and, if you don't have Cycle mode on, they define the start and end of Drop mode. If you do have Cycle mode on, an additional Locator Display window replaces the Logic Pro logo to the right of the Locator Display, as shown in Figure 6.13. This new window is where you set the Drop start and end points.

Figure 6.13
If both Cycle mode and Drop mode are activated, a new window for the Drop Locators replaces the Logic Pro logo.

As with the Position Display, if you double-click the numeric values, a text box appears in which you can enter the position of each Locator.

The Tempo/Free Event Memory Display

To the right of the position display is the Tempo/Free Event Memory Display box, shown in Figure 6.14.

Figure 6.14
The Tempo/Free Event Memory Display box.

The tempo value displays the tempo of the current song in either beats per minute (BPM), frames per second, or quarter notes per minute. You can choose how tempo will be displayed in the Display Tempo As pull-down menu in the General tab of **Logic Pro > Preferences > Display,** as shown in Figure 6.15.

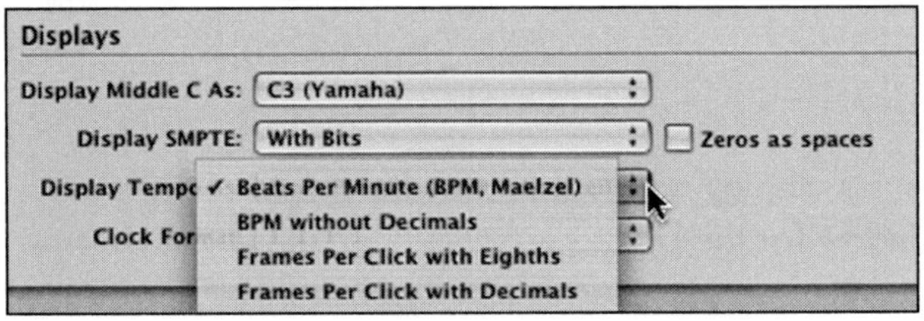

Figure 6.15
The Display Tempo As pull-down menu in **Logic Pro > Preferences > Display (General tab).**

Logic offers a BPM range of 0.5–9,999 BPM, with four decimal place precision, which should be enough tempo range for most users! You can change the tempo of the song inside the Transport in two ways: first, by double-clicking the tempo value to bring up a text box, then entering the new value; and second, by clicking on the tempo number and dragging the mouse up or down. Logic allows for more complicated tempo programming and changes using either the Tempo track in the Global Tracks discussed in Chapter 5, or the other tempo functions explored in Chapter 15, "Advanced Tempo Operations."

The free event memory number shows you how much RAM you have left to store events in your Logic song. If you ever find this number getting too small, you can double-click on this value to choose Reconfigure Memory. Logic then optimizes your song to save RAM. Logic automatically optimizes your song every time you save it, so you will rarely, if ever, need to use this feature—it is really just a relic from older versions of Logic in which users had to optimize songs manually.

The Time Signature/Division Display

To the right of the Tempo/Free Event Memory Display is the Time Signature/Division Display, as shown in Figure 6.16.

Figure 6.16
The Time Signature/Division Display.

The time signature value represents the time signature at the currently selected measure in the song. You can add as many time signature changes as you like to your song using the Signature track as described in Chapter 5, or the Score Editor, which will be explained in Chapter 9. If you want to remove a time signature change, simply change the time signature back to its original value.

The division value lets you determine what note value will get the third position in the bar—beat—division—tick display. This also will affect the resolution of the Bar Ruler in the Arrange window. You can also assign key commands to allow you to raise and lower this division value quickly.

The MIDI Monitor/Song End Display

To the right of the Time Signature/Division Display and Logic Pro logo/Drop Locator Display is the MIDI Monitor/Song End Display. Figure 6.17 shows this display window as it appears in the Transport.

Figure 6.17
The MIDI Monitor/Song End Display.

The MIDI monitor gives you visual feedback as to whether Logic is sending or receiving MIDI events. If the MIDI events being sent are a chord, Logic's Auto Chord Recognition feature will show you the proper name for the chord, rather than showing you all of the individual notes. If your MIDI devices get stuck notes (in other words, they can't stop playing) or are otherwise unresponsive, you can click in the MIDI monitor to send a MIDI Reset command to them. If that doesn't work, you can double-click to send a MIDI Panic Off—basically, this will send individual note off commands for every note on every channel.

The song end box below the MIDI monitor shows you the final bar in the song. When the SPL reaches this measure, Logic stops playback. You can double-click in this box to display a text box in which you can change the value. The maximum song length in Logic is 8,550 quarter notes; exactly how many bars this will add up to depends on the time signature of your song, but in 4/4 time it will be 2,137.5 bars long.

In between the MIDI Monitor/Song End Display, the Transport displays the name of your song. This is mostly for looks, but it does have a function if you have more than one Logic song open at a time: The name on the Transport will indicate to which song that Transport window belongs.

The Transport Window Display Menu

If you click on the down-arrow button at the bottom-right of the Transport, Logic displays the Transport Window Display pop-up menu shown in Figure 6.18. This menu allows you to customize the display of the Transport.

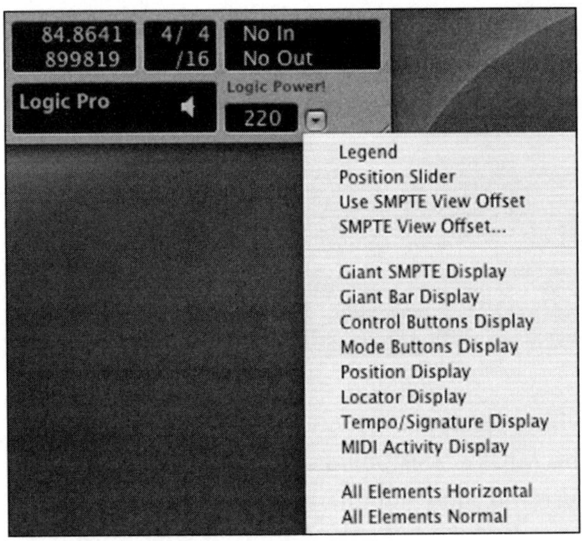

Figure 6.18
Click on the button at the bottom-right of the Transport, and this menu of display options for the Transport appears.

Here is a brief explanation of the menu options:

- **Legend.** This option adds text labels to the various buttons and displays in the Transport. Figure 6.19 shows a Transport bar with this option turned on.

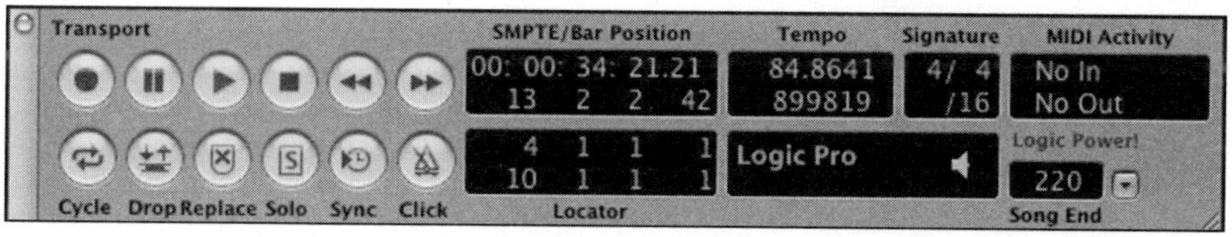

Figure 6.19
Selecting Legend in the pull-down menu adds text labels to the Transport.

- **Position Slider.** If you select this option, Logic creates a monochromatic progress bar at the bottom of the Transport. The solid gray color moving through the progress bar represents how far into the song the SPL has traveled. Figure 6.20 shows a Transport with a position slider.

  You can click-drag the gray bar and move it forward or backward to move the SPL in the song.

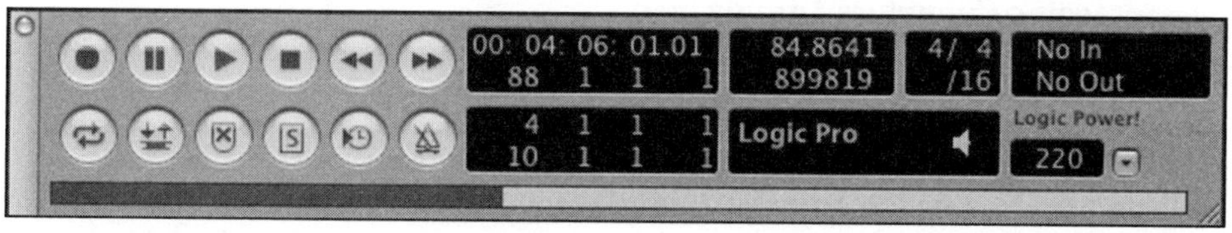

Figure 6.20
A Transport with a position slider displaying the current position of the SPL in the song.

- **Use SMPTE View Offset/SMPTE View Offset.** This option allows you to display a different SMPTE time for the start of your song than the true SMPTE start time that an external device is sending to Logic. For this to work, you need to check the box in the **SMPTE View Offset** option, then choose **Use SMPTE View Offset**. Synchronizing to external SMPTE is explained further in Chapter 15.
- **Giant SMPTE Display.** Selecting this option changes the Transport window into simply a very large display of the current SMTPE position. Figure 6.21 shows this display.

Figure 6.21
The Giant SMPTE Display option of the Transport.

- **Giant Bar Display.** Selecting this will change the Transport window into simply a very large display of the current bar-beat-division-tick position. Figure 6.22 shows this display.

Figure 6.22
The Giant Bar Display option of the Transport.

If you choose any of the following options, you will view only the selected portion of the Transport, and the other portions of the Transport will not be available:

- Control Buttons Display (Transport buttons only)
- Mode Buttons Display (Mode buttons only)
- Position Display
- Locator Display
- Tempo/Signature Display
- MIDI Activity Display

If you select more than one of these options, then you will view only each selected portion of the Transport. In other words, if you only had Position Display and Control Switches Display selected, your Transport would only include the Transport buttons and the position display.

- **All Elements Horizontal.** This option aligns all the selected elements of the Transport horizontally in a single row, instead of the standard two-row Transport.
- **All Elements Normal.** This option returns the Transport to the standard two-row view.

> **EXPERT TIP: OPENING MORE THAN ONE TRANSPORT WHEN USING GIANT DISPLAYS**
>
> If you select the Giant SMTPE Display or the Giant Bar Display option, you will lose all the other functions of the Transport. But never fear: Logic allows you to open as many of each kind of window as you like, so you can also open up multiple Transports if you want. This way, you can open one Transport and configure it as a Giant Bar Display, for example, and then open a second, fully featured Transport.

Resizing the Transport

To resize the Transport window, click-hold the mouse on the lower-right corner and drag the Transport to the desired size, as shown in Figure 6.23.

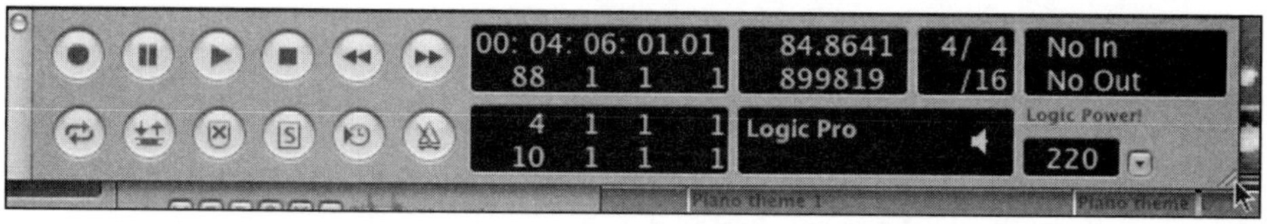

Figure 6.23
To resize the Transport window, simply drag the lower-right corner with your mouse.

Recording

Logic Pro offers a large number of recording modes and options. First of all, to record in Logic, you need to select a MIDI track or record-enable some Audio Tracks (this is explained further in the next chapter). To activate the normal Record mode, simply click the **Record** button. After the count-in that is set in the Metronome Settings dialog box, Logic begins capturing data. If you hold down the Record button, however, Logic displays the pop-up menu shown in Figure 6.24.

Figure 6.24
You access this pull-down menu by clicking and holding down on the Record button in the Transport.

Here is an explanation of the menu options:

- **Record.** This starts the normal Record mode. Selecting this is the same as simply clicking the Record button without accessing the Record pull-down menu.
- **Record Repeat.** This option starts recording at the previous Drop or record-start point.
- **Record Toggle.** Record Toggle switches between Record and Playback mode. Accessing this command using the mouse during recording is very awkward; if you find yourself wanting to use this command, do yourself a favor and assign and use a key command for the action instead.
- **Recording.** This brings up the Recording Settings dialog box. You can also access this dialog box by pressing the key command **OPTION + R** or by selecting **File > Song Settings > Recording**. The Recording Settings dialog box is explored further in the next section.

- **Punch On The Fly.** If you are recording audio, normally you set up a track and start recording from the beginning of the song, or set recording to begin at predetermined Drop Locators. If you turn on Punch On The Fly, you can be in Play mode and simply switch into Record mode immediately. This is punching "on the fly" because you did not previously configure Logic to record at the specific location you chose. You should record on the fly sparingly, because it's pretty taxing on your computer's resources to punch in completely cleanly without clicks or gaps. Instead, you should use the Drop Locators to set locator points in advance so that Logic can allocate and conserve the resources ahead of time. Also, keep in mind that even though you are punching in on the fly, you'll still need to have an Audio Track record-enabled in order to record your punch-in.

WHY CALL IT PUNCH-IN?

The term "punch-in" comes from the fact that when recording to tape, in order to start recording on the fly, engineers would "punch in" (not literally) the recording head while the playback head was operating. With digital recording, there are no tape heads to punch, but Logic still has to switch instantly from Playback to Record mode, which in itself is quite a task.

- **Auto Input Monitoring.** This allows you to monitor in Logic what is coming in through the hardware inputs when Logic is stopped and in Record mode. When in Playback mode, Logic plays any prerecorded Audio regions on the Audio Track that are record-enabled. You'll almost always leave this option on unless your audio hardware has a special monitoring mode or you want to free additional resources in the host computer. As I discussed in Chapter 2, keep in mind that whenever monitoring audio through software, there is some latency.
- **Set Audio Record Path.** Selecting this option brings up a dialog box in which you choose the directory into which you will save the audio files for your song. The audio record path is saved with each song, so you don't have to define it more than once per song unless you want to change it. If you have not set an audio record path when you attempt to record your first Audio Track in a song, it will bring up the Set Audio Record Path dialog box automatically. Keep in mind that you should not set an audio record path in your Autoload song; otherwise, Logic will automatically use that folder for all the audio you record for any subsequent songs. **<A>**

Recording Options Parameters

The Recording Settings dialog box, shown in Figure 6.25, presents a number of options to customize how you record with Logic.

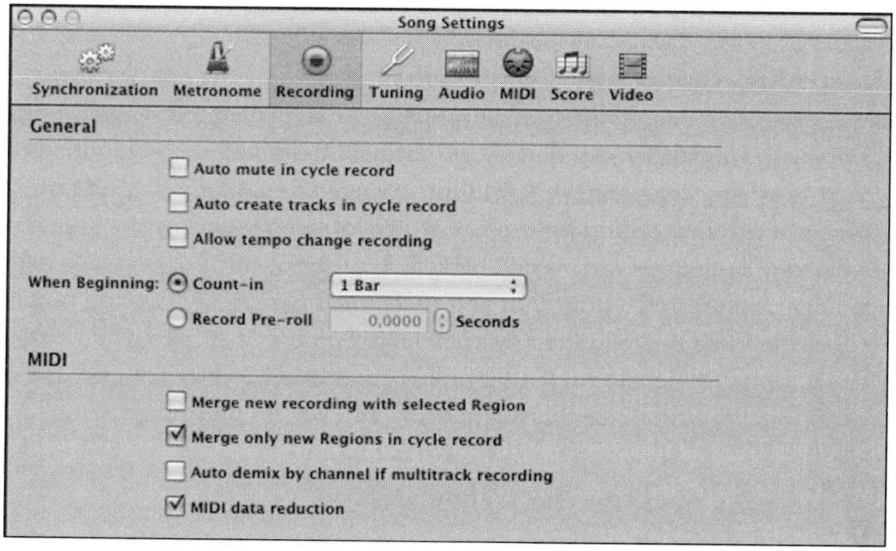

Figure 6.25
The Recording Settings dialog box.

Some of these parameters are explained elsewhere in the book, and some parameters appear in other windows as well. The following are brief descriptions of some of these parameters:

- **Auto Mute in Cycle Record, Auto Create Tracks in Cycle Record, Merge New Recording with Selected Region, and Merge Only New Regions in Cycle Record.** These options all control how Logic records when in Cycle mode. These parameters are defined in the "Cycle Mode" section of Chapter 7.
- **Allow Tempo Change Recording**. This option allows you to record tempo changes.
- **Count-In/Record Pre-Roll.** Use these radio buttons to determine how many bars or seconds Logic will rewind the SPL when you start recording.
- **Auto Demix by Channel If Multitrack Recording**. If this option is selected and you are recording on more than one MIDI Channel at a time, Logic will automatically create a new MIDI track for each MIDI Channel that is recorded. Each MIDI track that is created will contain a single MIDI region with all of the information recorded from that channel.

- **MIDI Data Reduction.** If this is checked, Logic filters MIDI information according to your specification. You can select which MIDI messages you want Logic to filter out by selecting **Files > Song Settings > MIDI Options** and configuring the MIDI Options dialog box's settings.

Recording Using Key Commands

While Logic's menus offer a large selection of recording modes and parameters, if you want to record quickly, you should assign key commands to all of the modes, functions, and options that you access regularly. In addition, some powerful recording functions are available only via key commands; for example, "retrospect recording," which is a special MIDI option with which you can capture MIDI data that you performed *before* you started recording, is available only via the key command Capture Last Take as Recording. As you are starting to see, the more key commands you assign and use while recording, the faster and more efficiently you will be using Logic.

> **METHOD TIP: HOW TO RECORD IN LOGIC**
>
> Don't let all these recording options confuse you into thinking that basic recording of audio or MIDI in Logic is difficult. It's not. The basic procedure couldn't be easier:
>
> - **To record audio.** Select one or more Audio Tracks in the Arrange window. Record-enable the Audio Tracks, and start recording (via Transport button, key command, control surface, and so on).
> - **To record MIDI.** Select a MIDI track and start recording.
> - **To record MIDI and audio at the same time.** Record-enable one or more Audio Tracks, and then **SHIFT + CLICK** a MIDI or Audio Instrument track. With all your Audio Tracks record-enabled and your MIDI track selected, start recording.
>
> More on record-enabling Audio Tracks will be discussed in the next chapter.

Transport Controls in Other Windows

Although this chapter has focused on the Transport window, you can also place the Transport controls directly into the Score Editor, Hyper Editor, and Arrange window. You won't have as much configuration control over the Transport as you do when it is a stand-alone window, but integrated Transports do include the same functionality.

Adding the Transport to the Score Editor and Hyper Editor is discussed in Chapter 9, "Working with MIDI." The next chapter discusses the Arrange window.

7 The Arrange Window

The Arrange window is perhaps the central window in Logic. Here you create and manipulate all the various tracks of your song, along with those tracks' adjustable parameters. You can record data onto tracks in the Arrange page, and that data is graphically represented in track lanes as one or more regions. These regions can then be arranged—meaning manipulated into new organizations that do not necessarily reflect the original data organization—processed, and automated. You can use Arrange to give you an overview of an entire song, or a sample accurate close-up of a few tracks. You can play your Logic song from beginning to end, or set up song Locators at any two points and just focus on your song from there. Figure 7.1 gives you a look at an Arrange window showing a selection of Audio and MIDI tracks along with their regions, some automation, and a Global Track (an expanded Marker track).

You will find that you spend much of your time using Logic in Arrange, so you'll need a solid understanding of what functions and features are available to you in here.

Local Menus

Every editor and window in Logic has its own local menus. These menus conveniently contain commands users need within that window and editor. Keep in mind that some commands that can be used in a given window will not be in local menus because they are already located in the global application menus, or because the given function is available only using key commands.

The following subsections describe the local menus in the Arrange window of Logic and the commands that they contain.

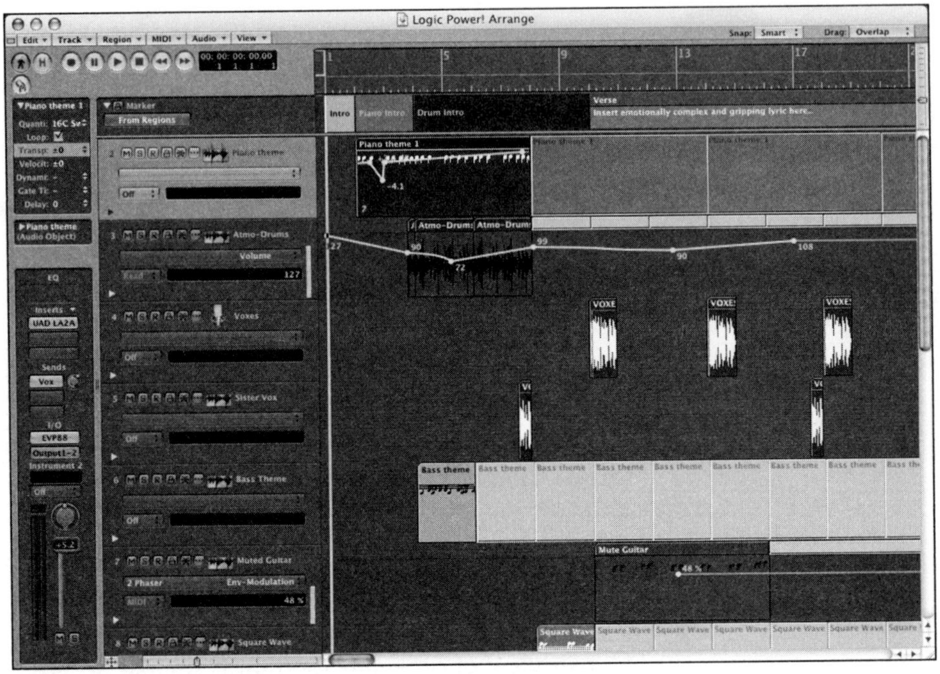

Figure 7.1

The Arrange window in Logic Pro 7. You will spend much of your time using Logic in this window, so getting comfortable with it will make your Logic experience a productive one.

The Edit Menu

The Edit menu, shown in Figure 7.2, is the first local menu in the Logic Arrange page. An explanation of its commands follows. Whenever a key command is defined by default, it is listed in brackets (< >) at the end of the definition. Remember that even for menu commands that do not have default key commands assigned, you can assign one yourself in the Key Commands window.

The following are descriptions of each command in the Edit menu:

- **Undo**. This command will undo the last action in Logic. Be careful about relying on Undo, however, since not every action can be undone. If an action cannot be undone, this command is grayed out and changes to Can't Undo. **<COMMAND + Z>**
- **Redo**. This will redo the option previously undone. Be careful about relying on Redo, however, since you cannot redo every option that you can undo. If an action cannot be redone, this command is grayed out and changes to Can't Redo. **<SHIFT + COMMAND + Z>**

- **Undo History.** Logic has more than a single level of Undo. Logic offers multiple Undo, meaning that Logic will maintain a list of undoable actions, and you can choose to undo any or all of them at any point. And this does mean at *any* point—your undo list is saved with your song, so the list of all your undoable actions is always available (unless you choose to delete it; see the description of Delete Undo History). You determine how many levels deep your Undo History will be via a preference found in the Editing tab of the Global preferences, which you can access by selecting **Logic Pro > Preferences > Global**. The default is 30 steps, but you can choose any number under 10,001 steps.

  When you select this command, you are presented with the Undo History window shown in Figure 7.3.

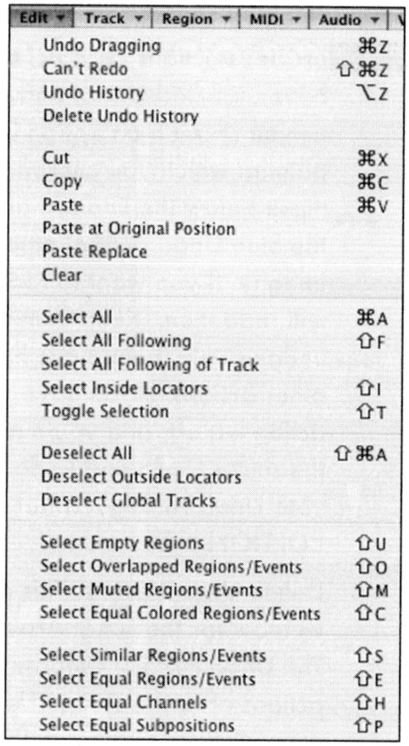

Figure 7.2

The Edit menu in the Arrange.

Figure 7.3

The Undo History window. In this example, you can undo action 20 and below by clicking the Undo button. If you undo these actions, you can redo them by clicking the Redo button.

The obvious features of the Undo History window are a list of your previous actions in Logic, and two glowing buttons on the left: a blue button labeled Undo, and a green button labeled Redo. Notice that as you click on an option inside the window, a red line moves to the point at which you clicked. The actions above the line are blue, and those below the line are green. This means that if you were to click the blue Undo button, all of the options below the line would be undone. If you want to redo those actions, clicking the Redo button will redo them. Keep in mind that you can redo what you have just undone only if you have not already gone ahead and performed other actions. If you have, these new actions start where your Undo action left off, and you'll no longer have Redo as an option. As with the single Undo and Redo commands, not every action will appear in your Undo History, as not every action can be undone or redone. **<OPTION + Z>**

- **Delete Undo History.** This option completely empties the Undo History window for the song. After this, no previous actions will be undoable. The Undo History window immediately starts recording all undoable actions after the Delete Undo History command, and those subsequent actions remain undoable until the next time you select Delete Undo History.
- **Cut.** The Cut command removes the contents of any selection you make in a text box or track lane of Arrange and places it onto the Clipboard. You can then use the Paste command to replace the Cut selection. **<COMMAND + X>**
- **Copy.** The Copy command copies the contents of any selection you make in a text box or track lane of Arrange and places it onto the Clipboard. The original data is not removed. You can then use the Paste command to insert a copy of the data on the Clipboard. **<COMMAND + C>**
- **Paste**. Paste inserts the data from the Clipboard at the current song location. Keep in mind that if you have text in the Clipboard, you have to paste it into a text window, and if you have a region from a track lane on the Clipboard, you cannot paste that into a text box. **<COMMAND + V>**

- **Paste at Original Position.** If you select Paste at Original Position, the regions on the Clipboard will always be pasted to the exact position they were cut or copied from, instead of being inserted at the current song location.
- **Paste Replace.** Instead of inserting the regions from the Clipboard at a given location, Paste Replace overwrites any regions that occur at the same point in the timeline with regions from the Clipboard.
- **Clear.** Clear erases any currently selected regions. **<DELETE>**
- **Select All.** This command selects all regions on every Arrange track lane. **<COMMAND + A>**
- **Select All Following.** If you select a region on Arrange, this command selects all other regions on every Arrange track lane beyond the selected region. This command does not select any region whose starting point comes before your originally selected region, even if the end of those regions extend to (or past) the selected region. **<SHIFT + F>**
- **Select All Following of Track.** If you select a region on Arrange, this command selects all other regions beyond the selected region on the same Arrange track lane. This command does not select any region whose starting point comes before your originally selected region, even if the end of those regions extend to (or past) the selected region.
- **Select Inside Locators**. This command selects all regions that are between the left and right Locators. **<SHIFT + I>**
- **Toggle Selection.** This powerful command toggles the selection status of regions on Arrange. In other words, if you currently have four regions selected, this command deselects those four regions and selects every other region on Arrange. **<SHIFT + T>**
- **Deselect All.** Any selected regions will be deselected with this command. **<SHIFT + COMMAND + A>**
- **Deselect Outside Locators**. When you select this command, any regions you've previously selected outside the left and right Locators will be deselected. Regions between the two Locators will be unaffected.

- **Deselect Global Tracks.** This command will deselect any Global Tracks, and/or global events on Global Tracks, that have been selected.
- **Select Empty Regions.** If you have regions that do not contain any data, this command selects them. Because empty regions don't often serve much purpose, this command is often used in tandem with Clear (or the **DELETE** key) to remove unnecessary regions from the Arrange window. **<SHIFT + U>**
- **Select Overlapped Regions/Events.** This command selects every region that is overlapping (or overlapped by) another region. **<SHIFT + O>**
- **Select Muted Regions/Events.** You can use this command to select all the regions that you have previously muted on Arrange. **<SHIFT + M>**
- **Select Equal Colored Regions/Events.** If you are using color to organize your tracks in the Arrange window, this command will select all the regions that have the same color. **<SHIFT + C>**
- **Select Similar Regions/Events.** If you select a region, this command selects regions that process the same type of MIDI data as the one you have selected. **<SHIFT + S>**
- **Select Equal Regions/Events**. If you select a region, this command selects regions identical to the region you have selected (for example, if you have copied and pasted a region a number of times, this will select each of the copied regions). **<SHIFT + E>**
- **Select Equal Channels**. This command selects all regions that are of the same type (Audio or MIDI) or on the same MIDI Channel as a region you have selected. **<SHIFT + H>**
- **Select Equal Subpositions**. To use this command, first select a region that is at the desired relative position in a bar of your song—for example, on the first downbeat. After that, if you choose Select Equal Subpositions, all regions at that relative position—in this example, at the first downbeat of a bar—will be selected. **<SHIFT + P>**

The Track Menu

The Track menu is the local menu on Arrange that contains many of the commands regarding the creation, deletion, and sorting of tracks. Figure 7.4 shows the Track menu of the Arrange window.

Explanations of the Track menu commands follow:

Figure 7.4
The Track menu of the Arrange window.

- **Create.** This command creates a track directly below the currently selected track. The track created is an exact duplicate of the selected track. For example, if you select Audio Instrument 1, Create then adds a second Audio Instrument 1 to the track list. **<SHIFT + RETURN>**
- **Create with Next Instrument.** This command creates a track directly below the selected track. The created track follows the selected Environment Object in sequence, even if the track list already contains a track that follows the selected instrument sequentially. In other words, if you select Audio 5, using this command creates Audio 6, even if the next track already on the track list is Audio 6. **<CONTROL + SHIFT + RETURN>**
- **Create Multiple.** This powerful and convenient new command gives users a dialog window in which to choose which type of Audio Track to create, which audio driver the Audio Tracks will be linked to, and how many tracks to create. More details about the Create Multiple command can be found in Chapter 4, "Creating Your Autoload Song."
- **Create for Overlapped Regions.** If you select a number of regions on a track lane that overlap, this command creates one new track for each region.
- **Create for Selected Regions.** Similar to the Create for Overlapped Objects command, this command creates a new track for each region you have selected. This command does not require regions to be overlapping, however.
- **Delete.** This command deletes a track from the track list.
- **Delete Unused.** This command deletes any track from the track list that does not have any regions in its track lane.
- **Delete Redundant Audio Tracks.** If you have a number of Audio Tracks pointing to the same Audio channel (for example, if you used the Create command to create four Audio 1 tracks), this command deletes all the repeated tracks that do not have any regions on them.

- **Create Track Name.** This command presents you with a text box to enter a name for the selected track.
- **Delete Track Name.** This command erases the name of the selected track.
- **Sort Tracks By.** This option opens a hierarchal menu of track sorting options, as shown in Figure 7.5.

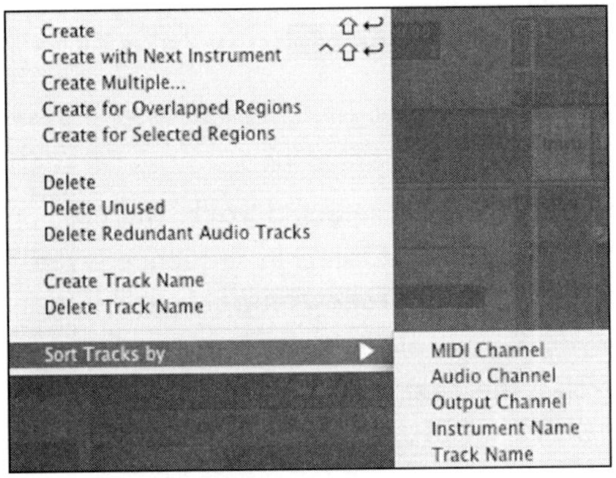

Figure 7.5
The Sort Tracks By submenu of the Track menu.

- **MIDI Channel.** If you choose this option, Logic sorts all the tracks in your track list in order of their MIDI Channel. Even Audio channels will be sorted in order of the MIDI Channel in their parameter box.
- **Audio Channel.** This option sorts Audio Object tracks by their Audio channel. MIDI Channels, which don't have an Audio channel, will be sorted to the top of your track list. This option also alphabetizes your Audio Object tracks by type, so, for example, your Audio Instrument tracks will come before your Audio Output tracks.
- **Output Channel.** This option sorts Audio Object tracks by their output channel. Tracks assigned to the same output will be sorted alphabetically. MIDI Channels, which don't have an Audio channel, will be sorted to the top of your track list.
- **Instrument Name.** This option sorts tracks alphabetically by instrument name. This option works only if you have selected **View > Instrument Name**.
- **Track Name.** This option sorts tracks alphabetically by track name. This option works only if you have selected **View > Track Name**.

The Region Menu

The Region local menu contains commands and subfolders of commands that act on regions in the Arrange window. Figure 7.6 shows the Region local menu.

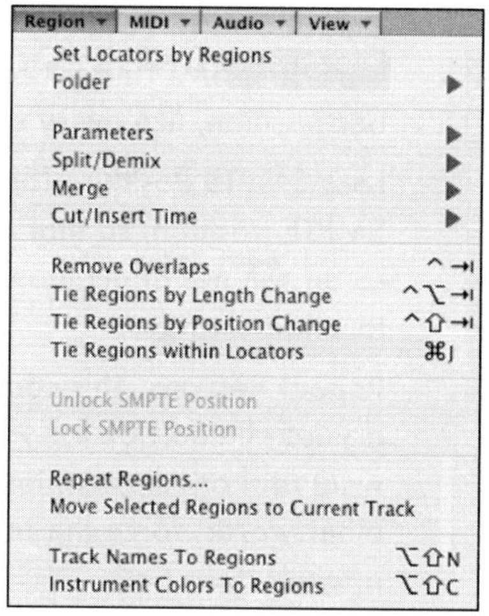

Figure 7.6

The Region local menu.

As you can see, this local menu contains a fair number of submenus filled with commands. Below is a description of the Region menu commands, as well as its submenus and commands.

- **Set Locators by Regions.** This command moves the left Locator to the leftmost boundary of the leftmost region you have selected, and the right Locator to the rightmost boundary of the rightmost region you have selected.
- **Folder Submenu.** See below.
- **Parameters Submenu.** See below.
- **Split/Demix Submenu.** See below.
- **Merge.** See below.
- **Cut/Insert Time.** See below.
- **Remove Overlaps.** If you have overlapping regions on your track, this command shortens the length of the earlier region to stop at the beginning of the later region. **<CONTROL + RIGHT ARROW>**
- **Tie Regions by Length Change.** This command extends all selected regions so that they end at exactly the beginning of the subsequent region on the track. For Audio regions, this only works if the audio file is long enough for the region to extend to the beginning of the subsequent region.
- **Tie Regions by Position Change.** This command does not alter the length of the first selected region, but Logic will move all subsequent sequences so that they begin precisely at the end of the previous region.
- **Tie Regions within Locators.** This command elongates all MIDI regions between the Locators so there are no gaps between them.

- **Unlock SMPTE Position.** This command unlocks the selected regions from their SMPTE position. At this point, these regions are tied to their bar position, like every other region.
- **Lock SMPTE Position.** This command locks any selected region to its SMPTE position, so that any changes in bar length, tempo, meter, and so on will not affect those regions' time positions, even as their bar location changes.
- **Repeat Regions.** This command repeats the selected region. It presents a small dialog box for you to select the number of repetitions, if you want real or Alias copies, and if you want to quantize the copies (in other words, force the repeats to end on an exact bar line, even if the original does not).
- **Move Selected Regions to Current Track.** If you have a track selected in the track list, and then select one or more regions on different track lanes, this command moves all the regions you have selected to the selected track.
- **Track Names To Regions.** When you select a track and then use this command, all of the regions on that track will be given the name of the track. **<OPTION + SHIFT + N>**
- **Instrument Colors To Regions.** When you select a track and then use this command, all of the regions on that track will be given the same color as the track. **<OPTION + SHIFT + C>**

Folder Tracks

Folder tracks are tracks that are containers for the data of one or more other tracks. This allows you to organize tracks into their own little Arrange window groups and move and edit the entire group as a single track. With Folder tracks, for example, you could keep your "main" Arrange window organized by creating Folder tracks for all your drum loops, synth lines, backup vocals, and so on. I will explain Folder tracks in more depth later in this chapter. The Folder submenu, shown in Figure 7.7, contains commands that operate on Folder tracks.

Figure 7.7
The Folder submenu of the Regions local menu.

The commands in the Folder submenu are as follows:

- **Pack Folder.** This command combines all the selected tracks into a single Folder Track. **<COMMAND + F>**
- **Unpack Folder (Create New Tracks).** When you select a folder track, this command removes each track from the folder and creates a new track in your track list for each track in the folder. **<SHIFT + COMMAND + F>**
- **Unpack Folder (Use Existing Tracks).** This command also removes each track from the selected folder. If you do not have any existing tracks on your Arrange that match the Folder track, it creates new tracks. If empty tracks already exist that match the name of the Folder track, it places the contents of each track on the matching empty track.

The Parameters Submenu

These commands relate to functions you can access inside a region's parameter box, such as looping. Figure 7.8 shows the Parameters submenu of the Region menu.

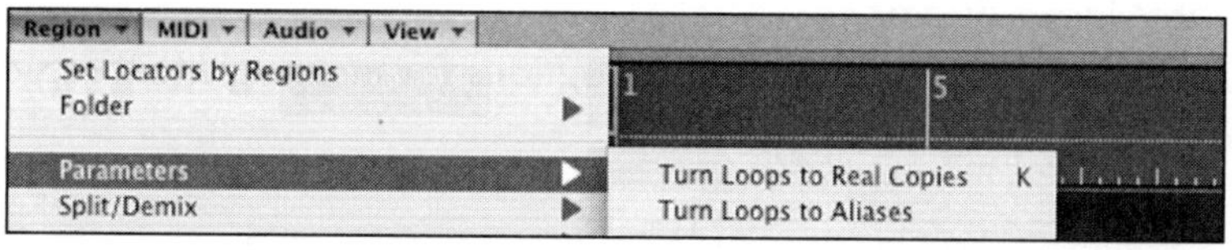

Figure 7.8
The Parameters submenu of the Regions local menu.

There are currently only two commands in the Parameters submenu:

- **Turn Loops to Real Copies.** This command turns any loops of the selected region into an actual copy of the selected region. **<K>**
- **Turn Loops to Aliases.** This command turns any loops of the selected region into Aliases of the selected region.

The Split/Demix Submenu

This submenu includes commands that divide regions in different ways. Figure 7.9 shows the Split/Demix submenu.

Figure 7.9
The Split/Demix submenu of the Regions menu.

An explanation of the four commands in the Split/Demix submenu follows.

- **Split Regions by Locators.** This command creates a split in any selected regions at the current Locator positions. **<COMMAND + Y>**
- **Split Regions by Song Position.** This command splits any selected regions at the current song position. **<CONTROL + Y>**
- **Demix by Event Channel.** If you have a MIDI track selected, this command creates a new track for each MIDI Channel used by events on that track. Each new track will contain the events from the original track that were on that MIDI Channel. This command is useful for recording many different MIDI parts on different MIDI Channels at once, then moving each part to its own track afterward. **<COMMAND + D>**
- **Demix by Note Pitch.** If you have a MIDI track selected, this command creates a new track for every MIDI note in the track. This command is especially useful for recording a MIDI drum performance, in which each note is a separate drum, and then placing each drum note on its own separate track afterward.

The Merge Submenu

This submenu offers a couple of options for merging MIDI regions together, as shown in Figure 7.10.

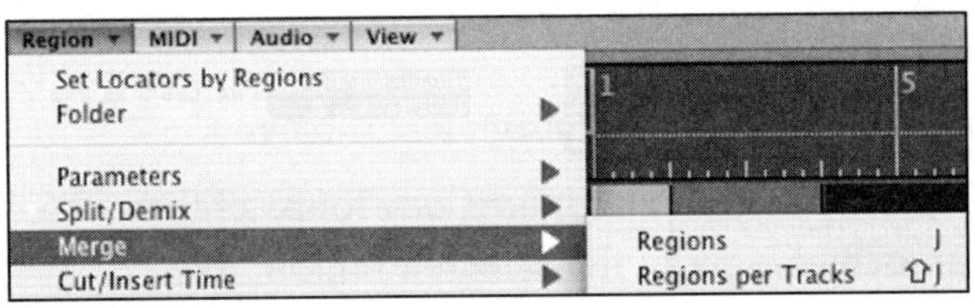

Figure 7.10
The Merge submenu of the Regions menu.

The submenu's two options are as follows:

- **Regions.** This command merges the data from any selected regions into a single region. The new object will be given the same name and be on the same track as the track of the first selected object. If you have MIDI regions on different tracks, the merged data will retain its position in time, but not its MIDI Channel; the MIDI Channel of the newly created MIDI region will be the MIDI Channel that the instrument on the selected track is using. If you use this command on non-contiguous Audio regions, Logic will create a new audio file containing the merged regions, just as if you had used the Glue tool (described later in the chapter).**<J>**

- **Regions per Tracks.** This is the same as the preceding option, except that if the selected objects are on different tracks, rather than a single region being created on the track of the first region, Logic will create regions on each track on which there are selected regions. This means that merged regions will retain the MIDI Channel of the events in the original regions because they are not changing MIDI Instruments. **<SHIFT + J>**

The Cut/Insert Time Submenu

This submenu includes a few commands that add or remove time from the song. Figure 7.11 shows the Cut/Insert Time submenu.

Figure 7.11
The Cut/Insert Time submenu of the Regions menu.

An explanation of the trio of options in the Cut/Insert Time submenu follows:

- **Snip: Cut Time and Move by Locators.** This command removes an amount of time determined by the song Locators. Regions after the right Locator move to the left Locator, and all information between the Locators is removed from the song to the Clipboard.
- **Insert Time and Move by Locators.** This command creates a gap of empty space between the two Locators. Any regions between the Locators move to the right of the right Locator.
- **Splice: Insert Snipped Part at Song Position.** This command inserts all the information cut by the Snip command back into the song at the current position. All regions to the right of the inserted objects are pushed back so they begin at the end of the inserted regions.

The MIDI Menu

The MIDI local menu consists of commands and submenus of commands relating to MIDI regions. The MIDI local menu is shown in Figure 7.12.

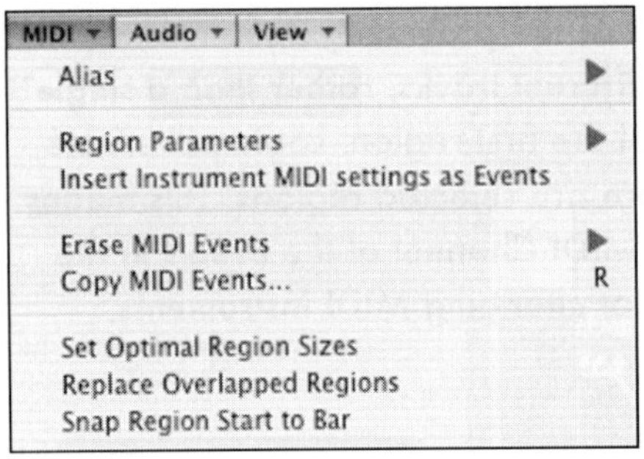

Figure 7.12
The MIDI local menu of the Arrange window.

The commands and submenus of the MIDI menu are described below:

- **Alias Submenu.** See below.
- **Region Parameters Submenu.** See below.
- **Insert Instrument MIDI Settings as Events.** When you select a MIDI track, choosing the Insert Instrument MIDI Settings as Events command creates MIDI events for program, volume, and pan if they are checked in the Object parameter box and places those events in the track.
- **Erase MIDI Events Submenu.** See below.
- **Copy MIDI Events.** This command opens the dialog box shown in Figure 7.13. From this box, you can select exactly where your data to copy is, if you want to copy it to the Clipboard or to another location on the Arrange, what type of copy mode (merge, replace, and so on) you wish for your MIDI data, and how many copies you want to make. This command is a very powerful way to move large amounts of MIDI data around your song. **<R>**

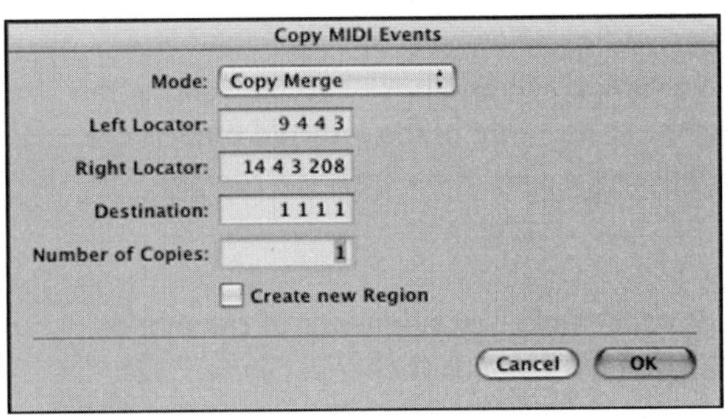

Figure 7.13
The Copy MIDI events dialog box. Use this command to copy or move large amounts of MIDI data around your song.

- **Set Optimal Region Sizes.** This command reduces or increases the length of a MIDI region to be just large enough to contain the MIDI events within it, rounded to the nearest bar. Most regions tend not to be too much larger than the amount of data inside them to begin with, so you are unlikely to need this command. Its main uses include if you record a MIDI part and don't stop recording quickly, leaving you with a large empty space in the MIDI region without notes, or if you are editing a MIDI region in a MIDI editor and delete notes at the beginning or end of the region.
- **Replace Overlapped Regions.** This command moves selected overlapping regions so that they no longer overlap. It does so by deleting the regions the selected region overlaps and lengthening the selected region to fill the space previously occupied by the deleted region.
- **Snap Region Start to Bar.** This command rounds your MIDI regions to start at the nearest bar.

The Alias Submenu

Aliases are regions that do not themselves contain data, but are pointers to other regions that contain data. This submenu offers a selection of commands relating to the creation and selection of Aliases. Figure 7.14 shows this submenu.

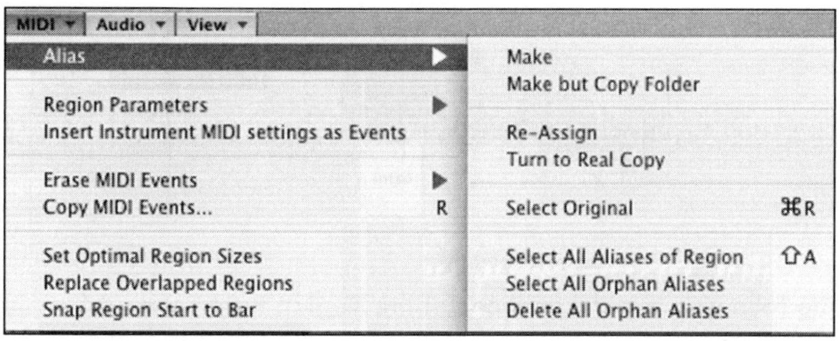

Figure 7.14
The Alias submenu of the MIDI menu.

An explanation of the commands in the Alias submenu follows:

- **Make.** This command makes an Alias of the selected region.
- **Make But Copy Folder.** If you select a Folder track and then choose this command, Logic creates a copy of the Folder track that contains Aliases of all the objects in the original folder. This command has no effect if no folder is selected.

- **Re-Assign.** By selecting an Alias and the desired region you wish to re-assign that Alias, this command reassigns the selected Alias to point to a different region than the initial region to which the Alias pointed.
- **Turn to Real Copy.** This command turns an Alias into a real copy of the original region, meaning it will now contain data identical to that of the original region, and not simply a pointer to the original region.
- **Select Original.** If you select an Alias and then choose this command, the original region to which the Alias is pointing is selected as well. **<COMMAND + R>**
- **Select All Aliases of Region.** If you select a region and choose this command, all the Aliases of the original region are selected as well. **<SHIFT + A>**
- **Select All Orphan Aliases.** If you have unassigned Aliases in your Arrange because you deleted the original region to which they pointed, this command selects those Aliases.
- **Delete All Orphan Aliases.** This command deletes all Aliases that point to deleted regions.

The Region Parameter Submenu

This submenu contains a number of commands that relate to the parameters specific to MIDI regions. Figure 7.15 shows the Region Parameters submenu.

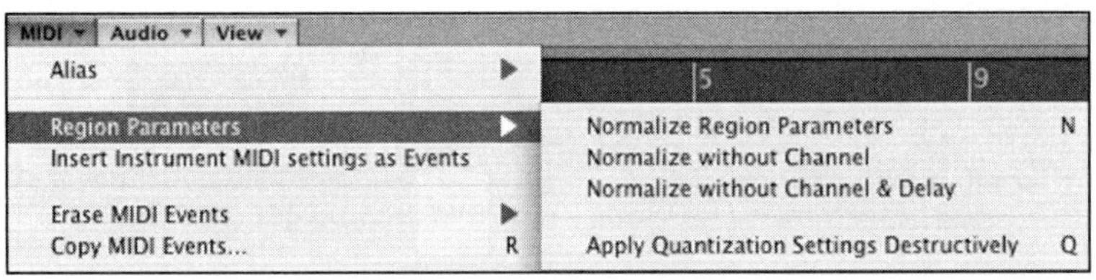

Figure 7.15
The Region Parameters submenu of the MIDI menu.

The following are descriptions of the Region Parameters submenu's options:

- **Normalize Region Parameters.** This command permanently adjusts the values in the parameter box of a MIDI region. **<N>**
- **Normalize without Channel.** This command normalizes the parameters of a MIDI region without normalizing the MIDI Channel value.
- **Normalize without Channel & Delay.** This command normalizes the parameters of a MIDI region without normalizing the MIDI Channel or the MIDI delay.

- **Apply Quantization Settings Destructively.** This command permanently applies the playback quantize value assigned to the MIDI region in its parameter box. **<Q>**

The Erase MIDI Events Submenu

This submenu contains different options for deleting MIDI events in a track. Figure 7.16 shows the Erase MIDI Events submenu.

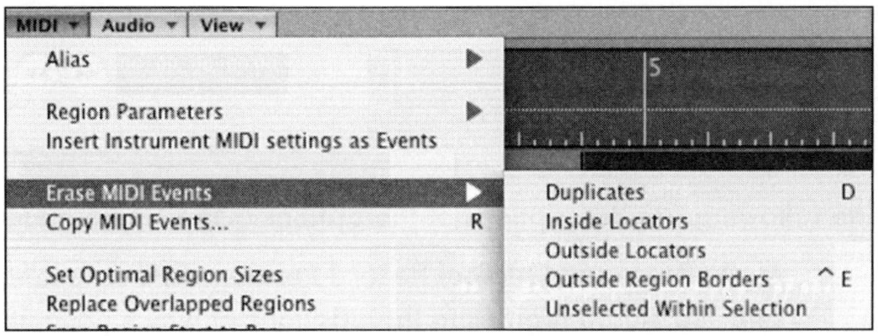

Figure 7.16
The Erase MIDI Events submenu of the MIDI menu.

Explanations of the commands in the Erase MIDI Events submenu follow:

- **Duplicates.** This command erases all duplicate MIDI events (meaning, similar events at the same time position in your song) in selected regions. **<D>**
- **Inside Locators.** This command erases all MIDI events in selected regions inside the left and right Locators.
- **Outside Locators.** This command erases all MIDI events outside of the left and right Locators in selected regions.
- **Outside Region Borders.** Use this command to erase all of the MIDI events outside the borders of a selected region. **<CONTROL + E>**
- **Unselected Within Selection.** This command erases all the unselected MIDI information inside an area you have selected.

The Audio Menu

The Audio local menu of Arrange contains commands that only affect Audio regions. Figure 7.17 shows the Audio menu. The next chapter, "Working with Audio and Apple Loops," explains the use of these functions in more depth.

Figure 7.17
The Audio menu of the Arrange window.

The following are descriptions of the options in the Audio menu:

- **Move Region to Original Record Position.** This command returns all selected Audio regions to the positions at which you initially recorded them. This works only for Audio regions consisting of audio recorded in Logic, or Broadcast WAV files that have embedded start information; because a region that you imported from a disk of audio samples would have no "original record position," this command would not have any effect.
- **Convert Regions to New Regions.** This command makes independent Audio regions in the Audio window for regions previously considered subregions of a "parent" Audio region (meaning, Audio regions carved from what was one initial Audio region). **<CONTROL + R>**
- **Convert Regions to New Audio Files.** This command can save all the Audio regions you select as separate audio files on your hard disk. This command is incredibly useful if you want to export specific regions to other audio applications. **<CONTROL + F>**
- **Strip Silence.** When you select an Audio region, you can choose Strip Silence to scan the Audio region for points in which the audio material is below a threshold and then create a number of new Audio regions out of those regions above the threshold. This command is extremely useful for removing any pauses in a recording. This command is covered in more detail in Chapter 8. **<CONTROL + S>**
- **Adjust Region Length to Locators.** When you select an Audio region and choose this command, Logic will time stretch or compress your

audio to the length of the Locators. Note that no Audio region can be stretched or compressed more than half of, or less than double, its original length.

- **Adjust Region Length to Nearest Bar.** This command results in Logic using time stretching or compressing to adjust the length of a selected Audio region to the nearest bar. Note that no Audio region can be stretched or compressed more than 100 percent of its original length.
- **Time Machine Algorithm.** When Logic time stretches or compresses an Audio region, it uses unique and high-quality algorithms created for its Time Machine in the Sample Editor, which is explored in the next chapter. The Time Machine Algorithm submenu is explained in the following subsection.
- **Show Selected Audio File(s) in Finder.** This command will bring up Finder windows showing you the actual file on your hard drive referenced by the selected Audio region(s).
- **Copy ReCycle Loop.** If you want to copy audio in your Arrange for use in Propellerhead's ReCycle, you can select the audio file and copy them to the Clipboard with this command.
- **Paste ReCycle Loop.** If you have copied a REX or REX2 loop onto the Clipboard, you can paste it at the current SPL position with this command.
- **Search Zero Crossings.** This command searches the selected Audio region for points at which the amplitude of the audio wave crosses the zero line. Any subsequent attempts to edit the length of an Audio region will be restricted to zero crossings. This is useful in matching up audio edits.

The Time Machine Algorithm Submenu

You can choose from several Time Machine Algorithms, each of which is optimized differently. Figure 7.18 shows the hierarchal menu of Time Machine Algorithm.

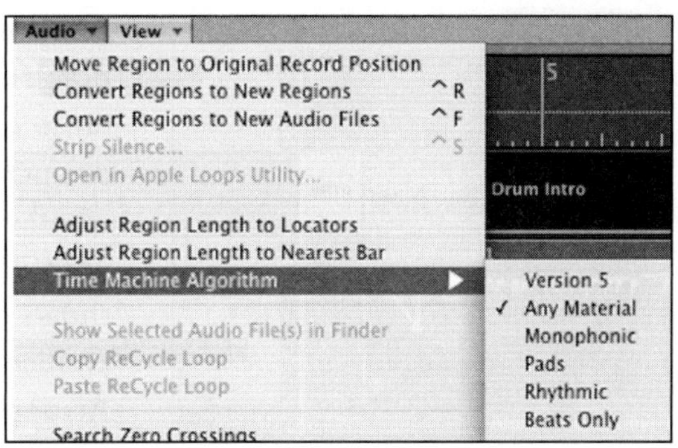

Figure 7.18
The Time Machine Algorithm submenu of the Audio menu.

You can select from the following algorithms:

- **Version 5.** This is the Time Machine Algorithm from Logic 5.
- **Any Material.** This algorithm has been designed to give high-quality results when stretching and compressing Audio regions containing any variety of material.
- **Monophonic.** This algorithm is optimized for material that uses only a single voice (such as a single singer, wind instrument, mono synthesizer, and so on).
- **Pads.** This algorithm is optimized for polyphonic material, such as pads, choirs, and so on.
- **Rhythmic.** This algorithm is optimized for instruments with dramatic rhythmic peaks, such as percussion, steel drums, pulsing rhythmic synths, and so on.
- **Beats Only.** This algorithm is designed for nonpitched material with strong rhythmic peaks, such as drums. You can use this algorithm to adjust the spaces between peaks, which produces excellent results on drums and such. However, the algorithm is often ineffective or unusable on melodic audio parts.

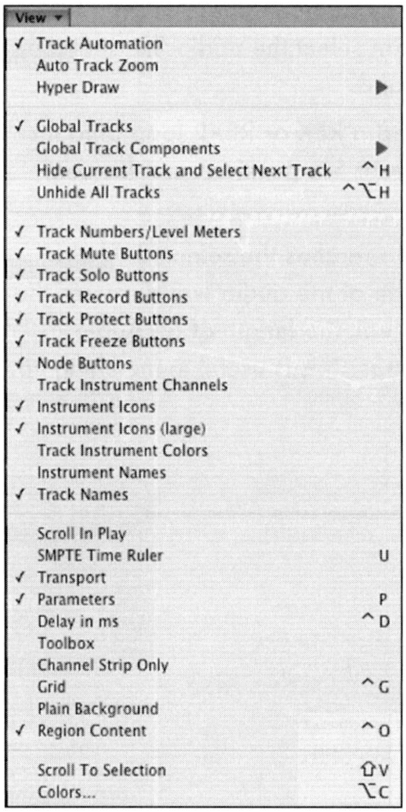

Figure 7.19

Use the View menu of the Arrange window to select which items you will view in your Arrange.

The View Menu

The last local menu in the Arrange window, View, is loaded with options you can use to specify what you will see as part of your Arrange page. Most of these options simply allow you to check or uncheck various items to determine whether they will appear or not on your Arrange window. Figure 7.19 shows all the various items that you can choose to view or not to view on your Arrange page.

Because these items are simply checked on or off and are described individually later in this chapter, this menu doesn't call for a definition of options here. The main thing to remember about the View menu is that when you need to toggle the view of any feature of Arrange, you use this local menu.

Track Classes

By now you realize that all tracks are not created equal. Logic provides several different track classes. Each track contains different sorts of data and has a different purpose. I'll briefly go over them:

- **MIDI Tracks.** A MIDI track is assigned to a MIDI Instrument, and contains MIDI data. You can only record and play back MIDI information from a MIDI track.
- **Audio Tracks.** An Audio Track is a track assigned to an Audio channel. It may contain, record, and play back audio information. An Audio Track doesn't have to contain audio data, however; you can create Audio Tracks to represent audio bus, auxiliary, output, input, and other tracks that do not actually contain information, but are assigned to an Audio channel. Reasons for creating these sorts of tracks are to access their channel strips from the Arrange window, to include the multiple outputs of a software synthesizer with its Audio Instrument track, to automate them using Track Automation, and so on.
- **Audio Instrument Tracks.** These are also Audio Tracks, but a special kind of Audio Track. An Audio Instrument outputs audio produced by the instrument through Logic's audio engine. So an Audio Instrument track uses an Audio channel and has a channel strip similar to the channel strips of the other Audio Objects. However, since Audio Instrument tracks contain instruments, the track itself contains only MIDI data that triggers the instrument. As such, the parameters and channel strip of an Audio Instrument track look like an Audio Track, but the regions on an Audio Instrument track look like that of a MIDI track.
- **Folder Tracks.** As explained previously, Folder tracks are containers for other classes of tracks. Tracks packed in folders can be arranged and edited as a single track. An advantage of this capability is that if you have a group of tracks that you want to keep together—for example, a full choir—you can put them all in a folder, and then when

you move, split, or otherwise change that Folder track, all of your choir tracks will be moved and edited together, so that you need not operate on each individual track. Folders are also great organizational tracks, in that packing tracks into folders can help keep your main Arrange window from becoming cluttered. There are commands in the **Region > Folder** submenu to both pack folders (load a folder with tracks) and unpack folders (unload all of the tracks in a folder onto Arrange). See the previous subsection, "Folder Tracks," for a description of those commands.

METHOD TIP: USES FOR FOLDER TRACKS

Len Sasso, author of *Emagic Logic Tips and Tricks* (PC Publishing: 2003), offers a few expert uses for Folder tracks:

> *"Create a screenset with two Arrange windows, one normal and the other floating. Click the floating window's Link button until it is yellow, indicating Contents-Link mode. Any folder you select in the normal Arrange window will now have its contents shown automatically in the floating Arrange window."*

Sasso also explains how to unpack only part of a folder:

> *"When you want to unpack only some of the regions in a folder, select the regions you don't want unpacked and pack them into a subfolder of their own. Then unpack the original folder and you will have the desired regions unpacked and the rest in their own folder. That's easier than trying to find and re-pack the desired regions in the full Arrange window."*

- **Metronome Track.** This is the track reserved for the Metronome in Logic, named MIDI Click by default. You can use this track to adjust the parameters of your MIDI Click to best assist your live performance. You will only want a single Metronome track per song. Keep in mind that you don't actually need to have a Metronome track in your Arrange to use the Metronome.
- **No Output Track.** This special track, as its name implies, does not output any MIDI data to MIDI devices or audio data to audio outputs. The No Output track option is mostly used for storing synth SysEx data you don't want to send, or as a temporary assignment for tracks you want to turn off momentarily.

You can change the class of a track and/or instrument of a track by click-holding the mouse over a track on the track list. A hierarchal menu then appears containing all of the previously discussed track classes, and all of your Instrument and Audio Object options divided into submenus based on the Environment layer in which they appear. Figure 7.20 shows this hierarchal menu of track classes.

To change the track, simply select a new track class or instrument.

Figure 7.20
When you click-hold the mouse over a track, a hierarchal menu appears of all available track classes and instruments on the various Environment layers.

EXPERT TIP: FOLDERS ON NONFOLDER TRACKS

There is an exception to the preceding rule, as aforementioned author Sasso points out:

> *"Normally folders are placed on special Folder tracks, which are not assigned to particular Environment Objects as are other tracks. That's what Logic does automatically when you create a folder, but you can reassign the track to any Environment Object and you can also move the folder to another track. When a folder is on a normal track, all of its output is routed to the Environment Object assigned to that track. That holds for the 'No Output' track as well."*

Adding Tracks to Arrange

I already discussed how to add tracks to Arrange in Chapter 4, and from the menu descriptions in this chapter, you have already seen the various commands relating to creating tracks in the Track local menu. You can also use the following two additional methods to add tracks:

- **Append Track to Track List.** If you want to append a new track to the very bottom of your track list, you can do so by double-clicking in the empty space below the final track in your track list. This creates a new track that is identical to whichever track you have selected in the track list. You can also define a key command for this function in the Key Commands window.
- **Append Track to Track List with Next Instrument.** If you want to add at the bottom of the track list a track that contains the next instrument from the track that you have selected, you can hold the **OPTION** key down while double-clicking in the empty space below the track list. You can also define a key command for this function in the Key Commands window.

Track Parameters

You've already seen the parameter boxes for Environment Objects and discussed parameter boxes when building your Autoload song, but it bears repeating that every single track has two parameter boxes. Figure 7.21 shows both parameter boxes.

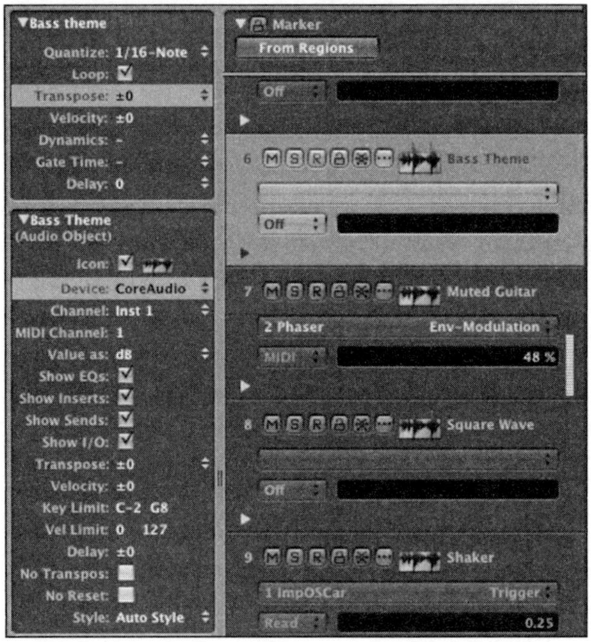

Figure 7.21

The Region parameter box and the Object parameter box of an Audio Instrument track. The Object parameter box should be familiar from Chapter 4. The Region parameter box contains playback parameters for MIDI regions.

The first parameter box contains Region Playback parameters that will apply for the entire track if no region is selected, or only for the selected regions if any are selected. The second box is the same parameter box for the object that you can access in the Environment. Chapter 4 explained the Object parameters, and the next section describes the playback parameters.

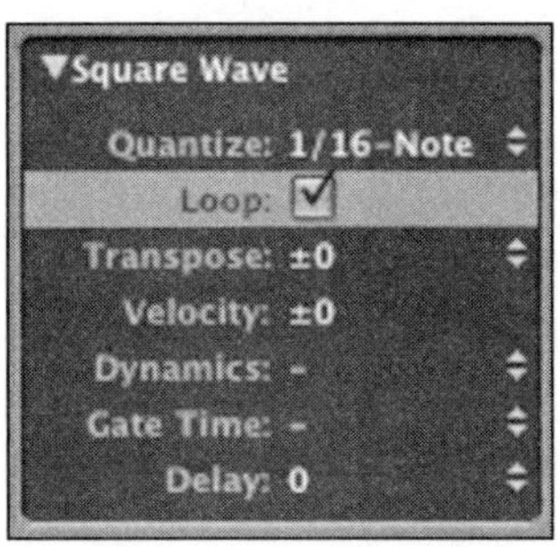

Figure 7.22

The Region Playback Parameters box of a MIDI or Audio Instrument track.

Region Playback Parameters

Figure 7.22 shows the Region Playback parameters that you will find for a MIDI or Audio Instrument track. They are called playback parameters because these settings do not affect recording, and they are not written to the region itself, but only affect the way Logic plays back the track unless you apply the Normalize Region Parameters command.

Descriptions of the parameters follow:

- **Quantize.** This is the quantize setting. To *quantize* MIDI data means to lock its playback to a beat count, so that regardless of the timing of the data, it will be played back with the exact timing selected in the Quantize parameter. If you click to the right of the parameter, a pull-down menu appears that offers you myriad beat and note options from which to choose. Quantizing is explored in more depth in Chapter 9, "Working with MIDI."
- **Loop.** Clicking in the box to the right of this parameter turns on "old style" looping for that track or region. When activating old style looping, the looped region will continually repeat for the length of the song, or until another region on the same track interrupts the looping. When old style looping is activated for a region, a number of solid gray regions representing the repeats of the looped region extend until the end of the song, or looping is interrupted by another region. Looping will be explained in more detail later in the chapter.
- **Transpose.** This parameter allows you to transpose the pitch of playback higher or lower by up to 96 semitones.
- **Velocity**. You can also offset the velocity of a MIDI track or region up or down. The range of velocity is the standard MIDI parameter range of 0–127, and you can add or subtract up to 100 to or from that value, up to the maximum value of 127.
- **Dynamics**. Adjusting the Dynamics parameter affects the velocity, except that instead of offsetting the maximum value, Dynamics offsets the distance between the loudest and softest velocities in the region. This can compress or increase the difference in volume between the notes, affecting the perceived volume. If you select this parameter, a pull-down menu opens that offers adjustment steps from 25 percent to 400 percent, with values below 100 percent increasing the dynamics, and values above 100 percent reducing the dynamics. The FIX option plays back all the notes at the same velocity.
- **Gate Time.** Gating literally opens or closes playback of the note that is being played, reducing or expanding its length. This scales the note duration, forcing playback to be staccato (shorter) or legato (longer). This parameter offers a pull-down menu of adjustment steps from 25 percent to 400 percent, with values below 100 percent reducing note duration, and values above 100 percent increasing note duration. The

FIX option enables you to specify the note length to a single value or to make all notes legato.

- **Delay.** This parameter offsets when a region plays back. The range of this parameter is –999 to 9999 ticks; a tick is the smallest time resolution in the sequencer, 1/3840th of a quarter note. You can turn on Delay in Milliseconds by choosing **View > Delay in Ms**, which displays this range in milliseconds instead of ticks. This parameter is useful if you are trying to align audio and MIDI data, and your MIDI seems to play back a tiny bit ahead or behind the audio.

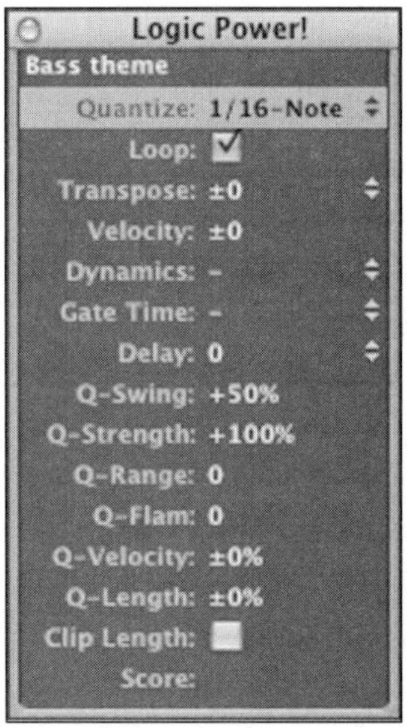

Figure 7.23

The Extended Region Parameters floating box for the track in Figure 7.22.

Extended Region Parameters

If you double-click on the parameter names, select **Options > Extended Region Parameters**, or press the key command **X**, you can access a floating parameter box that offers more selections than the standard Region Playback Parameters box in the Parameters column of the Arrange window. The Extended Region Parameters box is shown in Figure 7.23.

As you will see in the following description of the Extended Region parameters, most of these parameters offer finer control over the Quantize function. Again, Chapter 9 explains quantizing in more detail.

The Extended Region parameters are as follows:

- **Q-Swing.** This controls how tightly the quantization feature locks every second beat to its quantization grid to give the MIDI part a more "pushed" or "laid-back" feel. You can adjust this parameter from 1 percent to 99 percent, with values under 50 percent resulting in an early beat, and values over 50 percent resulting in a delayed beat.
- **Q-Strength.** This parameter determines how close to move each note to the nearest quantization grid position. You can adjust the value from 0 percent to 100 percent, with 0 percent resulting in no movement of the note at all, and 100 percent moving the note completely to the grid.

- **Q-Range.** If you set this parameter, notes that are farther away than the number of ticks you set are not quantized. The range can be from –3,840 to 3,840 ticks. There are some exceptions to this, however. A negative setting means that only those notes farther away are quantized; this is useful to quantize only those notes farther away from the grid than you would like. Also, a value of 0 basically turns off the Q-Range function, in which case all notes are quantized.
- **Q-Flam.** This parameter spreads out notes that fall on the same point; in other words, it rolls the chords. A positive value creates an upward roll; a negative value creates a downward roll. You can set the range from –3,840 to 3,840 ticks.
- **Q-Velocity.** This parameter sets how much the velocity values of a template MIDI region will affect the velocity of the notes. You can adjust this parameter from –99 percent to 127 percent, with negative numbers and numbers over 100 percent creating the greatest velocity deviation from the template MIDI region, 0 percent leaving the notes unaffected by the note velocities of the template MIDI region, and 100 percent meaning the notes adopt the note velocities of the template MIDI region completely.
- **Q-Length.** This parameter determines how the note lengths of a template MIDI region affect the note length of your MIDI region in Arrange. You can adjust this parameter from –99 percent to 127 percent, with negative numbers and numbers over 100 percent creating the greatest note length deviation from the template MIDI region, 0 percent leaving the notes unaffected by the note lengths of the template MIDI region, and 100 percent meaning the notes adopt the note lengths of the template MIDI region completely.
- **Clip Length.** When the end of a MIDI region is reached, this parameter determines whether any notes that sustain past the end of the region will be played back to their completion or cut off. If the parameter is *checked*, any sustaining notes are stopped. If the check box is *unchecked*, the notes continue playing normally.
- **Score.** This parameter determines whether the MIDI region is available in the Score Editor or not. Check this box to make the region available in the Score Editor. This parameter is of use when a MIDI region contains only nonmusical MIDI information, such as controller messages, and you don't need to display the region in the Score Editor.

Figure 7.24
The parameter box of an Audio region.

The Audio Region Parameter Box

If you select an Audio region, a different parameter box appears that contains parameters specific to Audio regions. Figure 7.24 shows this parameter box.

The parameters are as follows:

- **Loop.** This setting is the same as that described for Region Playback parameters.
- **Fade In.** You can adjust this parameter to determine the length of a fade-in at the beginning of an Audio region.
- **Curve.** This setting determines the strength and shape of the curve of the fade-in, if any.
- **Fade.** This parameter determines which kind of fade there will be at the end of your Audio region. The options are Out (for fade out), X (for crossfade), EqP (for equal-power crossfade), or X S (for equal-strength crossfade).
- **Curve.** This setting determines the strength and shape of the curve of the final fade, if any.

> **A WORD ABOUT FADES**
>
> Don't worry if you are completely unfamiliar with the concept of audio fades right now; you'll learn more about this in Chapter 8, "Working with Audio and Apple Loops."

- **Delay.** This setting is the same as that described for the Region Playback parameters.

The Arrange Channel Strip

To make mixing and accessing mixing parameters more convenient, Logic displays the channel strip for the selected track below the parameter boxes. You need to have parameters turned on in the View menu (**View > Parameters**) in order to see the Arrange channel strip. Figure 7.25 shows the Arrange channel strip of an Audio track.

The Arrange channel strip takes up a lot of vertical space, so depending on how large your Arrange window is, and how many items you are viewing, the channel strip may not fit in the window and may appear "cut off" at the top of its frame. To fit the entire channel strip in the window you might need to close either or both of the parameter boxes by clicking on their disclosure triangles in the top-left of each box. You may also want to make sure that the Toolbox and Transport are turned off in the View local menu to increase your amount of vertical space further. If you are content with only seeing the channel strip in the Parameters column, you can select **View > Channel Strip Only**.

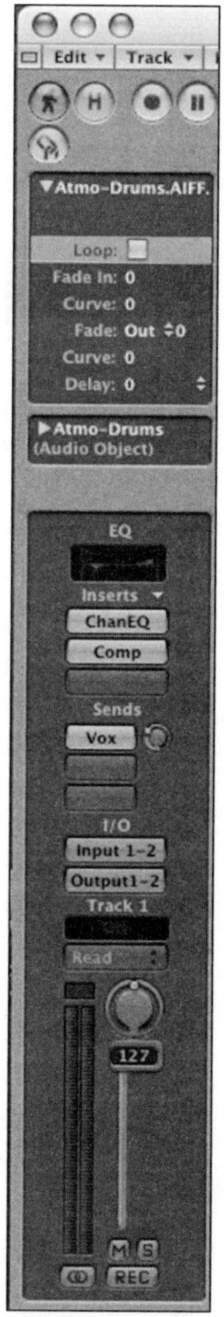

Figure 7.25

The Arrange channel strip of an Audio track. Note that you need to close the Audio Object parameter box to fit the entire strip on the page.

Track Icons

Every track may have an icon associated with it if you have Instrument Icons and Instrument Icons (Large) turned on in the View menu. This track icon represents the channel strip and/or Environment Object to which the track is linked. Logic features excellent, high-resolution icons, as you can see in Figure 7.26. These icons are scalable from 128 × 128 pixels downward.

Track icons are not only aesthetically pleasing, but functional as well. If you click on the track icon in the Track button bar, it selects the object or channel strip that your icon represents in the appropriate window. If the appropriate window is not already open, Logic Pro 7 will open it for you. In other words, if you click on the track icon of an Instrument icon, it will open an Environment window with that MIDI Instrument selected. If you click on an Audio Track icon, it will open the Track Mixer with that channel strip selected. If you prefer to use the Environment Audio Mixer and have an Environment window open, clicking on the track icon on an Audio Track will select the channel strip in the Environment mixer instead of the Track Mixer. You can also choose to open the Environment mixer instead of the Track Mixer by holding down the **CONTROL** key while double-clicking an Audio Track (more on the

Figure 7.26

Here you can see both the mini-icon in the Audio Object parameter box and the large icon in a fully zoomed-out track lane.

two mixers can be found in Chapter 12). This can be a convenient way to access the Environment mixer or Instrument Objects to adjust Environment cabling and so on.

You are not limited to the icons that ship with Logic Pro 7. You can also create your own unique icons for use within Logic. The icons you create must be 128 × 128 pixels in size, have an alpha channel for transparency, and be saved in the Portable Network Graphic format with the file extension .png. Filenames for Logic icons must include a three-digit number so Logic knows where in its icon list to place the new icon. Be aware that if you choose a number under 325, your icon might replace a Logic icon that is named with the same three-digit number; however, many numbers aren't used, and you may want to replace an older Logic icon, so you have that option.

For Logic Pro 7 to use your homespun icons, you need to place them in an Icons folder at the following directory: ~/Library/Application Support/Logic/Images/Icons. If folders named Images or Icons do not yet exist inside your Applications Support/Logic folder, you will need to create them yourself. After placing your properly formatted icons in this folder, they will appear in the pull-down menu of icons alongside all of Logic's other icons.

A QUICK WORD ABOUT LOGIC PRO 7 AND OS X FILE PATHS

Upgraders from different versions of Logic might initially be confused by the standard Mac OS X directory organization method. Often I hear new users complain that older versions of Logic were more convenient because they consolidated all of Logic's support files in one Logic folder. "It was easier to find and copy all of my Logic related files the old way" upgraders often feel.

The thing is, *so does Logic Pro 7*. The main difference is that now the Logic folder isn't in the local *Applications* directory, but it's in the user's *Application Support* directory—a directory specifically set aside by Mac OS X for files and folders that an application may need to access, without cluttering the main Applications folder. As Figure 7.27 shows, all the files you need are still in one place, easy to get at.

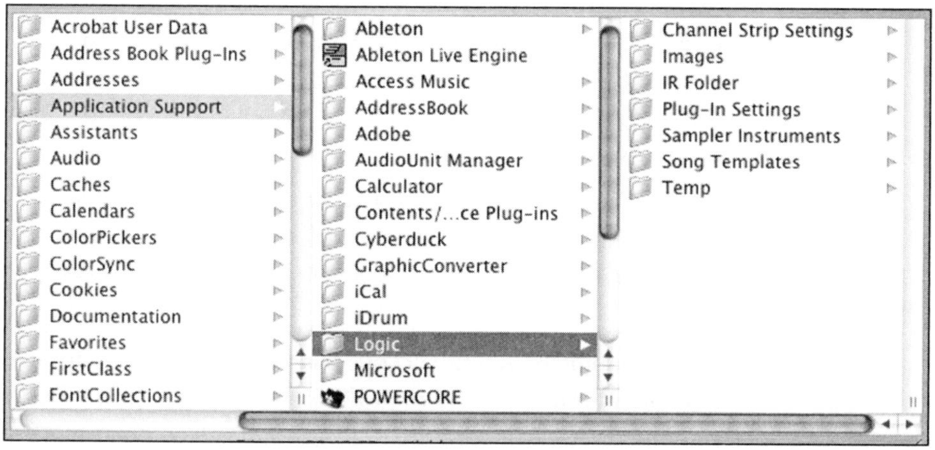

Figure 7.27
This is the ~/Library/Application Support/Logic directory. As you see, this has all the goodies you would expect in the old Logic folder, just in a new, more organized location.

I will go more in depth into file paths in Chapter 13, but since I've started talking about file paths already with adding icons, now is a good time to get comfortable with the new, OS X–compliant directory organization of Logic Pro 7.

Track Buttons

Each track contains a number of buttons that allow for easy access to a few track-related functions. You determine which of these buttons you would like to be visible in the View menu of Arrange. Figure 7.28 shows a track lane with all of its track buttons activated.

Figure 7.28
A track lane with all buttons visible. You can turn these buttons on or off in the View menu of Arrange.

All of these functions will be explained in detail later in the book. For now, here is a quick description of the functions that each button represents:

* **M.** Track Mute. This button mutes (silences) the track. When you click this button, the track is muted, the regions colors will become grayer, and the button glows turquoise. Clicking again unmutes the track.
* **S.** Track Solo. This button will solo all the regions on the selected track, and enable Solo mode in the Transport. When you engage the Solo button, only other tracks with their Solo button engaged, or regions that have been soloed, will play back. With Solo engaged, the Bar Ruler will become yellow, and a yellow outline surrounds all the regions in the soloed track.
* **R.** Record-Enable. This button allows the track to receive audio as soon as you begin recording. When you click the button, the track is record-enabled and the button glows red. Clicking again disables record-enable.
* **Lock.** Track Protect Switch. When clicked, this button locks the regions on the track in time, and disallows recording on that track (the R button vanishes). The icon glows turquoise and changes to an image of a closed lock. When you click the button again, the track is no longer protected and the icon returns to the image of an open lock.
* **Track Freeze.** The button with a snowflake icon is the Track Freeze switch (Audio Tracks and Audio Instrument tracks only). Clicking this button freezes Audio Tracks or Audio Instrument tracks (see the section "Freeze Tracks" later in this chapter). The button glows turquoise when the Track Freeze switch is active for that track. If you click the button again, the track unfreezes.
* **Node.** Nodes are a powerful and elegant new feature of Logic Pro 7 that allow you to distribute the processing of Logic's built-in plug-ins and synthesizers to other Node computers. If you engage this button, the built-in plug-ins and synthesizers on an Audio or Audio Instrument track will be processed on your Logic Node computers. The Node feature is explained in detail in Chapter 12, "Mixing in Logic."
* **H.** Hide Track. This icon is not turned on or off in the View menu, but appears when you click the Hide Track button at the top of Arrange. When you click this button, the button glows turquoise, and the next time that you press the Hide Track button, the track will disappear from the track list. Hide Tracks is explained in depth in the next section.

> **METHOD TIP: QUICKLY TOGGLING MULTIPLE BUTTONS**
>
> If you want to toggle on or off multiple buttons of the same type, navigating to each track one by one to click its relevant track button will become quite time-consuming. Luckily, you can click-hold the mouse over a button, and then mouse up or down over the other similar track buttons to activate or deactivate multiple buttons at the same time. For example, let's say that you wanted to mute 10 tracks. Rather than selecting each track individually and clicking each individual Mute button, you could click-hold the first Mute button, then slide your mouse over the other nine Mute buttons to mute the rest of the tracks.
>
> You can only use this feature on the same type of button—in other words, you can't click-hold on the Mute button of one track, and then slide over the Solo button of another. Nonetheless, you'll find this feature to be a massive time-saver!

Hide Tracks

Let's say that you have tracks in the track list that have song-related MIDI data, such as SysEx data, that you do not need to see on Arrange. Or perhaps you created a number of tracks for Audio Objects that you wanted to appear in the Track Mixer, but which you do not need to display in the track list. For those situations where you have tracks in the track list that you do not need or want to have visible, Logic offers the Hide Tracks feature.

There is a new global Hide View button at the top of Arrange. It appears to the right of the Link button and looks like a large *H*, as you can see in Figure 7.29.

Figure 7.29
The global Hide View button. It is currently blue, indicating you can click on the Hide button on individual tracks to hide them.

When you click on the Hide View button, it glows turquoise and Hide buttons on the individual tracks become available. You can now activate the individual Hide buttons on the desired tracks, which will also glow turquoise when activated. When you deactivate the global Hide View button, all those Arrange tracks with Hide activated will no longer be visible, and the Hide View button will glow orange to let you know that the track list includes hidden tracks. When you want to see the hidden tracks again, simply reactivate the Hide View button.

Several key commands relate to the Hide Track feature. Even when the global Hide View button is deactivated, you can still hide an individual track by assigning a key command for Hide Current Arrange Track and Select Next Track or selecting **View > Hide Current Track and Select Next Track**. You can toggle the state of the Hide View button with the key command Toggle Hide View. Finally, there is a key command to Unhide All Tracks that resets the Hide buttons of each track, making them all visible. Note that these key commands do not appear in any menu; you'll need to assign them to keys yourself in the Key Commands window.

Keep in mind that hiding a track does not affect its playback in any way. Also, you can link the Hide functions of all the tracks belonging to a group if you select Hide in the Group Property settings. I will discuss groups in Chapter 12, "Mixing in Logic."

Freeze Tracks

Freeze Tracks is one of the most powerful features in Logic. Now most applications have some form of "freeze," but Logic was the first major sequencer to add Freeze Tracks. Freeze Tracks can extend the power of your computer if you find your CPU beginning to strain under the processing load of your song. If you use audio or Audio Instruments, you will want to use Logic's Freeze Tracks function.

What Is Freeze Tracks?

When you start using audio effects, Audio Instruments, and plug-ins, you'll quickly realize that realtime effects and synth processing take up a large amount of CPU power. Each effect and synth takes up different amounts of CPU power, of course, but the more you use, the higher the load on your CPU. What happens when you reach the limit of your Mac's CPU capability? You get a "System Overload" error message, your song stops playing, and you need to turn off some of the synths or effects you have turned on.

This is where Freeze Tracks comes in. With the simple click of the Freeze Tracks button, Logic will make a temporary audio file of your Audio or Audio Instrument track, including all effects and effects automation, and then link that track to the temporary audio file, bypassing all the effects (and the Audio Instrument, if the track is an Audio Instrument track). This means that instead of your CPU having the heavy load of realtime synths and effects, the CPU only has the lighter duty of playing back the referenced audio file. All of the processing power required by the synth and the effects utilized by that track are now released.

You may want to use Freeze Tracks if you want to use effects and/or softsynths after you've run out of CPU power. Or, if you are trying to play back a Logic song created on a computer with greater power (or that used a number of Logic Node computers for extra processing muscle), you can use

Freeze Tracks until the CPU load is reduced to the point that the song will play back. Keep in mind that if your song's realtime processing demands are not causing any processing problems, you do not need to freeze any tracks.

The Freeze Tracks Procedure

Freezing Tracks is an incredibly easy procedure. First, make sure that the Freeze Tracks button, which looks like a snowflake, is visible on your track. If it isn't, you can turn it on by selecting **View > Track Freeze Switch**.

Once the button is visible, simply click on it. The button glows white, as shown in Figure 7.30. Repeat this procedure for all the tracks in your song that you want to freeze. If you want to freeze many tracks at once, you can use the Method Tip above for toggling multiple buttons. The next time you issue the Refresh Freeze Files command (via key command or found in the global menu at **Audio > Refresh Freeze Files**) or the Play command (via the Transport, a key command, or a software controller), instead of beginning playback of your song, Logic freezes all of the tracks that you have selected. That's it!

Figure 7.30

An Audio track with Freeze Track turned on. This button tells you that the plug-ins on this track will not be played back in realtime, but instead the track is playing an audio file that is an exact duplicate of the track.

When you freeze a track, you can no longer edit the track or add additional effects and plug-ins, or adjust the automation of your effect or Audio Instrument parameters, since the track is no longer playing back the regions in the track lane in realtime, but linking to the recorded file. If you attempt to edit any of these parameters, Logic displays the error message, "Current track or object is frozen. Do you wish to unfreeze it?" As this message informs you, if you want to make further changes or edits to the regions, effects, or effects automation, just click the Unfreeze button in the message, or click the Freeze Track button again to unfreeze the track. When you are finished editing your track, simply reactivate the Freeze Track button, and then the next time you activate Play, the track will refreeze with your changes.

Not every function of the track is frozen, however; you can still adjust the effect send level and destination, the pan and surround parameters, the volume, and toggle the channel strip's mute and solo (as well as automation for these features).

The Freeze process always attempts to freeze for the full length of the song; however, if your track contains only audio (or MIDI data for an Audio Instrument) for a portion of the song, you may want to stop the Freeze procedure manually. Even though the Freeze Tracks procedure happens faster than realtime, Logic does allow you to stop it. When tracks are freezing, Logic displays a dialog box with a progress bar showing you how much is left to freeze, and you will see the SPL speed through the song, showing you visually how much of your song has been frozen. You can interrupt the Freeze Tracks procedure by pressing **COMMAND + . (period key)** when Logic passes the point at which you want to freeze. The partially frozen track will now play back the Freeze file (see following note) to the end of the file, and then the track will fall silent.

Keep in mind that since Freeze Tracks operates by printing files faster than realtime, in order for Freeze to work, the audio engine and processors you are using must be capable of working faster than realtime. All native plug-ins, and most DSP accelerator cards (such as the Universal Audio UAD-1 and the PowerCore) have no problem with this. But if you are using a Digidesign TDM system, the DAE audio engine, which can only run in realtime, cannot freeze tracks. Also, if you are using the I/O plug-in to access external hardware in realtime, you cannot use Freeze Tracks.

The Transport Within the Arrange Window

I have already discussed the Transport in the previous chapter. However, I wanted to bring it up again because you can choose to activate the transport in the Arrange window instead of its own floating window. You can view the transport in the top-left of Arrange by selecting **View > Transport**. Figure 7.31 shows an Arrange window with the Transport active.

There are a number of advantages to activating the Transport view in Arrange instead of having the Transport window visible. If you do most of your recording in the Arrange window, this setup is very convenient. If you are short on screen real estate, this might fit better in your workspace. And you may simply prefer to lock down the location of the Transport rather than leaving it floating.

When the Transport is active in Arrange, you'll have less room for parameters, and you might not be able to fit the entire Arrange channel strip on screen without closing some parameter boxes, as you can see in Figure 7.31. If you prefer not to record from the Arrange window at all, instead spending

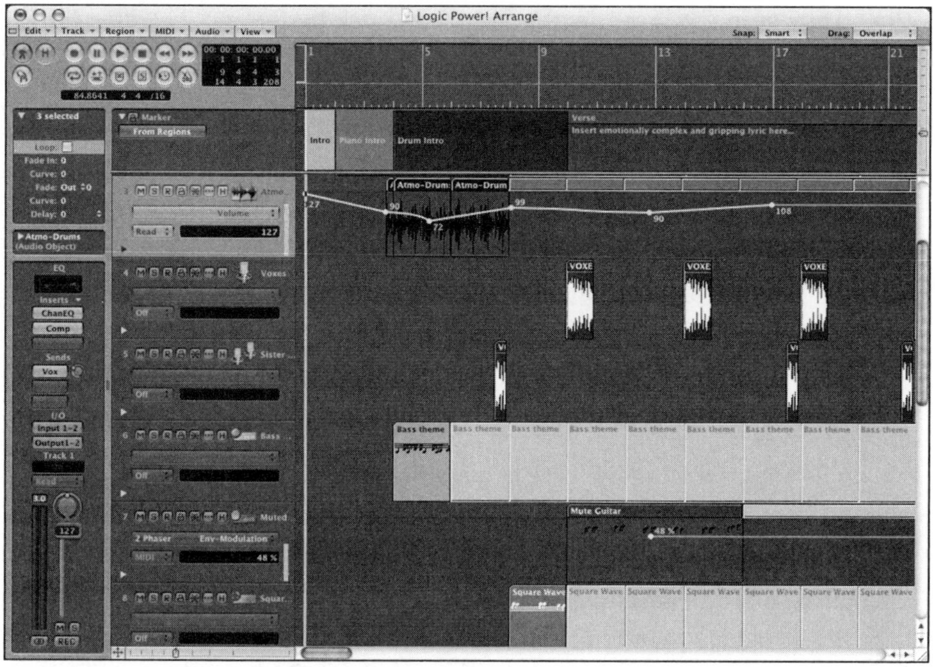

Figure 7.31
This Arrange window has the Transport view on. As you can see, the controls from the Transport window are now integrated into Arrange.

most of your time in the Track Mixer, having a Transport in your Arrange may not appeal to you. Personally, I do like having the Transport active in Arrange because it has all the controls I normally use and saves me from needing a floating Transport window. That doesn't mean it's better or worse. It is, however, another option, and one that you should be aware of.

Cycle Mode

I touched on Cycle mode in Chapter 6, but now I'll go into it in detail. As you recall, Cycle mode allows you to loop a predefined section of your song continually. You might want to do this to listen critically to a specific section of your song, to practice performing a specific part of your song, to edit events only in a given section, and so on.

You can turn on Cycle mode a number of ways:

- Click the Cycle button on the Transport
- Press the Cycle key command
- Click the top of the Bar Ruler
- Define the Cycle region

When Logic is in Cycle mode, the SPL plays back the song only within the Cycle region. When the SPL reaches the end of the cycle, it immediately returns to the beginning of the cycle, interrupting playback of whatever sound is at the end of the cycle.

Combining Cycle Mode and Recording

One of the most powerful combinations of features in Logic is to use Cycle mode with recording. This can greatly facilitate creativity and frees you to improvise parts over a section of your song without worrying about creation and organization of tracks and so on. The Recording tab of the Song Settings dialog box offers a number of preferences as to how Cycle recording will operate within a given song. You can access these parameters by selecting **File > Song Settings > Recording**, click-holding the Record button in the Transport, selecting Recording Options, or pressing the key command **OPTION + R**.

You already saw the Recording tab of the Song Settings window in Figure 6.25 of Chapter 6. Please refer back to Chapter 6, "The Transport Window," if you would like more information on the Recording tab as a whole—here are short explanations of each parameter that relates to Cycle mode recording:

- **Merge New Recording with Selected Regions.** This parameter merges the data from each recording pass into a single region on the track to which you are recording. If you do not check this box, Logic will create a new region for each recording pass.
- **Merge Only New Regions in Cycle Record.** This setting allows you to record the first pass as a unique region. Then Logic merges all subsequent recording passes into another region. If you do not check this box, Logic will create a new region for each recording pass.
- **Auto Mute in Cycle Record.** If you check this box, each pass will be muted as soon as it is finished recording, so you will not have to listen to it when recording subsequent passes. This setting is independent from whether Logic is creating new tracks or merging tracks for each pass; regardless of whether your data is being recorded to one region or separate regions, you will hear only the current recording pass.
- **Auto Create Tracks in Cycle Record.** This option not only creates a new region for each recording pass, but creates a new track as well. The newly created tracks appear sequentially beneath the original track to which you began recording. Obviously, this function deactivates the merge options.

Defining the Cycle Region

There are a number of different ways to set the Cycle region in Logic. The most straightforward method is to click in the top third of the Bar Ruler, then drag your mouse to the point at which you want the cycle to end. As you drag the mouse, a white bar travels behind your mouse to the point at which you stop. This white bar represents the Cycle region. Figure 7.32 shows a defined Cycle region.

You can grab one of the lower corners of the ends of the Cycle region to redefine it—even during playback! You can also click in the middle of the Cycle region to move it over. If you want to reset one of the Cycle region boundaries to a specific point near that boundary, you can click on that point while holding down the **SHIFT** key. You can also drag a Marker from the Marker track (or Bar Ruler) into the upper portion of the Bar Ruler to set the Cycle region.

In addition to setting the Cycle region graphically, you can set it by directly inputting the measure numbers into the position display of the Transport. You might also define several key commands to set the Cycle region. If you do a key command search for *Locators*, you will find a host of key commands that can set the Cycle regions by objects, Markers, and so on. None of these key commands are defined by default—it's up to you to decide which ones you want to use and then to define them.

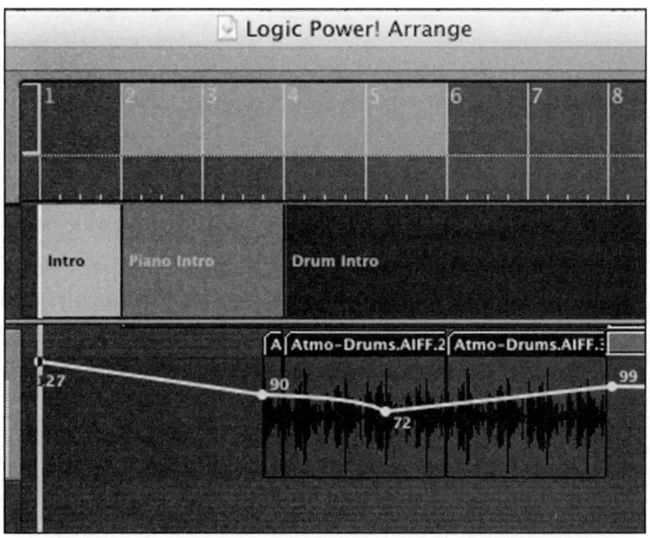

Figure 7.32

The green bar between measure 2 and measure 6 represents the defined Cycle region.

Using Skip Cycle

Skip Cycle is a variation of Cycle mode. Skip Cycle mode allows you to define a region that will be skipped over rather than used during playback. You can create a Skip Cycle region by dragging from the right to the left boundary of the region you want to skip, by dragging the left Locator of a Cycle region to the right of the right Locator, or by defining the Swap Left and Right Locators key command. A Skip Cycle region is defined by a thin white bar at the top of the Bar Ruler, as shown in Figure 7.33.

When a Skip Cycle region is defined, the song simply ignores that section of the song during playback or editing. The SPL jumps from the beginning of the Skip Cycle region instantly to the end, and continues as if the section did not exist. When Skip Cycle mode is turned off, the region plays back as normal.

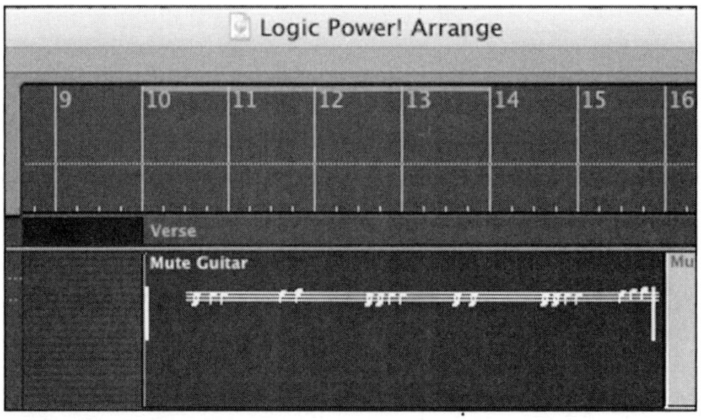

Figure 7.33
Here a Skip Cycle region is defined between measures 10 and 14.

Looping Regions in Arrange

I've already touched on the Loop parameter in the Region parameter box, and you've seen some of the commands related to looping in Arrange local menus. If you loop a region, Logic repeats that region again as soon as it ends. You will be able to see this visually on the track lane as well; gray boxes with the identical length of your original region will emanate from the end of your original region. This is illustrated in Figure 7.34.

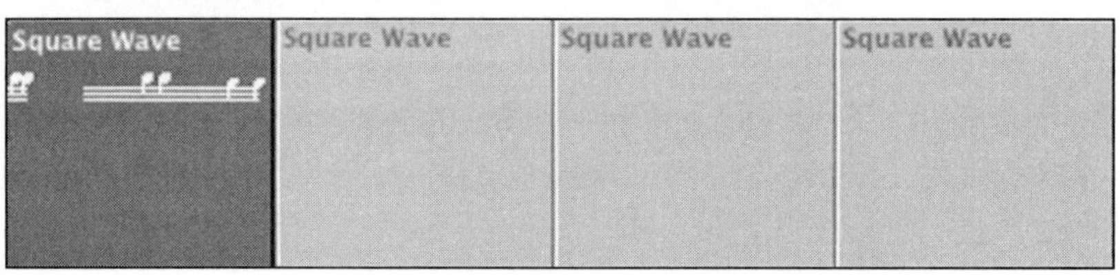

Figure 7.34
The gray boxes attached to the MIDI region offer visual feedback on the track lane that the region is looped.

Looping Regions in Logic Pro 7

The traditional method, or "old style," of looping in Logic consists of clicking the check box of the Loop parameter in the Region parameter box. You can also use the key command Toggle Loop to turn the Loop parameter on and off for a selected region. Once looping is engaged, gray boxes representing *loops*—repeats of your region—will extend from the selected region until it reaches either the end of the song or another region in the same track lane. If you don't want the loop to extend to the end of the song, the old style method of controlling how many measures a region will loop is to use the Pencil tool to create an empty region at some point in the track after a region that you want to loop; when you turn on looping for the original region, it loops until it reaches that empty region, and then the looping ends. As you move that empty region around, you can extend or reduce the number of loops for that original region. You will also notice that as you extend or reduce the length of your song, those loops that extend to the end of your song will be extended or reduced along with the song length. You could also cut loops using the Marquee tool (which is covered later in this chapter).

Logic Pro 7 introduces a new, simply intuitive looping method, which for distinction's sake, I will call "new style" looping. Users of GarageBand or other ACID-loop style applications will be familiar with this method of looping. For users of previous versions of Logic, you are in for a treat, because it couldn't be easier. Here's how it works:

First, move the cursor to the upper-right edge of a region. The pointer becomes the Loop tool, as shown in Figure 7.35.

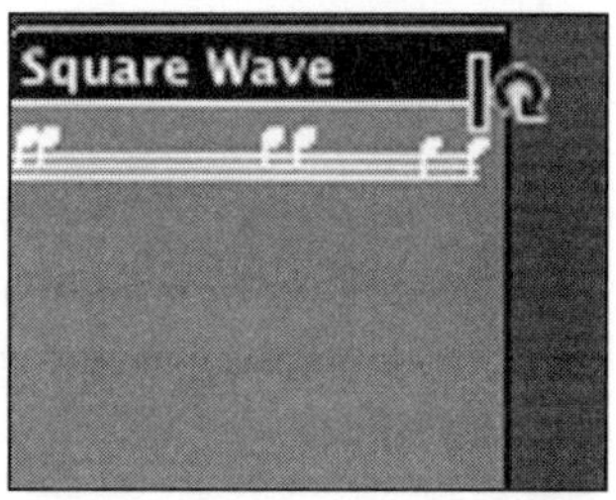

Figure 7.35

When you move the Pointer tool to the upper-right edge of a region, it becomes the Loop tool.

Then click-drag the loop out as many measures as you wish, as you can see below in Figure 7.36. The cursor info tag will indicate which region you are looping, where you are in your song, and how many times the region has been repeated.

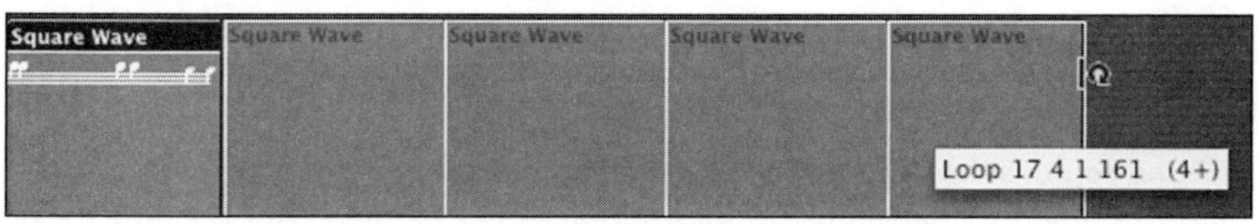

Figure 7.36

To loop your region, simply click-drag the region as far to the right as you would like your region to loop.

That's it! Looping in Logic couldn't be simpler! If you want a loop to continue for an entire song, or for so many measures that manually dragging the loop would be tedious, that's where the old style of looping comes in.

Logic Pro 7 introduces another way to edit loops; if you simply move the pointer to the upper-third of a loop, it will turn to the Loop tool, as shown in Figure 7.37.

Figure 7.37
Moving the cursor to the upper-third of any loop will turn the pointer into the Loop tool, and you can then split and drag the loop.

You can then click on the loop to stop looping at that point. You can also drag the new endpoint exactly as you would a new style loop. You can cut loops with the Loop tool regardless of whether they were looped using old or new style looping.

If you wish to operate on a loop that resides on a track in which the Automation Lane is showing, you will have to **OPTION + CLICK** and **OPTION + DRAG** the loop. The reason is that when the Automation Lane is in view, there is a very small area that must be shared by both looping and resizing functions. You will read more about resizing and Track Automation later in this chapter.

OLD VERSUS NEW STYLE LOOPING

One more time, just to be clear: There is no actual distinction made by the application between the previously existing loop methods and those introduced in Logic Pro 7. I simply call the previous methods "old style" and the recently introduced methods "new style" for the sake of upgraders who are familiar with traditional looping in Logic, but unfamiliar with the updates to looping in Logic Pro 7.

Clicking on a loop selects the looped region and all its loops. Click-holding on a loop turns the cursor to a "rubber band," like normal, and it will not select any looped sequences or the original region, only subsequent non-looped regions that you select. The exception to this is if you have selected the Marquee tool, which is described later in this chapter. The Marquee tool is capable of making "rubber band" selections of portions of a loop.

The Turn Loops to Real Copies command changes all the loops from a selected region into new, independent regions that are identical to the original region. The Turn Loops to Aliases command will change all the loops from a selected region into new, independent regions that contain no data but point to the original region.

> **EXPERT TIP: FOLDERS AND LOOPING**
>
> Sasso, author of *Emagic Logic Tips and Tricks*, offered some tips on using Folder tracks earlier in the chapter. He also has some tips specifically regarding using Folder tracks for looping. "When you want to create a composite loop incorporating several regions," he explains, "pack the regions into a folder and loop the folder." In fact, if you use Propellerhead's ReCycle (REX) files, you will see that they use this same concept—REX files in Logic are folders packed with individual audio slices.

The Arrange Toolbox

The Arrange window Toolbox contains a collection of tools for use in Arrange. These tools each have a different function when graphically manipulating and editing regions. You can use the **View > Toolbox** menu option to have the Toolbox appear as part of the Parameter bar, you can press the **ESC** key to create a floating Toolbox at the current cursor position, or you can right-click with your mouse if you have set right-click to open the Toolbox in the editing tab of **Logic Pro > Preferences > General**. Figure 7.38 shows the Toolbox.

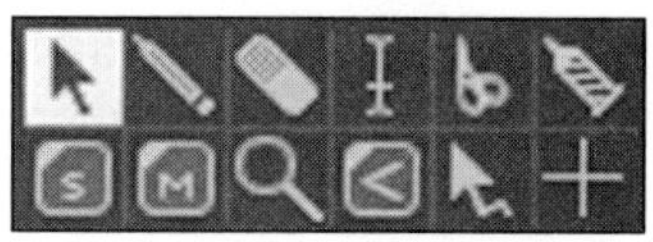

Figure 7.38
The Toolbox in the Arrange window. Each window and editor contains its own set of tools.

Brief descriptions of each tool follow—first the top row, then the bottom row, from left to right:

- **Pointer.** This tool looks like an arrow pointing upward and left. The pointer should be familiar from most other computer applications and is the default tool in Logic. You can use it to select regions by clicking on one or more regions, or click-dragging over a group of regions to create a "rubber band" or "lasso" that will select them all.
- **Pencil.** The icon for this tool resembles—surprise, surprise—a pencil. It is used to add or alter the length of regions.
- **Eraser.** This tool looks like an eraser. It is used to remove ("erase") any regions you have selected from Arrange.

- **Text Tool.** This tool looks like a text-entry bar. It is used to name regions.
- **Scissors.** The Scissors tool conveniently looks like a pair of scissors. It is used to split regions. You hold the **OPTION** key down while splitting regions to divide the entire region into multiple equally spaced regions the same length as your initial split.
- **Glue.** This tool looks like a tube of glue. It is used to join selected regions into one single region, which is given the name and track position of the initial object. When the Glue tool is used to glue Audio regions that were not originally next to each other, Logic will need to create a new audio file.
- **Solo.** The Solo tool is represented by the letter *S* in a box. This tool solos any selected regions.
- **Mute.** The Mute tool is represented by the letter *M* in a box. This tool mutes any selected regions.
- **Magnifying Glass.** This tool resembles a magnifying glass. When you use this tool to select an area containing regions, Logic zooms in on that area.
- **Crossfade.** This tool looks like a less-than symbol (<) in a box. This tool, when dragged over two adjacent Audio regions, creates a cross-fade between them. See the next chapter for an explanation of cross-fades.
- **Automation.** The Automation tool resembles a bent arrow pointing upward and left. You can set the Automation tool to Curve mode, where it can create curves between two automation notes, or Select mode, where it can select automation data in the automation lane. Chapter 11, "Using Automation in Logic," discusses automation in depth.
- **Marquee.** This tool looks like a crosshair. The Marquee tool is a unique and powerful tool, as you'll see in the next subsection. Briefly, the Marquee tool is not limited to selecting entire regions, but can make selections within regions for subsequent editing. (The name *Marquee* was adopted from graphics applications, in which some selection boxes featured moving, broken selection lines often resembling an old theater marquee with rotating lights.)

> **EXPERT TIP: USE KEY COMMANDS TO BRING UP TOOLS**
> Logic offers key commands to accomplish the function of many of these tools and offers key commands that enable you to select tools without having to use the Toolbox. If you want to get as fast with Logic as you can, be sure to assign and use those key commands!

Creating Regions

At first, your tracks will not have regions on their track lanes. There are basically three ways for you to create regions on Arrange:

- You can record audio or MIDI onto your various tracks (see Chapter 6 for more information on recording). Logic will create Audio regions and MIDI regions consisting of what you record.
- You can use the Pencil tool to create regions. If you click the Pencil tool in a MIDI track lane, an empty region 1-bar long will be created. If you click the Pencil tool in an Audio Track, you will be presented with the Add File dialog for you to choose an audio file to add to Arrange at the current cursor location. The created Audio region will be the length of the audio file you select.
- Finally, you can create regions on Arrange by adding audio or MIDI files to your Arrange either by choosing the Add menu command or by dragging them onto the Arrange window. You can drag MIDI files from the Finder directly into Logic, and you can drag audio files from the Finder, the Audio window (discussed in Chapter 8, "Working with Audio and Apple Loops"), or the Project Manager (discussed in Chapter 13, "Working with Files").

Editing in the Arrange Window

Like most of us, it was probably the ability to cut, resize, and rearrange musical segments graphically that initially attracted you to using computers to produce music. After you create your track list and you've got some regions on Arrange, you most likely will want to edit and rearrange them. As you would imagine, the Arrange window is ideal for rearranging regions. Every region displayed in the track lanes of Arrange is ready and waiting for you to manipulate using Logic Pro's powerful tools and features.

Making Selections

The first step in editing your song is to select one or more regions, or portions of regions, that you want to edit further. Selected regions will have darker outlines and black title bars. Figure 7.39 shows a number of selected regions on Arrange.

Logic offers a number of methods for selecting regions.

Selecting Regions Using Commands

You can use many menu commands to select regions, such as the Select...Object commands. These commands were previously listed in the Local menu earlier in this chapter. And, if you do a search in the Key Commands window, you will also find many selection commands, some of which are unassigned.

The two most common key commands for selecting regions are the Select Next Region and Select Previous Region commands. These keys move you to the following or previous region, depending on the direction of the arrow. Only the region that the command moved you to will be selected. If you want to use the arrow keys to select more than one region, hold down the **SHIFT** key while navigating to the various regions with the arrow keys.

If you select a track using the Select Previous Track or Select Next Track key commands, you select every region on that track. If Cycle mode is enabled, only the regions within the cycle range are selected.

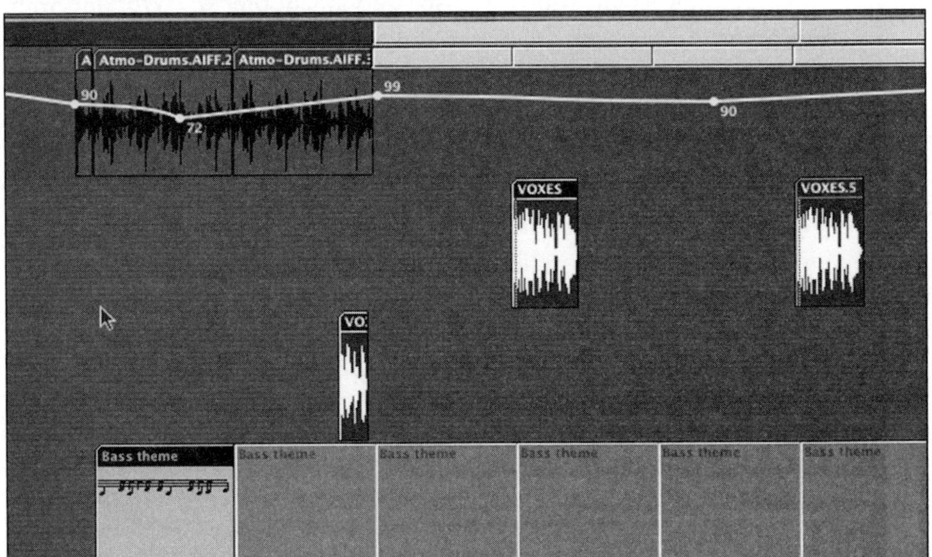

Figure 7.39

An Arrange with several regions selected. The dark color and title bar indicate which regions are selected.

Finally, you can choose the **Edit > Toggle Selection** command (or key command) to reverse the selection status of the regions you have selected, so everything you select will become unselected, and instead all the rest of the regions in your song will be selected.

Selecting Regions Using the Pointer Tool

Clicking on any region in the Arrange window with the Pointer tool will select that region. Perhaps the most popular method of selecting regions is by using the Pointer tool to "rubber band" a group of regions. To do this, simply click the Pointer tool on an empty spot on Arrange near the objects you want to select, then drag a selection square over all the regions you want to select.

You can also click on a track name to select every region in that track. If you hold down **SHIFT** and click on multiple track names, you can select all the regions in multiple tracks.

Making Selections with the Marquee Tool

The Marquee tool is unique in that instead of selecting a number of entire regions, it can select a *portion* of regions, as shown in Figure 7.40.

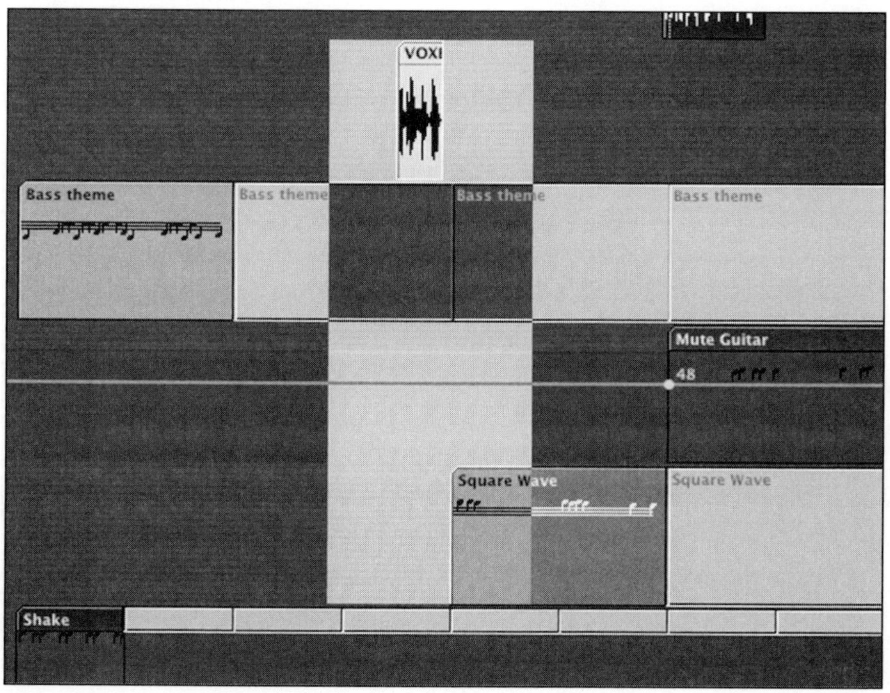

Figure 7.40

A Marquee selection spanning a number of objects and tracks. The area in which the colors of the tracks are inverted is the Marquee selection.

To use the Marquee tool, select the tool and then drag it over a portion of one or more regions. When you release the mouse button, the colors inside your selection area are inverted; this is the selected area. By holding down **SHIFT**, you can adjust the borders of the current Marquee selection from either the left or right side (not up or down). Almost every editing function that is available when you select entire regions is available when you select portions of regions with the Marquee tool, as you will learn later in this chapter.

The Arrange Grid

Most of what you'll be doing in the Arrange window will be editing and moving regions. For many users, using the SPL and the Bar Ruler offers enough of a guide. If you want more obvious guidelines, you're in luck! If you select **View > Grid** (or press **CONTROL + G**), you will activate the Arrange Grid. This tool puts guidelines at every bar of your song; the resolution of the Grid depends on your current zoom level, and the numerator of the time signature of your song. Figure 7.41 shows an Arrange with the Grid turned on.

The Grid is a purely visual tool; it does not affect region movement or editing at all. If the Grid makes working in Arrange easier for you, turn it on whenever you need it.

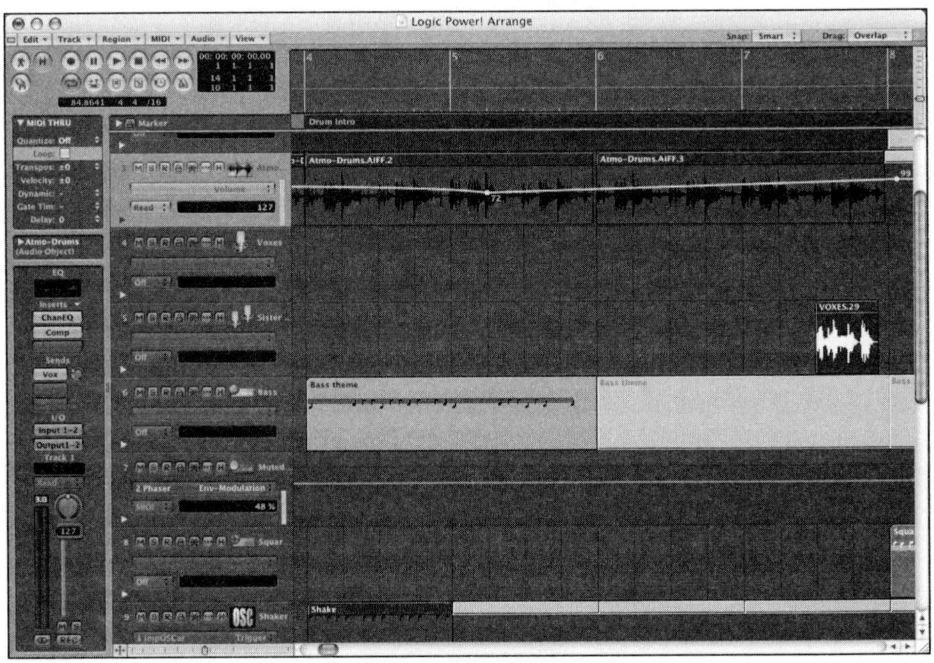

Figure 7.41
This Arrange window has the Arrange Grid activated. Due to the zoom level and the 4/4 time signature, you can see a grid line every quarter note.

Zooming in Arrange

As you begin moving and editing regions, you'll find that some times you'll want an overview of a portion of the song, and other times, you'll want to focus in on a very small area. To do this, you'll want to zoom in and out.

I already discussed in Chapter 4 using the zoom sliders in the top-right of the Arrange window to adjust the vertical size of the track lanes. It follows that using the horizontal zoom increases or decreases the number of bars that are visible on screen at a time. When your song is fully zoomed out, you can easily fit the entire length of the song on your monitor at once for arranging regions, and if you zoom in all the way, you'll be able to view each individual sample of your audio to enable very precise editing. Figure 7.42 shows a song zoomed out and zoomed in completely.

By now, it should be no surprise that Logic offers a full complement of key commands to facilitate zooming in addition to the telescopes. By default, pressing **CONTROL + ARROW** zooms in and out, horizontally or vertically, depending on the arrow key. But there are also key commands to zoom in and out for individual tracks, to change instantly to user-definable zoom settings, to zoom to fit selection, and more. Be sure to do a search for *zoom* in the Key Commands window; you'll find a lot of fantastic time-saving key commands just waiting to be assigned.

Finally, you can select Auto Track Zoom either via key command or by selecting **View > Auto Track Zoom**. This command automatically increases the vertical zoom of the selected track for as long as that track is selected. This command is useful if you want to keep your tracks vertically short in order to fit more tracks on the screen, but you want the specific track you are working on to be larger for more precise moves and edits.

Splitting and Resizing Regions

Two operations that go hand in hand with zooming are splitting and resizing regions. You can zoom out or in to get the optimal view of a section of song, and then edit that section to suit your taste. This is one of the most important uses for sequencers, and Logic's Arrange window offers users powerful and intuitive tools and commands for this purpose. This section describes some of the most popular commands, functions, and tips for splitting and resizing regions.

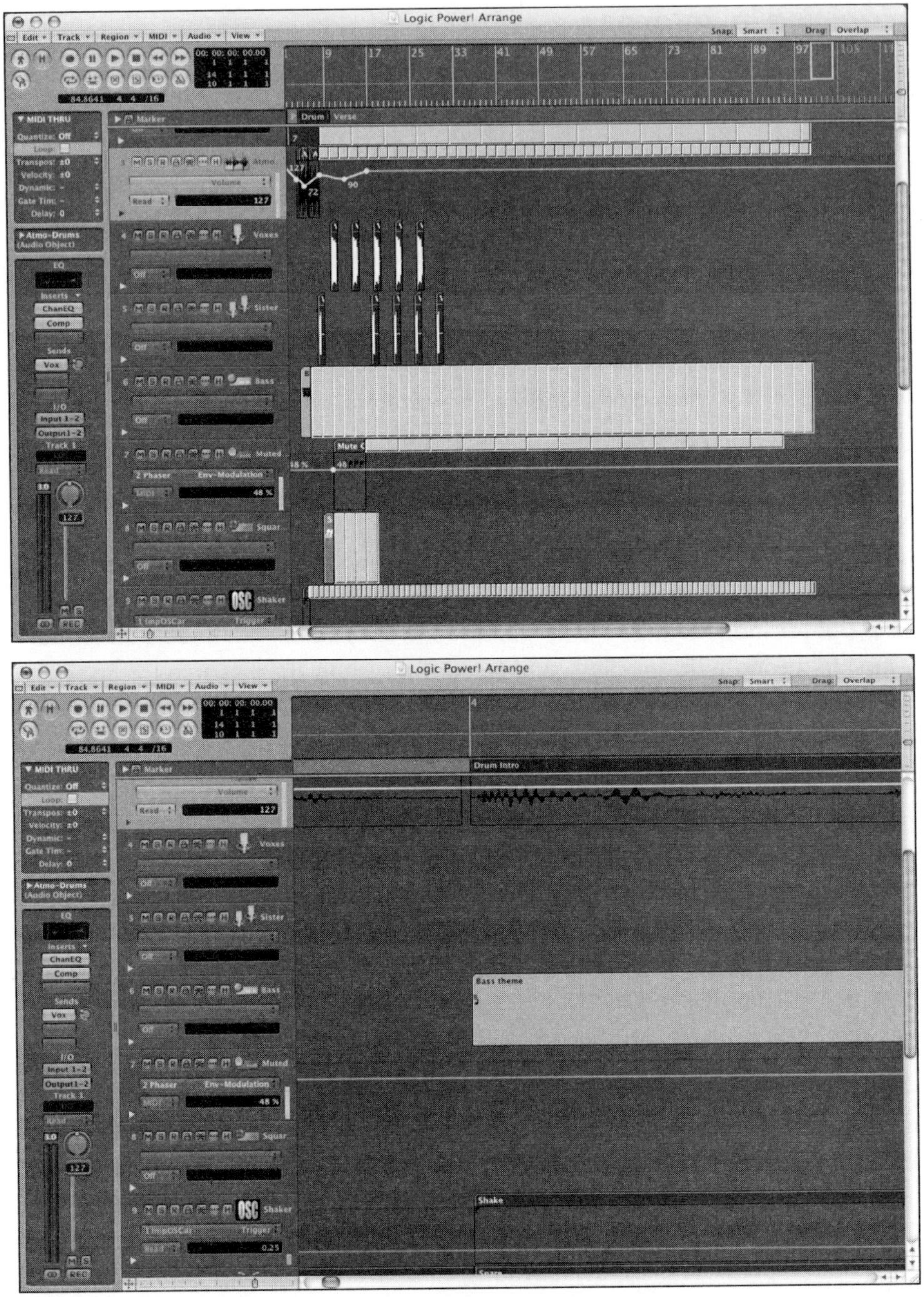

Figure 7.42

Using the zoom in Logic: (a) a song where the Arrange window was zoomed out far enough to show the entire song; (b) the same song, but with maximum zoom, so you can see each sample of audio.

Splitting Regions

Logic offers a number of different functions and methods to split one region into two or more regions. Perhaps the most graphically intuitive way to split a region into two parts is to select the Scissors tool from the Toolbox, then click on a portion of a region. Logic then splits that region into two regions at the point at which you clicked. Figure 7.43 shows a region that has been split into two regions using the Scissors tool.

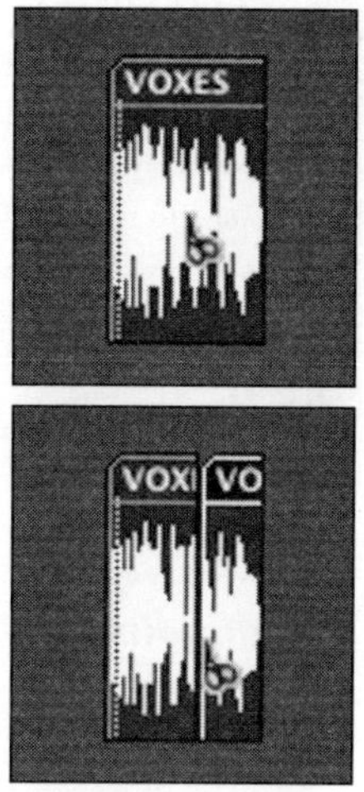

Figure 7.43
Splitting a region with the Scissors tool: (a) the Scissors tool over a region in Arrange; (b) the resulting two regions after clicking with the Scissors tool.

If you try to split a MIDI region that has a note that overlaps the split by more than 1/16 notes, Logic will display a dialog box asking if you want to Keep, Shorten, or Split those notes. Keep, the default option, leaves the note lengths unaltered, and you will simply have notes in the first region that play past the end of the region. If Clip Length in the Extended Region Parameters box is checked, however, the note will still be cut off. If you select Shorten, the overlapping notes are truncated at the end of the first region. Finally, selecting Split creates two notes to represent the original overlapping note: one note in the first region that is truncated at the end of the first region and a new note at the beginning of the second region that consists of the remainder of the original note. Click the option you prefer in the dialog box to choose your preferred option.

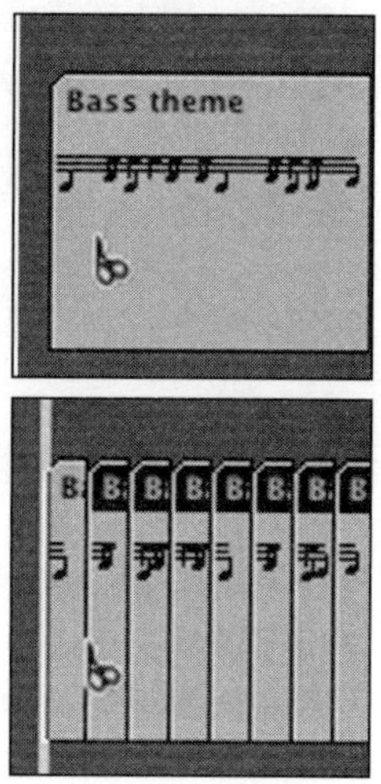

Figure 7.44
Using the Scissors tool to split a region into multiple regions: (a) the Scissors tool about a 1/4 note into a MIDI region; (b) the results of clicking with the Scissors tool and while pressing the **OPTION** key.

Logic also enables you to split a region into multiple regions with the Scissors tool. If you hold down the **OPTION** key while splitting your region, the Scissors tool will appear with a "+" sign above the teeth of the scissors, and it will split the region into multiple regions of equal size. Figure 7.44 illustrates this.

You can also use a number of commands to split regions. As explained previously, the **Region > Split/Merge** submenu offers the commands Split Region by Locators and Split Region by Song Position. These commands split a selected region by using the Locators in the Bar Ruler or by using the SPL, respectively. You can also use the key commands for these commands, as well as the key command for Split Region by Rounded Song Position, which splits the region at the bar line nearest to the SPL.

> **SPLITTING REGIONS THAT ARE LOOPED: SMARTLOOP**
>
> If you split a region that has been looped, the loop immediately following the split region is turned into a copy, and then that region is split. This is a special feature in Logic called Smart-Loop. Logic does not assume that just because you want to split a looped region you necessarily intend to split every single loop that comes after it. So, Logic automatically keeps the loop identical to how it was before you split the looped region, by creating a copy that can be the new original for the loops. This procedure of creating a copy, looping the copy, then splitting the original used to take a number of steps and a fair amount of time; now, Logic takes care of it for you automatically!

Resizing Regions

Splitting isn't the only way that you can alter a region in Arrange; you can also resize it. Logic offers a few simple ways to resize regions. The most straightforward way to resize a region is simply to move the pointer to the lower half of the edge of a region; the Pointer tool will become the Resize tool, and you can now drag to the right or left to expand or shorten the region. The info tag beneath the cursor will display your action and position. Figure 7.45 shows a region being resized in this manner.

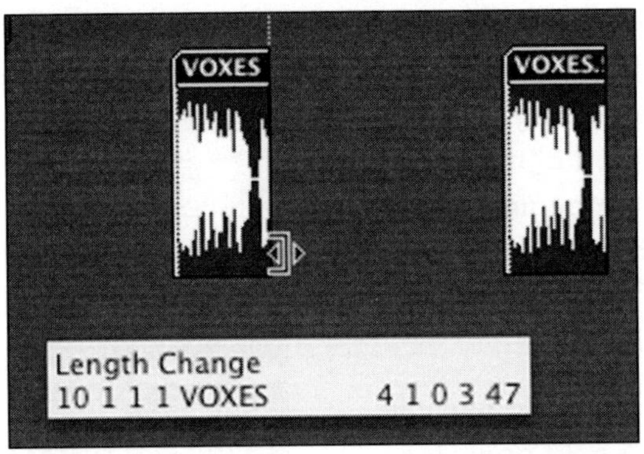

Figure 7.45
When you move the pointer to the lower half of the right or left edge of a region, the pointer turns into the Resize tool, and you can drag right or left to lengthen or shorten selected regions. The info tag displays what you are doing.

You can also resize multiple regions this way: Simply select a group of regions, click on the lower-right corner of one of the selected regions, and then Logic will lengthen or shorten all the regions by the amount you adjusted the region that you clicked. If you want to adjust multiple regions to the same absolute length (meaning the same Bar Ruler position) even if they were originally of varying length, hold down the **OPTION + SHIFT** keys while resizing.

There are some limitations as to your ability to resize regions, however. You cannot shorten a region out of existence—Logic will always retain at least a sliver of the region. Also, if you are expanding an Audio region, you cannot lengthen it past the end of the audio file itself, since there is no audio after that point. However, you can expand a MIDI region past existing MIDI data. You cannot shorten a region to cover up its original starting point. This means that you will usually find that you're limited to extending a region outward to the left. Remember, you cannot extend an Audio region beyond the original audio file.

If you shorten a boundary of a region that includes data, Logic will no longer consider that data part of that region. The data will not be deleted or modified in any way, however, and if you later lengthen the region, the original data will still be there, exactly as it was before you shortened the region.

Sometimes, however, when you adjust the length of a region, you may want to compress or expand the data inside to fit the new region boundary. If you have selected a MIDI region, you can do this by holding down the **OPTION** key while dragging the right region boundary. A dialog box appears asking whether you want to time/compress the region. Click OK and Logic will stretch or compress all the MIDI data to fit within the resized region.

You have to use a different procedure to resize an Audio region and to compress or stretch its contents to fit. You'll need to use the Adjust Region Length to Locators and Adjust Region Length to Nearest Bar commands from the Audio local menu. This command invokes the chosen Time Machine Algorithm to adjust the length of your Audio region.

Other local menu functions such as Set Optimal Region Sizes, Remove Overlaps, and Tie Regions, are also useful for resizing regions. Review that subsection to learn about these commands. There are also unassigned key commands that will allow you to nudge the length of regions shorter or longer by varying degrees. If you find any of them useful, remember to assign key commands to them.

Splitting and Resizing Regions Using the Marquee Tool

The Marquee tool is a special tool, perhaps one of the most powerful editing methods available in Logic Pro, and thus gets its own subsection here. As described in the "Making Selections with the Marquee Tool" subsection above, you can use the Marquee tool to select portions of regions, not just entire regions. Once you have made a selection with the Marquee tool, you can perform most Arrange edit options, such as the following:

- Erase (press **DELETE** or click with the Eraser tool).
- Move (drag the selection) or copy (hold down **OPTION** while dragging the selection) using the Pointer tool (see "Moving and Copying Regions" below).

- Cut and copy (press **COMMAND + X** for cut, and press **COMMAND + C** to copy).
- Paste at the SPL (press **COMMAND + V**).
- Copy and paste using the Pencil tool (this operation is quantized to the current format value).
- Cut at the selection border (click inside the selection with the Scissors tool).
- Mute (via either a key command or the Mute tool; this results in a cut at the selection borders with the regions inside the selection borders muted).
- Solo (via either a key command or the Solo tool; this results in a cut at the selection borders with the regions inside the selection being soloed).

Moving and Copying Regions

Now that you've split and resized some regions in Arrange, you probably want to, well, *arrange* them! Moving regions around is perhaps the central function of the Arrange window, and it couldn't be simpler. Just select a region or regions, hold down the mouse button, drag your selection anywhere you want, and then drop the region or regions in the new location. Done!

Of course, Logic gives you many more options for moving regions. If you want to restrict the movement to either the horizontal or vertical axis (depending upon if you initially move the region horizontally or vertically) there is a check box preference to Limit Dragging to One Direction in Arrange in the Editing tab of the Global preferences, accessible through **Logic Pro > Preferences > Global**. You can also toggle this feature on and off by pressing the **SHIFT** button while dragging (in other words, if you've checked the preference, pressing **SHIFT** will allow normal movement, and if the preference is unchecked, you can press **SHIFT** to limit region movement to one axis). There are also unassigned key commands that you can use to nudge a region forward or backward by varying amounts. If you find any of them useful, be sure to assign keys to them.

Sometimes you may want to duplicate the data in a given region or regions in another location. Logic allows you to copy regions very easily. To move a copy of your selected region(s) instead of the original region(s), hold the **OPTION** key while moving the region, leaving the original regions in their original positions. If you want the copied regions to be *Aliases* (see following Method Tip) that point to the original regions instead of actual copies, press

OPTION + SHIFT when moving the regions. You can also make multiple duplicates that will follow your selected region or regions by using the Repeat Regions command either via key command or by choosing **Regions > Repeat Regions**. This command presents you with a dialog box in which you may select the number of copies you want and specify whether you want them to be Aliases or copies.

METHOD TIP: ALIASES VERSUS COPIES

Copying a region creates a completely new region, with its own MIDI notes or audio data. It is a duplicate of the original region, but you can edit the original region without affecting the copy, and vice versa. An *Alias*, however, looks like a copy of the original region, but it doesn't contain any data of its own; instead, it is just a reference to the original region. This means that any editing you do to the original will be reflected in the Alias.

Aliases are perfect for when you want to ensure that each instance of your copied region exactly reflects the original region, since any edits and changes to the original affect all the Aliases as well. And if you want to edit an Alias without affecting the original, you can always turn your Alias into a real copy. Trust me, you will find Aliases a major help when arranging your music!

Moving and copying operations snap automatically to the Snap menu setting, which I discuss in the next section. If you want to drag regions at a finer resolution, you can hold down the **CONTROL** key while dragging. This enables you to drag your regions at the single-tick level.

METHOD TIP: COMPILING MULTIPLE TAKES OF THE SAME TRACK

Producer/engineer Don Gunn uses the editing features of Logic to construct a single performance from multiple recordings. As he explains:

> *"When recording, it's not uncommon to want to capture the same part multiple times, either to allow the performer to try different nuances in the performance, or if they are a little unsure of their abilities, compiling takes allows the 'perfect take' to be created after the fact from bits of the various attempts. To greatly simplify the compiling, or 'comping,' of these multiple takes, use the same Audio Object on multiple tracks in the Arrange window for each pass.* ***CONTROL + RETURN*** *will create a duplicate track using the same Audio Object under the original, allowing you to record a second take (and third, and fourth, etc.).*
>
> *Once you have recorded audio onto the various tracks, use the arrow keys to move among the takes. By using your key command for Mute Objects (or the Mute tool), you can mute and unmute the various takes as they play back. Setting a cycle for a couple of measures can allow you to scrutinize each take thoroughly."*

Figure 7.46 shows this in action.

(Continued)

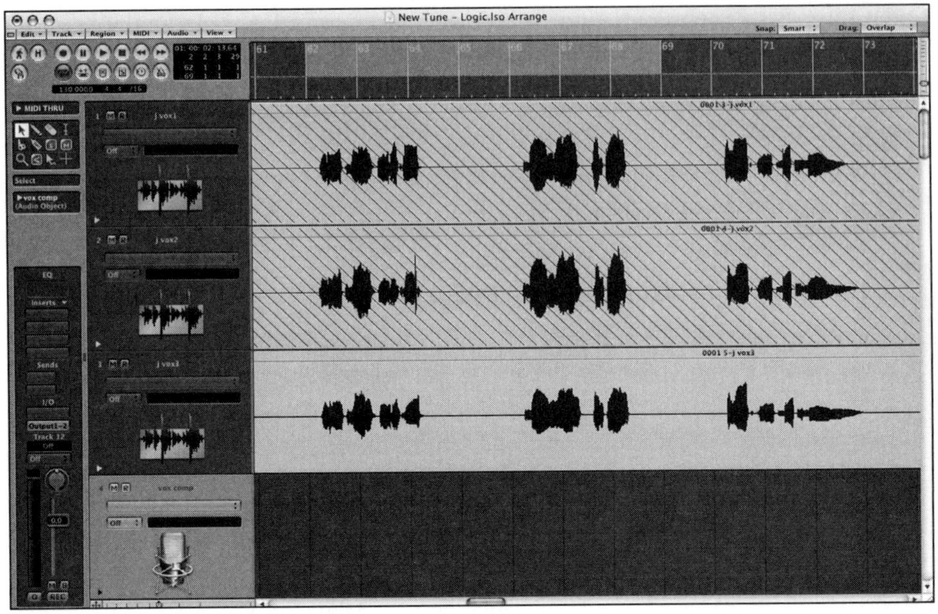

Figure 7.46
Gunn uses Cycle mode to focus on a portion of his takes, and mutes the takes that he isn't currently auditioning (screenshot courtesy of Gunn).

Gunn continues:

> *"As you go through the takes, when you find a part that you like, either create a new track that will be the destination for the edits, or make another duplicate of the original track. The benefit to using a new track is that you can change the name of the track to reflect that it is a new and different track from the original. As you select parts of the takes to use, either cut them with the Scissors tool or use the Marquee tool to define the new object. You may find it helpful to change the color of the selected regions (**OPTION + C**) as they are created, making it easier to know which ones to move to the new track."*

Figure 7.47 illustrates this.

Don finishes his comping tips with the following suggestions:

> *"Holding the **OPTION** key down when selecting and moving the new objects will make a copy of them to the destination track, rather than simply moving them from the original. This can be beneficial if you need to return to the original at some future point in time. Once the selected objects have been copied to the new track, you may want to apply a crossfade between any adjoining object to smooth the transition between them."*

(You'll learn about crossfades in Chapter 8.) Figure 7.48 shows the final results of Gunn's compiling. He's now left with a single perfect performance compiled from the various tracks.

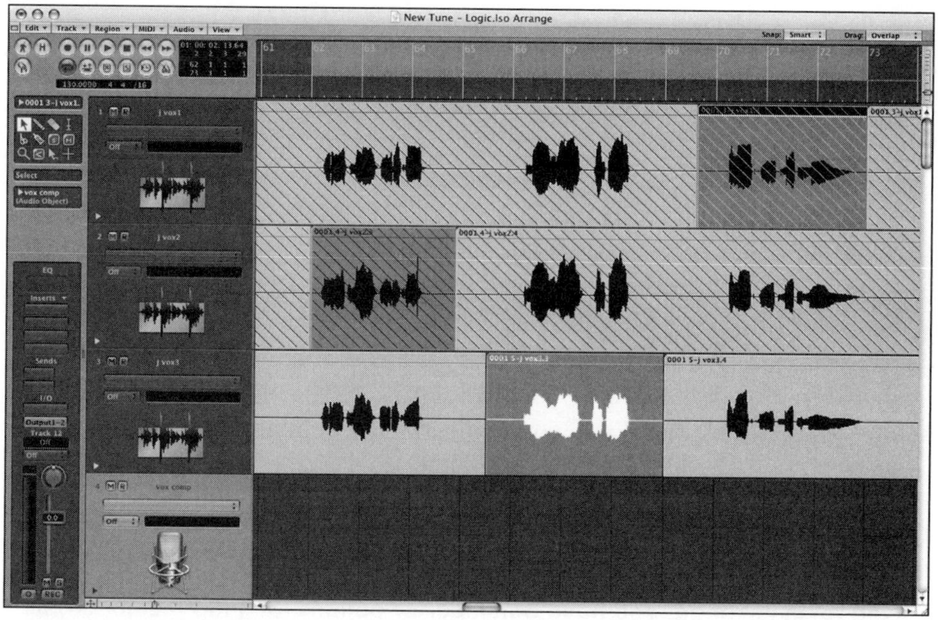

Figure 7.47
Here Gunn has split his various takes into regions. To highlight the regions he intends to keep, he changes their color (screenshot courtesy of Gunn).

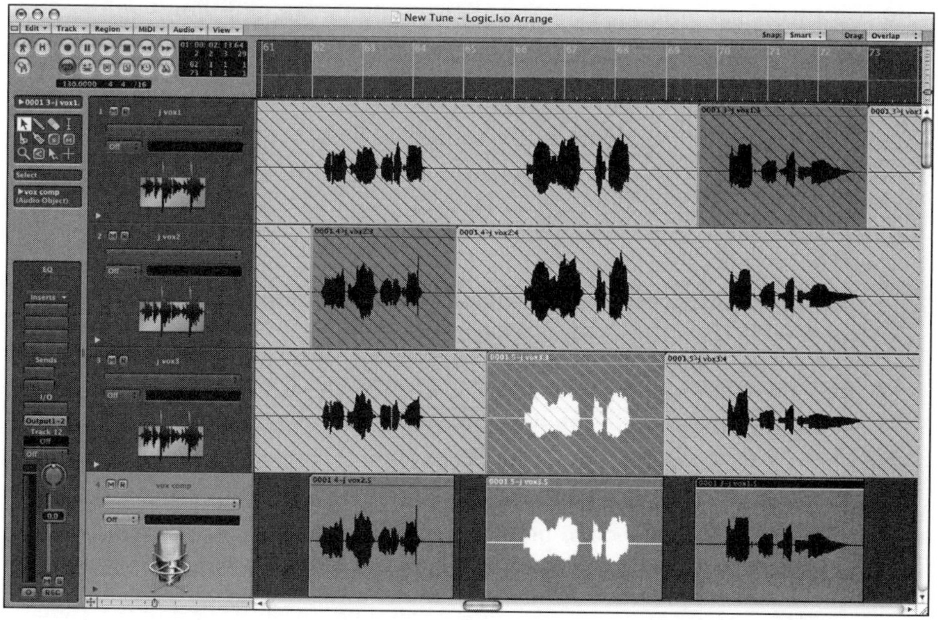

Figure 7.48
The results of the comping procedure. Gunn has created a single performance from the original three recordings that represents the best moments from each (screenshot courtesy of Gunn).

The Snap and Drag Menus

Logic Pro 7 adds two completely new pull-down menus to the right side of the Arrange window: the Snap menu and the Drag menu. Figure 7.49 shows these two Arrange menus.

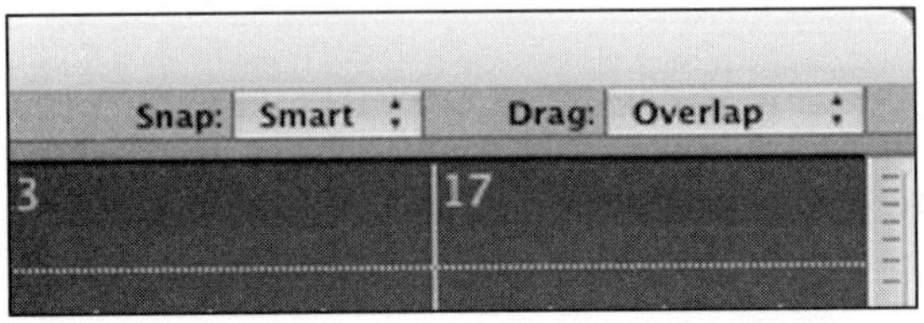

Figure 7.49
The Snap and Drag menus of the Arrange window.

Both of these menus affect the way you can move regions around Arrange in Logic Pro. The following subsections explain each menu in more detail.

The Snap Menu

The Snap menu affects precisely where a region you move will "snap," or be affixed to, in Arrange. You have a number of options for snap resolutions in this pull-down menu, designed to give you the ultimate say on where you want Logic to place your region. Your Snap options are as follows:

- **Smart.** Smart snap determines the snap resolution based on the zoom level of Arrange. For example, if you are zoomed out to see all 200 bars of your song, if you move a region, Smart snap will snap to even bars. However, if you are zoomed in so you can accurately see 32nd notes, Smart snap will snap to 32nd notes. The limit, of course, is the single-tick level.
- **Bar.** This option will always snap every region you move to the nearest bar division, regardless of zoom level.
- **Beat.** This option will snap to the denominator of your time signature (which determines the beat) regardless of the zoom level. For example, if your song is in 4/4 time, Beat snap will snap your measures to quarter notes; if your song is in 6/8 time, Beat snap will snap to eighth notes. If you have time changes in your Signature track, Beat snap will follow those signature changes and snap to the correct beat.
- **Format.** Format snaps to the note Format value displayed in the Division Display of the Transport window (1/16th notes, 1/8th notes, and so on) regardless of the zoom level.

- **Ticks.** This option will always snap to ticks, the finest resolution possible in Logic, regardless of the zoom level.
- **Frames.** Frames snap to SMPTE frames regardless of the zoom level. The exact snap will depend on which Frame rate you have set in your synchronization options (see Chapter 16, "Synchronizing Hardware with Logic Pro").
- **QF.** This option will always snap to Quarter Frames (one quarter the length of a full SMPTE frame) regardless of the zoom level.

The Drag Menu

The majority of the Drag menu options determine how regions will react when two regions are moved into the same space, called overlapping (as the regions will then overlap each other). The exceptions are the Shuffle modes, which determine how regions respond when dragged or cut. The Drag menu options are as follows:

- **Overlap.** In this mode, two regions can overlap, as shown in Figure 7.50. Be careful not to lose one region behind another in this mode! You can always move regions to expose a region hidden due to overlapping.

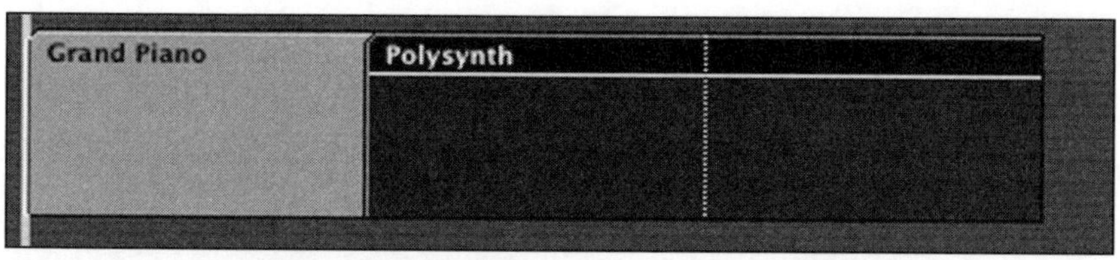

Figure 7.50
Two regions that overlap in Overlap mode. The dotted white line represents where the Grand Piano region ends underneath the Polysynth region.

- **No Overlap.** In this mode, two regions are not allowed to overlap. If you move a region into a position in which it would overlap another, the region that would be overlapped is simply cut and the hidden portion discarded, as shown in Figure 7.51.

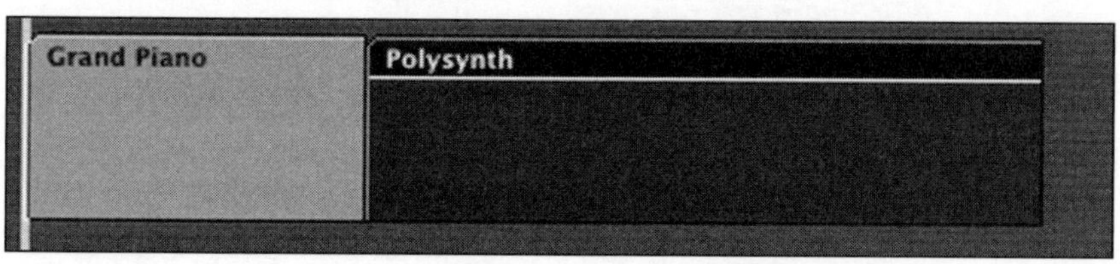

Figure 7.51
In No Overlap mode, you can see that the portion of the Grand Piano region that would have been hidden underneath the Polysynth region was simply removed.

* **X-Fade (Crossfade).** This mode acts like Overlap mode for MIDI regions. However, if you overlap two Audio regions together, Logic Pro automatically generates a crossfade between the two regions, as shown in Figure 7.52. See Chapter 8 for more information on audio crossfades. The dotted white line represents where the overlapped region ends.

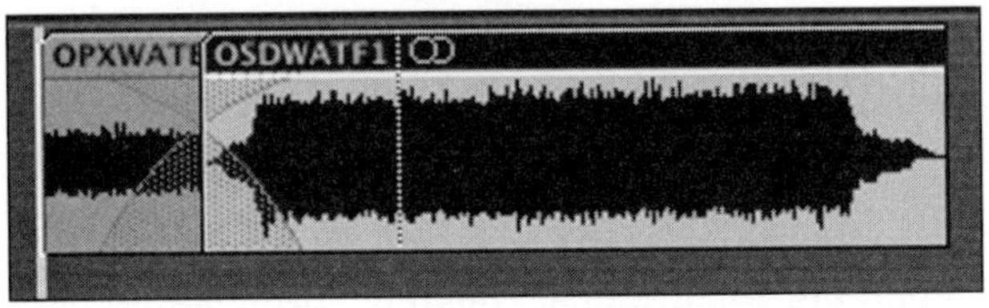

Figure 7.52
Logic Pro 7 will automatically create crossfades for overlapping Audio regions with the Drag mode set to X-Fade.

* **Shuffle R.** With Shuffle R mode enabled, if you move a region any distance to the right, it automatically snaps to the region to its immediate right, as shown in Figure 7.53. Obviously, if there is no other region to the right of the region you are moving, this will not happen.
* **Shuffle L.** Shuffle L mode operates identically to Shuffle R mode, with the difference that if you move any region to the left, it will snap to the region to its immediate left. Shuffle L operates the same as the Pro Tools Shuffle mode. (Pro Tools does not have two shuffle modes, only one, that operates like Logic Pro's Shuffle L.)

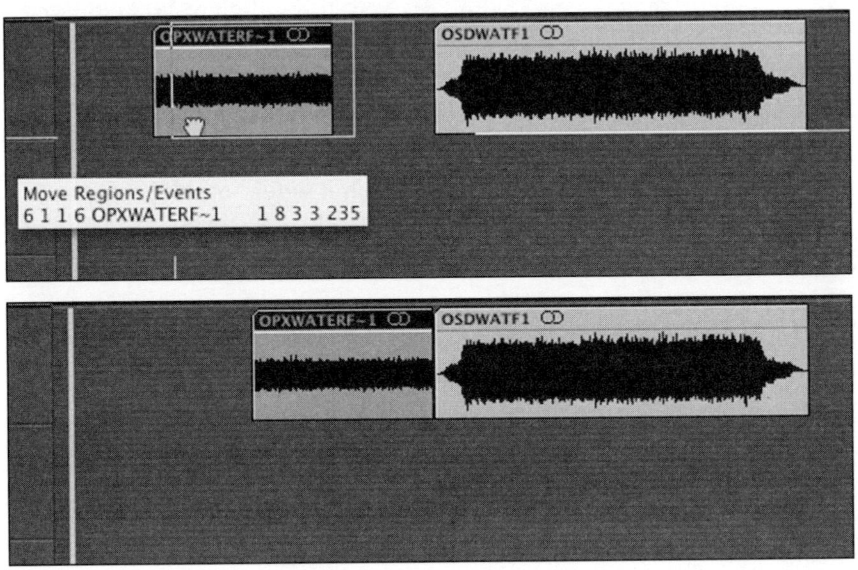

Figure 7.53
As you can see from the two figures, in Shuffle R mode, if you (a) move a region even a slight distance to the right, it will snap to the nearest region to its right. (b) Shuffle L mode is identical, but for regions you move left.

Adding Files to the Arrange Window

As noted previously, recording audio and MIDI is not the only way to create regions. You can also add preexisting files into the Arrange window in Logic. There are a number of ways to add files:

- As already explained above, if you click the Pencil tool in an Audio Track, Logic presents you with the Add File dialog box to select an audio file to add at the clicked position.
- By choosing **File > Import**, you can import audio or MIDI files into Logic. If you use the Open dialog box to navigate to an audio or MIDI file, this command imports the file into Logic. If you selected a MIDI file, this command creates one or more regions on Arrange; if you selected an audio file, this command imports it to the Audio window, from which you can drag the audio file into a track in Arrange to create a region for it.
- You can drag audio or MIDI files from your computer's desktop (or any file directory) onto your Arrange. This method drops the dragged audio or MIDI file directly onto a track on Arrange. If it is an audio file, this method also adds the file to the Audio window.
- You can drag audio or MIDI files from the Project Manager to Arrange. The Project Manager is explained in detail in Chapter 13, "Working with Files."
- If you are working with an audio file, you can add it to the Audio window using the Add Audio File command, then drag that file from the Audio window into Arrange. This method is explained in more detail in the next chapter.

EXPERT TIP: USING FOLDERS WHEN IMPORTING STANDARD MIDI FILES

Sasso has another great tip for how Folder tracks can assist when importing Standard MIDI Files into Logic:

> *"If a Standard MIDI File (SMF) has multiple tracks, dragging it to the Arrange window will create a separate region for each track. To keep them together and well organized, first create an empty folder, then open it and drag the SMF into the Arrange window displaying the folder's contents. If some of the resulting regions contain multiple channels, use 'Demix by MIDI Channel' to further separate them."*

Automation

Automation is one of Logic's more extensive features, and Chapter 11, "Using Automation in Logic," will examine automation in depth. However, since most automation functions are in the Arrange window, a brief explanation of automation follows.

Track-Based Automation

Track-Based Automation (TBA) is the most powerful, accurate, and modern automation in Logic. With TBA, your automation is not connected to the regions on a particular track lane, but to the actual track lane itself. This is how automation would function with an actual hardware mixer, in which you automate a mixer channel, not the material that is playing through the channel. It is possible, however, to tie TBA to the regions on a track, which is explained in Chapter 11.

When you turn on Track-Based Automation by choosing **View > Track Automation** or by using the key command, the track lane expands and you will see the various automation options. Figure 7.54 shows a track with Track-Based Automation visible.

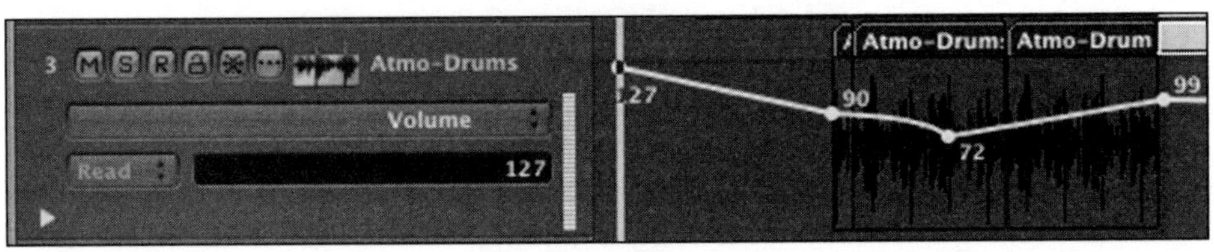

Figure 7.54
This track has Track-Based Automation turned on, and you can see Volume automation data in the track lane.

Because the automation lane takes up the majority of the track lane, when you want to edit, move, and resize regions, you'll need to be careful to click only in the top label portion of the region above the automation data—otherwise, Logic assumes that you are trying to edit your automation data, not the region.

Region-Based Automation (Hyper Draw)

Before Logic introduced TBA, the only method of automation was called Hyper Draw. Hyper Draw uses standard MIDI messages to automate MIDI data. These MIDI messages are directly tied to the region for which they were created; hence, Hyper Draw is also known as Region-Based Automation (RBA). Figure 7.55 shows a track with RBA information visible.

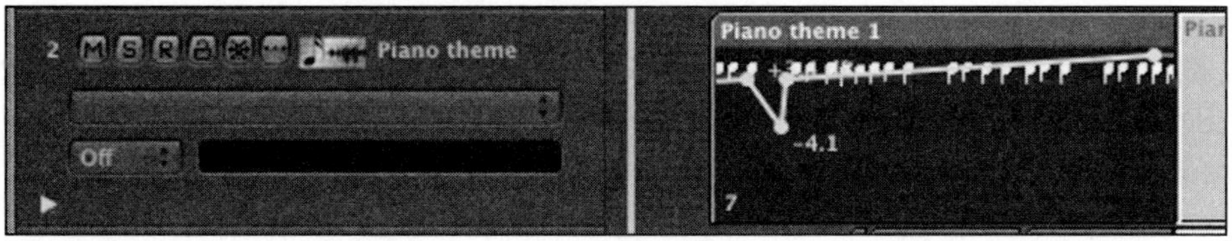

Figure 7.55

This track has volume Hyper Draw (Region-Based Automation) data displayed. The track list does not show as much information for the RBA data as for the TBA data in Figure 7.54. Notice also that the RBA information is included as an actual part of the region itself, unlike TBA information, which is connected to the track.

One of the main advantages to RBA is that as you move regions around, RBA automatically moves with it. In general, however, RBA does not have the high resolution, or show you as much information on the track list, as does TBA. You can turn RBA data into TBA data, as you will explore in Chapter 11.

Caps Lock Keyboard

Finally, while this isn't technically a part of the Arrange window, since you may want to use it to record Audio Instrument performances I will mention the Caps Lock keyboard here. The Caps Lock keyboard is new to Logic Pro 7. If you have the Enable Caps Lock Keys checked in the Caps Lock Keys tab of the Global Preferences window, pressing the **CAPS LOCK** key will bring up the onscreen keyboard shown in Figure 7.56.

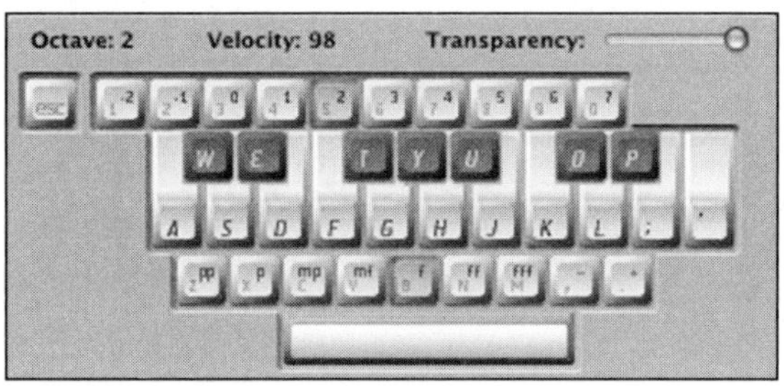

Figure 7.56

The Caps Lock keyboard.

The Caps Lock keyboard is a realtime MIDI keyboard with a maximum of 6 notes of polyphony. You can use it to audition Audio Instruments without having to reach for your MIDI controller, or you can even use the Caps Lock keyboard to record a MIDI performance in realtime! The numeric keys can select from among the 10-octave range of the Caps Lock keyboard, you can use the **SPACE BAR** as a sustain pedal (also set in the aforementioned Preference window), and it is velocity sensitive! Obviously, you toggle the Caps Lock keyboard by pressing the **CAPS LOCK** key.

The Caps Lock keyboard clearly doesn't replace a full MIDI keyboard controller. But if you are in a plane, train, or automobile with no access to a real keyboard, Logic 7's Caps Lock keyboard is very convenient. If you want to record a MIDI performance using it, just select your Audio Instrument track in Arrange, press the **CAPS LOCK** key, start recording, and play!

The Arrange window is perhaps the most complex window in Logic; there's a lot of information to digest here, but when you're comfortable with Arrange, you'll be far along the path to being comfortable with Logic as a whole. The next chapter specifically explores using audio and Apple Loops in Logic.

8 Working with Audio and Apple Loops

Now that you've explored manipulating and editing regions, it's time to address manipulating and editing the data within those regions. Logic's handling of audio has always been one of its most lauded features. Now, Logic adds support for a special kind of audio file developed by Apple Computer that can contain pitch, tempo, genre category, and even MIDI and channel strip information: the *Apple Loop*. In this chapter, I'll examine how Logic Pro 7 handles audio and Apple Loops, as well as some useful and creative tips and tutorials for using these features.

First, it's important to remember what's been discussed about Audio Objects. I already discussed that Audio Objects expand to channel strips, or virtual representations of hardware audio mixer channels. That said, let's start by going into greater detail about the various Audio Objects available in Logic Pro 7.

Types of Audio Objects

Logic offers many different kinds of Audio Objects. These different types represent the different mixer functions, or in some cases, applications, of a particular Audio Object. You can assign all of these Audio Objects to an Arrange track, and they will appear as channel strips in the Arrange parameter area, in the Audio Mixer, and the Track Mixer. A brief description of the different Audio Objects follows:

- **Audio Track Object.** This Audio Object is analogous to the standard Audio Track on a hardware mixer. You record and play back audio files on Audio Tracks. You will normally record or place audio onto an Audio Track in Arrange, and then use the Audio Track as a playback track. Audio Tracks can be mono, stereo, or surround. Depending on your version of Logic, Logic offers from 48 (Logic Express) to 255 (Logic Pro) Audio Tracks.

- **Bus Objects.** This Audio Object does not play or record audio files at all—it is more of a "patch bay" track. Traditionally, busses on mixers were often push buttons that sent the audio on an Audio channel to an auxiliary track or auxiliary output. Bus Objects in Logic serve a similar purpose of being a patch bay between destinations for your audio, although in Logic, you can also use a Bus Object as a destination itself. You can have a Bus Object route audio from other Audio Objects to hardware outputs. Aux Objects (see below) may use busses (Bus Objects) as their input source. You can also put effects directly in the channel strip of a Bus Object if you want. In addition, other Audio Objects can use their Sends (see "Channel Strip Components" below) to route signal to a Bus Object. Bus Objects do not have Sends on their own channel strips, as Bus Objects are the destination of Sends from other channel strips. Bus Objects can be mono or stereo. Logic offers from 16 (Logic Express) to 64 (Logic Pro) Bus Objects.
- **Input Objects.** Input Objects are used as a "live audio play through" track in Logic. Unlike Audio Tracks, on which you record audio and then play back Audio regions, tracks with Input Objects are used for tracks that are always live—for example, a hardware synthesizer that you want to mix with the rest of your tracks in the Logic mixer, but you do not want to record onto an Audio Track. Input Objects can be mono or stereo. The number of hardware inputs on your audio interface determines how many Input Objects are available in Logic.
- **Aux Objects.** Aux (auxiliary) Objects in Logic, like Bus and Input Objects, do not record or play back Audio regions. Instead, Aux Objects are routing destinations that can accept their input from a number of sources. They can accept the input of a bus (Bus Object), becoming a Send destination for your other Audio Objects. Aux Objects can accept their input from a Multichannel Audio Instrument, so each Aux Object becomes the destination of a different output from the Audio Instrument. Finally, Aux Objects can take their inputs from your audio interface, allowing for complex routing of live audio. Aux Objects, unlike Bus Objects, have Sends on their channel strip (in

other words—Aux Objects can serve as Bus Objects with sends). Aux Objects can be mono or stereo. Logic supports from 16 (Logic Express) to 64 (Logic Pro) Aux Objects.

- **Output Objects.** Output Objects are used to send audio to your external hardware. They are usually the output destination of your Audio Objects. You can use Output Objects to "bounce" audio—which means to create an audio file that contains the summation of all the Audio Objects routing their output to the Output Object. Output Objects can be mono, stereo, or surround. The number of hardware outputs on your audio interface determines how many Output Objects are available in Logic.
- **Audio Instrument Objects.** Audio Instrument Objects are unique among Audio Objects, as they are the only ones that contain MIDI regions instead of Audio regions. Audio Instrument Objects allow you to access the built-in or third-party plug-in software synthesizers that can be integrated into Logic. When you play back the MIDI regions of an Audio Instrument, those MIDI regions will trigger the DSP algorithms of the Audio Instrument to generate sound. Audio Instruments can be mono, stereo, or multichannel. Multichannel Audio Instruments use Aux Objects for their additional outputs (see Chapter 10, "Working with Audio Instruments in Logic"). Logic offers from 16 (Logic Express) to 128 (Logic Pro) Audio Instrument Objects.
- **Rewire Objects.** Rewire Objects are related to Audio Instrument Objects. With an Audio Instrument, built-in or plugged-in software synthesizers generate the DSP algorithms of the Audio Instrument, allowing one object to both receive the MIDI data and trigger sound generation. The Rewire 2 protocol syncs multiple programs inside the computer, not inside of Logic. This means that the Internal Rewire Instrument Object is required to send the MIDI data out of Logic and into the Rewire 2 application, and then the Rewire Object accepts the audio data from the Rewire 2 application. Because the Arrange track assigned to the Internal Rewire Object contains the MIDI regions that trigger the Rewire 2 application, Rewire Objects do not contain any regions. Rewire Objects can only be mono, so for a stereo signal, you'll need to create two Rewire Objects (hopefully, this limitation in Logic will be addressed in the future). The number of Rewire Objects you may access depends on the specific Rewire 2 applications you have installed on your computer. Chapter 10 provides more information on using Rewire Objects.

- **Master Fader.** Finally, Logic offers a Master Fader Object. This object does exactly what it says—it serves as a "master volume" for your song. To be honest, I don't like these, because I would rather use the Output Objects, which are far more functional, as my "master volume" objects. On the other hand, if you are doing a surround mix with many Output Objects, or you are sending each track to a hardware mixer and using many Output Objects, having a Master Fader offers a convenient way to adjust the overall level.

Figure 8.1

An Audio Object channel strip.

Channel Strip Components

You've seen the channel strip in previous chapters. Now that I've described the different types of Audio Objects, I'll go over the components of the channel strip, and the subtle differences in the strips for various Audio Objects. The channel strip is mostly utilized during mixing, which is covered in Chapter 12, "Mixing In Logic." However, editing audio and using the Audio window described in this chapter require some knowledge of the channel strip. You can use the channel strip in Figure 8.1 as your reference.

Each of the components of this channel strip can be toggled on or off in the Audio Object parameter box, as has been mentioned previously. The following descriptions of the various components of the channel strip explain any differences that exist for a specific type of Audio Object:

- **EQ.** If you double-click inside this rectangle, you will enable a thumbnail of the Channel EQ effect graph (using Logic's EQs is discussed in Chapter 12, "Mixing in Logic") inside the rectangle, and the Channel EQ effect is instantiated in the first Insert (Inserts are described next). If you hold the **OPTION** key down while double-clicking inside the rectangle, the Channel EQ will be instantiated in the 2nd Insert. If you have instantiated the Linear Phase EQ, then the EQ graph from this effect will be shown in the EQ rectangle. If the thumbnail image of the Channel or Linear Phase EQ is already showing in the channel strip, double-clicking on the thumbnail opens the respective EQ's Editor window. In previous versions of Logic, the EQ section contained parameters for Logic's built-in EQ effects. All Audio Objects contain the EQ section.

- **Inserts.** These rectangles represent slots into which you can "insert" effects into the channel strip. Logic comes with up to 70 built-in effects (depending on your version of Logic), and you can also use various third-party plug-in effects (this is discussed further in Chapter 12). You add effects to Inserts by clicking and holding the button until a pull-down menu of effects appears. When you select an effect, it appears in that Insert slot, and the Insert glows blue indicating the effect is functioning. You can have up to four Inserts in Logic Express, and eight Inserts in Logic Pro. If you see fewer than the maximum number of Insert slots on your channel strip, don't worry; when you fill the last Insert slot on screen, another slot will appear beneath it, and this will continue until you reach your version's maximum number of Inserts. All Audio Objects have Inserts except the Master Fader.
- **Sends.** Send knobs are used to route (send) a variable amount of the audio signal from channel strips to busses (Bus Objects). When empty, Sends appear to be empty rectangles (slots). When you click-hold on a Send rectangle and add a Send destination, not only does the destination appear in the slot, but a small dial appears to the right of the Send for you to adjust the Send level. If you see fewer than the maximum number of Send rectangles on your channel strip, don't worry; when you fill the last Send slot on screen, another rectangle will appear beneath it, and this will continue until you reach the maximum of eight Sends (four in Logic Express). Because Bus Objects are the destinations of Sends, Bus Objects do not have Sends themselves.
- **I/O.** There are two rectangles under I/O; the upper rectangle is for selecting the Input of the Audio Object, the lower rectangle is for selecting the Output.
- **Input**. Each Audio Object features a different method of handling its Input slot:
  - **Audio Track Objects.** You may select any of your audio interface's physical inputs as the Input for this slot.
  - **Audio Instrument Objects.** You may select any available software synthesizer as the Input for this slot.

- **Aux Objects.** You may select your hardware inputs, Bus Objects, or Multichannel Instrument outputs as the Input for this slot.
- **Rewire Objects.** The input for Rewire Objects is the Rewire 2 channel selected using the Channel parameter, so the Input slot does not appear in the Rewire Object's channel strip.
- **Input Objects.** Input Objects have their Input determined by the selected hardware input in the Input Object's Channel parameter, so the Input slot does not appear in the Input Object's channel strip.
- **Output Objects and Bus Objects.** These objects do not have rectangles for Input, since they can only be used as destinations for other Audio Objects.

- **Output**. The Output for all Audio Objects except Output Objects can be any available bus (Bus Object) or Output Object. The hardware output selected in an Output Object's parameter box determines its output, so Output Objects do not have an Output rectangle.
- **Group Slot.** This window shows the group number of the selected Audio Object. If the Audio Object is not assigned to a group, this window displays "Off." Groups are explained in Chapter 12. All types of Audio Objects may belong to groups.
- **Automation Slot**. This window shows whether the channel strip is currently using Logic's Track-Based Automation or not. If the channel strip is utilizing automation, the window displays whether the track is currently reading automation data, or which mode it is using to write automation data. Automation is explained in Chapter 11, "Using Automation in Logic." All Audio Objects have Automation slots.
- **Pan Knob.** The large rotary knob below the Automation slot is the Pan knob. This knob allows you to adjust the panorama—or stereo position—of the Audio Object in the stereo field. If you are in Surround mode, you may adjust the Audio Object's panorama on more than two axes. All Audio Objects have Pan knobs.
- **Volume Slider.** This long slider below the Pan knob, directly to the right of the channel strip Audio Meter, allows you to adjust the volume of the Audio Object. All Audio Objects have Volume sliders.
- **Audio Meter.** This meter displays a bar line that represents the volume of the Audio Object. It changes with each variation in volume of your

Audio Object. The small box above the Audio Meter displays the highest volume peak that the Audio Object has hit up to that point in the song. The channel strip Audio Meter has a range from –20dB to +6dB. All Audio Objects have Audio Meters.

- **M.** This is the Channel Mute button. Clicking on this button mutes the Audio Object (and all the tracks in the Arrange window assigned to the muted Audio Objects are silenced). All Audio Objects have the Channel Mute button.
- **S.** This is the Channel Solo button for the Audio Object. Pressing this button silences all other currently unsoloed objects (and only those Arrange tracks assigned to the soloed track will be heard). All Audio Objects have Solo buttons.
- **Mono/Stereo Button.** The single or double circle icon underneath the Audio Meter is the Mono/Stereo button. If the button is a single circle, the Audio Object is in mono. If the button is a double circle, the Audio Object is in stereo. Clicking the button toggles between mono and stereo. Rewire Objects do not have this button, as Rewire Objects are always mono. Audio Instrument Objects do not have this button because the type of software synthesizer you selected will determine whether the Audio Instrument Object is mono or stereo.
- **REC.** This is the Record-Enable button. If you click this button, the Audio Object is ready to record audio through your audio interface. Only Audio Tracks have REC buttons, as they are the only Audio Object that can record audio.
- **Bounce.** The Bounce button is only on Output Objects. Clicking this button brings up a dialog box enabling you to create a mono or stereo audio file from all the Audio Objects routed to that Output Object. Bouncing is discussed further in Chapter 12.

The Audio Window

The Audio window is in a sense a repository for recorded and imported audio files. You do not have to use every audio file listed in the Audio window in your song, but every audio file used in your song will be listed in the Audio window. The Audio window is far more than a simple list of files, however. First of all, the Audio window also keeps track of every Audio region into which an audio file has been split. You can drag Audio regions from the

Audio window directly onto an Audio Track on Arrange. The Audio window itself offers many ways to manage, group, and manipulate audio files and Audio regions as well. Figure 8.2 shows an Audio window filled with audio files and Audio regions.

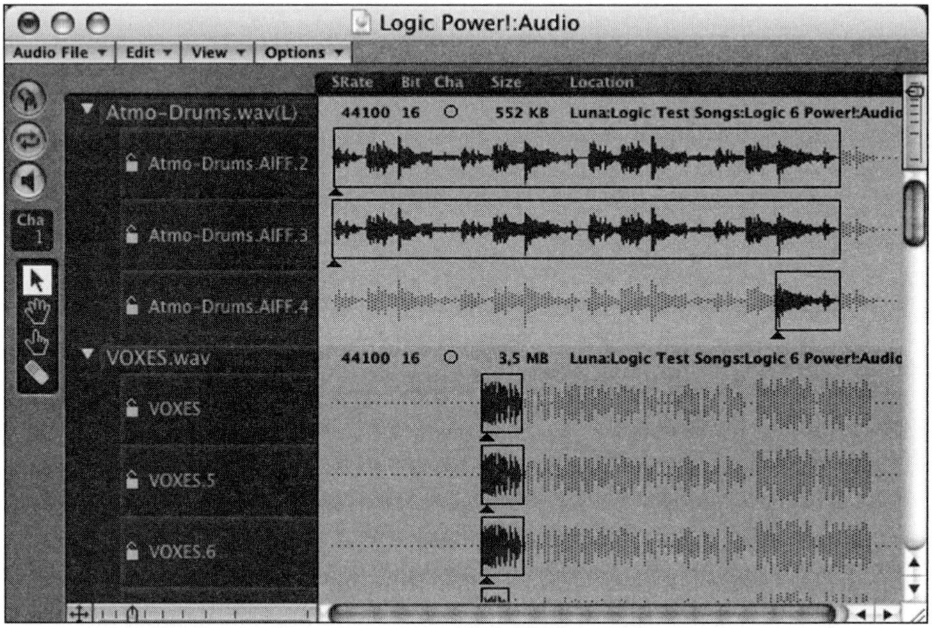

Figure 8.2
The Audio window.

The Audio window consists of local menus, buttons, and a Toolbox around its perimeter, an Audio List in which the names of all your audio files and Audio regions are listed, and then the Audio Window Graphic Overview window (usually just referred to as the Audio window). In this section, which is the majority of the Audio window, you not only see your Audio regions represented in relation to the entire audio file that they are part of, but you can see sample rate, bit depth, size, and location information for all your audio files.

You can start your exploration of the Audio window with the local menus.

The Audio Window Local Menus

Like all windows and editors in Logic, the Audio window features its own local menu containing commands that specifically affect audio and audio files. Keep in mind that for those commands that do not have key commands assigned by default, you can assign keys to them in the Key Commands window.

The Audio File Menu

The Audio File menu contains commands that operate on the audio files themselves. Figure 8.3 shows the Audio File menu of the Audio window.

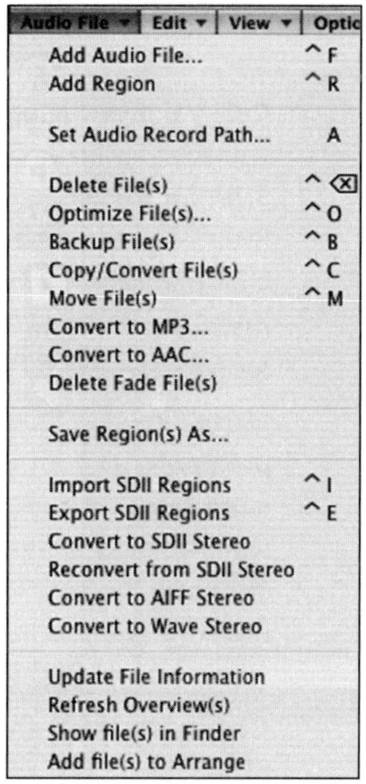

Figure 8.3
The Audio File menu of the Audio window.

An explanation of the Audio File menu commands follows.

- **Add Audio File.** This command brings up an Open File dialog box, which allows you to import audio files from your hard drive into the Audio window of your Logic song. You can then drag your file into the Arrange window or process it further in the Audio window. Logic is capable of importing files in WAV, Broadcast WAV, AIFF, or SDII (Sound Designer II), mp3, or AAC format. **<CONTROL + F>**
- **Add Region.** If you select an audio file in the Audio List, this command creates a new Audio region for that audio file. The new Audio region will initially be the full length of the audio file, but you can adjust this length. **<CONTROL + R>**
- **Set Audio Record Path.** This is the same command discussed in Chapter 6. It allows you to set the location of audio files recorded in that song. **<A>**
- **Delete File(s).** This command deletes all selected files.
- **Optimize File(s).** This command deletes sections of audio files that are not used in your song. You can use this command to save hard drive space by eliminating unnecessary data, but beware you don't accidentally erase a piece of audio that might prove useful. Because of this, you should use this command only when you are reasonably sure that you are completely finished with a given song. **<CONTROL + O>**
- **Backup File(s).** This command creates a duplicate of all selected audio files. These files are given the extension .dup. Generally, since any edits to regions are nondestructive (that is, they don't touch the file), this command is mostly useful if you are processing time and pitch

processing or editing samples, which each affect the actual audio file itself. <**CONTROL + B**>

- **Copy/Convert File(s).** This command brings up a dialog box in which you can duplicate your selected audio file or files into WAV, AIFF, or SDII; for example, you could copy an AIFF file into a WAV file, or an SDII file into an AIFF file. You can of course choose the original format, and simply make duplicate WAV files. This function is particularly useful when you want to export one or more files into a different format. <**CONTROL + C**>
- **Move File(s).** When you choose this command, a dialog box appears prompting you for a new location on your hard drive to move one or more selected audio files in the Audio window. If you move audio files without using either this command or the Project Manager, Logic will not know the new location of your audio file and will prompt you to find it. If you use this command, Logic will be able to keep track of where you moved your audio files. <**CONTROL + M**>
- **Convert to MP3.** This converts any audio files you have selected into MP3 files.
- **Convert to AAC.** This converts any audio files you have selected into AAC files. AAC is the format of music used by the iTunes Music Store, and generally sounds a bit more robust than MP3 at the same compression level. On the other hand, AAC is not as widely supported as MP3 by non-Macintosh media players.
- **Save Region(s) As.** This command allows you to save one or more specific Audio regions as separate audio files. This is very useful if you want to export only those selected regions to another application.
- **Import SDII Regions.** This command imports SDII format Audio regions from your hard drive. If audio files that you want to import are in SDII format, the advantage of using this command is that you can then automatically use the time stamp included in those SDII regions (assuming the other application time stamped those regions) to place the imported SDII regions in the proper place in the Arrange window. <**CONTROL + I**>
- **Export SDII Regions.** This command enables you to export the Audio regions from one or more selected audio files as SDII regions for importing as SDII regions in another audio application. <**CONTROL + E**>

- **Convert to SDII Stereo.** Most applications that work with SDII files cannot actually work with SDII files that contain data for both audio streams (right and left) in the same file; instead, they use two files for each stereo file—one with the extension .L for left, and the other with the extension .R for right. This is known as a *split stereo* SDII file. Since Logic is capable of utilizing true stereo SDII files, this command converts a split stereo SDII audio file into a single stereo SDII file.
- **Reconvert from SDII Stereo.** This command takes the selected stereo SDII file or files and creates a split stereo SDII file for every stereo SDII file. This is useful when exporting SDII stereo files for use in applications that cannot handle true stereo SDII files.
- **Convert to AIFF Stereo.** This command converts your selected audio file or files into a stereo AIFF file. This is mostly useful if you need to export stereo AIFF files, or, if you generally record using AIFF format, you imported some stereo audio files in a different format and need to convert them to AIFF.
- **Convert to Wave Stereo.** This command converts your selected audio file or files into a stereo WAV file. This is mostly useful if you need to export stereo WAV files, or, if you generally record in WAV format, you imported some stereo audio files in a different format and need to convert them to WAV.
- **Update File Information.** If you find one or more of your Audio regions are grayed out, that means Logic couldn't find the original audio file used by that Audio region. When you select those grayed-out Audio regions and choose this command, Logic presents a dialog box prompting you to navigate to the missing audio files. After using this command (and saving your song), Logic will remember the new file information.
- **Refresh Overview(s).** If the preference to Create Overviews After Recording is active, for every audio file, the Arrange window will display an image of the audio inside the region or file. If you have one or more Audio regions or audio files for which the Arrange window doesn't display an image, you can use this command to refresh (redraw) the overviews of any Audio regions or audio files you select.
- **Show File(s) in Finder.** If you select one or more Audio regions, this command will then open Finder windows showing you the actual audio file on your hard drive that these regions point to.

- **Add File(s) to Arrange.** You can select one or more Audio regions and use this command to place them in the Arrange window. See the section "Adding Audio to the Arrange Window" below for more details.

The Edit Menu

This menu consists of some standard application editing functions and some functions specific to Logic. Figure 8.4 shows the Edit menu of the Arrange window.

The first four commands in this menu—Undo, Redo, Undo History, and Delete Undo History—are the same commands as the Arrange window's local Edit menu. See the previous chapter for detailed information. Definitions of the rest of the commands follow:

- **Cut.** This command removes the selected audio files and Audio regions from their locations on the Audio List and places them in the Clipboard. **<COMMAND + X>**
- **Copy.** The Copy command places a copy of the selected audio files and Audio regions onto the Clipboard. **<COMMAND + C>**
- **Paste.** This command pastes the contents of the Clipboard beneath the currently selected Audio region or audio file in the Audio List. **<COMMAND + V>**
- **Clear.** The Clear command removes any selected Audio regions or audio files from the Audio window.
- **Select All.** You can select every audio file and Audio region in the Audio window with this command. **<COMMAND + A>**
- **Select Used.** This command selects all the Audio regions that are currently used in your song.
- **Select Unused.** This selects all the Audio regions that are not currently used in your song. **<SHIFT + U>**
- **Select files.** This submenu allows you to select all audio files in the Audio List that are used in other songs, used in EXS24mkII Sampler Instruments, or both.
- **Info.** The Info command displays a dialog box with basic information about how many audio files, Audio regions, fade files, and fade regions are part of your song, and how many are actively being used in your song.

- **Search Zero Crossings.** A "zero crossing" occurs when the amplitude of the audio wave is at the zero line. If you turn this option on, all adjustments to Audio regions fall at the nearest zero point. The advantage to this option is that you are far more likely to have seamless playback between two adjacent Audio regions, since the amplitude of both Audio regions will be at the zero crossing when they meet. The disadvantage is that this will sometimes interfere with where you want to make an edit if there doesn't happen to be a zero crossing at that point. Keep in mind that if you turn this option on, it also holds true for Audio region resizing and splitting in the Arrange window.

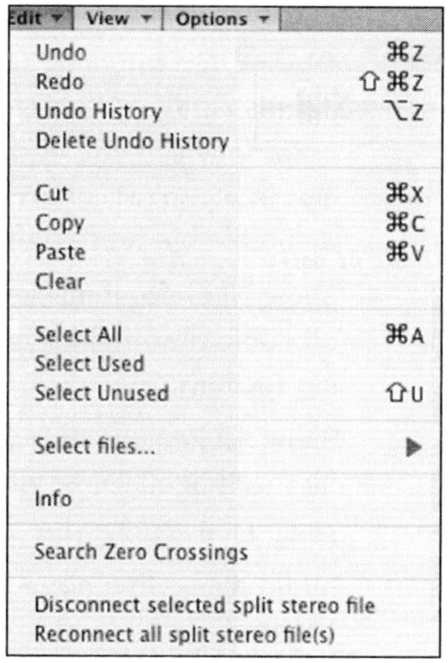

Figure 8.4
The Edit menu of the Audio window.

- **Disconnect Selected Split Stereo File.** This command converts a split stereo SDII file into two unlinked mono audio files.
- **Reconnect All Split Stereo File(s).** This command reconnects all unlinked mono SDII files that used to be part of a split stereo SDII file. This is especially useful when you import Audio Tracks that were originally split stereo SDII files, but their link was broken in the process of exporting them from their original application.

The View Menu

The View menu offers options for viewing and sorting Audio regions and audio files in the Audio window. Figure 8.5 shows the View menu of the Audio window.

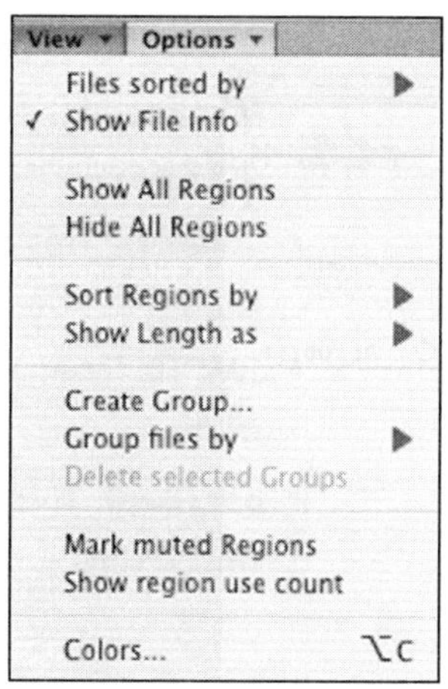

Figure 8.5
The View menu of the Audio window.

The various options in the View menu are as follows:

- **Files Sorted By.** This entry opens a hierarchal menu, which allows you to check one of six options for sorting audio files in the Audio List: None, Name, Size, Drive, Bit

Depth, and File Type. When you re-sort your audio files, all the Audio regions that originate from that file always move with the file. The default category is None, meaning your audio files are sorted by the order in which you added them. If you find it useful to have all your files in alphabetical order, or in order of their file size, hard drive, or audio file bit depth, select the appropriate option.

- **Show File Info.** If this is checked, Logic displays the file information for all audio files in the Audio List. This is described further in the following sections.
- **Show All Regions.** This command expands the view triangle of all audio files so that all Audio regions are displayed in the Audio window.
- **Hide All Regions.** This command contracts the view triangle of each audio file so that none of the Audio regions appear in the Audio window.
- **Sort Regions By.** This entry opens a hierarchal menu, which allows you to check one of three options for sorting Audio regions used by a given audio file: Start, Length, or Name. This sorts only the Audio regions attached to each audio file; the files themselves do not change position in the Audio List.
- **Show Length As.** If you want to display the length of each Audio region above the graphic representation of the region in the Audio window, you can choose one of the Show Length As options that you are offered in the hierarchal menu that opens when you select this command. These are your options:
  - **None.** This is the default. The Audio region length is not displayed above the region.
  - **Min:Sec:Ms.** This displays the length of the region in the format *minutes: seconds: milliseconds.*
  - **Samples.** This command displays the number of samples in the region.
  - **SMPTE Time.** This displays the length of the region in SMPTE timecode.
  - **Bar/Beat.** This command displays how long the region is in bars and beats.

- **Create Group.** This command allows you to create a new grouping of audio files in the Audio window. Audio groups are discussed further in the chapter in the section "Audio Window Groups" below.
- **Group Files By.** Logic Pro 7 can automatically create Audio window groups by grouping files by Location, File Type, or Arrange selection. Audio groups are discussed later in the chapter.
- **Delete Selected Group.** This command will delete any selected Audio window group(s).
- **Mark Muted Regions.** If this option is checked, for every Audio region that is muted in Arrange, this command will place a dot before its name in the Audio window.
- **Show Region Use Count.** If this option is checked, beneath the name of every Audio region in the Audio window will be a number representing how many times that region appears in the Arrange window.
- **Colors.** This command brings up the color palette so you can color your Audio regions.

The Options Menu

The final local menu in the Audio window is the Options menu. This last menu contains a few more esoteric commands that don't fit logically in the other Audio window menus. Figure 8.6 shows the Options menu.

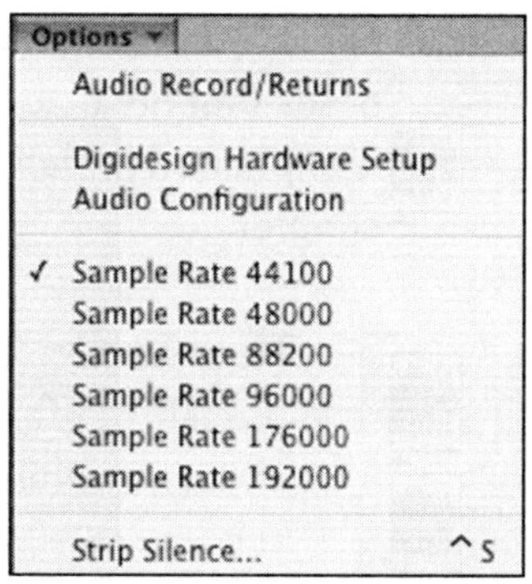

Figure 8.6
The Options menu of the Audio window.

Brief descriptions of the commands in this menu follow:

- **Audio Record/Returns.** In case you need to reference an Audio Object's channel strip while working in the Audio window, you can choose the Audio Record/Returns command to open the Environment's Audio Mixer to the current channel strip that is selected in Arrange. Frankly, this command is of dubious value, and you will likely never need it.
- **Digidesign Hardware Setup.** If you need to access your audio hardware drivers while working in the Audio window, you can choose this command to open the Audio Preference dialog box to the Drivers tab.

The command name Digidesign Hardware Setup is a throwback to when Digidesign hardware was the sole audio hardware available.

- **Exchange Digidesign Hardware.** For all practical purposes, this does the same thing as the previous command—open the Audio Preference dialog to the Drivers tab.
- **Audio Configuration.** This command will open the Audio Configuration window, discussed below in the "Audio Configuration Window" section.
- **Sample Rate (44100–192000).** These are not so much commands as options for the sample rate. The checked option represents the sample rate for your song. If you need to change the sample rate of your song, check a different setting. Be careful not to select a different sample rate for your song than for your audio files. You can also access the sample rate options in a submenu of the Global Audio menu by choosing **Audio > Sample Rate**.
- **Strip Silence.** Strip Silence was briefly mentioned in the last chapter's subsection on the Arrange window's local Audio menu; it is also available here. Strip Silence allows you to remove the silence in Audio regions, creating many new Audio regions that include only those areas that have content. Strip Silence is a very valuable function and is explained in detail in the section "Using Strip Silence" later in this chapter.

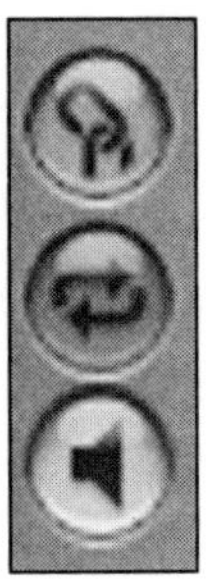

Figure 8.7
The Audio window's buttons.

The Audio Window Buttons

The left border of the Audio window houses three buttons that affect how the Audio window operates. Figure 8.7 shows those buttons.

In order from top to bottom, the buttons do the following:

- **Link Button.** As with other windows, the chain link icon is the Link button. If this is glowing purple, the Audio window is linked to the Arrange window, meaning that the most recently selected Audio region will be selected in the Audio window. If this button is not glowing, the Audio window does not reflect Arrange at all.

- **Loop Button.** With this button glowing green, the selected Audio region loops continuously. This is especially useful when you are adjusting loop points in the Audio window (see the section "Using Looping in the Audio Window" later in this chapter).
- **Playback Button.** When the speaker icon is glowing green, the selected Audio region plays back. If you have an audio file selected, the first Audio region of that audio file plays back. If you have nothing selected at all, you cannot activate the button. If you click-hold the mouse button over any Audio region, the cursor itself becomes a speaker icon, your Audio region plays back as long as you hold the button down, and the Playback button remains lit during playback.

The Audio Window Channel

When you are working in the Audio window, any Audio region you play back will always play back through the same Audio channel. This Audio channel is selected in a text box below the Audio window buttons. Figure 8.8 displays the Audio window's Channel box.

Figure 8.8
The Audio Channel box below the Audio window buttons displays the Audio channel on which your Audio regions will play back when being auditioned or adjusted in the Audio window.

It is important to keep in mind which channel you choose for the Audio window to use, since Logic will apply all the EQ, Inserts, Sends, and similar settings of the channel strip for that Audio channel to every Audio region that you play back from the Audio window. At first, this might seem counterintuitive—why doesn't the Audio window simply play back each region using the Audio channel to which that region is already assigned?

Remember, the Audio window is a repository for all the audio files and regions that you have imported or recorded for your song, whether you use them or not. This means that a good number of your Audio regions are likely not assigned to any Audio channel. Moreover, since you can move Audio regions on Arrange from track to track, and from Audio Object to Audio Object, their channel assignment is fluid. Also, since you can jump around in the Audio window selecting and playing back regions at will, the Audio window would need to be able to switch Audio channels continually and seamlessly—and it would need to keep all the EQ, Inserts, Send levels, and similar settings of each individual channel strip in sync as well. This would be rather costly in CPU resources.

By limiting the assignment of a single track for playback of everything in the Audio window, Logic ensures that each region, whether it is currently used in the song or not, will be able to play back. It also ensures that the Audio window is far more resource-efficient than if it had to use resources constantly to enable it to switch to any Audio channel, turn on new effects processing, and so on.

What you can do, of course, is manually switch the Audio channel. If you have looped playback on, playback will continue as you change Audio channels. If you change Audio channels while the Audio window is stopped, the next time you audition an Audio region, it will play back on the new channel.

Another question that arises is why Logic doesn't simply have a dedicated Audio window playback channel instead of using an Audio Track Object to play back audio. This would definitely solve the problem of how unassigned Audio regions could play, but it wouldn't allow you to audition regions in the context of the channel you intend to place them on. You can easily approximate the "dedicated playback channel" by setting the Audio window to play back on a channel that you will not otherwise use, such as channel 96. Or, since Logic defaults to using channel 1 as its playback channel, you can dedicate channel 1 as a monitor channel (personally, this is what I do). That way, you'll never need to worry about any processing interfering with your auditioning. If you want to hear a region on its assigned track, you can temporarily reassign the Audio channel to the Audio channel of the selected region, then return it to your usual monitoring track.

The Audio Window Toolbox

The Audio window, like most other windows in Logic, has its own Toolbox. It contains four tools geared to help you select and manipulate audio in the Audio window. Figure 8.9 shows you the Audio window Toolbox.

From top to bottom, these four tools are as follows:

- **Pointer.** As you would expect, the Pointer tool selects audio files and Audio regions in the Audio window. Click on the name of an audio file or Audio region in the Audio List, or on the actual region in the Audio window, in order to select it. You cannot use the pointer to "rubber band" more than one audio file or region; however, you can hold down the **SHIFT** key while making multiple selections in the Audio List to select multiple regions. You can also use the Pointer to drag audio regions to the Arrange window.

- **Grab.** This tool enables you to grab audio files and Audio regions and drag them onto tracks in the Arrange window. See "Adding Audio to the Arrange Window" below.
- **Finger.** This tool lets you to slide the boundaries of an Audio region around the audio file. If you click in the middle of a region, right and left arrows appear indicating that you can slide the entire region box around the file. If you click the pointer on either the right or left boundaries, the tool turns into a horizontal pointer allowing you to adjust that boundary. You can resize your region this way to anything from a thin sliver to an entire audio file.
- **Eraser.** This tool removes (deletes) Audio regions and audio files from the Audio window. This is the same as using the **DELETE** key.

Figure 8.9

Located under the Audio window channel, the Audio window Toolbox contains four tools to help you work in the Audio window.

Zooming in the Audio Window

The Audio window includes two Zoom horizontal sliders. These are identical to the zoom sliders in the Arrange window (and, indeed, all other windows with zoom sliders). You can also use the Zoom-related key commands if you want to zoom in or out.

Adding Audio Files to the Audio Window

Every time you record using Logic, the resulting audio file is automatically placed in the Audio window. Sometimes, however, you'll want to use audio in your song that you didn't record. If you want the audio to be in the Arrange window of your song, you can of course open an audio file from Arrange, or drag audio from the Finder to the Arrange window. Sometimes, however, you'll want to have a number of prerecorded audio files available for your song, but not placed in Arrange yet; in these circumstances, you'll need to add it to the Audio window yourself. Luckily, this is very easy to do.

The easiest way to add audio to your song is simply to drag the audio files from your desktop into your Audio window. At that point, Logic creates an overview for the file, and it appears in your Audio List like all the rest of your audio. You can select as many audio files as you want on your desktop, and when you drag them onto the Audio window, all of them will be added.

You can also use the Add Audio File command described previously. This command opens an Open File dialog box with one Logic-specific addition: a Play button. This button auditions the selected audio file on the same channel that you have selected in the Audio window Channel box. You can select one or more files to add, and when you click Open (or press **RETURN**), Logic will add any selected files to the Audio List in the Audio window.

Exporting Audio from the Audio Window

Sometimes, you may want to use an audio file you have recorded in Logic in another application. In these cases, you'll want to export your audio. The usual way to export audio is to do a bounce, which is discussed in Chapter 12, "Mixing in Logic," or to export one or more tracks, which is discussed in Chapter 13, "Working with Files." However, this section discusses a couple of options for exporting audio directly from the Audio window.

You can use the Copy/Convert commands (Copy/Convert File(s), Convert to MP3, Convert to AAC) to save your file in the same or a different format. When you select one of these commands, the resulting dialog box prompts

EXPERT TIP: EXPORTING SDII REGIONS WITH THEIR TIME STAMP

Unlike with standard AIFF or WAV files, you can export an SDII region from Logic with a time stamp. This means that you can import the file into another application and that application can read the SDII time stamp to place the audio file in the same place in time the file occupied in Arrange in Logic. This doesn't happen automatically, however; you'll need to configure Logic a bit first.

In the Arrange window of Logic, first select all the Audio regions that you want to export. Select **Convert Regions to New Regions** from the local Audio menu of the Arrange window. This not only creates separate entries in the Audio List in the Audio window for those regions, but includes the individual name and time stamp for that Audio region as well.

At this point, you can select those Audio regions in the Audio window, then choose **File > Export SDII Regions**. This command saves those selected regions to your hard drive.

Exactly what steps you follow after this command depends on the specific audio program that you are using. For example, in Logic Pro, first you would open the SDII regions, drag the imported regions to the Arrange window, and then select **Audio > Move Regions to Original Record Position**. Regardless, you next want to ensure that you have enough tracks set up in that application to accept the exported SDII regions, then import them into the new application. This application should give you some option, either in a preference box or in the import dialog box itself, to place the region according to a "user time stamp." Choose this option, and your exported Audio region should appear at the same point in the new song as it did in Logic.

you for a name and location for your file, and then exports the audio file in the format you have selected.

Sometimes, you want to export only individual Audio regions from various tracks for use in other applications. In this case, you can choose **File > Export SDII Regions** from the Audio window (or press the key command **CONTROL + E**). This command works only if you are using SDII files.

Using Strip Silence

Early in this chapter, I mentioned Strip Silence; now it's time to give this essential function a closer look. When you record an audio performance of an instrument that does not play constantly throughout the entire performance—for example, a vocal that weaves through the music, or instruments that come and go during the duration of a song—your audio file will play back with moments of silence. At best, these moments take up unnecessary CPU cycles as Logic plays and processes segments of an audio file that are empty. At worst, the portions where your instrument or vocal aren't performing aren't truly silent at all, but filled with background noise, guitar amplifier hiss, and the like. The Strip Silence command is designed to search your audio file for these segments of low-to-no audio and remove them from your song.

Strip Silence does not actually remove anything from the audio file on your hard drive. Because Logic plays Audio regions in the Arrange or Audio windows, Strip Silence divides the selected Audio region into several Audio regions, leaving out those portions in which it did not detect any audio. The command allows you to set the threshold or minimum level for audio to be considered "not silence," so you have a certain amount of control over how many new Audio regions the command will create. Figure 8.10 shows the Strip Silence window for a selected Audio region.

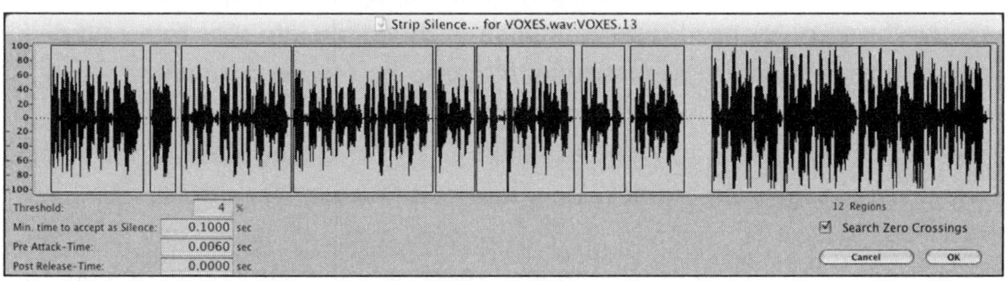

Figure 8.10
In the Strip Silence window, you can fine-tune the Strip Silence function.

The Strip Silence window gives you a number of settings:

- **Threshold.** This is the amplitude above which Strip Silence detects the audio as audio and not as silence. Logic's default value is 4 percent, which is good for removing the silence in quiet tracks. If you have a noisier performance, such as a vocal that recorded a fair amount of background noise when there was no singing, or a guitar amplifier with a loud hum or hiss when it wasn't playing, you will get better results if you set the threshold higher.
- **Min. Time to Accept as Silence.** You wouldn't want Strip Silence to detect any moment below a threshold as silence, or else Logic will split up those nanoseconds between notes into their own Audio regions! This parameter allows you to set how much time must pass before Logic detects silence. The default is 0.1 seconds, which is generally a very good setting. You might want to raise the setting if you find that Strip Silence is chopping off the decay of very quiet notes.
- **Pre Attack-Time.** This parameter ensures that Strip Silence will not cut off the attack of notes with slower amplitudes (or "rise times"). If you find that Strip Silence is cutting off your notes, raise this value.
- **Post Release-Time.** Similar to the preceding parameter, this setting is used to ensure that the decay of notes isn't removed. If you find that Strip Silence is cutting off your notes, raise this value.
- **Search Zero Crossings.** This command ensures that Logic always begins and ends Audio regions at the point that the amplitude crosses the zero line. This way, no glitches or clicks will be audible at the beginning or end of newly created regions. You'll pretty much always want this option to be checked.

As you can see, Strip Silence is a powerful tool for quickly splitting the musically relevant portions of a performance or audio file into separate Audio regions. If you want the silenced audio to also be removed from your hard drive, you can use the **Audio Files > Optimize Files** after using the Strip Silence command. You can also use this function as a creative tool. For example, you can set the Pre Attack-Time and Post Release-Time parameters specifically to cut off audio for a unique gated audio effect, or split different beats from a drum loop apart and then rearrange them to create an entirely new rhythm. Don't be afraid to experiment with Strip Silence—creativity is the name of the game, and remember, you can always undo it later!

METHOD TIP: USING STRIP SILENCE AND FOLDER TRACKS TO LOOP AUDIO

I've placed this tip in the "Working with Audio and Apple Loops" chapter instead of "The Arrange Window" chapter so as to follow the section on the Strip Silence function, but this really should be done completely in the Arrange page. Remember that the Strip Silence function appears in the Arrange window in **Audio > Strip Silence** as well as in the Audio window.

Sometimes you might want to use Strip Silence to remove the irrelevant segments of an Audio region, but still retain the ability to manipulate the result as a single region. For example, let's imagine you have a 4-bar drum performance you want to loop throughout the choruses of a song. You want to use Strip Silence to eliminate the noise between the beats, but trying to loop eight tiny Audio regions representing a part of a whole would interfere with your looping. Once again, Folder tracks to the rescue! After using Strip Silence, you can place all resulting Audio regions in an Audio T rack in the Arrange window, and then use the **Region > Folder > Pack Folder** command in Arrange to pack that track into a folder. You can now manipulate the Folder track as you would any other Arrange track.

Also, as you get more familiar with Logic, you can expand on this trick. For example, you could put each of the Audio regions on a separate track, being careful not to alter their spacing from one another. In fact, you'll find there's even an assignable key command, Tracks for Selected Objects, that is really handy for this. You would select the rightmost new region, use the key command to assign that region to a new track, then move to the previous region, select it, then use the key command to assign it to its own track, and so on. This way you would end up with each Audio region on its own track. Since each Audio region in the folder gets its own channel strip, you could have different effects on every Audio region, as well as submix the Audio regions in the Folder track (more on mixing in Chapter 12).

Using Looping in the Audio Window

As mentioned previously, you can turn on looping by clicking the Loop button on the Audio window, selecting an Audio region, then clicking on the Playback button (the one represented by the speaker icon). That Audio region will now repeat until you disengage the Playback button. This may not seem particularly useful at first, but let's look at how you can use this in tandem with the Arrange window.

If you have an Audio region in Arrange that just doesn't seem to begin and/or end where you'd like it to, and your attempts to resize it in the Arrange window are not giving you the desired results, the Audio window is your answer. If you've turned on the Link button of the Audio window, it should already have the region you're working on selected. Click the Playback button, and your region will repeat. Now select the Finger tool from the Audio window Toolbox and use it to adjust the start and end points of your Audio region. As soon as you hold the mouse button down over the edge of your region, you'll see the cursor change into the Resize cursor, same as resizing regions in Arrange. You can even use the zoom sliders (or key commands) to make the regions larger in the Audio window for more accurate dragging of start and/or end points. The Arrange window immediately reflects any changes you make, so you need not drag or move anything between windows.

Using this method to adjust regions not only can be a time saver, but if you have painstakingly set the Locators, Cycle, and/or Autodrop points in Arrange, this method gives you a way to loop the Audio region you need to adjust without affecting any other aspect of your Arrange window setup. Give it a try—you'll find using looping in the Audio window is a great way to resize individual Audio regions.

Audio Window Groups

New in Logic Pro 7 is the ability to organize audio files into groups inside the Audio window. You'll find this to be a great organizational help if you have lots of different types of audio material. For example, you could create one group called Guitars, one called Drums, one called Synths, and so on, and use this to keep your audio files organized within the Audio window.

Creating groups in the Audio window couldn't be easier. Simply select those audio files (not regions representing segments of a larger file, but regions representing a complete file) in the Audio window that you wish to group together and then select the Create Groups command. A text box will appear for you to name the new group, and the selected audio files will be placed inside it. You can also use the Create Groups command without any audio files selected in the Audio window, and then simply drag audio files into the group later. Finally, Logic Pro 7 can automatically group your audio files together by their location on your hard drive, their file attributes, or it can group those files selected in Arrange with the group files by command (if you already have groups created, you will be prompted if you want them to be deleted).

The names of Audio file groups will be italicized, and the Audio List will identify the group as an Audio file group (if you double-click this text, however, you can add your own comment). Figure 8.11 shows an Audio window with two Audio file groups created.

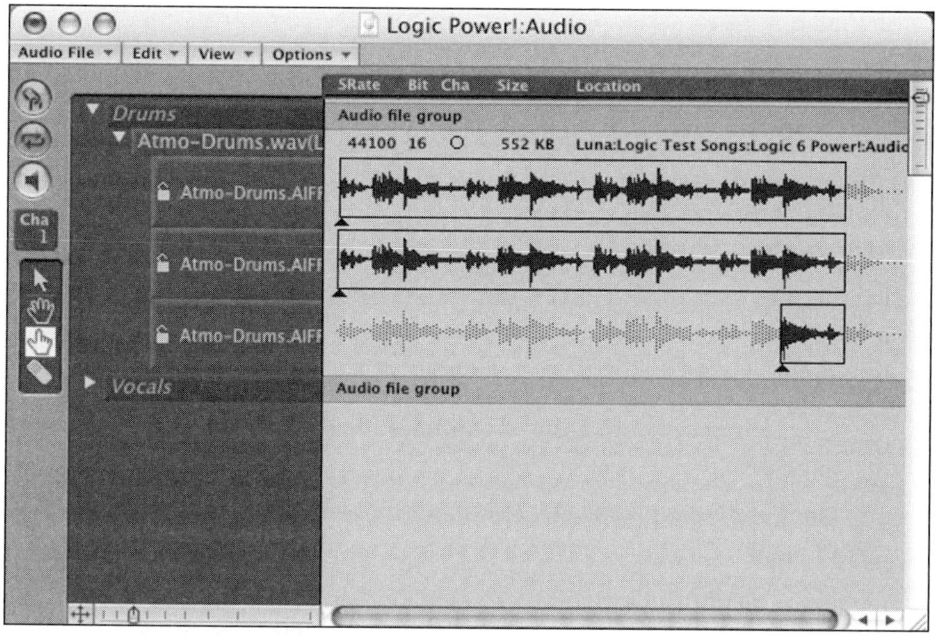

Figure 8.11
This Audio window has two Audio file groups: Drums and Vocals. You can see the Audio regions in the expanded drums group; the Vocals group has been collapsed, so its audio files are not displayed.

You can open and close Audio file groups by clicking on their expansion triangle. You can also **OPTION + CLICK** on a group triangle to open or close all groups. You can **OPTION + CLICK** on a group name to select all the files in that group.

Keep in mind that Audio file groups are strictly organizational groups. Grouping audio files does not affect their location on your hard drive, their use in the Arrange window, and so on.

Adding Audio to the Arrange Window

The Audio window is a great organizational and processing window for audio, but to actually use your audio in a song, you'll need to add it to the Arrange window. You can do this by either selecting one or more Audio regions and dragging them to the Arrange window, or by using the Add Audio File(s) to Arrange command.

If you use the Add Audio File(s) to Arrange command, or drag multiple audio files/regions from the Audio window (or the Finder) to Arrange, you will be prompted with the dialog window shown in Figure 8.12 so that you can instruct Logic how to handle the Audio region(s).

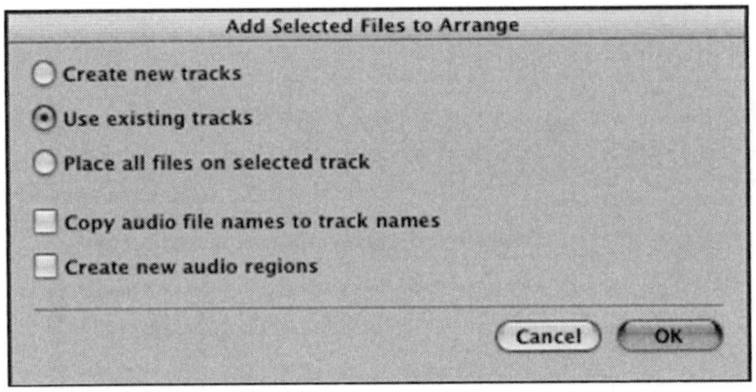

Figure 8.12
The Add Selected Files to Arrange dialog.

Depending on your radio button and/or check mark selections, Logic Pro will

- Create a new Audio Track in Arrange for each Audio region you wish to add.
- Use the existing Audio Tracks on Arrange and add one Audio region to each.
- Place all the Audio regions you are adding to Arrange on the selected Audio Track.
- Copy the names of the audio files to the track names.
- Create brand new Audio regions in the Audio window for each region you are adding to Arrange.

As you can see, Logic makes adding audio from the Audio window to the Arrange window simple and intuitive, as well as giving you plenty of options to make sure it handles the audio the way you want it to.

The Sample Editor

Sometimes, resizing or editing Audio regions won't be enough; you'll want to alter the audio data itself permanently. This is where the Sample Editor comes in. The Sample Editor operates on the actual data in the audio file. This means that the Sample Editor's edits are *destructive*, because they forever alter the contents of the file, unlike edits to Audio regions, which are *nondestructive*, meaning that the audio data itself is never touched. Figure 8.13 shows the Sample Editor window.

Double-clicking any Audio region in either the Arrange or the Audio window launches the Sample Editor with that region already inside the Waveform overview and detailed Waveform Display. You can also launch the Sample

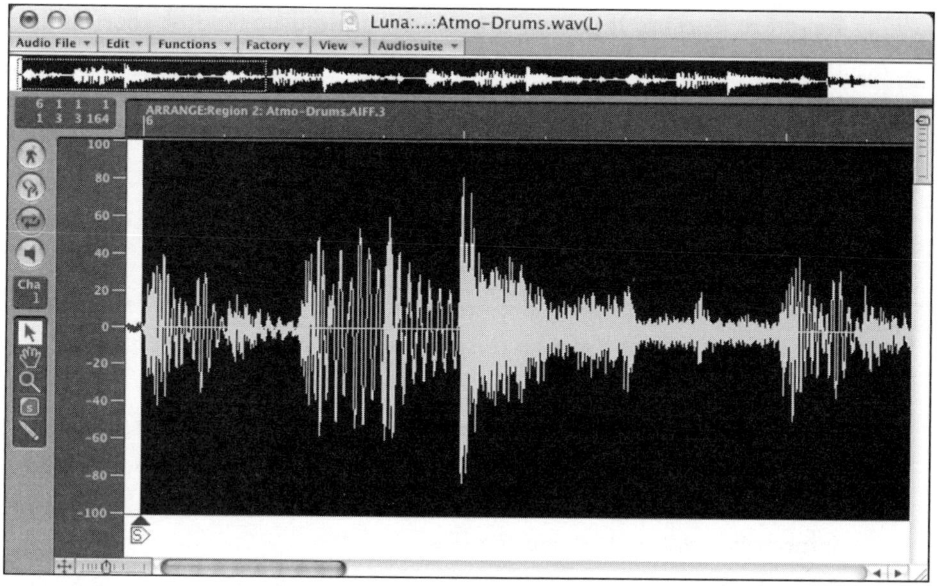

Figure 8.13
The Sample Editor window.

Editor by choosing **Audio > Sample Editor** or by pressing the key command (the default is **COMMAND + 0**).

As with the other windows, I'll start with a discussion of the Sample Editor's local menus.

Local Menus

The local menus provide file, editing, and processing commands specific to the Sample Editor. A description of the local menus follows.

The Audio File Menu

This menu contains the file operations that are possible from the Sample Editor. Figure 8.14 shows the Audio File local menu of the Sample Editor.

Figure 8.14
The Audio File menu of the Sample Editor.

An explanation of the commands follows:

- **Create Backup.** Because the actions that you make in the Sample Editor are permanent, you may want to make a backup of your file, so that if you do something you don't like, you still have your original audio. **<COMMAND + B>**

- **Revert to Backup.** If you've previously made a backup of your audio file, this command replaces your current processed and edited audio file with the backup. You can use this command if you've made a backup and are not happy with the changes you've made to your audio file. **<COMMAND + SHIFT + B>**
- **Save a Copy As.** You can create a copy of audio file using this command.
- **Save Selection As.** Using this command, you can save only the portion of your file that you have selected with your mouse. **<SHIFT + COMMAND + S>**
- **Update File Information.** This updates the information that Logic has stored for the file you are editing. The normal file-saving routine performs this updating, but you can use this command to update the file information without saving the file.
- **Refresh Overview(s).** This command refreshes the Waveform overview of the Audio region you are editing in the Sample Editor.

The Edit Menu

The Edit menu contains functions that involve the selection and manipulation of audio and Audio regions. Figure 8.15 shows the local Edit menu of the Sample Editor.

The following are details about the commands in this menu:

- **Undo.** This command undoes the last action made to your audio in the Sample Editor. You can have as many levels of undo as you set in the **Preferences > Audio > Sample Editor tab.** **<COMMAND + Z>**
- **Redo.** This command will redo the last undone action in the Sample Editor. Note that the Sample Editor Undo and Redo functions are unique to the Sample Editor (meaning you can't undo an Arrange action in the Sample Editor, while in a MIDI editor for example, Undo will include windows outside the MIDI editor).
- **Cut.** This command removes a selected area of audio and places it on the Clipboard. **<COMMAND + X>**
- **Copy.** This command copies a selected area of audio and places it on the Clipboard. **<COMMAND + C>**

- **Paste.** This command pastes audio from the Clipboard at the current Locator position. <**COMMAND + V**>
- **Clear.** This command removes the selected audio from your audio file.
- **Select All.** This command selects your entire audio file. <**COMMAND + A**>
- **Region > Selection.** This command selects the entire Audio region that you are currently editing. <**SHIFT + R**>
- **Selection > Region.** This command replaces the original Audio region that you are editing with the selected audio. <**SHIFT + COMMAND + R**>.

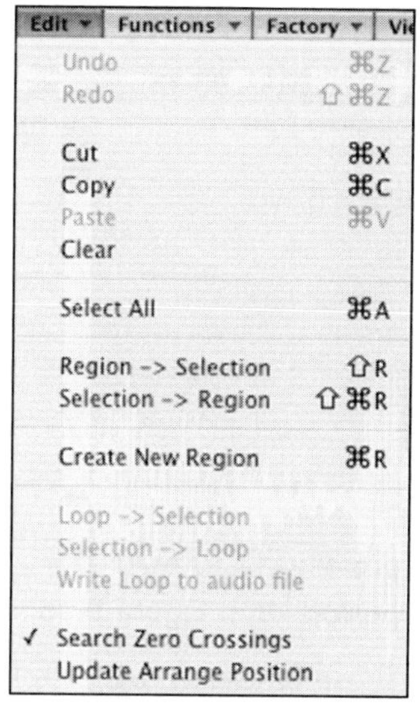

Figure 8.15
The Edit menu of the Sample Editor.

- **Create New Region.** This creates a new Audio region from your current selection. The original Audio region you are editing remains unchanged.
- **Loop > Selection.** This function turns a loop you have loaded into the Sample Editor from Emagic's EXS24 Sampler into a normal audio selection that you can edit.
- **Selection > Loop.** This turns a selection of audio into a loop for use with Emagic's EXS24 Sampler.
- **Write Loop to Audio File.** This command saves an audio file from the contents of an EXS24 loop.
- **Search Zero Crossings.** You learned about zero crossings earlier in this chapter. If you select this command, Logic always looks for the point at which the amplitude crosses the zero mark while you are editing. This is to ensure glitch- and click-free playback, but it might restrict you from making edits at the exact location you want.
- **Update Arrange Position.** With this command engaged, the left boundary of an Audio region will stay fixed in the Arrange window regardless of any changes you make to an Audio region in the Sample Editor. If this is not engaged, anchor points will remain fixed in the Audio regions in Arrange.

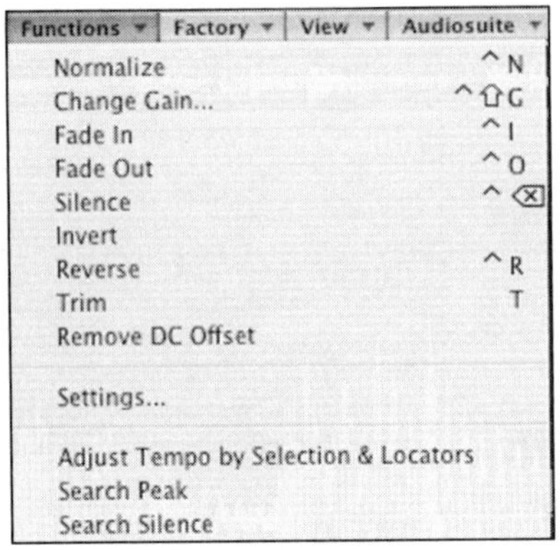

Figure 8.16
The Functions menu of the Sample Editor.

The Functions Menu

The Functions menu consists of Sample Editor functions that process your audio in one way or another. These processes are destructive, so you should definitely back up your audio before using them. These functions only operate on the area of your Audio region that is selected. If you want to process your entire file, be sure to choose **Edit > Select All** first. You can generally cancel any process in progress by pressing **COMMAND + .** (that is, press **COMMAND** in combination with the period key). Figure 8.16 shows the Functions menu of the Sample Editor.

These functions are as follows:

- **Normalize.** To "normalize" audio means to increase its level as much as possible without changing the dynamics or distorting the audio file. Logic does this by finding the loudest point in the currently selected audio, determining its distance from the maximum attainable level for the audio passage, and then increasing the audio for the entire selection to that level. This way, the dynamics are preserved, the audio is not maximized to the point it distorts, and the entire selection is louder by a specified amount. You can set the desired maximum level in the Settings dialog box. **<CONTROL + N>**
- **Change Gain.** This command raises or lowers the level of the selected audio by a specified amount. You can determine this amount in the dialog box that appears when you select this command. You can choose to change the gain by either inputting a percentage of the current level or entering absolute decibels. If you click Search Maximum, Logic finds the highest peak in the selection and calculates how much it can safely raise the gain (much as it does with the Normalize function). You can also view the Results in Absolute, which shows you an absolute value rather than a percentage. Keep in mind that if you raise the gain more than 100 percent, you will clip your file, producing a very nonmusical digital clipping. **<CONTROL + SHIFT + G>**
- **Fade In.** This allows you to create a destructive fade-in at the front of your selection. This is in contrast to creating a fade-in on Arrange, which only affects how the Audio region is played back and is

nondestructive. You can adjust the curves of the fade-out in the Settings dialog box. **<CONTROL + I>**.

- **Fade Out.** With this command, you can create a destructive fade-out at the end of your selection. This contrasts with creating a fade-out on Arrange, which only affects how the Audio region is played back and is nondestructive. You can adjust the curve of the fade-out in the Settings dialog box. **<CONTROL + O>**
- **Silence.** Silence removes all audio data inside your selection. **<CONTROL + DELETE>**
- **Invert.** This inverts the phase of the audio selection. In other words, what originally was the peak of the amplitude of the waveform becomes the bottom, and so on. This command doesn't affect the sound, but can help fix phase cancellation problems with your audio file that become apparent during mixing.
- **Reverse.** This command reverses the audio in your selection (in other words, the audio plays backward). **<CONTROL + R>**
- **Trim.** Trim erases any area of the current region you haven't selected. Make sure you don't delete any areas that you'll need for your song! If you try to trim away portions of a region you are using in the Arrange window, a warning screen appears asking you to confirm that you want to do so. **<T>**
- **Remove DC Offset.** When you are using lower-quality audio hardware, often stray direct current (DC) is layered over your audio signal, which causes the waveform to look like it's not centered around the zero line, but shifted vertically up or down. This can cause crackling and artifacts at the beginning and end of Audio regions. This command removes the effect of DC and centers the audio around the zero bar.
- **Settings.** Settings isn't a function itself, but rather a dialog box of parameters for other functions. Figure 8.17 shows the Function Settings dialog box.

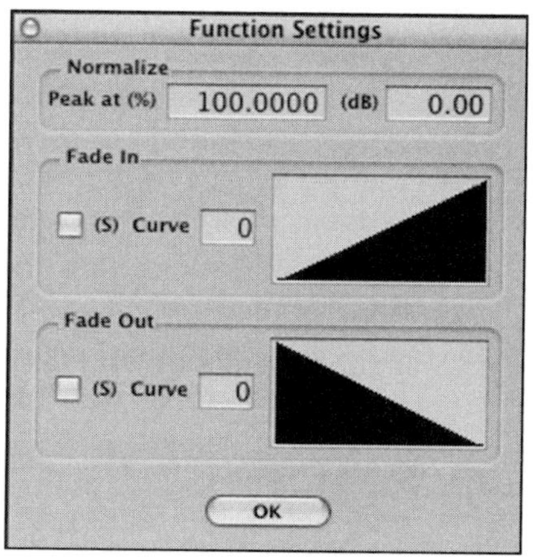

Figure 8.17
The Function Settings dialog box offers settings for the Normalize, Fade In, and Fade Out functions.

Here you can set the maximum value to which you want the Normalize function to increase the selection's level, either as a percentage of the maximum amplitude or in decibels. The dialog box also presents options to adjust the curves for the Fade In and Fade Out functions. If you check their boxes and adjust the curve value from –100 to +100, the graphic display changes to illustrate the current shape of the curve.

- **Adjust Tempo by Selection & Locators.** This command adjusts the tempo of your audio by stretching or compressing it to fit the length of the current Locator positions. This is very similar to the Arrange option to Adjust Object Length by Locators, except that in Arrange, the function operates on Audio regions, whereas in the Sample Editor, the command works on the tempo.
- **Search Peak.** If you select this, Logic searches the currently selected audio for the sample with the greatest amplitude value, and centers the cursor in the Waveform Display around this point.
- **Search Silence.** With this option, Logic searches the currently selected audio for silence, and places the cursor at the start of the first section of silence detected.

The Factory Menu

Most of the options on the Factory menu allow you to choose one of the available functions in the Digital Factory, Logic's built-in audio processing tool. The remaining options in the Factory menu are functions from the Quantize Engine. All of these operations are destructive. Figure 8.18 shows the Factory menu.

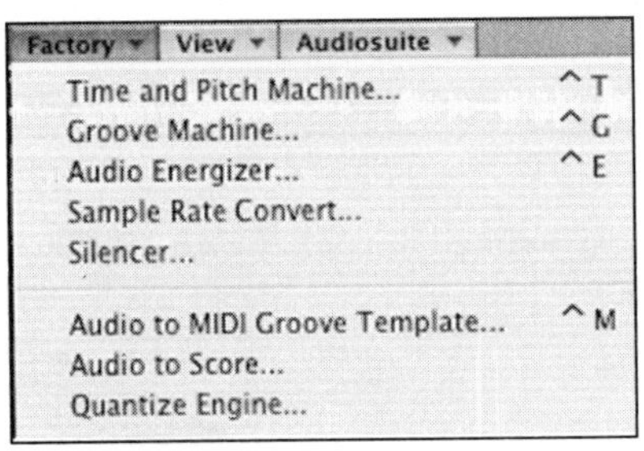

Figure 8.18
The Factory menu of the Sample Editor.

The Digital Factory and Quantize Engine are both given individual subsections later in this chapter. However, the contents of the Factory menu are described briefly here:

- **Time and Pitch Machine.** The Time and Pitch Machine enables you to independently adjust the tempo and pitch of your selected audio. **<CONTROL + T>**
- **Groove Machine.** This allows you to "regroove," or alter the rhythm and feel of your audio. **<CONTROL + G>**

- **Audio Energizer.** The Audio Energizer attempts to raise the perceived loudness of audio. **<CONTROL + E>**
- **Sample Rate Convert.** This allows you to convert the sample rate of the selected audio to a different sample rate.
- **Silencer.** The Silencer, which is the last component of the Digital Factory on this local menu, allows you to reduce the level of noise and/or volume spikes (such as pops or clicks) in your audio.
- **Audio to MIDI Grove Template.** This powerful feature allows you to extract the rhythm and feel of an audio selection for use as a "groove template" that you can apply to MIDI notes. **<CONTROL + M>**
- **Audio to Score.** Audio to Score works best using a mono audio file with monophonic content (audio content that includes only one note at a time, such as a vocal, horn, kazoo, and so on). Audio to Score converts that audio data into MIDI data. You can use this MIDI data in the Score Editor or as another MIDI region in Arrange assigned to a MIDI Instrument or Audio Instrument.
- **Quantize Engine.** This attempts to lock your specific points you specify in your audio file to a quantize grid, just as MIDI quantize locks MIDI notes to a grid.

The View Menu

The View menu offers you a number of options for changing the units of measurement on the Waveform Display and the way the audio wave itself is displayed. Figure 8.19 shows you the View menu of the Sample Editor.

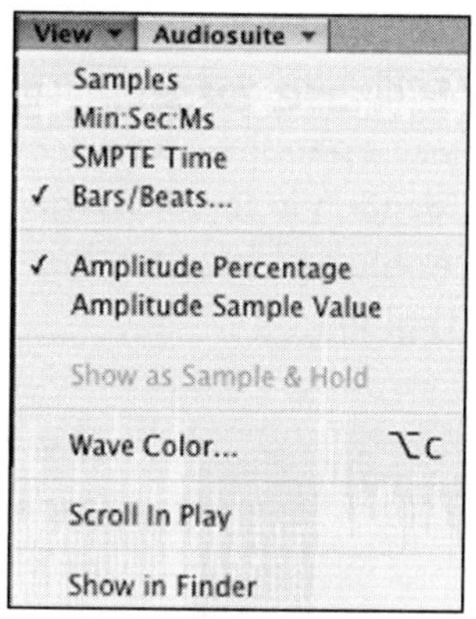

Figure 8.19

The View menu of the Sample Editor.

The Samples, Min:Sec:Ms, SMPTE Time, and Bars/Beats options determine the units that the Bar Ruler displays. The Samples option displays the actual number of the sample or the samples you are currently viewing. Min:Sec:Ms shows the elapsed time on the Bar Ruler. SMPTE Time displays the SMPTE position, and Bars/Beats shows the musical location of the audio. By choosing **View > Amplitude Percentage** or **View > Amplitude Sample Value**, you can specify whether the vertical axis of the Waveform Display measures the amplitude of the audio wave as a percentage of the maximum amplitude, or as a number of samples.

A few more options determine how a waveform will be displayed. Show as Sample & Hold displays the actual data structure of the waveform (that is, the wave appears blocky, not rounded). This is very useful if you are using the Pencil tool to remove pops and clicks (see the section "The Sample Editor Toolbox" later in this chapter). Wave Color brings up the now-familiar color palette, where you can assign a color to your waveform. Scroll in Play moves the audio file past a stationary SPL, instead of moving the SPL across your audio file. Finally, Show in Finder opens a Finder window displaying the location on your hard drive of the audio file being edited.

The Audiosuite Menu

This local menu is only of interest if you are using Digidesign hardware and the DAE audio engine. It allows Audiosuite plug-ins to be applied destructively in the Sample Editor. If you have any Audiosuite plug-ins, they will appear here. If you don't (as most users will not), then simply ignore this menu. Refer to your plug-in's manual for how to apply any specific Audiosuite process.

The Sample Editor Region Locators Display

Below the local menus is a position display that shows you the start point and length of the Audio region in the Sample Editor using the unit display you selected in the local View menu above. You obviously cannot place Audio regions graphically using the Sample Editor, only numerically. When you open the Sample Editor from Arrange, the Bar Ruler reflects the region's location in the Arrange window; when you open the Sample Editor from the Audio window, the Bar Ruler instead measures from the start of the Audio region.

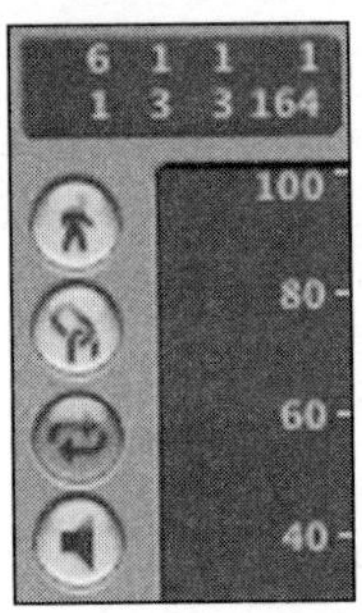

Figure 8.20

The Sample Editor buttons.

The Sample Editor Mode Buttons

Under the Region Locators display are the Sample Editor's four mode buttons. Figure 8.20 shows the Sample Editor buttons under the Region Locators display and the Sample Editor Channel.

The functions of the Sample Editor buttons are as follows:

- **Catch Mode.** The "walking man" button enables Catch mode. If this button is lit, the Sample Editor is linked to the current song position. If there is no audio, the SPL simply stops at the end of the Audio region.
- **Link Mode.** This button enables Link mode. This means that the Audio region selected in the Arrange window also appears in the Sample Editor.
- **Cycle Playback Mode.** If you enable Cycle Playback mode, playback of the selected portion of audio repeats continuously if the Playback button is also enabled.
- **Playback Mode.** The speaker icon represents Playback mode. If the Cycle Playback button is also enabled, Logic will continuously play back your selection from start to finish. If the Cycle Playback button is not also enabled, it will play through your selected audio one time. If the Playback button is not enabled, your selection will not play back.

The Sample Editor Channel Window

Like the Audio window, the Sample Editor always auditions the audio in the Sample Editor through one preselected channel (the same preselected channel as the Audio window). The Channel window is directly below the mode buttons, and you can change it by dragging the mouse up or down or by entering text directly. You should choose an unused track, usually one with a very high number. You may want to use the same track you use for auditioning audio in the Audio window, and simply consider that track to be your auditioning track.

The Sample Editor Toolbox

Under the Channel window is the Toolbox containing the five tools available to you in the Sample Editor. Figure 8.21 shows the Sample Editor Toolbox.

Figure 8.21
The Sample Editor Toolbox.

A description of how each tool functions in the Sample Editor follows:

- **Pointer Tool.** Drag the Pointer tool across the audio in the Waveform Display to select audio.
- **Move Tool.** The hand represents the Move tool. This tool allows you to reposition a selection box (made previously with the pointer) to the right or left.

- **Magnifying Glass Tool.** Drag the selection "rubber band" over a portion of audio to increase the magnification of the selected audio down to the single-sample level. Double-click anywhere outside the magnified selection to return the selection to its original zoom resolution. If you have already used the Zoom rectangles or key commands to zoom in on your audio, this tool has no further effect.
- **Scrub Tool.** This tool will scrub (play back slowly) a selection of audio.
- **Pencil Tool.** This tool will allow you to redraw the audio waveform. The main use for this tool is to smooth out sudden sharp peaks in your audio, as these sudden sharp peaks are usually pops or clicks. This tool works well in tandem with Show as Sample & Hold, which enables you to see exactly which samples are peaking. Be very careful when redrawing waveforms, however—if you don't know what you are doing, you are likely to redraw a waveform incorrectly and compromise the sound of your audio.

The Waveform Display

The main feature of the Sample Editor is the Waveform Display. This is the main window you use to edit your audio in the Sample Editor. You can use the Zoom rectangles in the top-right of the Sample Editor (as well as key commands) to zoom in and out on your audio, and display and edit your Audio region down to single-sample accuracy.

Beneath your audio on the Waveform Display are three important positions on your audio waveform: the *start point,* which is represented by an *S* in a pointer, the *end point,* represented by an *E* in a pointer; and the *anchor point,* represented by a black triangle. Figure 8.22 shows a waveform with the start, anchor, and end points clearly visible.

The anchor point represents the first musically relevant point on which you want the Audio region to pivot. It is the anchor point that gets placed at a specific time position when you drag regions around the Arrange window. For example, if your Audio region begins with a fade-in, you might want to place the anchor point at the end of the fade-in, so that the audio past the fade-in falls exactly on the bar as you move the region in the Arrange window.

As you use the Digital Factory or otherwise process or edit your audio, the Waveform Display reflects your changes. Use the Bar Ruler to ensure that the Audio region is still positioned where you want it to be as you process and edit your audio.

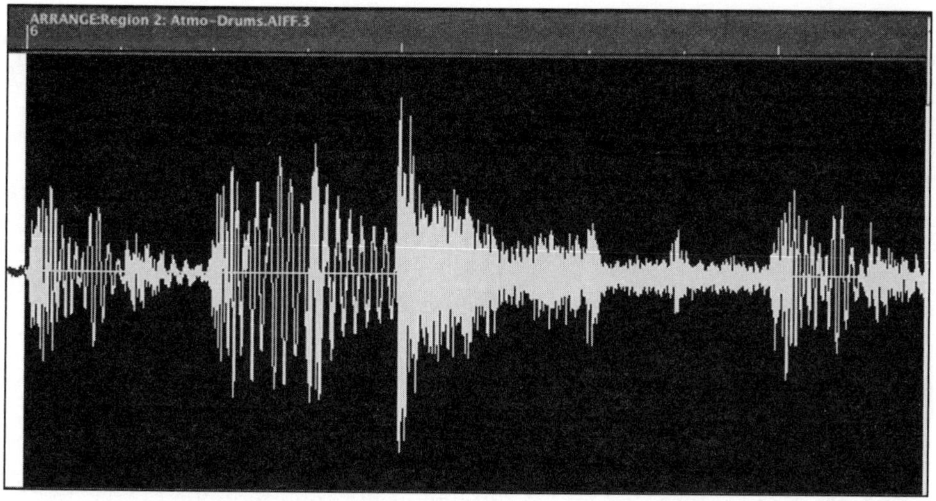

Figure 8.22
The Waveform Display of the Sample Editor. Notice the start, anchor, and end points of the Audio region under the waveform.

The Digital Factory

The Digital Factory is a repository of destructive offline processes that Logic offers to process audio. As the local Functions menu illustrated, five different processes compose the Digital Factory: the Time and Pitch Machine, the Groove Machine, the Audio Energizer, Sample Rate Converter, and the Silencer. Each of these components is detailed in this section.

Time and Pitch Machine

The Time and Pitch Machine can change the tempo of audio by stretching or compressing that audio. In fact, when you stretch and compress audio in the Arrange window, you are technically invoking the tempo-adjusting function of the Time and Pitch Machine. When you access the Time and Pitch Machine from the Sample Editor, you can also transpose audio up or down in pitch. You can link these functions together, or they can be independent. Figure 8.23 shows the Time and Pitch Machine dialog box.

The left of the dialog box is taken up with a three-dimensional graph with Tempo, Timbre, and Pitch on the X, Y, and Z axes respectively. The graph has a sphere representing the current settings of the Time and Pitch Machine. You can adjust most of the settings by dragging the ball in the graph.

If you know the specific numeric values you want to use for your parameters, however, you can enter those numbers in the parameters to the right. Most parameters include a text box for the original (current) value of the audio, and a text box to input the desired new value. Any changes you make in text

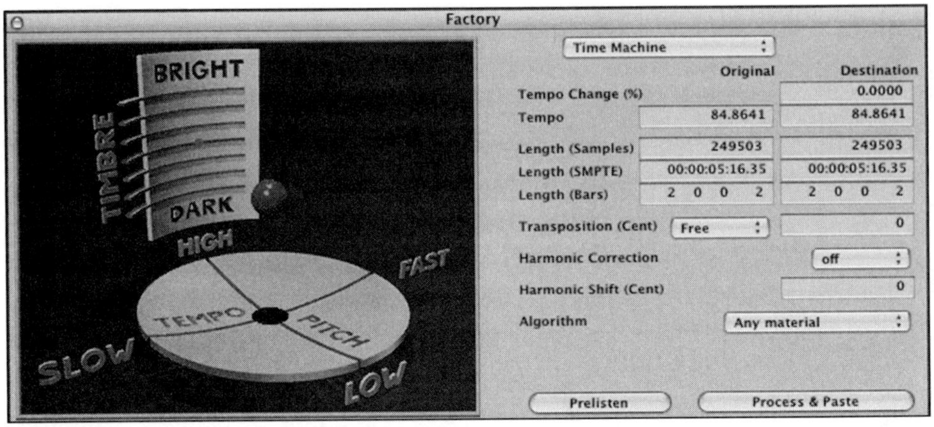

Figure 8.23
You can access the Time and Pitch Machine via the Sample Editor.

boxes are also represented by the position of the sphere on the graph. The parameters are as follows:

- **Tempo Change (%).** This parameter tells you how drastic your tempo change will be by giving you the percentage of change from the original tempo. For example, if the tempo of your original Audio Track was 120BPM and you change the tempo to 240BPM, the parameter will indicate a 100 percent tempo change. Logic will not increase the tempo more than twice the original value (100 percent) or reduce the tempo by more than half (–50 percent).
- **Tempo.** The Original box lists the current tempo of your audio. You can input a new tempo in the Destination box. The new tempo can be as much as twice the current tempo or as little as half the current tempo.
- **Length (Samples).** This is the exact length of the audio in samples. If you know exactly how many samples you want your processed audio to be, you can enter that value in the Destination box. You cannot adjust the number of samples so drastically that the result would be beyond the boundaries of the tempo restrictions mentioned for the Tempo setting (no more than half or double the original tempo).
- **Length (SMPTE).** The length of your audio in SMPTE frames is listed here. If you know exactly how many SMPTE frames you want your processed audio to be, you can enter that value in the Destination box. You cannot adjust the SMPTE frames beyond the boundaries of the Tempo setting's restrictions (no more than half or double the original tempo).

* **Length (Bars).** This is perhaps the most musically useful setting, and the closest to the way the Time Machine is used in the Arrange window. Here you see how long your audio is in bars. You can enter the number of bars you want your audio to be in the Destination box. Again, you cannot adjust the bar length beyond the Tempo setting's restrictions (no more than half or double the original tempo.
* **Transpose (Cent).** Now you are getting into the transposition settings that affect *pitch*, not tempo. First, Logic offers a pull-down menu from which you can select to transpose in Free or Classic mode. *Free* mode indicates that tempo and pitch adjustments are independent. *Classic* mode means that pitch and tempo are adjusted together, like an old tape machine, which gets higher in pitch when the tape speeds up, and lower in pitch as the tape slows down. The text-entry box allows you to enter the number of *cents*, or hundredths of a semitone by which you want to adjust your audio. Positive numbers raise the pitch, whereas negative numbers reduce the pitch.
* **Harmonic Correction.** As you adjust the pitch of audio, its *formants* (timbre) are also changed. This means that not only the pitch of the audio changes, but the sonic character of the sound as well. If you turn on harmonic correction, Logic attempts to adjust the harmonics of the pitched audio so that the formants remain the same as the original audio. If Harmonic Correction is off, Logic makes no such correction, and the formants change along with the pitch.
* **Harmonic Shift (Cent).** If you activate Harmonic Correction, you can use Harmonic Shift to adjust the formants of the audio independently. A Harmonic Shift setting of 0 means that Logic will attempt to keep your formants in the pitched audio identical to the original audio. If you input any other number, Logic shifts the formants by that number, regardless of the Transpose (Cent) setting. In fact, you can choose to only alter the formants of audio by not transposing the audio at all, but turning on Harmonic Correction and inputting a value for Harmonic Shift. This value is also adjusted in cents (hundredths of a semitone).
* **Algorithm.** This selects which algorithm the Time and Pitch Machine uses to adjust the tempo of the audio. These options are already detailed in "The Time Machine Algorithm Submenu" section in Chapter 7, "The Arrange Window."

Because using the Time and Pitch Machine is a destructive process, Logic offers a Prelisten button to the left of the Process & Paste button. Prelisten gives you a sample of what your new audio will sound like before you commit to processing your audio and pasting the newly processed audio into your song. Once you process and paste your audio into your song, you cannot undo it after you continue working on your song (the Sample Editor has only one level of Undo), so it's important to have a clear idea of what you want before you process your audio.

The Groove Machine

The Groove Machine allows you to "regroove" or change the feel of your audio by adjusting the level and placement of the up and down beats. Figure 8.24 shows the Groove Machine.

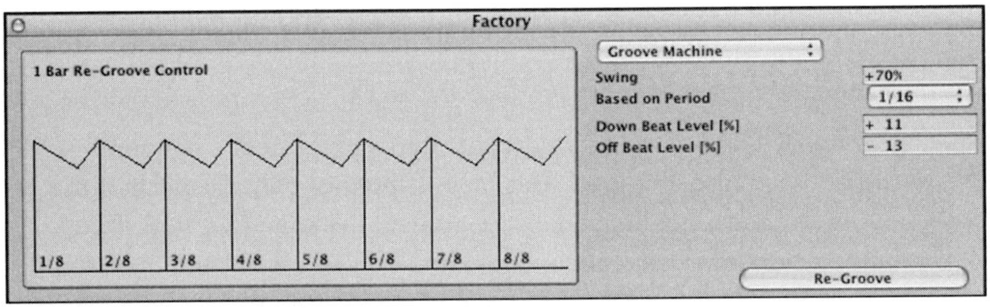

Figure 8.24
The Groove Machine, part of the Digital Factory of the Sample Editor.

The left of the Groove Machine offers you a graphic representation of how the changes are affecting your audio. The parameters of the Groove Machine are as follows:

- **Swing.** This allows you to adjust how far from the beat the change in level occurs. A value of 50 percent means the level change occurs directly on the beat, and you can adjust the value to +70 percent from that value. In general, subtler settings are most useful.
- **Based on Period.** You can choose whether the regroove will be based on eighth notes or 16th notes. Select the period most relevant to your audio material.
- **Down Beat Level (%).** This allows you to raise or lower the level of the down beat (the beat on the bar) from –100 percent to +100 percent.
- **Off Beat Level (%).** This setting allows you to raise or lower the level of the off beat (the beat between the bar) from –100 percent to +100 percent.

The Audio Energizer

The Audio Energizer attempts to raise the perceived loudness of audio by reducing the distance between the peaks and valleys in the audio wave, resulting in audio with less dynamic range but more consistent loudness. This is the same idea as that of the maximizer and loudness maximizer plug-ins that work in realtime in Logic's mixer. Figure 8.25 shows the Audio Energizer dialog box.

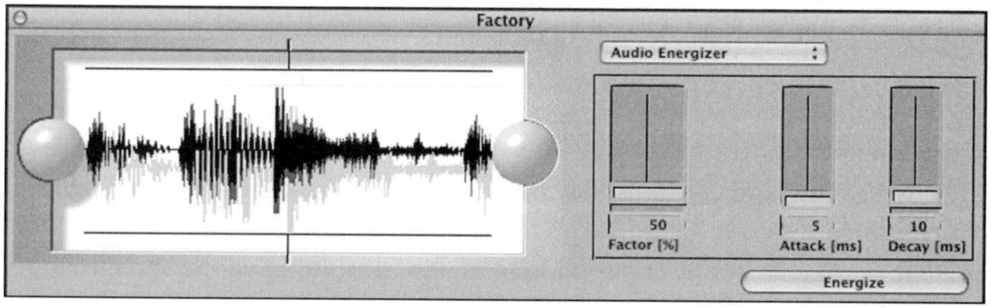

Figure 8.25
The Audio Energizer of the Digital Factory.

The Audio Energizer has only three parameters, and the display to the left of them shows you graphically what adjustments are being done to the audio waveform. The parameters are as follows:

- **Factor [%].** Factor is the main parameter. This is the average level boost. High values flatten out your audio at the maximum possible amplitude for the waveform. Lower values have little effect.
- **Attack [ms].** This affects the steepness of the effect's onset. Low values mean a very quick, steep onset of the Energizer. High values result in a more gradual ramp up.
- **Decay[ms].** This affects the steepness of the effect's release. Low values stop the Energizer's effect very abruptly after making an adjustment. High values result in a gradual decline of the effect.

Since realtime limiters and maximizers that you can insert in the channel strips of your audio offer more control and are nondestructive processes, you will most likely not find yourself using the Audio Energizer often, if at all.

Sample Rate Conversion

Selecting the Sample Rate Convert option of the Digital Factory opens a new dialog box that simply presents a text entry box containing the original sample rate of your audio, and another box for the destination sample rate.

When you choose Convert, Logic converts the sample rate. This option is mostly useful when you have a song at a particular sample rate, such as 44.1kHz, and you import an audio file at a higher sample rate. The Sample Rate Convert function gives you a quick way to change the sample rate from within Logic.

Converting the sample rate often leaves artifacts and degrades the sound quality, whether you are increasing or decreasing the sample rate. Luckily, Logic Pro 7 added a world-class sample rate conversion algorithm to Logic. Even so, be careful when converting sample rates, because even the best algorithm doesn't always work well on all source material.

The Silencer

You can use the Silencer to reduce noise and audio spikes destructively. It offers selector buttons for adjusting the strength of each function, and another parameter for configuring how gentle or aggressive the spike reduction will be. Figure 8.26 shows the Silencer.

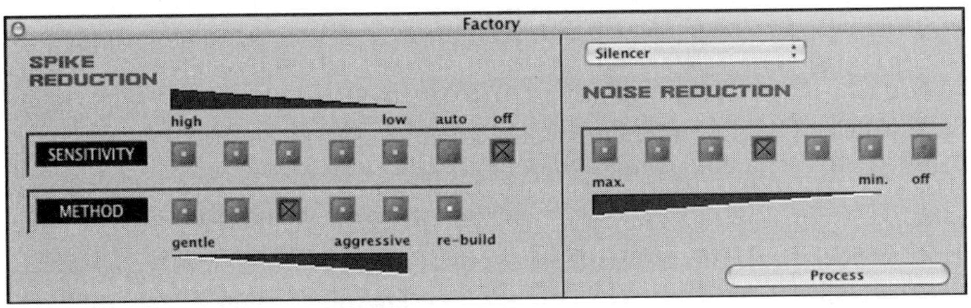

Figure 8.26
The Silencer, the final function of the Digital Factory.

Simply click the button representing the level of noise or spike reduction you want, and choose how gently or aggressively the spike reduction algorithm should be in detecting noise. If you choose values too low, the Silencer might not have a noticeable effect. If you choose values too high, you risk adversely affecting your audio.

Logic's Silencer is convenient and of acceptable quality, but there are many plug-ins and stand-alone applications devoted to high-quality noise and spike reduction. If you find yourself doing a significant amount of noise reduction, you would be best served by using one of those applications, such as TC Electronic's Restoration Bundle for the TC PowerCore card, Bias's Sound Soap Pro, or Waves' Restoration Suite.

The Quantize Engine

The Quantize Engine, beyond simply offering quantization (locking the timing to a grid), offers functions that relate to the interaction and interchanging of audio and MIDI. There are three options: Audio to MIDI Groove Template, Audio to Score, and the Quantize Engine. Each of these is described in its own subsection.

The Audio to MIDI Groove Template

This function takes the rhythm and feel of an Audio Track and creates a Groove Template to superimpose that feel onto MIDI data. To use this feature, you'll need a one-bar drum part displayed in the Sample Editor. (You can either have recorded one bar of drums, or used Add Audio File in the Audio window to add a one-bar drum file.) Then select **Factory > Audio to MIDI Groove Template**. When you select this command, the dialog box shown in Figure 8.27 appears.

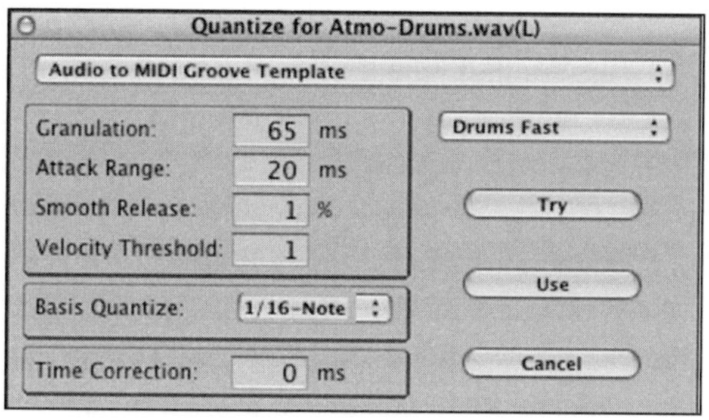

Figure 8.27
The Audio to MIDI Groove Template dialog box. Adjust these parameters to capture more accurately the rhythm of your audio selection.

You use the first four parameters on the left that appear in their own box to set the analysis algorithm:

- **Granulation.** To make a Groove Template, Logic must analyze segments of your audio. This parameter determines the length in milliseconds of the slices that Logic will use to derive "velocity points" in the Groove Template. How long you want to set this depends on the tempo of your audio, and how distinct each beat and rhythmic element in your audio is. More distinct and loud elements do not require as much time to analyze, but softer or less distinct elements do. Generally, you'll want to keep this parameter between 50 and 200 milliseconds.

- **Attack Range.** Use this setting to specify the length of the attack times (in milliseconds) of the audio's rhythmic elements. Generally, drums and percussion have very short attack times (1ms to 10ms), and other instruments have longer attack times (10 ms to 40 ms).
- **Smooth Release.** This smoothes out the analyzed release times of instruments with long fades, which generally don't make as good Groove Templates as instruments with short decay times.
- **Velocity Threshold.** Logic ignores any sound whose value falls below that which you set in the Velocity Threshold parameter. In general, you want to raise this from the default 1 only if you have very loud material and want Logic to ignore the background noise.

You use the remaining parameters to fine-tune the MIDI Groove Template created by the analysis algorithm that the preceding settings generated:

- **Basic Quantize.** This is a pull-down menu that contains all of Logic's usual MIDI quantization options. You can select one of these to ensure that your Groove Template has a standard groove as a basis, in addition to any audio hits that are saved to the Groove Template.
- **Time Delay.** You can use this setting to compensate for any noticeable delay when playing MIDI tracks or Multichannel Audio Instruments. Compensating for delay is addressed in more detail in Chapter 12, "Mixing in Logic."
- **Instrument Type.** The Audio to MIDI Groove Template dialog box comes with a number of presets for different types of material. This pull-down menu contains a list of those parameters.

As you adjust the parameters of the Audio to MIDI Groove Template window (or any of the Audio Quantize functions of the Digital Factory), you will notice your settings being reflected in a quantize ruler that appears below the Waveform Display in the Sample Editor, as shown in Figure 8.28.

If you click Try, Logic applies your MIDI Groove Template to any selected MIDI regions so you can audition your new template. If you like the template, you can click Use to save your Groove Template and install it in the current song. You can now access your Groove Template from Arrange in the Quantize pull-down menu in the parameter box of MIDI regions and MIDI Objects.

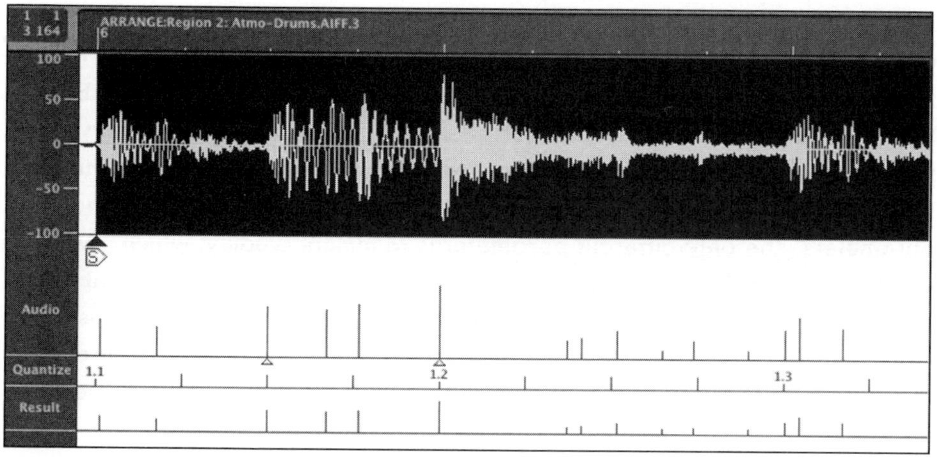

Figure 8.28

The Audio Quantize ruler above appears below your audio waveform when you select the Audio to MIDI Groove Template function of the Digital Factory.

Audio to Score

Usually, audio data and MIDI data never have anything to do with each other. MIDI data will not make sound, and audio data doesn't send messages to MIDI devices. Logic has a unique and powerful function, however, that tries to convert audio data to MIDI data using the same underlying Quantize Engine as the Audio to MIDI Template function.

This is a very difficult procedure—Logic tries to estimate MIDI notes from the shape of an audio waveform—and the function is limited. You should use this function only with monophonic material—that is, material in which only one note sounds at a time. Still, few other applications even attempt to provide this function, so Logic is definitely ahead of the curve on this one!

When you select Audio to Score, the dialog box shown in Figure 8.29 appears.

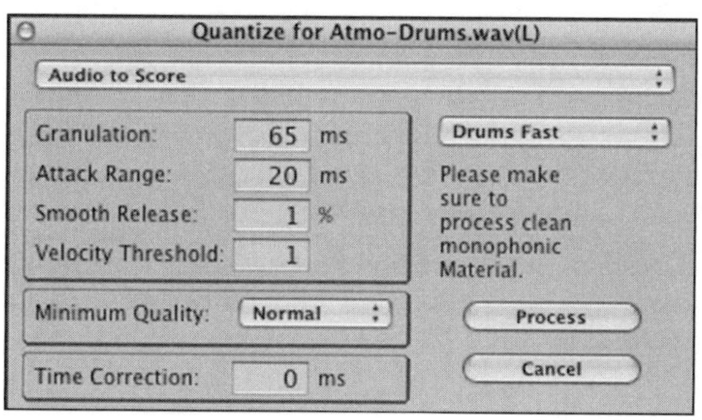

Figure 8.29

The Audio to Score dialog box.

As you can see in Figure 8.29, almost all of these parameters are the same as those in the Audio to MIDI Groove Template dialog box. The Audio to Score function brings up the same Audio Quantize ruler in the Sample Editor Waveform Display as shown in Figure 8.28. Logic uses the same analysis parameters and the same analysis engine for both functions. Refer to the section "The Audio to MIDI Groove Template" above for descriptions of these parameters. The only different parameter is Minimum Quality, which gives you two options, Normal and High. The Normal setting is more tolerant of notes slightly off pitch, but may capture wrong notes. The High setting is far more exacting, but it only converts those notes that it can discern accurately, so it may miss notes. Experiment with both settings to see what works better for any given audio selection.

When you are ready, click **Process**. Logic then converts your audio into MIDI data and opens up the Score Editor with the newly created MIDI region. Logic uses the Score Editor because this function was initially conceived as a method of writing sheet music from audio. This is why the function is called Audio to Score instead of Audio to MIDI. Don't worry; you can copy and paste the data into any editor or a new MIDI region, however you see fit.

The Quantize Engine

Quantizing audio isn't as easy a process as it is with MIDI data, where you can simply change numeric values, so the results are usually not perfect—but depending on the source material, Logic can achieve good results. If you choose Quantize Engine, the dialog box shown in Figure 8.30 appears.

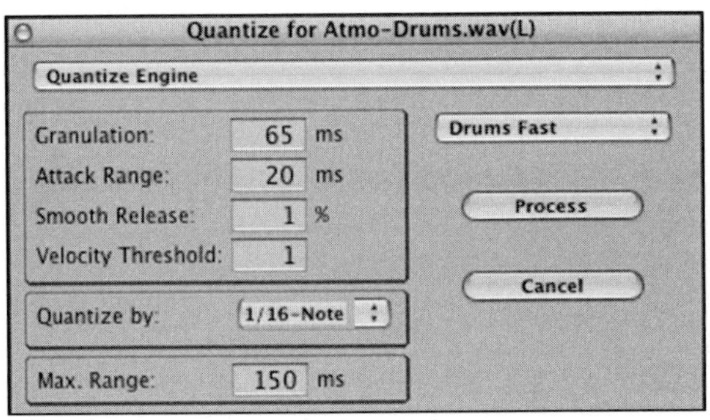

Figure 8.30

The Quantize Engine dialog box.

Once again, most of the parameters are the same as the other Quantize Engine functions, and the Audio Quantize Bar Ruler shown in Figure 8.28 appears. The only new parameters are Quantize By, which opens the standard Quantize pull-down menu from the MIDI Region parameter box, and Max. Range, in which you set the maximum number of milliseconds that a peak in the audio material is allowed to diverge from the quantization grid. To get a tighter quantization, set this value as small as possible; for a looser quantization, use a larger value.

METHOD TIP: QUANTIZING ONE AUDIO REGION TO MATCH ANOTHER AUDIO REGION

If you have two audio segments, and you want Segment #2 to adopt the rhythm of Segment #1, you can accomplish this by using the Quantize Engine functions in tandem.

First, load Segment #1 into the Sample Editor and select **Factory > Audio to MIDI Groove Template.** Create a MIDI Groove Template from this audio. Then load Segment #2 into the Sample Editor and select **Factory > Quantize Engine.** The Groove Template that you made from Segment #1 should appear at the bottom of the Quantize By pull-down menu along with any other Groove Templates you have made.

You'll want to experiment with different settings to capture the best Groove Template you can, but the procedure itself is very simple.

If these Digital Factory functions have you thinking that adjusting the timing and pitch of audio material seems too involved, you're going to love Apple Loops, which are explored later in this chapter!

The Audio Configuration Window

The Audio Configuration window should perhaps more accurately be called the Audio Mixer Configuration window or Audio Channel Strip Configuration window since this window offers functions to label audio inputs, outputs, and busses, and configure the effects and outputs slots of your channel strips. Nonetheless, since this window only affects Audio channels and can be called from the global Audio menu and the Audio window, it makes sense to include it here. Figure 8.31 shows the Audio Configuration window open to the I/O Label screen.

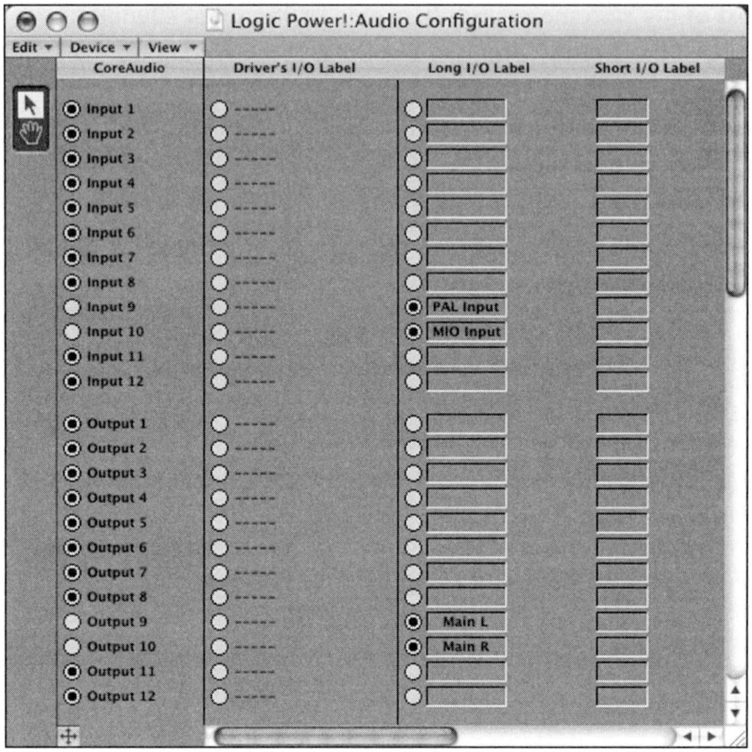

Figure 8.31

The Audio Configuration window, open to the I/O Label screen.

There are three local menus in the Audio Configuration window, each with a few options:

- **Edit.** The Edit menu contains standard editing options such as Cut, Copy, Paste, and so on, along with options to remove all the effects on all channels, and to remove all the labels you have set.
- **Device.** This menu allows you to switch between audio drivers, for those using both DAE and Core Audio. This menu will be of no use to anyone else.
- **View.** You can switch the view to the I/O Labels screen, to view only those channel strips you are using in your song, or to view all your channel strips in your Environment.

The Audio Configuration window also includes two tools—a Pointer tool for selecting radio buttons and channel strip slot, and a Hand tool for moving effects around the various channel strip slots. The following subsections briefly explain how to use the Audio Configuration window.

Labeling Inputs, Outputs, and Busses in the Audio Configuration Window

Figure 8.31 above shows you the I/O Labels screen of the Audio Configuration window. Showing are all the mono input and output channels available on the selected audio interface (which in this examples offers 12 channels of input and 12 channels of output). This screen also shows a listing for each Bus Object, and for stereo inputs and outputs as well. The number of inputs, outputs, and busses shown depends on the number of inputs and outputs available on your audio interface, and the number of Bus Objects in your Environment.

Each listing has a column for Driver's I/O Label (in case the manufacturer ships OS X compatible I/O labels with their Core Audio drivers, which is unlikely), Long I/O Label, and Short I/O Label. If you wish to write in a label for an input, output, or bus, simply click the radio button next to the text box, and then double-click with the Pointer tool in the text box to bring up a text field. Type in what you would like to name that input, output, or bus, and press **RETURN**. From now on, that input, output, or bus destination will show the label you have assigned.

Moving Effects and Changing Output Assignments in the Audio Configuration Window

The Components screen of the Audio Configuration window shows you all the Inserts, Outputs, Sends, and Audio Instruments used in the slots of your channel strips. Figure 8.32 shows an Audio Configuration window open to the Components screen (with Used Components selected).

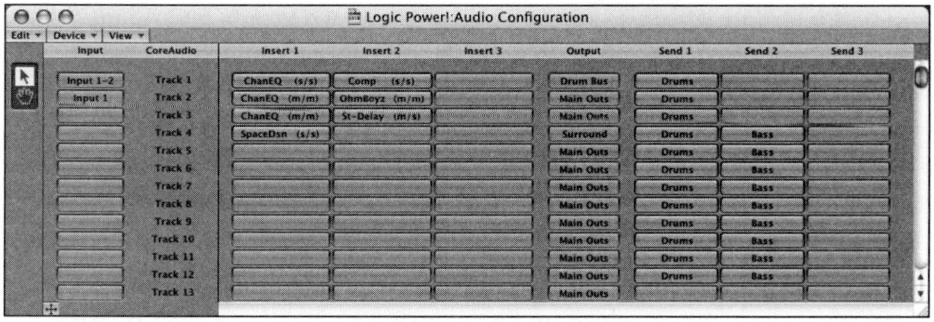

Figure 8.32

The Components screen of the Audio Configuration window shows all the Inserts, Outputs, Sends, and Audio Instruments in your channel strips.

If you want to use the Audio Configuration window to change the Output Object assignment of your channel strips, you can click-hold either the Pointer or Hand tool over the output slot. You will be presented with a pull-down menu of all available outputs to choose from. Because this is exactly what you can do on the actual channel strips in the Mixer or Arrange, it is doubtful you will want to use the Audio Configuration window for changing output assignments.

You will, however, want to use the Audio Configuration window to move around your Inserts and Sends from one slot to another on the same channel strip or between channel strips. You can move them using the Hand tool. Simply select the Hand tool on the left side of the Audio Configuration window, and then drag effects between slots on the same or different channel strip. You can also hold **OPTION** down while dragging to make a copy of the effect you have chosen rather than move the original effect. Figure 8.33 shows the Audio Configuration window being used to move Insert effects.

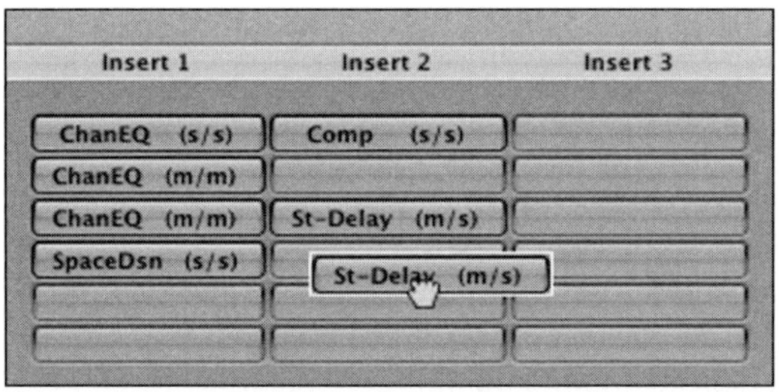

Figure 8.33
If you want to move around your Insert effects or quickly copy an effect, you can use the Hand tool in the Audio Configuration window.

You can use this same procedure to configure both Insert and Sends, however you cannot move Insert effects to Sends, and Send destinations to Inserts.

In a future update of Logic, you will be able to move Inserts and Sends around directly from the mixer. In Logic Pro 7, however, the only window in which you can move Inserts and Sends around your channel strips with the Hand tool is in the Audio Configuration window.

Audio Fades and Crossfades

There are three types of audio fades: a fade-in, in which audio "ramps up" in volume, a fade-out, in which audio ramps down in volume, and a crossfade, in which two Audio regions fade into each other. Many times, fading is used as a creative effect, such as fading out a song over a 20-second coda, building in an effect, or crossfading between two songs. But sometimes you will want to use fades as tools to cover up clicks at the beginning or end of Audio regions, or clicks caused by overlapping two Audio regions. These fades, rather than being seconds long, are usually measured in milliseconds. For these micro-fades, Logic allows each Audio region to have one fade-in and one fade-out or crossfade associated with it. When a fade is associated with an Audio region, the length of the fade will appear in the Region parameter box, and the fade will appear as green shading on the region itself, as shown in Figure 8.34.

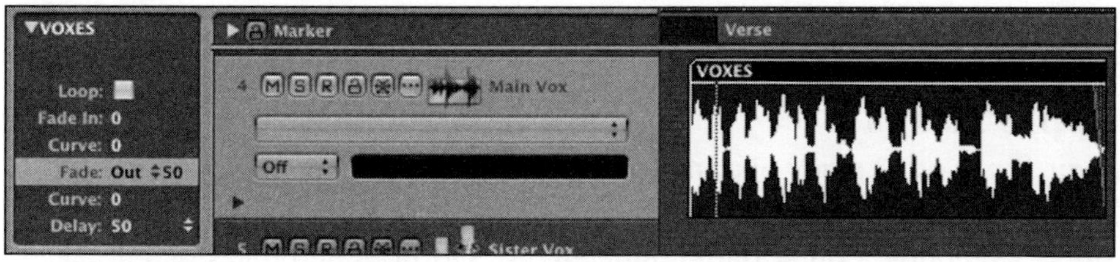

Figure 8.34
The Audio region above has a fade-out 50ms long, as you can see on the region, and in the Region parameter box.

Creating Audio Fades

There are three ways to create fades in Logic:

- Typing fade settings into the Region parameter box
- Using the Crossfade tool in the Arrange Toolbox
- Setting the Arrange Drag mode to X-Fade, and overlapping two Audio regions

Fade Files

Whenever you set up a fade, Logic creates a Fade file. This is a very short temporary audio file that contains just the faded segment. This file is stored in a Fade Files folder in your Project folder, or next to your song file if you have not saved your song as a project. These files cannot be edited. Whenever you adjust a fade in Arrange, the Fade file will be recreated.

Adjusting Audio Fades

Logic doesn't offer too much in the way of adjusting fades. If you want your fade to have a curve (in other words, instead of a linear increase or decrease in volume, a logarithmic increase or decrease) you can adjust the curve parameter from –99 to 99 to create various symmetrical curves in the Region parameter box. This number determines the strength and direction of the curve. You can also select if the right region fade will be a fade-out, a linear crossfade (X), an equal power crossfade (EqP) for crossfading between two regions that are not phase coherent (for example, two completely different instruments), or an S-shaped crossfade (X S) for material that is hard to crossfade with a standard-shaped crossfade. Generally, just sticking to a straight crossfade (X) will work in most common situations, and you should only try the other curves if you find yourself getting audio dropouts with a linear crossfade. The Time and Curve parameters for the X-Fade drag mode's crossfades can be set in the General tab of the Audio Preferences dialog.

Apple Loops

Logic Pro 7 adds many exciting features, but perhaps the most exciting for many users will be the addition of Apple Loop support. Those familiar with Apple Computer's other audio applications, GarageBand and Soundtrack, will already be familiar with Apple Loops. Users familiar with ACID-ized WAV files will already have an idea of what Apple Loops can do, although Apple Loops go much further than ACID-ized WAVs.

To put it simply, Apple Loops are special Audio or MIDI regions that contain embedded pitch, tempo, channel strip, and even sample information.

Real Instrument Apple Loops

Real Instrument Apple Loops (which I will refer to as *Audio Apple Loops*) are AIFF audio files with specially embedded tempo and pitch information. Audio Apple Loops

- Automatically play at the current song tempo, regardless of the tempo that the audio was originally recorded at.
- Automatically adjust to the key of the current song, regardless of the key of the original performance.

Audio Apple Loops behave just like normal Audio regions—you can loop them, resize them, cut them, and so on. They even appear in the Audio window like other Audio regions. However, you *cannot* edit an Apple Loop in the Sample Editor, as this would compromise the embedded information in the Apple Loop. If you want to edit an Apple Loop, make a copy of it that is a normal audio file, and edit that.

To add an Audio Apple Loop to your Logic song, simply drag it into an Audio Track in Arrange as you would any other audio file. That's it! You don't need to set up anything—Logic automatically will handle it as an Apple Loop.

Software Instrument Apple Loops

Software Instrument Apple Loops (which I will refer to as *MIDI Apple Loops*) are MIDI files with specially embedded information. In addition to their MIDI notes, MIDI Apple Loops include

- **Channel strip information**. Means that the Audio Instrument and effects that the loop uses will be instantly recalled as soon as you add the loop to an Audio Instrument track!
- **Sample information**. If the MIDI Apple Loop uses a sample-based instrument, all the samples it uses will instantly load and be ready for use.
- **Audio information**. If you drag a MIDI Apple Loop to an Audio Track, it will behave exactly as an Audio Apple Loop!

To use a MIDI Apple Loop, just drag it into a MIDI, Audio Instrument, or Audio Track. Remember that unlike Audio Apple Loops that only work on Audio Tracks, MIDI Apple Loops also contain an Audio version of the Apple Loop embedded as well and can be used on either MIDI or Audio Tracks.

The Loop Browser

Because Apple Loops are a special kind of file, there is a special kind of window to organize them. Those of you who are used to Soundtrack or GarageBand are already familiar with the concept of a Loop Browser. Basically, the Loop Browser allows you to search and audition your loops by various criteria. The Loop Browser can index more than just Apple Loops; if you have many ACID loops, for example, you can use the Loop Browser to index them as well. Figure 8.35 shows the Loop Browser window.

Browsing Loops

Searching for loops couldn't be simpler. You can either type in search words in the search field, press the category buttons to limit your search to various instrument categories and genres, or both. If you prefer lists of categories instead of buttons, the buttons in the top-left of the Loop Browser will switch you between Button view and Column view, as shown in Figure 8.36. You can also select a scale and time signature of Apple Loop to look for.

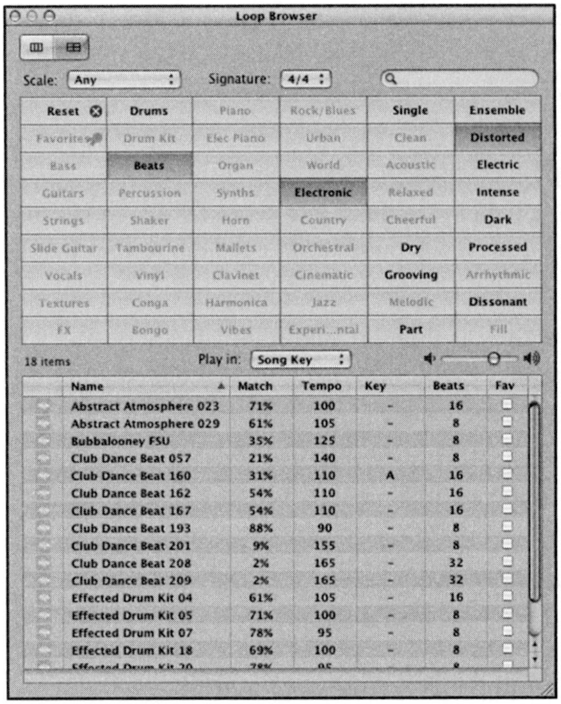

Figure 8.35

The Loop Browser allows you to search for your Apple Loops via category, text search, and more.

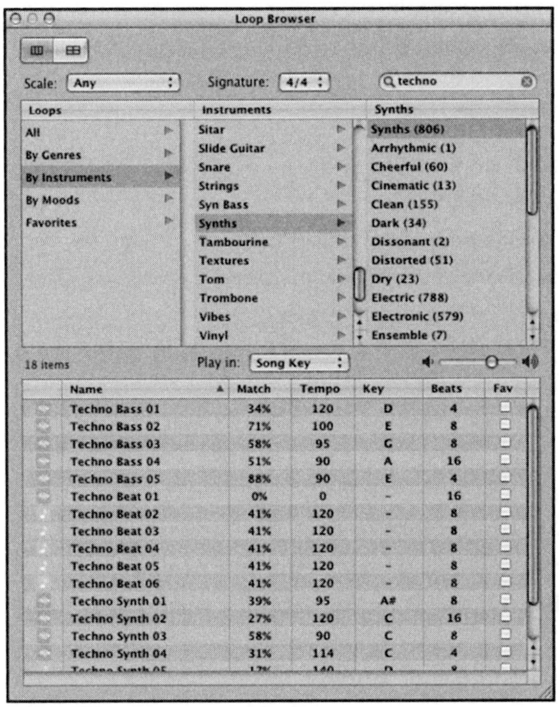

Figure 8.36

The Loop Browser in column view. Notice that there is also text in the text search field, further restricting the results.

The left-hand column in the results window will display either a blue audio wave or a green MIDI note to indicate if the loop is an Audio Apple Loop or a MIDI Apple Loop. To the right of the loop name is a Match column letting you know how close the loop is to your search criteria. To the right of that is the Tempo column, displaying the original tempo of the loop. The Key column tells you the original key of the loop, if any. The Beat column tells you how many beats are in the Apple Loop. Finally, if you want to store a loop in your Favorites category in the Loop Browser, just check the box in the Fav column.

Auditioning Loops

To audition a loop, simply click the name of the loop (or anywhere on the same line). The loop will play back using Audio Channel 1, with the volume determined by the volume slider, and the key determined by the key pull-down menu. To stop the loop from playing, click the loop again.

Adding Loops to the Loop Browser

You add new loops to the Loop Browser by dragging them from the Finder to the results window of the Loop Browser. You will be asked if you want to copy the loop to Loop Browser's default loop location, or if you'd rather the Loop Browser just indexed your loop in its current location on your hard drive. After making your selection, your loop will be entered into the Loop Browser's database and is ready for use in Logic. If you are adding ACID loops, be sure to drag the entire folder (or CD) containing the ACID loops onto the Loop Browser, because with Apple Loops, the folder name is used as the category name.

Adding Loops from the Loop Browser to Your Logic Song

If you find a loop you want to use in your song, simply drag it to an appropriate track on the Arrange window—an Audio Track for an Audio Apple Loop (or other kind of loop, such as an ACID loop) or a MIDI Apple Loop, or a MIDI or Audio Instrument track for a MIDI Apple Loop. The loop will now be part of your song, and if it's an audio loop, it will be added to the Audio window as well.

If, for example, you want a number of audio loops in your song, but not necessarily placed on Arrange yet, you can also add audio loops directly to your Audio window. Just drag the audio loops to the Audio window like any other audio file.

Creating Your Own Apple Loops

If you're like me, you're very excited by the potential of Apple Loops! It won't be long until you'll want to make your own Apple Loops. Unfortunately, there is currently no way to make MIDI Apple Loops—those have to be purchased from Apple in expansion packs such as the GarageBand JamPacks. But you *can* make your own Audio Apple Loops. To do this, first select the Audio region you want to turn into an Apple Loop in Arrange, then select the command Open in Apple Loops Utility from the Arrange local Audio menu. If your Audio region is an exact number of bars, Logic will then launch the Apple Loops Utility. If your audio isn't quite an exact number of bars, you will be asked to select how many bars or beats long your Audio region is, as shown in Figure 8.37.

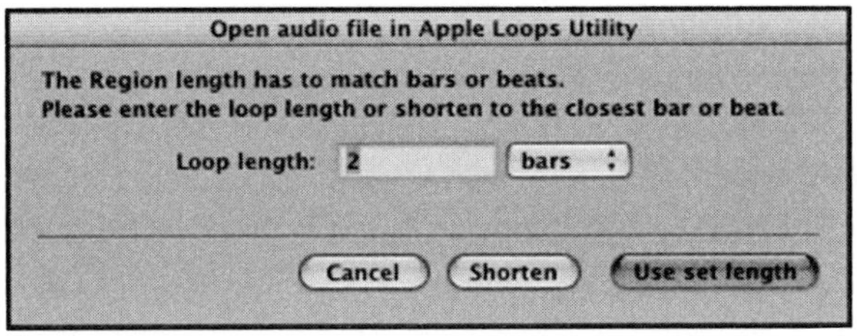

Figure 8.37

If your Audio region doesn't fall exactly on the beat, you will be prompted to tell the Apple Loops Utility exactly how long your Audio region is.

Set the number of bars or beats that your audio material currently is in the box, and select **Use Set Length**.

The Apple Loops Utility is a separate application much like Propellerhead's ReCycle application, if you are familiar with that program. Your selected Audio region will be loaded into the Waveform Display, and you will be able to reselect how long you want your loop to be, and to manually set transient points. Figure 8.38 shows you the Apple Loops Utility.

It is beyond the scope of this book to delve into the art of transient setting and making the perfect Apple Loop using the Apple Loops Utility. But the basic process is that you adjust the tempo and transient points in the Transient tab of the Utility, and then in the Tags tab, select genre and other information, as shown in Figure 8.39.

After you save your Apple Loop, it should be in the same Project folder as your song. You'll need to manually add it to your Audio window or drag it back into Arrange, and then you will have access to your selected Audio region as a brand new Apple Loop.

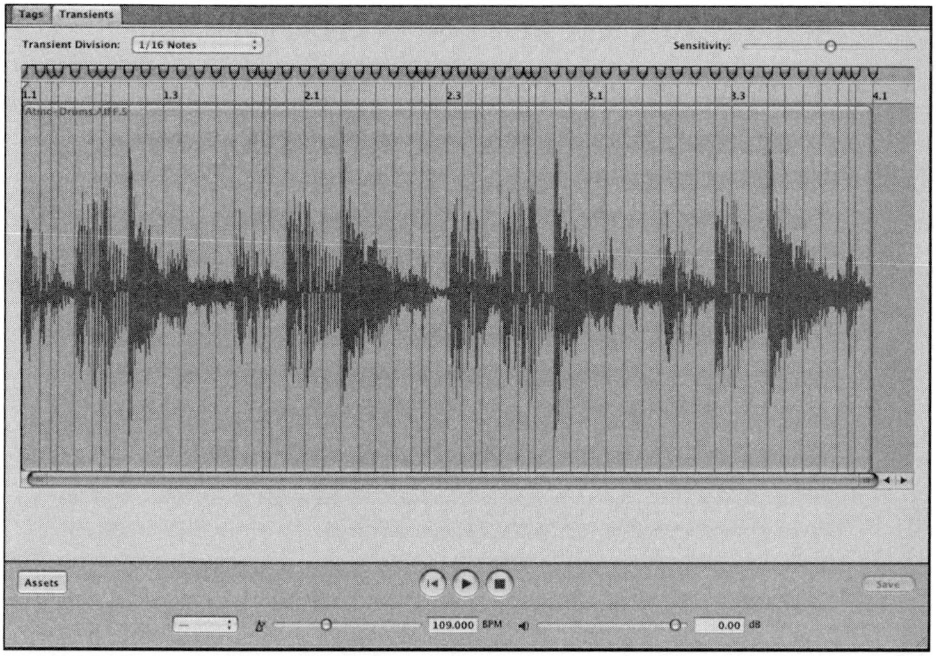

Figure 8.38

The Apple Loops Utility is where you can turn an Audio region into an Audio Apple Loop.

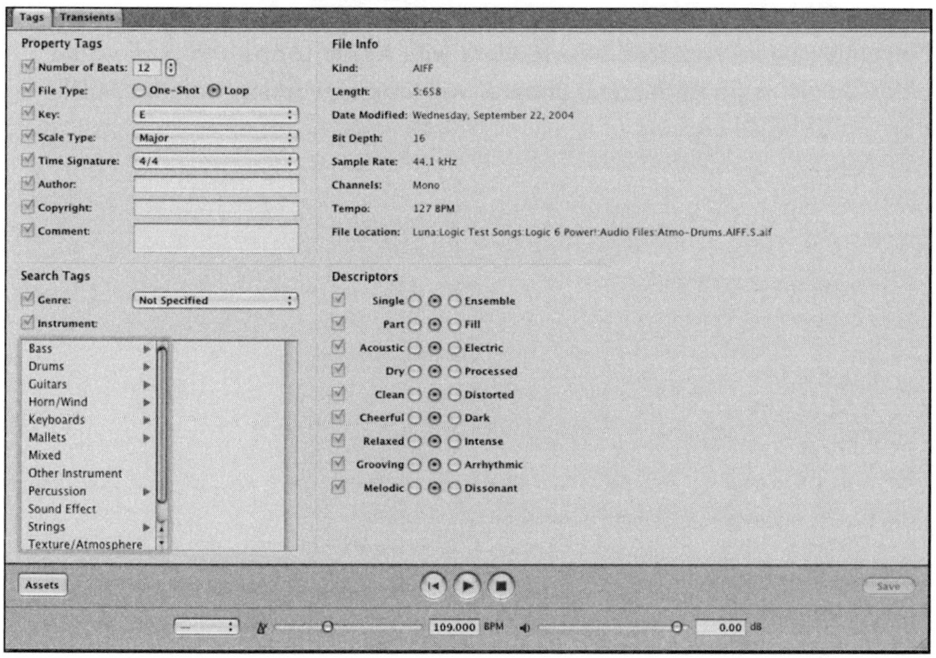

Figure 8.39

In the Tags tab of the Apple Loops Utility, you can set the beats, tempo, categories, and other information for your Audio Apple Loop before you save it.

IS THERE AN EASIER WAY TO CREATE AN AUDIO APPLE LOOP?

Well. . . no. Apple Loop technology is brand new, and Apple is just getting started with it. In the future, creating your own Apple Loops and integrating them into your song should get much easier. But for now, this is the process. Personally, I find it easier to load AIFF files into the Apple Loops Utility manually, and when I'm done with the loop drag it into the Loop Browser. But there's no seamless way to create Apple Loops in Logic yet.

EXPERT TIP: CONVERTING AUDIO TO APPLE LOOPS TO FIX TIMING ISSUES

One of my favorite uses of Audio Apple Loops is to fix slight timing issues with audio files. Say that you have a 3-bar acoustic guitar part that was performed a bit too fast for the song's tempo of 130 BPM. The part sounds out of time and is only 2.7 bars long. Audio Apple Loops to the rescue! Load the audio into the Apple Loops Utility (either manually or via the Open in Loops Utility command) as a 3-bar loop. You'll notice when the audio is in the Apple Loops Utility, it will identify the tempo as something like 133.35BPM because your audio is a bit fast. Now set the transient points to the musically relevant points in your performance, and save the loop. When you load it back into Logic, the loop will instantly adjust itself to the Logic tempo of 130 BPM, with the stretching occurring only at the transient points you set. Voilá! Your acoustic guitar part is perfectly in time!

Now that you've explored how to work with Apple Loops and audio data inside Audio regions, the next chapter will look at working with the MIDI data inside MIDI regions.

9 Working with MIDI

Because MIDI messages are simply numerical messages instead of actual sound, like an audio file, you can move, alter, program, and view those MIDI messages in many different ways. Thanks to these advantages, and Logic's origins as a MIDI-only application, there are far more editors and windows relating to MIDI information than audio. Each MIDI editor offers its own unique view of MIDI data, and allows you the choice of working with your MIDI information in whichever way is most comfortable for you. Logic offers perhaps the most comprehensive and powerful MIDI editing and re-imagining functions of any sequencer, and these obviously take some time to master.

This chapter is not going to explore every possible detail and use of every possible option in all the editors, but it will go over the functionality, operation, and potential of each specifically enough for you to explore deeper on your own.

MIDI Editors and MIDI Regions

I've previously discussed MIDI regions. Just as double-clicking an Audio region brings you to the Sample Editor in which you edit your audio, double-clicking a MIDI region opens the MIDI editor of your choice. You can choose which MIDI editor will open automatically when you double-click a MIDI region by clicking **Logic Pro > Preferences > Global** and selecting the Editing tab. If you click on the pull-down menu beside the Double-Clicking a MIDI Region Opens preference, Logic presents you with a menu of the four MIDI editors in Logic, as shown in Figure 9.1.

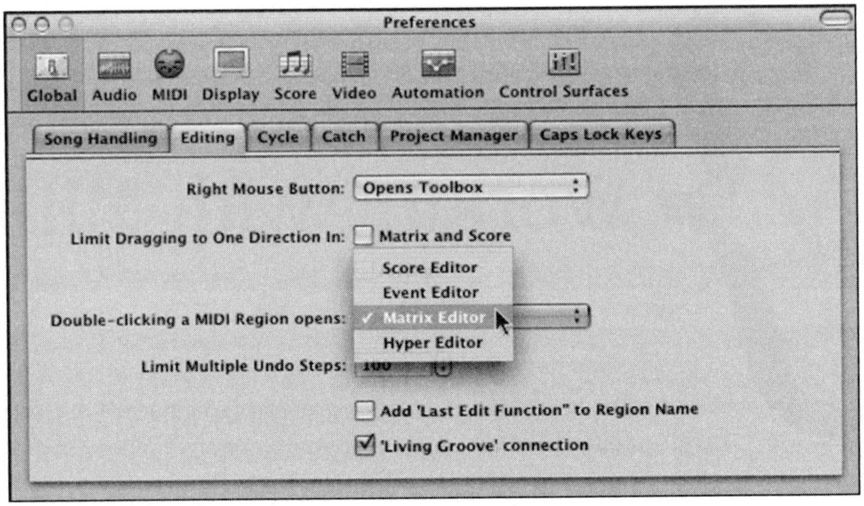

Figure 9.1
You can choose any of the four MIDI editors as the default editor in Global Preferences.

Logic defaults to the Matrix Editor opening up with a double-click because, these days, graphically editing MIDI is the most popular form of MIDI editing and programming. Others may like to use the Event Editor or another editor. When you get used to the various editors and how you like to use Logic, you can change the default to reflect your personal working method.

MIDI regions can be viewed in the MIDI editors in ways besides simply double-clicking the region in Arrange. All the MIDI editors have Link buttons, which allow you to keep one or more MIDI editors in your screenset, and those editors automatically contain the data from any MIDI regions selected on Arrange (except the Hyper and Event Editors, which can only display a single region at a time). There are also key commands you can use when selecting regions to open specific editors.

And of course, you can always open the various MIDI editors by using menu and key commands, regardless of what is selected on Arrange.

The Matrix Editor

The Matrix Editor offers a graphic "piano roll" view of MIDI data. It displays MIDI notes as colored bars in different positions, with different lengths, colors, and velocities. You can even use the Matrix Editor to visually edit MIDI controller data (called Hyper Draw data), as you'll see later in this section. Figure 9.2 shows the Matrix Editor.

Figure 9.2
The Matrix Editor allows you to edit your MIDI notes graphically.

The Matrix Editor contains now-familiar elements of buttons, a position display, and a Toolbox, but its most striking feature is the large window that displays the MIDI notes. The SPL moves across all the notes of the MIDI region as you play the song, much like a piano roll spins as the song plays. You not only can use the Matrix Editor to edit notes, but also to create MIDI parts as well. The Matrix Editor also has a Bar Ruler display complete with Global Tracks to help you navigate and edit.

This section explores the various elements of the Matrix Editor and how you can use them.

Local Menus

The Matrix Editor contains three local menus: the Edit, Functions, and View menus. Figure 9.3 shows the local menus of the Matrix Editor.

Figure 9.3
The local menus of the Matrix Editor.

The following subsections contain descriptions of each local menu.

The Edit Menu

The Edit menu contains options for moving and selecting data. Figure 9.4 shows the Edit menu of the Matrix Editor.

The commands in this menu are as follows:

- **Undo.** This undoes your last action in the Matrix Editor. **<COMMAND + Z>**
- **Redo.** This command redoes your last action in the Matrix Editor. **<COMMAND + SHIFT + Z>**
- **Undo History.** This command opens the Undo History window. See the Arrange local menu for details. **<OPTION + Z>**
- **Delete Undo History.** Choose this command to delete Undo History. See the Arrange local menu for details.
- **Cut.** This removes all selected notes from the grid and places them in the Clipboard. **<COMMAND + X>**
- **Copy.** This command copies any MIDI notes onto the Clipboard. **<COMMAND + C>**
- **Paste.** Paste places any MIDI notes in the Clipboard on the grid at the current SPL position. **<COMMAND + V>**
- **Paste at Original Position.** This command places MIDI notes from the Clipboard back into the notes' original location. This is useful if you cut notes and decide you still want them where they were, or if you copy notes, subsequently delete them, and decide you want them back.
- **Paste Replace.** This command replaces notes you select in the Matrix Editor with those from the Clipboard. It pastes notes at the current SPL and replaces all notes within the time-range of the pasted notes.
- **Clear.** Clear removes the selected MIDI information from the Matrix Editor.
- **Select All.** This selects all the notes in the Matrix Editor. **<COMMAND + A>**
- **Select All Following.** Use this command to select all the notes after the currently selected note. **<SHIFT + F>**
- **Select Inside Locators.** This command selects all the notes inside the two Locators. **<SHIFT + I>**

- **Deselect Outside Locators.** You can deselect any selected notes outside the Locators with this command.
- **Toggle Selection.** This command toggles the selection status of all the notes in the Matrix Editor. In other words, if you have a single note selected, this command toggles between that single note and every note except that selected note. If you had previously used the Select Inside Locators command, Toggle Selection alternates between all notes inside the selected Locators and those outside those Locators. **<SHIFT + T>**
- **Deselect All.** This command deselects any selected events. **<SHIFT + COMMAND + A>**

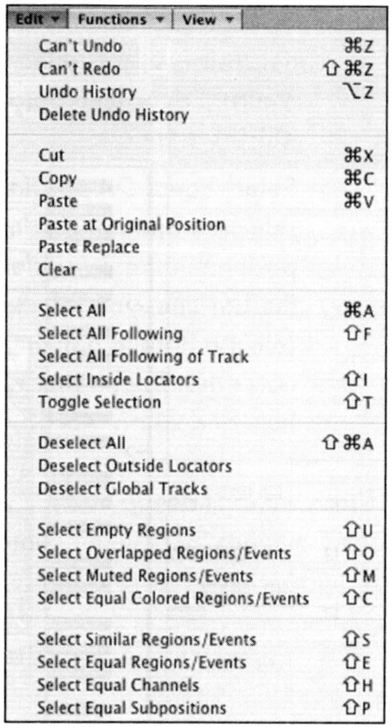

Figure 9.4
The Edit menu of the Matrix Editor.

- **Deselect Outside Locators.** This command deselects any selected events outside the right and left Locators.
- **Deselect Global Tracks.** This command deselects any selected Global Tracks.
- **Select Empty Regions.** This is one of the selection commands common to a number of edit windows, but since Matrix Editor notes are never empty, this command has no real effect. **<SHIFT + U>**
- **Select Overlapped Regions/Events.** You can use this command to select all notes that overlap each other in time, such as chords.
- **Select Muted Regions/Events.** This command selects all notes that you have muted. **<SHIFT + M>**
- **Select Equal Colored Regions/Events.** This command selects all notes with the same color. **<SHIFT + C>**
- **Select Similar Regions/Events.** This selects all notes that are the same (for example, all D#4 notes). **<SHIFT + S>**
- **Select Equal Regions/Events.** Select Equal Regions usually selects the same notes you would select by using Select Similar Regions. **<SHIFT + E>**

- **Select Equal Channels.** This selects all notes on the same MIDI Channel. This is useful when viewing more than one MIDI track in the same Matrix Editor (see below for details on viewing options in the Matrix). **<SHIFT + H>**
- **Select Equal Subpositions.** Select Equal Subpositions is a powerful selection option—it selects all MIDI notes that have the same relative position in the Bar Ruler. This means if you select a note directly on the bar line, you select all notes that fall on a bar line as well; if you select a note in between the third and fourth bar, you also select all notes that fall on that relative position between the third and fourth bar; and so on. **<SHIFT + P>**

The Functions Menu

The Functions local menu contains commands that operate on MIDI notes, or require MIDI notes to operate. Figure 9.5 shows the Functions local menu.

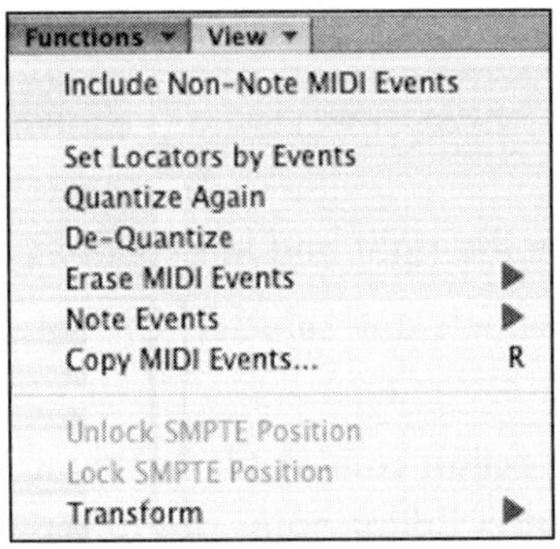

Figure 9.5
The Functions menu of the Matrix Editor.

The functions included in this menu are as follows:

- **Include Non-Note MIDI Events.** If you check this option, editing and moving notes also edits and moves any controller data acting on those notes.
- **Set Locators by Events.** This sets the left Locator by the leftmost selected note, and the right Locator by the rightmost selected note.
- **Quantize Again.** In case you have moved or edited notes, this applies the previous quantization to the selected notes.
- **Dequantize.** This removes any quantization that may have been applied and returns the selected notes to their original location.

- **Erase MIDI Events.** If you select Erase MIDI Events, the submenu of options shown in Figure 9.6 appears.

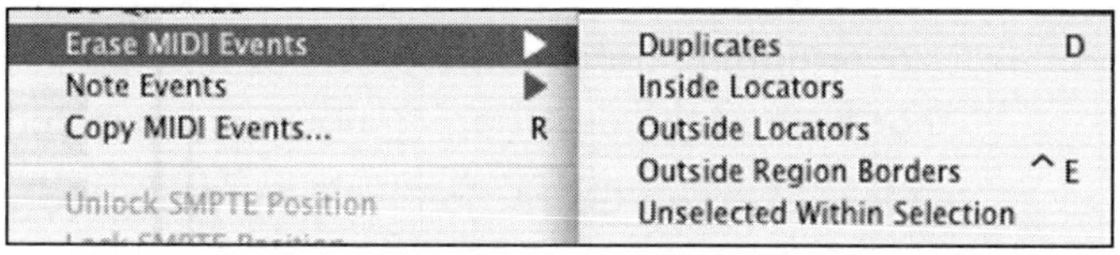

Figure 9.6
The Erase MIDI Events submenu of the Functions menu.

These commands offer different options for erasing groups of MIDI events in the Matrix Editor. Here is a brief description of each:

- **Duplicates.** This erases the second instance of all MIDI events that are duplicated (in other words, same pitch, time, controller number, and so on) by other MIDI events. **<D>**
- **Inside Locators.** This command erases all MIDI events between the Locators.
- **Outside Locators.** This erases all MIDI events not between the Locators.
- **Outside Region Borders.** If you are editing more than one MIDI region in the Matrix Editor, this command erases MIDI events inside the selected region, but outside the current region boundaries. The other regions will not be affected. **<CONTROL + E>**
- **Unselected Within Selection.** If one or more notes/events are unselected between the first and last selected note, this command erases those MIDI events.

- **Note Events.** Choosing Note Events opens a hierarchal menu of options, as shown in Figure 9.7.

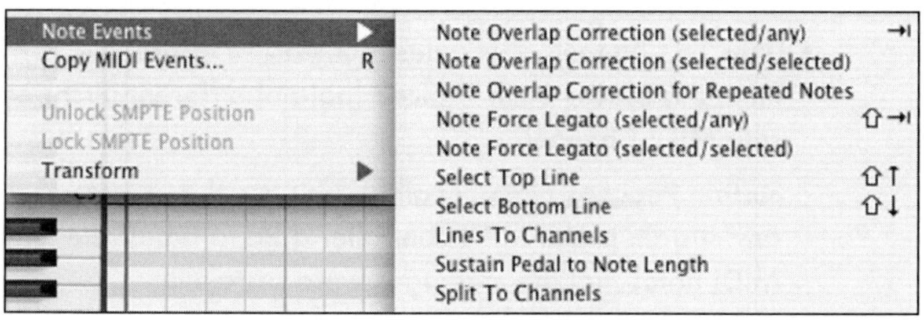

Figure 9.7
The Note Events submenu of the Functions menu.

These commands give you different ways to affect the position and length of notes. A description of each follows:

- **Note Overlap Correction (selected/any).** This shortens any selected overlapping notes so they do not overlap. It does not matter if one or both of the overlapping notes are selected. **<TAB>**
- **Note Overlap Correction (selected/selected).** This command shortens any selected overlapping notes so they do not overlap. You must select both of the overlapping notes to correct a given pair of overlapping notes.
- **Note Overlap Correction for Repeated Notes.** This shortens any repeated overlapping notes of the same pitch so they do not overlap. The first note in the overlap must be selected in order for this command to work.
- **Note Force Legato (selected/any).** This command lengthens any note to extend to the beginning of any following notes (this sort of smooth transition from one note to another without space in between is called *legato*). The initial notes to be extended must be selected. **<SHIFT + TAB>**
- **Note Force Legato (selected/selected).** This lengthens any note to extend to the beginning of any following notes. You must select both the initial notes to extend and the notes to which they will extend.
- **Select Top Line.** This command selects all the topmost notes across the length of your MIDI region. **<SHIFT + UP ARROW>**
- **Select Bottom Line.** The Select Bottom Line command selects all the bottommost notes across the length of your MIDI region. **<SHIFT + DOWN ARROW>**
- **Lines To Channels.** For notes that start at approximately the same time, this places each "voice" (note of different pitch) on a separate MIDI Channel.
- **Sustain Pedal to Note Length.** If you use this command, Logic uses any sustain pedal MIDI controller data to adjust the lengths of the MIDI notes that the messages were sustaining.

- **Split To Channels.** This splits selected notes to different MIDI Channels, based on the Auto Split Pitch setting in the Score Preferences—notes above get one channel, notes below another.

- **Copy MIDI Events.** You can copy all MIDI events with this command. You will be presented with a dialog asking you the range of notes to copy, and how you want them to be copied. **<R>**
- **Unlock SMPTE Position.** This releases the MIDI events from being tied to their current SMPTE positions.
- **Lock SMPTE Position.** This command locks the MIDI events to their current SMPTE position.
- **Transform.** One of Logic's most powerful MIDI tools is its Transform feature, which lets you literally "transform" data in nearly unlimited ways. If you select this command, a hierarchal menu of Transform presets appears, as shown in Figure 9.8.

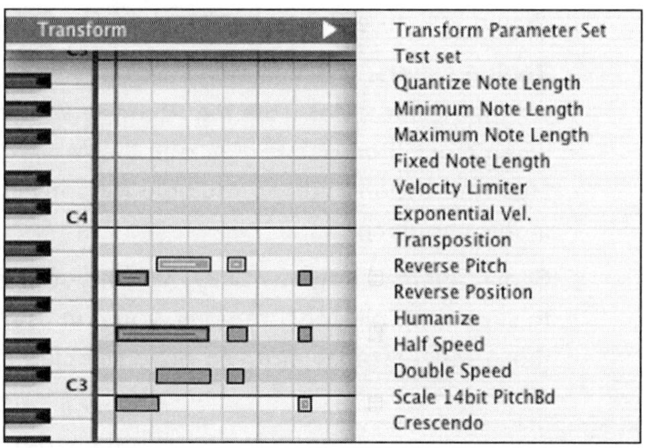

Figure 9.8
The Transform submenu of the Functions menu.

If you select one of these presets, you launch the Transform window, which is configured to run the task you have chosen. The Transform window is one of the more complex aspects of Logic, and is examined further in this chapter in the section "The Transform Window."

The View Menu

The View menu allows you to alter the appearance of the Matrix Editor and gives you access to the Hyper Draw functions. Figure 9.9 shows the View menu of the Matrix Editor.

The View menu options are as follows:

- **Scroll In Play.** If you select Scroll In Play, instead of the SPL scrolling across the Matrix Editor window, the SPL remains stationary in the center of the window, and the MIDI data scrolls horizontally past it, from right to left.
- **SMPTE Time Ruler.** This changes the Bar Ruler into an SMPTE Time Ruler. **<U>**
- **Parameters.** This command toggles the button, Toolbox, and Note Division display at the left of the Matrix Editor. **<P>**
- **White Background.** This toggles between the light matrix background shown in Figure 9.2 and a black background.
- **Region Colors.** This command displays the notes of each MIDI region with the same color from the Arrange window. This is most useful when more than one region is in the Matrix Editor at the same time (see the section "Editing Multiple Regions in the Matrix Editor" later in this chapter).
- **Show Selected Regions Only.** When you are using the Matrix Editor to show multiple MIDI regions, you can use this option to show only those MIDI regions that you have selected in the Arrange window.
- **Scroll To Selection.** You can have the Matrix Editor scroll only until it reaches a specific selection in the Arrange window with this option. **<SHIFT + V>**
- **Global Tracks.** You can toggle the Global Tracks on or off with this check box.
- **Global Track Components.** This pull-down menu lets you toggle on or off individual Global Tracks you wish to view.

Figure 9.9
The View menu of the Matrix Editor.

- **Track Protect Buttons.** If this is checked, Track Protect buttons will appear on the Global Tracks.
- **Event Float.** This launches a small, one-event tall Event List that floats above the Matrix Editor. The list displays and allows you to numerically edit text information regarding the specific note you are editing. **<OPTION + E>**
- **Matrix Colors.** If you choose this command, a dialog box appears presenting different color choices for the Matrix Editor background and grid lines.
- **Hyper Draw.** As I mentioned briefly in Chapter 7, "The Arrange Window," Hyper Draw enables you to enter and edit MIDI controller data to automate a MIDI region (Hyper Draw is also called RBA, Region-Based Automation). Since the MIDI controller data is part of the region itself, when you are editing a region in the Matrix Editor, you can edit the controller data as well. This command displays a hierarchal menu that offers a selection of possible MIDI controllers you may wish to view alongside your note data, as shown in Figure 9.10.

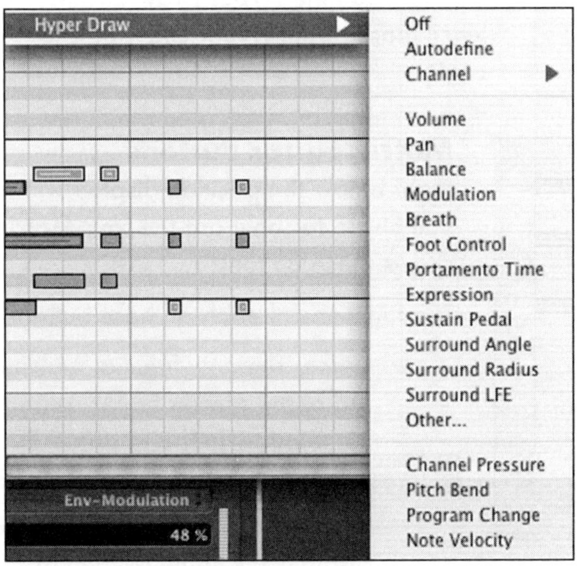

Figure 9.10
The Hyper Draw submenu of the View menu.

If you select one of these options, a controller data lane opens in the bottom half of the Matrix Editor. This blue window is filled with any existing controller messages that you already have in the region, as shown in Figure 9.11.

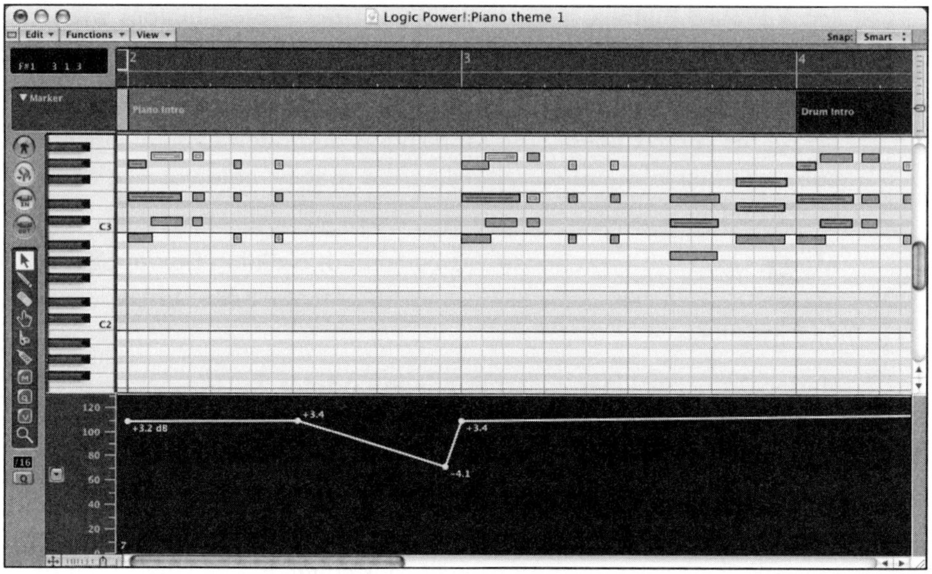

Figure 9.11
A Matrix Editor showing the Hyper Draw window. Currently, the Volume MIDI controller data is showing.

You can adjust the height of the Hyper Draw window by dragging the bar between the Hyper Draw and Matrix windows up or down. You'll learn more about Hyper Draw in Chapter 11, "Using Automation in Logic."

Figure 9.12
The Matrix Editor buttons.

Matrix Editor Buttons

Right below the position display window and any Global Tracks you chose to show are the four Matrix Editor buttons. Figure 9.12 shows those buttons.

The functions of each of these buttons are as follows:

- **Catch.** The now-familiar walking man icon is the Catch button of the Matrix Editor. With this button engaged, the visible window in the Matrix Editor always follows the SPL position. You will almost always want this button engaged.
- **Link.** Engaging the Link button ensures that the editor always displays the same content as the topmost window. Double-clicking the Link button while the Catch button is also engaged activates Contents Catch mode, which means that the Matrix Editor will always show the contents of the currently playing region as the song plays.

- **MIDI IN.** When the MIDI IN button is engaged, you can use your MIDI controller to directly input MIDI into the Matrix Editor. This is very useful for Step Input, which is explained later in this chapter, in the section, "MIDI Step Input."
- **MIDI OUT.** With this engaged, you hear each note as you select and edit it. This is useful if you want to monitor what you are doing as you work in the editor.

The Matrix Editor Toolbox

Because the Matrix Editor is designed for graphic editing, it makes sense that the Matrix Editor would have a rather extensive Toolbox of graphic editing tools. Figure 9.13 shows the Matrix Editor Toolbox.

Figure 9.13
The Toolbox in the Matrix Editor.

Here is a description of the tools, in order from top to bottom.

- **Pointer.** This tool is the standard pointer for selecting and making "rubber band" selections of multiple notes.
- **Pencil.** The Pencil tool allows you to draw new notes into the Matrix Editor. You'll learn how to use the Pencil tool later in this chapter in the section "Inserting and Deleting Notes in the Matrix Editor."
- **Eraser.** This tool removes notes from the Matrix Editor.
- **Finger.** This tool allows you to resize notes.
- **Scissors.** The Scissors tool splits notes into multiple notes.
- **Glue.** This tool merges adjacent notes together, forming one note from multiple notes.
- **Mute.** The Mute tool mutes or unmutes notes in the Matrix Editor.
- **Quantize.** The Quantize tool allows you to quantize only selected notes, leaving the rest of the region unquantized. This is very useful if you have a great performance with only one portion in which the timing is slightly off. You can use this tool to quantize just those few notes and leave the rest of the performance alone.
- **Velocity.** The bar inside each note indicates the relative velocity of that note. With the Velocity tool, you can raise or lower the velocity of one or more notes graphically, by selecting the note and then scrolling up or down with the mouse to shorten or lengthen the velocity bar

inside the note or notes. When you adjust the velocity of all selected notes at once by clicking on a single note and moving the mouse, every note retains its relative values compared to the other notes (so if you raise the velocity of a loud note and a soft note, both will get louder, but the soft note will still be the same amount softer). You can hold down **OPTION + SHIFT** to adjust all selected notes to the same velocity.

- **Magnifying Glass.** To zoom in on a particular group of notes, use the Magnifying Glass tool to "rubber band" them to zoom in to the maximum zoom level. Click anywhere there are no notes to return to the original zoom level.

Inserting and Deleting Notes in the Matrix Editor

You may already have a region filled with MIDI information from recording a keyboard performance. If, however, you want to enter MIDI data without recording and performing a keyboard part in its entirety, and working with your music graphically appeals to you, the Matrix Editor is *the* place to create MIDI performances in Logic. There are two ways to insert notes in the Matrix Editor: You can use a MIDI controller or onscreen keyboard to "step input" MIDI, or you can use the Pencil tool to draw your MIDI performance on screen.

To use either method of inserting notes, first you must have an open MIDI region in the Matrix Editor. This can be an empty region that you created in the Arrange window just so you could fill the region in the Matrix Editor, or it could be a region that already contains MIDI data. In the following subsections, you'll learn how to use each method of inserting notes.

MIDI Step Input

The Matrix, Score, and Event Editors allow you to use your hardware MIDI controller to input MIDI in what is known as "step input" or "step recording" mode. In this mode, you enter your MIDI performance one step at a time. This is useful if you want to create a MIDI performance that is beyond your technical ability to play in realtime, or if you know precisely which notes you want to input and want to insert them quickly. Step input in Logic is fast and intuitive once you understand the basics, and is a powerful tool when you know how to use it.

First, make sure you have the MIDI IN button engaged so that the Matrix Editor can receive external MIDI. Next, set the Note Division for the length of notes you'll be playing. The Note Division display is directly under the toolbar, as shown in Figure 9.14.

Figure 9.14

The Note Division display. Either double-click this number to enter a number from your keyboard, or drag the mouse up or down to raise or lower the Note Division.

You can either double-click the Note Division to enter a new value directly, or drag the mouse up or down to raise or lower the value. Another option you have is to quantize your input automatically by pressing the Q button in Figure 9.14. Since step input automatically places your notes exactly on the Note Division line, you shouldn't need to set a quantize value.

At this point, start playing your controller. Logic considers any notes you hold down at the same time to have been input at the same point, so you can play either single notes or chords. As soon as you release the key or keys, the SPL advances by one division, and you will see the notes you performed (complete with the velocity with which you pressed the keys) on screen. It's as simple as that!

As you'd expect, Logic offers more control over step input than the basic procedure I have just described, however. You can adjust the Note Division using the Note Division display or key commands, throughout the step input process. So you could, for example, step input a few 1/8 notes, then a passage of 1/16 notes, then two 1/4 notes, then back to 1/8 notes. You can lengthen notes that you have just input by using the sustain pedal or Sustain Inserted Notes key command. You can also insert a rest by depressing the sustain pedal without inputting notes, or using the Rest key command. You can also step forward and backward via key commands, or press the **DELETE** key to erase what you have just input and thus move the SPL backward.

I've made references to some of the key command options for step input; in fact, you can use step input entirely by means of key commands. In the Key Commands window, look for the Keyboard Input section. You will find key commands for everything, from all the notes and divisions to different velocity settings.

If you would rather use step input completely with the mouse, you can use Logic's Caps Lock Keyboard (described in Chapter 7) or the Step Input Keyboard. You can launch the Step Input Keyboard either by selecting **Windows > Step Input Keyboard** or via key commands. The Step Input Keyboard shown in Figure 9.15 appears.

Figure 9.15
Use the Step Input keyboard window to step input MIDI notes onscreen with the mouse.

This window includes buttons representing the various Note Divisions, velocity ranges, advance SPL, and so on. As with MIDI hardware or keyboard input, you can adjust these features at any point while inputting, so you can create complex MIDI performances with the Step Input keyboard.

> **STEP INPUT VERSUS CAPS LOCK KEYBOARD FOR STEP INPUT RECORDING**
> As mentioned in the text, you can use both the Caps Lock keyboard or the Step Input keyboard to step input MIDI notes. Because the Step Input keyboard has so many more options relating to MIDI step input, I highly recommend you use it for step recording instead of the Caps Lock keyboard. The Caps Lock keyboard is designed more for onscreen input of live performance from the Arrange window.

All of these step input methods and key commands offer you rich and creative tools to create and develop MIDI performances. Feel free to experiment with them, and be sure to check out the available key commands. Don't think that step input is only for those who are not piano virtuosos—even the best performers may just need to add a few notes to a MIDI region, and there's nothing faster than using step input key commands!

Entering MIDI Notes with the Pencil Tool

You can also "draw" your MIDI performance with the Pencil tool. If you know exactly what you want, this is a great way to create MIDI parts quickly. When you click the Pencil tool, it creates a note at the current SPL. The created note will be the same length and velocity of the previously created note; so, if you created a 1/8 note, then used the Finger tool to lengthen it to a whole note, the next note you create will be a whole note. If you select a note with the Pointer tool, and then use the Pencil tool to create notes, all subsequent notes will have the length and velocity of the previously chosen note.

Deleting Notes in the Matrix Editor

You can delete notes in the Matrix Editor by pressing the **DELETE** key to delete any selected notes, or by using the Eraser tool. If you want to restore notes that you have deleted, you can undo the action.

Resizing and Moving Notes in the Matrix Editor

After creating notes, resizing and moving notes are what you will use the Matrix Editor for most often. Because the Matrix Editor is designed for graphic editing, it's no surprise that it includes tools to make these tasks as easy as possible. This section explores some of the methods for moving and resizing notes in the Matrix Editor.

Resizing Notes

You can resize notes using a number of tools. To resize notes from the front, leaving the end point the same, you can grab a note from the lower-left corner, hold down the mouse button, and drag right or left to move the beginning of the note forward or backward in the region. If you select multiple notes, when you click on the lower-left of one note, you adjust the beginning point of all the selected notes.

The Finger tool is designed to allow you to adjust the length of one or more notes quickly. You can either click on a single note to resize, or you can drag over a group of notes and resize them all. As you hold down the mouse and drag right and left, the note becomes longer or shorter. You can resize a note to be as long as the entire MIDI region in the Matrix Editor, or as tiny as the smallest possible Note Division. Keep in mind that the smallest Note Division to which you can graphically reduce a note depends on the zoom resolution of the Matrix Editor. You can change the zoom level with the Magnifying Glass tool, the zoom sliders in the top-right of the Matrix Editor, or via key commands.

If you hold the **SHIFT** key down while using the Finger tool to resize multiple notes, every selected note will then end at the same point as the note you are resizing. If you hold the **SHIFT + OPTION** keys down, every selected note will be made the exact same length as the note you are resizing.

Moving Notes

You can move notes around the Matrix Editor by selecting them with the Pointer tool and dragging them around to a new location. When you hold the mouse button down with one or more notes selected, the Pointer turns into a hand to give you a visual cue that you can now move your notes around the Matrix Editor. You can move at the highest resolution possible for the current zoom level by holding down the **CONTROL** key as you move your notes. To move at the single-tick level (the finest resolution possible in Logic) regardless of zoom level, you can hold down the **CONTROL + SHIFT** keys.

To move a copy of one or more notes but not the original notes themselves, you can hold down the **OPTION** key while dragging your notes.

> **EXPERT TIP: ADJUSTING PITCH AND VELOCITY USING A MIDI KEYBOARD**
>
> If you select a note in a MIDI editor, you aren't limited to using the computer to move that note or alter its velocity. If you double-click the MIDI IN button, every time you select a note in a MIDI editor in Logic, you can move that note and change its velocity by pressing a note on the keyboard. The note in the editor will change pitch and velocity based on which MIDI note you trigger and its velocity, and the note will retain the timing and length it already had.

Editing Multiple Regions in the Matrix Editor

The most common use of the Matrix Editor is to open a single MIDI region for editing. However, sometimes you may want to view and/or edit more than one region in the Matrix Editor simultaneously. You can accomplish this very easily.

To view all regions in the Matrix Editor, simply double-click in any empty area in the window, and all your MIDI regions will appear in the Matrix Editor. Lines delineating the start and end points of MIDI regions in the Arrange window will appear as thick vertical lines in the editing window. If you have Show Sequence Colors engaged, the notes of the various regions will have the same colors in the Matrix Editor as their regions do in the Arrange window. If you have Show Selected Sequences Only engaged, instead of all the MIDI regions on the Arrange appearing in the Matrix Editor, only those MIDI regions selected in the Arrange window appear.

When showing multiple regions, you can make selections, resize, and move notes from more than one region as if they were all in the same region.

To return to showing only a single MIDI region at a time, simply double-click on a MIDI note; the Matrix Editor then displays the region to which the double-clicked note belongs; and the rest disappear. You can of course bring them all back simply by double-clicking an empty area on the window, as described previously.

The Event List Editor

The Event List Editor (usually referred to as either the Event List or the Event Editor) is the oldest method of recording, storing, and entering MIDI data, both in general and in Supertrack, Logic's earliest predecessor. Given this long heritage, the Event Editor is extremely robust and feature-laden while admittedly looking a bit anachronistic. Put simply, the Event Editor features a scrolling text window containing MIDI information. You view, edit, and modify this information by changing the text in the list. Figure 9.16 shows an Event Editor.

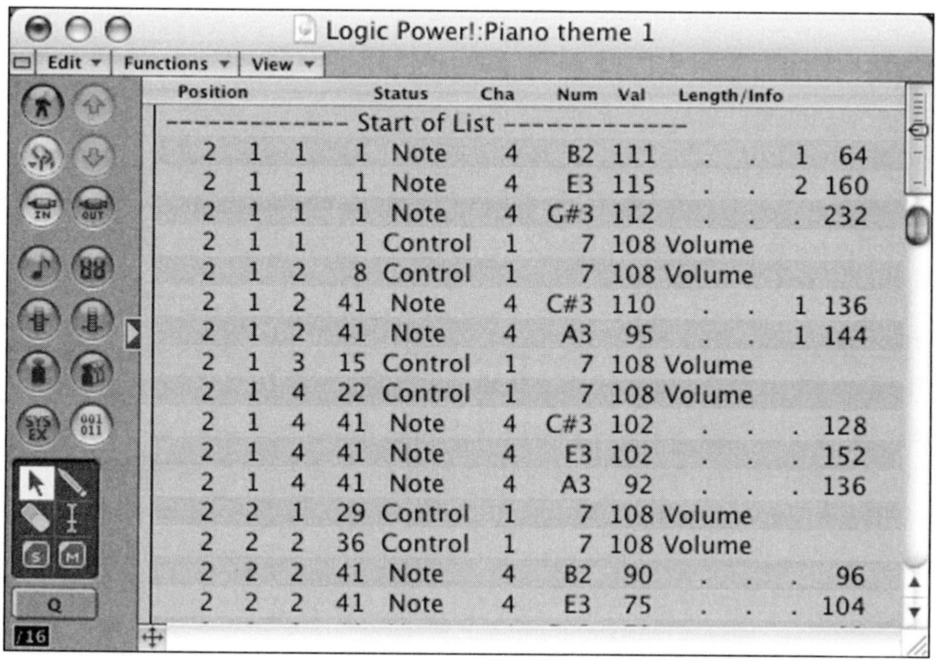

Figure 9.16

In the Event List Editor, you can view and edit your MIDI data as text.

The Event Editor displays the position of events, the specific type of event it is (which the editor labels as "status"), the MIDI Channel of the event (Cha), any numerical values associated with that event, and the length or other relevant information about that MIDI event.

At first blush, it might seem that editing music as text would be more tedious than creative. When you get used to the Event Editor, however, you'll find this is far from the reality. Many times, you'll want to have a linked Event List even when using another editor or the Arrange window, simply to view the detailed information available in the Event Editor. In some cases, some MIDI information, such as note release velocity, can be viewed and edited only in the Event List. And you may just find that when you know what you are doing, being able to quickly find and replace MIDI data as text is the most efficient method of editing available.

Let's start looking at this vital and powerful tool by going through its local menus.

Event Editor Local Menus

Like the Matrix Editor, the Event Editor has three local menus: Edit, Functions, and View. Figure 9.17 shows the local menus of the Event Editor.

Figure 9.17
The local menus of the Event Editor.

The similarities between the Matrix Editor's and the Event Editor's local menus don't end there. Since all the MIDI editors are essentially working with the same data, many of the commands are also shared, as you will see in the following subsections.

The Edit Menu

The Edit menu of the Event Editor is shown in Figure 9.18.

As you can see, this menu is exactly the same as the Edit menu in the Matrix Editor. Refer to the descriptions of the commands in that subsection.

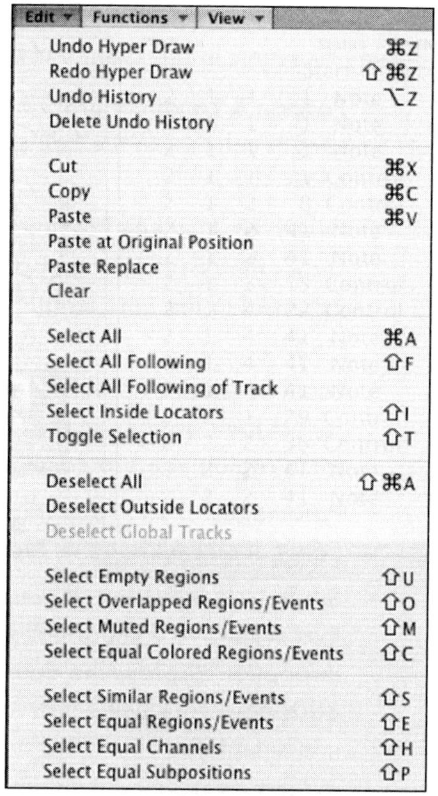

Figure 9.18

The Event Editor's Edit menu is identical to the Matrix Editor's Edit local menu (the Undo option is different, but that changes with each action).

The Functions Menu

Once again, take a look at the Functions menu of the Event Editor in Figure 9.19 and compare it to the Functions menu from the Matrix Editor.

Refer to the description of the commands in subsection "The Functions Menu" in "The Matrix Editor" section.

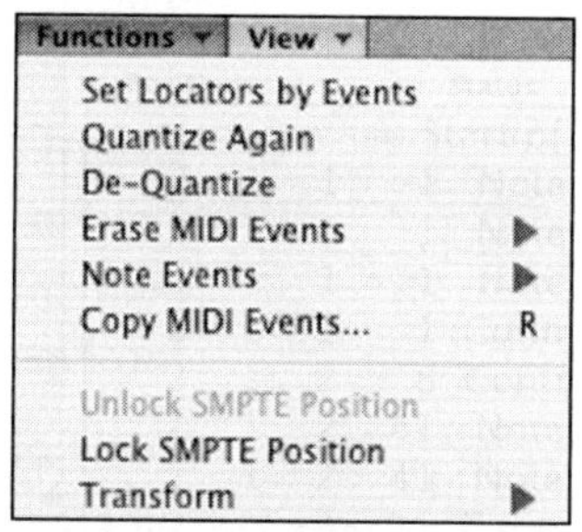

Figure 9.19

Like the Event Editor's Edit menu, the Functions local menu in the Event Editor shares the same options as the Matrix Editor's Functions menu.

The View Menu

Unlike the other two local menus in the Event Editor, the View menu offers selections unique to this editor. Figure 9.20 shows the View menu of the Event Editor.

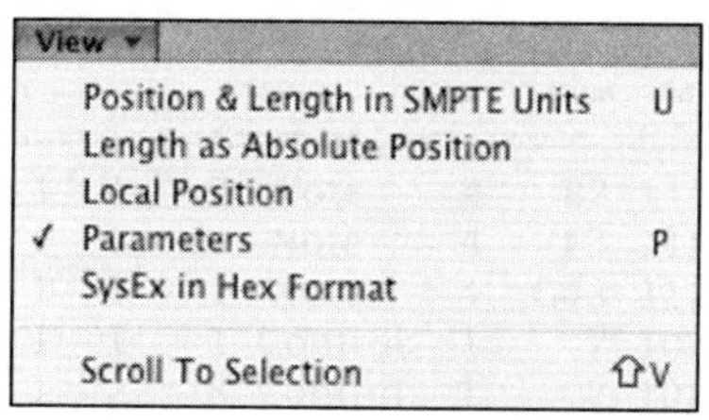

Figure 9.20

The View menu in the Event Editor.

This menu offers a selection of commands that allow you to customize the display of events in the Event List:

- **Position & Length in SMPTE Units.** With this engaged, the Position and Length columns in the Edit List display SMPTE units instead of bar units. **<U>**
- **Length as Absolute Position.** If this is engaged, the length display shows the absolute song position of the "note off" message, as opposed to the note length (which is the usual way of displaying length).
- **Local Position.** With this engaged, the position of notes does not reflect their position in the song, but their relative position inside the MIDI region you are editing.
- **Parameters.** If you keep this option engaged, the left side of the Event Editor shows all buttons, toolbars, and so on. **<P>**
- **SysEx in Hex Format.** If your Event List is displaying any System Exclusive (SysEx) information for a hardware MIDI device, engaging this option displays the data in hexadecimal format. Consult your MIDI hardware unit's instruction manual for details of its SysEx implementation.
- **Scroll To Selection.** With this engaged, the Event List scrolls to the region selected in the Arrange window. **<SHIFT + V>**

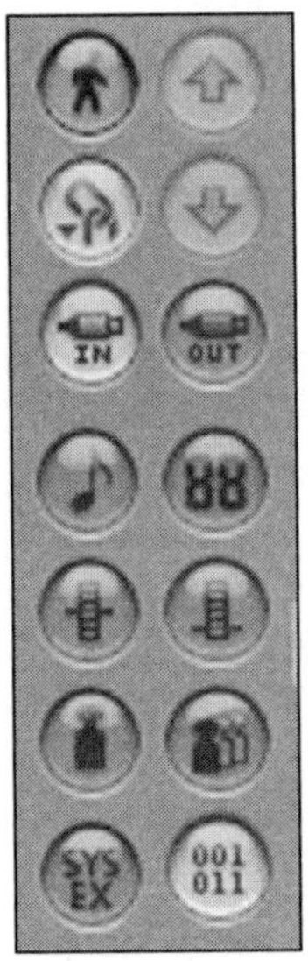

Figure 9.21

The Event Editor buttons allow you to select which data to show and which to filter out.

Event Editor Buttons

The Parameter bar at the left of the Event Editor holds many more buttons than any window you have explored so far. Figure 9.21 shows the Event Editor buttons.

Some of these buttons are familiar from other windows, but others are unique to the Event Editor, and allow you to display only those specific types of MIDI messages with which you want to work. Descriptions of each button follow, moving from left to right and top to bottom through all the buttons:

- **Catch Button.** With this button engaged, the visible window in the Event Editor always follows the SPL position. You will almost always want this button engaged.

- **Up Arrow.** Use this button to navigate backward one MIDI message at a time in the Event List.
- **Link Button.** Engaging the Link button ensures that the editor always displays the same content as the topmost window. If you do not have a MIDI region selected and the topmost window is an Arrange window, a list appears of the folders and regions in Arrange rather than the MIDI messages inside the regions. Double-clicking the Link button while the Catch button is also engaged activates Contents Catch mode, which means that the Event Editor always shows the contents of the currently playing region as the song plays.
- **MIDI IN Button.** When the MIDI IN button is engaged, you can use your MIDI controller to input MIDI directly into the Event Editor. This is described in the previous subsection "MIDI Step Input."
- **MIDI OUT Button.** With this engaged, you hear the currently selected MIDI note that you are editing.
- **Note Button.** With this engaged, the Event List displays the MIDI notes in the MIDI region that you are editing.
- **Program Change Button.** The dual digit icon represents the Program Change button. With this button engaged, the Event List displays any program change messages in the MIDI region that you are editing.
- **Pitch Bend Wheel Button.** The button below the note is an iconic representation of the pitch bend wheel of a hardware synthesizer. With this button engaged, the Event List displays any pitch bend messages in the MIDI region that you are editing. Keep in mind that if your region has pitch bend information, you may find literally *hundreds* of pitch bend messages representing every instant the pitch bend wheel was touched, so this button comes in very handy!
- **Modulation Wheel Button.** To the right of the Pitch Bend Wheel button is a very similar iconic representation of a modulation wheel (the marker is on the bottom of the wheel, as opposed to the middle of the wheel for the Pitch Bend Wheel button). With this button engaged, the Event List displays any control change messages in the MIDI region that you are editing.
- **Channel Pressure Button.** Underneath the Pitch Bend Wheel button is an iconic representation of a single weight. This is the Channel Pressure button. Engaging this button displays any aftertouch messages in the MIDI region that you are editing.

- **Polyphonic Aftertouch Button.** The button to the right of the Channel Pressure button is an iconic representation of multiple weights; this is the Polyphonic Aftertouch button. Engaging this button displays any polyphonic key pressure messages in the MIDI region that you are editing.
- **SysEx Button.** The button that says "SysEx" is—appropriately enough—the button to toggle display of any System Exclusive (SysEx) data in the MIDI region that you are editing.
- **Full Message Button.** To the right of the SysEx button is a button labeled with 0's and 1's. This is the Full Message button. As the name implies, if this button is engaged, it will display extra information (the "full message") about the displayed MIDI message.

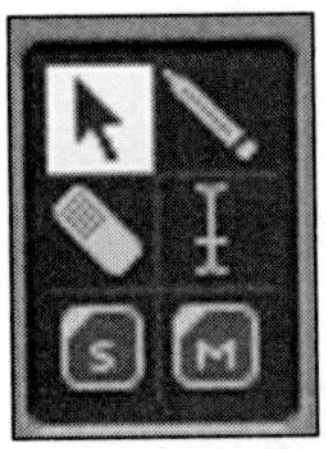

Figure 9.22
The Toolbox of the Event Editor.

The Event Editor Toolbox

Because the Event Editor is designed for text, not graphic, editing, its Toolbox contains fewer tools than the other MIDI editors. Figure 9.22 shows the Event Editor Toolbox.

A description of the tools in the Toolbox follows, starting from the top-left and moving clockwise through the tools:

- **Pointer Tool.** The Pointer tool is the standard tool for selecting single or multiple MIDI events. To make multiple selections with the Pointer tool, hold the mouse button down over an area in the Edit List that doesn't contain a note and drag over a group of notes to make a "rubber band" selection, or hold down the **SHIFT** key while clicking on individual messages.
- **Pencil Tool.** You can click in the Edit List to create a new MIDI event. This is described in more detail in the next section, "Inserting and Deleting MIDI Messages in the Event Editor."
- **Eraser Tool.** The Eraser tool removes one or more MIDI messages from the Event List. This has the same effect as selecting MIDI messages and pressing the **DELETE** key.
- **Mute Tool.** You can click on one or more MIDI notes in the Event List to mute them. Click again to unmute the muted notes.

- **Solo Tool.** The Solo tool works the same way as the Mute tool, only it will solo, not silence, the note or notes. It only functions as long as the mouse button is held down.
- **Text Entry Tool.** If your Event List is not showing MIDI notes, but instead is showing the names of regions and folders from the Arrange window, you can use this tool to rename them.

Inserting and Deleting MIDI Messages in the Event Editor

As with the other MIDI editors, you can insert and delete MIDI information. Since the Event Editor is a text editor, you do not have the visual cues that you do in the Matrix Editor, or the musical notation cues you have in the Score Editor. Still, some people may find it convenient to add notes directly while using the Event List, and you can employ a number of methods.

First of all, you can use the same process described in the previous "MIDI Step Input" subsection to input MIDI information into a MIDI performance one note at a time. The major difference is that you will not see a graphic representation of the note you have performed, but a line of text information instead.

You can also insert an event using the Pencil tool. Simply click in the Event List and it adds a new event, identical to the currently selected event, at the current song position. You can duplicate an existing event by clicking on it with the Pencil. A text input box appears in which you can type in the position where you want to place the duplicate event. Type in the desired position and press **RETURN**. If you press **RETURN** without specifying a new position, the duplicate appears in the same position as the original event (although since this is a text list, it appears right under the original event but with the same position value).

If you are pasting events from the Clipboard, a text-entry box also appears in which you can enter position values; follow the same procedure of entering their position, and the editor will paste them in the new location.

You can delete MIDI events by clicking on them with the Eraser tool, or by selecting them and then pressing the **DELETE** key. If you are not happy with any insertions or deletions you have made, you can always use the Undo command, or open the Undo History window if you have made a number of edits you dislike.

> **EXPERT TIP: CREATING NEW MIDI MESSAGES USING EVENT EDITOR BUTTONS**
>
> In addition to the aforementioned methods of creating MIDI events, you can **COMMAND + CLICK** any of the Event Editor buttons to create a new MIDI message of the same type as the button you clicked. **COMMAND + CLICKING** the Full Message button creates Meta-Events. The new events will be added to the Event List at the current SPL position.

Moving and Adjusting the Values of MIDI Messages in the Event Editor

Even though you do not have the graphic bar to move, lengthen, or shorten for each note, you can easily accomplish these things in the Event Editor, and with even more precision. The important thing to remember is that you are accomplishing everything through text entry, so you need to know the precise values of how much you want to resize a MIDI note, or the exact position to which you want to move a MIDI event.

First of all, to move a single event, simply double-click its position data with the Pointer. A text-entry box appears in which you type the new value. You can skip between the various parts of the position and length parameters by using the **TAB** key. When you press **RETURN**, the event moves to the new location. If you select multiple MIDI messages, they all move relative to the event whose position you changed. So if you selected three MIDI notes that occurred on Bar 1, Bar 2, and Bar 3, and you double-clicked on the note at Bar 2 and changed its position to Bar 3, the note at Bar 1 would move to Bar 2, and the note at Bar 3 would move to Bar 4.

The procedure for adjusting any other value, such as a MIDI event's length or velocity, is basically the same: You simply double-click the desired data with the Pointer tool, enter a new value in the text box, and press **RETURN**. If you select more than one MIDI event, they all maintain their values relative to each other, just as previously described; all selected events maintain their relative length.

You can also adjust values and move events without entering text, but by selecting one or more events and then using the mouse as a vertical slider to adjust values up or down.

When adjusting values for a group of MIDI events with the mouse this way, when any event reaches its maximum or minimum value (remember, MIDI values are between 0 and 127), no further adjustments in that direction will be possible for any event in that group, so that each event may maintain its relative value. If you want to change one single event more than this, however, you can do so by holding the **OPTION** key down while dragging that specific event, or by using the text-entry box for that specific event instead of dragging with the mouse. If you want to set the same value for all selected events, hold down the **OPTION + SHIFT** keys while dragging or entering a text value for one of the events.

The Hyper Editor

The Hyper Editor is another MIDI editor with a heritage that goes back to the early versions of Notator. It offers a unique way to build drum parts and to edit MIDI controller data graphically. It looks a bit like a cross between an Arrange window and a Matrix Editor, with lanes for different notes or controller messages like Arrange, but bars representing MIDI events. You can also view Global Tracks in the Hyper Editor. Figure 9.23 shows a Hyper Editor window.

The Hyper Editor not only offers a step-entry graphic editor for drums and controller messages, but it also allows you to save combinations of event definitions and drum note names as hyper sets, which you'll explore later in this chapter. Due to the uniqueness of the Hyper Editor, it is often overlooked. After reading this section, I hope you will feel comfortable enough to integrate it into your working method.

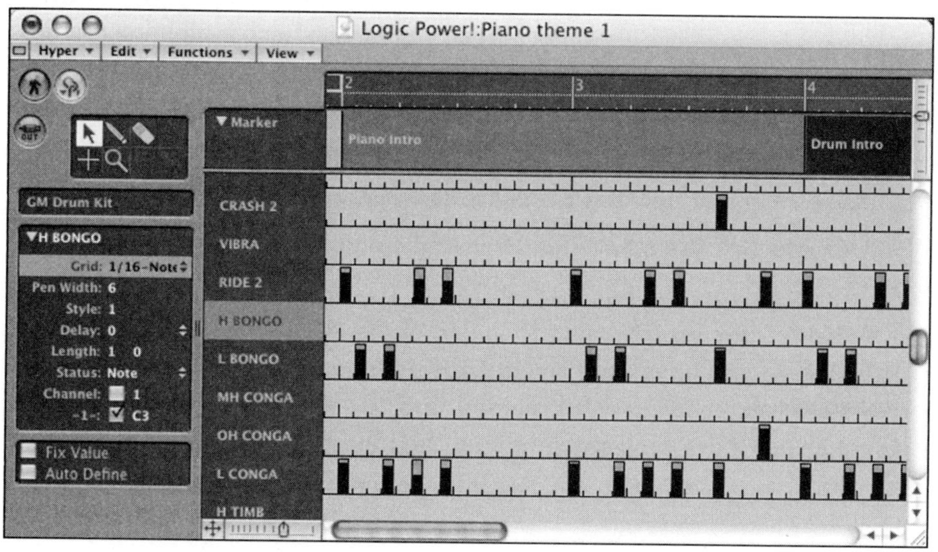

Figure 9.23
You can use the Hyper Editor as a MIDI drum or controller editor; here it is being used as a drum editor.

> **HYPER EDITOR AND HYPER DRAW**
>
> It's tempting to confuse the Hyper Editor with Hyper Draw. While they may share the word "hyper" in their names, they are not referring to the same thing, although they both can operate on MIDI control messages. *Hyper Draw* is the name for the automation-like protocol in which you can enter MIDI control data in the Arrange window or Matrix Editor. The *Hyper Editor* is a grid-based editor that also allows for the input and editing of MIDI control data, but its grid-based editing does not allow for the smoothness of changes of Hyper Draw. Hyper Draw is not suited for "one off" and noncontinuous MIDI control—Hyper Draw wants to connect control messages together. The Hyper Editor, on the other hand, you'll find is far too tedious if you are trying to create automation-like effects—you'd be far better served using Hyper Draw. Finally, there's no way to use Hyper Draw as a drum editor, whereas the Hyper Editor's grid-based edit window is uniquely suited for drum programming.

Hyper Editor Local Menus

Like the Event Editor, the Hyper Editor shares some local menus that the other MIDI editors offer. The unique menus and commands are as follows:

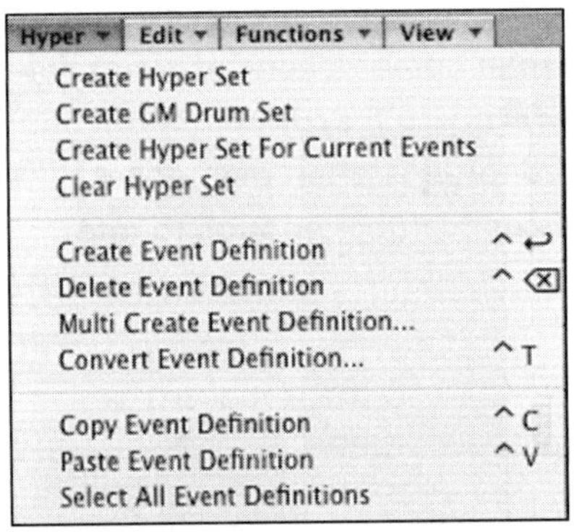

Figure 9.24
The Hyper menu of the Hyper Editor.

The Hyper Menu

As you might have guessed, the local Hyper menu includes commands unique to the Hyper Editor. Figure 9.24 shows the Hyper menu.

This local menu contains most of the commands related to using hyper sets. The "Hyper Sets" subsection later in this chapter explains in detail how to use hyper sets. The following are descriptions of these commands:

- **Create Hyper Set.** This creates a new hyper set.
- **Create GM Drum Set.** This command creates a new GM Drum Set.
- **Create Hyper Set For Current Events.** This creates a hyper set using the events currently selected in one of the MIDI editors. This is very useful if you have used Hyper Draw in other windows to add controller messages to MIDI regions, and you want to create a hyper set with just those previously defined messages (events) represented.
- **Clear Hyper Set.** This command empties the current hyper set.

- **Create Event Definition.** This command creates a new Event Definition on the selected lane of the Hyper Editor. Event Definitions determine which MIDI event a given lane of the Hyper Editor will edit. **<CONTROL + RETURN>**
- **Delete Event Definition.** This erases the Event Definition of the selected lane or lanes in the Hyper Editor. **<CONTROL + DELETE>**
- **Multi Create Event Definition.** You can automatically create Event Definitions for either all MIDI events or all selected events. When you choose this command, a dialog box appears asking whether you want to create a new set with definitions only for those events you have selected or for all events. Select the option you desire, press **RETURN**, and all those Event Definitions will appear to the right of the lanes in the Hyper Editor.
- **Convert Event Definition.** This redefines the selected Event Definition, as well as all the events in its lane. The events retain their values after conversion. **<CONTROL + T>**
- **Copy Event Definition.** This command copies an Event Definition onto the Clipboard. **<CONTROL + C>**
- **Paste Event Definition.** This pastes an Event Definition from the Clipboard. **<CONTROL + V>**
- **Select All Event Definitions.** This command selects all the Event Definitions in the current hyper set.

The Edit Menu

Figure 9.25 shows the Edit menu of the Hyper Editor.

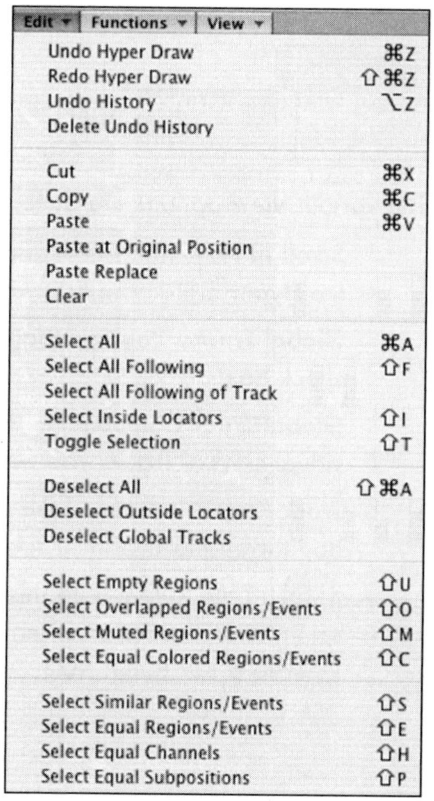

Figure 9.25
The Edit menu from the Hyper Editor is the same as the Edit menus of the Matrix Editor and Event Editor.

As you can see, the Hyper Editor also shares its Edit menu with the Matrix Editor. Refer to the previous subsection covering the Edit menu of the Matrix Editor for descriptions of these commands.

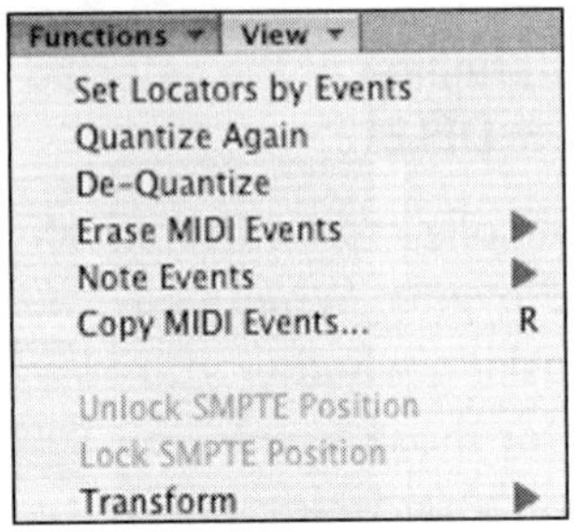

Figure 9.26
The Functions menu of the Hyper Editor is also the same as that of the Matrix Editor and the Event Editor.

The Functions Menu

Figure 9.26 shows the Functions menu of the Hyper Editor.

Once again, this menu is also the same Functions menu as that of the Matrix Editor and the Event Editor. Refer to the previous subsection covering the Matrix Editor's Functions menu for descriptions of these commands.

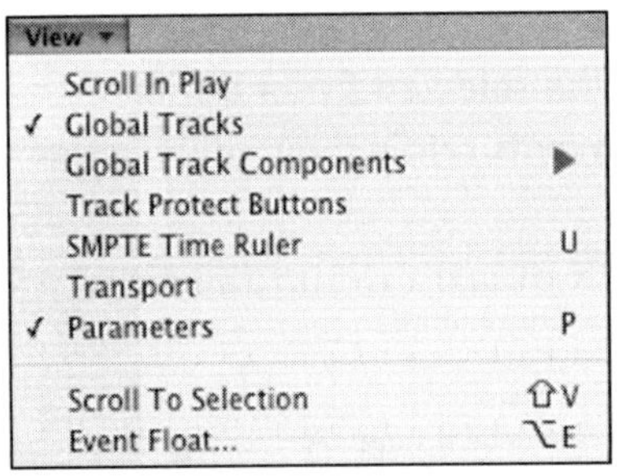

Figure 9.27
The View menu of the Hyper Editor.

The View Menu

The View menu for the Hyper Editor offers unique options. Figure 9.27 shows the View menu of the Hyper Editor.

The various view options are as follows:

- **Scroll In Play.** If this is engaged, instead of the SPL scrolling through the Hyper Editor, the Edit window scrolls past the stationary SPL.
- **Global Tracks.** You can toggle the Global Tracks on or off with this check box.
- **Global Track Components.** This submenu lets you toggle on or off individual Global Tracks you wish to view.
- **Track Protect Buttons.** If this is checked, Track Protect buttons will appear on the Global Tracks.
- **SMPTE Time Ruler.** With this option engaged, the Bar Ruler becomes an SMPTE Time Ruler. Disengaging this option returns the SMPTE Time Ruler to a Bar Ruler. **<U>**

- **Transport.** You can view the Transport controls in the top-left corner of the Hyper Editor, just as in the Arrange window. This is particularly useful when you use the Hyper Editor as a drum editor.
- **Parameters.** Keep this engaged to view the buttons, Toolbox, and other controls on the left side of the Hyper Editor. **<P>**
- **Scroll To Selection.** The Hyper Editor scrolls to a selected MIDI region in Arrange when this control is engaged. **<SHIFT + V>**
- **Event Float.** This command launches a small, one-event tall Event List that floats above the Matrix Editor and displays text information regarding the specific note you are editing. **<OPTION + E>**

The Hyper Editor Buttons and Toolbox

Since the Hyper Editor is unique in its functions, it relies less on the standard Logic window components such as buttons and toolboxes. As you can see in Figure 9.28, the Hyper Editor has far fewer buttons and tools than the other MIDI editors.

Figure 9.28

The buttons and Toolbox of the Hyper Editor.

The next two subsections briefly describe the functions of the buttons and tools.

Hyper Editor Buttons

The Hyper Editor has three basic function buttons common to the other MIDI editors:

- **Catch Button.** With this button engaged, the visible window in the Hyper Editor always follows the SPL position. You will almost always want this on.
- **Link Button.** Engaging the Link button ensures that the editor always displays the same content as the topmost window. Double-clicking the Link button while the Catch button is also engaged activates Contents Catch mode, in which the Hyper Editor always shows the contents of the currently playing region as the song plays.
- **MIDI OUT Button.** With this engaged, you will hear the currently selected MIDI note or event change (if you are working with pitch bend data, for example) while you are working.

The Hyper Editor Toolbox

The Crosshair tool is unique to the Hyper Editor, but the other four tools are standard. Descriptions of the five tools, moving clockwise from the top-left, follow:

- **Pointer Tool.** This is a standard Pointer for selecting and making "rubber band" selections of multiple notes.
- **Pencil Tool.** The Pencil tool allows you to draw in new drum notes if you are using the Hyper Editor as a drum editor, or new controller information if you are using the editor to edit controller data. You learn how to use the Pencil tool later in this chapter in the subsections that cover editing.
- **Eraser Tool.** This tool removes notes and controller data from the Hyper Editor.
- **Magnifying Glass Tool.** To zoom in on a particular area, use the Magnifying Glass tool to "rubber band" them. You then zoom in to the maximum zoom level. Click in any empty space in the Edit window to return to the original zoom level.
- **Crosshair Tool.** This tool is valuable if you want to make linear changes in your data. To use this tool, click the mouse on the note or controller message that you want to begin your line, drag the vertical line until you reach your end point, then click the mouse again. The velocity or controller data in any event between the line's end points will snap to the value at which the line bisected the event. In other words, if you wanted to fade up the velocity of drum hits slowly, you could click the crosshair on the first drum hit at the very bottom of the hit; then, at the end of the measure, click the mouse again, drawing a diagonal line up through your drum hits. The velocities of your drum hits now have the upward ramp formed by the Crosshair tool, giving you an even, linear fade-in.

The Hyper Editor Event Parameter Box

Unlike the Matrix Editor or Event Editor, the Hyper Editor has a parameter box. This box contains parameters to define that note or event. Every Event Definition has its own parameter box. Figure 9.29 shows a parameter box for the Volume lane.

The functions of these parameters are as follows:

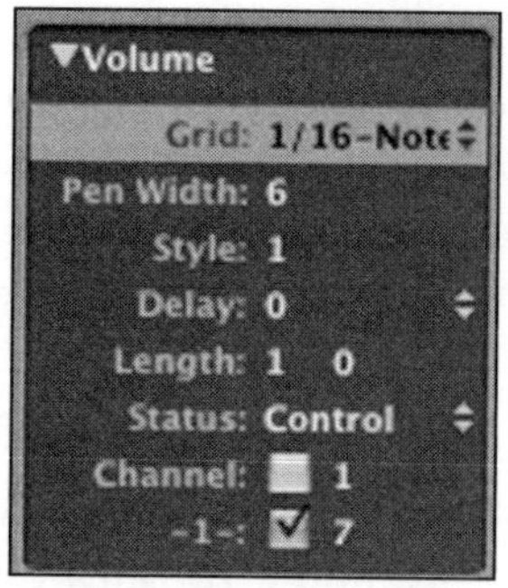

Figure 9.29
The parameter box for the Volume events in the Hyper Editor.

- **Grid.** This determines the grid, meaning how many events will fit in one bar in the edit window. The size of the grid determines the resolution of the events.
- **Pen Width.** With this parameter, you can adjust the width of the bars that appear in the Edit window. You can adjust this parameter between 1 and 16. In general, you'll want to find the value that almost completely fills the grid space, but which still leaves a few pixels so you can differentiate the different bars. You need to determine the correct value based on your chosen grid resolution.
- **Style.** This parameter adjusts the shading style of the Hyper Editor. You have eight styles from which to choose. Styles 5–8 are the same as 1–4, except that the lane flashes when selected.
- **Delay.** With this parameter, you can offset all the events in a lane by a number of ticks. Simply double-click the right edge of the parameter box across from the word "Delay" and enter a value in the text box. Positive values delay events, negative numbers advance events. If you click between the parameter name and the number, a pull-down menu appears in which you can select your Note Divisions.
- **Length.** The Length parameter determines how long added notes will be. The first number is measures, the second is ticks. You will not normally need to set this, unless you have some particularly long or short drum samples.
- **Status.** Here you can change the Event Definition from one type of message (note, volume, pitch bend, and so on) to another.
- **Channel.** Normally, the Hyper Editor displays all matching MIDI events in the region being edited. If you set the MIDI Channel (Cha) parameter and check the box, the Hyper Editor shows only those events on the selected channel. If the box is unchecked, the parameter is ignored.
- **-1- (First Byte).** With this box checked, this parameter determines what the initial byte (note pitch for notes, controller type for MIDI control messages) must be for the lane to display data. In other words, if the

First Byte parameter is set for C#2, the editor displays only those notes that fall on C#2. Generally, for drum editing and specific MIDI control message events, you'll want this box checked. For more generic columns (such as the All Velocities option), you'll want to leave this box unchecked.

Hyper Sets

Hyper sets are unique to the Hyper Editor. They are basically stored lists of MIDI notes, or MIDI Control Message Definitions, complete with parameters for each lane. Hyper sets allow you not only to configure the editor for your specific needs, but also to then save that configuration, with all of your parameter settings, note names, and so on, and recall that configuration at will. You can have a hyper set for your specific MIDI drum kit, and whenever you want to program drums, the exact setup on the grid that you need will be waiting for you. Or if you like to use a few specific MIDI control events, you can create a hyper set of only those Event Definitions.

Hyper sets not only are powerful tools, but they are also very easy to use. You can access your available hyper sets from a pull-down menu between the Toolbox and parameter box. Simply pull down the menu and select the hyper set you want to use. Figure 9.30 shows the Hyper Set selection field.

Logic offers hyper sets for MIDI controls and GM (General MIDI) drums, which you can use as they are, or you can use them as templates for your own hyper sets. Simply adjust each lane using the Hyper local menu and key commands, set the parameter box for the Event Definitions to taste, use the **Select All** command, then choose **Create Hyper Set for Current Events** to create a hyper set of your current configuration. If you'd prefer to start from a blank slate, you can always start the process by using the Create Hyper Set command. You can name your hyper set by double-clicking in the Hyper Set selection field, which presents you with a text box in which to enter a new name for the hyper set. You need not worry about saving anything—Logic automatically saves each new hyper set in Logic's preferences, so it's available in any of your songs.

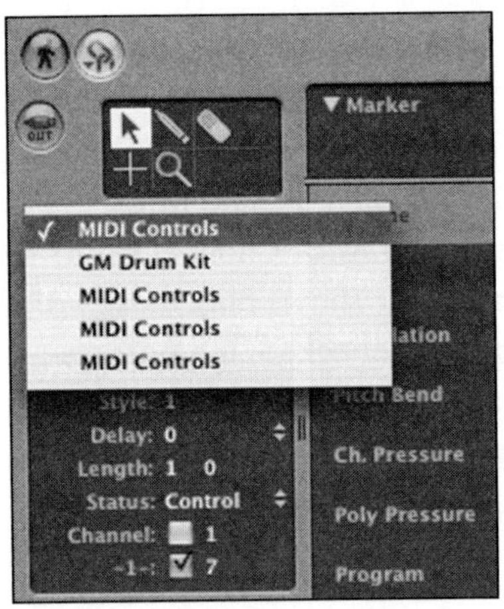

Figure 9.30

All the hyper sets you create are available in the Hyper Set selection field.

Editing MIDI Control Messages Using the Hyper Editor

The Hyper Editor is ideal for editing situations in which you want to see your controller data in a grid or in vertical bars. You can also view many different MIDI messages in one hyper set, and get an overall view of how your various MIDI messages are interacting with each other (such as how Volume and Pan messages are interacting).

You can use the Pencil tool to place MIDI events directly on the grid where you want them. If you want to create many messages, simply hold the button down and move across the grid. As you move the mouse up or down, you draw in higher or lower values for your data. The bar for each note is solidly colored to represent how high the value of the event is. (A solid event means the event has a value of 127, the highest MIDI value. If the solid portion of the bar is only a third of the way up the bar, the value may be only 42.) After creating your data with the Pencil, use the Crosshair tool to make smooth value adjustments across an entire lane.

If you are used to viewing messages as continuous, viewing them instead in the shape of static bars might seem tricky at first. But what you might think is continuous is actually nothing but a series of individual messages, each assigning a given controller a value. After using the Hyper Editor to edit those individual messages and values, you might just fall in love with having that level of control over your data!

Editing MIDI Notes (Drums) Using the Hyper Editor

A MIDI note is actually just a form of MIDI control message that tells a sound module to play a sound. Because the Hyper Editor allows you to place notes directly on a grid, using the Hyper Editor as a drum editor is a natural fit. If you enjoy programming drums in the computer, rather than via a performance on a MIDI keyboard, drum controller, or MIDI percussion set, the Hyper Editor offers you the ability to draw notes on a grid quickly, exactly where you want them. Thanks to hyper sets, you can even name each lane with the name of the drum instrument that lane triggers.

The procedure for using the Hyper Editor to program drums is exactly the same as described previously for MIDI control messages: You draw in the event you want, in the lane you want, at the velocity you want. You'll see a bar line representing your drum hit and the velocity you selected. You can hold the Pencil down and roll over many positions to create multiple notes, and you can use the Crosshair tool to create fade-ins, fade-outs, steady velocity at a particular value, and so on. If you like programming drum parts directly into Logic, you'll find the Hyper Editor especially suited to your needs.

> **EXPERT TIP: HYPER EDITOR ISN'T LIMITED TO DRUM PROGRAMMING**
>
> Clearly, the Hyper Editor assumes if you want to program notes in its grid, they will be for drum parts—as its inclusion of a GM Drum Hyper Set and commands to create them illustrates. However, that doesn't mean that you *must* use the Hyper Editor for drum tracks. If you are programming heavily quantized MIDI parts and looking for an "analog step sequencer" style of grid in which to place your arpeggiated synth pulses and techno hits, you just might find that the Hyper Editor suits your needs as well.
>
> Simply create a GM Drum Hyper Set, which will give you a hyper set with all notes, then erase the drum name in the parameter box and give each event its standard note name. You'll end up with a hyper set of notes without drum names. Rename the hyper set and you now have a MIDI Step Sequencer Hyper Set, ready for you to program synths right to the grid!

The Score Editor

As cutting edge as Logic is, traditional musicians are not left out in the cold. One of the most powerful editors in Logic is the Score Editor, which offers traditional music notation recording, editing, and score printing. Even if you don't feel at home with using computers to manipulate MIDI performances, you will find the Score Editor to be the "digital music notation paper" you always wanted, where you can perform, move, erase, redraw, and print out notes with the ease that only a computer can bring. Figure 9.31 shows the Score Editor.

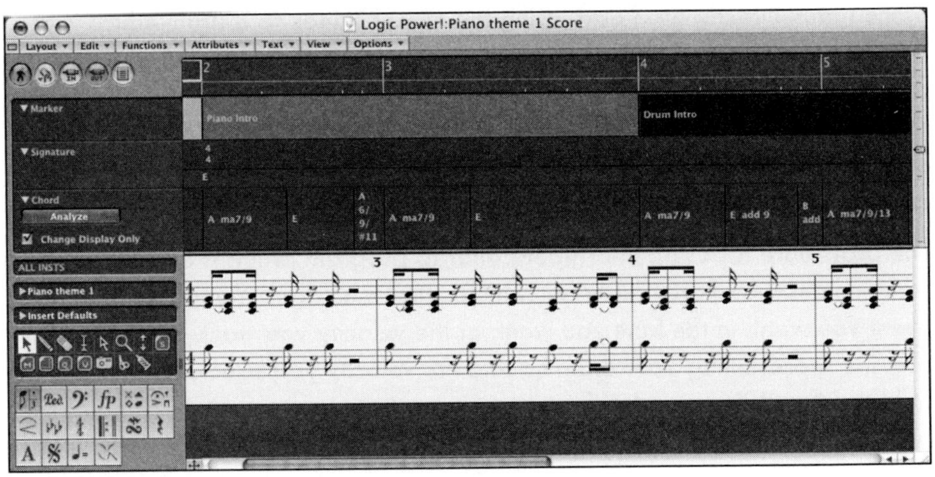

Figure 9.31
The Score Editor.

If you do not read and write music notation, you may find this editor superfluous to your working method. However, if you do use—and sometimes even think in—music notation, you'll find the Score Editor to be one of Logic's most important features, with advantages over other sequencers that do not offer nearly the power and flexibility of Logic's notation facilities.

> **THE SCOPE OF THIS SECTION**
>
> This section is not intended to teach music theory or the reading and writing of music notation. Instead, the purpose is to introduce those already familiar with these concepts to the way that Logic allows users to write and edit music in notation form. And I do mean *introduce*—the Score Editor is perhaps the deepest editor in Logic, because music notation itself is truly an advanced symbolic language, with all the inherent complexity and options that implies. If this chapter inspires you to explore music notation on your own, *great!* Music theory will always help your music productions, even if you're a DJ building techno backing tracks and don't feel any music notation skills are necessary.

Score Editor Local Menus

Because of the comprehensive nature of music notation, the Score Editor has a lot of commands relating to how to format, layout, and enter notes. To accommodate this, the Score Editor has more local menus than the other MIDI editors. A couple of the local menus are shared with the other MIDI editors, but most are unique to the Score Editor. The subsections that follow describe the various options available in the local menus.

Layout Menu

The Layout local menu contains options for how to format your score. Figure 9.32 shows the Layout menu.

Figure 9.32

The Layout menu of the Score Editor.

The various options are as follows:

- **Score Styles.** This command opens the Score Styles window, which allows you to access Logic's predesigned Score Styles as well as create your own. The Score Styles window is described in the subsection "Score Styles" later in this chapter. **<CONTROL + COMMAND + S>**

- **Instrument Sets.** This command brings up a window that allows you to select which MIDI Instruments from the Arrange tracks you want to appear in your score. **<CONTROL + COMMAND + I>**
- **Global Format.** This command opens the Score Song Settings window to the General tab, which allows you to configure the page setup for printing, the spacing of your score, the chord symbols, and so on. You can also access this dialog box by choosing **File > Song Settings > Score**. Figure 9.33 shows this window. **<CONTROL + COMMAND + F>**

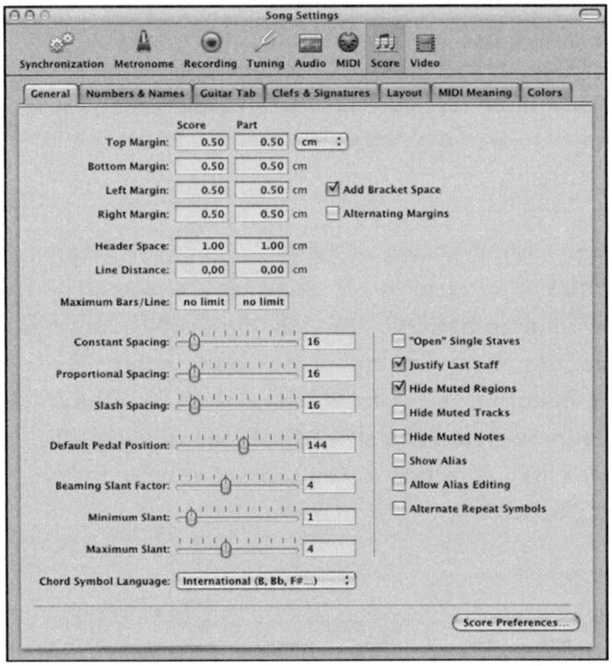

Figure 9.33
The Score Song Settings window open to the General tab.

- **Numbers & Names.** This command opens the Score Song Settings window to the Numbers & Names tab, in which you can configure page numbers, bar numbers, and instrument names for printing and so on. You can also access this dialog box by choosing **File > Song Settings > Score**. Figure 9.34 shows this window.
- **Guitar Tablature.** This command opens the Score Song Settings window to the Guitar Tab dialog which allows you to configure how Logic will format guitar tablature and similar features. You can also access this dialog box by choosing **File > Song Settings > Score**. Figure 9.35 shows this window.

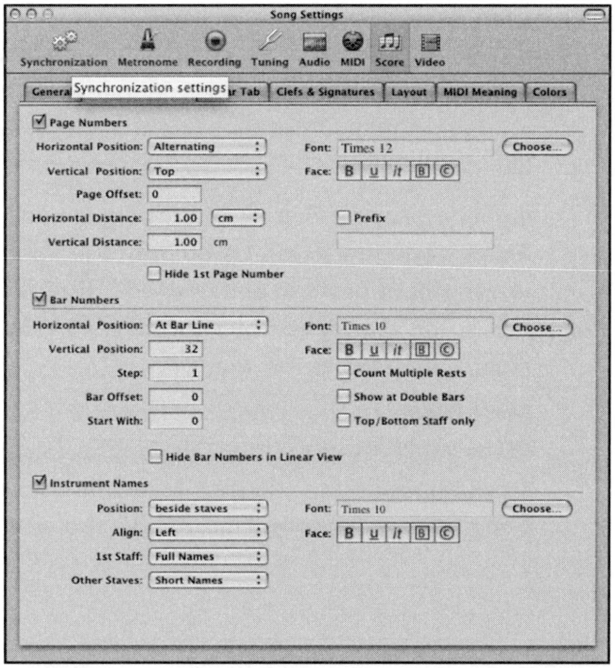

Figure 9.34

The Score Song Settings window open to the Numbers & Names tab.

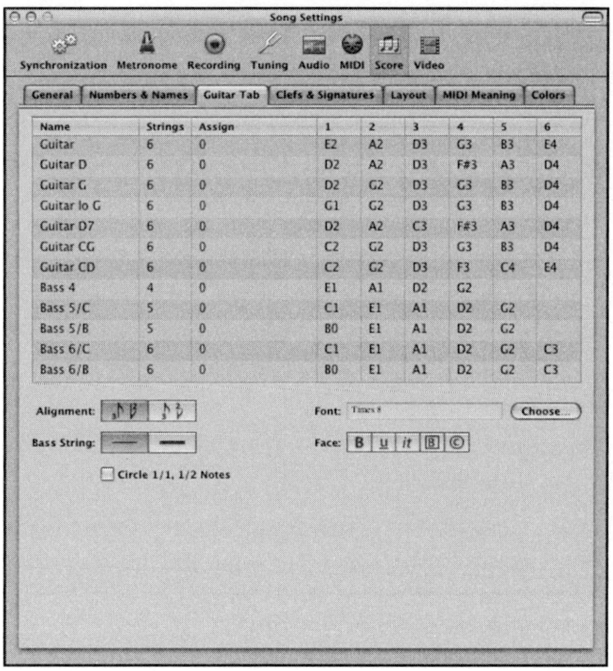

Figure 9.35

The Score Song Settings window open to the Guitar Tab dialog box.

- **Clefs & Signatures.** This command opens the Score Song Settings window to the Clefs & Signatures tab. This window offers parameters for how Logic displays clefs, key signatures, time signatures, and octave symbols. You can also access this dialog box by choosing **File > Song Settings > Score**. Figure 9.36 shows this window.
- **Extended Layout Parameters.** This command opens the Score Song Settings window to the Layout tab. This window offers extra parameters for more esoteric and aesthetic display options. You can also access this dialog box by choosing **File > Song Settings > Score**. Figure 9.37 shows this window.
- **MIDI Meaning.** This command opens the Score Song Settings window to the MIDI Meaning tab. This window lets you assign MIDI values to score symbols. You can also access this dialog box by choosing **File > Song Settings > Score**. Figure 9.38 shows this window.

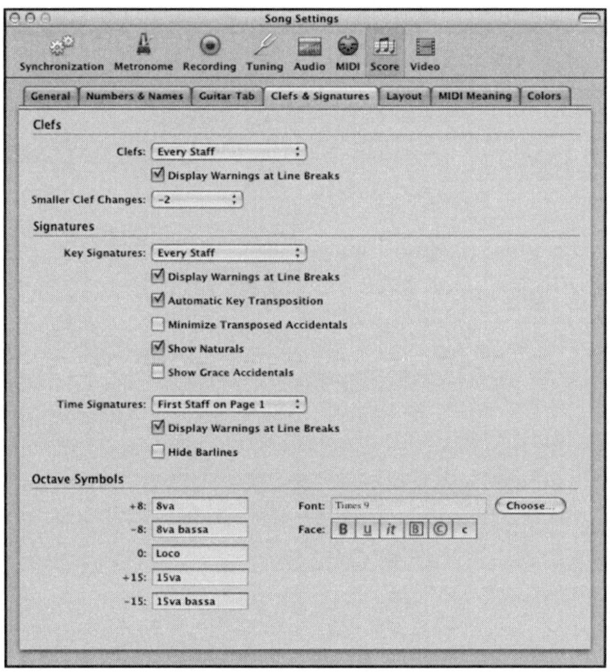

Figure 9.36

The Score Song Settings window open to the Clefs & Signatures tab.

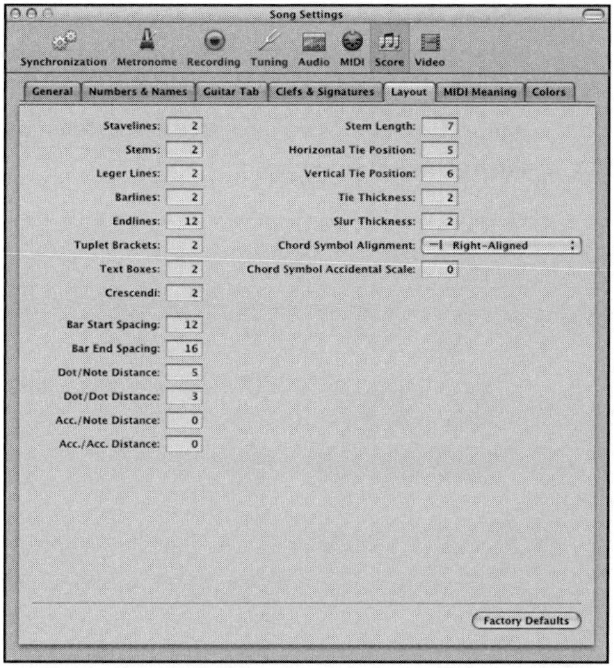

Figure 9.37

The Score Song Settings window open to the Layout tab.

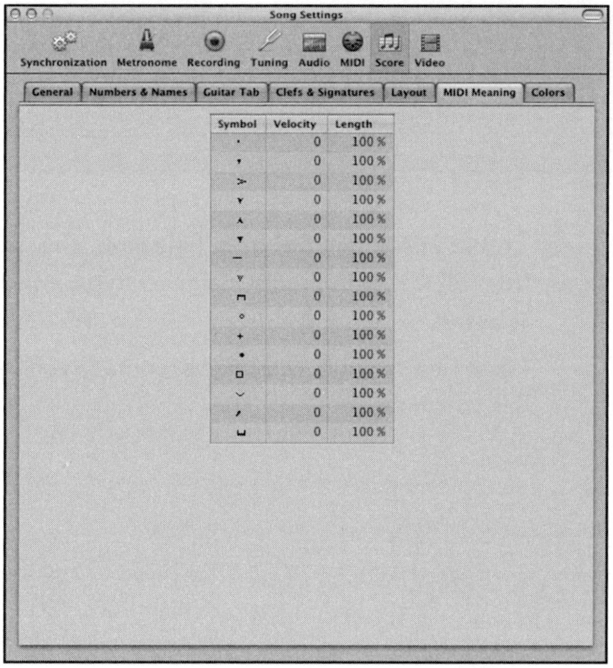

Figure 9.38

The Score Song Settings window open to the MIDI Meaning tab.

- **Colors.** This command opens the Score Song Settings window to the Colors tab. This window lets you assign colors to pitch and velocity, as well as construct your own user palettes. You can also access this dialog box by choosing **File > Song Settings > Score**. Figure 9.39 shows this window.

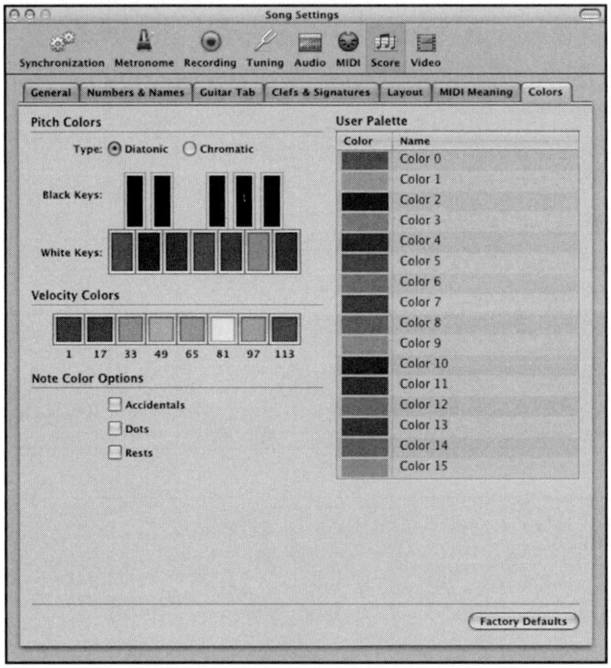

Figure 9.39
The Score Song Settings window open to the Colors tab.

- **Create Instrument Set from Selection.** This creates a new instrument set from all the instruments assigned to the MIDI regions you have selected.
- **Reset Line Layout.** You can reset the layout of the notation lines with this command.

PRINTING A SCORE THAT INCLUDES BOTH A TRANSPOSED AND NON-TRANSPOSED INSTRUMENT

Noted film and television composer Jay Asher is a longtime Logic user who, as he puts it "lives in the Score Editor." Asher shares with us a very helpful tip he learned for printing scores that begin on a non-transposing instrument and switch to a transposing instrument:

"Let us say you need to print out a part that begins on a non-transposing (C) instrument—for example, the oboe—and then switches to a transposing instrument—for example, the English horn, which transposes up a 5th (+7). You could highlight all the notes in one of the editors and manually transpose them, but the result would be that the notes would sound different when played back. Here's how you can do it without changing the sound:

1. Make sure that your Score Editor is showing the default instrument set ALL INSTS.
2. If your oboe and English horn parts are already different MIDI regions on the same Arrange track, you can skip to step 4.
3. Cut the MIDI region into two MIDI regions and put them on the same Arrange track.
4. Make sure that both have the proper transposition, in our example none for the oboe sequence, +7 for the English horn.
5. Open the Score Editor. Make sure that you are in Full Score mode in Page Edit View and select both MIDI regions by holding the **SHIFT** key while selecting.
6. In the Layout local menu choose **Create Instrument Set from Selection**. This will create a new Instrument Set (which you can rename if you would like).
7. Then double-click anywhere in the white area around the MIDI regions.
8. Switch to Print View.

The result is [a single] score part with both MIDI regions properly transposed for a [professional musician] to read, and your MIDI parts will sound [as they did originally]. Remember of course to insert text to [inform] the player...when he is playing one instrument (oboe in our example) and when he switches (to English horn in our example)."

The Edit Menu

As Figure 9.40 illustrates, the Edit menu in the Score Editor is the same as the other MIDI editors.

Refer to the subsection covering the Matrix Editor's Edit menu to learn about the various functions of the Edit menu.

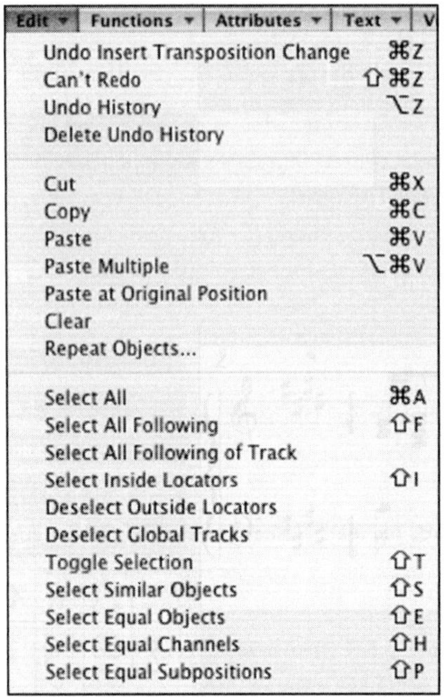

Figure 9.40

The Edit menu in the Score Editor is identical to the Edit menu in all the other MIDI editors in Logic.

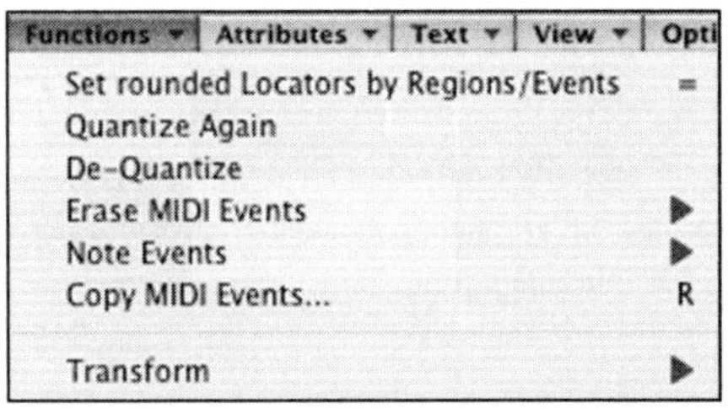

Figure 9.41

The Functions menu in the Score Editor is the same as the other MIDI editors' Functions menus.

The Functions Menu

The options of the Functions menu, shown in Figure 9.41, are also shared with the other MIDI editors.

Refer to the subsection "The Functions Menu" in the section "The Matrix Editor" for descriptions of the commands in the Functions menu.

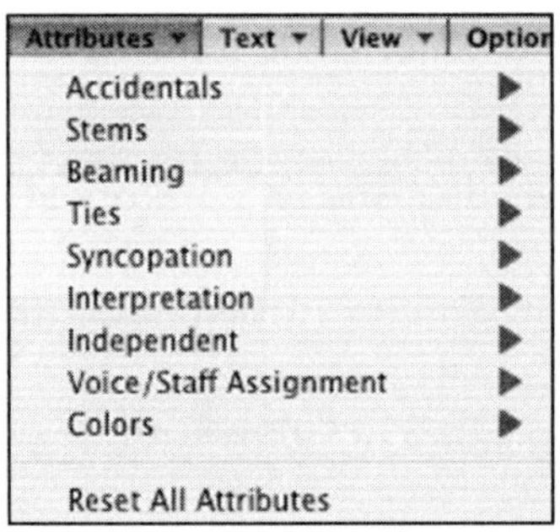

Figure 9.42

The Attributes menu of the Score Editor. This local menu contains different options to change the attributes of a selected note or symbol.

The Attributes Menu

The Attributes menu is filled with note and score symbol display parameters that you can set individually per note, regardless of your settings in other menus. Figure 9.42 shows the Attributes menu.

The Attributes menu contains nine hierarchal menus with over 37 options for altering the attributes of the selected note or notes. To apply any of these options, select one or more notes and/or symbols in the Editor display, then choose the desired option from this menu.

It's beyond the scope of this book to cover all 37 possible note and symbol attribute alterations. If you write music notation and need to alter note attributes, you should find it easy to locate the desired attributes in this menu.

The Text Menu

The Text menu should look familiar to anyone used to word processing and desktop publishing applications. It offers a standard selection of text formatting menus from which to choose any of your installed fonts, size, style, left/right alignment, and so on. Figure 9.43 shows the Text menu.

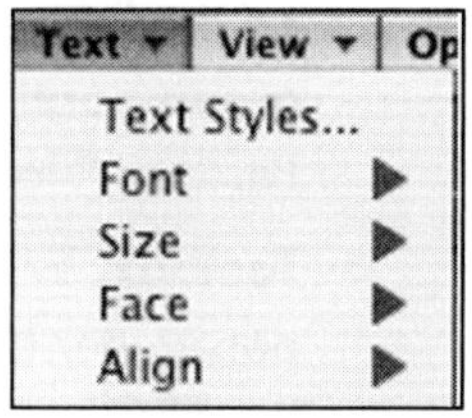

Figure 9.43

The Text menu of the Score Editor offers you the use of your currently installed fonts, and basic style options, for score text.

You can use this menu to select which one of your installed fonts you would like to use for lyrics, notes on your score, and more.

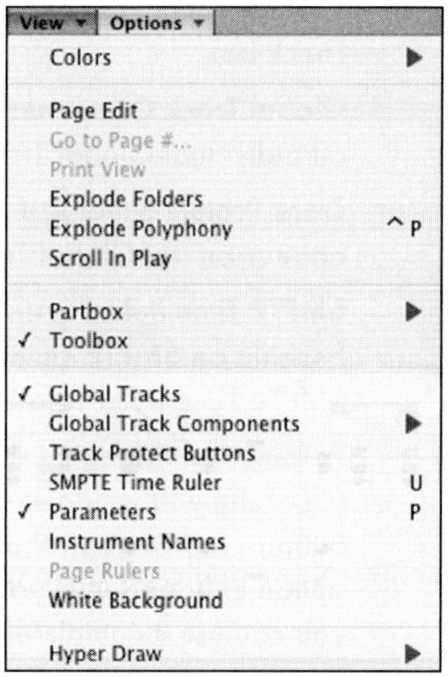

Figure 9.44

The View menu of the Score Editor.

The View Menu

The View menu contains options for configuring your view of the Score Editor. Figure 9.44 shows the View menu.

The various options available in the View menu are as follows:

- **Colors.** This View menu option allows you to colorize notes either by pitch, velocity, or voice assignment. You can also force a note to be black and white instead of colorized. The different choices are available in the hierarchal menu that opens when you select this menu option.
- **Page Edit.** This switches to Page Edit view, where you can edit your printable score page.
- **Print View.** This command switches to Print view, where you can see your score as it will print.

- **Explode Folders.** This separates Folder Tracks into their component tracks.
- **Explode Polyphony.** This command separates the various separate voices playing together into separate staves. **<CONTROL + P>**
- **Scroll In Play.** If this is engaged, instead of the SPL scrolling through the Score Editor, the edit window scrolls past the stationary SPL.
- **Partbox.** In this hierarchal submenu are two options: one is to view all the groups in the Partbox (the box of notes, staffs, and other symbols on the left of the Score Editor), and the other option is to lock the group positions. The Partbox is described in its own subsection, "The Partbox," later in this chapter.
- **Toolbox.** With this engaged, you will see the Toolbox as part of the parameter bar. Otherwise, you can still view the Toolbox by pressing the **ESC** key; the Toolbox appears at the current cursor position.
- **Global Tracks.** You can toggle the Global Tracks on or off with this check box.
- **Global Track Components.** This pull-down menu lets you toggle on or off individual Global Tracks you wish to view.
- **Track Protect Buttons.** If this is checked, Track Protect buttons will appear on the Global Tracks.
- **SMPTE Time Ruler.** With this option engaged, the Bar Ruler will become an SMPTE Time Ruler. Disengaging this option returns the SMPTE Time Ruler to a Bar Ruler. **<U>**
- **Parameters.** Engaging this option displays the parameter bar to the left of the edit window; without engaging this, you will not see your buttons, the Toolbar, the Partbox, and so on. You should keep this option engaged until you are so familiar with the Score Editor that you can use it completely via key commands.
- **Instrument Names.** This determines whether the name of the instrument to which your MIDI region is assigned is displayed or not.
- **Page Rulers.** You can toggle the Page Rulers on and off with this option.
- **White Background.** With this selected, the background color changes from yellow to white.

- **Hyper Draw.** Just as with the Matrix Editor View menu option, this command creates a track lane beneath the Score Editor where you can view, edit, and create Hyper Draw, or MIDI control message, information. Figure 9.45 shows a Score Editor displaying the Hyper Edit lane.

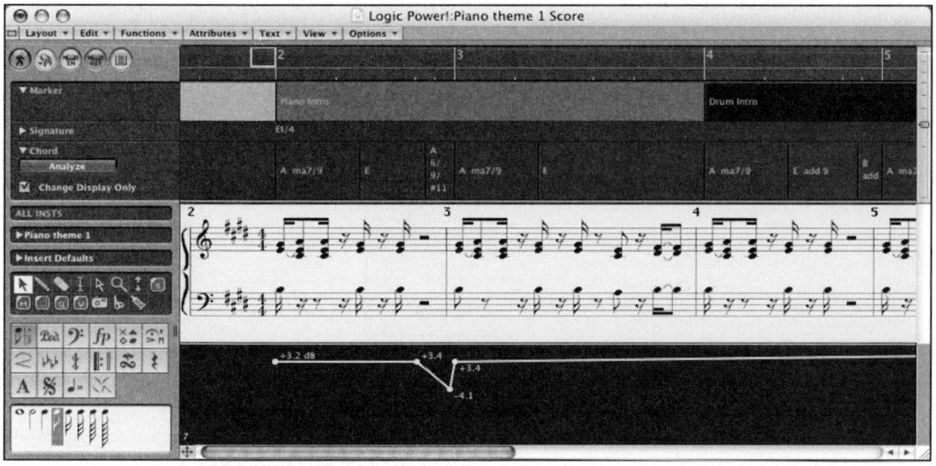

Figure 9.45
The Hyper Draw view option selected in the Score Editor.

The Options Menu

This short local menu has just a few miscellaneous commands. Figure 9.46 shows the Options menu.

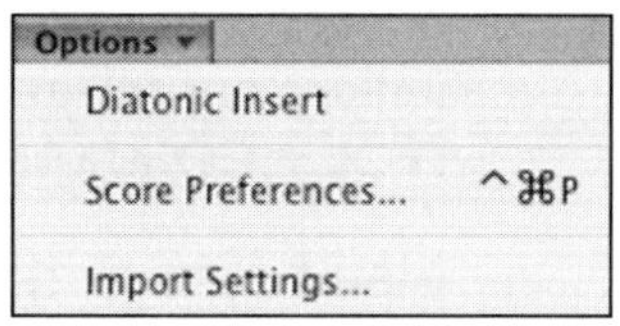

Figure 9.46
The Options menu of the Score Editor.

The functions of these commands are as follows:

- **Diatonic Insert.** When you are using the Pencil tool, engaging Diatonic Insert limits you to inserting only notes that are diatonically correct for the current key. You can alter the notes chromatically once they have been inserted, however. Also, this function does not work for MIDI input notes, only drawn notes.
- **Score Preferences.** This command launches the global Score Preferences dialog box. You can also open this dialog box by choosing **Logic Pro > Preferences > Score** and by pressing the key command **CONTROL + COMMAND + P**. Figure 9.47 shows the Score Preferences dialog box.

Figure 9.47

The Score Preferences dialog box is accessible in many different ways, including by choosing the Options menu in the Score Editor.

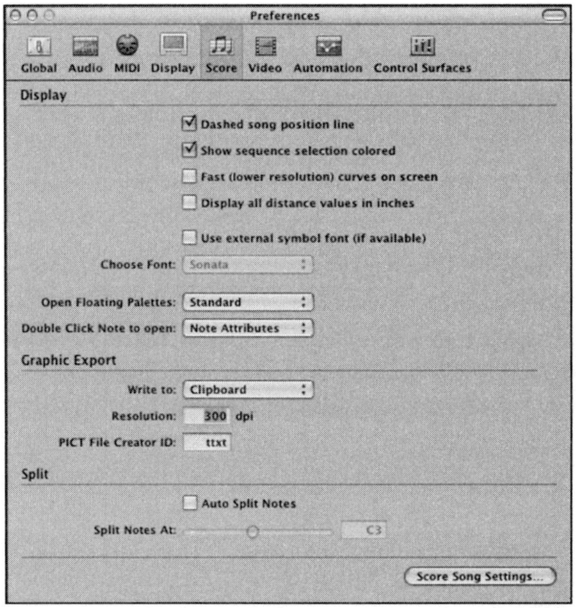

The Score Preferences dialog box includes preferences for how you want the Score Editor to operate. The specific settings that you will want will depend completely on how you use the Score Editor—for example, do you use it more for editing, or just for printing? The menu options are self-evident if you are familiar with music notation. **<CONTROL + COMMAND + P>**

- **Import Settings.** This options allows you to specify how many score and MIDI elements you want to import from another Logic song.

The Score Editor Buttons

The Score Editor offers five buttons, four of which are common to the other MIDI editors. Figure 9.48 shows the Score Editor buttons.

Figure 9.48

The Score Editor buttons.

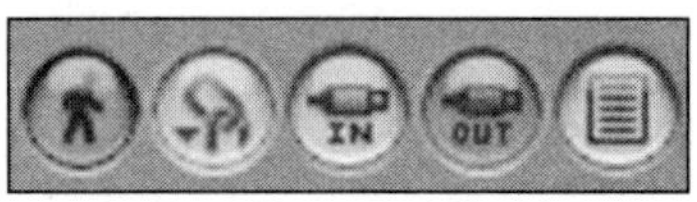

The following are descriptions of the buttons, moving from left to right:

- **Catch Button.** With this button engaged, the edit window in the Score Editor will always follow the SPL position. You will almost always want this on.
- **Link Button.** Engaging the Link button ensures that the editor always displays the same content as the topmost window. Double-clicking the Link button while the Catch button is also engaged activates Contents Catch mode, in which the Score Editor always shows the contents of the currently playing MIDI region as the song plays.
- **MIDI IN Button.** The MIDI IN button engages Step Input mode, described earlier in the section "The Matrix Editor."
- **MIDI OUT Button.** With this engaged, you hear the currently selected MIDI note or event change (if you are working with pitch bend data, for example) while you are working.
- **Page View.** This button toggles between the Edit view—the normal Score Editing mode seen in Figure 9.31—and Page Layout view, a full-page overview of how your score will print out. Page Layout view is far less responsive than Edit view, since it was not designed for realtime input or editing operations, but for final finishing touches before printing.

The Score Editor Parameter Boxes

As you can see in Figure 9.31, the Score Editor is loaded with boxes. Two of them are parameter boxes for the region being edited in the Score Editor. The following subsections describe these parameter boxes.

The Display Parameter Box

The Display parameter box, located directly underneath the Instrument Set selection box, contains parameters that configure the rhythmic display of the selected MIDI region. Figure 9.49 shows the Display parameter box.

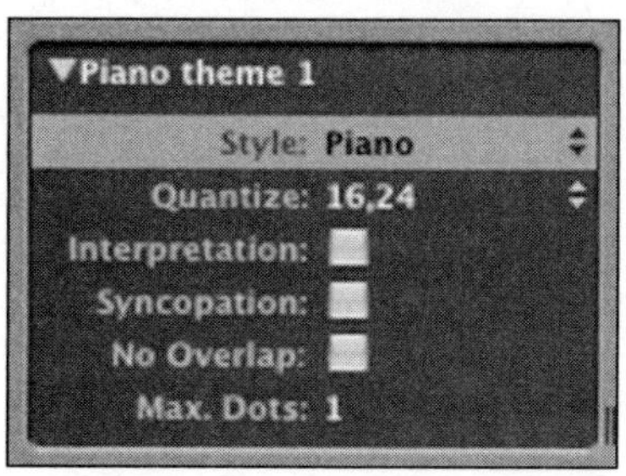

Figure 9.49
The Display parameter box.

Descriptions of the parameters follow:

- **Style.** This parameter indicates the Score Style used for the score display of the selected MIDI region. Clicking to the right of the parameter name opens a pull-down menu of all available Score Styles from which you can choose.
- **Quantize.** The Display Quantization parameter determines the shortest note value that the currently selected region can display. The value can either be a single number, called a *binary quantization*, or two numbers (a binary and a ternary value), called a *hybrid quantization*. As with the Style parameter, you choose your desired value from the pull-down menu that appears when you click to the right of the parameter name.
- **Interpretation.** With Interpretation on, the Score Editor displays notes with length values that fall on the beat, to make the score easier to read during realtime recording. The display is far less precise than when Interpretation is off and the Score Editor shows notes at their true length. You can also turn this feature on or off on a per-note basis by choosing the appropriate option in the Attributes menu or via a key command. Generally, you might want to leave Interpretation on if you have the Score Editor open while you are recording in the Arrange window, but otherwise you'll want it off.
- **Syncopation.** If Syncopation is turned on, instead of displaying syncopated notes as several tied notes, the Score Editor displays syncopated notes as a single note. As with Interpretation, you can turn this feature on or off per note by choosing the appropriate option in the local Attributes menu or via the key command.
- **No Overlap.** This prevents the overlapping of notes in the display. Except when you want to display visually repeated and overlapping notes, you will want to keep this option on.
- **Max Dots.** The Max Dots option determines how many dots that Logic allows a single note to display. You can change unwanted dotted notes by inserting User Rests.

Event Parameter Box

Each event in the Score Editor gets its own parameter set. The Event parameter box displays those parameters for each individual event (note, rest, time signature, and so on) in your score. Figure 9.50 shows the Event parameter box.

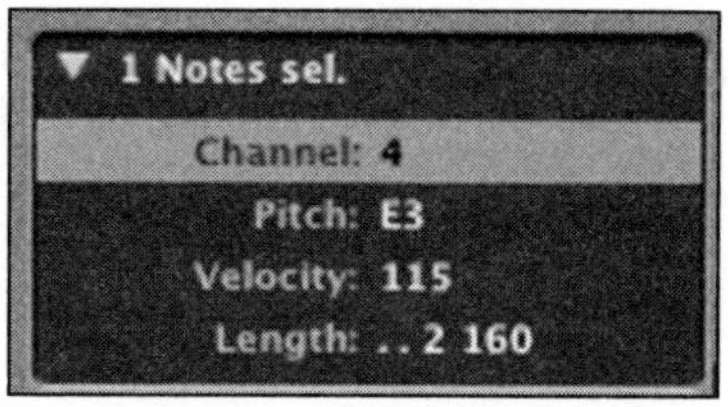

Figure 9.50
The Event parameter box.

Depending on whether you have selected a note or non-note event, the Event parameter box displays different options. The following are all the possible parameters that can appear in this box:

- **Channel.** The selected event is on the MIDI Channel set in this parameter. In general, your entire MIDI region should send all of its notes on the same channel, but you might want to send a few notes to other devices. An exception is if you are working on a drum score, and you are sending different drum instruments on different MIDI Channels.
- **Pitch.** This sets the pitch of the selected note. This parameter appears only when notes are selected.
- **Velocity.** This parameter is for setting the MIDI velocity (volume of the event). If the event is a rest, even though the parameter contains a value, it is still sending silence.
- **Length.** This parameter sets the length of the note. This parameter appears only when notes are selected.
- **Text.** Use this parameter to select a Text Style from the pop-up menu of text styles that appears when you click on this parameter. You'll learn about Text Styles later in this chapter. This parameter does not appear for note events.
- **Lyric.** You should check this box if you are writing lyrics above this event, or leave it set to off if you are not. This parameter does not appear for note events.

The Score Editor Toolbox

Because the Score Editor is geared toward both graphic editing and printing, its Toolbox is the largest of all the MIDI editors, housing 15 tools. Figure 9.51 shows the Score Editor Toolbox.

Figure 9.51
The Score Editor Toolbox.

Many of these tools are familiar, but a few are unique to the Score Editor. The following are descriptions of these tools, moving from left to right, starting in the top row and then to the bottom row.

- **Pointer Tool.** The standard Pointer tool is for selecting and making "rubber band" selections of multiple notes.
- **Pencil Tool.** The Pencil tool allows you to insert new notes into the Score Editor.
- **Eraser Tool.** This tool removes notes from the Score Editor.
- **Text Input Tool.** With this tool, you can enter text into your score.
- **Layout Tool.** Use this tool to move objects around in your score without actually affecting the timing of the actual MIDI event.
- **Magnifying Glass Tool.** If you want to zoom in on a particular group of notes, use the Magnifying tool to "rubber band" them. You then zoom in to the maximum zoom level. Click anywhere there are no notes to return to the original zoom level.
- **Voice Splitter Tool.** This tool allows you to separate polyphonic voices into different staves by drawing a dividing line. For this tool to be effective, you must be using a polyphonic style.
- **Solo Tool.** This tool solos or unsolos notes in the Score Editor.
- **Mute Tool.** The Mute tool mutes or unmutes notes in the Score Editor.
- **Sizer Tool.** This tool can adjust the size of objects in the Score Editor.
- **Quantize Tool.** The Quantize tool allows you to quantize only selected notes, leaving the rest of the region unquantized. This is very useful if you have a great performance with only one portion in which the timing is slightly off. You can use this tool to quantize just those few notes and leave the rest of the performance alone.
- **Velocity Tool.** The bar inside each note indicates the relative velocity of that note. With the Velocity tool, you can raise or lower the velocity of one or more notes graphically, by selecting the note and then scrolling up or down with the mouse to shorten or lengthen the velocity bar inside the note or notes. When you adjust the velocity of all selected notes at once by clicking on a single note and moving the mouse, every note retains its value relative to the other notes (so, if you raise the velocity of a loud note and a soft note, both become louder, but the soft note becomes the same amount softer). You can hold down **OPTION + SHIFT** to adjust all selected notes to the same velocity.

- **Camera Tool.** Use the Camera tool to select sections of your score and export them into graphics files.
- **Scissors Tool.** The Scissors tool splits notes into multiple notes.
- **Glue Tool.** This tool merges adjacent notes together, forming one note from multiple notes.

The Partbox

The Parameter view of the Score Editor contains a unique notation toolset underneath the Toolbox called the Partbox—so named because it contains various parts you might like to use in a score. Figure 9.52 shows a Score Editor Partbox.

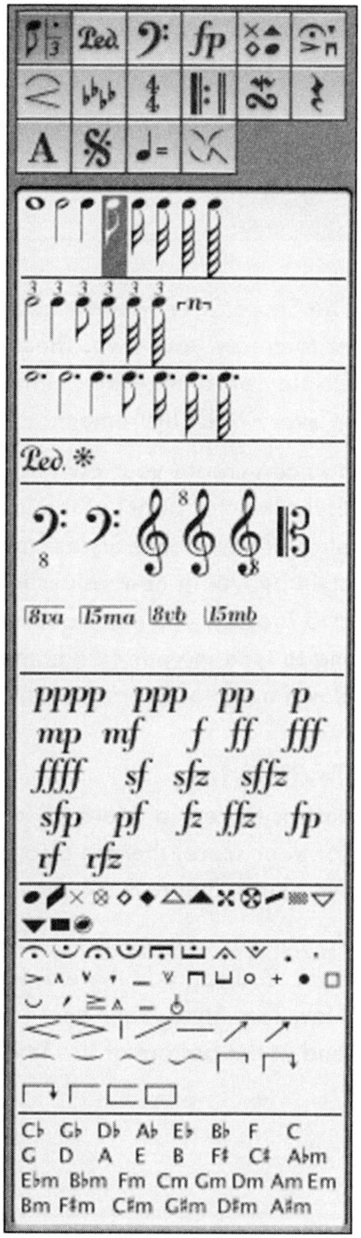

Figure 9.52

The Score Editor Partbox.

The Partbox is so expansive that the entire box fits into the Score Editor only at the highest resolutions of your display. This isn't a problem, however, as the top portion of the Partbox consists of 14 Group buttons. As you press different buttons, different sections of the Partbox move to the top of the box under the Group buttons, so the specific section of the Partbox you need is always no more than one click away.

Inserting parts from the Partbox couldn't be easier: Simply click on a part, then drag it into the location of your score where you want to place it. You can also click and hold one of the Group buttons, and all the parts in that group will appear in a pop-up menu below the Group button. If you want a group to appear as a floating menu, you can double-click the Group button. And of course, you can use key commands to switch between parts in the Partbox.

Score Styles

Score Styles can be thought of as similar to style sheets in word processor or desktop publishing applications: They each contain a set of formatting and layout preferences for you to apply when needed. You can access Score Styles from the Layout local menu or via key command. Figure 9.53 shows the Score Style window.

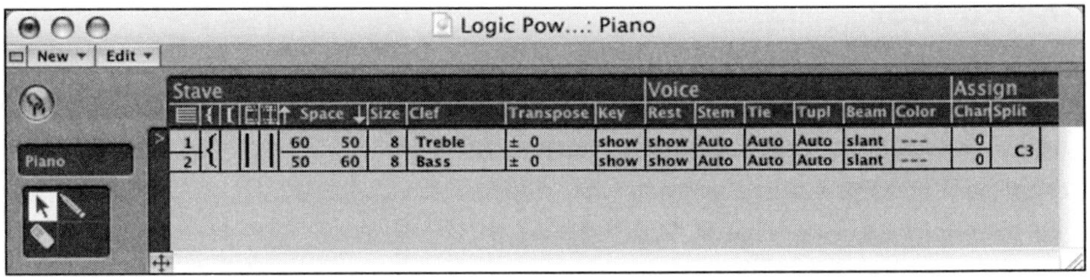

Figure 9.53

The Score Style window.

The Score Style window allows you to select one of the default Score Styles or to create your own. These Score Styles are then accessible through the Display parameter box in the Score Editor or the Instrument parameter box in every MIDI Instrument.

You can create your own Score Styles by selecting **DUPLICATE** from the Style selector panel at the left of the window, or by choosing one of the varieties of new Score Styles from the New local menu. After designing your style by typing new values in and/or using the basic tools (Pointer, Pencil, and Eraser), you can double-click the name of the style you have been creating to type in your own name. That Score Style then appears in every pull-down menu of Score Styles.

Text Styles

Just as there is a Score Style window to create format and layout templates for your score, there is also a Text Styles window for creating text formatting templates. Figure 9.54 shows the Text Styles window.

As you can see, each Text Style lets you select a font, size, and formatting style. You can edit the existing styles, or create your own by choosing **New > New Text Style**. Your new Text Style will appear at the bottom of the window and at the bottom of the Text Style pull-down menu.

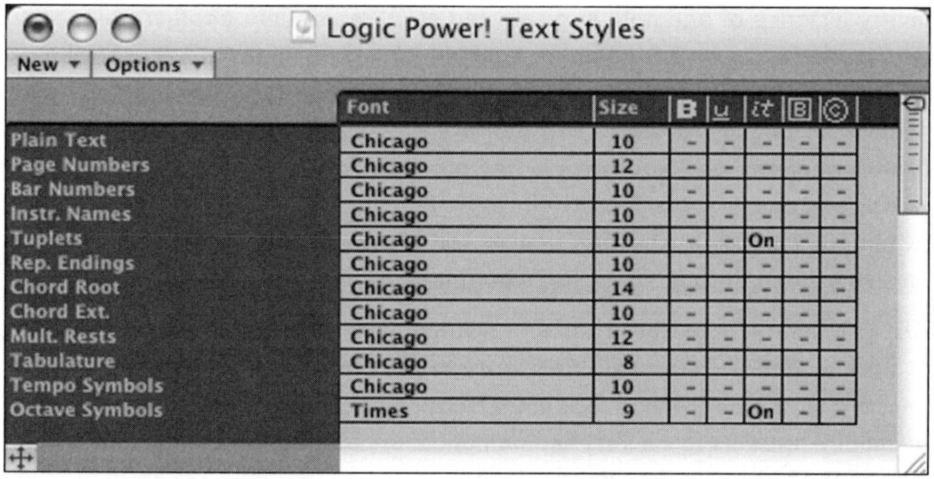

Figure 9.54

The Text Styles window.

> **FOR FURTHER SCORE EDITOR INFORMATION**
>
> The Score Editor is the deepest MIDI editor in Logic, and there is far more to delve into than space allows. As you see, just the preceding explanation of the surface functionality of the Score Editor has already taken more figures and pages of this book than any other MIDI editor! Going into minute detail could easily fill half this book. Instead, let me point you to two resources for further information on the Score Editor. The first of course is the Logic Pro manual itself, which includes 120 pages on the Score Editor. But for a really excellent guide on how to use the Score Editor, I recommend Johannes Prischl's *Logic Notation Guide*, which has over 200 pages of explanation, tutorials, valuable Logic Environments, and more, to help you get the most out of the Score Editor. The book is available only electronically through the author's Web site: http://members.aon.at/prischl/LNG. Prischl wrote this guide for an earlier version of Logic, but the Score Editor hasn't changed much over the years—his examples will look different, but the methodology and procedures are the same, and his Environments still work. I cannot recommend his book highly enough for those who want a complete Score Editor reference.

The Transform Window

The Transform window is not exactly a MIDI *editor*, but it offers you the ability to alter (or "transform") large amounts of MIDI data at once. You can consider it a "MIDI event batch processor window" if you want. And if that sounds a bit complicated, that's because its functionality can be incredibly far-reaching. You can use it for processes as straightforward as changing every instance of one note in a selected MIDI region into another note, or you could set up a very complex map, which would filter out only specific notes of a specific velocity and map them to selected new notes. Logic comes with a number of Transform Sets that are preconfigured for many popular transformations, and you can create your own Transform Sets. The Transform window is one of those features in Logic that you won't use constantly, but when you can use it, knowing how to will allow you to automate transforming your MIDI data in ways that would take forever manually.

Users often overlook the Transform window. First of all, it's not an editor, so it's not a window absolutely necessary to the basic recording and editing of music. But another reason that users frequently overlook the Transform is that it initially appears to be very mathematical in nature and not very intuitive. Figure 9.55 shows a Transform window.

Unless you already have a mathematical understanding of MIDI data and values, the Transform window doesn't seem very inviting, does it? Despite its initial complexity, however, it is a very powerful tool to have in your arsenal. My goal for this section is to demystify the Transform window for you!

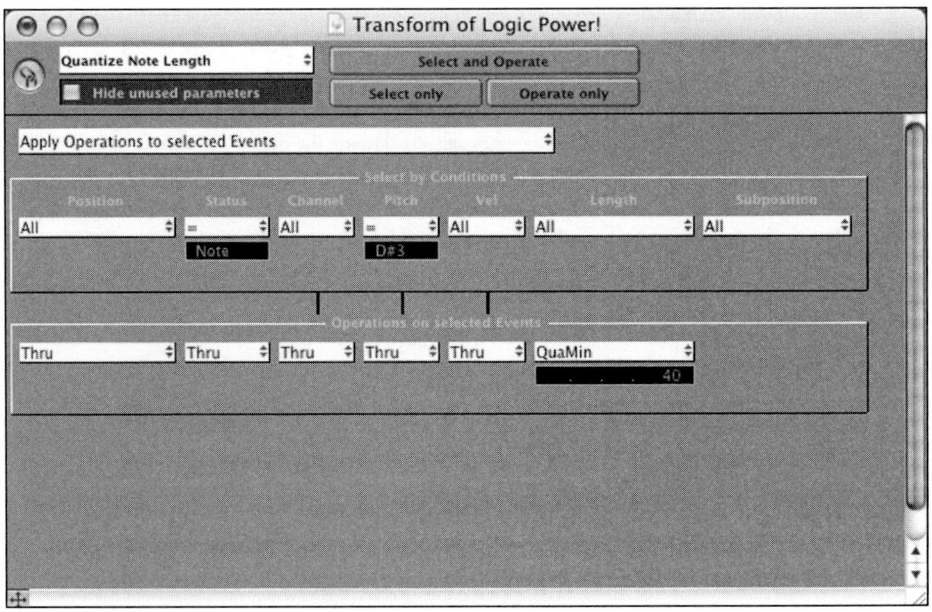

Figure 9.55

You can use the Transform window to make batch transformations of MIDI data.

How the Transform Window Works

The Transform window becomes easier to grasp once you have a general idea of how the Transform window works. Remember that at its root, MIDI represents musical ideas mathematically, and the Transform window uses the form and flow of a mathematical formula to operate on your data.

You'll start by setting the Operation mode from the pull-down menu below the buttons and Transform Set menu at the top of the window (**Quantize Note Length** is the Transform Set showing). The mode you choose determines how the transformation will affect the selected events. The different modes are described in the "Setting the Transform Mode" section below.

Next, you set up the conditions for the transformation. Here you define which events to transform. You set up these conditions in the box labeled Select by Conditions. You learn how to do this in the section "Setting Up Transform Conditions" later in this chapter. Once you have set up your conditions, you define the operation that you want to execute. You can select the various parameters of your operation in the box labeled Apply Operations to Selected Events. You'll learn how to set these parameters later in this chapter in the section "Setting Up Transform Operations."

Finally, you perform your transformation by clicking on one of the Action buttons at the top of the window. The different buttons are described in the "Action Buttons of the Transform Window" section later in this chapter.

Setting the Transform Mode

Beneath the Transform Set menu (**Quantize Note Length** is the Transform Set showing), the Action buttons, and the Hide Unused Parameters check box is the Mode pull-down menu (**Apply Operations to Selected Events** is the mode showing). Figure 9.56 shows the Transform Mode pull-down menu.

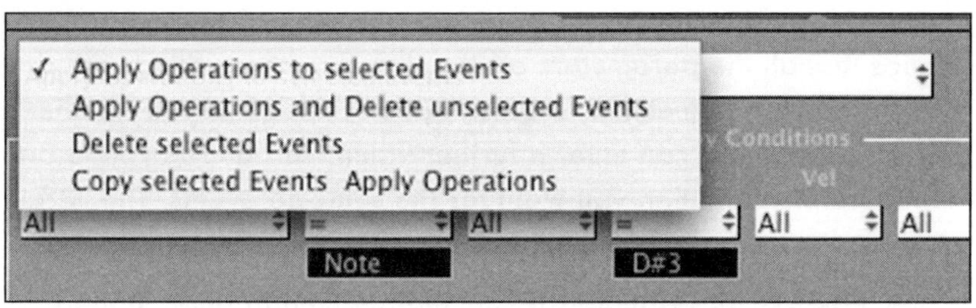

Figure 9.56
In the Transform Mode pull-down menu, you shape how the transformation will affect your selected events.

The modes available from this menu are as follows:

- **Apply Operations to Selected Events.** In this mode, the operation that you set up in the Transform menu is applied to the events you select via the conditions you set. This is the default mode.
- **Apply Operations and Delete Unselected Events.** When the only events you want to remain after the transformation are those events that are operated on, choose this option. It operates on the selected events and deletes any other events in the region.
- **Delete Selected Events.** In this mode, you can use the Transform window as a programmable delete function. You set up which events to select in the Conditions box, and when you apply the transformation, those events are deleted.
- **Copy Selected Events Apply Operations.** If you don't want to modify your original events but you want to add transformed events to your region, you can do so in this mode. This mode copies your selected events, then operates on those events, so you retain the original events and add the transformed copies of those events.

Setting Up Transform Conditions

The Select by Conditions box in the Transform window gives you seven parameters with which to define those events you want to select. Figure 9.57 shows you the Select by Conditions box.

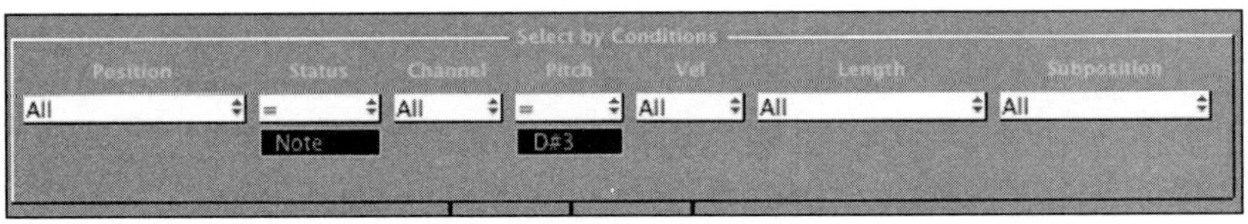

Figure 9.57
The Select by Conditions box in the Transform window allows you to focus precisely on the exact events you want to transform.

Notice that all the parameters offer pull-down menus filled with options for that parameter. Sometimes, a given option then gives you another pull-down menu in which you can enter a further value. This allows you to precisely configure the condition you want for the selected events. The various parameters and your options for setting them are as follows:

- **Position.** This option is for setting the time position in the song of your selection relative to the conditions you set. In other words, should Logic select only those notes that happen at an earlier or equal time to your conditions, or should it also select those that are unequal to the time position you are setting? Or should it select those events that are equal, or those events inside a specific time range (map) of values? Figure 9.58 shows the pull-down menu of all your options.

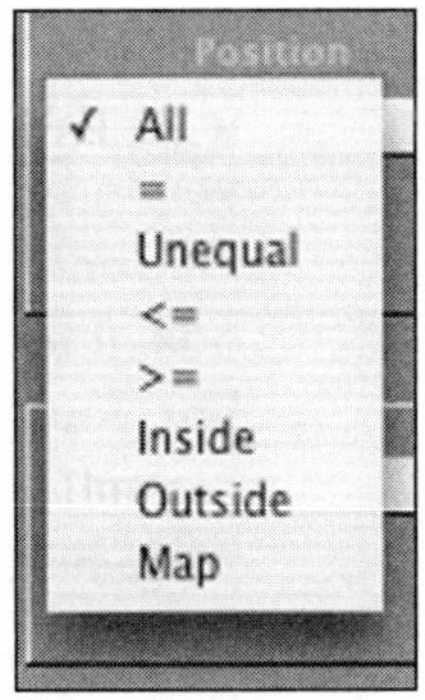

Figure 9.58
The pull-down menu of Position options. Use this menu to determine where to place the selected notes relative to the value determined by your conditions.

Remember that your MIDI data is mathematical at its base, so it's easy to create mathematical relationships between the conditions you set up and to specify how you want those conditions to determine which notes to select.

- **Status.** First, the pull-down menu allows you to choose whether you want your conditions to be equal to a specific kind of MIDI event or apply to all MIDI events. If you choose to limit your conditions to one type of MIDI event, another pull-down menu appears, this one with a black background and blue text, from which you can choose your event type. Figure 9.59 shows the pull-down list of event types.

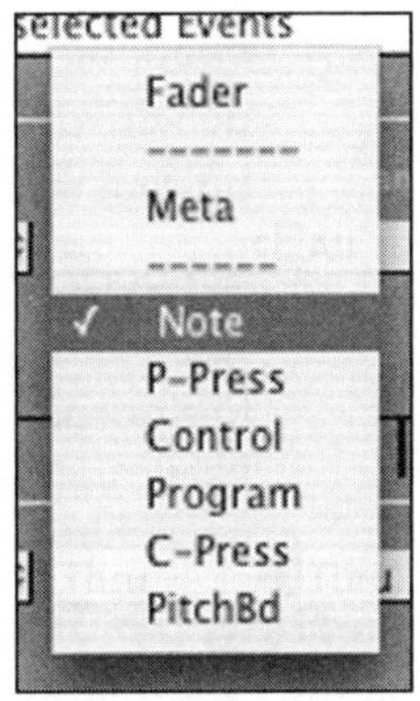

Figure 9.59
In this pull-down menu, you can choose the event type to which you want to limit your conditions.

  Note events are the most commonly chosen, but you can also choose Fader (automation) events, Meta events, MIDI program changes, or other common MIDI performance events.

- **Channel.** Here you can specify whether you want the conditions to apply to events on all MIDI Channels, only channels equal to or less than the recorded MIDI Channel of the event, and more. The pull-down menu has the exact same options as the Position pull-down menu.
- **Pitch.** The white pull-down menu under the title is the same menu as displayed for the Position and Channel parameters; this menu allows you to specify the range of pitches, controller number, value, and so on, of the selected notes or controller numbers relative to the conditions you are setting. Underneath this menu is a text-entry box. If the event you selected in the Status menu is a note, then in this box you type in the note you want. If you selected a control message type in the Status menu, you input the controller number here.

- **Vel.** The white pull-down menu under the title is the same menu as displayed for the Position, Cha, and Pitch parameters; this menu allows you to specify the range of the velocity or controller value relative to the conditions you are setting. Underneath this menu is a text-entry box. If the event you selected in the Status menu is a note, then in this box you type in the velocity you want for the note. If you selected a control message type in the Status menu, you input the controller value here.
- **Length.** Here you can determine what the relative length of the event selected by your conditions should be, whether they all need to be equal or unequal in length, and more. This option presents the same pull-down menu as displayed for the Position, Cha, Pitch, and Vel parameters. This field is irrelevant except for note events.
- **Subposition.** This parameter determines whether events must have the same subposition inside a bar as other selected notes. Once again, this parameter features the same pull-down menu as the Position, Cha, Pitch, Vel, and Length parameters.

Setting Up Transform Operations

In the Operations on Selected Events box, shown in Figure 9.60, you can specify any changes that you want executed on those MIDI events that match all the conditions you set in the Select by Conditions box.

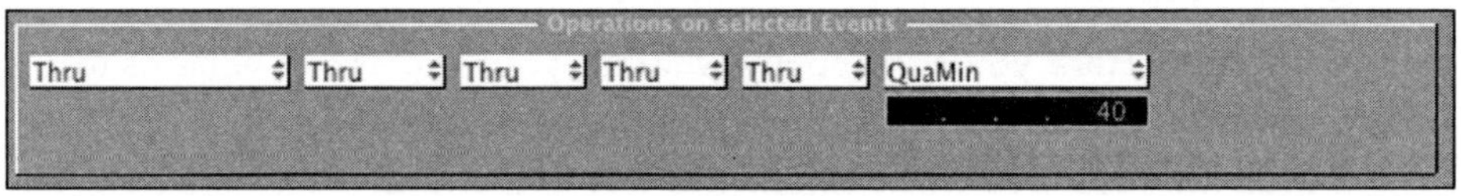

Figure 9.60
The Operations on Selected Events box is where you specify which transformations you want to perform on the events selected by the conditions you set.

Notice the pull-down menu in the Operations box directly beneath each parameter in the Conditions box. Each pull-down menu in the Operations box directly affects the parameter above it (you can refer back to Figure 9.55 for a view of the whole Transform window). In other words, if you want your transformation to operate on the pitch of a note, you would use the pull-down menu under the Pitch condition. The default for each of the pull-down menus is Thru, which specifies that no operation is performed. Figure 9.61 shows the Operations pull-down menu and all of the possibilities for transformations it offers. This Operations pull-down menu is the same menu for every column in the Operations box except Status.

Figure 9.61 shows all the ways in which you can operate on your data. As soon as you select an option, a text box appears below for you to type in the value that you want for the operation. A brief explanation of the options follows:

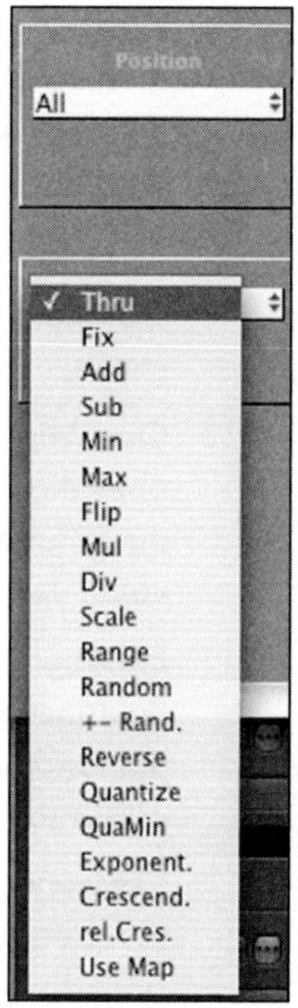

Figure 9.61
The Operations pull-down menu. Every column but Status uses this same menu.

- **Fix.** The parameter is fixed (changed) to the value you choose.
- **Add.** This option adds the value you choose to the event.
- **Sub.** This subtracts the value you choose from the event.
- **Min.** If any events that met your conditions have values in this column less than the number you set for this parameter, Logic changes the event values to the number you set here.
- **Max.** If any events that met your conditions have values in this column that exceed the value you set, this value replaces those event values.
- **Flip.** You can "flip," or reverse, data around a set point. If the value of the event in this column is above the "flip" value, Logic reduces the value below the flip point by the same amount it was originally over it. If the value in the selected event is below the flip point, Logic raises it above the flip point by as much as it originally had under it.
- **Mul.** The event is multiplied by the value you choose.
- **Div.** The event is divided by the value you choose.
- **Scale.** In this complex action, two text-entry boxes appear underneath the Operations box, one above the other. Logic first multiplies the value of events that match your conditions by the top number, then adds the bottom number to the result.
- **Range.** If any events are outside the range specified by these text boxes, Logic flips those values around a flip point of 63.5.
- **Random.** This generates random values for the events that match the conditions, within limits that you set.

- **+ – Rand.** This adds to the event a random number between zero and a value that you set. You can use either a positive or negative number as a value.
- **Reverse.** This option reverses the value of the event within its parameter range (so a velocity of 13 becomes 31, for example).
- **Quantize.** This quantizes the event to a multiple of the value you chose.
- **Qua Min.** This is a combination of the Qua and Min operations. The operation quantizes the event, but if the quantized value falls below the value you choose, Logic replaces the value with the minimum value you chose.
- **Exponent.** This scales the parameter value according to an exponential function. The value you choose shapes the curve of the exponential function. A positive value scales exponentially, a negative value scales logarithmically.
- **Crescend.** If you have selected "inside" as your value for your condition above, this operation creates a smooth alteration between the set boundaries.
- **rel.Cres.** This has a similar effect to Crescend., except it takes the original values of your selected event into account to create a more natural crescendo and preserve the original feel of the MIDI event.
- **Use Map.** When you select this option, the map at the bottom of the Transform window becomes interactive, and you can select, deselect, and map different values as you see fit. Figure 9.62 shows the Universal Map under a Velocity operation.

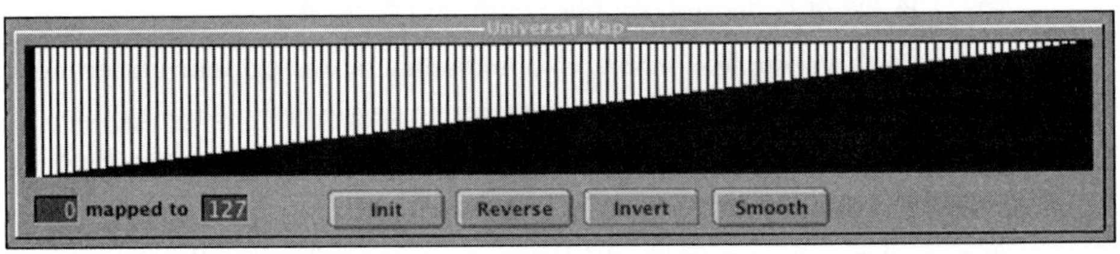

Figure 9.62
The Transform Universal Map can be used to map one parameter value to another, only operate on specific values within the map, and more.

You use this map by either typing a value in each text box in the lower-right (such as 81 in the first box, and 67 in the second box), scrolling the numbers in the text boxes, or by clicking in the map itself. The vertical columns represent every permissible value, and the black lines represent the location to which that value is currently mapped.

Action Buttons of the Transform Window

The top of the Transport window contains a few general controls—the Link button to link the Transform window to the top window in your screenset, the Transform Set pull-down menu, and the parameter to hide any menus you aren't using in the Conditions and Operations boxes—and the Action buttons. These three rectangular buttons give you a number of different ways to use the Transport window. Figure 9.63 shows the three Action buttons of the Transport window.

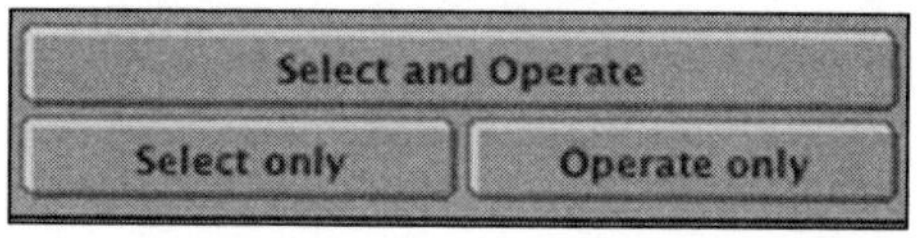

Figure 9.63
The Action buttons of the Transform window.

Once you have your conditions and operations defined, you must click one of these buttons to begin the transformation. These buttons are as follows:

- **Select and Operate.** This button selects events according to your Conditions settings, and processes those events according to Transform mode and your Operations settings.
- **Select Only.** This selects all the events that fulfill your conditions, but it will not operate on them. This is useful if you want to use Transform as a programmable selection tool, or if you want to verify that your conditions select the right events.
- **Operate Only.** This button processes any selected events according to the Operations settings, regardless of the Conditions settings. This is useful if you have already manually selected all the events you want to be operated on.

Transform Sets

As mentioned previously, in the top-left corner of the Transform window is the Transform Sets pull-down menu. These Transform Sets are already configured for many popular transformations in order to save you the trouble of having to set up each transformation from scratch. You can simply select the

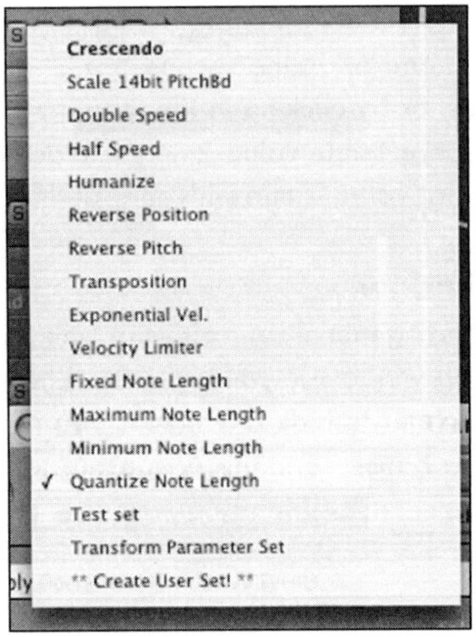

Figure 9.64
The pull-down menu of available Transform Sets. At the bottom of the menu is the option to create your own Transform Set.

Transform Set and modify any specific parameters to suit your needs, and you're ready to process your data. Figure 9.64 shows you the pull-down menu of available Transform Sets.

You may also find that there are specific transformations that you like to do regularly. Logic allows you to save your own transformations as Transform Sets. Notice the last item on the Transport Sets menu is named **Create User Set!** If you select this option, a fresh Transform window appears with a new Transform Set named Transform Parameter Set. You can now configure your transformation any way you want, and Logic will automatically save your settings in this new Transform Set. You can rename it by double-clicking the name and changing it to anything you want.

10 Working with Audio Instruments in Logic

One of the most exciting developments in the world of computer music, without a doubt, is the software synthesizer. Knowing a bit about the development of software synthesis will help you understand the philosophy, uses, and limitations of Audio Instruments, so the next few paragraphs will explain how Audio Instruments came to be and what they are.

From the late 1960s through the 1980s, synthesizers were electronic devices that used oscillators and filters to make sound. These devices sounded spectacular (at least to synthesizer enthusiasts!) but were incredibly bulky and expensive. Starting at the end of the 1970s and into the 1980s, the first steps in digital synthesizers were being made—in effect, a dedicated computer chip that had specially written software to control sound production. Digital synthesizers took over in the 1980s and 1990s, and even though these synthesizers were housed in rackmount boxes in keyboards, it was in fact the software that was doing the synthesis.

With the rise of home computers in the 1980s and 1990s, programmers began to experiment with writing programs that used the built-in sound potential of the computer for making music. While fun and innovative, these initial forays into desktop software synthesis were limited by the primitive sound delivery components, CPU power, and memory. As the 1990s progressed, however, computers became more powerful, and more sophisticated. DSP (digital signal processing), programmers began to try to bring their understanding of programming hardware digital synthesizers to bear in the desktop computer world. Some of the stand-alone software synthesizers developed in those days, while rudimentary, were orders of magnitude better than anything previously available. In the late 1990s, Steinberg blew the computer music world off its collective feet when the second version of its audio plug-in format, Virtual Studio Technology (VST), allowed for not only audio processing plug-ins, but also synthesizer plug-ins. These were small pieces of code that could be "plugged in" to the host audio sequencer, accepted MIDI data, and translated that MIDI data into sound—just like any hardware synthesizer, but completely inside the computer, with no cabling required, sample-accurate timing, and total integration into your software mixing environment. The computer music world has never been the same.

As time passes, software synthesizers keep getting better and better, both reaching the quality of hardware synthesizers and in many cases surpassing them in terms of ease of use and integration into computer recording environments. There is a downside to all of this, however; the more processing we ask our computers to do, the sooner they run out of power. For example, let's imagine that simply playing back, editing, and mixing your 32-track audio and MIDI song requires 30 percent of your available CPU power. Now suppose that you want to add your favorite software synthesizer plug-in, which requires 25 percent of your available CPU by itself. As you can see, your computer could only comfortably handle two such processor-intensive software synthesizers with your song.

Logic is very efficient with CPU resources and offers the Freeze function described in Chapter 7 to help manage CPU resources even further. This enables you to get even more power out of your computer than ever before. But as you can see, although software synthesizers are a spectacular new development in the computer music world, they require compromises and careful resource management.

Logic and Audio Instruments

Emagic embraced the idea of software synthesizers very early. In fact, Emagic's release of its ES1 synthesizer and EXS24 24-bit software sampler were two of the very first integrated synthesizers available for any sequencer. Unlike VST plug-ins, Emagic's own software synthesizers are not additional programs that can be integrated into Logic; Logic's software instruments are actual extensions of the main Logic application and are already 100 percent integrated into the application. In addition to offering Emagic's own software synthesizers, Logic can also accept third-party software synthesizers compatible with Apple Computer's Audio Units format.

These plug-ins will be called "components" on your hard drive, since Audio Units are technically a "component" of the audio architecture of the Macintosh OS X operating system.

To best integrate software synthesizers into Logic, the Audio Instrument Object is unique among DAWs. It allows for a single Arrange track that allows you to insert a software instrument and enter MIDI data onto the track, and then produces audio from the software instrument. Logic Pro 7 includes a sizable number of very useful and high-quality software instruments for free, so every Logic Pro user can take advantage of the software synthesizer revolution!

Accessing Emagic Audio Instruments

Emagic's own software instruments don't need any installation at all—they are part of the Logic code itself. This means there's no procedure necessary to install them, other than making sure you're using the most current update of Logic.

To instantiate any of Logic's Audio Instruments into an Audio Instrument Object, simply click and hold the mouse on the input box of the channel strip. A hierarchal menu appears from which you can select the Mono, Stereo, or Multichannel Instrument menus. Each menu is divided into two additional hierarchal menus; one labeled Logic for Emagic's built-in software instruments, and another labeled Audio Units for third-party software instruments. Simply select the Logic instrument you want to use, and it will be loaded into that Audio Instrument Object. Figure 10.1 shows Logic's ES1 being installed into an Audio Instrument channel strip in the Arrange window.

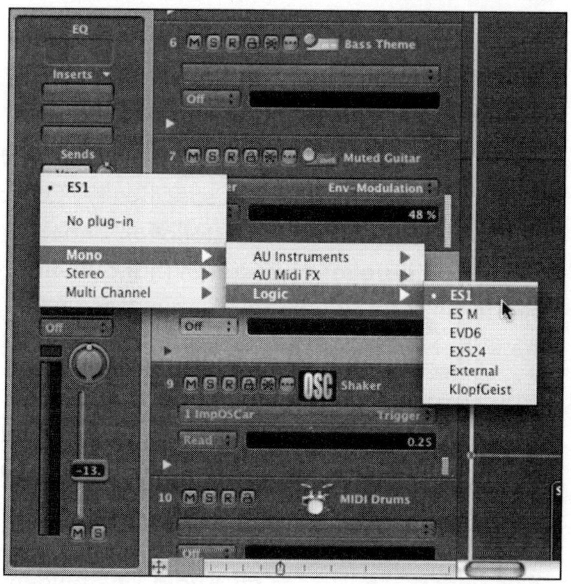

Figure 10.1

This Arrange channel strip for an Audio Instrument track shows Emagic's ES1 monophonic software instrument being selected from the Input hierarchal menus.

If you want to access the Audio Instrument Editor, double-click on the input box displaying the name of the Audio Instrument. The Audio Instrument graphic editor launches, giving you full access to all the parameters and functions of the instrument. Figure 10.2 shows the graphic editing window of an Emagic Audio Instrument.

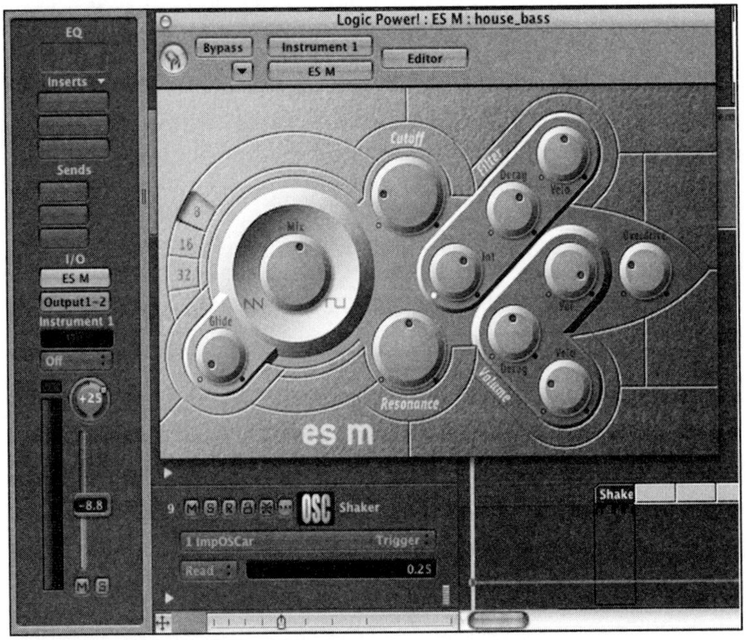

Figure 10.2

The channel strip of an Audio Instrument with Logic's built-in ES M Audio Instrument instantiated. If you double-click on the input box displaying the name of the instrument, you launch the graphic editor for that instrument.

Installing and Accessing Non-Emagic Audio Instruments

You need to install any third-party software instruments into either the local (system wide) or user (yours specifically) Components folder of your Macintosh. The exact method of installation depends on whether the developer included an installer application that automatically places files where they need to go, or if you need to move the plug-in application manually to where it belongs.

If you have to install the plug-ins manually, the local Components folder resides at /Library/Audio/Plug-ins/Components, and the user Components folder at ~/Library/Audio/Plug-ins/Components. Personally, I keep all my components in the local directory. It shouldn't make a difference, however, which one you choose, or if your components are split among both Components folders. Logic sees all Audio Unit plug-ins in both folders.

You instantiate third-party Audio Instruments into Audio Instrument channel strips using the same procedure as with Emagic Audio Instruments except that you use the Audio Units portion of the hierarchal menu. The Audio Units menu contains additional hierarchal menus that divide Audio Instruments into groups based on the manufacturer of the instrument. Figure 10.3 shows the ImpOSCar software synthesizer by GMedia Music being selected.

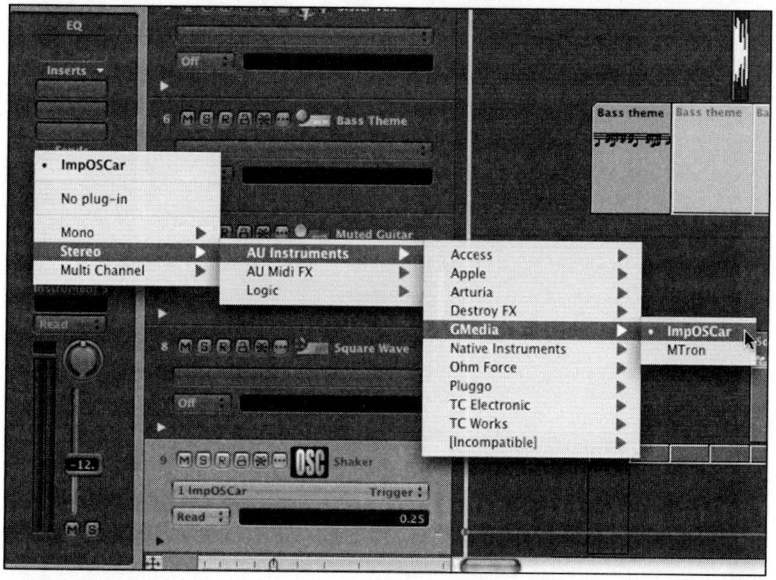

Figure 10.3
A third-party synthesizer—in this case, ImpOSCar by GMedia Music—is being instantiated on this Audio Instrument channel strip.

THE [INCOMPATIBLE] GROUP IN THE AUDIO UNITS MENU

In Figure 10.3 you'll notice that below all the names of Audio Unit synthesizer developers, there is a group called "[Incompatible]." If you are new to Logic Pro 7, you will not have this group in your menu. If all of your Audio Units have passed the validation scanning from the Logic AU Manager mentioned in Chapter 5, you will not have this menu. How Logic handles managing Audio Units, and your options within Logic Pro's AU Manager are explained in greater detail in Chapter 12. But for now, just know that if you install an Audio Unit Audio Instrument and it doesn't appear in your list of available instruments, you can launch the AU Manager by selecting **Logic Pro > Preferences > Launch AU Manager**, check the box next to that deactivated instrument, and the next time you go to an Audio Instrument channel strip, the instrument will be in the [Incompatible] menu.

Just as with the Emagic Audio Instrument, double-clicking the input box displaying the name of the Audio Instrument launches the instrument's graphic editor. Figure 10.4 shows the ImpOSCar's graphic editor launched next to the channel strip in which the instrument is instantiated.

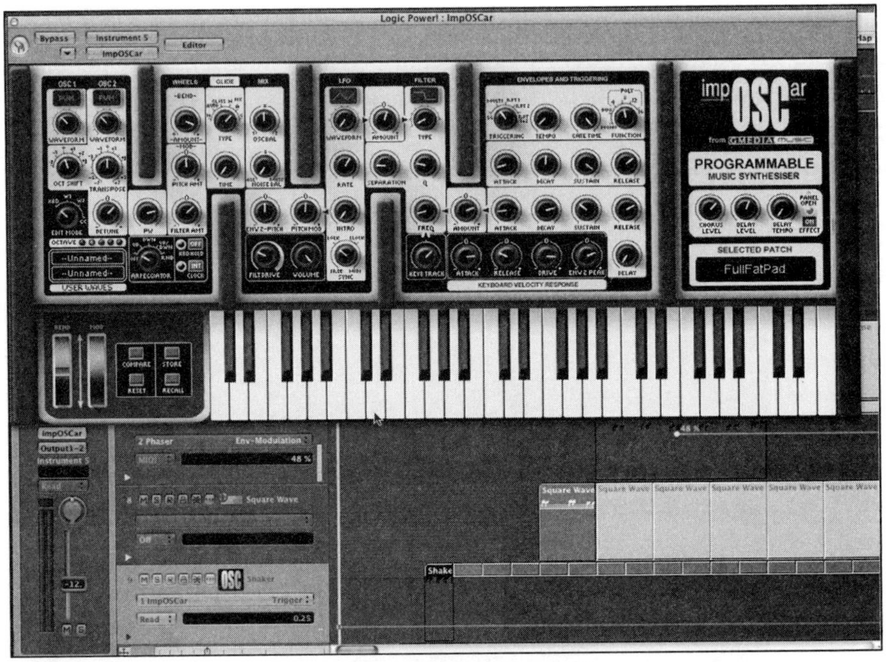

Figure 10.4

Just as with Emagic's own Audio Instruments, you can double-click the input box of an Audio Instrument channel strip with a third-party instrument to launch its graphic editor.

METHOD TIP: USING THE EXTERNAL INSTRUMENT TO CONNECT MIDI SYNTHESIZERS

Considering how many Audio Instruments and effects Logic comes with, it is impossible for this book to go into them. However, there is one of Logic's Audio Instruments that is so special, it warrants going over. And it's not even a true Audio Instrument in that it makes no sound itself.

Many times, you may want to send MIDI performances to an external MIDI device, such as a MIDI sound module or MIDI synthesizer, and then send the stereo audio from your MIDI hardware back into the Logic mixer to be processed and summed with all your other tracks. Before Logic Pro 7, this took a fair amount of preparation. You needed to create an Instrument or Multi-Instrument Object for your MIDI hardware device in the Environment. This object would then need to have a track created for it on the Arrange in order for Logic to record MIDI from and send MIDI to the device. Then you needed to instantiate Audio Objects (either Audio Track Objects or Audio Input Objects) for the audio outputs of your MIDI device.

Logic Pro 7 offers a brand new, completely unique Audio Instrument, called the External Instrument, designed expressly for the situation described above. You still need to have created an Instrument, Multi-Instrument, or Mapped-Instrument Object for your MIDI device. Then, instantiate an Audio Instrument Object and set its mono or stereo instrument to **External**. The plug-in editor gives you only a few options: set its MIDI destination to your Instrument, Multi-Instrument, or Mapped-Instrument. Then set its input to the input(s) on your audio interface into which you plugged your MIDI hardware device.

That's it! You now have a single track that both sends and receives information from your hardware MIDI device. Keep in mind that you can only use one (mono) or two (stereo) outputs of your MIDI hardware with this instrument—there is not a multichannel option.

Plug-In Window Controls

Audio Instruments and audio effects (which I discuss in Chapter 12, "Mixing in Logic") use the same basic form of plug-in window. Each plug-in window features a Link and Bypass button, and either four or five pull-down menus, as shown in Figure 10.5.

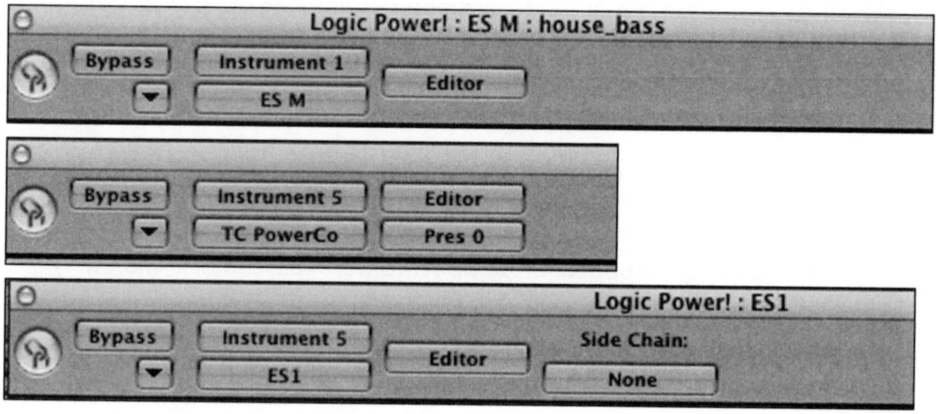

Figure 10.5

The two varieties of controls you'll find on Audio Instrument plug-in windows. They are identical except for the number of pull-down menus: (a) Audio Instrument windows for Emagic Audio Instruments, such as the ES M, have four pull-down menus; (b) some Audio Instrument windows for third-party instruments, such as this Audio Instrument Object featuring the TC PowerCore 01 software instrument, have five pull-down menus; finally, some Emagic Audio Instruments have "side chains," which gives them five pull-down menus, with the Side Chain menu offset from the others.

The elements of the plug-in window in which your Audio Instrument will open are described below.

Plug-In Window Buttons

There are two buttons at the top of the plug-in window:

- **Link.** By default, the Link button is disengaged, so multiple plug-in windows can be on the screen simultaneously. If the Link button is engaged, only a single plug-in window at a time is allowed onscreen. This is useful if you have a limited amount of screen space. You can also open a number of windows with the Link button disengaged, and then engage the Link button on one of the open plug-in windows so that all subsequent plug-ins will appear in this window.
- **Bypass.** The Bypass button turns the plug-in on and off. This has the same effect as pressing **OPTION + click** in the plug-in's box in the channel strip in which the plug-in is instantiated.

Plug-In Window Menus

The plug-in window contains either four or five pull-down menus in its top bar, depending on whether it is an Emagic or third-party plug-in:

- **Arrow.** The first pull-down menu looks like a downward arrow. This menu has commands for loading and saving Logic plug-in setting files. These files store the current parameter conditions of your plug-in, which you can then reload later, and even re-use in other songs. This is useful for creating your own unique collection of commonly used settings for your various plug-ins. As you save your settings, they appear in this pull-down menu for easy access. The presets for Emagic's own instruments and effects are listed at the bottom of this menu as well. Plug-in settings are stored in the Plug-In Settings folder inside the Logic Application Support folder. You can also manually add settings collected from other users by copying them to this folder.
- **Object Menu.** The top menu lists the current Audio Object in which you are viewing a plug-in, as well as all the other Audio Objects used in the current Logic song. To switch to a different Audio Object, just select it.
- **Plug-In Menu.** Below the Object menu is the name of the plug-in you are currently viewing. The pull-down menu contains all the other plug-ins used by this Audio Object. To change the current plug-in window to that of another plug-in being used by the same Audio Object, you can use this menu to select the new plug-in.
- **Editor Menu.** This menu contains two options. Editor, which offers the standard graphic editor view of plug-ins, and the Control view, which simply lists the parameters of the synth and offers a slider for each. Most plug-ins have too many parameters and offer useful graphic feedback, so you'll almost always want to use the Editor view.
- **Preset Menu.** For some third-party plug-ins, Logic offers an additional pull-down menu that lists the built-in presets for that plug-in. Note that many third-party plug-ins have their own methods for loading and saving presets and do not rely on the host application for preset handling. Plug-in windows for these plug-ins might lack this additional pull-down menu.
- **Side Chain Menu.** Some Emagic synthesizers are capable of processing the audio from an Audio Track. To do this, you will need to use the Side Chain menu to select which Audio Track to process. Side Chains are discussed in detail in Chapter 12.

METHOD TIP: ACCESSING MULTIPLE MIDI CHANNELS ON MULTITIMBRAL AUDIO INSTRUMENTS

Some software instruments allow for multichannel operation, meaning they'll allow you to load completely different plug-in settings, presets, and so on for each different MIDI Channel the instrument can receive. Not all instruments allow for this—in fact, Emagic doesn't currently make any Audio Instruments that are multichannel—but if you do have some Audio Unit instruments that allow this function, here's how you would access them from within Logic.

One method is to simply have the MIDI regions on your Audio Instrument track send different MIDI events to different MIDI Channels. For example, you could create a single MIDI region with a bass line sending to MIDI Channel 1 and a high lead part sending to MIDI Channel 2. Your software instrument will take care of routing the different notes to the proper MIDI Channel. This technique comes in handy for scoring, where you may want several voices in a single MIDI region going to different channels. However, if you want separate tracks for each MIDI part being routed to different channels, you can use the following method.

In the Arrange window, instantiate the software instrument you want on Audio Instrument Track 1. Now create a MIDI region with the MIDI part you want for your software instrument to play on one channel. After that, choose the same Audio Instrument for Audio Instrument Track 2. You'll notice that the channel strip and region parameters will be identical to the instrument's settings on Audio Instrument Track 1—that's because it is the exact same Audio Object being used on both Audio Instrument tracks. Now you can create new MIDI regions on this track and send those MIDI regions to a different MIDI Channel of your multichannel software instrument. This way, you have the MIDI parts for each channel separated on different tracks. You can repeat the above procedure to have as many different AI tracks access the same multichannel software instrument as you want.

This could be useful if, for example, you had each channel of a multichannel sampler loaded with a different sample set, and you wanted separate tracks for each sample set. Keep in mind that you don't have to set the different Audio Instrument tracks to send their parts to different channels—there is no relation between the specific track lane and where the MIDI data is routed. You could create 16 AI tracks using the above method and have them all routed to the same track if you wanted to. Keep in mind that for this method to work, you need to have the Channel parameter for the Audio Instrument set to All.

Audio Instruments and the Environment

As I've already discussed, an Audio Instrument Object is both an Audio and a MIDI Object. As such, you can route Audio Instrument Objects to other MIDI Objects to create unique MIDI effects and routings just like you can any other MIDI device. You'll learn about the Environment routing and macro construction possible in Logic in Chapter 14, "The Environment," but for now, keep in mind that you can use Audio Instrument Objects just like MIDI Instrument Objects for any sort of Environment work.

Using Multiple Output Audio Instruments

The vast majority of the Audio Instruments you use will be either mono or stereo instruments. Moreover, you'll probably only need stereo outputs from Audio Instruments that allow for more than two outputs. However, sometimes you may want to have an independent output for each sample from a sampler, each voice of a synthesizer, or each drum from a drum instrument, to allow for more precise mixing, processing, or automation control. For these situations, you can instantiate a Multichannel Instrument in an Audio Instrument Object.

Logic is far more efficient than other DAWs in the management of resources when using Audio Instruments. The price for this efficiency, unfortunately, is that accessing the additional outputs of Audio Instruments takes a bit more thought and a few more steps than in other applications. Other applications automatically create every allowable output channel for multiple output instruments as soon as you instantiate the plug-in. This is very convenient, because there are no steps required to access the additional outputs. There are two drawbacks to this, however. The first is that if your instrument is set up to allow 32 outputs, your mixer will be cluttered with 32 additional output channels, making it huge and unwieldy—especially if you only wanted to use four outputs! The other drawback is that all of those unused outputs may drain your computer's CPU power and RAM. Logic allows you to activate only those additional outputs that you will actually use, conserving both screen real estate and computer resources. But giving you this flexibility means that activating the additional outputs requires some configuration.

The first step is to make sure that your software instrument is configured to allow multiple outputs. Many software synthesizers do not need any additional configuration, but some require you to select multiple output operation in its preferences or configuration screen. For details, consult the documentation for your specific software instrument.

The next operations you will most likely want to do in the Environment window, where you have access to all your Audio Objects at once, and you can create new Audio Objects as you need them. It is possible to use the Arrange channel strip if you have enough Audio Objects created, but this will be slower and less intuitive.

After confirming that your software instrument is configured to allow multiple outputs, in an unused Audio Instrument Object, select the desired Multichannel Instrument from the Audio Instrument's input box. Figure

10.6 shows a Multichannel Instrument being selected in an Audio Instrument Object.

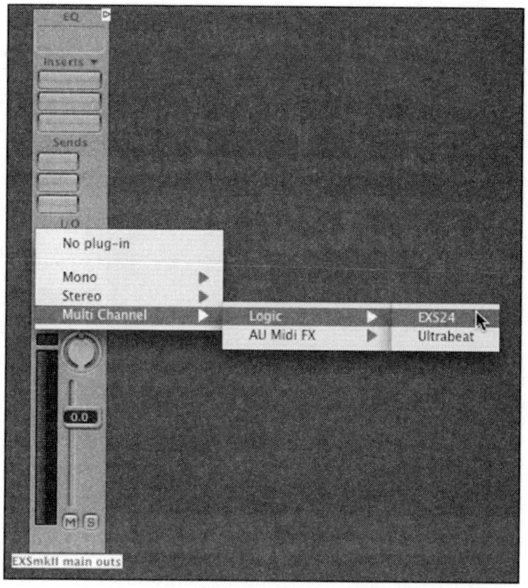

Figure 10.6

To use multiple outputs from software instruments, the first step is to select a Multichannel Instrument for the Audio Instrument Object. Here, a multichannel instance of the Emagic EXS24mkII Sampler is being selected.

The Arrange track for this Audio Instrument Object is the track in which you will record, program, and edit the MIDI data that will operate the software instrument. The Audio Instrument Object's own outputs will be the "master outputs" for the multichannel software instrument. This means that depending on how the specific software instrument you are using operates, it may serve as your master stereo output, or it may be a summation output of all the other outputs for the entire instrument. You'll need to consult your instrument's documentation for specifics on how it utilizes its master outputs.

For each additional output you want to access, you need to add a different type of Audio Object—the Auxiliary (or Aux) Object. In the pull-down menu for the input of your Aux Object, in addition to your hardware inputs and available Bus Objects, you will find a hierarchal menu of all the outputs available for your Multichannel Instrument. If the Stereo button shows a single circle, mono outputs are displayed, and if the Stereo button is pressed so it shows two overlapping circles, stereo outputs are displayed. Choose the multichannel output (or outputs if you are using stereo) that you want this Aux Object to use as its input. Figure 10.7 shows an Aux Object being assigned a Multichannel Instrument's output as its input.

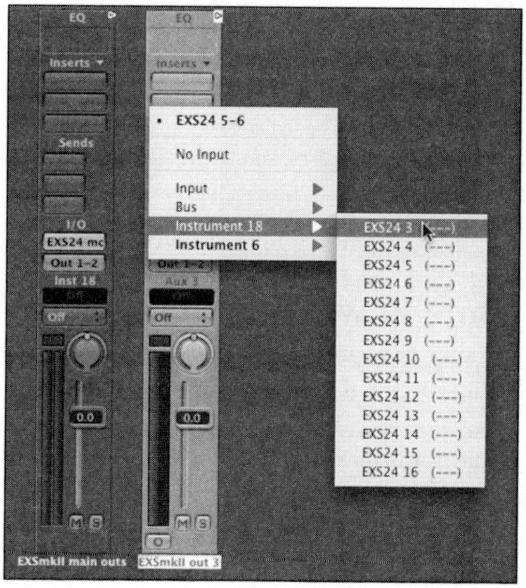

Figure 10.7

To access the additional outputs of Multichannel Instruments, create an Aux Object and select the desired output from its input menu. Here Output 3 is being chosen as the input for this Aux Object.

Figure 10.8
The multichannel EXS24mkII has now been configured to include the main outputs, two additional mono outputs, and an additional stereo output. If you needed more outputs, you could easily continue creating Aux Objects and choose more EXS24mkII outputs, to the limit of the instrument's capacity.

Now you simply repeat the preceding process for each additional output or outputs you will need in your song. Figure 10.8 shows the EXS24mkII Multichannel Instrument after the previous procedure. Note that in addition to the main Audio Instrument Object that serves as the main stereo output pair, the Multichannel Instrument has two additional mono Aux channel strips and then a stereo Aux channel strip. This is the power of Logic—only 6 of the EXS24mkII's 16 outputs were needed, and the configuration matches exactly the user's desired combination of mono and stereo outputs.

This is a perfect example of the "Logic way"; it may take some initial learning, but when you understand how it works and how to do it, not only is it simple, but you can really take advantage of the power and flexibility it offers over other applications!

DON'T FORGET: USE YOUR AUDIO INSTRUMENTS IN ARRANGE!

Because I discussed setting up your Multichannel Instruments and their additional outputs in the Environment, I just wanted to remind you one more time that, while you can *create* Audio Objects for Audio Instruments in the Environment, to actually *use* those instruments, you still need to create an Audio Instrument track on Arrange and assign your instrument to that track. For Multichannel Instruments, you won't need to have any of the additional outputs on Arrange if you don't want them there, but personally, I like to put them all on Arrange so that I can automate those tracks, if I want to. Automation will be discussed in the next chapter, "Using Automation in Logic."

Using Rewire 2 Instruments

I briefly described how to create Rewire Instruments in Chapter 4, but now I'll go into more detail. As mentioned previously, Rewire 2 is a protocol, developed by Propellerhead Software, through which two music software programs running in the same computer can be used together. Rewire 2 applications are software instruments since all their processing is being done inside the host computer, but they are different from Audio Instruments in the sense that they are not part of the Logic application (like Emagic's instruments) or literally "plugged in" to the Logic application like third-party plug-ins. So while all the connections that Logic needs to make are "virtual connections" that do not require hardware interfaces and cables, Logic must still create these connections *out* of Logic *into* another application. The Environment's Rewire Instrument, therefore, is the "virtual MIDI cable" between Logic and the Rewire 2 application, and the Rewire Audio Object is "virtual audio cable" between Logic and the Rewire 2 application. This section explains how to configure these objects in order to use a Rewire 2 application with Logic.

Working with Rewire 2 Applications

Rewire 2 has two modes: Master mode and Slave mode. Generally, the application that is launched first is the default Rewire Master, and the Rewire 2 application launched subsequently is the Rewire Slave. The Master application is the one that controls the synchronization between the two applications, and the sound from the Rewire Slave application plays through the Rewire Master application. Logic is only capable of being a Rewire Master, so be sure that the Rewire 2–capable application you want to use is capable of operating in Rewire 2 Slave mode.

No special configuration is required to initialize Rewire operation. Be sure to launch Logic first, then launch your Rewire 2 Slave application. The application should automatically load in Rewire Slave mode.

Creating Rewire Instruments for MIDI Transmission

To have a MIDI connection to and from your Rewire 2 application, you need to create Rewire Instruments in your Environment. You can do this from the Environment local menu by selecting **New > Internal > Rewire**. Figure 10.9 shows a newly created Rewire Instrument and its parameter box.

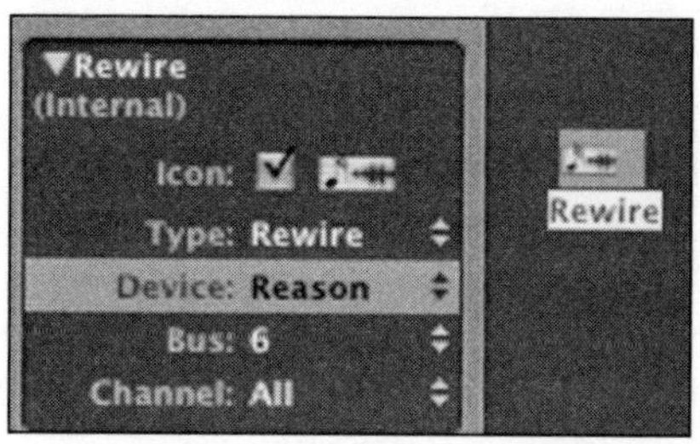

Figure 10.9
A Rewire Instrument and its parameter box. This MIDI Object allows you to send and receive MIDI data from Rewire 2 applications.

As with any other MIDI Object, to configure your Rewire Instrument properly, you may need to change the settings in the parameter box. The following are descriptions of each parameter:

- **Device.** This refers to the specific Rewire 2 application to which the Rewire Instrument is connecting. For example, if you were using three different Rewire 2 applications, all three applications would appear in this pull-down menu, and you could select which of the three applications to which to connect this Rewire Instrument.

- **Bus.** This parameter allows you to choose which Rewire bus to use from your available Rewire busses. For the Propellerhead application, Reason, the Bus parameter allows different functions depending on the value. Bus 1 addresses only the instrument chosen as the Live instrument in Reason. Busses 2–5 address busses A–D of Reason's MIDI IN Device. And busses 6 and above address the individual instruments inside the Reason Rack (these devices appear by name in busses 6 and above).
- **Channel.** The Channel parameter specifies the MIDI Channel on which you want your Rewire Instrument to send and receive MIDI data.

In the Driver tab of the Audio Preferences dialog box, accessible from **Logic Pro > Preferences > Audio**, you will find a pull-down menu for Rewire mode with two options: Playback and Live mode. For normal use, you will leave this setting in Playback mode. If you have your Rewire Instrument's bus set to 1 to enable live performance of instruments over the Rewire connection, you will want to put Rewire mode into Live mode. This setting diverts extra CPU resources to ensure the best possible synchronization between Logic and your Rewire application during live performance. If you use Rewire applications extensively, even if it's not strictly for live use, you will want to keep this option on.

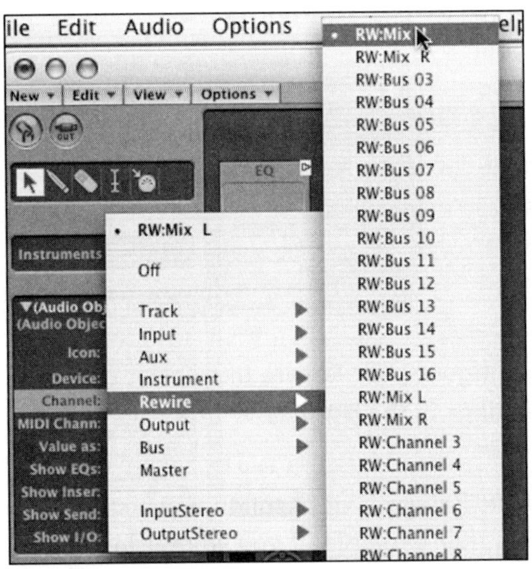

Figure 10.10
To create a Rewire Audio Object, choose one of the Rewire channels from the Rewire menu of the Audio Object's Channel parameter.

Setting Up Rewire Audio Objects for Audio Transmission

As stated previously, the Rewire Instrument is the MIDI connection between Logic and your Rewire 2 application, but you need to create a Rewire Audio Object to receive the audio from the application. To turn an Audio Object into a Rewire Audio Object, simply open the pull-down menu for the Audio Object's Channel parameter, and then select one of the available Rewire channels in the Rewire hierarchal menu. Figure 10.10 shows an Audio Object with its Rewire menu open.

That's it! Logic will automatically receive any audio that a Rewire 2 application sends on that Rewire channel. How many Rewire channels are available to you depends on the Rewire 2 applications you are working with, and how many outputs they offer.

CREATING STEREO REWIRE CHANNELS USING REWIRE, BUS, AND AUX OBJECTS

You may not mind the fact that Rewire Objects in Logic Pro can only be mono. But many people wish that Logic allowed for stereo Rewire Objects so that they could use the same inserts, sends, and so on for both sides of a stereo pair of tracks. Luckily, Logic's flexibility allows you to use the existing object types to build a stereo Rewire object with inserts and sends using Bus and Aux Objects. Basically, the procedure is to pan each mono track to a stereo Bus Object, then use that Bus Object as the input for an Aux Object.

For example, say that you are using two Rewire Objects, Reason Mix L and Reason Mix R, and you wish both Rewire Objects could be a single stereo track so you could use the same insert and send effects on both left and right signals. To combine them into a stereo Aux Object, follow these steps:

1. Turn the Pan knob on the Reason Mix L Object completely to the left and set its output to an unused stereo Bus Object.
2. Turn the Pan knob on the Reason Mix R Object completely to the right and set its output to the same stereo Bus Object you used above.
3. Set the output of the Bus Object to **No Output**.
4. On an unused stereo Aux Object, set its input to the Bus Object above.

That's it! Both mono Rewire Objects have been sent to one channel of a stereo Bus Object, which serves as the patch bay; the stereo Aux object can then accept the stereo Bus Object, which includes both Rewire Objects, as its input. The result is a single stereo Aux Object with each mono Rewire Object being sent to one channel. You can use the inserts and sends on the Aux Object exactly as you would the inserts and sends on any other Object type. You can do this with any two Rewire Objects, of course, not just Reason Mix L and Reason Mix R.

Using QuickTime Instruments

QuickTime (Apple Computer's multimedia technology) comes with its own Roland-licensed soundset, which you can also access within Logic. Since the QuickTime Synth is a software instrument that is inside your computer but outside of Logic, just like a Rewire application, the QuickTime Object looks almost identical. In fact, you create a QuickTime Instrument almost the same way as a Rewire Instrument: by choosing it from the New local menu in the Environment window via the path **New > Internal > QuickTime**. Figure 10.11 shows a QuickTime Instrument.

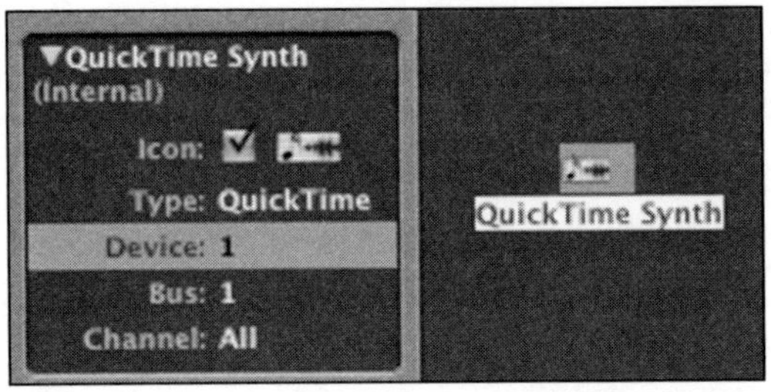

Figure 10.11
The QuickTime Instrument. This is an internal instrument that makes virtual MIDI connections like the Rewire Instrument.

Notice the QuickTime Instrument has the same parameters as the Rewire Instrument. Refer to the section "Using Rewire 2 Instruments" for a description of the parameters. You'll likely never need to adjust them, with the exception of the Channel parameter if you are using more than one QuickTime Instrument.

The QuickTime Music Synthesizer offers you a complete collection of Roland GS General MIDI sounds. You can double-click on the QuickTime Instrument to bring up the QuickTime Instrument interface shown in Figure 10.12. You can use the various pull-down menus to select the specific sound you want to use for your QuickTime Instrument.

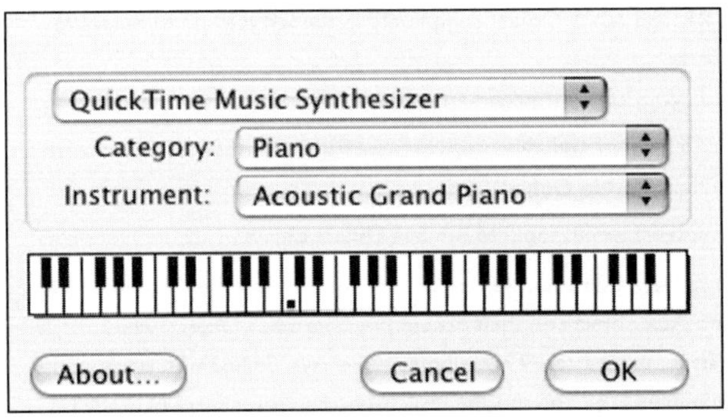

Figure 10.12
You can use the pull-down menus in the QuickTime Instrument interface to access the various installed sounds of the QuickTime Synth.

You will probably not want to use the QuickTime Synth much at all. Its sounds are very basic, and in most cases, you will be better off using one of Logic's included Audio Instruments.

11 Using Automation in Logic

In the early days of recording, if you wanted to capture the sound of moving one of the controls—for example, to create a wild stereo panning effect with an instrument, to have sound fade out gradually, or simply to level out the volume of a track that fluctuated wildly in level—you would need to move the control carefully by hand while the mixdown was happening. Any error in movement meant starting the whole thing over from scratch, and there was no way to exactly repeat anything. If you wanted to repeat the move for a new mixdown, the only option was to do it again manually and hope that the result was close to that of the original mixdown. In the 1970s, large mixing consoles began to offer automation—a way to write, rewrite, and save these moves in memory so that as you mixed your material, it would automatically make your move for you. This was not only more convenient, but it meant that you could audition, change, and repeat any move an infinite number of times, and it would be the same each time. This opened the door not only for more accurate mixing, but also for much more creative mixing by experimental artists who wanted to use the studio itself as an instrument.

With the advent of computer sequencers, automation has become an even more powerful tool, available to all. You can use automation to turn static effects into living, dynamic instruments, you can tailor the volume of a track exactly to the source material, you can perfect mixes to previously unimaginable accuracy, and you can use your sequencer not only as a tool, but as an instrument in its own right. Logic 5 introduced a powerful, modern automation system into Logic that is truly world class. Logic's automation system is fairly intuitive, but it still takes a while to get used to its "logic"!

Types of Automation

As I introduced in Chapter 7, "The Arrange Window," there are two ways to automate your song data in Logic. Both types are useful, and very similar in many ways, but each has distinct advantages and disadvantages.

The first method is called Track-Based Automation (TBA), so named because the automation data is stored with the Arrange track lane. This paradigm of storing the automation data with the track harkens back to the days of hardware mixing consoles, where you automated a specific channel of the mixer. TBA allows for incredibly high (sample-accurate) resolution, which allows you precise control over automation points and lines. One of its limitations is that when you move around your regions, the automation doesn't move with them. Nonetheless, since TBA is the more recent and powerful automation system, you will most likely use TBA for most of your automating in Logic.

Unlike using a hardware mixing console, in which the console doesn't know what type of audio you are sending through that channel, a computer *does* know what sort of data you have in your song. This means that unlike a hardware console, a computer sequencer doesn't need to automate a channel, but it can instead include automation information as part of the Audio or MIDI region itself. This type of automation in Logic is called Hyper Draw, or Region-Based Automation (RBA). Emagic developed Hyper Draw long before TBA, back when all automation of MIDI hardware and Audio Tracks was based on MIDI (hence the term "Hyper Draw," as it is basically a "hyper set" of the MIDI control messages). This means that RBA is limited to controlling parameters that have MIDI control message values, and that RBA's values are limited to the standard MIDI range of 0–127 (as opposed to TBA's 14-bit resolution). While RBA is definitely limited compared to TBA, it still has its uses. RBA's main feature is that if you want to move your regions around, your Region-Based Automation moves with you. This is very important if you like to automate as you create, as opposed to using automation as a final mixing step.

Both forms of automation can be used together, so you can have a region in which you've automated some plug-in parameters using Hyper Draw as well as done some Track-Based Automation. When you have Track Automation view enabled, there will be a disclosure triangle in the bottom-left corner of the track; if you click on the triangle, you can get as many additional lanes for Hyper Draw and Track Automation as you need. Figure 11.1 shows a track that has Track-Based Automation turned on, while the MIDI region itself has some RBA on it as well, and two automation lanes visible to view them

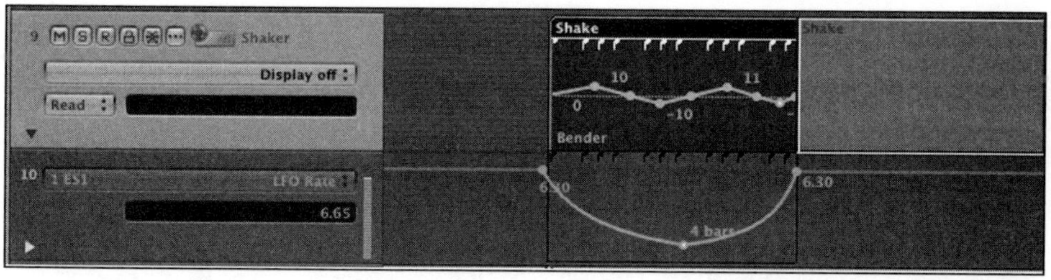

Figure 11.1
This screenshot shows both Hyper Draw (Region-Based Automation) and Track-Based Automation. The Matrix Editor shows the Shake region with Pitch Bend RBA, and Arrange is showing the same region with TBA automating the LFO Rate for an ES1 Audio Instrument. You can use both of them interchangeably, depending on your needs. Since TBA is the newer and more robust automation system, you will most likely use TBA more often.

both. You can even turn RBA into TBA, and vice versa, as you'll explore later in this chapter. Be careful not to use TBA and RBA for the same parameter—the results will be random and unusable.

Using Track-Based Automation

Using TBA couldn't be simpler. If you've already turned on Track-Based Automation in the local View menu of Arrange, the Automation Display is visible for all your tracks. If you haven't done that, select **View > Track Automation** and your tracks will all enlarge to fit the Automation Display data (unless you have already zoomed the tracks). Figure 11.2 shows an Arrange track list with the Automation Display visible in each track.

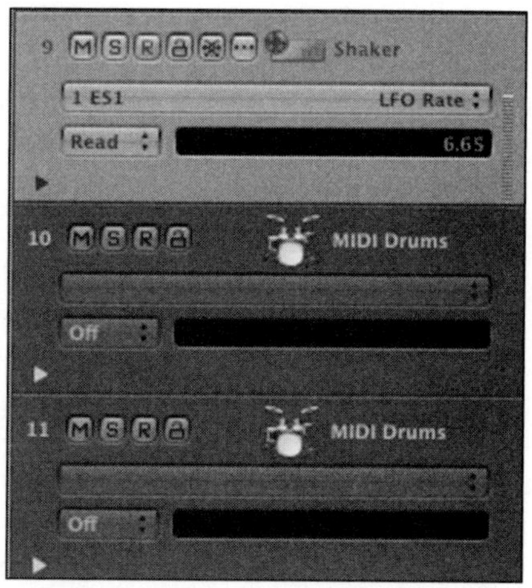

Figure 11.2
By choosing **View > Track Automation**, you ensure that each track in the track list contains the pull-down menus for Track-Based Automation. Note that only the first of the three visible tracks actually has automation data visible in the track lane, but all three tracks are ready to be automated.

The first pull-down menu is the Parameter Display. Here you can select from all the available parameters for all the automatable elements of the track itself (volume, pan, solo, mute, send, insert bypass, and so on), as well as each automatable plug-in and software instrument parameter. Choose from this menu the parameter you want to automate. Figure 11.3 shows the pull-down menus in the Parameter Display.

As you automate more parameters, they appear in the automation lane behind the currently "live" parameter. Volume appears as a dark beige line, Pan as a dark green line, and everything else in dark blue. How easy the dark colors are to see depends on the Automation Transparency value you set by choosing the Arrange tab in **Logic Pro > Preferences > Display**.

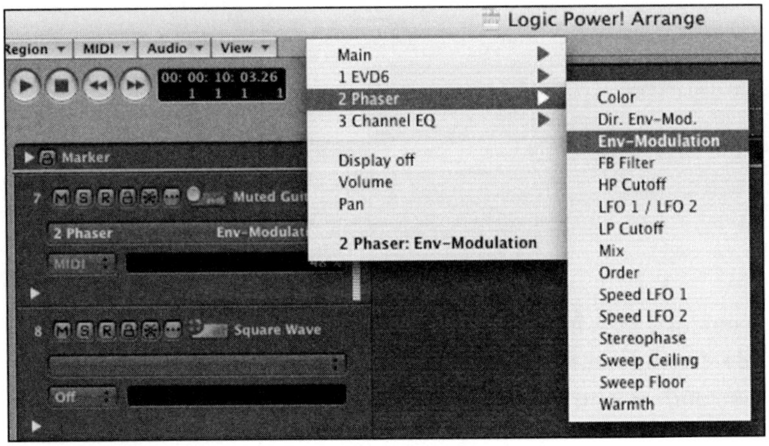

Figure 11.3
You can see from the Parameter Display box of this track that in addition to the shortcuts to Display Off, Volume, and Pan, there are hierarchal menus to choose to display parameters from the main track, software instrument, or effects.

Then you need to choose the automation mode. There are six automation modes:

- **Off.** To disable automation, set the mode to Off. This doesn't erase any existing automation data, but any existing data will not play back, and you cannot write any new data. If you already have automation data on the track and you edit that data while in Off mode, the mode switches to Read, so that the next time you play your song, Logic will play back the automation data you just edited.
- **Read.** This mode tells Logic to "read" the automation data on the track. When you play your song, Logic automates your track. You cannot write automation data in realtime in this mode, but you can create and edit automation data in the track lane itself (as explained below in the section "Manipulating Automation Data").
- **Touch.** In Touch mode, if you "touch" an element of the channel strip with your mouse or a software control surface such as the Logic Control, Logic starts writing automation data for that element. This is realtime, live automating, so any move you make is recorded live into Logic's Track Automation, although you can of course edit the data later. As soon as you release the mouse, the control surface, or stop "touching" the onscreen element, Logic stops writing automation data. For example, if you are in Touch mode and during playback you click the mouse on the Pan knob and move it, you will write pan automation data in real time. When you release the mouse button, you will stop writing pan automation data. Keep in mind that if you already

had pan data written in that specific place in which you wrote new data, the new data recorded in Touch mode will overwrite the previous data. Touch mode is the standard mode for realtime on-screen or software controller automation.

- **Latch.** Latch mode is like Touch mode except that once you click your mouse or move your control surface to start writing automation, Logic continues to write new data for that parameter even after you release the control. Only when playback stops will Logic stop writing automation for that parameter. Latch mode is desirable when you know that after a certain point in your song, you want to overwrite all the remaining data for a particular parameter.
- **Write.** Write mode deletes all existing Track Automation as the SPL passes it. If you write new data, the new data is recorded. If you do not write new data, Write mode acts as a "realtime eraser" of previous automation data, which it replaces with nothing. Write mode is useful only if you want to start your mix over without using any of the delete commands described later in this chapter. You will find this mode to be less useful than the other automation modes.
- **MIDI.** As mentioned previously, RBA performs MIDI automation. You can thus use your channel strip to record RBA instead of having to select **View > Hyper Draw** to choose a Hyper Draw parameter. While the other modes that write automation work when Logic is playing, MIDI mode only works when Logic is in Record. If you want to record MIDI Automation this way on an Audio track, Logic must be in Record, but the track must *not* be record-enabled.

After setting the parameter you want to display and the automation mode, all that's left to do is actually write the automation data! There are basically two ways to do this: realtime or in the track lane (non-realtime).

You can automate in realtime by clicking the mouse on the various elements of the channel strip (Volume fader, Pan knob, Solo button, Mute button, insert and send slots) or the graphic interface of a plug-in or Audio Instrument, then adjusting those elements by dragging them with the mouse (or just clicking on them, if a button) as your song plays. As you change the location of various elements, you will create *automation nodes,* which are points in which the value of an automatable parameter has changed. When you do realtime automation, as you might imagine, you may create hundreds of these nodes at a time in a mix with lots of complex motion.

You can also use a control surface such as the Mackie/Logic Control, SAC-2k, or any other MIDI hardware controller that you have set up using the Learn Controller Assignment function described in Chapter 4. In this case, you would use the hardware controls on your controller to manipulate the on-screen channel strip and plug-in elements. If you are used to hardware mixers, automating the use of a controller will seem more natural to you. Also, unlike a mouse, using hardware controllers gives you the ability to manipulate more than one parameter at the same time.

If you don't want to automate in realtime, you can also directly add automation nodes (points) and drag them up and down with your mouse in the track lane itself. This offers more precise placement of automation data than realtime mixing, but also less feedback, as you can't hear what you're doing as you make the move.

PARAMETER DISPLAY VERSUS PARAMETER WRITE

Although you need to select a parameter for the automation lane in order to write automation data, in fact you can write automation data for any parameter that is automatable, even if it is not currently being displayed. For example, let's say you select Volume to be the parameter displayed in the automation lane. Then while in Touch mode, you write some Volume automation data, but you also make some panning moves. Logic will write both the volume and the pan moves, even though the automation lane will reflect only the volume moves while you are recording automation data.

Keep in mind that you are not limited to one or the other method of writing automation data—you can use the mouse to automate volume in a track, then add a few more points and adjust them in the track lane. I discuss this further in the "Expert Automation Editing" section below.

METHOD TIP: VIEWING MULTIPLE AUTOMATION LANES

A track's automation lane only lets you choose one "live" parameter to display; however, you can automate more than one parameter at a time with a software controller. What if you want to view more than one parameter that you are automating? As mentioned above, you can view multiple parameters on separate displays by clicking the small disclosure triangle at the bottom-left of a track displaying automation to open a new track lane to display another automation parameter. The new automation display lane will also contain a disclosure triangle. You can use this technique to open as many new automation display lanes as you need for the number of tracks you are automating. You can also **OPTION + Click** on the triangle to open up one new automation display lane for each parameter currently automated, and then **OPTION + Click** the triangle again to close all those automation lanes. Figure 11.4 shows a track that is displaying more than one automation lane this way.

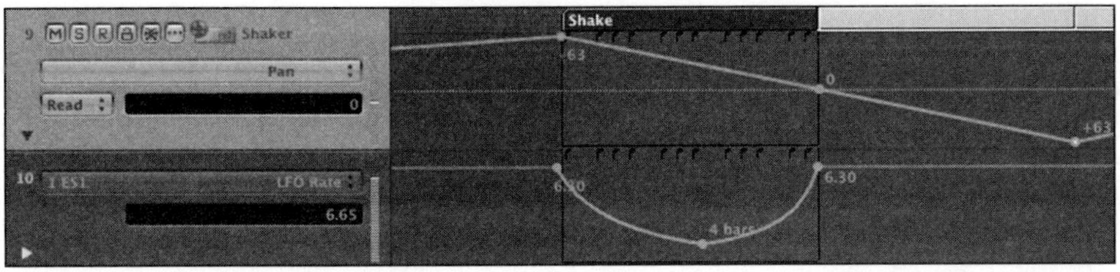

Figure 11.4

This track displays pan automation on its track lane, but then by clicking the triangle in the lower-left, the user created an additional automation display lane for LFO Rate automation.

Manipulating Automation Data

Because you can write automation either by using the mouse or a hardware controller in realtime or by simply adding it to an Arrange track while not playing back, you can use the methods in this section either to alter existing data or to create new data. All that you need to do is turn on Track-Based Automation and select a parameter in the Parameter Display.

Using the Pointer Tool

To move a node, simply grab it with the Pointer tool and then move the node in any direction you want. Notice that the position line representing the continuous parameter value simply shifts positions and values depending on wherever you move the node. If you click on a point in the automation lane in which there isn't currently a node, Logic creates a node in that location, which you can manipulate as described previously.

The Pointer tool can manipulate automation data in additional ways. Short-clicking on a node deletes it. Long-clicking on a line between two nodes enables you to move the line. Long-clicking while holding down the **SHIFT** key enables you to select a length of automation data (from one tick away to the entire song). Pressing **COMMAND + Short-Click** selects all the automation data in the song for the current parameter. Pressing **OPTION + Click** enables you to copy a node or selection. Finally, pressing **OPTION + CONTROL + Click** on a node or line enables you to set curves, like the Automation tool in Curve mode (see the following section).

To change the value of a group of nodes, simply alter the value of one of the selected nodes. All the selected nodes then change by the same amount. If you click outside of a line or node but inside a selected area, you raise the values proportionally to where you clicked, but the values do not change by the same absolute amount. Pressing **COMMAND + Long-Click** allows you to scale all the automation data in the track for the current parameter.

Using the Automation Tool

You can also use the Automation tool described in the section, "The Arrange Toolbox," in Chapter 7. The Automation tool has two modes: Curve and Select. You change the automation mode in the pull-down menu beneath the Toolbox. Figure 11.5 shows the Automation tool and Mode box.

Figure 11.5
The Automation tool is the arrow with the jagged stem. The Automation tool mode menu is below the Toolbox. Currently the Automation tool is set to Curve mode.

In Curve mode, you can use the Automation tool to grab the line between any two nodes and bend it into a curve. Logic offers a number of preset curve types: convex, concave, and S-curves. Which variety of curve you create depends on where on the line you start your bend and in which direction you bend the line.

In Select mode, the Automation tool can make "rubber band" selections in the automation lane. If you click outside the automation lane into a region title bar, you select all the automation that falls within that region. You can make noncontiguous selections of automation with this tool by holding down the **SHIFT** key while selecting additional automation data on the track. You can also extend a selection by pressing **SHIFT + Click** on a node in front of or behind an existing selection; everything from the selected area to the node you clicked on is then selected. Finally, if you select one or more regions and then **OPTION + Click** the Automation tool on the region above the Automation lane, Logic will place one node at the beginning and one node at the end of each selected region.

Expert Automation Editing

As you would expect, Logic offers myriad key commands to control various automation functions. Figure 11.6 shows all the automation key commands.

Feel free to assign keys to any of the options you want—you'll find using Logic's automation even faster and more natural when you master the key commands. But notice one option in the middle can only be accessed via key commands: Automation Event List. These views of automation data are normally invisible. I call the Automation Event List an "expert option" because, unless you know what you are doing, you will find this window too confusing to be of much use. If you want to explore it, however, the following subsection describes it briefly.

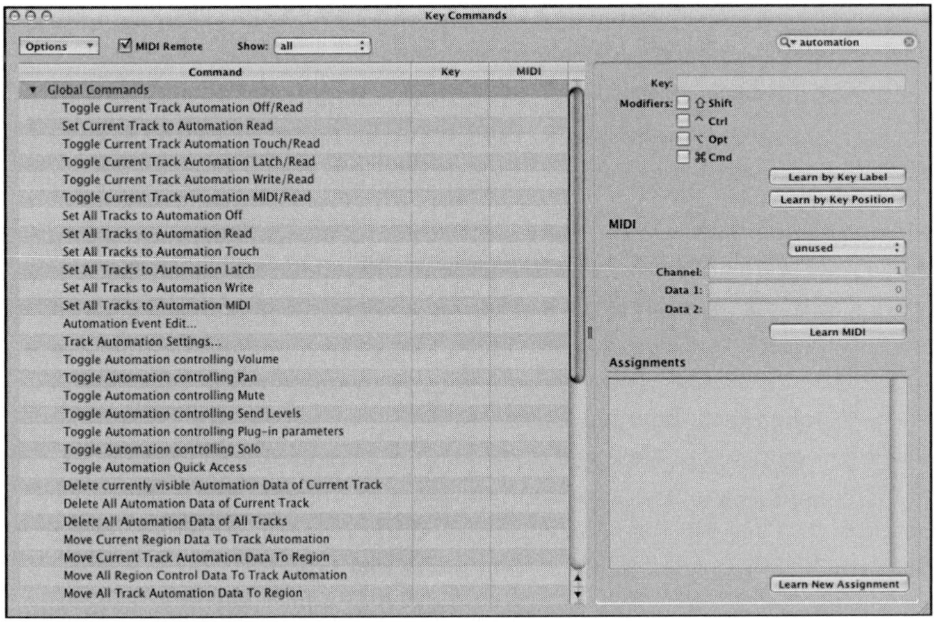

Figure 11.6

The Key Commands window showing the automation-related commands.

Automation Event List

You can view automation data in an Event List, just like other command data such as MIDI control messages. Because automation data is technically a special proprietary type of data known as Fader messages, you'll notice that the Automation Event List consists exclusively of Fader and Control data, depending on what the entry is automating. Figure 11.7 shows an Automation Event List.

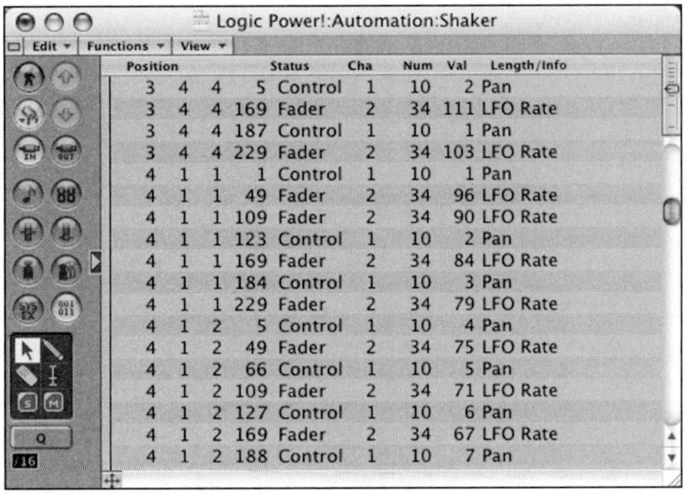

Figure 11.7

An Automation Event List. Because this is a standard Event List Editor, you have all the options previously described in Chapter 9 to edit your automation data.

As you can see, the Automation Event List is an Event Editor like any other, and you can use all the options and techniques described in Chapter 9 regarding the Event Editor to edit your MIDI automation. You may find the Automation Event List useful if you know exactly what you want to edit, or if you are more comfortable editing data numerically rather than graphically.

Moving Automation Data from One Parameter to Another

If you have automation data written for one parameter but you'd like to move it to another parameter—say you automated a filter cutoff for a software instrument, and now you want that data to control the envelope level—you can do this easily. With the parameter you want to move displayed in the automation lane, hold the **COMMAND** key while opening the Parameter Display pop-up menu. Now when you choose a destination parameter, a dialog box appears asking whether you want to convert (move) the current automation to the new parameter or copy and convert it, which leaves the data you have recorded in the current parameter but also adds it to the new parameter. Select the option you prefer, and that's it!

Deleting and Converting Automation Data

Eventually, you may find yourself wanting to get completely rid of all the automation for a given parameter you have recorded and start over. Or perhaps you want to attach your Track-Based Automation to those regions. Or perhaps you'll want to convert MIDI control information into TBA. Luckily, Logic allows you to delete automation and convert between RBA and TBA easily. You can find the basic commands to convert automation data by choosing **Options > Track Automation**. Figure 11.8 shows the submenu that appears.

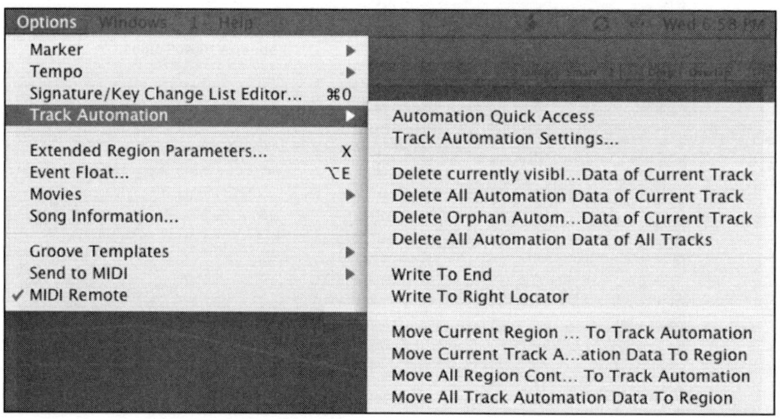

Figure 11.8

The Track Automation submenu in the Options menu.

Here is a brief description of these commands:

- **Automation Quick Access.** This turns on Automation Quick Access, which is explained in the next section.
- **Track Automation Settings.** In the Track Automation Settings dialog box, you can choose whether Logic moves automation automatically when you move the regions that are being automated. Also in this dialog box, you configure Automation Quick Access, which is described in the next section.
- **Delete Currently Visible Automation Data of Current Track.** This command erases all the automation data on the selected track for the parameter in the Parameter Display.
- **Delete All Automation Data of Current Track.** This command erases all automation data on the selected track.
- **Delete All Automation Data of All Tracks.** This command erases all automation data on all tracks.
- **Write To End.** With this command, you can zero (erase) all automation data on the selected track from the current SPL location to the end of the song.
- **Write To Right Locator.** Like the preceding command, this command zeroes all automation data on the selected track, but only as far as the right Locator.
- **Move Current Region Data To Track Automation.** This command converts the Hyper Draw information currently displayed into TBA data. When you use this command, TBA data in the automation lane replaces the blue Hyper Draw display inside your region.
- **Move Current Track Automation Data To Region.** You can convert your currently displayed TBA data to Hyper Draw with this command. When you use this command, your TBA data turns into Hyper Draw information that is part of the region.
- **Move All Region Control Data To Track Automation.** This command converts all of a region's Hyper Draw information into TBA data. When using this command, TBA data in the automation lane replaces the blue Hyper Draw display inside your region.
- **Move All Track Automation Data To Region.** You can convert all your current TBA data to Hyper Draw with this command. When you use this command, your TBA data turns into Hyper Draw information that is part of the region. Since Hyper Draw is MIDI, keep in mind you'll need a MIDI region under the TBA for this to work. (For Audio Tracks, you can always create a MIDI region on a MIDI or Audio Instrument track, then move it under the TBA with your mouse.)

Automation Quick Access

Sometimes, you may want to record a single parameter live to Track Automation as part of a MIDI performance—for example, let's say that you want to perform a synthesizer track, but you want to record your pitch-shifting as TBA instead of Hyper Draw information. You can of course record the information as normal MIDI and then convert it to TBA using one of the commands discussed previously, but Logic offers you an even more elegant shortcut: Automation Quick Access. This feature allows you to use any single hardware controller able to send MIDI data to write Track-Based Automation data. Automation Quick Access is very easy to set up, thanks to Logic's very intuitive Learn function explained next.

To configure and engage Automation Quick Access, open the Automation Preferences dialog box that contains the Automation Quick Access controls shown in Figure 11.9 by choosing **Options > Track Automation > Track Automation Settings**. You can of course also access this window via **Logic Pro > Preferences > Automation**.

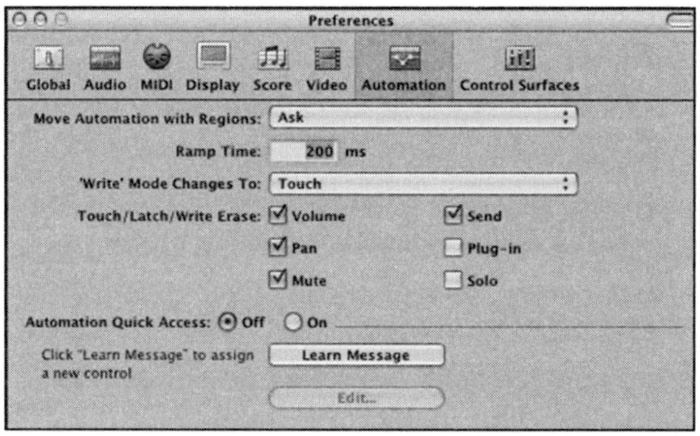

Figure 11.9
The Automation Preferences window contains the options to configure Automation Quick Access.

You'll immediately notice the bottom of the Automation Preferences window consists of settings for Automation Quick Access. All you need to do is click the large Learn Message button at the bottom of the window. As soon as you engage this button, Logic is ready to "learn" the specifications of the controller you want to use as your Automation Quick Access control. The text to the left of the button now reads, "Slowly move/turn the control up and down you want to assign." In other words, simply take hold of the control you want to assign, slowly adjust the control to its maximum value, and then adjust the control to its minimum value.

That's it! Click Done, and you're ready to use your control to input TBA data. So much for the myth that everything in Logic is too difficult—Automation Quick Access couldn't be easier!

12 Mixing in Logic

Whenever you have more than one track in your DAW, you will have to "mix together" the different tracks that you have so that you can hear all the various tracks out of the same set of external speakers. The simplest form of mixing is when you simply "sum" (in other words, add the different audio streams of) all of your audio to the same outputs so all your different tracks of audio play from the same speakers. For example, you could take a song with material on 16 different Audio channels and combine them into a single stereo output so you can listen to all 16 channels through your stereo monitors. After doing the above, your audio has been "mixed" together. But mixing music is far more of an art than simply that. You can adjust the volume and position of your audio in a stereo or surround panorama for each track. You can process your tracks through effects individually or in groups. You can process the song as a whole through effects. And of course, you can "bounce"—or print—the mix to an audio file.

Logic offers some of the most comprehensive and intuitive options and features for mixing that are available in the digital realm. Logic can build a mixer for you from the tracks you have in your Arrange window, or you can build your own mixer in the Environment. You can route your audio directly to your outputs or use myriad creative methods to allow you to group tracks together for mixing and processing. You can insert effects directly into a given Audio Track, send your audio to other channels for processing, or change the output of your track to group them with others for processing. You can bounce your audio down to a file in realtime, so you can hear exactly what is going into the file, or bounce the audio offline when you know exactly what you have and don't need to hear it again. And Logic does all this using channel strips that are both visually appealing and perhaps the most efficient provided in any application, offering you a complete view of each track's settings at a glance.

This chapter will not teach you how to create a professional radio-ready mix of your music; it will, however, explain how you can use Logic to achieve the best mix you can, and offer some techniques for using Logic to mix in creative and exciting ways.

Track Mixer or Environment Mixer?

As discussed previously, the Audio Objects in Logic, when expanded, show a complete channel strip reminiscent of a hardware mixer channel strip. Logic gives you two options for how you can arrange these channel strips. The first method is to allow Logic to put together your mixer for you. As mentioned in Chapter 4, Logic creates a mixer, called the Track Mixer, based on the tracks you have in the Arrange window. The other way you can create a mixer is to create one manually by creating your own Audio Objects in the Environment window and organizing them yourself. Each method has its advantages and disadvantages, and they are not mutually exclusive; because any channel strips in the Track Mixer represent Audio Objects in the Environment, both mixers co-exist together in the same project. You may prefer to access either or both, depending on your preferences and the specific project you are working on. The specific features of each mixer are described in this section.

The Track Mixer

As already noted in Chapter 4, the Track Mixer reflects all the tracks in the Arrange window. You can access the mixer from the Windows global menu by selecting **Windows > Track Mixer** (or by pressing the key command **COMMAND + 2**). The Track Mixer includes channel strips for all the various tracks you have in the Arrange window, and it continually adapts itself to any reorganization and additional tracks that you add to the Arrange window. Figure 12.1 shows the Track Mixer for a song.

One of the best features of the Track Mixer is that Logic automatically configures it for you—there is no setup at all to do. You never have more channel strips to scroll through than you have tracks in your Arrange, and you never will find yourself short a channel strip. Also, the Track Mixer is the only mixer that shows MIDI channel strips. So if you use a fair number of

Figure 12.1
The Track Mixer reflects all the tracks you have in the Arrange window.

MIDI tracks, the Track Mixer allows you to see channel strips for your MIDI tracks alongside your Audio Object channel strips.

You can use the buttons at the side of the Track Mixer to access only one type of channel strip (just the Audio Tracks, Instruments, Outputs, MIDI tracks, and so on). You can also use the Global button to view every channel strip in your Environment Mixer if you want to.

The strength of the Track Mixer is also its weakness; since it contains channel strips only for those tracks in Arrange, if you want to route your audio to various Bus and Aux Objects, those busses and auxes are part of your mixer only if you add those tracks to your Arrange window. And, if the type of object or instrument you want to add to your Track Mixer isn't created in the Environment, you still need to access the Environment at least to some degree. Also, your options for the shape of the Track Mixer are limited to only a single horizontal row of channel strips. You could, however, open multiple Track Mixers, each set to a different Audio Object type. Finally, if you want to rearrange the order of tracks in the Track Mixer, you'll need to reorganize the tracks in the Arrange window.

Environment Audio Mixer

You create Audio Objects in the Environment, so by simply adding and expanding Audio Objects in the Environment window, you can create your own custom-configured Audio Mixer. The Audio global menu includes a command to open the Audio Mixer; this command opens an Environment window to the Audio layer of the Environment. Normally, this is where Logic keeps channel strips of your Audio Objects, but if you put your own mixer on a new layer, the Audio Mixer command will not open your Audio Mixer. The Audio Mixer in the Environment can have any shape you want, and can include as many or as few Audio Objects in any given layer as you want (with the caveat, of course, that all the tracks in your song will have objects created for them on some Environment layer). Figure 12.2 shows an Environment Audio Mixer for the same song as in Figure 12.1.

The biggest advantage of building Audio Mixers in the Environment is that you can create and organize them however you like, allowing your mixer to reflect exactly how you want to work. The Environment Audio Mixer does not reflect your Arrange window at all, however. This can create extra navigation headaches; for example, if your Audio Mixer contains 64 Audio Track channel strips and then three Audio Instrument channel strips, but your song uses only 16 Audio Tracks and two Audio Instruments, you'll have to scroll from Audio Track 16 through 64 empty Audio Tracks to your two

Figure 12.2
The Environment Audio Mixer offers great flexibility, but doesn't automatically adapt to the tracks in your Arrange window like the Track Mixer.

Audio Instruments—or continually create Environment Mixers reflecting what your song looks like. By contrast, the Track Mixer only contains your 16 Audio Tracks, so you'll have no extra tracks to navigate. On the other hand, in the Environment Audio Mixer, you can instantly rearrange any of the objects, so you can simply move your mixer around or open new layers for different Audio Objects. Of course, as is self-evident from the name *Audio Mixer*, it does not show you any of the MIDI tracks in your Arrange window.

> **USING THE STRENGTHS OF BOTH MIXERS**
>
> As I said at the beginning of this section, the mixers are not mutually exclusive—you can design a custom mixer in the Environment and use the Track Mixer. You can use Logic's flexibility regarding mixers to configure the ideal workspace for yourself. One way that I like to do this is by creating my ideal "big mixer" in the Environment, with all the Audio Tracks, Bus tracks, Aux tracks, Audio Instruments, Rewire tracks, and such that I'll ever need. I make sure to check the "icon" parameter for each, so that I can access them from the Arrange window. This way, I use the Environment Mixer as a sort of "set and leave" mixer with everything that I might possibly want in my song.
>
> At this point, I build my song track by track in the Arrange window, and use the Track Mixer so my mixer contains only those channel strips I'm using and includes my MIDI Channels. If I need an Aux or Rewire track in my Track Mixer, I add it to my Arrange window so it appears in the Track Mixer. At first blush, it might seem a bit unnecessary to have tracks in the Arrange that don't have regions on them just so they appear in the Track Mixer, but I find that there are other advantages to having my Aux, Rewire, Output, and other tracks in Arrange. When they are in Arrange, I can automate them, I can access their channel strip directly in Arrange, and so on.

The Track Mixer Local Menus

Like all windows in Logic, the Track Mixer includes its own local menus with commands specific to itself. The following subsections describe the two Track Mixer local menus and their options.

The Options Menu

The Options menu consists of a few miscellaneous functions you may want to use. Figure 12.3 shows the Options menu of the Track Mixer.

Figure 12.3

The Options menu of the Track Mixer.

Here are brief descriptions of these functions:

- **Send All Mixer Data.** This command sends all the mixer-related information that is on MIDI tracks to your MIDI devices.
- **Change Track in Record Mode.** With this checked, you can change the selected track during recording. This can be dangerous—if you're not careful, you might interrupt your recording—so you'll most often want to keep this option unchecked.
- **Change Track in Play Mode.** This command enables you to change and edit the selected track while in Playback mode. This is exceedingly useful when mixing, and you usually will want this option checked.
- **Add GS/XG Effects.** This check box adds rotary knobs to MIDI tracks. These knobs can control the built-in effects that use the Roland (GS) or Yamaha (XG) General MIDI parameters.

The View Menu

The View menu offers a number of options that relate to MIDI tracks and the overall look of the Track Mixer. Figure 12.4 shows you the View menu.

The various options in the View menu are as follows:

- **Parameters.** If you check this box, the Track Mixer displays the buttons on its left side.
- **Follow Control Surface.** If you have a hardware control surface connected to Logic, checking this box ensures that the track selected in the Track Mixer always reflects the channel that you have selected on your control surface.
- **Scroll To.** This hierarchal submenu includes options that allow you to jump to various track types in your mixer. The submenu includes the same group of track types as the Track Mixer buttons. These navigation options can be very useful if you have a large Track Mixer and keep your track types organized together. If your Track Mixers are small, or you mix up your track varieties, you most likely will not use these options. You can also assign key commands for these options, of course, with which you can navigate among the track varieties even faster.

* **Folder Tracks.** Check this view option if you want Folder Tracks to get channel strips in the Track Mixer. Uncheck this view option if you do not.
* **Other Tracks.** Check this view option if you want channel strips for other types of tracks not specifically named in buttons and menu options, such as the Master Fader and Rewire channels, to get channel strips in the Track Mixer.

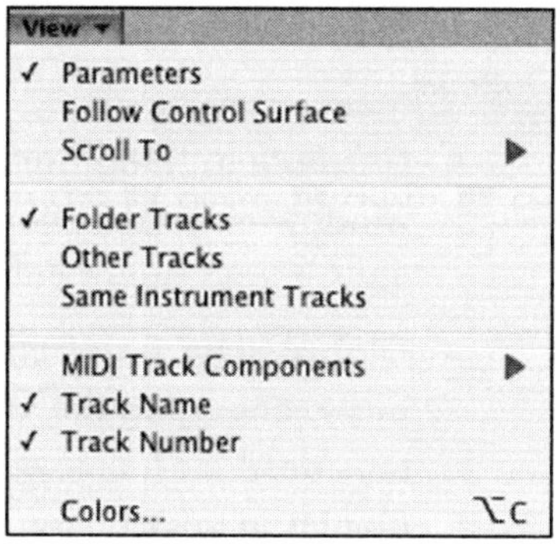

Figure 12.4
The View menu of the Track Mixer.

* **Same Instrument Tracks.** The Same Instrument Tracks option, if checked, gives you a separate channel strip in your Track Mixer for each track that accesses the same object. With this unchecked, if more than one track is assigned to the same object, you will only see a single channel strip for that instrument in the Track Mixer.
* **MIDI Track Components.** This submenu allows you to check or uncheck individual components within the MIDI track. You can toggle the Program, Bank, Assign 1–5, Pan, and Volume fader for MIDI track strips by checking or unchecking the relevant component.
* **Track Name.** If checked, this option displays the names of each track at the bottom of each channel on the Track Mixer.
* **Track Number.** If checked, the Track Number option displays the number of each track at the bottom of each channel on the Track Mixer.
* **Colors.** This opens the Color window, so you can assign colors to the various tracks in the Track Mixer. Any colors you assign to a channel strip in the Track Mixer will also apply to any tracks and regions in the Arrange window assigned to that channel strip.

Track Mixer Parameters

The Track Mixer has a Parameter bar along its left side that has a number of options. Figure 12.5 shows the Track Mixer Parameter bar.

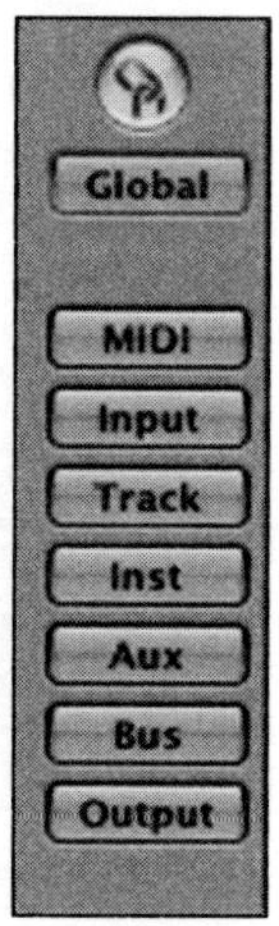

Figure 12.5
The Parameter bar of the Track Mixer.

The function of each element of the Parameter bar, from top to bottom, is as follows:

- **Link Button.** If this button is lit, the Track Mixer follows your Arrange window track selections. The Track Mixer will also follow your selections in and out of Folder tracks in Arrange.
- **Global View.** This button engages Global view. As mentioned previously, engaging the Global View button in conjunction with the buttons described below allows you to view all of the selected types of objects in your entire song, as opposed to just the selected track type in your Arrange window.
- **MIDI through Output Buttons.** If you click on any of these buttons, the Track Mixer displays only the selected track type. To return to viewing all of your tracks, just click the button again, or click the Global View button to enter Global view.

Recording Audio from the Mixer

Throughout the rest of this chapter, everything discussed applies to either the Track Mixer or an Environment Audio Mixer. First, you likely need to set up your audio recordings directly from your mixer. This process consists of two steps.

Figure 12.6
From the Input pull-down menu, choose the hardware input you want to use for this track.

The first step is to select the physical input you want to use from the Input box of your channel strip. When you click and hold the box, a pull-down menu of all available inputs will appear, as Figure 12.6 illustrates. From this menu, select the input you want to use.

Next, click the REC button at the bottom of the channel strip. The REC button flashes red, as you can hopefully somewhat discern from Figure 12.7. This indicates that when you press Record on the Transport, the track will record audio.

Figure 12.7

When you click the REC button at the bottom of an Audio Track channel strip, it flashes red to indicate that the channel is now armed for recording.

If this is the very first track of audio that you are recording for your song, then Logic may ask you to set the record path for the recording you are about to make. This record path is also where all subsequent audio for this project will be recorded. You'll know that this is the first recording, or that there is no record path set, if a dialog box such as the one in Figure 12.8 appears.

Repeat the preceding two steps for each track on which you want to record audio. After that, just press the Record button on the Transport (via mouse, hardware controller, or key command) and record away!

Basic Mixing: Summing Volume and Panorama

The most basic mixing that you'll want to do is simply to adjust the volume of one track in comparison to another, and to place mono tracks at different points in the stereo field, or panorama. If this is all you'll ever want to use Logic's mixers for, then this section will tell you all you'll ever need to do.

Figure 12.8

If you haven't recorded any audio yet, when you record-enable a channel, a file dialog box appears in which you can select the record path for the song.

Volume Summing

Because each individual track is usually recorded with an ear toward getting the best recording of that specific source material, you almost never will initially record your tracks at the perfect level in relation to each other. This is why, since the beginning of recorded music, engineers have brought the level of one track up in a mix, while perhaps bringing another track down. The result is to create the perfect balance among all the various sounds in the mix.

You adjust the volume of a channel by moving the onscreen Volume fader on its channel strip. If you are using a mouse, you'll generally be able to adjust only one fader at a time, but if you have a hardware control surface, you may be able to adjust many faders at once. The numbers inside the fader represent either how many decibels you have added or subtracted from the initial volume of the track or the current MIDI volume, from 0 to 127. Figure 12.9 shows a Track Mixer in which the volume faders have been adjusted to different levels to create a pleasing overall volume balance.

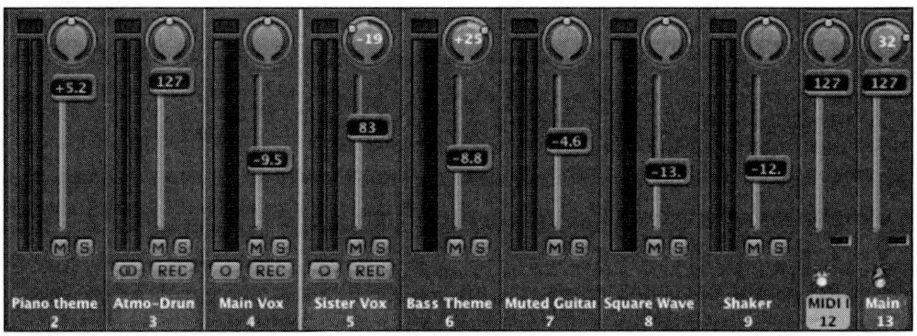

Figure 12.9
Mixing the volume of your tracks is as easy as sliding the Volume faders with your mouse or controller. You can also adjust the volume numerically.

OPTION + Clicking a Volume fader sets it to its *null value,* or the center point at which no adjustment is made. This is 0dB for decibel faders, and 90 for MIDI data faders.

Panning

The other basic mixing technique you'll find yourself wanting to do is to place monophonic tracks at different spots in the stereo panorama. This is known as *panning*. Panning can make tracks more distinct by placing them in a stereo location in which there is no other sound "competing" for the space. The technique can make mixes come alive by making the material sound as if it is coming from all over the stereo spectrum, instead of all sounds originating from the exact middle of the listening field. The Pan rotary knob is right next to the Volume fader, and you can adjust the pan value for any track by moving the knob to the right or left with either your mouse or a hardware control surface. Pan values range from −64 (full left) to +64 (full right), with 0 being the exact middle. Figure 12.10 shows a pair of tracks that have been panned differently to enhance the mix.

Figure 12.10

To adjust the pan of a track, rotate its Pan knob to the desired setting. You can also directly enter a pan value numerically.

You can double-click the Pan knob to enter a pan value numerically, and **OPTION + Clicking** on the Pan knob returns the pan value to the center. Keep in mind that you can automate these parameters as explained in the last chapter so that your mix can be dynamic, with automatic changes happening exactly on cue.

METHOD TIP: PANNING STEREO TRACKS USING THE DIRECTION MIXER EFFECT

If you adjust the Pan knob on a stereo track, you aren't really panning the signal between left and right, since the stereo signal already exists in both channels. Instead, you are adjusting the balance between the two channels. Sometimes this can work like panning, but sometimes, it won't. If you want more control over the track's stereo panorama, check out Logic Pro's built-in Direction Mixer (or DirMixer) effect. It will allow you to not only adjust the balance of the signal, but to adjust the width of the stereo image and its location between the two channels. It's a fantastic little plug-in—give it a look!

Bussing Tracks in Logic

When you play back your audio material in Logic, the most direct signal path your audio can follow in order for you to hear it is for the channel strip of the source Audio Object to output its audio directly to the Output Object connected to your hardware. Logic offers you more signal path options than this, however. As I discussed when introducing Bus Objects in Chapter 8, "Working with Audio and Apple Loops," these are basically "parallel mixers" that allow you to send a portion of your signal to another channel strip, or that allow you to output a track into another mixer channel strip for further grouping and processing instead of having to output that track immediately to your hardware. Aux tracks can also serve the same purpose as Bus tracks, and have some additional features as well. The subsections that follow explain how you can use Bus and Aux Objects in Logic for creating bussing, grouping, and signal processing.

Figure 12.11

A Bus Object channel strip.

Using Bus Objects

As you can see from the Bus Object in Figure 12.11, Bus Objects do not have Send or Input boxes. That is because audio does not originate from Bus Objects, unlike Audio Track or Audio Instrument Objects, which contain audio data (or MIDI data that the instrument will use to trigger audio). Bus Objects do not have a REC button for this same reason. Bus Objects do not have a BNCE button because a Bus is not a final destination, like an Output Object.

Think of a Bus Object as a "patch bay" between your source material (Audio or Audio Instrument track) and your ultimate destination (Output Object). You can use a bus in two ways: You can have a channel strip with Send slots send a variable amount of audio to your Bus Object for processing, or you can set the output of a channel strip to a Bus Object, sending all of the audio to that Bus Object.

Using a Send to Feed a Bus Object

If you want to use a Send to feed audio to a Bus Object, simply click and hold a Send box, and a pull-down menu of all your available Bus Objects appears. Select the Bus Object you want, then turn the Send knob to send to the Bus Object the amount of audio you want. Figure 12.12 shows the pull-down menu of a Send box with all the busses available for you to choose.

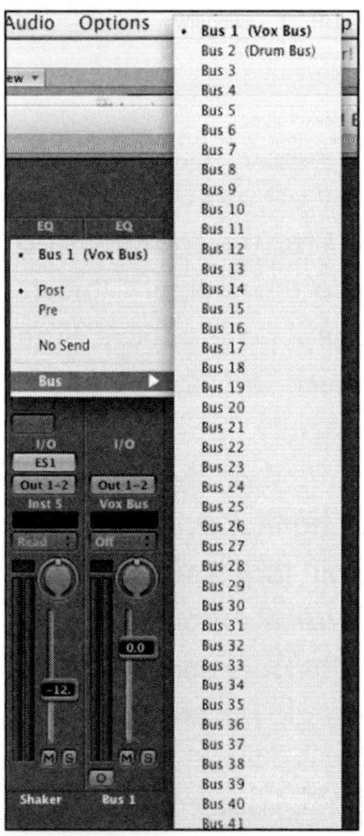

Figure 12.12

To send audio to a Bus Object using a Send, simply select the Send you want from the Send box pull-down menu, then adjust the Send knob to send the desired amount of signal to the Bus Object.

The Send pull-down menu includes options for Post and Pre. If you select Post, Logic feeds your audio through the Send *after* the volume fader has adjusted its level. If you select Pre, Logic feeds the audio through the Send to the Bus Object *before* the fader adjusts the volume of the channel. To turn off a Send, you can click on it with the **OPTION** key held down. Your Send box will stop glowing, indicating that it is turned off. It still retains the Bus Object you chose for it, so **OPTION + Clicking** again on the Send will reengage it.

Bussing audio to Sends is especially useful when you want to use time- and modulation-based effects such as delay, chorus, and reverb to process your audio. Because you rarely want to process all your audio using these effects, you can insert the effect into the Insert box of a Bus Object, then send a variable amount of your audio to that Bus Object, adjusting the Send knob until you get just the right balance for your music. Figure 12.13 shows an Audio Instrument that is using a Send to add a reverb that is inserted in a Bus Object. Inserting effects is discussed in more detail later in this chapter.

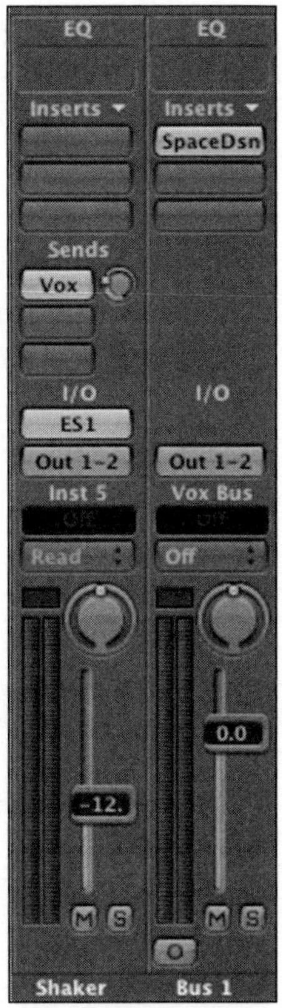

Figure 12.13
The channel strip on the left is for an Audio Instrument, in this case Logic's own ES1. The Audio Instrument is using a Send to feed the second channel strip, which is a Bus Object in which Logic's built-in Space Designer impulse response reverb is instantiated. By adjusting the Send knob on the AI channel strip, you can control how much reverb is added to the Audio Instrument.

Outputting a Channel to a Bus Object

You can select a Bus Object as the output for all Audio Objects except Output Objects. To do this, select a Bus Object as an output, click on the Output box of the Object's channel strip until the Output pull-down menu appears, then select the desired bus from the menu. Figure 12.14 shows the Output pull-down menu of a channel strip.

Outputting channels to Bus Objects can have a number of valuable uses in mixing. You can set the output of a number of tracks to a Bus Object, and use that Bus Object as a sort of Master channel strip for the entire collection of channels (you can use this in tandem with the Groups feature in Logic to create a complete "submixer" in your mixer; the Group feature is discussed later in the chapter in the section "Mixer Groups"). You can use your bus as an additional fader, or to do additional processing, much like you can with Sends, but this way all of the source channel's audio goes to the Bus Object, and if the source channel is stereo, Logic preserves the channel's stereo image when outputting the audio to a Bus Object.

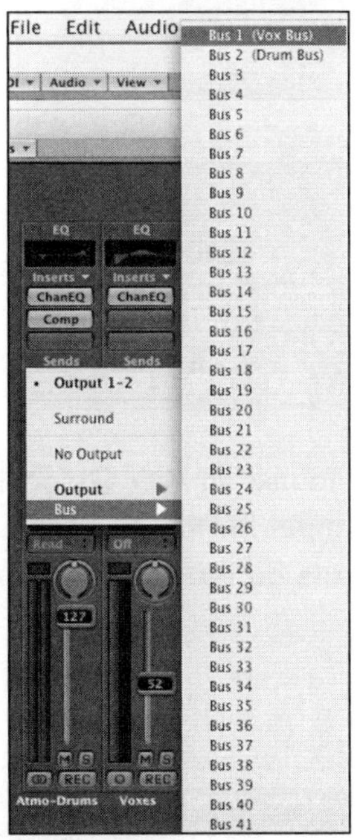

Figure 12.14
To set the output of an Audio Object to a Bus Object, click on the Output box to access the Output pull-down menu and choose an available Bus Object.

Or perhaps you want to send a channel to an Aux track; to do so, you set the output of the channel to a bus, and the input of the Aux Object to the Bus Object. The following section discusses the functions and flexibility of Aux Objects.

Using Aux Objects

Aux Objects are another kind of parallel, "auxiliary" mixer much like a Bus Object, but with some unique features and limitations. Unlike Bus Objects that are basically patch bays and extra faders, Aux Objects can directly accept source audio. This means that Aux Objects have two features that Bus Objects do not: Aux Objects can have live inputs, and they have Sends to feed Bus Objects.

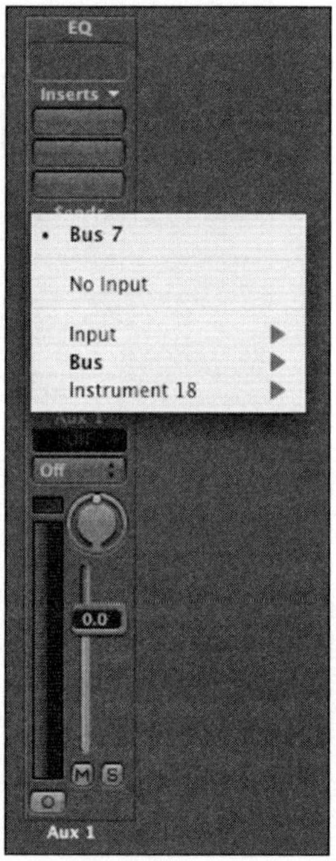

Figure 12.15
When you click on the Input box of an Aux Object, you access its Input pull-down menu.

When you click the Input box of an Aux Object, you'll access the Input pull-down menu for the Aux Object, as shown in Figure 12.15. Notice that the object can accept a hardware input, a Bus Object, or a multichannel output from an Audio Instrument.

Using an Aux Object for Multichannel Audio Instruments was already discussed in Chapter 10, so the next section addresses using Aux Objects with live inputs and Bus Objects.

Using Aux Objects with Live Inputs

Sometimes you may want to record some audio without effects, but hear your source audio while recording with some effects on it. One way to do this is by setting up an Aux Object with a live input as its Input source. This allows you to use an Aux Object as a true "auxiliary mixer" in which one set of audio goes to your hard disk and another goes to the speakers or headphones.

To use an Aux Object this way, simply select one of your live inputs as the input for the Aux Object. As soon as the source starts to play, you will hear the audio through the Aux Object as well as any Audio Track or Input

Object through which the audio is routed. Figure 12.16 shows an example of a setup with both an Audio Track and an Aux Object using the same input for a source.

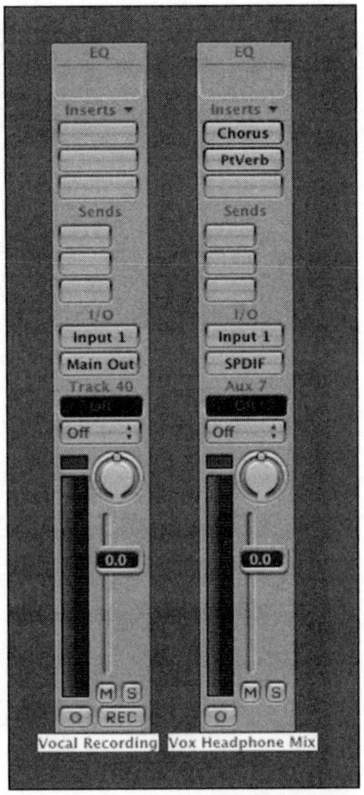

Figure 12.16
Here an Audio Track will record using audio hardware interface Input 1, and an Aux Object is also getting its input from Input 1. The Aux Object is being used to add chorus and reverb effects.

Such a setup is particularly useful when you have software monitoring turned off so that Logic is not monitoring the actual track doing the recording, and only the Aux Object is playing back the source material during recording. This is also very useful if your vocalist likes to hear some effects, for example, a bit of reverb or chorus, while recording; by setting up an Aux track with effects, the vocalist will hear the performance through the Aux with effects, but Logic will record the performance on the Audio Track without effects.

Using Aux Objects as Busses

This is my favorite use of Aux Objects! Often you might want to assign a group of channels to a bus so you can use the Bus Object to process all the tracks together and serve as a master fader for the group. In other words, say your song has 12 tracks of drums (a full drum kit, mic'd with 12 microphones). In addition to having individual controls for each track, you may want a master fader, or to apply effects to all the drums at once (such as putting them all through the same compressor). Now, you can use a Bus Object for this as well, however, you might also want to include Sends on your master group fader so that you can use effects into which you would rather send a variable amount of audio. Logic allows you to set up an Aux Object to serve basically as a "Bus Object with Sends" by using a Bus Object as a patch bay between your source channel and the Aux Object.

To do this, first you need to set the Output setting of your source channels to a Bus Object. Then set the Output setting of your Bus Object to No Output—otherwise you'll get output from the Bus Object *and* the Aux Object. Finally, set the Input of your Aux Object to the same Bus Object to which you have

Figure 12.17

Here the two channel strips on the left are guitar tracks with their output set to Bus 10. Bus Object 10, in the middle, is set to No Output, and the final channel strip (on the right) is an Aux Object with its input set to Bus 10. The Aux Object is now acting as a Bus Object with Sends by using Bus 10 as a patch bay between the Audio Tracks and the Aux Object.

set the output of the source channels. Figure 12.17 shows a simple setup in which one track is using an Aux track as its Bus Object with Sends.

If you end up using Aux Objects as master group faders like I do in Figure 12.17, I highly recommend you use Aux Objects as described here—having the option to use Sends on your master group fader is definitely worth it!

Keep in mind that you'll need to have the Bus Object in your Environment in order to change its output to No Output; but after that, it's safe to delete it from your Environment, since you're not using it. In fact, it's probably safer to delete it so that you don't accidentally use it as well, and wonder where your "double signal" is coming from! (I'll admit, I've done that a couple of times. . . .) Also, multiple Aux Objects can use the same Bus Object as their input, so you can create some complex and creative parallel routings if you desire.

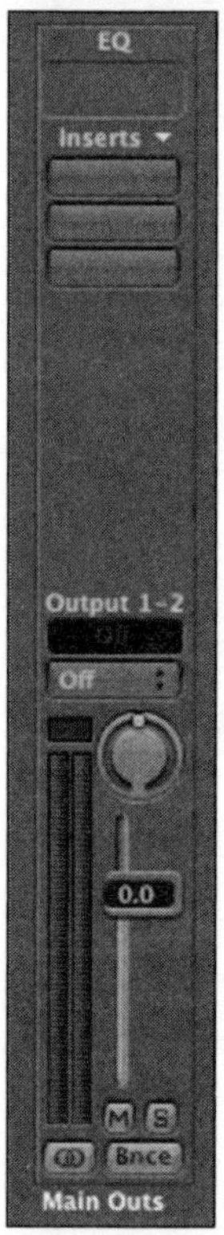

Figure 12.18

This Output Object is hard-wired to Outputs 1–2, the main stereo outputs for the hardware interface used with this project.

Output Objects

Finally, I should talk a bit about Output Objects. These objects are the final destination for your audio; Output Objects connect directly to your hardware audio interface. You can have as many Output Objects as you have physical outputs on your audio hardware. Output Objects have Insert slots for effects, but no Sends, since Output Objects portion out audio to hardware, not to additional processing channels within Logic. Output Objects also don't have Input boxes, as they are destinations for any audio that they receive. These objects include the BNCE button, which allows you to sum all the audio going to that Output Object into a file on your hard disk.

Usually, a song has only a single Output Object, which represents the hardware output that leads to your speaker system. Figure 12.18 shows an Output Object for the main outputs to the audio hardware.

Sometimes you may want to use more than the main Output Object. If you are mixing surround audio, for example, you may need 6–12 outputs, each sending to a discrete input on a hardware surround encoder. Perhaps you are not doing all your mixing in Logic, but sending tracks from Logic into a large studio mixing console. Or maybe you are sending out various tracks to various hardware processors and mixing your song on a tape deck. Whatever your use, you will use Output Objects to interface Logic with your audio hardware.

Using Effects

Mixing is not simply a matter of bringing together multiple source signals. Sometimes, you'll want to process them as well. You can process audio in all sorts of ways—you can compress and distort audio; add EQ, delays, modulation, and reverb; link a track to external hardware for additional processing; and more. In traditional hardware studios, you need to cable an Audio channel to a hardware effects processor in order to process a channel with effects. Just as software sequencers feature software mixers, they also feature software effects.

Effects in Logic generally have their own graphic editor that displays the parameters of the effect, and often gives you some visual representation of the current effect settings. This is called the Editor view. Figure 12.19 shows the Editor view of a Logic effect.

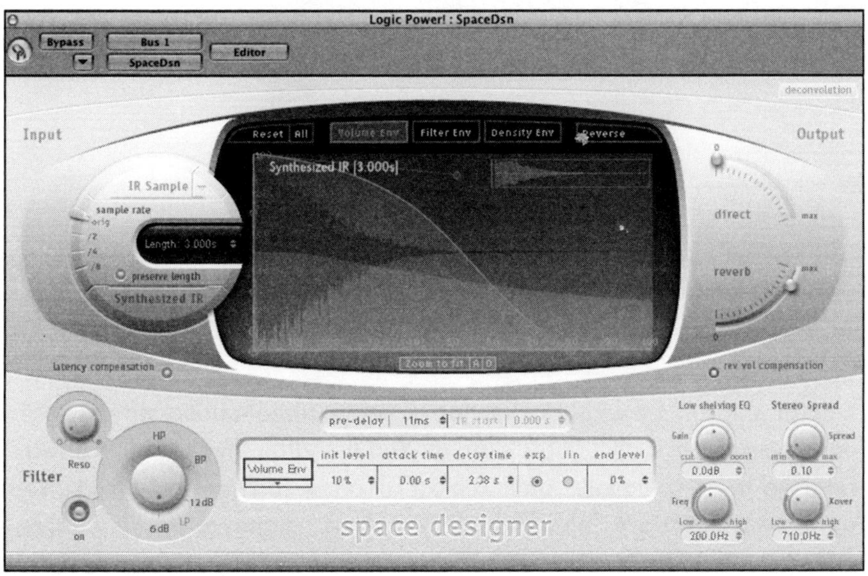

Figure 12.19

This is the graphic control window of Logic's built-in reverb effect, Space Designer. Notice that not only are the parameters given graphic controls, but the impulse response audio file and volume envelope are represented graphically.

Notice that the plug-in window for effects has the same controls already discussed in Chapter 10 regarding software instruments. You will most often want to use Editor mode to work with your effects as this is where you get the most pleasing user experience, as well as graphical feedback. Sometimes, however, if you know exactly what you want and just want to adjust a parameter numerically, or if you are working with older effects without graphics, you might want to use Control mode. As Figure 12.20 shows, when an effect is in Control mode, no graphics other than a slider for each parameter are displayed. You still have full control over your effect, but do not get the aesthetic experience or graphical feedback that the Editor mode offers.

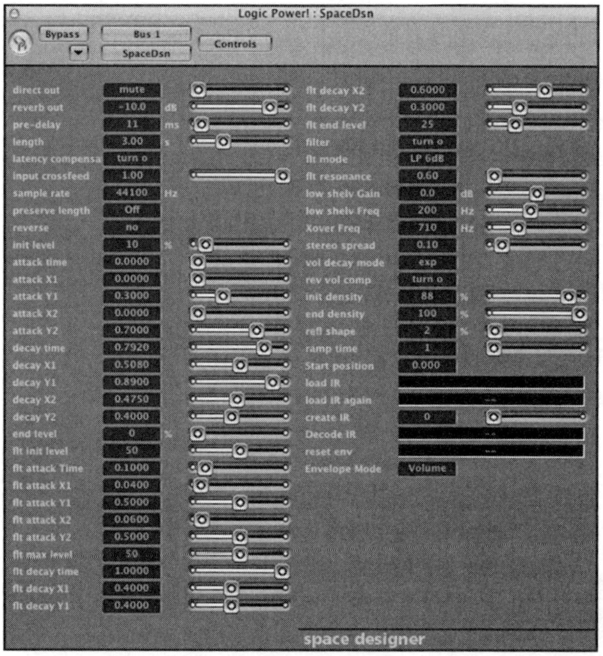

Figure 12.20
This is the Control window of the Space Designer from Figure 12.19. It displays only a slider for each parameter.

This section explores using audio effects within Logic's mixer, and also offers some tips and suggestions for using effects in a mix.

Logic Effects

Emagic ships Logic with a collection of professional-quality effects, which you can access from within Logic's mixer. You will often hear Logic's effects referred to as "plug-ins," since almost all other software effects are separate applications that are "plugged in" to a "host" digital audio sequencer, such as Logic. Logic's effects, while accessed the same way as third-party plug-ins, are in fact built in to the code of the application itself. This is why you cannot access Logic's effects in other applications that allow effects plug-ins.

To access a Logic effect, click-hold on an Effects slot in a channel strip. If the channel is mono, a hierarchal menu appears offering you the choice of Mono or **Mono > Stereo** effects. If your channel is stereo, your only option is the Stereo hierarchal menu. After making your menu selection, additional hierarchal menus appear allowing you to choose from either Logic effects or Audio Units. To instantiate a Logic effect, simply choose the Logic hierarchal menu, then a Logic effect from the menus offered. After selecting the effect you want and releasing the mouse button, the effect appears in the Effect slot in the channel strip, and the effect Editor window opens, ready to be configured. Figure 12.21 shows a Logic effect being selected.

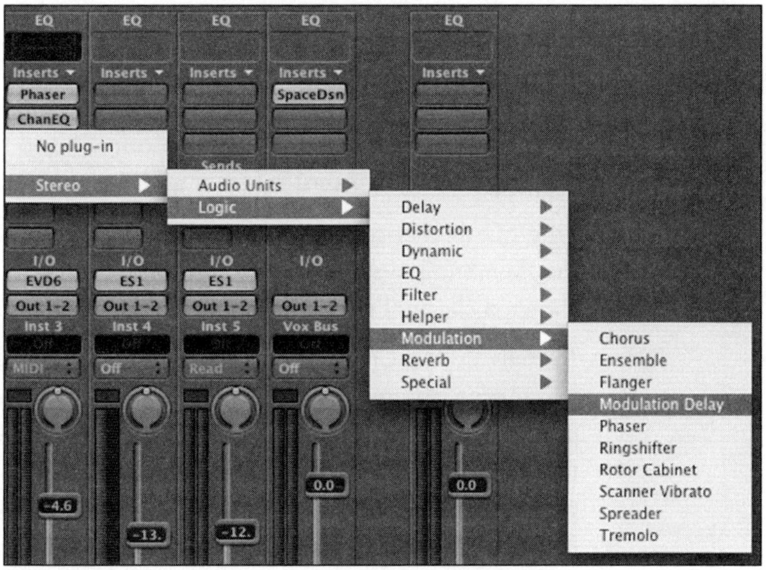

Figure 12.21

To select a Logic effect, follow the hierarchal menus and select the Logic effect you desire—in this case, the Modulation Delay effect.

Logic gives you a complete selection of all the effects that you will need in modern music production, including all the standard dynamics-based effects (compression, limiting), time-based effects (delay, reverb), modulation effects (chorus, flange), and many completely unique offerings (Spectral Gate, AutoFilter). A full list of Logic's effects is given in Appendix A.

Using the Channel and Linear EQ

There is not enough space in this book to go over how to use each effect included with Logic Pro 7. However, there are two plug-ins that interact with the channel strip differently than the others: the Channel EQ and the Linear Phase EQ. Therefore, this unique interaction is explained in this subsection.

As stated above, Logic Pro 7 includes two professional-quality equalizer plug-ins: the Channel EQ and the Linear Phase EQ. Both are filters that can adjust the frequency response of your audio; the two EQs look and operate identically. The main difference is that the Linear Phase EQ maintains the exact phase relationship of the frequencies of your audio material, which at extremes non-linear phase algorithms can alter. The price of this advanced linear phase algorithm is both increased CPU overhead and increased processing delay. I will discuss processing delay later in this chapter. But the point is, you'll want to be judicious in your use of Linear Phase EQs. The Channel EQ is actually just another effect, like any other of Logic's effects. The Channel EQ offers a few special features beyond other plug-ins worth noting.

Figure 12.22

A channel strip's EQ thumbnail box above the Inserts parameter. This box is where you can access your Channel EQ and see the current EQ curve.

If you have the EQ parameter turned on in an Audio Object's parameter box, the top of the channel strip has a rectangular box labeled EQ, as in Figure 12.22. This EQ thumbnail box offers you both easy access to the Channel and Linear Phase EQ plug-ins and a visual reference of the current EQ curve.

If the EQ thumbnail box is empty, you simply see the outline of the thumbnail over the channel strip background. Figure 12.23 shows a channel strip with an empty EQ thumbnail box.

Figure 12.23

An EQ thumbnail box for a channel strip that does not have a Channel EQ instantiated.

To activate the Channel EQ, double-click inside the thumbnail box. Logic opens a new window with the Channel EQ plug-in, places a thumbnail of the grid display of the new Channel EQ in the EQ thumbnail box, and instantiates the Channel EQ plug-in into the topmost available Insert slot. You cannot click into the box to instantiate the Linear Phase EQ, but if you add a Linear Phase EQ effect on your own, it also will show its grid in the EQ thumbnail box. As you adjust the parameters in the Channel or Linear Phase EQ, this thumbnail box reflects the EQ curve that is created in the plug-in window. This offers you a quick visual reference as to how you have EQ'd that channel. If you need to make an adjustment, you can double-click the EQ thumbnail box to open the Channel or Linear Phase EQ (depending which you have instantiated).

If you have multiple Linear Phase or Channel EQ effects in one track, only the topmost EQ will have its grid showing in the EQ thumbnail box.

All the effects, including the Channel EQ, are listed in Appendix A.

Effects Side Chains

Some effects, such as Logic's Compressor, Expander, and AutoFilter, as well as some third-party plug-ins, have what is called a "side chain" input. A side chain is an input to an effect or plug-in that allows another Audio Track to trigger that effect or plug-in. You can use side chains to configure an effect to activate only when another signal is present. One example of this would be to have a compressor on a bass track triggered by a kick drum on another track, so that the bass is compressed only when the kick drum sounds in order to create a tighter feel for the rhythm. Side chains are also very useful for "ducking" (making a signal softer when another signal is present), for vocoder effects and instruments (where an Audio channel is sent into the side chain of a vocoder software instrument to "play" the vocoder), and so on. The side chain input looks like an additional pull-down menu on the plug-in window control bar, as shown in Figure 12.24.

Figure 12.24

The side chain input can be seen on the Compressor effect in Logic as a new pull-down menu on the far right of the control bar.

To select a track to use as the side chain input, simply select an available audio source from the pull-down menu, as in Figure 12.25. The track that you choose triggers the operation of the effect.

Not all plug-ins or effects have side chain inputs, but for those that do, it opens a whole new creative way to use effects.

Figure 12.25
To use one of these available tracks as the side chain trigger, select it from the pull-down menu.

EXPERT TIP: USING THE SIDE CHAIN INPUT TO RESCUE LACKLUSTER KICK DRUMS

Producer and Logic guru Don Gunn offers his expert method for how you can use the side chain input feature to add "guts" to a kick drum performance that isn't punchy enough:

> "If you find yourself mixing a song and the kick drum just isn't providing the bottom end you'd like, there's an easy way to create low-frequency content. This tip utilizes Logic's software instruments as well as the side chain feature on the Noise Gate plug-in."
>
> "With your kick drum track in the Arrange window, assign an unused bus to one of the sends; as you can see in Figure 12.26, I've used Bus 23."
>
> "Next, create an Audio Instrument track and assign the track a software instrument of your choice for generating low tones. In Figure 12.27, I've used the ES2 in this example, but any of the built-in Logic synthesizers (ESM, ESE, ESP) will work as well. You can see that to create the tone, I'm using one oscillator set to generate a sine wave, as well as the secondary sine sub-oscillator for additional fatness."
>
> "Now insert a Noise Gate plug-in on the Audio Instrument track and assign the side chain input to the bus that was assigned to the Send on the kick drum track, as shown in Figure 12.28."
>
> "If you play this track as it is currently set up, you will still only hear the original kick drum; for the instrument to produce sound, it needs a note that is affected by the incoming signal via the Noise Gate side chain. You can see in Figure 12.29 that I have inserted the note A1 and made its length be the duration of the kick drum region that needs reinforcement. One benefit to this technique is that you can have the kick drum trigger a note that is in key with your song, helping to reinforce the notes being played by the bass part."

"At this point, when the song is played back, the kick drum will trigger the side chain on the Noise Gate to open, allowing the tone of the synthesizer to go to the output. Using the envelope controls in the Noise Gate (Attack, Hold, Release), you can make the tone of the synthesizer longer or shorter, give the note a short, clipped attack, or have the low-frequency material swell in behind the original kick drum. You can also adjust the sensitivity of the Noise Gate with the Threshold and Reduction parameters. Experimentation is the key!"

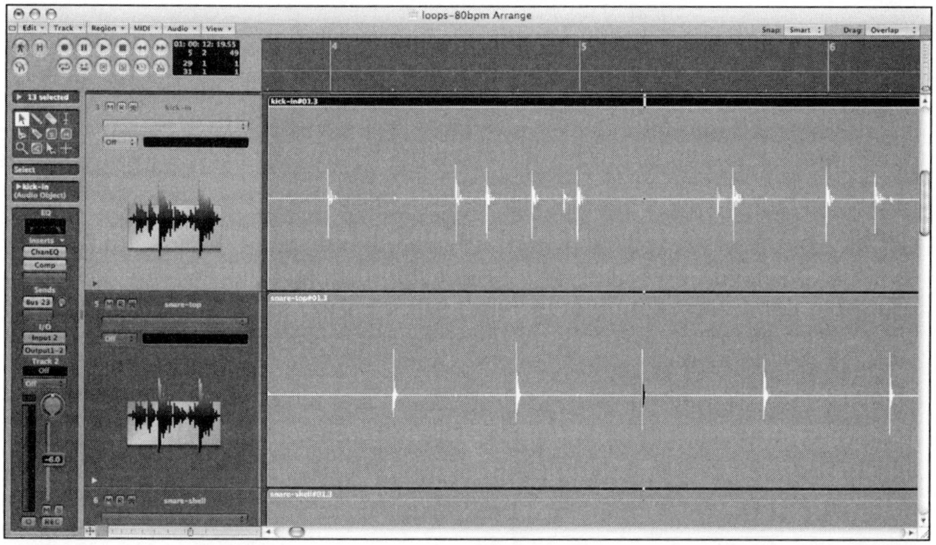

Figure 12.26

To begin the process of adding low-frequency content to a lacking kick drum, assign an unused bus to a Send; here, Bus 23 is assigned.

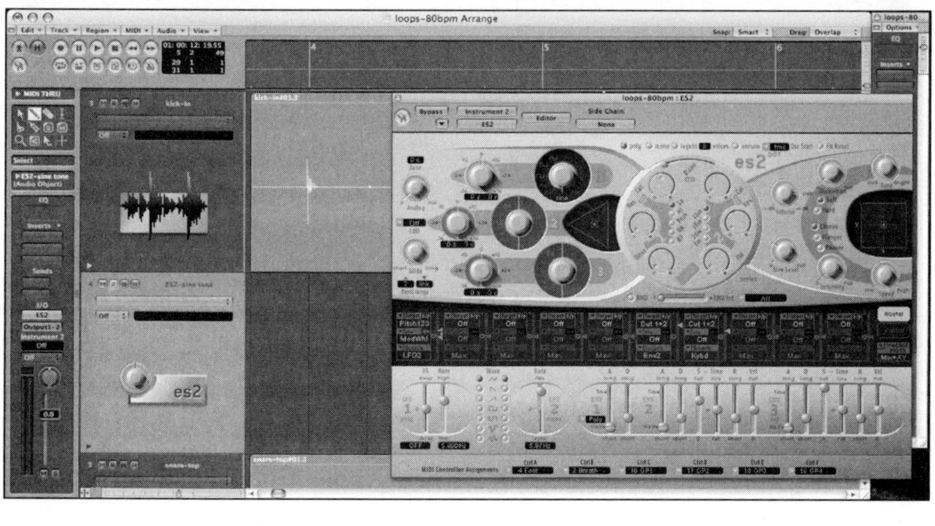

Figure 12.27

Next, Emagic's ES2 synthesizer is instantiated in a new Audio Instrument track. This instrument actually generates the new low-frequency content. If you have not purchased Emagic's ES2 synthesizer, you can substitute one of the synthesizers included with Logic.

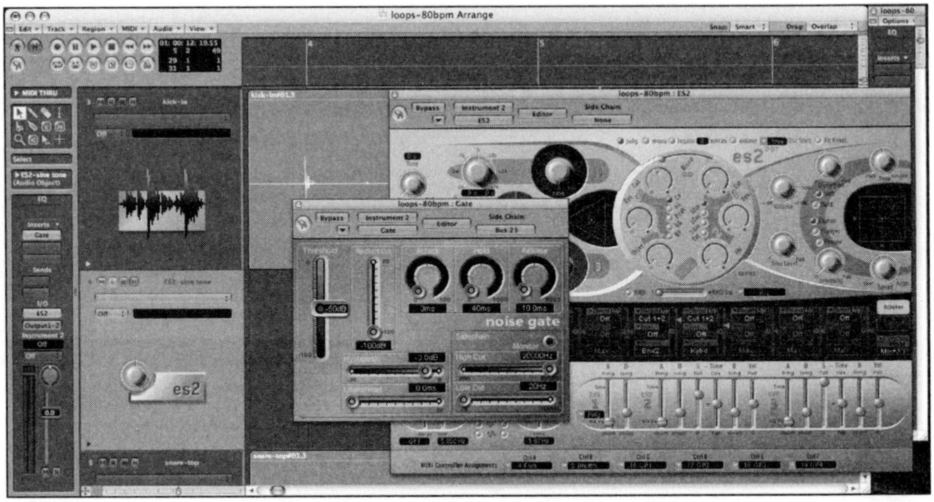

Figure 12.28
A Noise Gate plug-in is inserted onto the Audio Instrument track with its side chain input set to the same bus used in Figure 12.27.

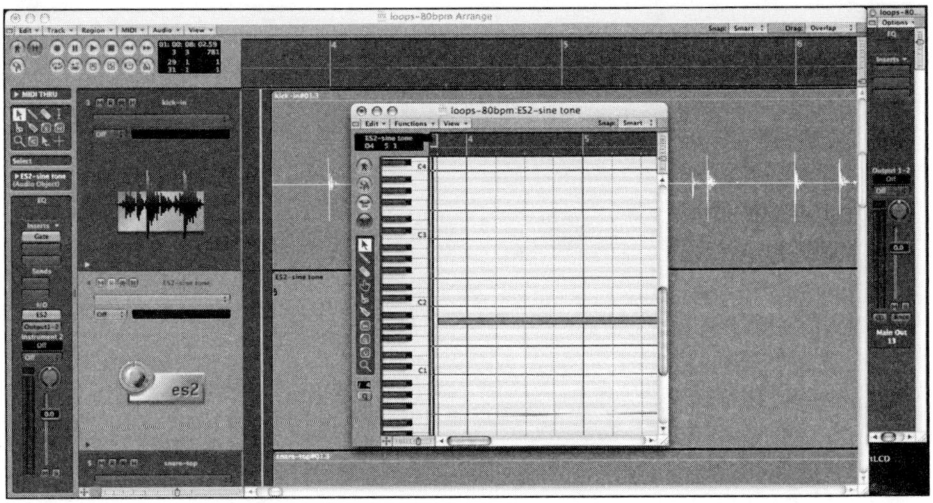

Figure 12.29
In the Matrix Editor, a single note that is the duration of the entire Audio region is used to trigger the Audio Instrument controlled by the Noise Gate side chain.

Audio Unit Effects

You may want to use an effect not included with Logic, or you may prefer to use a different version of an effect than the one that Logic includes. Toward this end, all versions of Logic allow you to use third-party effects plug-ins within the mixer as well. As discussed previously, these third-party applications literally "plug in" to the Logic mixers and offer extended processing functionality from within Logic. There are a number of different plug-in formats that different sequencers are compatible with, and Logic Pro 7 is compatible with Apple Computer's native Audio Unit format.

To access third-party effects, you follow the same basic procedure as you use with Logic effects. The difference is that instead of selecting Logic effects, you select Audio Units and then choose your effect from the list of manufacturers. Figure 12.30 shows a third-party Audio Unit effect being selected.

Figure 12.30
To select a third-party Audio Unit effect, you follow the same general procedure as when selecting a Logic effect, except that you follow the hierarchal menu of Audio Units plug-ins.

> **EXPERT TIP: PLUG-IN FORMAT CONVERTERS**
> What if a third-party effect that you really want to use within Logic is not available in the format that Logic supports? Well, in most cases, you are simply out of luck. However, if the plug-in you wish to use is available for the Mac OS X VST format, you can use the VST–AU Adapter from FXpansion to convert Mac OS X–compatible VST effects to Audio Units. Unlike "wrapper" plug-ins that basically require you to run two plug-ins (the original third-party plug-in and the wrapper plug-in) so that you can use an additional format, the FXpansion VST–AU converter actually creates a working Audio Unit from those third-party plug-ins with which the adapter is compatible. Be sure to check out http://www.fxpansion.com for the latest third-party plug-in compatibility charts and pricing if you are interested in this.

The Logic AU Manager

As you can imagine, there are hundreds of third-party Audio Units effects available, some of which come in bundles that are quite inexpensive. You may find that in no time flat your lists of available Audio Units will become huge! Thankfully, Logic Pro 7 includes a much requested feature: an integrated way to manage your Audio Units plug-ins. This is called the Logic AU Manager. You launch the AU Manager by selecting **Logic Pro > Preferences**

Figure 12.31

The Logic AU Manager. You can check and uncheck the Use boxes to select which AUs will be available in the plug-in menus in Logic Pro 7.

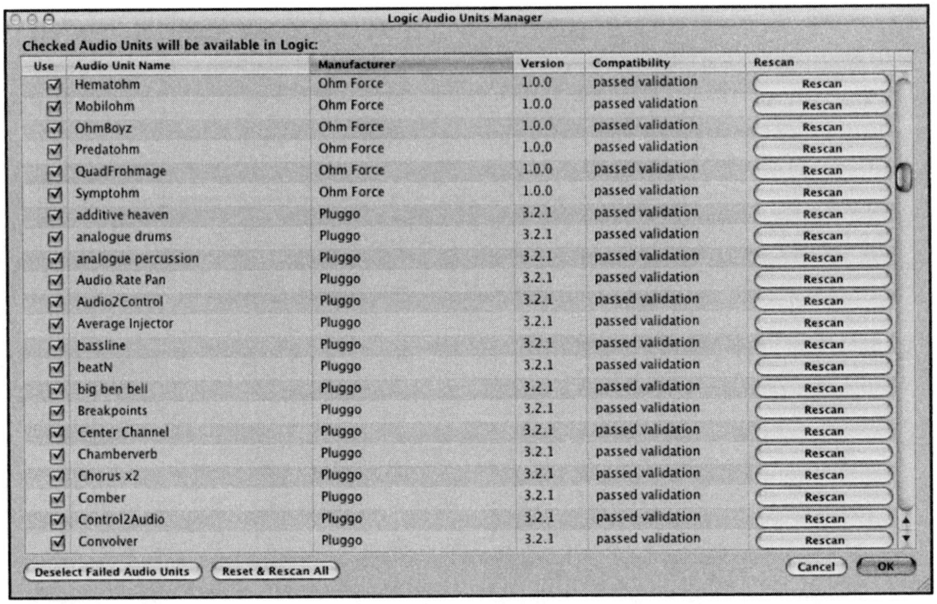

> Start Logic AU Manager. This will close Logic and start the Logic AU Manager, which you see in Figure 12.31.

The Logic AU Manager displays each of your Audio Unit plug-ins in a row, one after the other. The Logic AU Manager contains six columns:

- **Use.** Check this box if you want a plug-in to appear in the plug-in menus within Logic. Uncheck this box if you do not.
- **Audio Unit Name.** The name of the Audio Unit plug-in.
- **Manufacturer.** The name of the developer of the Audio Unit plug-in.
- **Version.** The version number of the Audio Unit plug-in.
- **Compatibility.** This column tells you if the plug-in passed, failed, or crashed Apple Computer's AU Validation scan. More on this below.
- **Rescan.** If you feel that there may have been an error in the initial scan of an Audio Unit, you can use this button to manually rescan the plug-in.

Using the Logic AU Manager couldn't be easier. If you don't need an AU to appear in the plug-in menus within Logic, uncheck the box in the Use column. If you want to reactivate a plug-in that you deactivated, re-click its box.

When you're done, simply click the OK button in the bottom right of the Logic AU Manager and Logic will relaunch.

The Logic AU Manager includes one additional, vital function besides Audio Unit management. It also scans your Audio Units for compatibility with the Audio Unit format, and deactivates them for you if they fail or crash validation. This is explained in more detail below.

Initial AU Scan

Apple Computer wants Logic Pro 7 to be the most stable audio application possible. To ensure this, they take pains to test the application rigorously before release. Unfortunately, third-party plug-ins, such as Audio Units, are not within Apple's power to test and debug. In the past, this has meant that plug-ins that didn't "play nice" with Logic could crash Logic, or in some cases, bring down your entire computer! So Apple Computer created a free test diagnostic application for developers—the AU Validation tool. This tool basically runs a number of diagnostic tests on an Audio Unit in an attempt to ensure that it properly complies with the Audio Unit format specifications and will not destabilize the host application.

When you first run Logic Pro 7, and every time you install a new Audio Unit plug-in, Logic will scan the plug-in with AU Validation to test it for compatibility and stability. Normally, all you will see is a progress bar indicating scanning is taking place, and that's it. When Logic Pro opens, your new plug-ins will be available in the appropriate menus.

Sometimes, however, you may find that a plug-in that you installed does not appear in the menu. This most likely means that the plug-in failed validation. At this point, if you open the Logic AU Manager, you will find that your plug-in is grayed out, along with the message that it failed or crashed validation. Figure 12.32 shows an AU plug-in that has failed the Logic AU Manager scan.

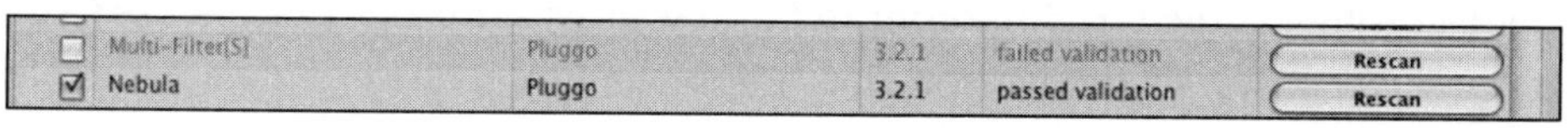

Figure 12.32

Here you see one Pluggo Audio Unit plug-in that passed the Validation scan, and is checked for use in Logic Pro, and another grayed-out plug-in that did not pass the Validation scan.

If you believe that the scan results were somehow incorrect, you have the option to hit the Rescan button. The Logic AU Manager will then rescan just the selected AU and present you with the results as shown in Figure 12.33.

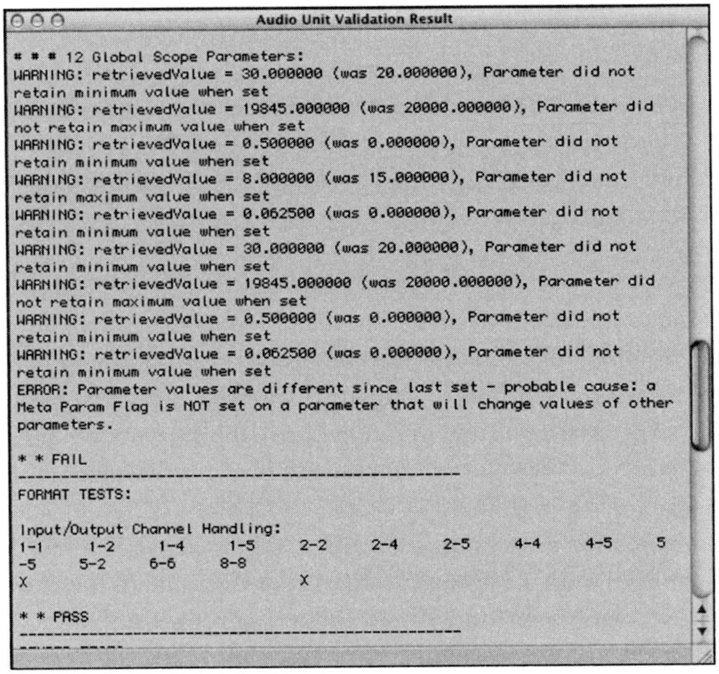

Figure 12.33

Here is the same Pluggo plug-in after being individually scanned by Apple's AU Validation tool in the Logic AU Manager.

If the plug-in still fails validation, I highly recommend that you contact the developer with the information that their plug-in fails AU validation. If you want to be extra helpful, you can even copy and paste the rescan results into an e-mail, and send it directly to the developer, saving them having to run it themselves. It is up to the developer to release an update that will comply properly with the Audio Unit specifications. When they do, Logic will scan the updated plug-in, it will pass the scan, the birds will sing in the trees, and everything will be right in the world. Or at least your plug-in will work properly!

Activating Incompatible AU Plug-Ins

But what if you absolutely, desperately need an incompatible Audio Unit plug-in within Logic Pro 7 in order to finish a previous project or the like? For these emergency situations, you *can*, if you want to, activate an incompatible plug-in within Logic. To do this, simply click its Use box, just like a compatible plug-in, as shown in Figure 12.34.

Figure 12.34

Even if a plug-in fails its AU Validation scan, you can still activate it at your own risk, as shown above.

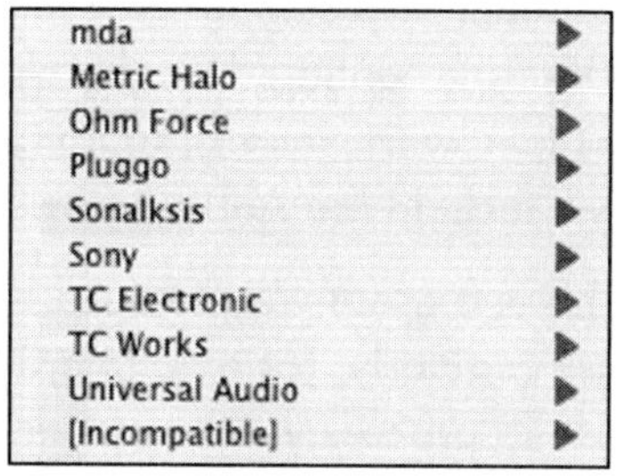

Figure 12.35

Any incompatible Audio Units that you activate will be available to you in the [Incompatible] submenu.

Audio Units that you activate this way are filtered into their own special hierarchal menu for incompatible plug-ins, as shown in Figure 12.35.

I *highly* recommend against activating incompatible Audio Units unless for some compelling reason you have no choice. The whole purpose of scanning Audio Units is to try to ensure that Logic Pro will not be destabilized by an errant plug-in. If you activate a plug-in that crashes or fails validation, you defeat the whole purpose of the scan! This is truly a feature of last resort.

Besides, most developers are very good at updating their software. In fact, at the time of publication, of the two Audio Units I used in the screenshots above, one has already been updated and is compatible with Logic, and the fix for the other is on the way.

Using Insert Effects

Insert effects are really simple to use as I have already discussed—simply select an Insert effect for a slot, and you're ready to use it! There are a couple of additional facts you might want to know, however. First, if you want a quick way to bypass an Insert effect, **OPTION + Click** on that insert. The Insert stops glowing, indicating the effect is bypassed.

To move an effect from one Insert slot to another, you have two options. One is to remove both effects and then re-instantiate them in the slots you want. This method is time-consuming as well as counterproductive, because it erases any parameters you have configured. A far more efficient method is to use Logic's Audio Configuration window, in which you can move and copy Insert effects from the Components view. This was discussed in the Audio Configuration window section of Chapter 8.

Saving or Loading Channel Strip Settings

Logic Pro 7 introduces the option to save and load entire configurations of channel strip inserts—including audio instruments. If you **Click + Hold** the small downward arrow next to the word "Insert" on a channel strip, a pull-down menu appears that offers you options to save, load, and navigate channel strip settings. These channel strip setting files include all the insert effects instantiated on the channel strip (complete with their effects settings as they were saved), and if you are on an Audio Instrument channel strip, it will include the Audio Instrument as well.

This is a great way to save configurations of channel strip inserts that you use regularly, for example, if you have a particular set of plug-ins you like to use to process vocals, guitar, and so on. Logic Pro comes with many factory preset channel settings for you to explore as well—give them a listen!

Note that currently, you can only save or load channel strip settings onto the same type of channel strip that the channel strip setting was designed for. In other words, a channel strip setting for an Audio Track can only be loaded onto an Audio Track channel strip, not an Audio Instrument channel strip.

Using Send Effects

Using a Send to add effects to a track is a bit more complicated than using Inserts, because Sends don't directly connect to effects; instead they connect to busses. So to use a Send to add effects, you assign a bus to a Send, then add the effect you desire in an Insert of the Send. You control how much of your audio signal is sent to the bus via the Send rotary knob. Keep in mind that you can then set up an Aux track with the bus for its input, and use the aux as a Bus with Sends, as explained above.

As with Inserts, you can also use the Audio Configuration window to move around and copy the busses assigned to Send slots.

Plug-In Delay and Logic's Plug-In Delay Compensation

Most effects do their processing nearly instantly. Some, however, do not. They may involve highly mathematically complex processes, like convolution reverbs such as Logic's Space Designer. They might have a "look ahead" feature, by which the effect increases its accuracy by literally scanning audio before it processes it, which requires that the effect hang on to the audio signal for a while instead of instantly processing it. Some Audio Unit plug-ins run on FireWire or PCI DSP devices, such as the UAD1 PCI card or the TC

PowerCore FireWire; it takes time to get the audio out to these devices. The point is that some devices and plug-ins will introduce a delay into your signal path if you use them. This can be a real problem. For example, if you have two tracks that are both in sync with each other, and set to play at bar 1.0.0.0, but one track has plug-ins that introduce 2000 samples of delay, that track will play late and out of sync. If you are not careful, plug-in delay can really ruin your song.

Luckily, Logic tries to make things a bit easier for us. There is a check box in the Audio Preferences window for Plug-In Delay Compensation. This should always be checked, in my opinion! It will automatically adjust any of your Audio and Audio Instrument tracks to be in sync with any other Audio and Audio Instrument tracks that have delay-causing effects on them. Unfortunately, as of Logic Pro 7.0, there is no delay compensation for Aux or Bus tracks—so I highly recommend that you simply choose effects that do not cause delay for those tracks.

Keep in mind that plug-in delay compensation only works during playback, not during recording—so be careful not to use any plug-ins that cause delay when you are recording audio!

Final Notes on Using Effects

Using effects is arguably one of the most dramatic ways to alter an audio mix. Sometimes, the effects become instruments themselves, and their processing is an integral part of the music. But like all things, it's very easy to get carried away, both musically and computationally, if you are not careful.

Keep in mind that your computer has only a finite amount of CPU power. If you try to process to death every track in a large song, you'll most likely overtax your computer to the point that your song no longer plays back. And if you *really* overdo it, you might so overextend your resources that your song won't play unless you engage Track Freeze for every track! Of course, this is exactly the situation for which you will want to use Logic Nodes, which are described below.

If you are using a fair amount of software instruments and effects in a given song, keep a close watch on your system performance to make sure your computer is up to your demands. You can get a gauge of Logic's Audio CPU and hard disk usage from the System Performance meter in the global Audio menu, which you can open by selecting **Audio > System Performance**. This is another advantage to using some effects on Bus Objects and having tracks access them via Sends—you can have more than one track access the same bus, thereby saving you from having to instantiate that same effect on more than one track.

Beware of the pitfall of EQing and effecting one track until it is perfect when played by itself, but muddies everything up when placed in the context of the mix. That infinite delay line that you love so much might just start getting jumbled when you bring in 24 more tracks and it's been repeating for 90 seconds! Even as you work on perfecting individual tracks, always try to keep a holistic view of what you want the completed song to sound like. Logic Pro's new signal analysis effects—Correlation Meter, Multimeter, and Level Meter—can help you get a better picture of your material, where there is too much "signal energy" and where you might want to adjust your mix to sound more open or less "overloaded." The saying "less is more" definitely applies to mixing!

Lastly, remember that there are no hard and fast rules as to how to add effects to a mix. Listen to effects on a lot of your favorite CDs, read magazines and books that discuss effects placement and usage in detail, and experiment!

Logic Nodes—Distributed Audio Processing

As explained above, if you use a lot of effects and Audio Instruments, it's very easy to run out of processing power. Even with a top-of-the-line PowerMac dual G5, if you run dozens of Audio Instruments, along with scores of effects, you're going to bring your computer to its knees. Freeze Tracks is a great solution for when you are finished with a song, or for when you want to load a song onto a computer that isn't beefy enough to run it normally—for example, if you want to open a song that you composed on your G5 on your iBook, you can freeze all the tracks on your G5, then copy the entire Project folder to your iBook. But freezing your whole song isn't very conducive to spontaneous composing or mixing. Enter one of the aces up Logic Pro's sleeve: Logic Nodes, also known as distributed audio processing.

The idea of using many computers to process audio is not new. People have been hooking up multiple computers for a long time. First, simply using audio and MIDI connections, users could configure an auxiliary computer as if it were simply another external sound module, just like a synthesizer. Steinberg raised the bar from there by developing VST System Link. This was a protocol that used an available digital Audio channel to send both audio and MIDI between VST plug-in hosts. It was a real breakthrough—the first time that users could legitimately harness the power of additional computers to run software plug-ins. But VST System Link was very clunky and inelegant, requiring multiple cables to get a two-way connection between computers. It required that users keep track of two Project files, one on each computer, and that users manually load all the VST plug-ins on the client computer that would be available on the host. And because it relied on the digital clock inside multiple audio interfaces for synchronization, it was very prone to sync errors.

Apple Computer may not have been the first to the table when it presented the Logic Node method of distributed audio processing, but they certainly developed the most elegant and intuitive implementation to date. Using only a single Gigabit Ethernet connection between computers, you can use any connected computer as a node to process Logic's effects and synthesizers. You can use a PowerBook G4 as your main Logic Pro computer and then attach it to a network of Logic Node G5s if you want. You could use a G5 as your main Logic Pro computer, and have an entire rack of Xserves for a truly monstrously powerful studio. As you will see below, the configuration is absolutely minimal. Simply install the Logic Node application on the Macintosh you wish to be the node, and then the rest is handled from within the Logic Pro application. Simple. Neat. Efficient. The way it should be!

Using Nodes

As explained previously, the first step is to have installed the Logic Node application onto the computer you wish to be a node. At this point, you're ready to turn on Nodes in Logic Pro. Open the Nodes tab via **Logic Pro > Preferences > Audio**, and you will see a simple check box to turn on Node processing and a list of all available nodes on your network, as shown in Figure 12.36.

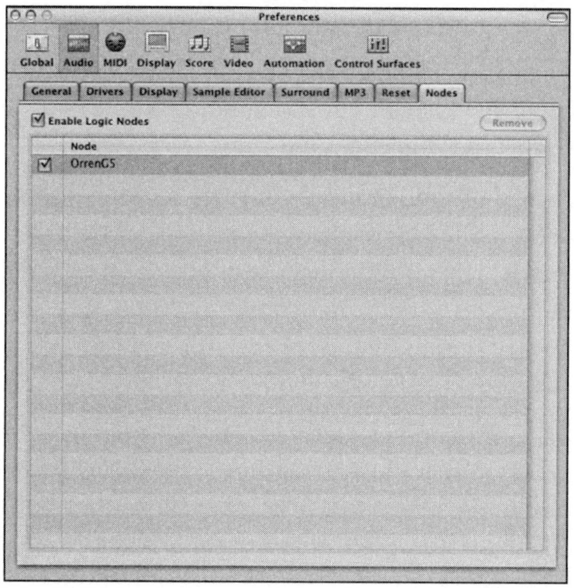

Figure 12.36
The Nodes tab of the Audio Preferences window. Here you can enable Logic Nodes and any Macintosh computers attached as nodes.

To enable Logic Nodes, simply check the box enabling Logic Nodes and any individual check boxes for attached Macintosh computers running the Logic Node application.

Figure 12.37

By clicking the Node buttons on the two bottom tracks, all of the Logic effects and plug-ins on this track will be processed on the active Logic Node.

After that, any time you want a node to handle the processing of the built-in effects and synthesizers on an Audio or Audio Instrument track, simply click its Node button, as shown in Figure 12.37. The button graphic will change from three dots to a right and left arrow, indicating the track is distributing its processing to the node.

That's all that there is to it! You send or stop sending each Audio and Audio Instrument track to a Logic Node by clicking the Node button. You can tell how heavy the load is on your various Logic Nodes by looking at the System Performance window. You'll notice that when Nodes are turned on, the System Performance window will expand to include a Nodes meter.

Current Limitation of Logic Node Technology

Logic Nodes make mixing huge songs more possible than ever—especially when you consider that you can have up to 128 nodes attached to one main Logic Pro system! But you should also be aware of the limitations of using Logic Nodes in Logic Pro 7.0.

First of all, you can only process Logic's own built-in effects and synthesizers, not the EXS24mkII Sampler or any Audio Units. Much of the reason for this is legal, rather than technical, based on complicated issues of sample library user rights, Audio Unit copy protection, and so on. So there is a good chance that as time goes on, Apple Computer and its third-party partners will clear that hurdle. But for now, this limitation stands.

Also, sending the audio across an Ethernet cable and back again takes time. Luckily, Logic Pro 7.0's automatic delay compensation for Audio Tracks and Audio Instrument tracks handles this seamlessly. It does mean, however, that until Logic Pro adds delay compensation for Bus and Aux tracks, it will not be possible to use nodes on busses and auxes.

Finally, Apple Computer lists a G5 and Gigabit Ethernet as the requirement for Logic Nodes. Does this mean that you can't hook up a Macintosh without Gigabit Ethernet such as the iMac G5? Or that you can't use a G4 as a node? Technically, you can use slower Ethernet and Macintosh computers as nodes; there is no technical reason that it wouldn't work. But the extra horsepower available from a G4 will be minimal. And not having Gigabit Ethernet reduces the throughput of your Logic Node. So while you can certainly try to hook up your old G4s and other computers to get a little more power for your system, you may find that the payoff is small.

Muting Channels

You're already familiar with the Mute button on each track of Arrange from Chapter 7. That button mutes or unmutes a single track. Each channel strip also has a mute button at its bottom, as shown in Figure 12.38. Pressing this button mutes or unmutes the channel in question.

Figure 12.38
The button with the M is the Mute button for this channel strip. If Mute is engaged, the button on the Audio channel glows light blue.

The main difference between muting a channel in the mixer and muting a track in the Arrange window is that you may have multiple tracks in Arrange all playing on the same channel. If you need to mute only a single track, note that muting one track in Arrange does not mute all the other tracks. On the other hand, if you want to mute all the tracks playing on a single channel, keep in mind that muting the channel silences all the tracks feeding that channel.

Soloing Channels

The Solo button on the channel strip operates differently than the Solo button on the Arrange tracks, just as the Mute button on the channel strip operates differently from the Mute button on the Arrange tracks. Each Audio Object except for Output Objects has a Solo button like the one in Figure 12.39. When the Solo button is engaged, all other Audio Objects, except Output Objects that do not also have their Solo button engaged, are silenced. When one or more tracks are soloed, the Mute buttons of the non-soloed tracks flash.

Figure 12.39
When the Solo button of a channel strip is activated, all non-soloed Audio Objects are silenced, except for Output Objects. The Solo button will glow yellow when activated.

Keep in mind that Solo does not silence Output Objects, since Output Objects are necessary for the soloed tracks to be heard. Also, soloing channels is strictly an audio function; MIDI tracks are not muted.

Solo Safe Mode

If you want to make sure that no matter which tracks are soloed you never silence certain tracks, effects, busses, and so on, you can make them "solo safe" to exempt them from being silenced. **CONTROL + Clicking** the Solo button turns on Solo Safe mode for a given Audio Object. You can tell whether a track is in Solo Safe mode because its Solo button will have a line through it, as in Figure 12.40. **CONTROL + Clicking** the Solo button a second time disengages Solo Safe mode.

Figure 12.40
When the unactivated Solo button of a channel strip shows a red line through it, that indicates the Audio Object is in Solo Safe mode.

Mixer Groups

Sometimes you may want to link some properties of different channel strips—for example, you may want the volume's Solo and Mute functions of all your drum tracks to change together as a group, or link the Pan control of a group of tracks that are all panned to the same location. The Group function allows you to do this and more. You not only can use the Group function to group mixer operations, but also to link Arrange window functionality for group editing.

The Group Display is the dark-blue display window directly below the channel label in each channel strip, as illustrated in Figure 12.41. This is where you can select and create groups. You can create as many as 32 groups, and channels can belong to multiple groups.

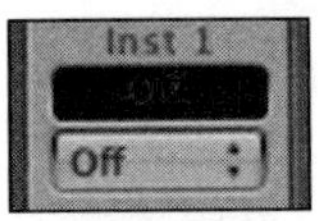

Figure 12.41
Directly under the channel label and over the Automation Display is the Group Display. In this figure, the channel strip is assigned to Group 1.

Assigning Channels to Groups

To assign a channel to a group, click in the Group Display on the channel strip. A pull-down menu appears with the numbers (and names, if assigned) of all 32 possible Mixer Groups, as well as the option to open the Group Settings window. Select the group number you want, and then release the mouse. The number of the group you have selected appears in the Group

Display of your channel strip. Figure 12.42 shows the Groups pull-down menu.

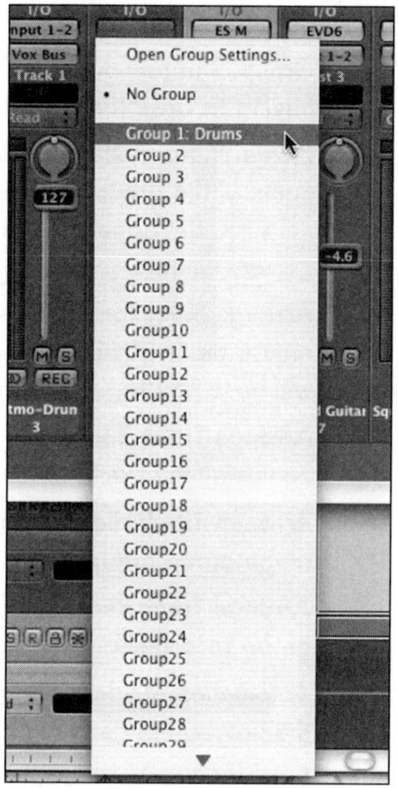

Figure 12.42

In the Groups pull-down menu, you can choose the number of the group to which you want to assign your channel, or you can open the Group Settings window.

You can assign a channel to more than one group by holding **SHIFT** down while selecting groups in the pull-down menu. If you **OPTION + Click** in the Group Display window, the last Group selection is applied to the current channel strip.

Group Settings

You can access the Group Settings window in two ways. If you assign a group to a channel, but you have not yet defined that group, the Group Settings window automatically opens. You can also select the Group Settings window from the Group pull-down menu if you want to define or change the settings of a group. Figure 12.43 shows the Group Settings window.

The window contains a list of options, each with a check box (except for the Name option). If you check the box next to an option, that option will be set to the group. So, if you adjust the control or do any editing or automation in one channel in the group, that action affects all channels in the group.

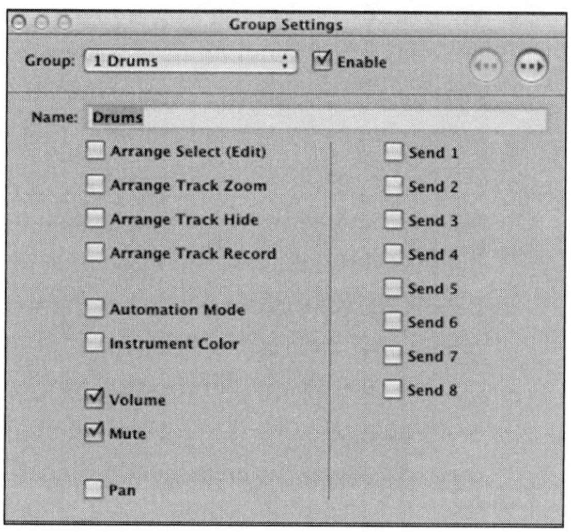

Figure 12.43

The Group Settings window.

The following list describes the various options:

- **Group.** This pull-down menu lets you switch to another group without having to close the Group Settings window and opening a new one.
- **Name.** In this text box, you can type a name for your group. The name of the group does not appear in the Group Display in the channel strip, but appears next to the number in the pull-down menu of group numbers.
- **Arrange Selection (Edit).** With this option selected, if you select a region on one track in the group in Arrange, every track in the group will have any regions at the same relative time in the song selected.
- **Arrange Track Zoom.** Adjusting the zoom of one track in the group zooms all the tracks in the group.
- **Arrange Track Hide.** If you hide one track in the group, all members of the group are hidden.
- **Arrange Track Record.** Record-enabling/disabling one channel in the group record-enables/disables all of them.
- **Automation Mode.** Changing the Automation mode of one member of the group changes all of them.
- **Instrument Color.** If you assign a color to one member of the group, all of them are assigned that color.
- **Volume.** Changing the Volume fader of one channel strip in the group changes all of them. Note that these are relative changes, so if two channels in the group are at different volumes, Logic raises or lowers both volumes by the amount of the change to the group, but they retain their relative difference in volume.
- **Mute.** If one channel in the group is muted/unmuted, every channel in the group is muted/unmuted.
- **Pan.** Logic adjusts the panorama of every channel in the group if you adjust one channel's pan. As with the Volume option, all channels retain their relative differences from each other.
- **Send 1–8.** As with the Volume and Pan options, if you check any of these Sends, Logic links them.

When you link the automation of a group, any track can be the "master" that you use to control the mode, and if you draw or write automation for any linked parameter, Logic writes the automation for each individual track in the group. Therefore, if you later ungroup your tracks, they will still have the automation you wrote. There is also a "clutch" to disable group links temporarily, if you want to adjust one single track without affecting the rest of the group: Simply assign a key command to the Toggle Group Clutch command. The readout in the Group Display changes colors from dark blue to yellow as a visual cue that the Group Clutch is engaged.

Temporary Groups by Selecting Multiple Channel Strips

There is also a very "down and dirty" way to make a change to more than one fader without going through the process of creating a group. If you just want to adjust the volume faders of four channel strips, for example, you can select them all, either by **SHIFT+Clicking** on them, or via a "rubber band" selection with the Pointer tool in the Environment. Logic Pro indicates which channels are selected by their color; they will all be light gray instead of dark gray. Once selected, you can adjust the volume fader on one of them, and all of the selected tracks will also adjust. You can click anywhere outside the selected channel strips to deselect the channel strips.

Bouncing Your Mix

At any point in the mixing process, you may want to "bounce" your mix down to a stereo (or surround) master mix. The term *bounce* originated from the days in which this process required you to play your audio from a multitrack tape machine and then rerecord your mixed audio onto a stereo tape deck—hence "bouncing" the audio from one tape deck onto another. With computer recording, however, bouncing to a file requires far less setup and effort, so you no longer need to wait until your mix is complete to bounce tracks—you can bounce mixes regularly during the mixing process to listen to them on different stereos, to share your mixes with others, and so on.

Figure 12.44
Press the BNCE button of an Output Object to display the Bounce dialog box and create an audio file of your mix.

Because bouncing consists of outputting your mix, Logic puts the Bounce button on the bottom-right of the channel strip of Output Objects. It is the button labeled BNCE, as shown in Figure 12.44.

There are two other ways to bounce your mix. You can select the global Bounce command from **File > Bounce**. This will only bounce outputs 1–2. If you have one or more Output Objects in the Arrange window, you can click the Record button on an Output Object to bounce from it.

The Bounce Dialog Box

When you select the command to bounce audio through any of the above means, the Bounce dialog box appears as shown in Figure 12.45. This window contains all your options to bounce your mix down to a file.

The top of this window consists of a standard Save As dialog box where you can type in a file name and navigate to the directory to which you want to save your bounced audio. Underneath the navigation bar on the left are your four file type selections in the Destination table:

- **PCM.** This option bounces a standard, noncompressed audio file into either AIFF, Broadcast WAV, or Sound Designer II format.
- **MP3.** This bounces to the MP3 compression format.

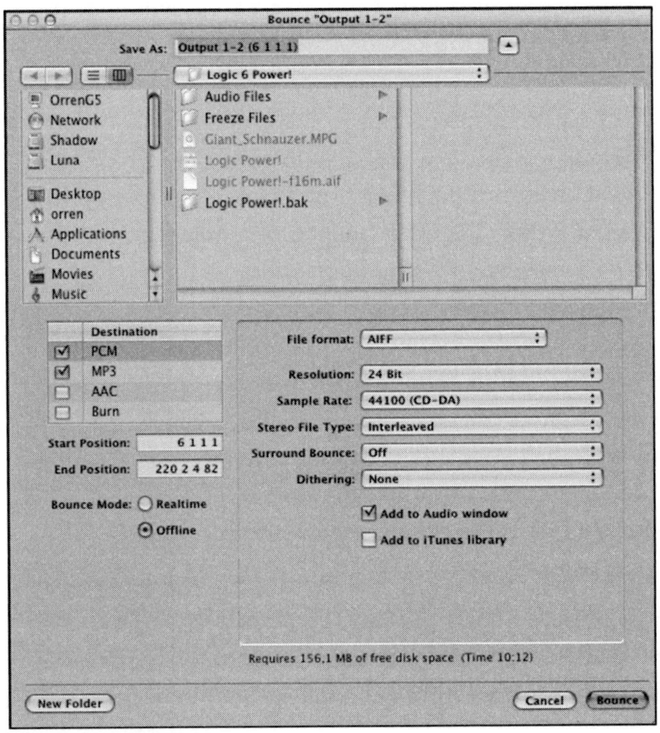

Figure 12.45
In the Bounce dialog box, you can set the parameters for how to bounce your mix.

- **AAC.** This bounces to the AAC compression format.
- **Burn.** This song burns your Logic Project onto a CDR or CDRW.

Below the Destination table, Logic lets you enter the start and end positions of your bounce, and allows you to select between Realtime or Offline Bounce mode. In Realtime mode, Logic plays the selection you want to bounce, and prints the file as it is playing. The advantage of this mode is that you get to hear exactly what the bounced file will sound like, and you can include the signal from Input Objects. But it can be slow if the file is long. In Offline mode, Logic bounces your mix internally. If your Logic song is not taxing your CPU, Offline bounce can be much faster than Realtime bouncing. If your song squeezes every last bit of your CPU to do complex processing, Offline bouncing will not be faster than Realtime bouncing. And if your song is too complex to play in Realtime at all, you can still do an Offline bounce—but it will take longer than if you played your song in realtime.

Below the Destination parameter box, Logic Pro informs you how much disk space you'll need for your bounce, and how long your file will be. You also have options to create a new folder for your bounces, to Cancel the operation, and to commence the bounce.

You can bounce to multiple destinations by checking the box to the left of more than one file type. The Bounce parameters to the right of the Destination table will change depending on which destination is selected. The parameters for each bounce destination will be explained in the following subsections.

Bounce to PCM

This bounce destination includes bouncing to uncompressed Sound Designer II, AIFF, or Broadcast WAV files. Figure 12.46 shows the PCM destination parameters.

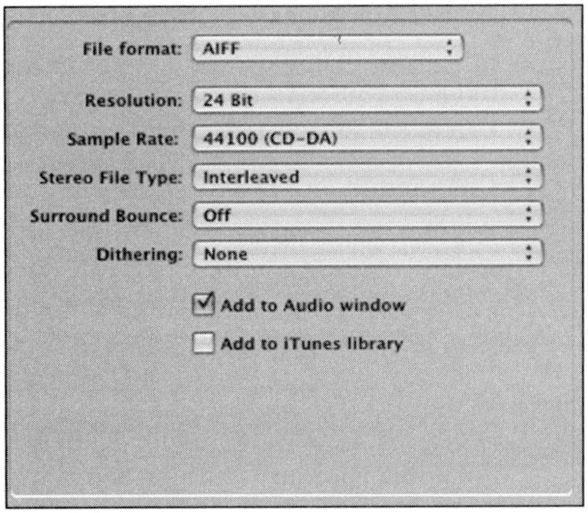

Figure 12.46
The PCM bounce destination parameters.

The parameters for this bounce are

- **File Format.** This is where you select Sound Designer II (SDII), Broadcast Wave (WAV), or AIFF format for your PCM bounce.
- **Resolution.** Here you can choose the file bit depth for your bounce. Your choices are 8-, 16-, or 24-bit. You will almost never want to print an 8-bit bounce. If you are going straight to CD, you might want to print a 16-bit file with dither (see the description of the Dithering option). Normally, you'll want to archive your mix at 24 bits, which is the highest bit rate that Logic currently allows.
- **Sample Rate.** You can select the sample rate for your bounced file here. Logic will default to the same sample rate as your Logic song, but you can change it to any of 12 different sample rate options between 11kHz and 192kHz. If you select a different sampling rate than the sample rate of your song, Logic will Sample Rate Convert your bounced file using its very high quality sample rate conversion algorithms.
- **Stereo File Type.** This option is available only if you are bouncing a stereo file. If your destination file is an SDII file, some applications cannot import interleaved SDII files and require Split Stereo files (meaning you bounce one file for the left track, and another for the right). Unless you know you need Split Stereo files, leave this set to Interleaved. If you are bouncing a mono file, this will be grayed out.
- **Surround Bounce.** If you are bouncing for a surround mix, you can select any of the 11 surround formats that Logic allows. If you turn on surround bounce, this grays out Stereo File Type. Logic doesn't do any surround encoding or decoding, so if you plan to do a surround bounce, you need additional hardware or software to play the bounced files in the proper format. Normally, you will leave this set to Off.
- **Dithering.** If you are bouncing your audio to a 16-bit file for CD, you'll want to turn on Dithering. Normally, when you save 24-bit audio into a 16-bit file, the 8 bits that don't make it to the 16-bit file are simply those that happen to be filling lowest bits of the audio stream; unfortunately, sometimes you have desired audio in those bits, and this "truncation" can end up sounding harsh. Dithering adds imperceptible amounts and frequencies of noise to your file, so that the noise "pushes" all the desired audio into the 16 bits that are

saved, and only the noise is eliminated. As you can imagine, not all dither is created equal. Logic includes the industry standard POW-r dithering algorithms. There are three algorithms—the first is plain, and the second and third have various amounts of "noise shaping" to attempt to tailor the dither even more to your audio material. Use the algorithm that sounds best with your material. If you are bouncing 24-bit files, leave Dithering off.

- **Add to Audio Window.** This check box allows you to add the bounced file to your Audio window, for re-use in your Logic song. This is very useful if you are only bouncing a small portion of audio to capture some effects processing, or doing a Realtime bounce to record audio from Input Objects, and want the result to be available for later use.
- **Add to iTunes Library.** This check box will add the bounced file to iTunes for you. This is a great time-saver if you like to audition your mixes in iTunes, or you want your song to be ready to add to your iPod, and so on.

Bounce to MP3

MP3 currently reigns as the ubiquitous compression format for sharing music across platforms. Figure 12.47 shows you the MP3 destination parameters.

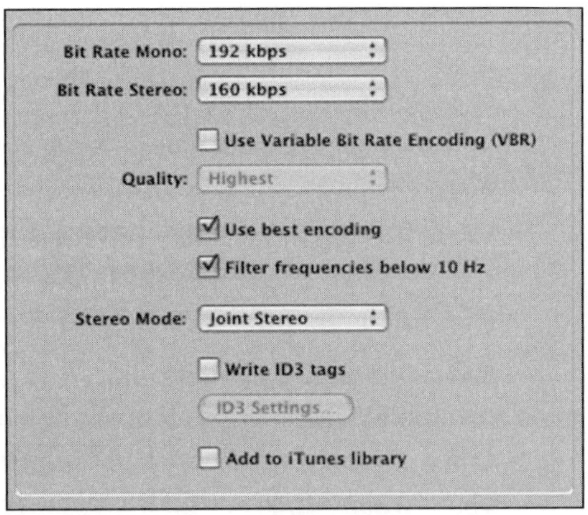

Figure 12.47 The MP3 destination parameters.

The parameters for this bounce are

- **Bit Rate (Mono/Stereo).** You can select bit rates between 8kbps and 320kbps. Personally, my favorite bit rates for MP3 compression are 160kbps or 192kbps. The quality improvement for bit rates above 192kbps is minimal.
- **Use Variable Bit Rate Encoding (VBR).** Check this box if you want to use Variable Rate encoding instead of Constant Bit Rate encoding. Variable Bit Rate encoding compresses simpler passages more heavily

than more harmonically rich passages, which in theory encodes better-quality MP3s. Unfortunately, not all MP3 players can accurately decode VBR-encoded MP3s, and often the results are not superior to an MP3 encoded at a consistently high bit rate—which is why this option is turned off by default.

- **Quality.** If you use VBR encoding, this pull-down menu allows you to select the quality of your Variable Bit Rate. My advice? Keep this set to Highest. Reducing the quality speeds up the conversion process, but at the expense of audio quality. Who wants that?
- **Use Best Encoding.** If you uncheck this option, you gain encoding speed at the price of audio quality. Again, you should always keep this setting checked.
- **Filter Frequencies Below 10Hz.** Frequencies below 10Hz are usually not reproduced by speakers and are not audible to human ears anyway. Such frequencies can, however, create a muddier MP3. If you check this box, Logic removes those frequencies, leaving slightly more data bandwidth for the frequencies that people can hear, and resulting in an improvement in perceived quality.
- **Stereo Mode.** You can select between Joint Stereo and Normal Stereo mode. The differences are very subtle, if any, so go ahead and experiment to see which sounds better on your source material. Don't be surprised if both sound the same. This option is not available for mono bounces.
- **Write ID3 tags.** MP3 files can have ID information, such as song title, artist, and so on encoded with the audio. If you want to enter this information for your bounce, check this box.
- **ID3 Settings.** If you check the Write ID3 Tags box, this button will be available; click it to open a window in which you can enter song title, artist, album, genre, and other information. ID3 tags are useful if you plan on sharing your MP3, or you want the information to display in iTunes. Otherwise, no need to bother.
- **Add to iTunes Library.** This check box will add the bounced file to iTunes for you. This is a great time saver if you like to audition your mixes in iTunes, or you want your song to be ready to add to your iPod, and so on.

Bounce to AAC

AAC, or Advanced Audio Coding, is the "next generation" of audio encoding, based in part on the MP4 format, the successor to MP3. AAC gets better audio quality at the same bit rate compared to MP3, but it is not as widely popular as MP3. AAC can be decoded by iTunes on both Mac and PC, as well as other media players, and is used by the iTunes Music Store for its commercially available songs.

When you select AAC in the Destination window, its only visible option is a check box for Add to iTunes Library. This will add your AAC file to the iTunes library. However, once you press the Bounce button, you are presented with the standard QuickTime AAC bounce dialog, as shown in Figure 12.48.

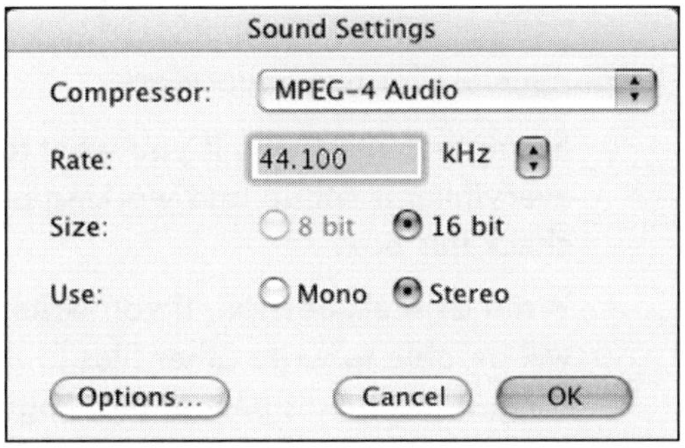

Figure 12.48
When you click Bounce, if you have selected AAC as a bounce destination, the dialog above, which is the same settings dialog from QuickTime, will appear.

Here you can select the sample rate of your audio, if it is 8- or 16-bit, and if the resulting file should be mono or stereo. You can also click the Options button for four more AAC encoding options:

- **Compressor.** In QuickTime, this lets you select from among its compression codes. In Logic, this has no effect.
- **Bit Rate.** You can choose the bit rate of your AAC file from between 8kbps and 320kbps. Personally, my favorite bit rates for AAC compression are 160kbps or 192kbps. The quality improvement for bit rates above 192kbps is minimal.
- **Output Sample Rate.** Generally, you will leave this at the default.
- **Encoder Quality.** You can choose Good, Better, or Best. Keep it on Best.

Bounce to CDR/CDRW (Burn)

This option lets you bounce your Logic song right to a CD. This option does not allow you the complete facilities for properly mastering a commercial

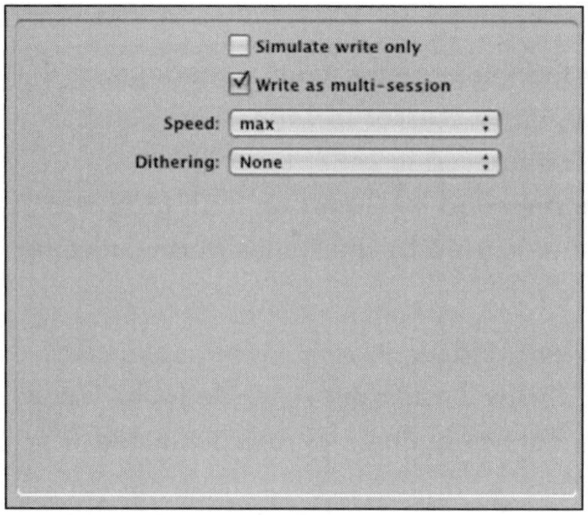

Figure 12.49
The Burn destination parameters.

CD—for that, you'll want to use WaveBurner, which came bundled with Logic Pro 7. But if you want to quickly bounce your Logic song to a CDR/CDRW to audition it in various stereo systems, to share with friends, and so on, this option will do the trick. Figure 12.49 shows the Burn destination parameters.

The parameters for this bounce are

- **Simulate Write Only.** If you want to try a "test run" to make sure that everything is set up and working properly to do a CDR/CDRW burn, check this box.
- **Write as Multi-Session.** If you write your session as multi-session, you will be able to write other files to the CDR after you burn your Logic song. If this box is unchecked, Logic will "close" the CDR when it is finished. If you want to use your CDR for more material, check this box. Otherwise, leave it unchecked.
- **Speed.** This allows you to select the maximum speed your CD drive can write a CD, or any lower speed your CD drive is capable of. How many options appear here will depend on your model of CDR drive.
- **Dithering.** If you are bouncing 24-bit audio to a 16-bit file for CD, you'll want to turn on Dithering. Normally, when you save 24-bit audio into a 16-bit file, the 8 bits that don't make it to the 16-bit file are simply those that happen to be filling lowest bits of the audio stream; unfortunately, sometimes you have desired audio in those bits, and this "truncation" can end up sounding harsh. Dithering adds imperceptible amounts and frequencies of noise to your file, so that the noise "pushes" all the desired audio into the 16 bits that are saved, and only the noise is eliminated. As you can imagine, not all dither is created equal. Logic includes the industry standard POW-r dithering algorithms. There are three algorithms—the first is plain, and the second and third have various amounts of "noise shaping" to attempt to tailor the dither even more to your audio material. Use the algorithm that sounds best with your material.

METHOD TIP: INCLUDING MIDI TRACKS IN YOUR BOUNCE

Clearly, bouncing your Audio Objects from an Output Object includes only audio. What if you want to include the output of your MIDI hardware modules in your bounce file?

There are basically two ways to go about this. The first method requires that before you do your final bouncing, you record the output of all your MIDI hardware into Audio Tracks in Logic. This takes extra time, but allows you to move and edit your newly recorded MIDI as you would any other audio performance, which you may enjoy. Once your MIDI has been committed to Audio Tracks, Logic bounces them with all your other Audio Tracks.

If you want to keep your MIDI hardware in the MIDI realm as long as possible and never record them as audio, you can instead create Input Objects for all of your MIDI hardware modules. Since Input Objects are Audio Objects, you can mix, process, and bounce them to a file just like the audio on any other Audio channel. Using Input Objects requires that you have as many physical hardware inputs as you have MIDI module outputs you want to use. Also, to compensate for your audio hardware latency, you may need to adjust the setting Delay All MIDI Output, which you can access by choosing **File > Song Settings > Synchronization Settings.** If you don't know exactly how much latency your audio hardware has, and its documentation lists no approximations in milliseconds, then you can use trial and error to determine the point at which your audio sounds in sync with your MIDI.

Surround Mixing

In addition to allowing for the usual stereo mixing, Logic also allows for basic surround mixing, with surround panning and bouncing functions available. Logic supports the most common surround formats (such as quad, Pro Logic, 5.1, and 7.1) and even some additional, more esoteric surround formats. To access Logic's surround functions, you must have audio hardware with more than two physical outputs. Logic doesn't offer any surround encoding or decoding, so you may need additional hardware or software as well.

Changing an Audio Object from a mono or stereo channel to a surround channel is very simple. Click the Output pull-down menu, then select Surround, as shown in Figure 12.50.

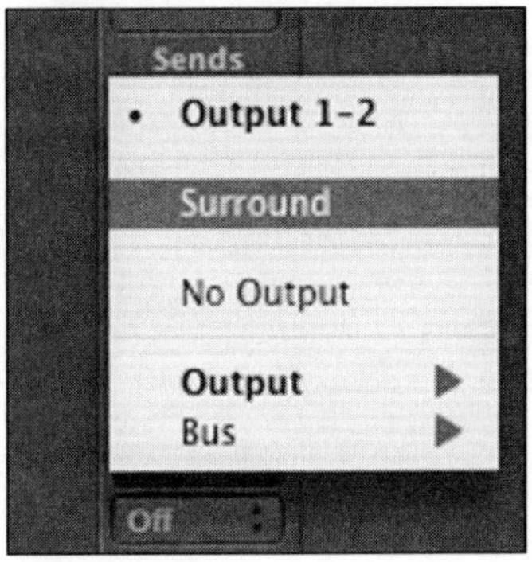

Figure 12.50

If you want an Audio Object to be a surround object, select Surround from the Output pull-down menu.

Figure 12.51

After placing an Audio Object into Surround mode, its Pan dial changes into a three-dimensional looking panorama control like this channel.

When an Audio Object is placed into Surround mode, its panorama dial is replaced by a three-dimensional-looking surround control, as shown in Figure 12.51. The speakers are represented by colored dots, and the pan position by a white dot. You can grab the white dot and rotate it anywhere around the surround control.

You can mix stereo and surround objects in the same Logic song with no restrictions.

The Surround Pan Window

If you double-click the surround control on a surround channel, you will open a Surround Pan window like the one shown in Figure 12.52. This gives you a more detailed view of the surround panorama, as well as access to the surround format, LFE Level, and Center Level.

The first thing you'll notice at the top of the window is a pull-down menu displaying the current surround format. Select any of the available formats you want, and the number of speakers included in the selected Surround mode appears in the graphic display.

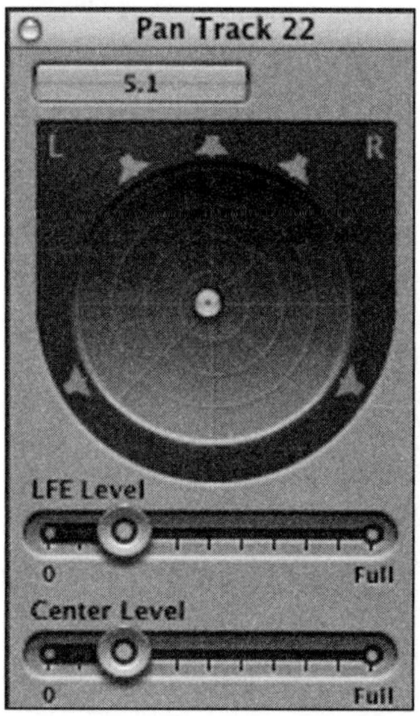

Figure 12.52

In the Surround Pan window, you can access the surround format, LFE Level, and Center Level, and also see a more detailed image of the surround panorama.

The Surround Pan window offers you more options when grabbing and moving your signal in the surround panorama. To lock the angle, you can hold **COMMAND** down while dragging the white dot. You can hold **CONTROL** down to lock the radius. And you can hold down the **OPTION** key to reset the angle and radius to the exact center.

The slider at the bottom of the window is the *Low Frequency Enhancement* Control, or LFE Control. Generally, the LFE channel is a subwoofer, but it doesn't have to be. This slider controls how much of the signal from this channel is directed toward the LFE channel. The Center Level determines signal level at the dead center of the surround panorama.

Assigning Surround Channels to Audio Outputs

You determine which physical output will correspond to which surround channel in the Surround tab of the Audio Preferences window. You can access this dialog box from the global menus, either by choosing **Logic Pro > Preferences > Audio** or from the Audio global menu by selecting **Audio > Surround**. Either way, you open the dialog box shown in Figure 12.53.

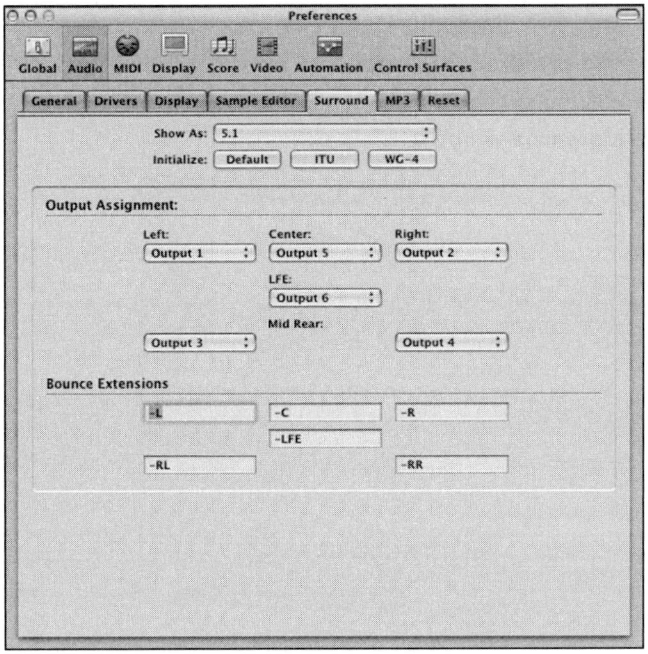

Figure 12.53

The Surround tab of the Audio Preferences window.

In the Show As pull-down menu, you can select which surround format you want to use. Be sure to use the same format you have chosen in your surround channels. At this point, pull-down menus for selecting one of your hardware outputs appear under the nine squares as dictated by your chosen surround format. Use these menus to select the hardware output you desire for each surround channel. You might want to place a Low Pass Filter effect into the Insert box of the Output Object that is your LFE, since that is the standard LFE cutoff for surround subwoofer channels. The three buttons on the right allow you to select the Default, ITU, or WG-4 configuration of hardware ouputs automatically without having to set each pull-down menu manually.

The Surround tab also tells you what file extensions will be added to your files when you do a Surround bounce, explained in the next section.

Bouncing in Surround

As mentioned in the preceding section describing the Bounce dialog box, you can choose to bounce in surround by selecting a format from the Surround Bounce pull-down menu. This creates as many files as your surround format has channels. Logic gives the files the extensions noted in the Surround preference window. Be sure to choose the same surround format for bouncing as you have selected in your surround objects and the Surround Preferences window.

13 Working with Files

At this point, you should have a pretty solid foundation in how to set up, compose, and mix a song in Logic. You're now ready to start learning about file management within Logic. Some general aspects of file management, such as creating new documents and opening and saving files, should already be familiar to you. Other unique features in Logic, such as the Project Manager, require a more thorough understanding in order to get the most out of them. This chapter should hit on everything you need to know to manage your projects' files properly in Logic.

Creating New Songs

As explained in Chapter 4, "Creating Your Autoload Song," Logic normally will launch to its default song or your Autoload. Normally, new songs are based off either of these songs. Your Autoload is your "virtual studio" representing an ideal configuration for the way you like to work. But what if you have a number of ideal configurations based on the specific project? Luckily, Logic lets you create new songs not only based off the default song or your Autoload song, but also off Song Templates.

Song Templates

I discussed Song Templates in some detail in Chapter 4. Because the Autoload is a special Song Template itself, having multiple Song Templates is just like having "multiple Autoload songs" at your disposal. For example, you might want one "virtual studio" set up for compositions with lots of Audio Instruments, one for recording lots of instruments simultaneously, one for different video setups if you do sound-to-picture, and so on. You may have more than one Macintosh and want different Song Templates based on the different monitor sizes and CPU power of each machine.

Logic Pro 7 comes with a number of Song Templates that are installed in the directory /Library/Application Support/Logic/Song Templates. You will notice that some are for TDM users, others for Rewire users, some for PowerBooks, others for G5s, and so on. You can also save any song you create as a template by selecting **File > Save As Template**. After you name the song in the dialog box, your song will be saved in the directory ~//Library/Application Support/Logic/Song Templates. Every time you create a new song from a Song Template, the Song Template you created will appear in the list of available Song Templates.

Using the New Command to Create New Songs

Obviously, the easiest way to create a new song is to simply start working in your Autoload (or the default) song, and then save it as a new song or Project later. However, if you set the preference in the Song Handling tab of **Logic Pro > Preferences > Global** to Automatically Open Most Recent Song on Startup, you will not get your Autoload or default song. Also, you may want to start a new song from one of your Song Templates. In these situations, you'll want to use the New command from the global File menu.

When you select the New command, you will get the New Song dialog box shown in Figure 13.1.

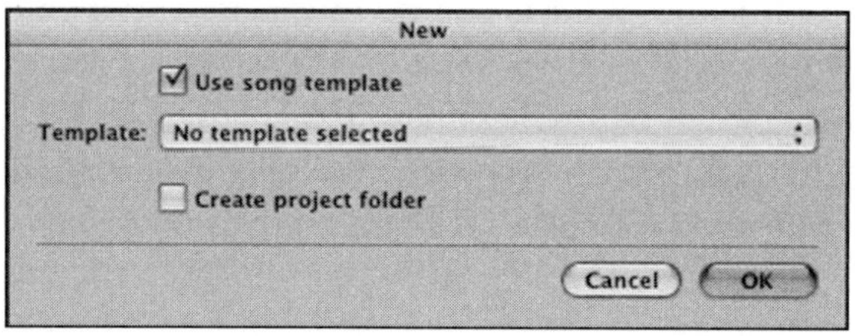

Figure 13.1

The New dialog box.

From here, you can select the Song Template you want from the pull-down menu of Song Templates, as shown in Figure 13.2.

Finally, if you want to set up your new song as a Project—which I cannot recommend highly enough—you can check the Create Project Folder box, and the dialog box will expand to show you the Project Folder settings, as shown in Figure 13.3.

These Project Folder settings are discussed below in the "Saving Your Song as a Project" subsection.

Figure 13.2

You can select which Song Template to use for your new song from the Song Template pull-down menu.

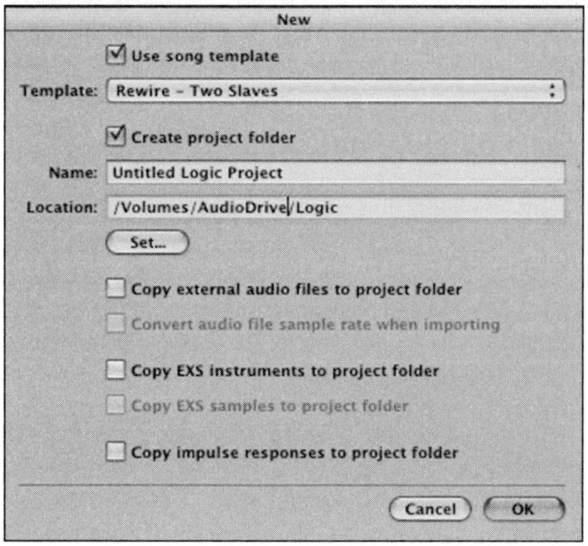

Figure 13.3

When you check the Create Project Folder box, the New dialog offers you the Project Folder settings.

Saving Logic Songs

To save your song in Logic, choose **File > Save** or press **COMMAND + S**. To save your Logic song with a new name or in a new directory, choose **File > Save As** or press **SHIFT + COMMAND + S**. You can also save a copy of your file by selecting **File > Save a Copy As**. A file dialog box appears in which you can type a new name for your file and select a directory in which to save your song. This is similar to other software applications.

Saving Backups of Your Song

Knowing how important it is to have backups of your songs, Logic has a preference in the Song Handling tab of **Logic Pro > Preferences > Global** to create an Auto Backup of your song every time you save your song. In the pull-down menu of the preference, you can choose for Logic to save the last song version every time you save a new version, all the way up to saving 100 previous versions of your song. Logic will place each backup into a backup song folder in the directory of the main song file. Each backup song is numbered and given the extension .bak to delineate that it is a backup.

Saving Your Song as a Project

Logic offers a unique file saving option, which in addition to saving your file also creates an entire Folder hierarchy for your song. When you select **File > Save as Project**, a dialog box appears that prompts you to name your song and choose a directory in which to save your file. As soon as you select the directory and name for your song, the Save as Project window, shown in Figure 13.4, appears.

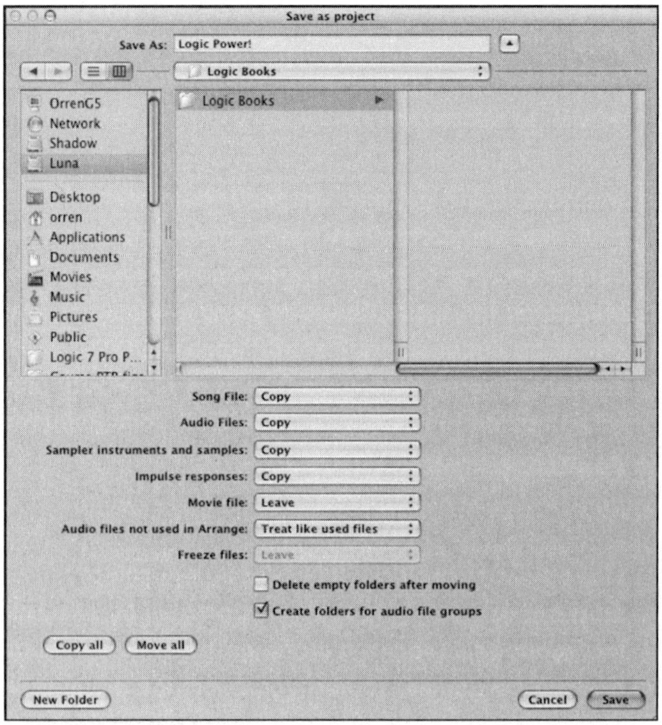

Figure 13.4

The Save as Project window.

This window allows you to determine exactly what to include in the Project folder created for your Logic song. The options are as follows:

- **Save As.** In this text box above the directory explorer, the name of your Logic song appears as the default Project folder name, but you can type in a new name for your Project folder if you want.
- **Song File.** You can choose to move the song file into the Project folder, place a copy of your song file into the Project folder, or leave the song file where it is on your hard drive.
- **Audio Files.** You can choose to move any audio files used by your song into this Project folder, create a copy of the audio files used in the song into the Audio subfolder of the Project folder, or leave the audio files used by this song in their current location.
- **Sampler Instruments and Samples.** You can choose to move any EXS24mkII sampler instruments and samples used by this song into this Project folder, create a copy of the sampler instruments and samples used and store them in the Sampler Instruments and Samples subfolder of the Project folder, or leave the sampler instruments and samples used by this song in their current location.
- **Impulse Responses.** You can choose to move any Space Designer impulse responses you use in the song into this Project folder, create a copy of the samples used and store them in the Impulse Response subfolder of the Project folder, or leave the impulse responses used by this song in their current location.
- **Movie File.** You can choose to move any QuickTime movies used by the song into this Project folder, create a copy of the movie and store it in the Movie subfolder of the Project folder, or leave the movie used by this song in its current location.
- **Audio Files Not Used in Arrange.** You can choose to move any audio files in the Audio window as part of the song but currently unused by the song into this Project folder, create a copy of the files and store them in the Audio subfolder of the Project folder, or leave the unused audio files in their current location.
- **Freeze Files.** If you have used the Freeze function to freeze tracks of your song, you can choose to move the Freeze files into this Project folder, create a copy of the Freeze files and store it in the Freeze Files subfolder of the Project folder, or leave the unused audio files in their current location.

- **Delete Empty Folders After Moving.** If Logic empties a folder in the process of executing the Save as Project command, that original folder will be deleted if you check this box.
- **Create Folders for Audio File Groups.** With this button engaged, if you create Audio Groups in the Audio window, they will be put into separate files on your hard drive.

You also have button options to set all the settings to Copy or Move. After you click OK, Logic saves your song to the new Project folder, closes the song, then opens the newly saved Logic Project song.

The Project Submenu

You have a number of Project-related options beyond simply saving Logic songs to Project folders and then opening the songs within them. Figure 13.5 shows the Project submenu.

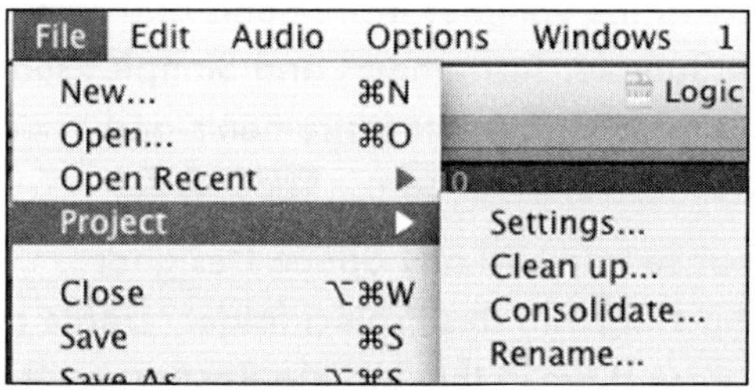

Figure 13.5
The Project submenu of the File menu.

Using Project folders gives you a number of very useful organization and workflow enhancements, as you will see below.

Project Settings

Every Project has a number of settings you can set even after you have created the Project folder itself. When you select **File > Project > Settings**, you bring up the Project Settings window, shown in Figure 13.6.

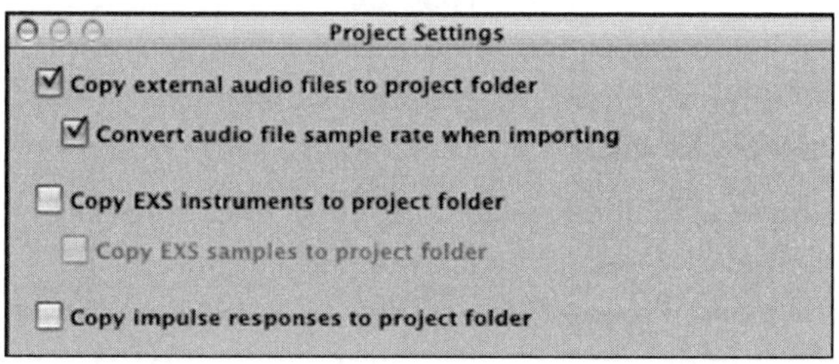

Figure 13.6
The Project Settings window.

You can check or uncheck the following settings:

- **Copy External Audio Files to Project Folder.** Checking this box will always copy audio files you add by dragging from the Finder to your Project folder. I highly recommend checking this.
- **Convert Audio File Sample Rate When Importing.** This option insures that any audio imported into your Logic Project will be automatically sample rate converted, if necessary, to match the sample rate of your Logic song. I highly recommend you check it; that way you won't have to worry about sample rate mismatches. (Logic Pro's sample rate conversion quality, by the way, is excellent).
- **Copy EXS Instruments to Project Folder.** This option will copy any Sampler Instruments used by the EXS in your Logic song to your Project folder.
- **Copy EXS Samples to Project Folder.** If you chose to copy the EXS instruments to your Project folder, this will insure that the used samples are copied as well. If you are copying your EXS instruments, I recommend you also copy the samples.
- **Copy Impulse Responses to Project Folder.** This option will automatically copy any impulse responses used by any instantiated Space Designer reverbs in your song to the Project folder.

Clean Up Project

You can clean up Project folders by deleting unused files with the Clean Up command. If you select **File > Project > Clean Up** you will open a window listing any files in the Project folder that are currently unused in your song, as shown in Figure 13.7.

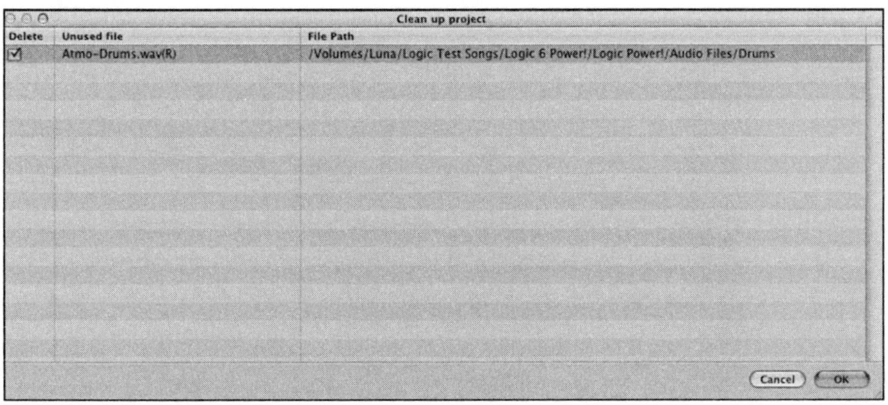

Figure 13.7
The Clean Up Project window allows you to delete unused files from your Project folder.

You can select which files to delete, and which unused files you wish to keep, then click OK and Logic will clean up your Project folder for you.

Consolidate Project

If you have been working with a Project that has managed to link to files all over your hard drive, or otherwise get unorganized, you can select **File > Project > Consolidate** to bring your Logic song and associated files together. After selecting this command, you will be presented with the Consolidate Project: Options dialog, that looks almost exactly like the Save as Project dialog, as shown in Figure 13.8.

Figure 13.8
The Consolidate Project: Options dialog.

After your Project is consolidated, you can use all the other Project-related functions (such as Clean Up and opening its Settings) to further operate on the consolidated folder.

Rename Project

If you want to rename a Project folder that already has songs and files in it, the **File > Project > Rename** command will allow you to rename your file and its included songs. Figure 13.9 shows the Rename Project dialog.

Figure 13.9
The Rename Project dialog.

You can choose to rename the Project folder only, the song only, or both the Project folder and the song file. This command is very useful if you save a Project before you name your song, and then want to rename it all in one go.

Opening or Importing Songs and Files

In Logic Pro, the Open dialog not only opens Logic and GarageBand songs, but also lets you import all the formats that Logic can import. When you select **File > Open** or press **COMMAND + O** Logic displays the Open dialog box. In this dialog you both select which file formats Logic will look for, and navigate to the file you wish to open. In Figure 13.10 you can see the Open dialog, with the Open File Type pull-down menu extended to show the various additional file types Logic can open.

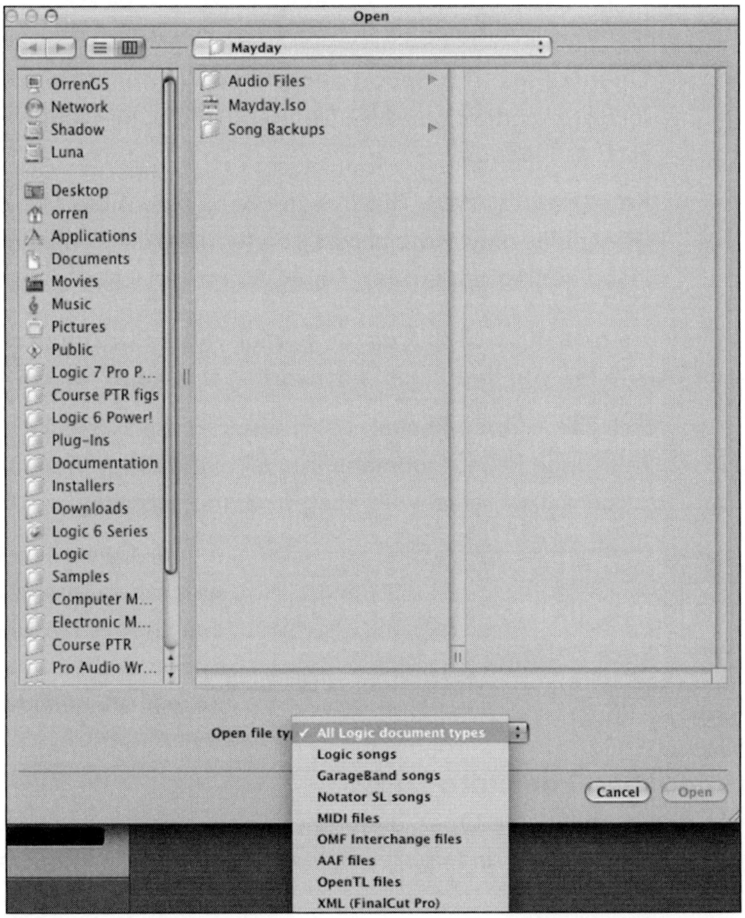

Figure 13.10

The Open dialog, showing the menu of all supported file types.

The options in the Open File Type menu are as follows:

- **All Logic Document Types.** This option will allow you to open a file in any of the formats Logic supports.
- **Logic Songs.** This option opens Logic songs only.
- **GarageBand Songs.** This option opens GarageBand songs only.
- **Notator SL Songs.** This option opens Notator SL songs only.
- **MIDI Files.** This option opens Standard MIDI Files (SMF) only.
- **OMF Interchange Files.** This option opens Open Media Framework (OMF) Interchange files only. OMF Interchange format was developed by Avid, parent company of Digidesign, and this format is currently supported by most major sequencers.
- **AAF Files.** This option opens Advanced Authoring Format (AAF) files only. This interchange format is currently supported by high-end professional audio applications such as Pro Tools HD.
- **OpenTL Files.** This option opens OpenTL format files only. The OpenTL format was developed by Tascam and is supported by applications such as Nuendo.
- **XML (FinalCut Pro).** This option opens Extensible Markup Language (XML) files only. XML allows you to integrate Logic Pro with Apple's video editing application FinalCut Pro.

If you are opening a song from an earlier version of Logic, a dialog box appears to tell you that Logic is converting the file to the newer song format.

If you click **File > Open Recent**, Logic displays the submenu shown in Figure 13.11. This Open Recent submenu lists all Logic songs that you have opened, and you can simply select your song from this submenu.

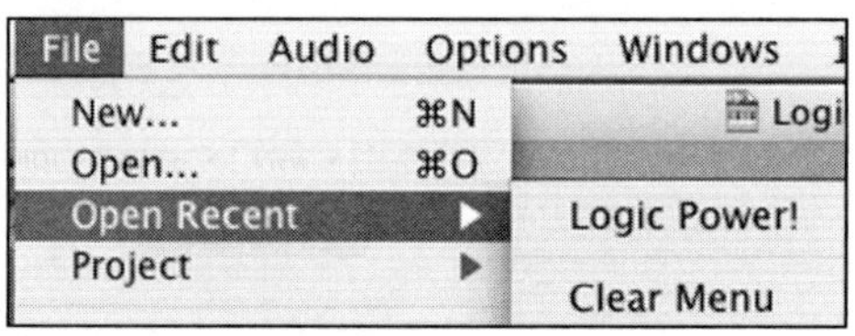

Figure 13.11

The Open Recent submenu in the global File menu.

If your Open Recent submenu gets too long and unwieldy, you can choose the Clear Menu option at the bottom of the Open Recent submenu to reset the list.

Importing Files into Logic

As stated above, the Open dialog both opens and imports files. However, Logic also contains an Import command, which you can access by choosing

File > Import. The main difference is that when you use Open, Logic Pro opens a new song, whereas with the Import command, Logic attempts to import the file into the currently open song (this only works for non-Logic songs). If it cannot add the imported material to the current song, it will open a new song, just like the Open command.

You can also import SMF files by dragging them onto the Arrange window in Logic. When you open an SMF file this way, Logic places it on your Arrange page; one track for each MIDI Channel is created, and any data on that track appears in the track lane as a single MIDI region.

Exporting Files from Logic

If you want to export your Logic song in a different format for use in a different application (or an earlier version of Logic), Logic offers an Export submenu in the global File menu. Figure 13.12 shows this submenu.

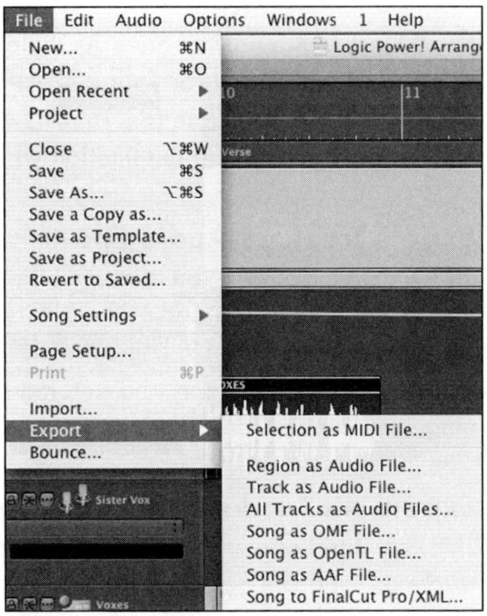

Figure 13.12
The Export submenu from the global File menu features your options for exporting files from Logic into different formats.

These export options are explained in the following sub-sections.

Export Selection as MIDI File

To export MIDI data from Logic, first select one or more MIDI regions (across as many tracks as you'd like), then choose this option. A file dialog box prompts you to choose a name and directory for your exported file, and then your MIDI selection is exported with a .mid extension to denote that it is a standard MIDI file.

Export Region as Audio File

This command allows you to export the selected Audio region as an audio file. When selected, this command opens the Region as Audio File dialog shown in Figure 13.13.

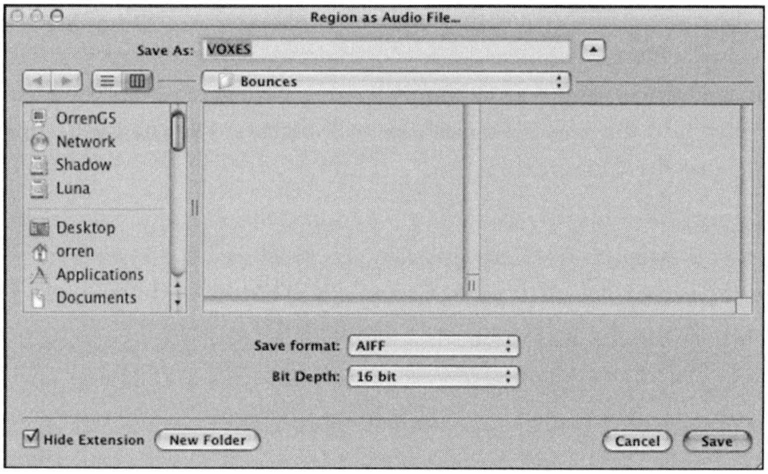

Figure 13.13
The Export Region as Audio File dialog.

In addition to the normal Save As dialog features, this window allows you to select the Save format for your file (AIFF, Sound Designer II, or Broadcast Wave), and the Bit Depth (8-, 16- or 24-bit). Logic will do an Offline bounce including all effects and automation when exporting your region.

Export Track as Audio File

This command allows you to export the selected Arrange Audio or Audio Instrument track as an audio file. Selecting this command brings up a dialog identical to Figure 13.13. Logic Pro will do an Offline bounce of the selected track, including all effects and automation, that begins at the song beginning, and ends at the song end.

Export All Tracks as Audio Files

This command allows you to export all of your Audio and Audio Instrument tracks as separate audio files. Selecting this command brings up a dialog identical to Figure 13.13. The Save format and Bit Depth you specify will be applied to every track you export (in other words, you can't choose different formats and/or bit depths for different tracks). Logic Pro will do an Offline bounce of each track, including all effects and automation, that begins at the song beginning, and ends at the song end.

While Logic has no specific command to only export a few tracks, the All Tracks as Audio Files command will not export any Arrange tracks or regions that have been muted, so you can mute those tracks/regions you do not wish to export. Alternately, if any tracks in Arrange are soloed, Logic will only export those tracks that are soloed, so if you only want to export a few tracks, you can solo them, then use this command.

Export Song as OMF File

To export a song in Avid's popular inter-application OMF (Open Media Format) Interchange file format, select this option. The OMF Export dialog box then appears, as shown in Figure 13.14.

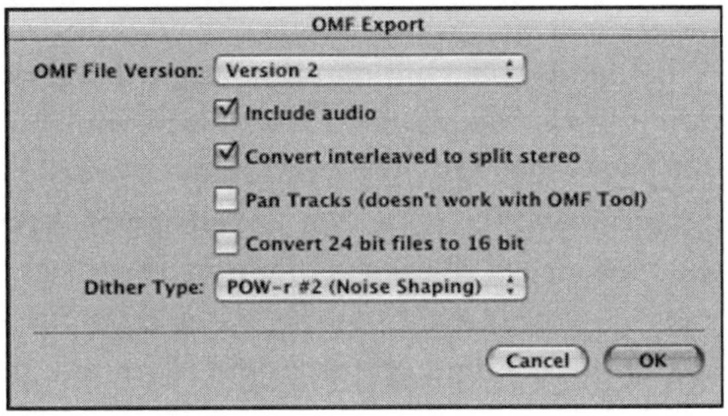

Figure 13.14
The OMF Export dialog. Here you can set the parameters for your OMF file.

The OMF Export options are described as follows:

- **OMF File Version.** You can select Version 1 or Version 2. Version 1 is an older version of OMF that was not as robust; you will nearly always use the default setting of Version 2 here.
- **Include Audio.** If you check this box, all of your Audio regions are integrated into the OMF file itself, resulting in a potentially very large file that will take longer to export. On the other hand, it is also the most compatible with other applications. If you uncheck this box, only the references to the used audio files are included, which some applications have a problem reading. As long as you have the disk space, you should include the audio in your OMF file.
- **Convert Interleaved to Split Stereo.** Some applications, such as ProTools and Digital Performer, are not capable of importing interleaved stereo files. If you intend to import your OMF file into an application that cannot use interleaved stereo files, you'll want to check this box. If you are not sure, it's always safer to leave it checked.
- **Pan Tracks (Doesn't Work with OMF Tool).** This option attempts to include the panorama information from the Logic channel strips with each Audio Track. The problem is that many applications (such as the ProTools OMF tool and others) cannot use this information. Therefore, although this option is good in theory, it is not very effective in practice.

- **Convert 24-Bit Files to 16-Bit.** If you know that the application to which you want to import your tracks cannot import 24-bit files, you may want to convert all your 24-bit audio files to 16-bit with this option.
- **Dither Type.** If you are converting your files down to 16-bit, you may want to use dither. This is the same Dither pull-down menu as from the Bounce dialog box described in Chapter 11.

When you have configured your OMF Export the way you want, clicking OK brings up a File dialog box in which you can choose the name and directory for your OMF file. After you select a location and name for your file, Logic begins the OMF export. A progress bar indicates the status of the process, as it will tie up Logic until the operation is complete. When you are finished, the result is a portable song file in OMF format (with a file extension of .omf) that contains all the Audio regions in your Logic song.

Export Song as OpenTL File

When you choose to export your song in Tascam's proprietary OpenTL file format, first a File dialog box appears in which to name your OpenTL file and choose a directory. Once accomplished, a dialog box appears asking whether you want to create a new folder to contain your OpenTL file and all relevant audio files. After you click either Yes or No, a new dialog box appears asking whether you want to make a copy of all audio files used in the song. Once you click Yes or No in response, the OpenTL exporting takes place, resulting in an OpenTL file (with a file extension of .tl) that you can import into any application that can import OpenTL files.

Export Song as AAF File

When you choose to export your song in the new, professional Advanced Authoring Format (AAF) file, you are presented with a specialized Save AAF File As dialog, shown in Figure 13.15.

In addition to the normal Save As options, this dialog offers four Audio File Export Settings:

- **Sample Rate.** You can select a sample rate from 44.1kHz to 96kHz.
- **Bit Depth.** You can select a bit depth of either 16- or 24-bit.
- **File Format.** You can select either Wave or AIFF format for your audio files.

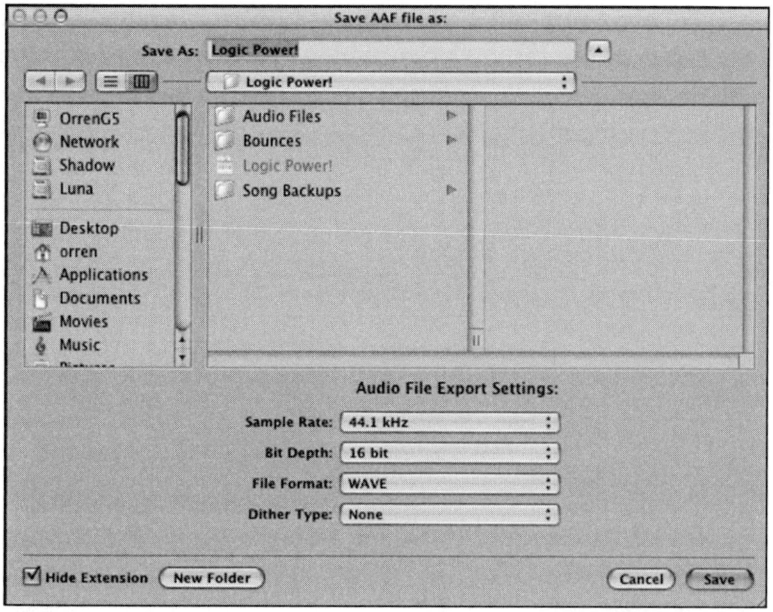

Figure 13.15
The Save AAF File As dialog.

- **Dither Type.** If you have selected 16-bit audio files from 24-bit originals, you should select one of Logic's three POW-r dither algorithms to dither your files.

Once you are finished setting up the AAF Audio File Export Settings, press Save and Logic will export your Logic song as an AAF.

Export Song to FinalCut Pro/XML

This option will save your Logic song in Extensible Markup Language (XML) for use in FinalCut Pro. When you select this option, it will present you with a standard Save As file dialog box. Simply name your file, choose where to save your XML file, and press **RETURN**. Logic will save your song as an XML file that you can then import into FinalCut Pro.

The Project Manager

One of the most powerful, yet perhaps underutilized, features of Logic Pro is its inclusion of a robust and powerful multimedia database management tool called the Project Manager. You can launch the Project Manager by selecting **Windows > Project Manager**, or by assigning Open Project Manager a key command.

Its initial appearance is slightly similar to that of the Audio window; the left side is a browser, displaying a catalog of files and file paths, and the right side displays the contents of selected items from the browser. The basic procedure of using the Project Manager is similar as well—you select a file or files displayed in the right side of the browser, and then operate on your selection. Figure 13.16 shows the Project Manager.

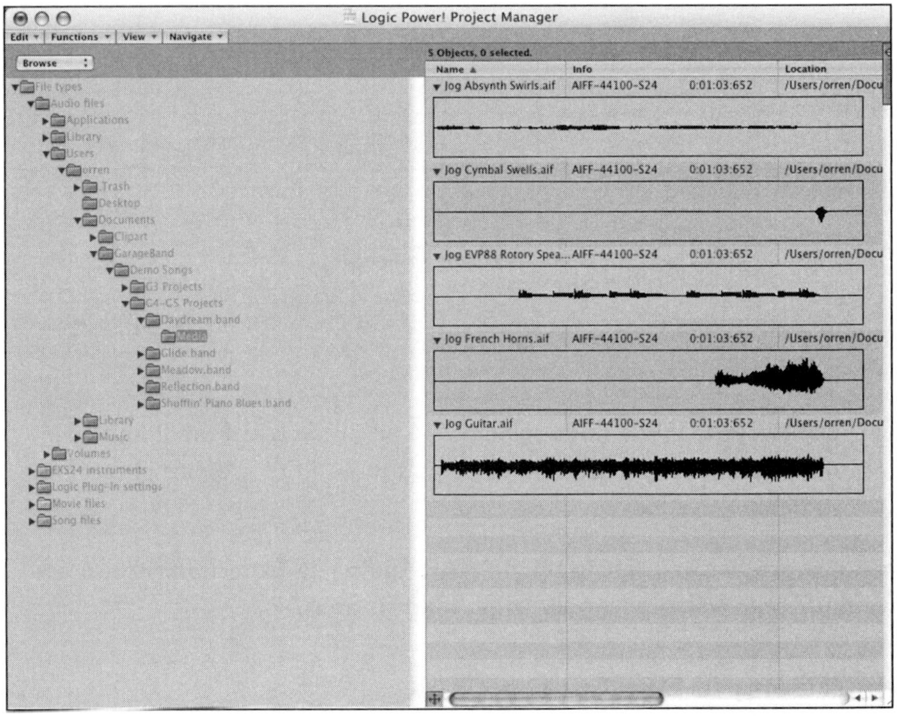

Figure 13.16
The Project Manager.

This is far more than simply a search engine for Logic songs. The Project Manager can audition files, remember relationships between files and various Logic songs, keep a database of all the media files on your local and network hard drives, and more. You can use the Project Manager not only to find and archive files, but to save, delete, and move them as well. The Project Manager can even keep track of plug-in settings for all your plug-ins across all your Logic songs. You can open audio files in the Sample Editor, move audio files to the Audio window or Arrange, move MIDI files to the Arrange window, and so on—all directly from the Project Manager window!

As you can imagine, with this much flexibility and power, the Project Manager initially may seem daunting. But once you understand it and experience what it offers you, you will find it a valuable part of Logic and an exceptional tool.

The Project Manager's Local Menus

The Project Manager's many commands are available in four local menus. Because the Project Manager shares few functions with other Logic editors and windows, most of the commands in the Project Manager are unique. The following subsections describe the various local menus.

The Edit Menu

The Edit menu contains commands geared toward making selections in the Project Manager. Figure 13.7 shows the local Edit menu of the Project Manager.

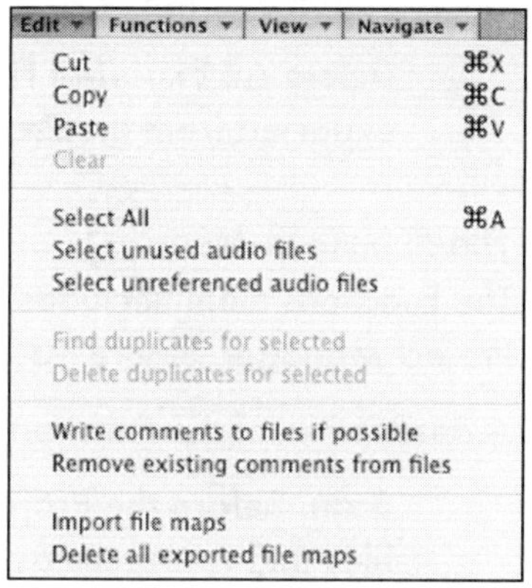

Figure 13.17
The local Edit menu of the Project Manager.

The commands are as follows:

- **Cut.** This removes an item from the Project Manager display and places it on the Clipboard.
- **Copy.** The Copy command places a copy of the selected item onto the Clipboard.
- **Paste.** This pastes the contents of the Clipboard into the currently selected path or location in the Project Manager.
- **Clear.** The Clear command clears the selection from the Project Manager.
- **Select All.** Select All selects the entire contents of the current location in the contents (right) side of the Project Manager.
- **Select Unused Audio Files.** This selects all audio files that are not used in a Logic song.
- **Select Unreferenced Audio Files.** This command selects audio files that are not referenced in any other song or Project.
- **Find Duplicates for Selected.** If you make a selection and then choose this command, Logic also selects all duplicates of your selection.
- **Delete Duplicates for Selected.** If you make a selection and then choose this command, Logic deletes all duplicates of your selection.
- **Write Comments to Files If Possible.** The Project Manager allows you to write two different comments for each file type it can catalog. With this command, the comments you have added to a file's entry in the PM database becomes a part of the file data, so the comments can

be recovered even if you erase and rescan the Project Manager database. If you haven't already written both comments, you can use this command to write a comment.

- **Remove Existing Comments from Files.** This removes comments from files for which you have written comments. The comments will still persist in the Project Manager database, however.
- **Import File Maps.** This command imports a Project Manager file map.
- **Delete All Exported File Maps.** This deletes all file maps that you have exported from the Project Manager.

The Functions Menu

The Functions menu includes commands relating to the unique features of the Project Manager. Figure 13.18 shows the Functions menu.

A description of the Function menu commands follows:

- **Scan.** Before the Project Manager can accurately manage the media files and resources available to Logic, it needs to scan all available drives to create a list of their contents. Scanning is delved into in more detail in the "Scanning" section below.
- **Expanded Scan.** Unlike Scan, which just looks for media files, Expanded Scan will scan absolutely every file. Scanning is delved into in more detail in the "Scanning" section below.
- **Scan Folder.** This command scans a specific folder.
- **Check for Modified or Deleted Files.** This command checks your drives to see what files have been modified or deleted since the last scan.
- **Abort Scan Process.** This command immediately stops the scan process.
- **Save Project Manager Data.** This saves all the data currently in the Project Manager. This doesn't actually save files, just data in the Project Manager database.
- **Clear Scanned Data.** This command clears all data from the most recent scan.
- **Consolidate Files of Selected Songs.** This command executes a Consolidate command (**File > Project > Consolidate**) for all of the Logic songs you have selected, putting each song in a new folder. This enables you to create subfolders to the folder, to move, copy, or

leave your referenced files, and more. This command is great either for archiving songs you're finished with, or for doing a Save As Project for older songs without having to load each one into Logic and choosing the Save As Project command.

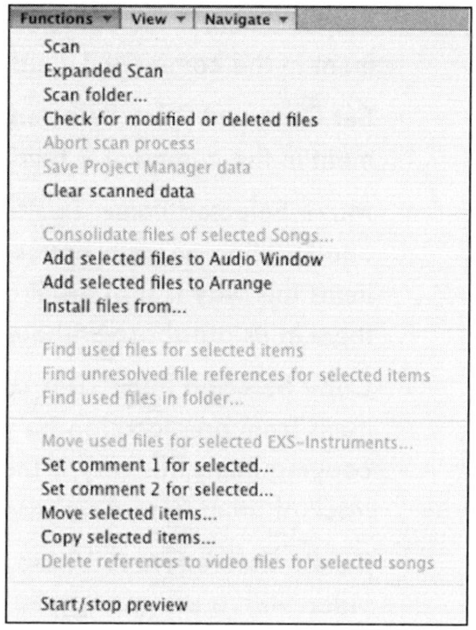

Figure 13.18

The local Functions menu of the Project Manager.

- **Add Selected Files to Audio Window.** This adds all the audio files you have selected in the Project Manager to the Audio window of the current Logic song.
- **Add Selected Files to Arrange.** This command adds all the selected files to the Arrange window of the open Logic song.
- **Install Files From.** You can use this command to install audio and EXS sampler files from a CD or hard drive into another location on your drive. If you select this, you get a file selector to choose what you want to install, and after you click Choose, Logic presents another file selector where you can set your destination directory for the installed files.
- **Find Used Files for Selected Items.** This finds every file referenced by the selected items.
- **Find Unresolved File References for Selected Items.** After you select a file or files, this command forces the Project Manager to analyze every file in an attempt to find any file that might refer to the selected files.
- **Find Used Files in Folder.** This selects all the files used by the selected items in a given folder.
- **Move Used Files for Selected EXS Instruments.** You can use this command to move the samples of selected EXS Instruments to a new location. The advantage of using this command to do this is that the EXS Instrument will not need to search for those samples again after the move.

- **Set Comment 1 for Selected.** This command allows you to type a comment in the comment 1 field of all selected files.
- **Set Comment 2 for Selected.** This command allows you to type a comment in the comment 2 field of all selected files.
- **Move Selected Items.** This allows you to move the selected items from one location on your drives to another. The advantage of moving items this way is that the Project Manager then can keep track of them in its database without having to rescan to find them.
- **Copy Selected Items.** This command allows you to copy the selected items from one location on your drives to another. The advantage of copying items this way is that the Project Manager can then keep track of them in its database without having to rescan to find them.
- **Delete References to Video Files for Selected Songs.** If you used a video with a song, and you no longer need it, you can delete the reference to the video file with this command so that Logic no longer prompts you for the video.
- **Start/Stop Preview.** If you are using the Program Manager to audition files, you can use this command to start and stop auditioning.

EXPERT TIP: AUDITIONING AND LOADING FILES USING THE PROJECT MANAGER

Len Sasso, author of *Emagic Logic Tips and Tricks*, weighs in with his suggestion of using the Project Manager for auditioning and loading audio files.

> "You can step through your whole library [of sound samples] or any part thereof, audition the samples, edit them in the Sample Editor, and load them into the Audio window and/or Arrange window as desired. Assign the Enter key to [the key command] Add Selected Files to Audio Window. Select any audio file in the Project Manager browser list, start playback (usually Spacebar), and arrow through the files. When you want one in your song, hit **RETURN** twice (once to transfer and once to confirm their dialog box telling you one sample has been added)."

The View Menu

The View menu offers you a few different options for which information to view and how to view it, in the Project Manager. Figure 13.19 shows the View menu of the Project Manager.

An explanation of the options follows:

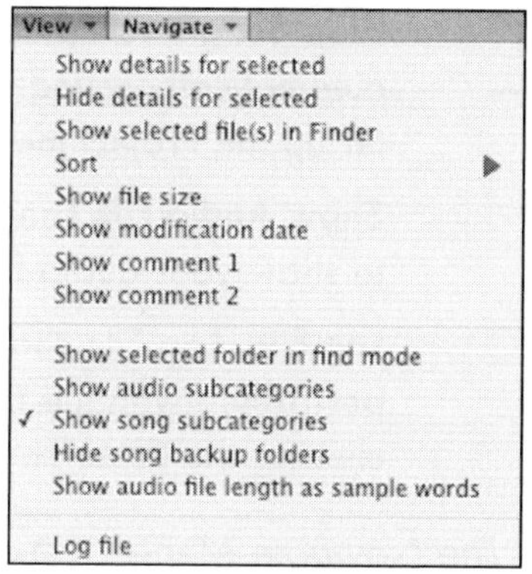

Figure 13.19

The local View menu of the Project Manager.

- **Show Details for Selected.** You can show the details of various files by clicking on the view triangle next to the filename in the contents window. When you select this command, Logic automatically expands the view of all selected items without your having to click on the view triangles individually.
- **Hide Details for Selected.** This retracts the view of all selected items in the contents display.
- **Show Selected File(s) in Finder.** This command will open one or more Finder windows showing the location of your selected file or files.
- **Sort.** This command gives you a hierarchal menu of options for how to sort the items in the Project Manager. You can choose to sort by Date, Size, Name, Info, Location, or Comment 1 or 2 by selecting the respective choice in the Sort submenu. You can also sort up or down, so that the items are ascending or descending.
- **Show File Size.** This option shows the file size of all files in the contents window.
- **Show Modification Date.** This option shows the modification date of the files in the contents window.
- **Show Comment 1.** This option shows the text in the comment 1 slot for each file.
- **Show Comment 2.** This option shows the text in the comment 2 slot for each file.
- **Show Selected Folder in Find Mode.** When you select this command, Logic displays in Find mode the folder you have selected in the contents window in Browse mode. The modes are described in the "Project Manager Modes" section below.
- **Show Audio Subcategories.** This displays the audio subcategories (AIFF, WAV, and so on) for audio files in the contents window.
- **Show Song Subcategories.** This command shows the subcategories for the Logic songs in the contents windows.

- **Hide Song Backup Folders.** This option hides folders that contain the automatically saved backup versions of Logic songs, so as not to clutter up the Project menu with duplicate songs.
- **Show Audio File Length as Sample Words.** You can select this option to show your audio file length in samples instead of in time.
- **Log File.** Log File shows you a simple log of every action you have performed with the Project Manager. You can also clear the log by clicking the Clear Log button.

The Navigate Menu

You can think of the Navigate menu as a sort of "bookmark" or "favorites" menu. It contains a few folder navigation commands, but its real value is as a bookmark menu. Figure 13.20 shows the Navigate menu.

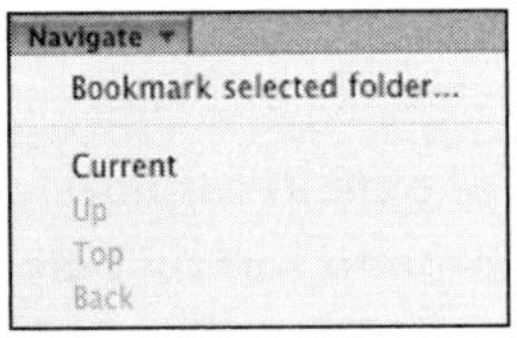

Figure 13.20
The local Navigate menu of the Project Manager.

As you can see, the menu includes commands to switch to the current folder, or to move up, to the top, or back in the directory structure. But it is the Bookmark Selected Folder command that is the most useful. With this, you can create a bookmark of all your commonly accessed folders. Then, without having to navigate through your directories in the browser window, you can simply choose the folder for instant access.

Project Manager Modes

Right under the Project Manager's local menus is the Mode pull-down menu. This menu includes a list of three operation modes for the Project Manager.

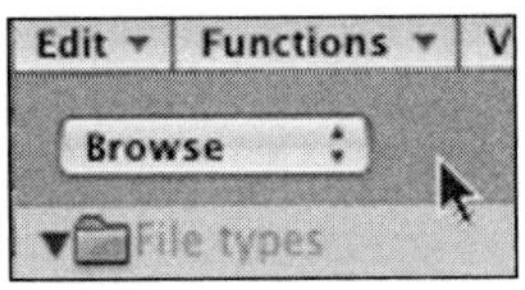

Figure 13.21
The Project Manager Mode pull-down menu, currently showing the Browse mode.

The four modes of the Project Manager are briefly as follows:

- **Browse Mode.** Browse mode is perhaps the main mode of the Project Manager. In this mode, Logic presents a catalog of directories on the left side of the Project Manager, and a list of the contents of those directories on the right side. The contents window shows the applicable information on each file that you have chosen to view in the local View menu; you can audition files, open them in Logic's Sample Editor, move them into the Arrange or Audio window, and more.
- **Find Mode.** This mode activates the Project Manager's powerful and configurable search engine. This mode is explored in the "The Project Manager's Find Mode" subsection later in this chapter.

- **Scan Paths Mode.** This mode allows you to configure the Project Manager's scan functions. This is covered as part of the following subsection, "Scanning."

Scanning

Before you can use the Project Manager, it first must scan all your drives to compile a database of all your available media files, plug-in settings, EXS samples and instruments, Logic songs, and so on. You can configure the Scan procedure in several ways, which are explained in this section.

To conduct a simple scan, make sure you are in Browse mode without any directory selected in the catalog window. Then select **Functions > Scan**. Logic then scans all connected drives looking for all relevant files. You can also select **Functions > Expanded Scan** to analyze absolutely every file, not just the files with relevant names or extensions.

As you can imagine, if you have a large amount of available drive space or an immense number of files, scanning absolutely every connected drive can take an exceptionally long time. The Project Manager allows you to expedite the scanning process by choosing to eliminate paths you know do not contain any relevant files, and include paths that you know you want scanned. To do this, you need to use Scan Paths mode instead of Browse mode. This mode presents you with new options on the left side of the window to customize your scanning paths, as shown in Figure 13.22.

As you can see in Figure 13.22, the left side of the Project Manager no longer features a directory catalog but instead offers buttons to add paths to include and exclude from scanning. After you click one of these buttons, a file dialog box appears in which you can choose the paths you want to include or

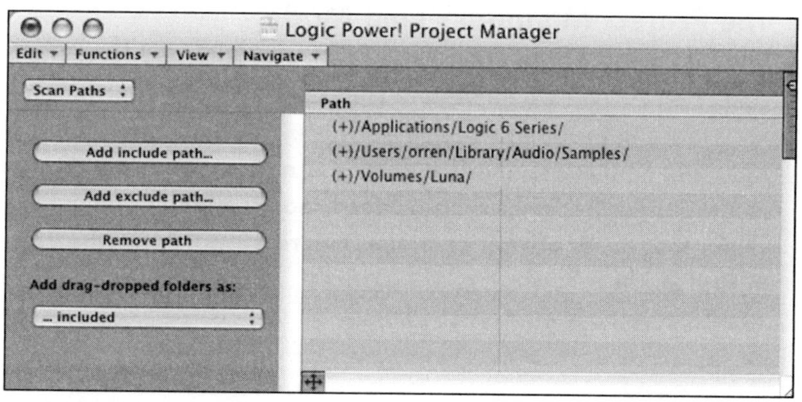

Figure 13.22
The Project Manager in Scan Paths mode.

exclude. The right side of the Project Manager then lists all those paths you have chosen to include or exclude. If a directory path is preceded with a plus sign (+), the path is included; a minus sign (–) indicates the path has been excluded. You can remove paths from the list by clicking the Remove Path button. You can also drag and drop folders directly into the Project Manager, which then adds the path to its list. The Add Drag-Dropped Folders As pull-down menu allows you to select whether you want Logic to include or exclude the paths of the directories you drag onto the Project Manager.

Selecting paths to exclude from scans reduces your scan time considerably by ensuring that the Project Manager doesn't spend time scouring directories that you know do not contain any relevant files. Keep in mind that you can include paths to network directories, that you can include specific subfolders from directories that have been excluded, and you can exclude specific subfolders from directories that have been included. If you have already organized your drives carefully, you can use the Scan Paths mode to hone in even further on exactly where your Logic-related media files are located.

Finally, the most severe way to restrict your scan is to choose **Functions > Scan Folder** while in Browse mode with a folder selected in the directory catalog. In this case, Logic scans only that folder. If you want to scan a folder that is not in the Project Manager database, do not select any folder, and a file dialog box appears in which you can choose which folder to scan.

Restricting the scan path is also a great idea if you use other audio applications besides Logic that create media files. Because the Project Manager's database won't reflect those files created by the other applications without a full rescan, you can use the Scan Paths and Scan Folder options to limit the Project Manager to those directories that you only use for Logic.

The Project Manager's Find Mode

One of the most frequent uses of databases is to find files. The Project Manager's powerful Find mode and Find options in the Functions menu allow for very thorough searches of relevant files. When you switch the Project Manager into Find mode, the first thing you notice is that the left side of the Project Manager becomes an advanced search engine, and the right side now shows the results of your searches. Figure 13.23 shows the Project Manager in Find mode.

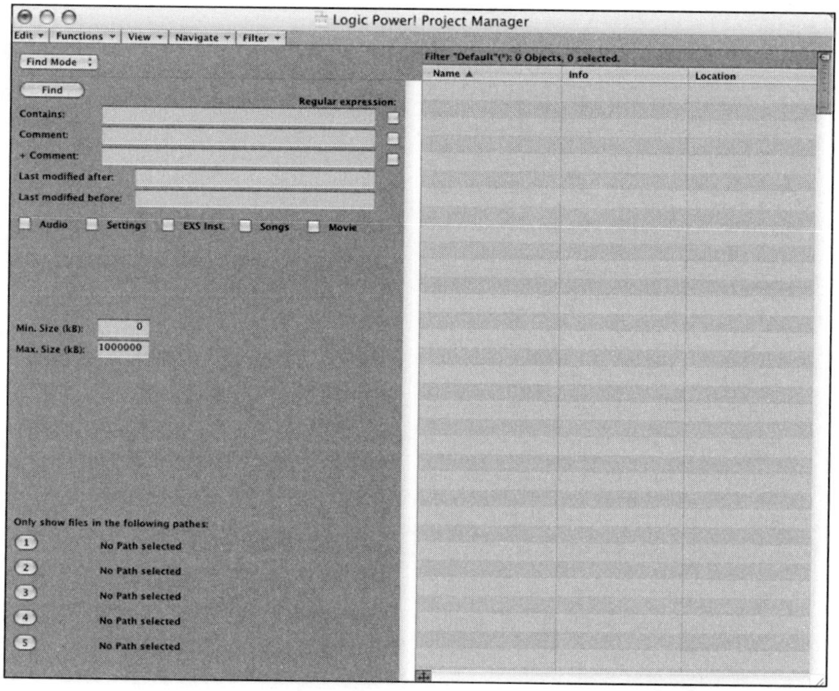

Figure 13.23
The Project Manager in Find mode.

You can use all the fields in the top half of the search engine's fields to enter variables such as key words, comments, modification dates, types of files, or the minimum and maximum size of the file. You can also check whether you are using English words or regular mathematic expressions. Depending on which file type you direct the Project Manager to search for, Logic may display additional check boxes of options. At the bottom of the Find field, you can also limit your search to as many as five paths. This is very useful if your Project Manager database covers many hard drives and a huge amount of data. If you've already restricted your Project Manager to scan only specific folders, you need not limit the search paths here.

After you have adequately specified your search, click on the Update File List button at the bottom of the Find field to begin the search. The Project Manager shows the results of the search on the right, along with all referenced files if you have specified those to be included. Figure 13.24 shows a completed search.

If you find that you want Logic to always search a particular path, you can speed up your search even more by setting the path of your search in one of

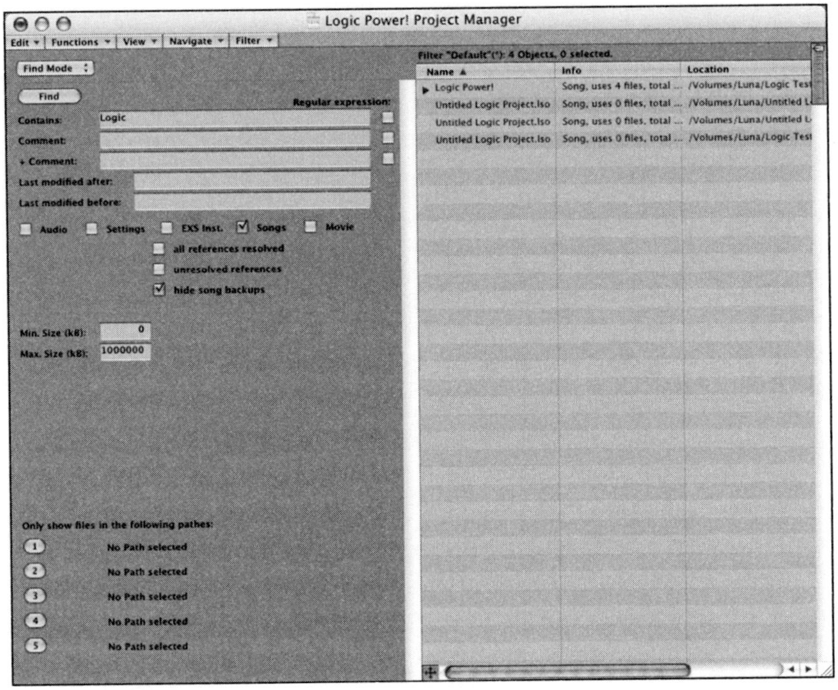

Figure 13.24

In this example, the Project Manager searched for all Logic songs with the word "Logic" in the title. All song backups were hidden. The screen shows the results on the right. Notice all the triangles that indicate the reference files.

the five buttons at the bottom of the window labeled Only Show Files in the Following Paths.

Find mode also introduces a new local menu to the Project Manager: the Filter menu. This menu allows you to save frequently used searches for easy recall. Figure 13.25 shows the Filter local menu.

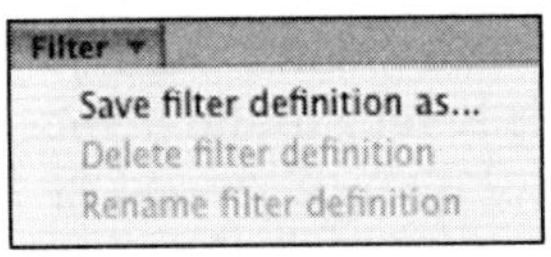

Figure 13.25

The Filter local menu of the Project Manager appears only in Find mode, and allows you to save your searches.

As you save definitions, they appear at the bottom of the menu. You can also delete and rename filter definitions that you have already saved. Figure 13.26 shows the Filter menu after the search from Figure 13.24 has been saved.

Figure 13.26

The search conducted in Figure 13.24 has now been saved as a filter definition and appears at the bottom of the Filter menu.

If you double-click on a file that you have found, the Project Manager switches to Browse mode so you can see the full path of the file, as well as audition the file, open it in the Sample Editor or Arrange window, and more. The Find mode of the Project Manager, as well as the three find commands described in the Functions menu, allow for a level of file searching that is truly best-in-class in music production applications.

14 The Environment

Do you wish you had a complete virtual model of your hardware synthesizer controls inside Logic for easy programming while sequencing? Do you have some great ideas for running the notes you perform through a couple of arpeggiators and delay lines to create amazing and unique rhythms that follow your playing dynamics? Have you thought about having single keys play unique chords, and then be delayed and play additional chords? Would you like to create structures in which the type of processing done to any data is conditional upon the notes you are playing, or the velocity of your notes, and so on? Would you like to be able to use Logic itself as a live performance tool? Then welcome to the Environment.

I have touched on the Environment in other chapters, but now it's time to dive into it in more detail. The Environment is perhaps the most unique and daunting aspect of Logic. There really isn't anything like it in the other commercially available digital audio sequencers. If the Environment seems like something you aren't ready to explore, don't worry—you can successfully use Logic without ever using the routing and transforming power of the Environment. Logic is highly competitive with the other sequencers simply by virtue of its audio and MIDI editing, recording, mixing, and arranging. On the other hand, if you want to use the power of the Environment, no other sequencer can possibly compete with Logic. The Environment puts Logic into a league all its own.

Understanding the Environment

By introducing parts of the Environment in several chapters previous to this one, you should be more comfortable with the concept. The Environment, as you know, is a virtual representation of your studio. Your available Audio

Objects represent your available Audio channels inside Logic as well as your available audio hardware. Your MIDI Objects represent your available MIDI hardware. There are Internal Objects that represent connections to software synthesizers that are running on your computer but outside the Logic application, such as the QuickTime Object and the Rewire Object. Hopefully, creating the objects to represent the external hardware you have and the virtual studio you desire has started making you comfortable with the Environment.

Let's take the "virtual studio" paradigm further. Just as in a hardware studio, you can cable different processors to different channels, you can have splitters that split up signals, you can monitor signals, and you can create entire racks of effects. By cabling objects, using transformer and splitter objects, and creating macros, you can do that in the Environment as well. This chapter is going to touch on the more complex types of routings and structures you can make with the Environment. No single chapter can cover everything you could possibly create with Logic's Environment, but hopefully you'll learn enough about what is possible to facilitate your own creativity and invention!

KEEP IN MIND: CAN DOES NOT MEAN MUST!

Unfortunately, the Environment plays a large part in why Logic is considered difficult. Users who cannot find anything they are familiar with in the Environment feel that Logic must require a degree in programming in order to do the simplest things. Hopefully, by this point in the book, you've already realized how false that idea is. To reiterate, just because the Environment will allow you to build complex constructions and macros that can do amazing MIDI processing, that doesn't mean that you *have* to do this! You don't need to use the Environment any more than you already have by creating your initial Audio and MIDI Objects. If you don't feel comfortable or interested in delving into the Environment yet, just put this chapter off for now.

Environment Local Menus

Like all windows in Logic, the Environment has its own local menus of functions. Unlike many local menus, since the Environment is designed to be a "graphical object workspace," not too many of them are accessible via key commands. Learning the options and functions available in the local menus is the first step toward understanding the potential of the Environment. The subsections below will detail the Environment local menus.

New Menu

The New menu contains all the various types of Objects you can create in the Environment. When you wish to add an Object, you will find it in this local menu. Figure 14.1 shows the New menu.

Figure 14.1
The New local menu of the Environment window.

You'll notice that a number of these Objects have already been discussed in previous chapters. Rather than describe each object in a short list, the next section will go into each object in detail.

Edit Menu

As with the Edit local menus in other windows, the Edit menu in the Environment window includes commands for selecting and editing selections. Figure 14.2 shows the Edit menu of the Environment window.

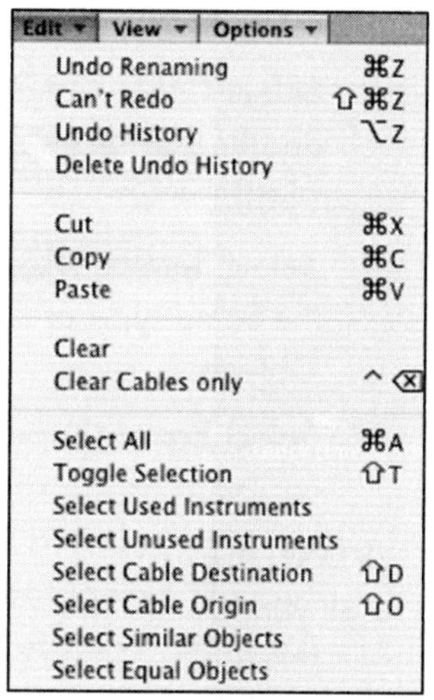

Figure 14.2
The Environment's local Edit menu.

A brief description of the available commands follows.

- **Undo.** This will undo the most recent action. **<COMMAND + Z>**
- **Redo.** This will redo the most recent action.
- **Undo History.** You can use this command to open the Undo History window. **<OPTION + Z>**
- **Delete Undo History.** This command will empty your Undo History window.
- **Cut.** You can use this command to remove the selected Object from the Environment window and place it on the Clipboard. **<COMMAND + X>**
- **Copy.** This command will place a copy of the selected Object onto the Clipboard. **<COMMAND + C>**
- **Paste.** You can paste the contents of the Clipboard into the Environment window at the current cursor position with this command. **<COMMAND + V>**

- **Clear.** This will clear the selected Objects from the Environment window.
- **Clear Cables Only.** This will clear all the cables running to or from the selected Objects but will not delete the Objects themselves. **<CONTROL + FORWARD DELETE>**
- **Select All.** This command selects everything in the current Environment layer. See the "Environment Layers" section later in this chapter for more information on layers. **<COMMAND + A>**
- **Toggle Selection.** This command will toggle between the selection you have made and everything in the current Environment layer except your selection. **<SHIFT + T>**
- **Select Used Instruments.** This command selects all instruments that are currently used in your song.
- **Select Unused Instruments.** This command selects all instruments that currently are not used in your song.
- **Select Cable Destination.** If you have an Object selected, this command will select the Object or Objects to which the selected Object is cabled. **<SHIFT + D>**
- **Select Cable Origin.** If you select an Object that is the destination of another Object's cable, this command will select the later Object. **<SHIFT + O>**
- **Select Similar Objects.** This will select Fader Objects similar (such as the same type of Object) to the currently selected Fader Object or Objects.
- **Select Equal Objects.** This will select additional Objects that are identical (such as the same type of Object with the same settings) to the currently selected Object or Objects. All objects of the same type are "equal" except faders. All faders are "similar," but only faders with the same style are "equal."

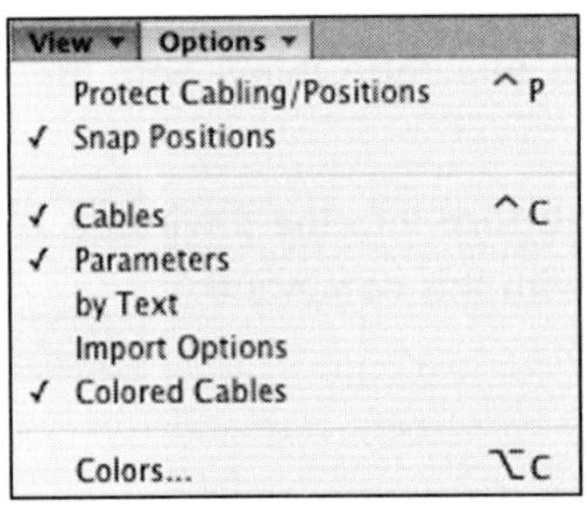

Figure 14.3
The local View menu of the Environment window.

View Menu

The View menu includes options for what will be displayed in the Environment window. Figure 14.3 shows the View menu of the Environment window.

A description of each View option appears below.

- **Protect Cabling/Positions.** With this checked, you will not be able to move Objects or remove any existing cabling between Objects. **<CONTROL + P>**
- **Snap Positions.** With this checked, Logic will snap newly created Objects to an internal grid to keep them more organized into rows and columns. Objects moved by dragging are also snapped to the grid.
- **Cables.** With this option engaged, you will be able to see the cabling between Objects; if it is unchecked, all cables will be hidden. **<CONTROL + C>**
- **Parameters.** This option shows the parameter box of the selected Object in the parameter bar at the left of the Environment window if it is checked.
- **By Text.** With this checked, Environment Objects will be displayed as text instead of as graphic Objects.
- **Import Options.** This option adds an entire new local menu to the Environment window, the Import window. This is useful when you are importing Environments from other Logic songs. This is discussed in detail in the "Environment Layers" section below.
- **Colored Cables.** With this option, cables will be the same color as the Environment Object.
- **Colors.** This launches the Color Palette window so you may color your Environment Objects.

Options Menu

The Options menu is a catchall local menu for additional Environment functions. Figure 14.4 shows the Options menu.

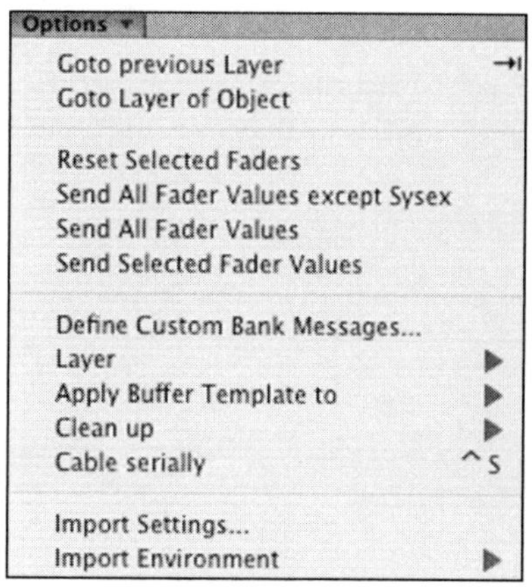

Figure 14.4
The local Options menu of the Environment window.

The various commands and submenus contained in the Options menu are detailed here.

- **Goto Previous Layer.** This will switch the current Environment layer to the previous Environment layer. **<ARROW + |>**

- **Goto Layer of Object.** If you have an Object selected in the All Objects layer, this command will switch the Environment to the layer that the selected Object is on.
- **Reset Selected Faders.** This command will cause all selected faders to return to their original values.
- **Send All Fader Values Except SysEx.** This will send all fader values to their recipient Objects except those faders sending SysEx data.
- **Send All Fader Values.** This will send all fader values to their recipient Objects, including those faders sending SysEx data.
- **Send Selected Fader Values.** This will send the fader values of selected faders to their recipient Objects.
- **Define Custom Bank Messages.** If you have a Multi-Instrument Object selected, and you double-click it to reveal its Multi-Instrument window, you can choose this option to launch a special Edit window in which you can define custom bank messages for each channel of your multi-instrument. Figure 14.5 shows the special Edit window.

  When finished, simply close the Edit window and your multi-instrument will have its custom bank messages defined.
- **Cable Serially.** This will cable all selected Objects. **<CONTROL + S>**

Figure 14.5
When you select and double-click a Multi-Instrument Object, you can use the Define Custom Bank Messages command in the Environment's local Options menu to launch this special Edit window to enter custom bank messages for your multi-instrument.

- **Import Settings.** This will open an open file window with additional options at the bottom of the window for you to select which elements of a Logic song you wish to import into the current Logic song. Figure 14.6 shows this dialog.

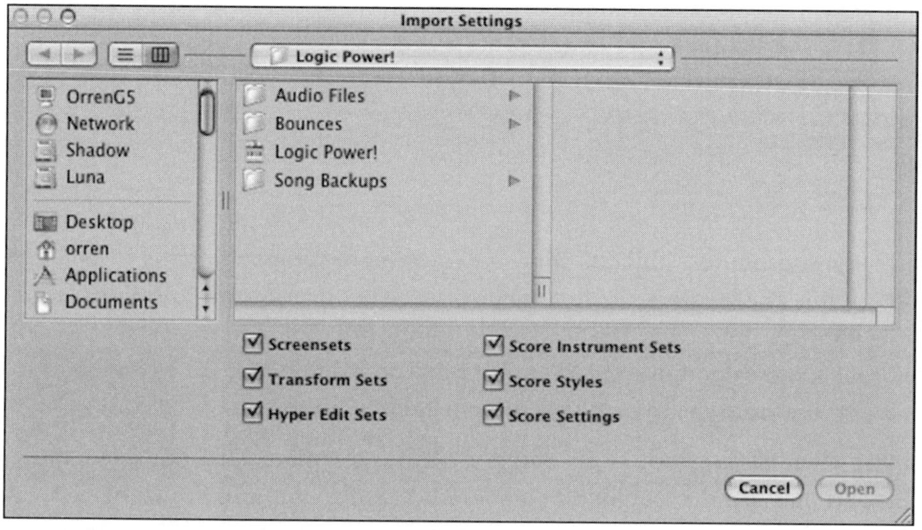

Figure 14.6
The Import Settings dialog is essentially an open file dialog with additional options for which song elements to import to the current Logic song.

Layer Submenu

The Layer submenu of the Options local menu includes two options, as shown in Figure 14.7: Insert and Delete. Insert will create a new, empty Environment layer that you can name anything you want by double-clicking on its name in the parameter bar. Delete will erase the current Environment layer.

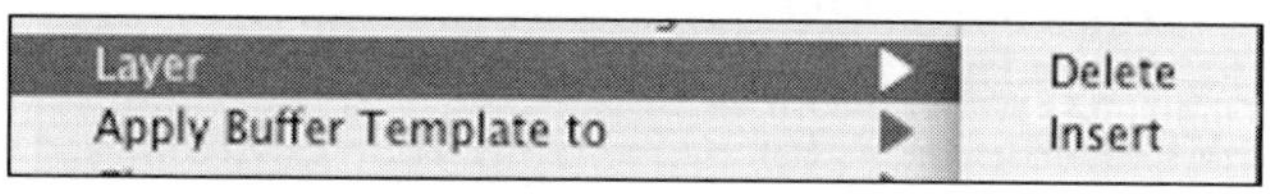

Figure 14.7
The Layer submenu of the local Options menu of the Environment window.

Apply Buffer Template to Submenu

When you build a virtual mixing desk or synthesizer controller in the Environment, you may find yourself using a significant number of Objects of the same type (such as a row of Fader Objects or Channel Splitters, all with the same spacing and settings). To save time defining and aligning all of these similar Objects, you may copy one or more Objects onto the Clipboard with either the Copy or Define Template command and use that Object (or group of Objects) as a template for the rest of your Objects in your construction.

The Apply Buffer Template To submenu, shown in Figure 14.8, consists of options to apply specific characteristics of your template Objects to the selected Objects.

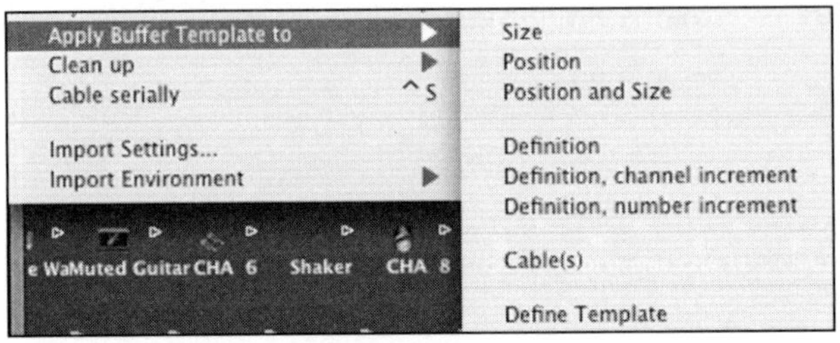

Figure 14.8
The Apply Buffer Template To submenu of the local Options menu of the Environment.

To align a group of Objects, choose two or more Objects in rows or columns whose horizontal or vertical alignment you want transferred to the rest of your Objects, and copy them onto the Clipboard. You can the select the rest of your Objects and use the Size, Position, or Position and Size command to transfer the positioning and size of your template Objects.

If you want to transfer the parameters of your template Objects, select the Objects and use the Definition command. You also can use the Definition, Channel Increment command to have the channel number of each Object increase from the top-left Object onward, or the Definition, Number Increment to increment the first data byte of whatever is being defined (such as a MIDI controller number). Definition, Definition Channel Increment, and Definition Number Increment apply only to faders. Finally, you can use your template to transfer the cabling of your template with the Cable(s) command.

Clean Up Submenu

The Clean Up submenu of the Options menu, as shown in Figure 14.9, contains three options for organizing your Environment window: Align Objects, Positions by Grid, and Size by Default.

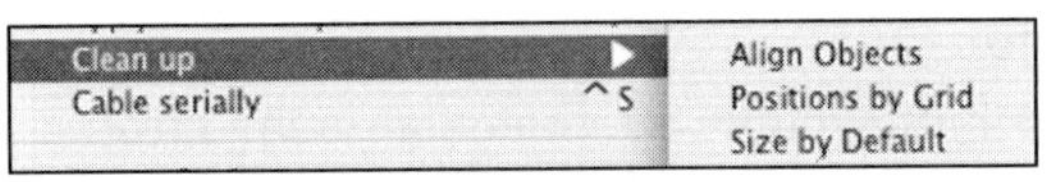

Figure 14.9
The Clean Up submenu of the local Options menu of the Environment.

The three options have the following effects on the currently selected Objects:

- **Align Objects.** This command will put all selected Objects into a row or column, depending on the orientation of the top or leftmost two Objects.

- **Positions by Grid.** This command will position all selected Objects in a grid pattern in case **View > Snap Positions** is not checked.
- **Size by Default.** This command will size all selected Objects to their default size.

Import Environment Submenu

The Import Environment submenu of the local Options menu, shown in Figure 14.10, contains seven options for importing Environments from other Logic songs. These options enable you to import some or all of another song's Environment in a number of different ways.

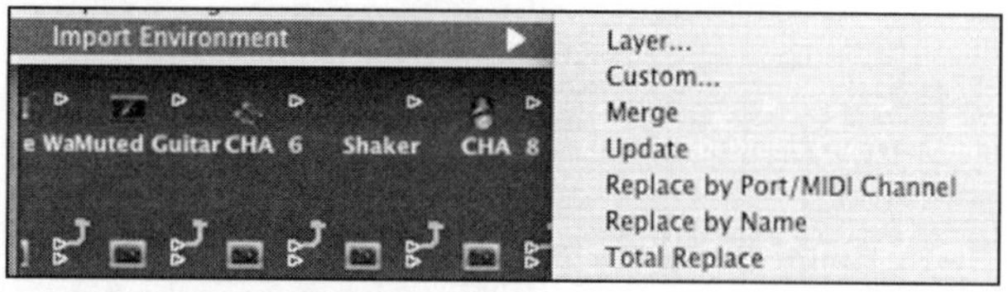

Figure 14.10

The Import Environment submenu of the local Options menu of the Environment.

The options in this submenu are explained below:

- **Layer.** If you have two Logic songs open, this option will present you with a dialog showing a pull-down menu of the other song's Environment layers to import. If you do not have two songs open, this option will first present you with a dialog box to select another Logic song from which you want to import an Environment. When you choose the Environment layer you want to import, it will be added to the Environment of your current song.
- **Custom.** This opens a special version of the All Objects layer of the song you want to import from and lets you pick which individual Objects you want to import. You will notice that this option creates the same Import local menu that the Import Options command in the local View menu opens. This menu enables you to mark each individual Object as one you want to keep, delete, reassign in some way as you import the Environment, and so on. Figure 14.11 shows the Environment window opened by the Custom command.

  When you are finished assigning each Object in the Environment you want to import, choose **Import Environment Using Current Assignment**, and your custom import will be complete.
- **Merge.** This will merge the Environment you want to import into the Environment of the current song.

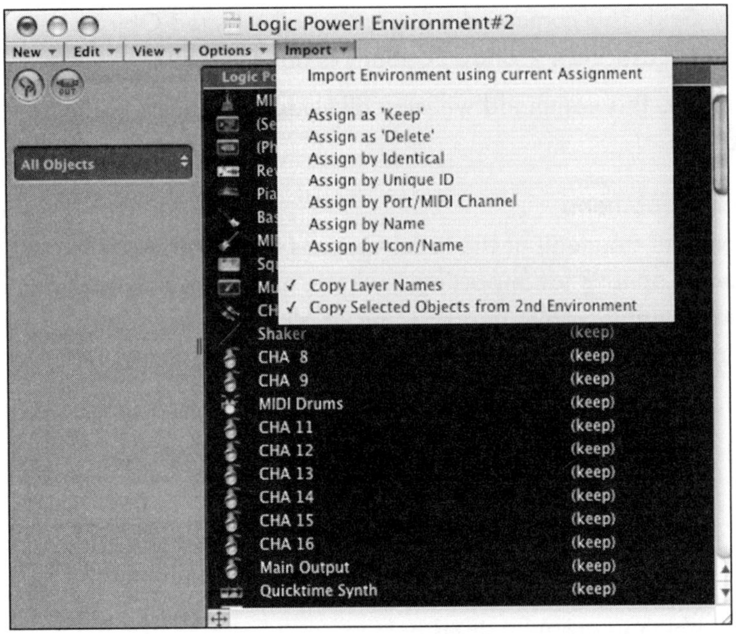

Figure 14.11

The specially colored All Objects Environment layer of the Environment to be imported. Use the Import local menu, also shown, to assign each Object, and then select Import Environment Using Current Assignment.

- **Update.** This is useful if you have a song with a very similar or identical Environment that you want to import. This will update your song's Environment with more recent changes made in the Environment you want to import.
- **Replace by Port/MIDI Channel.** This will import Objects from another Environment by replacing only those Objects that are set to similar ports and MIDI Channels as Objects in the current song.
- **Replace by Name.** This will replace only Environmental layers in the current song with Environment layers with the same name.
- **Total Replace.** This command completely replaces the Environment of the current song with the Environment you are importing.

Environment Window Buttons

The Environment window has two buttons in its parameter bar, as shown in Figure 14.12: a Link button to link the Environment to the frontmost window in the screenset and a MIDI OUT button to enable MIDI to be sent from the Environment. You will generally want to leave both of these buttons engaged.

Figure 14.12

The Environment window buttons.

Environment Toolbox

Directly under the Environment buttons is the Environment Toolbox, as shown in Figure 14.13.

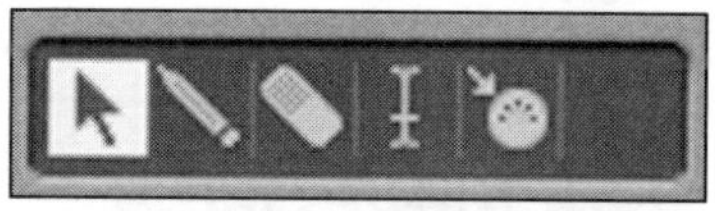

Figure 14.13

The Environment Toolbox.

The tools in the Environment's Toolbox are described below, from left to right:

- **Pointer.** This is the standard pointer for selecting, dragging, and rubber-banding Objects.
- **Pencil.** The Pencil tool will add a duplicate of the most recently created Object to the Environment. Dragging with the Pencil tool will create multiple Objects.
- **Eraser.** With this tool, you can delete any Object you click.
- **Text Entry.** You can enter text in text boxes that you click on with this tool. Simply click the text at the bottom of an Object to type a new name for it.
- **MIDI Connector.** When you click on a MIDI Instrument with this tool, the selected Arrange track will immediately change its assignment to the Object you clicked on.

Environment Objects

Objects are the building blocks of the Environment. Objects represent the devices and processes that you construct your virtual studio from. Some Objects do not themselves do anything other than give you a view of what data is being transferred. The subsections below offer some details about each Object not already discussed in previous chapters. As always, remember that these descriptions are designed to get you started, not to cover every single possible setting and option for each Object.

You create Objects by choosing them from the New local menu in the Environment. Refer back to Figure 14.1 for all of the Objects available in this menu.

Instrument Object

The Instrument Object was covered in detail in Chapter 4, "Creating Your Autoload Song."

Multi-Instrument Object

The Multi-Instrument Object was covered in detail in Chapter 4.

Mapped Instrument Object

The Mapped Instrument Object was covered in detail in Chapter 4.

Touch Tracks Object

The Touch Tracks Object, shown in Figure 14.14, enables you to use Logic as an interactive live sequencer, not simply a recording tool. With Touch Tracks, you can play an entire MIDI region (or even a Folder Track full of MIDI regions) live from a MIDI controller (a keyboard, guitar synthesizer, etc.). This is really useful for groups and artists with sequenced tracks in their music that want to be able to trigger entire sequences during a live performance.

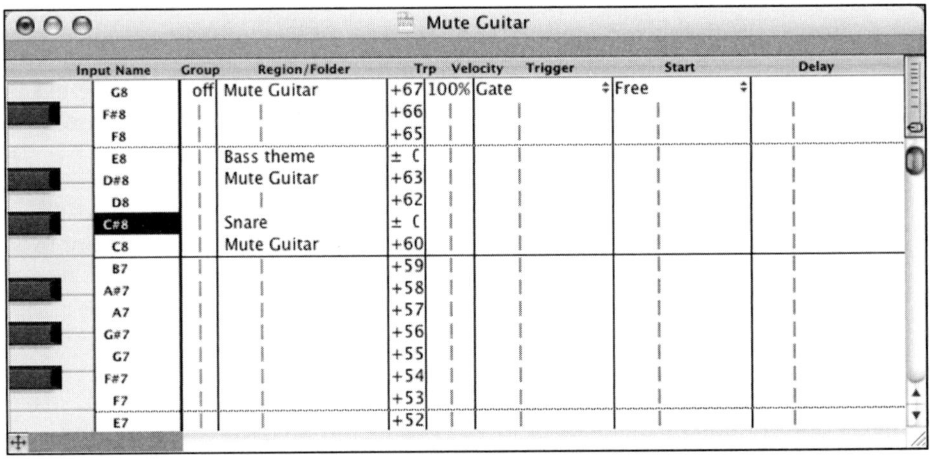

Figure 14.14
The Touch Tracks Object, including its expanded Touch Tracks window and parameter box.

Setting up a Touch Tracks Object couldn't be easier—after you create and double-click your Touch Tracks Object, simply drag your MIDI regions (or folder with MIDI regions inside) to the key that you want to trigger that region. You also can drag a MIDI region into the Environment, and Logic will create a Touch Tracks Objects automatically configured for every key on the keyboard to trigger your MIDI region.

Notice that the parameter box of the Touch Tracks Object includes the same basic MIDI parameters that are defined for Instrument Objects in Chapter 4. Keep in mind that even though the Touch Tracks Object has an output triangle to cable it to other Objects, you cannot actually cable Touch Tracks to anything else.

When you use Touch Tracks live, you'll want to mute those regions and folders in Arrange assigned to the Touch Tracks Object to ensure that those regions only play when you trigger them, and not as part of your pre-programmed sequence. Of course, if you *want* your MIDI regions to play exactly as programmed in addition to being available for you to perform live via Touch Tracks, do not mute those regions in the Arrange.

You can see in Figure 14.14 that the expanded Touch Tracks window shows the name of the MIDI region or folder assigned to a given note. There are a number of parameters across the top bar of the window that are defined below:

- **Input Name.** This is the name of the note. If you select a number of notes by dragging on them and then drag a MIDI region into the Touch Tracks Sequence column, the MIDI region will be assigned to the selected notes.
- **Group.** As in the Hyper Editor, if you assign a number of MIDI regions to the same group, when you trigger one of them, all the other regions in the same group will stop playing.
- **Region/Folder.** This is where the name of the MIDI region or folder will appear. If the notes below a given region are assigned to that region, you will see a vertical line instead of a name.
- **Trp.** This column lets you know how many steps your part is transposed at that note. If your region is played across the entire keyboard, the transposition at the extreme ends will be pretty severe. If your region is not transposed at all, this column will be blank.
- **Velocity.** This determines how much the velocity at which you trigger a region will affect the velocities already in the region you are playing. 100% means your trigger velocity will affect the velocity that the region plays back at significantly, 50% means there will be some effect, and Off means there will be no effect on the region's velocities.
- **Trigger.** This column determines how playback will be handled. There are a number of different trigger modes:
    - **Multi.** Playing the trigger note will start playing the MIDI region; playing the note again starts a second playback of the region without stopping the original region's playback.
    - **Single.** Playing the trigger note starts the MIDI region playing; playing the note again restarts playback of the MIDI region.
    - **Gate.** The MIDI region plays until the note is released or the end of the MIDI region is reached.
    - **Gate Loop.** The MIDI region loops until the trigger note is released.

- **Toggle.** Playing the trigger note starts playback; playing it again stops playback.

- **Start.** You can quantize how playback will begin and end with this parameter. Free means there is no quantization. Next 1/16, 1/4, or 1/1 will start the next region you trigger playing at the next 1/16, 1/4, or bar interval, depending on your selection.
- **Delay.** This enables you to set a delay for when playback will begin. The left side of the column sets the delay in note values, the right side sets delay in ticks.

> **EXPERT TIP: USING TOUCH TRACKS TO TRIGGER AUDIO**
>
> Touch Tracks work only with MIDI regions, not Audio regions. But you can still use Touch Tracks to trigger audio parts if you have a sampler. Record the audio parts you want to be triggered as samples, and then trigger those samples from a MIDI region in Logic. If you don't own a hardware sampler with enough memory to handle all the audio you want to trigger, you can use software instruments such as the Emagic EXS24mkII sampler to stream samples directly from your hard drive. You may need to adjust the delay parameter if you notice some latency. This way, the Touch Tracks Object will allow you to trigger a sampler that will in turn trigger your audio!

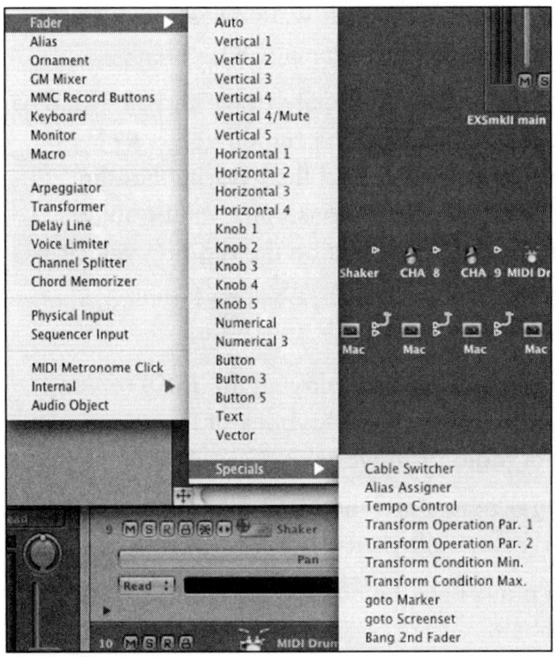

Figure 14.15
The submenus of fader types in the New local menu of the Environment. Despite how many varieties of faders there are, they all do basically the same thing—send MIDI events to Objects.

Fader Object

Fader Objects enable you to send MIDI events to different Objects. There are many different fader varieties, as Figure 14.15 shows.

All faders have the same parameters, as shown in Figure 14.16. All of them can be set to accept various MIDI message types as inputs or outputs, can be set to different values, and can be adjusted by the user.

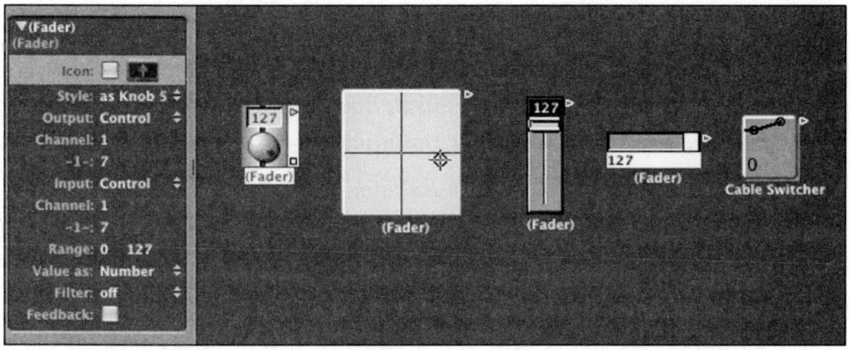

Figure 14.16
Despite the varieties of faders, all have the same parameter box.

The parameter box of Fader Objects, from top to bottom, includes the following parameters:

- **Object Name.** You can name your fader by clicking in this text box.
- **Icon.** You can select an icon for your text box. This is of limited use, as you'll rarely want a fader to show up in the Arrange window.
- **Style.** You can use this to change the style of your fader; for example, you can turn your knob fader into a horizontal fader or change your cable switcher to look like a knob.
- **Output.** This enables you to select what sort of event will be output from the fader. Your choices are various MIDI events: Switch (for a cable switcher), Fader (to send automation data to Logic), or Meta (for sending Logic's internal Meta messages to other Environment Objects or to Logic's sequencer).
- **Channel.** This determines the MIDI Channel on which the fader will output.
- **-1-.** This determines the control message the fader will output. It is the note number if the fader definition is Note or P-Pres, the MSB if the fader definition is Pitchbend, and has no meaning for C-Pres and SysEx.
- **Input.** For faders that accept input such as cable switchers, this determines the type of input message that it will accept. All faders accept input. The In definition and its components determine which MIDI messages will control the fader remotely. The special thing about the cable switcher in this context is that the message corresponding to the In definition will switch the switch rather than passing through it.

- **Channel.** For faders that accept input, this determines the MIDI Channel on which the fader looks for input.
- **-1-.** For faders that accept input, this determines the MIDI message number the fader looks for on input.
- **Range.** The minimum and maximum MIDI values for the fader. Full range is 0 to 127, but you can narrow the range for your fader if you wish.
- **Value As.** You can choose your fader to display its value as a number, dB value, Hz value, pan value, and so forth, depending on the type of data the fader is handling.
- **Filter.** Usually, this is used to filter which type of incoming messages the fader responds to, in order to prevent MIDI doubling or feedback for MIDI hardware devices that do not have a Local Off or MIDI THRU Off function. When used properly, the filter parameter can be one of the fader's most useful features, but because it deals with advanced MIDI meta data and hardware MIDI functioning, it is far beyond the scope of this book. It is better to ignore this parameter, which is why the default is Off.
- **Feedback.** The Feedback check box enables you to create cabling feedback loops (which Logic otherwise prevents). Leave it unchecked unless you know what you're doing.

As you start creating your own macros and Environment construction in Logic, you can cable Fader Objects to other Objects so that you can send data and change parameters with the mouse. As your Environment creations become more advanced, you will find Fader Objects to be a very important Object in your arsenal.

Alias Object

If you select an Object and then choose **New > Alias** from the local New menu of the Environment, you will create an Alias—or duplicate—of your original Object. Figure 14.17 shows an Alias of a MIDI Instrument Object next to its parent Object.

The Alias Object is effectively identical to the original, but it does have a parameter box that allows you to rename it, choose a new icon, set which Object it is referring to, and choose whether you want it to share its name and size with its parent object. The main use for Alias Objects is when you

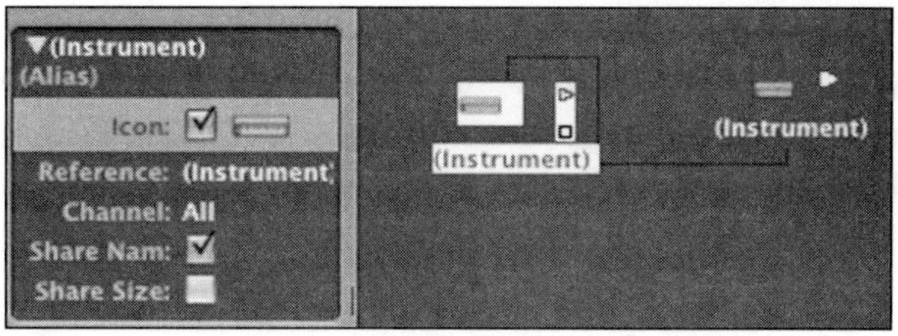

Figure 14.17
An Alias Object next to its parent Object.

need many identical faders. You can configure a single Fader Object and then create as many Alias Objects as you need. Each will be set to the proper style, channel, MIDI event, and so on automatically, and each fader can be adjusted independently.

Ornament Object

This Object is simply an empty box. Seriously. The color parameter has no effect on the Ornament Object. Its sole purpose is to be background behind an Environment construction. You can perhaps use the Ornament Object as an organizational aid by putting a boundary around your Environment construction. If you seem a little doubtful as to the value of this object, join the club!

GM Mixer Object

The GM Mixer Object is designed to control the 16 MIDI Channels of a MIDI hardware device that conforms to the GM, XG, or GS standard. The Object appears as a self-contained mixer consisting of MIDI channel strips from the Track Mixer, as Figure 14.18 shows.

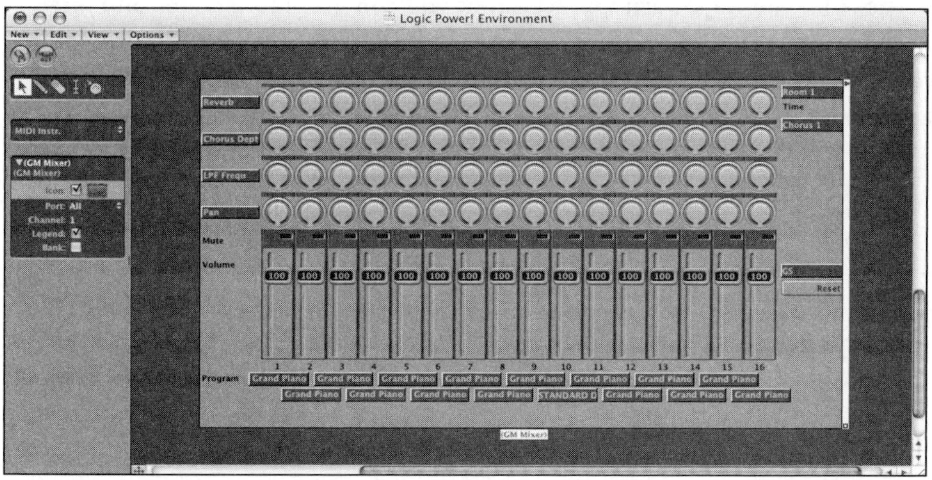

Figure 14.18
The GM Mixer. You'll need this only if you are using Logic to control 16 MIDI Channels of a General MIDI device.

This mixer should be pretty straightforward to operate, since I've discussed channel strips in detail previously. You will most likely never use this object unless you use an external General MIDI sound source, and even then, I'd highly recommend you use the simpler, more intuitive, and more powerful Track Mixer for mixing your MIDI tracks.

MMC Record Switches Object

The MIDI Machine Control (MMC) Record Switches Object gives you 21 memory buttons (or switches) that you can use to trigger various setups on your MIDI hardware. Not many hardware boxes use MMC, and for those that do, usually the most important functions are the Transport functions, which do not require this object.

Keyboard Object

The Keyboard Object, as shown in Figure 14.19, creates a virtual MIDI keyboard in the Environment.

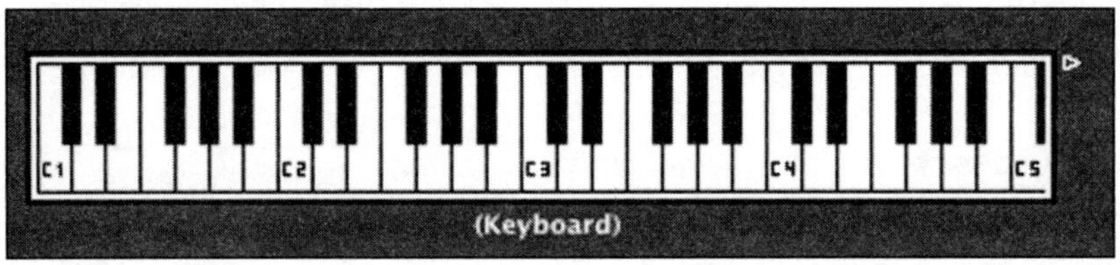

Figure 14.19
The Keyboard Object. You can cable this to other Objects in order to send them MIDI notes.

This keyboard can then be cabled to Environment Objects, and when you click on a key in the virtual keyboard, that MIDI note will be sent. The main purpose for the Keyboard Object is that you can use it to monitor and test your Environment constructions to ensure that they react properly when receiving MIDI notes. This saves you from needing an external keyboard hooked up if you just want to test something quickly.

Monitor Object

The Monitor Object is a window that displays all events passing through it. It is a very useful testing tool, and it also can be used to branch cables because it accepts input from one source but can output to many sources. Figure 14.20 shows a Keyboard Object feeding a Monitor Object.

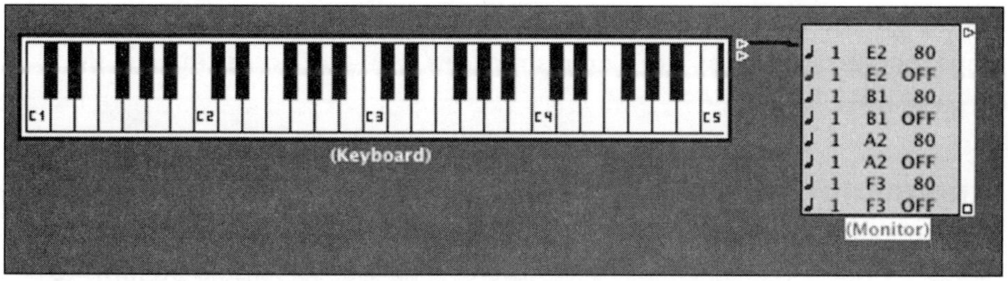

Figure 14.20

A Monitor Object displaying all the notes being sent by the Keyboard Object.

Macro

Macros are not actually Objects, but collections of Environment Objects and their cabling. You create a macro by selecting all the Objects that you have in your construction and then choosing **New > Macro** from the New local menu of the Environment. Figure 14.21 shows an Environment construction that has been packed into a macro. If you wish to create a macro that cannot be unpacked, select **New > Macro** with the **CONTROL** key pressed.

You can cable macros to other Objects just like any other, you can check their Icon parameter to have them available in the Arrange window's track hierarchical menus, and so on. You can even nest macros within macros! Be aware that there is a limit to the number of Objects you can have in a macro, based on how much processing they are doing (roughly 60 Objects is the maximum).

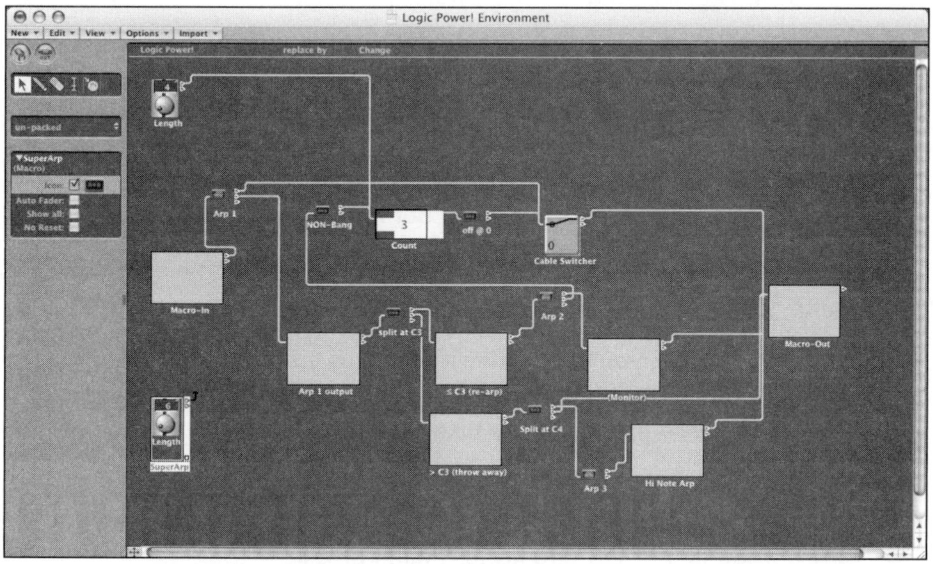

Figure 14.21

In this figure, you can see a complex construction of signal splitters, monitors, and arpeggiators that has been packed into a macro, at the bottom of the Environment window, called Super Arp.

The advantage of macros is that they are more portable to other Logic songs, and because they are single structures, you can access them in the Arrange track list.

Arpeggiator Object

The Arpeggiator Object will "arpeggiate" chords by cycling through all held notes in a user-selectable pattern. To be used, the Arpeggiator Object must be cabled to a MIDI device, and Logic's Transport must be running. You can use the arpeggiator to arpeggiate MIDI data in realtime, or you can record its output by cabling it to the Sequencer Input Object (be sure to record to a No Output track so you don't hear everything doubled!). Figure 14.22 shows the Arpeggiator Object and its parameter box.

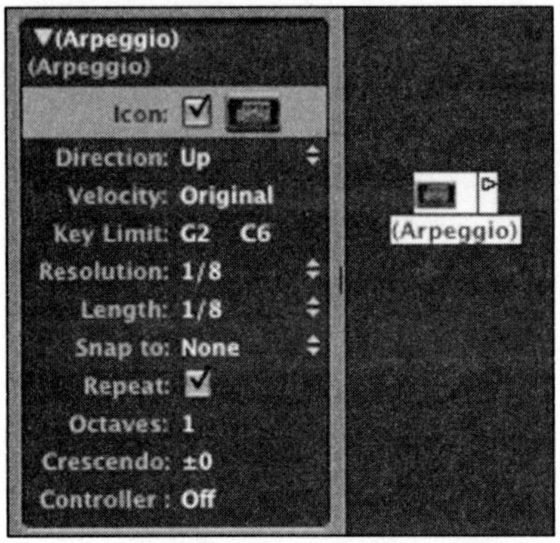

Figure 14.22
The Arpeggiator Object and its parameter box.

The Arpeggiator Object offers the following parameters:

- **Direction.** You have seven options for the direction of your arpeggio.
  - **Up.** Lowest note to highest note.
  - **Down.** Highest note to lowest note.
  - **UpDn.** Up and down; low to high, then high to low. Notes repeat after each cycle.
  - **Auto.** Up or down, depending on whether the second note in the chord is played before or after the first note.
  - **UpDn2.** Similar to UpDn above, but the notes do not repeat.
  - **Rand.** Notes play in random order.
  - **All.** All notes play at the same time.
- **Velocity.** This lets you choose the velocity of the arpeggiated notes. Orig will retain the original velocities of the notes, and Rand will randomize the velocities between 1 and the original value, or you can select a fixed velocity between 1 and 127.
- **Key Limit.** You can define the pitch limits of the arpeggiator here, down to a pitch of G2 and up to a pitch of G8.

- **Resolution.** This lets you set the note resolution of the arpeggios. All note divisions are represented in the pull-down menu. A value of none means the arpeggiator is switched off.
- **Length.** This lets you set the length of each arpeggiated note. This parameter offers a pull-down menu with all the note divisions represented. Orig will keep the same length as the performed notes for the arpeggiated notes.
- **Snap To.** If you want the arpeggiator to start and end arpeggiations only on a specific note division, you can set that here. This can be helpful in trying to sync the arpeggiator to other MIDI data.
- **Repeat.** If this is set to ON, the arpeggiator will continue as long as you hold the chord down. If this is set to OFF, the chord will stop as soon as all notes in the arpeggio have been played one time.
- **Octaves.** You can set the arpeggiator to repeat over up to 10 octaves.
- **Crescendo.** This will add or subtract the given velocity value each time the arpeggio is repeated.
- **Controller.** This will enable the parameters of the arpeggiator to be controlled remotely by controller events if the parameter is set to ON. The setting for this parameter is a number representing the lowest MIDI CC# used to control arpeggiator settings. That CC# controls the top parameter (Direction), and consecutive CC#s control the remaining parameters, counting down from the top.

You can use more than a single Arpeggiator Object in a single Environment construction, so even if you don't feel Logic's arpeggiator offers the most cutting-edge options, you can build your own cutting-edge arpeggiator macro or structure. That's the power of the Environment!

Transformer Object

The Transformer Object enables you to cable a realtime Transform window into your Environment creations. As you can see in Figure 14.23, when double-clicked, the Transformer opens up to a smaller Transform window that is functionally similar to the Transform window discussed in Chapter 9, "Working with MIDI," with the exception that there are no time-based parameters because the Transformer Object works in realtime.

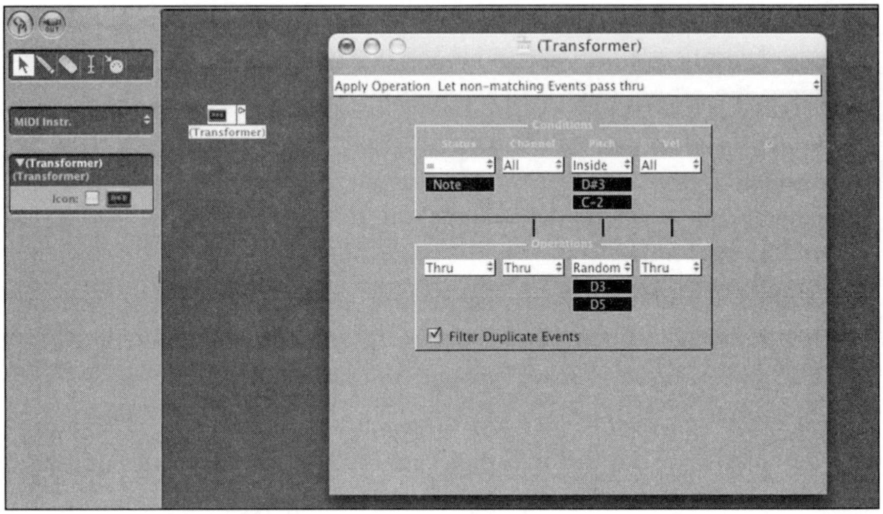

Figure 14.23
The Transformer Object is an Environment Object version of the MIDI Transform window. Use this to make complex transformations of your MIDI data in your Environment constructions.

As your Environment creations become more complex, you can use the transformer to select and transform MIDI data running through your Environment as you would use the Transform window to modify your region data. Please refer to the Transform window section in Chapter 9 for more on the full power of this Object.

Delay Line Object

This Object creates a "MIDI echo" effect by adding multiple repeats of MIDI data. Figure 14.24 shows the Delay Line Object and its parameter box.

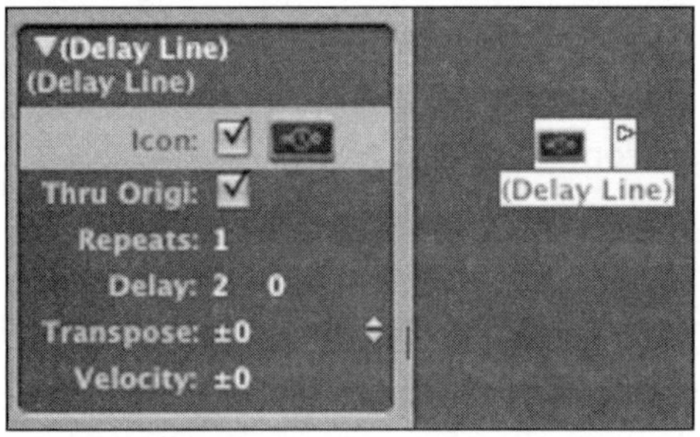

Figure 14.24
The Delay Line Object and its parameter box.

The Delay Line Object offers the following parameters:

- **Thru Original.** If this box is checked, the original signal also will pass through the delay line along with the repeats. If this box is unchecked, the original MIDI data will not pass through.

- **Repeats.** This is the number of repeats, from 0 to 99. (No repeats means the delay line is off).
- **Delay.** The delay time between repeats. The left value is divisions, the right value is ticks.
- **Transpose.** You can choose to transpose the repeats with this parameter, either up or down 99 semitones.
- **Velocity.** You can change the velocity values of the notes by adding or subtracting a MIDI value of up to 99 per repeat.

If you feel like experimenting, you can cable together the arpeggiator and delay line to create some very wild and interesting MIDI repeats! However, if you use multiple outputs of the delay line, individual repeats will cycle through them. Also keep in mind that the delay line repeats all messages, not just notes.

Voice Limiter Object

The Voice Limiter Object restricts the number of voices that are sent to a MIDI Object by turning off any MIDI notes over a selected limit. You can restrict a MIDI Instrument to between 1 and 32 notes. There are only two parameters: Voices, where you define how many voices the Voice Limiter will limit the instrument to, and Priority, where you decide which notes will be turned off first—the highest (Bot, giving low notes priority), lowest (Top, giving high notes priority), or first performed (Last, giving most recently performed notes priority).

If you are making a MIDI Environment that sends out more notes than your MIDI devices can handle, this can be useful. If you have older synthesizers that do not have the high voice counts (64 or more) of modern instruments, you may find this Object useful.

Channel Splitter Object

The Channel Splitter Object, as shown in Figure 14.25, routes MIDI events according to their MIDI Channel. It offers one output for each of the 16 MIDI Channels and an additional SUM output that combines all channels not specifically routed to other Objects.

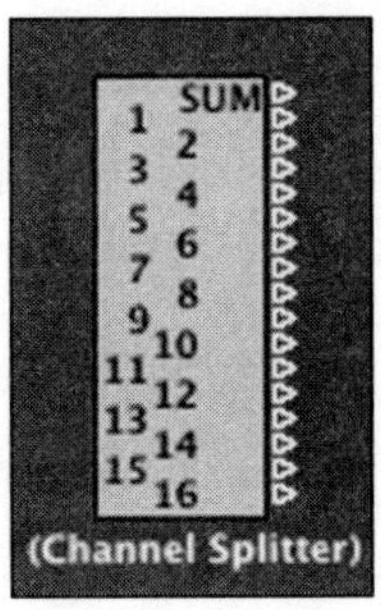

Figure 14.25
The Channel Splitter Object enables you to route individual MIDI Channels to different locations.

This Object is great for constructions in which you want to route specific MIDI Channels to specific destinations. You can process each MIDI Channel separately this way, or you can separate only a few channels, and the rest will appear at the SUM output.

Chord Memorizer Object

The Chord Memorizer Object has a number of functions. It can map single notes into chords. The chords can contain 12 notes or fewer. The chord memorizer also can be used as a "scale filter" by mapping out-of-scale notes to nothing. The Chord Memorizer window consists of two keyboards: one for inputting/incoming the note to map to a chord, and a second for inputting the chord. Figure 14.26 shows the Chord Memorizer Object, its parameter box, and its window.

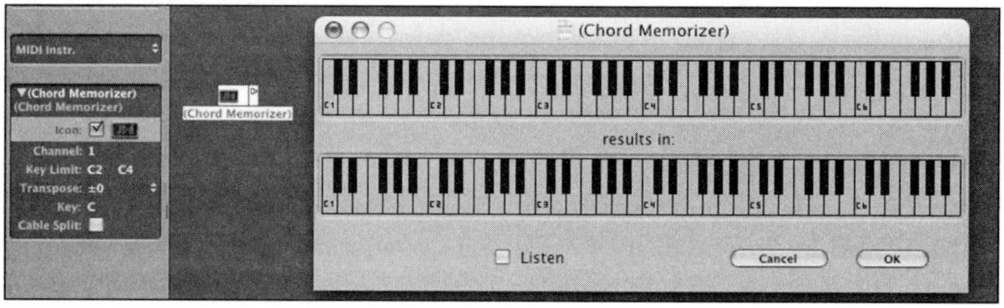

Figure 14.26
The Chord Memorizer Object, its parameter box, and the Chord Memorizer window.

The parameter box of the Chord Memorizer contains the following parameters:

- **Channel.** The Chord Memorizer will output all notes to this MIDI Channel.
- **Key Limit.** The notes within this range will be mapped to chords. Notes outside this range pass through the Chord Memorizer unchanged.
- **Transpose.** You can transpose the chords that are output up or down 99 semitones with this parameter.
- **Key.** The entire chord map will be transposed to the key you set here.
- **Cable Split.** This parameter, if ON, will split each note of the chord down a different cable, if you have enough cables.

The easiest way to configure the Chord Memorizer is to click on an input note in the top keyboard, and then click on the notes on the bottom keyboard until the entire chord you want has been played. If you click a key by mistake and turn on a note you do not want in your chord, a second click will turn that note off. When you are finished with the chord, click the OK button or another input note to configure another note in the same Chord Memorizer.

You can have a single Chord Memorizer memorize only one chord for each input note—so if you input a C and then selected a chord, then input a D and selected a chord, and then input C again and input a final chord, the only chords that would be stored in the Chord Memorizer would be the chord for the D note and the second chord for the C note. Of course, you can create as many Chord Memorizer Objects as you'd like.

All octaves within the CM range use the same chord, and the relations between the input note's octave and the output chord notes' octaves are preserved.

Physical Input Object

This Object has an input for up to 64 physical MIDI interface channels. In general, the only Physical Input Object you will need is the one created with your initial song. This is normally connected to the Sequencer Input Object so that the MIDI hardware can be recorded by the sequencer.

You can have only one physical input. If you create a new one, the old one is deleted along with all its cabling. If you have no physical input, all MIDI input is automatically routed to Logic's sequencer.

Sequencer Input Object

This Object represents the input to Logic's sequencer (in other words, the Arrange tracks). You will generally have a single Sequencer Input Object in a song, and that will be enough. Logic automatically creates one with each song.

You can have only one sequencer input. If you create a new one, the old one is deleted along with all its cabling.

The only reason to have the physical input/sequencer input combination is to insert other processes between them. Otherwise, you can do without either.

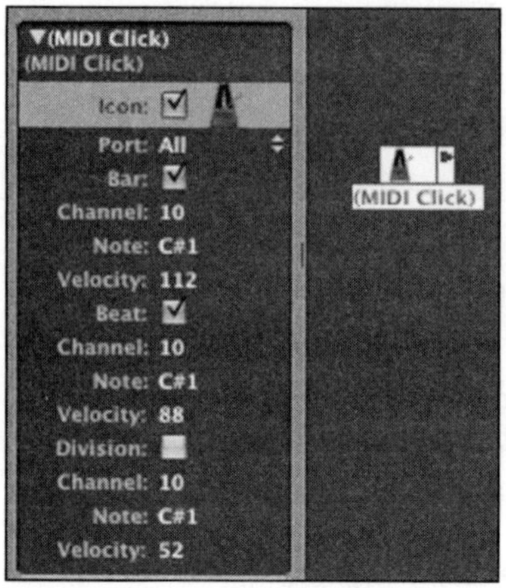

Figure 14.27
The MIDI Metronome Object and its parameter box. You can set up which MIDI note the Object will send to your MIDI device for different beats.

MIDI Metronome Object

The MIDI Metronome Object was previously discussed in Chapter 6, "The Transport Window." It enables you to use an external MIDI device to act as the metronome by generating a click in time with Logic's tempo. Figure 14.27 shows the MIDI Metronome Object and its parameter box.

The MIDI Metronome Object is pretty complete. As you can see in Figure 14.27, it enables you to send different notes for up to three beats and lets you set the note, channel, and velocity for each. However, MIDI timing can never be as accurate as the Klopfgeist software click, which is sample accurate. Therefore, I recommend that you do not use this object.

Another use for the MIDI Metronome Object (made more convenient by the addition of the Klopfgeist) is as a timer for other Environment processes. For example, you can use it to drive a MIDI LFO made from arpeggiators or delay lines.

Internal Objects

These Objects were discussed in Chapter 10, "Working with Audio Instruments in Logic."

Audio Objects

Audio Objects have been discussed in depth starting in Chapter 1 and continuing through chapters 2, 4, 8, and 12. Please feel free to re-read anything you're not clear on, and return to this point at your leisure.

Cabling Environment Objects

Now that you have an overview of the Objects you can cable together to create your own unique Environment constructions, let's talk about cabling. The basics of cabling are extremely simple: As you grab the small triangular outlet in the top-right of every Object and click the mouse, the mouse pointer will turn into a patch cord plug. You simply drag that patch cable to the Object you want to cable your initial Object to, and when you release the mouse, a gray line will connect the two Objects, indicating they are cabled together. Figure 14.28 illustrates a very simple cabling.

Figure 14.28

Here you see an Instrument Object being cabled to the Arpeggiator Object. After clicking on the triangle in the top-right of the Instrument Object, the pointer turned into the patch plug, and when the mouse is released on the Arpeggiator Object, the two Objects will be cabled together. At that point, the arpeggiator can be selected on an Arrange track, and when you hit Play in Logic and perform with your MIDI Instrument, the result will be arpeggiated.

As Figure 14.28 shows, creating a basic Environment structure is very simple. As you've no doubt already surmised, you can cable far more than two objects together. In fact, you can cable an unlimited number of cables into an Object. All incoming MIDI data is simply mixed at the input of the Object. You can also notice from Figure 14.28 that as soon as one output cable was used, another output triangle appeared directly beneath the first triangle. Again, this is so you can output as many cables from an Object as you wish. Keep in mind the limit mentioned above of about 60 Objects in a macro, however, so your constructions don't get too out of hand! To delete cabling, simply click on a cable with the Eraser tool or press **DELETE**.

You can cable Objects serially by selecting **Option > Cable Serially**. You might want to do this to cable all the faders in a synthesizer mixer you are constructing, for example. You can use the **Apply Buffer Template To > Cable(s)** function if you want to cable many Objects to the same destination. And if you want each cable to be the same color as the Object from which it originated, choose **View > Colored Cables**. You can even cable Objects between more than one Environment layer; layers are discussed in the next section.

Special Cable Outputs

Certain Objects—Channel Splitter, Cable Switcher, Delay Line, Chord Memorizer in CableSplit mode, Transformer Object in Condition Splitter, Alternating Split, and TA Splitter modes, and Physical Input—have functionally different outputs, as opposed to normal Objects where each additional output sends the same data. When using one of these special Objects, if you want to route a signal from a single output to more than one destination, you'll need to use a Monitor Object. The Monitor Object itself doesn't do anything to the data (other than give you a window to view it), but like other Objects, it can have as many outputs as you need.

Environment Layers

Layers are different display windows of the Environment. They enable you to organize your Environment so that you are not flooded with too much information at a time, and you can create layers to house only those constructions you want to use at a given time. You can easily switch from one Environment layer to another by choosing the **Options > Go to Previous Layer** command or by using the pull-down menu of Layers directly under the Toolbox in the parameter bar of the Environment. Figure 14.29 shows you the Layer pull-down menu in the parameter box.

Figure 14.29
The Layer box, inside the parameter bar of the Environment. Here you see the MIDI Instrument layer. If you click on the box, the pull-down menu of all available layers will appear.

To create a new layer, you have two options. You can choose **Options > Layer > Insert** to insert a new layer above the current layer. You can also select the last option in the Layer box pull-down menu, **Create!**. This will create a new layer at the end of the Layer list. You can then name the layer by double-clicking the Layer box to open a text window for you to type into. All newly created layers are devoid of Objects, waiting for you to fill them with your constructions.

Specialized Layers

You can do anything you want with all the layers in your Environment—even the layers automatically created for you by Logic—except for two protected layers: the All Objects layer and the Global Objects layer.

The first layer in the Environment is always the All Objects layer, with one exception (noted below). This layer lists every object in the Environment. You can use this layer to quickly get an overview of all the Objects you are using or to navigate to a specific Object. You can also select an Object, choose **Options > Goto Layer of Object** in order to switch from the All Objects layer to the layer on which your selected Object resides.

The other protected layer is the second one, the Global Objects layer. In this layer you can place Objects that you wish to appear in every layer in your Environment. This is useful if you want particular output ports on every layer, for example. Be very sparing in the Objects you place here, however, because they can clutter up your Environment layers pretty quickly.

Objects and Layers

Layers are purely an organizational and aesthetic partition; they do not actually separate the Objects from each other in any way. You can move an Object from one layer to another by selecting an Object, then choosing a new layer from the Layer box while pressing the **OPTION** key. You also can use the Clipboard to cut, copy, and paste Objects from one layer to another. Since you can open more than one instance of any window in Logic, you can also open multiple Environment windows and simply drag an Object from a layer in one Environment window to a different layer in the second Environment window.

Not only can you easily move Objects between layers, but you can cable Objects between layers as well. As above, you can simply open two Environment windows and drag a cable from an Object in one Environment window to an Object in the other Environment window, regardless of the layer each window has visible. You can also hold down the **OPTION** key while clicking and dragging on the output triangle of an Object to bring up a pop-up menu of available instruments to which you may cable your Object simply by selecting it. A cable connection between layers looks like a cable that goes through a hole in the ceiling, as shown in Figure 14.30.

Figure 14.30
An Object cabled to an Object on a different layer of the Environment.

Building Your Own Environments

Everyone ends up with a completely customized workspace in Logic, thanks to the power and flexibility of the Environment. Hopefully, the details provided in this chapter are enough to get you started cabling your own Environment constructions together. Go ahead and experiment—that's the best way to learn!

Space requirements mean that since this chapter is already nearing the 30-page mark, there aren't as many tips, tricks, and tutorials as you might have liked. Luckily, the author of *Emagic Logic Tips and Tricks* wrote an entire book in the form of PDF tutorials and prebuilt Environments called *The Environment Toolkit*—and it's free! You can obtain it directly from his Web site: http://www.swiftkick.com. This Web site is perhaps the best Environment support site on the Internet, with hundreds of free Environments and

Multi-Instrument Objects created by Logic users and freely offered to the Logic community. In fact, the "Super Arpeggiator" that I designed (see Figure 14.21) is available for free download on that site as well as a myriad of others. Have yourself a look around the site, get the Environment Toolkit (I did when I started with Logic), and enjoy creating your virtual studio!

15 Advanced Tempo Operations

Tempo, meaning speed and timing, is one of the most important elements in music. Tempo management can be as simple as agreeing on the timing of a song and asking all the musicians to play in time. It can be as complicated as keeping track of multiple tempo changes throughout a musical movement—or even continuous tempo changes. With digital audio sequencers being the nerve center for both electronic and acoustic, programmed and performed tracks, it becomes vital that the sequencer keep everything synchronized and give the user the tools to fully implement whatever tempo requirements he has.

Luckily, Logic is up to the task. Logic offers many different tempo functions and, in typical Logic fashion, many ways to use them, depending on your own personal style. It can sync with external hardware through a number of common protocols, and it keeps perfect internal sync.

I have already discussed the most innovative and intuitive controls Logic gives you over tempo—the Tempo track, discussed in detail in Chapter 5, "Global Elements of Logic." By contrast, in this chapter, you'll explore Logic Pro's other tools to work with tempo and synchronization.

The Tempo Display

The first step in tempo management is to know what the tempo is. As I discussed previously in Chapter 6, "The Transport Window," the tempo is displayed in the Tempo display in the Transport, along with the Free Event Memory. Figure 15.1 shows this.

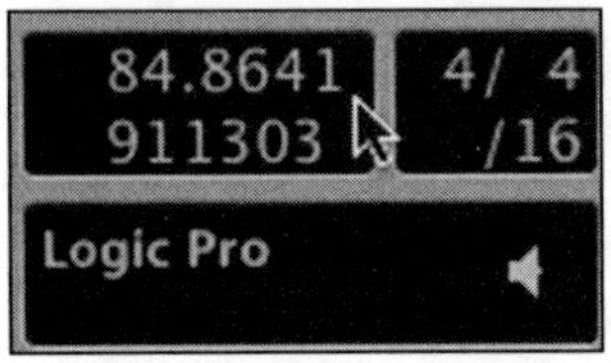

Figure 15.1
As you recall from Chapter 6, the Tempo/Free Event Memory display on the Transport shows the current song tempo. Chapter 5 also explains how to change the display preferences for the Tempo display if you want.

The Tempo display will show the current song tempo even if an external device to which Logic is synched is determining the tempo. If your Logic project has only a single tempo and Logic is the master of any external devices (or if you have no external devices, and Logic is the only tempo master), the easiest way to set the tempo is simply to double-click the tempo in the Tempo display, set it to the correct number, and then save your song. For more involved tempo manipulations, Logic offers a number of methods to edit tempo.

Recording and Editing Tempo

Whether you want to add only a few subtle tempo changes or a complex set of evolving tempos for different movements, Logic gives you a number of methods to record and edit tempo changes. This section will discuss the variety of ways you can either perform or program tempo changes.

Programming Tempo Changes on the Tempo Track

The Tempo track discussed in Chapter 5 not only displays any tempo changes in your song, but gives you an intuitive track on which to enter your tempo changes as well. Please refer to the "Tempo Track" section of Chapter 5 for the complete details.

Recording Tempo Changes

To record tempo changes while you are performing (for example, by inputting new tempos into the Tempo display on the fly or adjusting a tempo slider on external hardware), make sure the Allow Tempo Change Recording box is checked in the **Song Settings > Recording** tab. You can access this window from **File > Song Settings > Recording** or by pressing **OPTION + R**. Figure 15.2 shows this preference turned on.

Figure 15.2

Check the Allow Tempo Change Recording preference in the Recording Settings window if you want to record tempo changes in realtime.

After you check this box, any tempo changes you make will be saved into the Tempo track, which is the internal list of tempo changes that Logic maintains to manage a song's tempo. The next subsections discuss the two ways to access, add to, and edit that Tempo track.

The Tempo Interpreter

If you want to record your tempo live, perhaps the best way to do it is to tap your tempo into Logic as you are performing. To accomplish this, Logic includes a Tap Tempo key command and a Tempo Interpreter window. You can access the Tempo Interpreter by selecting **Options > Tempo > Tempo Interpreter**, by clicking and holding the Sync button on the Transport to reveal its pull-down menu and selecting Open Tempo Interpreter, or via key command. Figure 15.3 shows the Tempo Interpreter.

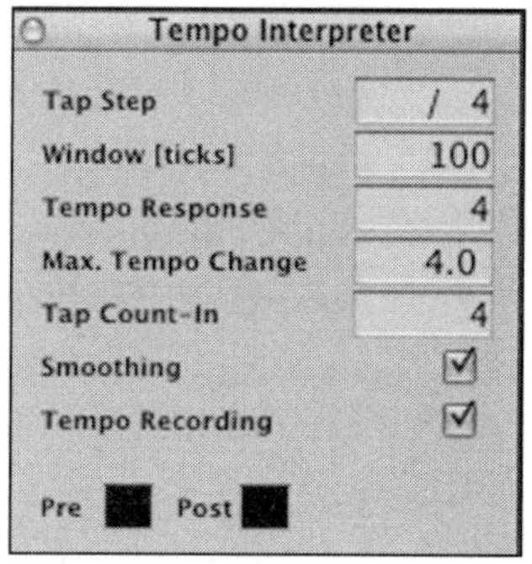

Figure 15.3

The Tempo Interpreter.

This window enables you to configure how Logic will interpret those tempos that you tap in with the Tap Tempo key command. A description of the parameters follows.

- **Tap Step.** This sets the note value that Logic will assign to each of your taps. Generally the best possible selection is 1/4 notes. Smaller figures will give you too much variation, and larger divisions will not accurately capture the tempo.
- **Window [ticks].** This adjusts how much of a window in time there is in which taps will be interpreted as tempo taps. In other words, if you set a huge window, only taps that are a very large number of ticks apart will be counted as a tap for determining tempo. If you set a tiny window, nearly every tick will be counted. In general, you'll want this

value to be large enough that double-clicks or ghost-clicks won't be counted but anything else will.

- **Tempo Response.** This sets Logic's internal sensitivity for tempo changes. The higher the value, the more responsive Logic will be—meaning, the more often Logic will change the tempo of the song. If you are hoping for a constant tempo, a value of 2 should work. If you are expecting some tempo changes, a value of 4 is recommended.
- **Max Tempo Change.** You probably don't want wild changes in your song. You should set as small a value as possible here so that any inconsistencies in your tapping don't result in outlandishly large tempo variations.
- **Tap Count-In.** This enables you to tap a count into your song. Type in the number of taps you want as a count (if any).
- **Smoothing.** If you check this box, any jumps in tempo will be smoothed out. If you want your taps to be followed exactly, do not check this box.
- **Tempo Recording.** This will create a realtime Tempo List if you are in Record mode. Normally, you will not need this because you won't be viewing the Tempo List at the same time you are performing, so you'll want to leave it off.
- **Pre and Post.** This has to do with how your taps are displayed on-screen. If you check Pre, every tap that is input will be displayed. If you check Post, only those taps that are in the accepted time frame defined in the Window parameter above will be displayed. Accepted taps flash yellow, unaccepted taps flash red. If you do not check either box, of course, no taps will flash at all.

Finally, remember that you must assign the Tap Tempo key command in order to record tempo this way!

Realtime Tempo Fader

One of the special Environment Fader Objects is a Tempo Fader. To create this object, in the Environment local menus select **New > Fader > Special > Tempo Control**. This fader can create realtime tempo changes in Logic by using the mouse to adjust the fader value. The range of this fader is 50 BPM–177 BPM.

If you simply want to adjust the tempo during playback, you do not need to cable the fader to anything. However, if you want to record your tempo changes or control the fader from a hardware MIDI device's pitch bend wheel (you can set this to another controller if you like, but it generally works best during a MIDI performance), you'll need to connect the fader between the Physical Input and Sequencer Input Objects.

Tempo List Editor

If you click and hold the Transport's Sync button (see Chapter 6), you can select Open Tempo List from the pull-down menu. This will open an Event List window dedicated to Tempo events. You also can access the Tempo List Editor from the global Options menu via **Options > Tempo > Tempo List Editor**, or the key command **OPTION + T**. Figure 15.4 shows the Tempo List Editor.

You will notice that this looks basically like a standard Event List, with a couple of exceptions. First of all, there is a large SMPTE display in the parameter bar. This is especially useful if you are synchronizing your Logic song via SMPTE. The other obvious difference is the Create button. As you would imagine, you can use this button to add a Tempo event to the current song location.

You can manipulate the events in the Tempo Event List similarly to how you would use a normal Event List as described in Chapter 9, "Working with MIDI." You can add Tempo events by clicking the word Tempo in an existing Tempo event with the Pencil tool. A new Tempo event will appear with a text box for you to enter its position. When you type in the song position for your

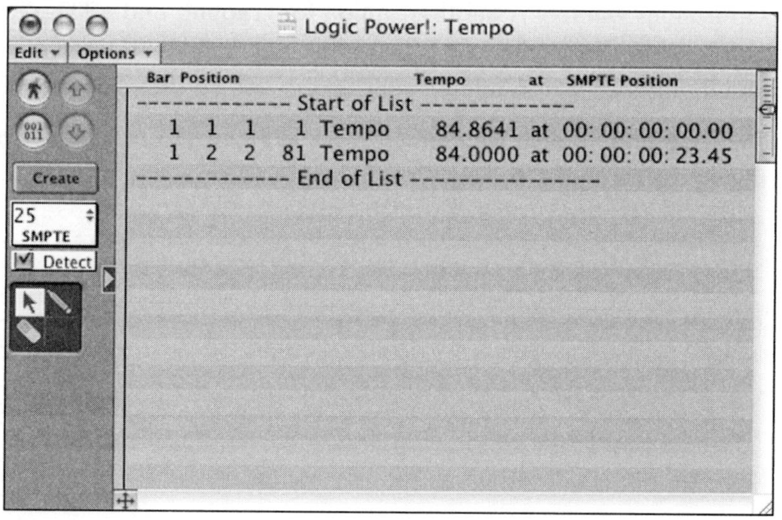

Figure 15.4
The Tempo List Editor.

new Tempo event, press **RETURN**, and the event will be positioned where you specified. You can delete Tempo events by pressing the **DELETE** key or using the Eraser tool. Lastly, you can edit the data in any event by adjusting the value using the mouse as a slider or by double-clicking the data and then typing a new value into the text box.

> **EXPERT TIP: KEEPING TRACK OF MULTIPLE TEMPO LISTS**
>
> Sometimes, you may want more than a single Tempo List in order to experiment with different tempos, changes in different places, and so on. To facilitate this, Logic allows you to store up to nine alternative Tempo Lists. In the Global Tempo Track or the Options local menu of the Tempo List Editor, select **Tempo Alternatives** and in the hierarchical menu you will be able to view any of your nine available alternatives. Remember that since the Tempo List Editor and the Global Tempo Track are showing the same information different ways, any changes you make to Tempo events in one editor will show up in the other editor.

Tempo Operations

You can access the Tempo Operations window a number of ways. From the two tempo editors above, you can access the Tempo Operations window from the local Options menu. From the global Options menu, you can choose **Options > Tempo > Tempo Operations**. You can open the Tempo Operations window from the pull-down menu accessible from the Sync button, again as with the tempo editors. And you can assign the key command Open Tempo Operations. Figure 15.5 shows the Tempo Operations window.

As with the Tempo track or Tempo List Editor already discussed, the Tempo Operations window is another option for creating and editing tempo changes. To use the Tempo Operations window, you'll need to make a selection in another tempo editor; your tempo will be shown in the window.

The Operation pull-down menu, shown in Figure 15.6, contains the six functions possible in the Tempo Operations window.

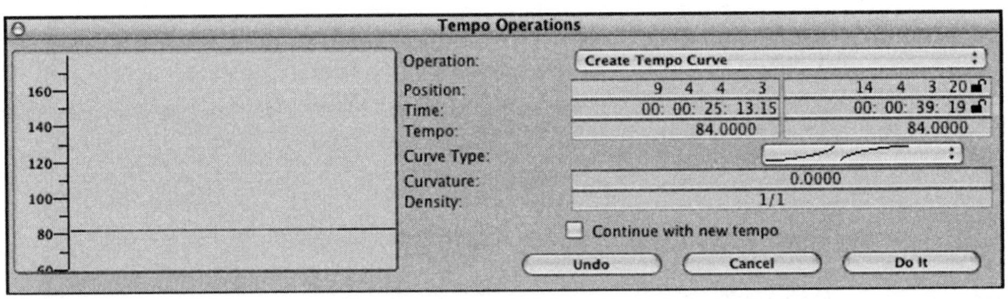

Figure 15.5

The Tempo Operations window.

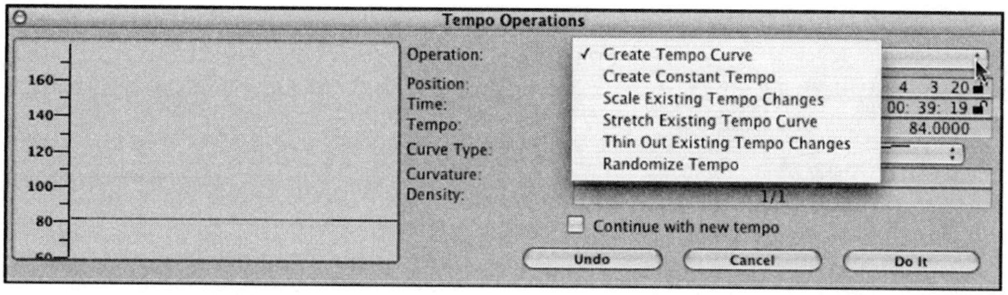

Figure 15.6

The Operation pull-down menu lists the six functions possible in the Tempo Operations window.

The following subsections describe each of the Tempo Operation window functions. You will find that most of these processes can be accomplished more quickly and intuitively in the new Tempo track.

Create Tempo Curve

This function enables you to create a tempo curve. To generate a curve, first choose one of the three curves available from the Curve Type pull-down menu, shown in Figure 15.7.

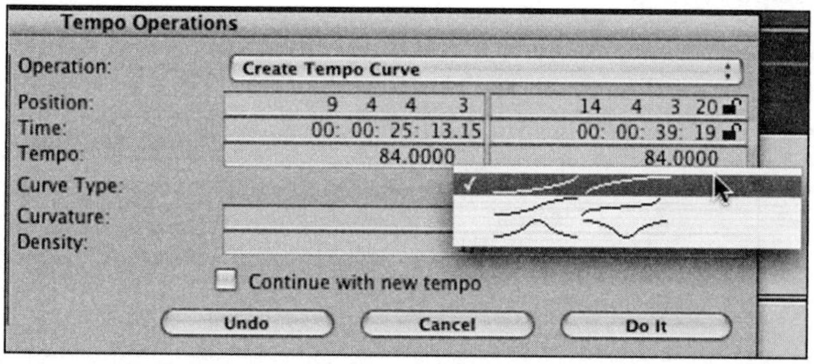

Figure 15.7

The Curve Type pull-down menu in the middle right of the Tempo Operations window contains the three curve shapes that you can choose for your tempo curve.

After you've chosen a curve, adjust the Position and Time settings to set the song position and length of your tempo change curve. Below those parameters, enter the starting and ending tempos you want in the Tempo track. Finally, set the Curvature parameter, which determines if your tempo will speed up or slow down, depending on if you enter a positive or negative number. Values between 1 and –1 are allowed. After that, pressing the Do It button will create your tempo curve.

If you need more Tempo events for a smoother curve, you can enter a smaller note denomination in the Density parameter, but don't do this just to make a prettier curve! Figure 15.8 shows an ascending tempo curve created using eighth notes.

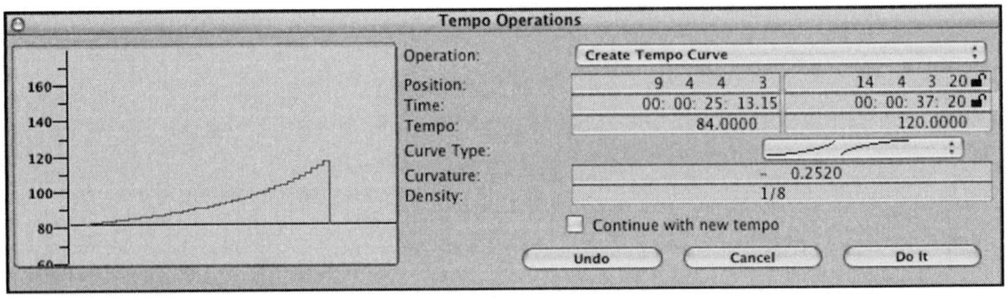

Figure 15.8
The above curve was created by the Create Tempo Curve operation generating one Tempo event every eighth note over the area specified by the chosen parameters.

You can check the Continue with New Tempo box if you want your song to maintain the tempo at which your curve ends. If you want to revert to the original song tempo after your curve, leave this option unchecked.

As you can see, creating tempo curves on the Tempo track is *far* simpler than using the Tempo Operations window for this!

Create Constant Tempo

If you want to eliminate all Tempo events for a given area and simply set one tempo for a given length of time, this operation will do it.

As you can see in Figure 15.9, the only options with this function are the Position and Time settings for where and how long your constant tempo should be set and the Tempo box to enter what the tempo should be.

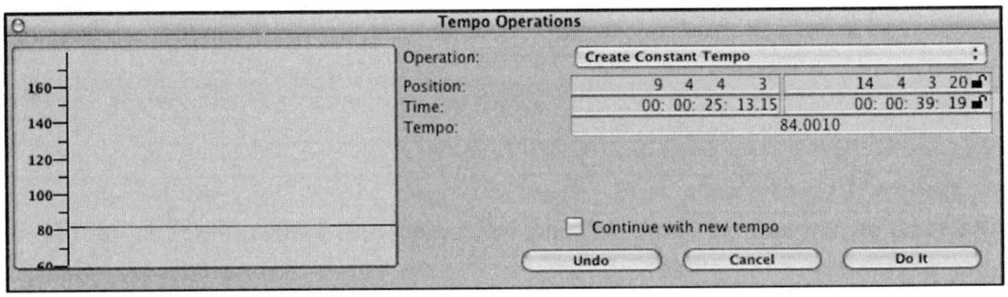

Figure 15.9
The Create Constant Tempo function display of the Tempo Operations window.

You can use the Continue with New Tempo box to either maintain this tempo for the rest of the song or revert to the original tempo after your section of constant tempo. Again, this process has been superseded by the Tempo track.

Scale Existing Tempo Changes

This lets you adjust currently existing tempo functions proportionally. You can set the Position and Time settings to determine where and how long you want your scaling to occur. You then enter the percentage of scaling you want to apply to the current Tempo events and the average tempo. Figure 15.10 shows the Scale Existing Tempo Changes function.

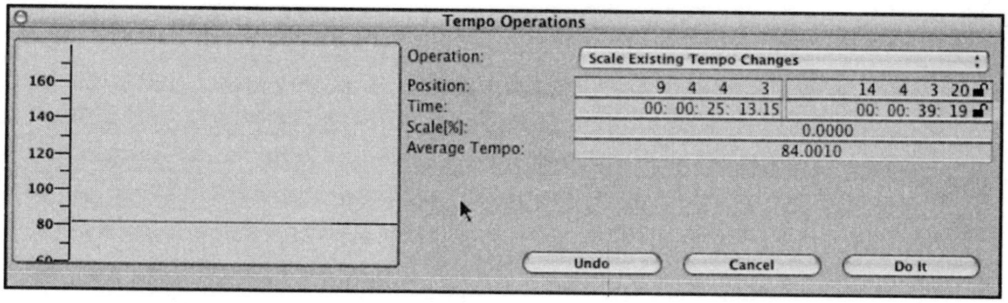

Figure 15.10

The Scale Existing Tempo Changes display.

Stretch Existing Tempo Curve

This enables you to shrink or elongate an existing tempo curve. You can set New End Position, New End Time, and the percentage of stretching you want as you adjust the length of the existing tempo curve. Figure 15.11 shows the Stretch Existing Tempo Curve screen.

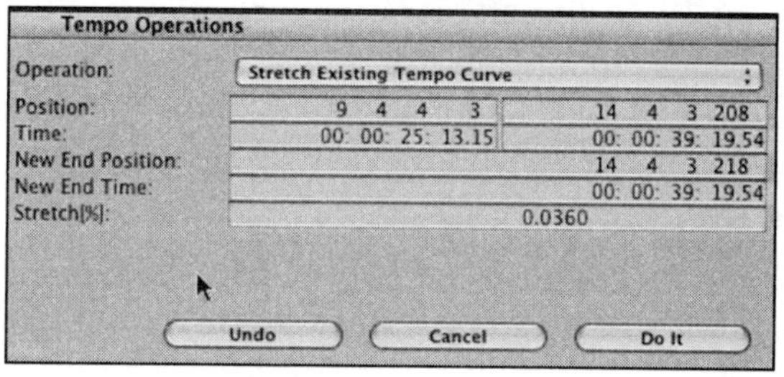

Figure 15.11

The Stretch Existing Tempo Curve display.

Thin Out Existing Tempo Changes

This lets you remove Tempo events from a given length of time. You can set the Position and Length at which you want the thinning to occur and the Density of events you want to remain after processing. Figure 15.12 shows the Thin Out Existing Tempo Changes screen.

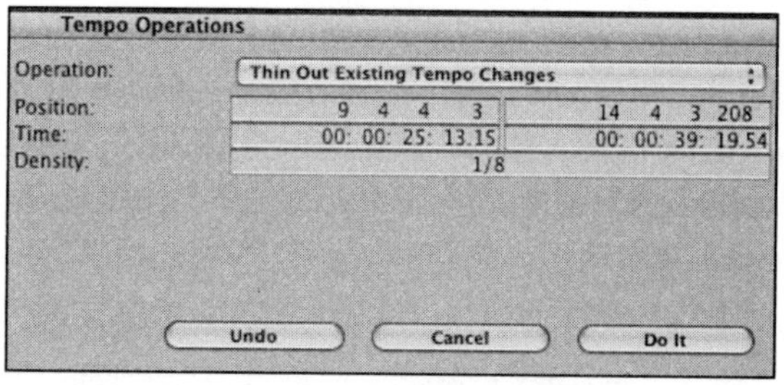

Figure 15.12

The Thin Out Existing Tempo Changes display.

This is something that the Tempo Operations window might come in handy for, since the Tempo track doesn't offer a simpler way to thin out specific tempo changes.

Randomize Tempo

Finally, you can randomize your tempo—create a random deviation in beats per minute (BPM) from your current tempo. The Position and Time parameters determine where and how long the section of random tempo deviation should be, and Density defines how many program changes will appear per bar.

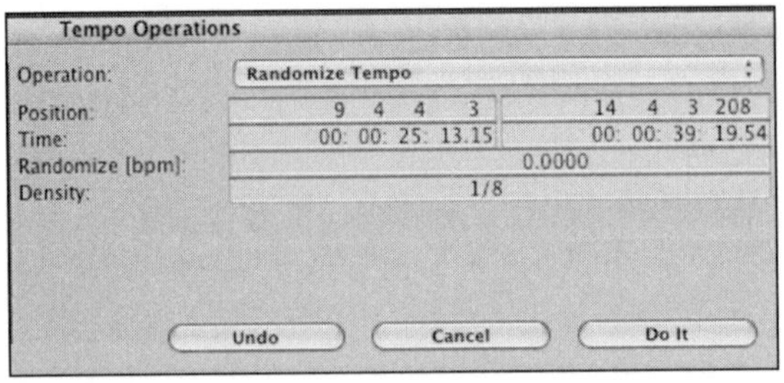

Figure 15.13

The Randomize Tempo display.

Figure 15.13 shows the Randomize Tempo screen.

This is something that you might want to use Tempo Operations for, as the Tempo track doesn't lend itself to randomizing tempo changes.

Reclocking Your Tempo Track Using the Old Logic Reclock Function

Perhaps the most drastic tempo option is to reclock your entire song. The promise of this option is that you can record without paying any attention to tempo at all—for example, recording a rock-and-roll group without setting the Logic song tempo or having the drummer play to a click track, or capturing a freestyle keyboard performance. The reality is that how accurately this promise can be achieved depends on how accurately the artist or artists keep time and how accurate a guide sequence you can create to assist the Reclock Song function. If you have a solid guide sequence, this command can deliver excellent results, but if you have no MIDI region to guide the Reclock Song function, and the performers didn't worry about keeping time themselves, don't be surprised if this function requires a fair amount of cleaning up.

The pre-Logic Pro 7 Reclock function has been completely superseded by the newer, intuitive, and more accurate Beat Mapping track. However, for those used to the "old way," or if you're not getting good results with the Beat Mapping track and want to try the old Reclock function just in case, I'll mention it here.

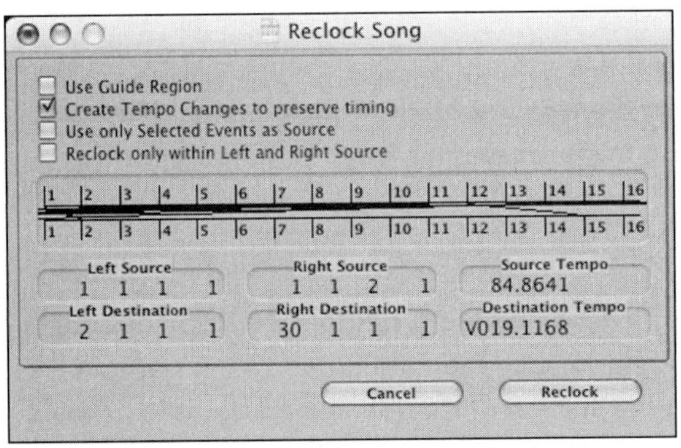

Figure 15.14

The Reclock Song dialog. Here you can create a new tempo based on a guide region or selected events.

To access the Reclock Song dialog, you must have at least one MIDI region selected, then from the global Options menu choose **Options > Tempo > Reclock Song**. Figure 15.14 shows the Reclock Song dialog.

The various check boxes and options are described next.

- **Use Guide Region.** With this checked, the Reclock Song function will use a MIDI region you select that has steady quarter notes (or whichever note division you choose) with the same timing as your recorded song (much like the Beats From Region function of the Beat Mapping track). In general, this gets the best results because the timing of your recorded MIDI or Audio regions may not be easy to detect. To generate the MIDI region you want to use, simply use a MIDI controller to record single notes in the same timing as the region to which you want to reclock your song. Then select it, open the Reclock Song dialog, and select the Use Guide Region option. You will notice the Left Source and Right Source boxes disappear, and after the Left Destination box, you'll have a new option for Step Increment, as shown in Figure 15.15. In the Step Increment box, enter the note division value of the notes in your guide region.

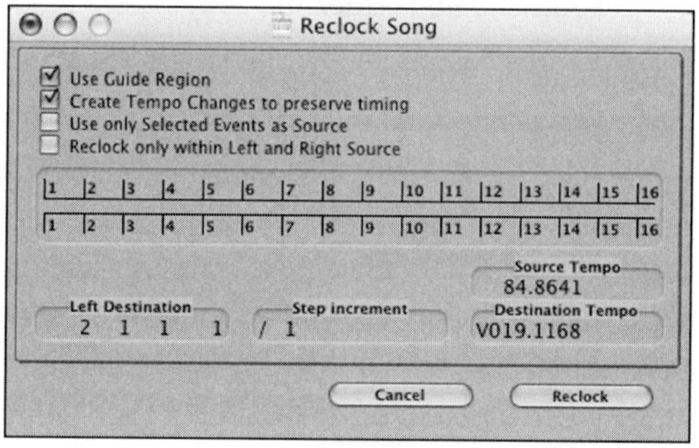

Figure 15.15

The Reclock Song dialog after the Use Guide Region option is checked.

- **Create Tempo Changes to Preserve Timing.** Unless your performers have perfect timing, it's very likely there will be fluctuations in tempo. If you have this checked, the Reclock Song functions will create Tempo events for each such fluctuation, so that the Logic song will preserve the timing of the performance. If this is unchecked, Logic will attempt to find a single tempo that's closest to the overall performance; this might very well change the timing of MIDI performances and make it very difficult to sync to audio performances.
- **Use Only Selected Events as Source.** If you don't want to use an entire MIDI region as your Reclock Song track (maybe the timing is too erratic past a certain point in the song), you can check this and the Reclock Song function will use only those specific MIDI events that you have selected to reclock by.

- **Reclock Only within Left and Right Source.** Let's say that your entire song is recorded to the current song tempo, but you have a freestyle performance you want to use as an introduction. Or perhaps the band stuck to a steady tempo for the entire song but then slowed down for the breakdown in the coda. In these examples, you do not need to reclock the entire song, but you may want Logic to generate new Tempo events just in that section that has the freestyle performance. In these and similar cases, you can check this option, and Tempo events will be created only inside the specified length of time.
- **Left/Right Source.** This is where you set the start and end points of the selected MIDI region that you are using for reclocking.
- **Left/Right Destination.** Here you set the points in time between which Logic should reclock the song.
- **Source Tempo.** This is the tempo Logic was set to when the part was recorded.
- **Destination Tempo.** This is what the song tempo will be after reclocking. You will not need to adjust it unless you already know exactly what it should be.

After configuring the Reclock Song dialog, click the Reclock button, and Logic will generate new Tempo events based on your settings and how accurately it could gauge the tempo from your selected MIDI region. You may find that you will need to open one of the tempo editors and make some manual adjustments to get it exactly right, but hopefully, this command got you close to where you wanted to be.

EXPERT TIP: RECLOCKING A SONG TO AN AUDIO TRACK

The Reclock Song command was designed to work with MIDI regions, but you also can use it to reclock your song to an audio performance. First of all, you'll need to have a monophonic audio performance that is in the same timing that you want your Logic song to have. The best track would be a steady kick drum, hi-hat, or percussion track. The first thing you'll do is use the Audio To Score function described in Chapter 8, "Working with Audio," to create a MIDI track with the notes of your mono percussion track. If you don't have a mono Audio Track that is steady enough to use as a guide sequence, you can always tap out on a MIDI controller a MIDI performance that is in the same timing as your audio and use that as a guide sequence. When you have your MIDI track, select it as the MIDI region to use as your guide sequence and reclock the song to that track. If the Audio Track you used for your guide track was accurate enough, your Logic song's tempo should now reflect the tempo of the audio being performed.

16 Synchronizing Hardware with Logic Pro

Some composers and producers do not want to produce an entire composition inside the computer. Other producers want to, but do not have access to a computer powerful enough for the most demanding projects. At the time of this writing, Logic Pro features performance optimizations for the PowerMac Dual G5, which offers the highest level of performance from any personal computer. As previously mentioned, you can also create an entire Distributed Audio Processing network, with additional G5s being used as Logic Nodes for nearly unprecedented processing capability. However, for those who want to use external hardware recorders and other devices, or have older computers, you still need a way to synchronize external recording hardware with Logic. Luckily, Logic Pro can sync with hardware using a number of different formats. This chapter will explain how.

The Synchronization Window

The main synchronization settings are located in the Synchronization window, which can be accessed from the Song Settings submenu via **File > Song Settings > Synchronization**, from the External Sync button on the Transport window, or via the key command **OPTION + X**. This will launch the Synchronization window, shown in Figure 16.1.

There are four different tabs across the top of the Synchronization window: General, Audio, MIDI, and Unitor (Emagic's own MIDI interface). The following sections deal with these tabs.

Figure 16.1

The Synchronization window, available from the Song Settings submenu.

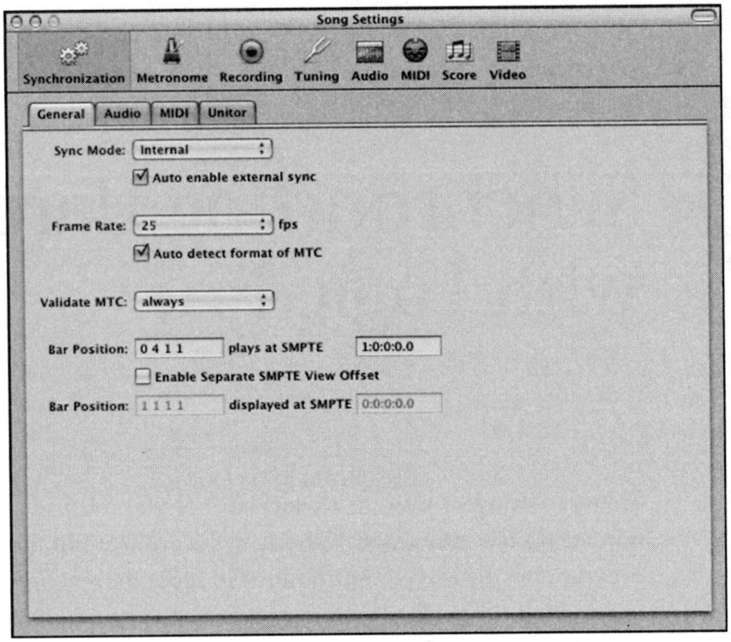

General Tab

As Figure 16.1 shows, the Synchronization window defaults to the General tab. These are the synchronization options you will most often need to configure—assuming you need to configure any of the default options. The list below offers an explanation of each option in the General tab of the Synchronization window, from top to bottom.

- **Sync Mode.** The Sync Mode pull-down menu lets you choose from four synchronization modes, as shown in Figure 16.2.

Figure 16.2

The Sync Mode pull-down menu.

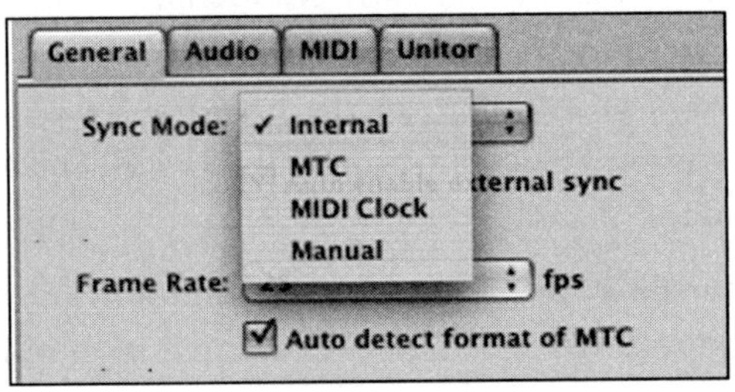

Each synchronization mode is described below:

- **Internal.** Logic will sync to its own internal clock—in other words, it will be the "master." Any external hardware connected to Logic can synchronize to Logic as a "slave" by using either MTC (MIDI Time Code) or MIDI Clock.
- **MTC.** Logic will synchronize to incoming MIDI Time Code (MTC) from an external device. The MTC can be generated directly by an external device, or the external device can generate a different time code format (such as SMPTE timecode), which a MIDI interface can translate into MTC for Logic.
- **MIDI Clock.** Logic will synchronize to the MIDI Clock of an external MIDI device.
- **Manual.** In this mode, Logic will synchronize to the Tempo Interpreter (described in the previous chapter). In this case, the Tempo Interpreter can base its tempo on external pulses as well as the computer keyboard.

- **Auto Enable External Sync.** With this enabled, Logic will synchronize to its own internal clock until it receives a synchronization signal from an external device in either MTC, MIDI Clock, or Tempo Interpreter format. Logic will automatically sync to the first synchronization signal it receives. This is very important—make sure Logic doesn't receive multiple synchronization signals simultaneously! That will cause Logic to synchronize to the wrong source (or throw up an error message if it is truly confused).
- **Frame Rate [fps].** Frame rate refers to how many frames per second are set. A *frame* is the basic unit because most often these formats were used to synchronize audio to picture, and pictures raced by at a certain number of frames per second, depending on the format. The pull-down menu for the Frame Rate option is shown in Figure 16.3.

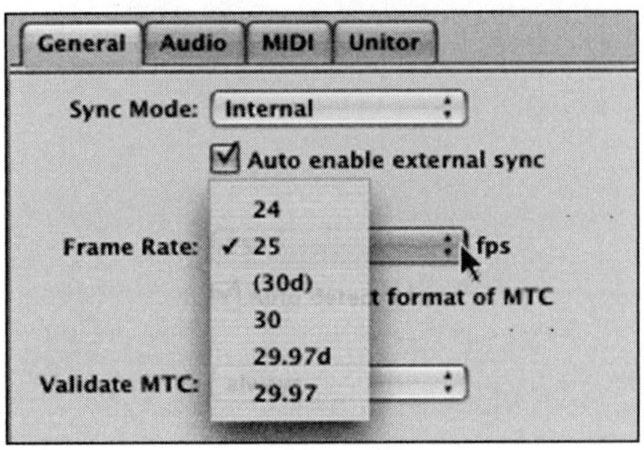

Figure 16.3
The Frame Rate pull-down menu.

The Frame Rate options include the following:

- **25.** This frame rate is common in Europe for PAL video and audio.
- **(30d).** This format stands for 30fps drop frame. This means that a certain number of frames are dropped from the normal 30 per second. This format is unusable in Logic because it cannot handle it in realtime. This is why the option is in parentheses.
- **30.** This frame rate is common in the United States for NTSC video and audio.
- **29.97d.** This is a more usable, realtime version of the 30d format. It is common in the United States for NTSC video and audio.
- **29.97.** As above, but without frame drop. This format is rarely used because the 29.97d format is far more accurate for synchronizing audio and video.

- **Auto Detect Format of MTC.** This option should almost always be engaged, because it usually chooses the correct frame rate. Why the qualifiers "almost" and "usually"? Unfortunately, the MTC standard does not provide a way for a host to make the distinction between the 29.97 and 30 frame rates. Logic generally will interpret both those rates as either 29.97d or 30, depending on if you are using a drop frame. If you know that you need either 30 or 29.97 as your frame rate, uncheck this option and set the frame rate manually.
- **Validate MTC.** This option enables you to select how often Logic will verify that it is getting the proper synchronization signal at the proper frame rate. The Validate MTC pull-down menu is shown in Figure 16.4.

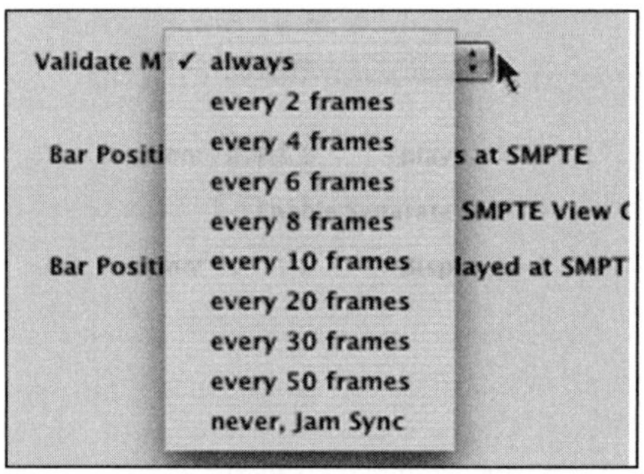

Figure 16.4

The Validate MTC pull-down menu.

In general, you always want to leave this option selected so that Logic will verify sync after every message. On the other hand, if you know that the sync will be erratic but want to use sync anyway, you might not want Logic to check the synchronization signal and simply accept whatever is thrown at it (which is known as "jam sync").

- **Bar Position/Plays at SMPTE.** These boxes enable you to enter a bar position or SMPTE time for Logic to start at instead of the very beginning of the song. This is known as *SMPTE offset* because it enables you to start running anywhere in your song that you want as soon as sync is received.
- **Enable Separate SMPTE View Offset.** With this engaged, the second set of text fields for entering bars and SMTPE values becomes available. Unlike the option above, in which you can set which bar position *plays* at which SMPTE location, in this field you can set which bar position will be *displayed* at which SMPTE location.

Audio Tab

The Audio tab of the Synchronization window reveals a number of displays that offer a more detailed view of the synchronization code being transmitted to Logic. Figure 16.5 shows the Audio tab of the Synchronization window.

What the different displays mean and how to interpret them are explained below.

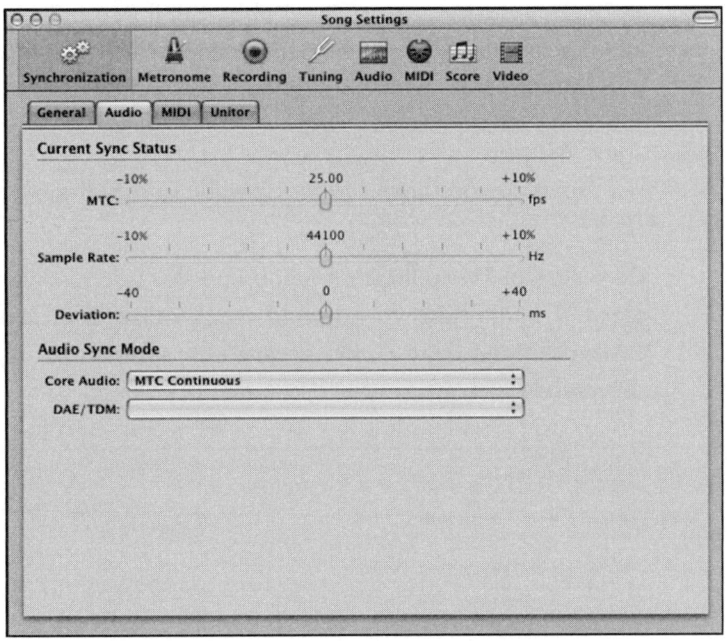

Figure 16.5
The Audio tab of the Synchronization window.

Current Sync Status

These items display the current status of your synchronization with your external hardware.

- **MTC [fps].** This display shows the percentage of deviation—if any—between the incoming MIDI Time Code and its nominal frame rate. Your goal, of course, is for the yellow line to be in the exact middle (meaning no deviation at all). If there is some deviation, adjust the speed of the master machine until the yellow line shows no deviation. If your deviation is too extreme, you might have chosen an incorrect frame rate in the General tab; try different settings to see if that eliminates the deviation.
- **Sample Rate [Hz].** This display shows any deviation of the sample rate from its nominal value. In general, if your synchronization signal is accurate, your sample rate will be. If there is a problem with your time code deviation, you may see your sample rate deviate as well. This can be particularly troublesome because some audio interfaces simply cannot handle any variation in sample rate.
- **Deviation [ms].** This will show you any deviation between Word Clock and time code, or in other words, any deviation between audio and MIDI. Tiny deviations are inevitable, but if you believe you have a major problem syncing your audio and MIDI, this display will enable you to determine the actual deviation in milliseconds.

Audio Sync Mode

These two submenus are linked to the specific audio driver you are using in Logic Pro.

- **Core Audio.** This pull-down menu enables you to determine how each piece of audio hardware should synchronize to an external time code master that the Core Audio engine can understand. Figure 16.6 shows the Core Audio pull-down menu.

Figure 16.6
The Core Audio pull-down menu.

Not all hardware can work in every synchronization mode; see your hardware manual for details. A description of each mode follows.

- **MTC Continuous.** In this mode, Audio regions start in sync, and the sample rate is regulated continuously according to the time code master to ensure constant sync of even very long Audio regions.
- **MTC Trigger + Auto Speed Detection.** In this mode, Audio regions start in sync but are then played at a constant sample rate regardless of any variations in the time code master. When Logic stops and restarts, it starts playback at the current sample rate of the time code master. This is useful when you must keep your audio playing at the same rate to maintain the absolute pitch of a recording.
- **MTC Trigger.** As above, Logic starts the Audio regions in sync, but they are then played at a constant sample rate regardless of any variations in the time code master. When Logic stops and restarts, however, the time code master is not queried again for the current sample rate. The initial sample rate Logic started playback in will continue.
- **External or Free.** In this mode, Logic completely relinquishes all influence over the sample rate to the external hardware. If you have a very high-quality external SMPTE/Word Clock synchronizer, this can be a valuable option. Otherwise, this can be a disaster.

- **DAE/TDM.** This pull-down menu enables you to determine how each piece of audio hardware should synchronize to an external time code master that the Digidesign Audio Engine (DAE) can understand. It is identical to the Core Audio submenu except for the addition of two settings (Digital and SSD/VSD Type) that are unique to TDM systems.

MIDI Tab

The MIDI tab includes options valuable when synchronizing external MIDI hardware to Logic. Figure 16.7 shows the MIDI tab of the Synchronization window.

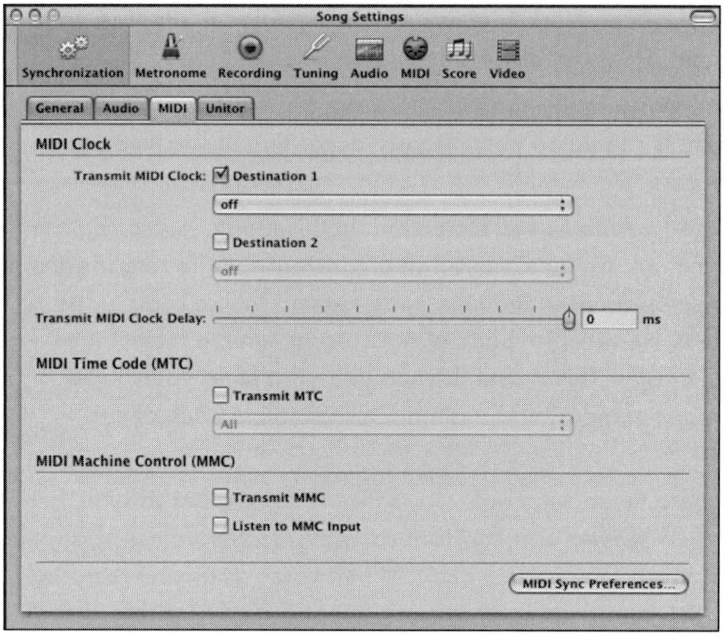

Figure 16.7
The MIDI tab of the Synchronization window.

The options in this window are explained in the following:

- **Transmit MIDI Clock.** With either of these check boxes engaged (for Destination 1 or Destination 2), you will send MIDI Clock to all external MIDI devices. The pull-down menus next to the check boxes include all the MIDI ports available. There are two check boxes with two pull-down menus, in case you have two MIDI interfaces and you want to send MIDI Clock via a port on each. If you do not have two MIDI interfaces connected, Destination 2 will have its pull-down menu grayed out. You will generally get the best timing by sending MIDI Clock to all ports instead of individual ports.
- **Transmit MIDI Clock Delay.** This command will delay the transmission of MIDI Clock. Setting a negative delay will start Logic transmitting MIDI Clock before the song begins playback. This will enable you to compensate for any reaction delays in your external hardware.
- **Transmit MTC.** This check box enables the transmission of MIDI Time Code (MTC) to one of your available MIDI ports from the pull-down menu next to the box. Unlike MIDI Clock, MTC is very data intensive and should not be sent to the ALL ports option. You will get the best performance if you transmit MTC on a port that is being used for nothing else.

- **Transmit MMC.** With this enabled, Logic will be able to transmit MIDI Machine Control (MMC). MMC enables Logic to control the Transport of an external device using MIDI commands. These commands will be transmitted whenever you operate Logic's Transport. Normally, MMC will be used if you are slaving Logic to an external MTC master, such as an ADAT machine, but you want to use Logic to control the Transport of the MTC master. Enabling this button will let Logic control the Transport of the MTC master device, even as Logic itself is slaved to that device.
- **Listen to MMC Input.** When you engage this button, Logic not only transmits MIDI Machine Control, but can itself be controlled by MMC commands. This is useful if you want to use your external hardware to control Logic's Transport, the record-arming of Audio Tracks in Arrange, and so on.

MIDI Sync Preferences

On the bottom-right of the Synchronization settings MIDI tab is a button to open the MIDI Preferences window to the Sync tab. This can also be accessed via **Logic Pro > Preferences > MIDI** and clicking into the Sync tab. Figure 16.8 shows the MIDI Preferences window open to the Sync tab.

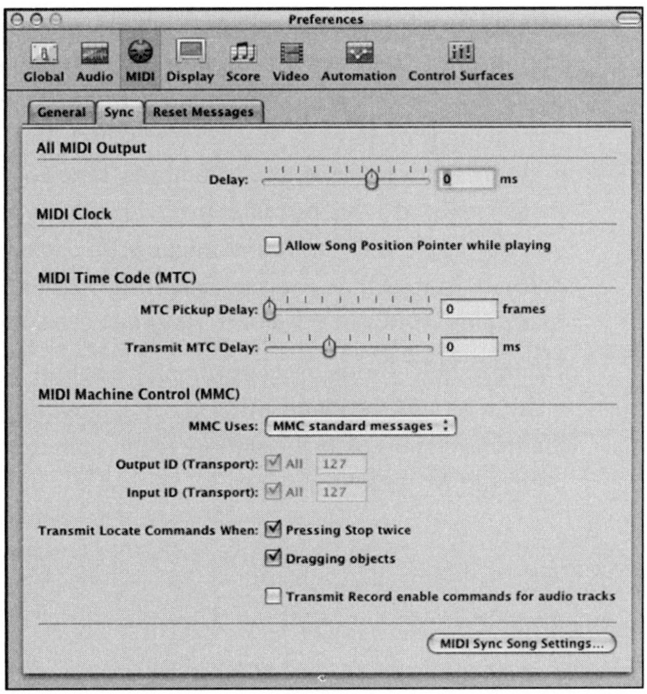

Figure 16.8

The MIDI Preferences Sync tab.

The MIDI Sync Preferences includes additional options that control synchronization with MIDI hardware, as described below.

All MIDI Output

- **Delay [ms].** In order for your MIDI hardware to play in sync with Logic, you'll probably need to delay the MIDI output by a certain amount. This is because your audio hardware will have a certain latency that depends on the audio buffer, as explained earlier in this book. By delaying the MIDI output by the same amount as your interface's buffer delays your audio, everything will play in sync. You will want to set a negative value in milliseconds, which in effect gives your audio a "pre-roll" so that everything will start together.

MIDI Clock

- **Allow Song Position Pointer While Playing.** Logic will also send Song Position Pointer (SPP) commands to your MIDI devices. However, many MIDI devices cannot process this message. If you know your device can process this message, go ahead and engage this option. If you aren't sure or if you know your device cannot process SPP messages, do not engage this option.

MIDI Time Code (MTC)

- **MTC Pickup Delay.** You will normally keep this parameter set to zero to ensure the quickest pickup time while Logic is in MTC sync mode. Some devices, unfortunately, take a while to get in sync and, as such, transmit imprecise MTC commands at first. This inaccuracy can result in an offset every time you attempt to sync Logic Pro to the device. In these cases, use this parameter to set a delay for MTC pickup. When you do, Logic will ignore the initial MTC commands for as long as the delay in frames that you set. Generally, 25 to 30 frames corresponds to a delay of about a second, depending on the selected frame rate.
- **Transmit MTC Delay.** This parameter enables you to delay the transmission of MTC. As with MIDI Clock Delay, negative values will start the transmission of MTC earlier, which can compensate for reaction delays in MTC slave devices.

MIDI Machine Control (MMC)

...ull-down menu if MMC will use
...d Fostex format. Only select Old
...e only format your device can

...you to set a specific MMC Output
...u can select any ID number from
...our external hardware to deter-
... MMC Output ID.

...ou to set a specific MMC Input ID
...can select any ID number from 1 to
...xternal hardware to determine if
...nput ID.

...gaged, pressing Stop on Logic's
...the MMC Locate command.

...bled, dragging regions in Arrange
...s to your external device with the
...on.

...**for Audio Tracks.** When this is
... Logic will send MMC Record-
...device. This works both ways, so
...nt to Logic will arm the Audio

...agic's Unitor8 MIDI interface. If
...chronization window in order to
...ons. If you have a different MIDI
..., it most likely came with its own
...terface.

DAY LOWEST PRICE GUARANTEE. Our goal is your total satisfaction.
ou're guaranteed the lowest price from Guitar Center. Period. If at any time within 30 days of your purchase om us, you find the identical item in stock and advertised by an authorized dealer at a price lower than hat you paid, Guitar Center will fully protect you. Just bring in the ad-even if it's our own-along with your riginal Guitar Center receipt, and we'll gladly refund the difference. Item must be advertised in a local or ational paper, magazine or catalog by an authorized U.S.dealer. Discontinued merchandise, demo and xclusive models, floor samples, factory seconds, vintage and used merchandise are exempt.

DAY SATISFACTION GUARANTEE. Our goal is your total satisfaction.
you're not satisfied, neither are we. If for any reason you're not completely satisfied with your purchase, mply return it in its original condition within 30 days, and we'll give you a full refund. Just bring it back to any uitar Center location, along with your receipt, manual, blank warranty card and all original packaging for xchange or refund. Restrictions: *Due to certain legal and health restrictions, computer software (copyright gislation mandates no returns on opened software), books, videos, CDs, harmonicas, internal earphones, arplugs, and microphones are exempt from this policy. Computers, DJ cartridges and styli, fog fluid, cleaning roducts, vintage items, demo gear, opened strings, tubes and leased purchases are also exempt, as are any ems special ordered from a manufacturer for a specific customer. Any other product exceptions will be oted on customer receipts at time of purchase. "All original packaging" includes cables, power adapters, man-als, blank warranty cards, etc., as well as the actual packaging.*

here is a 14 day return period and 15% restocking fee on open-box returns within the following product cat-gories:
• Recording devices - multitrack and mixdown
• Studio monitors
• Rackmount signal processors
• DJ mixers, turntables, and CD Players
• Pro workstation keyboards
• Fog machines and lighting effects

roducts that are defective may be exchanged for an identical product without the assessment of a restocking fee.

REPAIR DISCLAIMER
t Guitar Center, we are committed to making the repair process as easy as possible for our customers. uitar Center does not own or operate repair service centers, however, we can refer you to a local ndependent repair service center. Guitar Center accepts no responsibility for loss or damage to any ustomer owned merchandise sent for repair and we do not guarantee the work performed by an ndependent repair service center. The customer is responsible for all charges incurred, including but not mited to, freight to and from the repair service center, parts, labor, local tax, and surcharge/ estimate fee (if any). Merchandise not picked up within 90 days after notification of completed repairs will be sold by Guitar Center for he cost of repairs.

CASH REFUND POLICY
Refunds for cash purchases over $25.00 will be made by check.

Guitar Center The Musician's Choice

30 DAY LOWEST PRICE GUARANTEE. Our goal is your total satisfaction.
You're guaranteed the lowest price from Guitar Center. Period. If at any time within 30 days of your purchase rom us, you find the identical item in stock and advertised by an authorized dealer at a price lower than what you paid, Guitar Center will fully protect you. Just bring in the ad-even if it's our own-along with your original Guitar Center receipt, and we'll gladly refund the difference. Item must be advertised in a local or

There are many great MIDI interfaces on the market, and the Unitor8 is one of them. Having its synchronization functions integrated into Logic does not give it any special features, however. It simply means that you will not need to access a separate application to configure it. Because this book is not going into how to configure specific hardware devices, please read the Unitor8 manual or the online help feature for more information about how to configure your Unitor8 MIDI interface using this tab.

Switching On External Synchronization

If you want Logic to synchronize with external hardware, simply engage the Sync button on the Transport, shown in Figure 16.9.

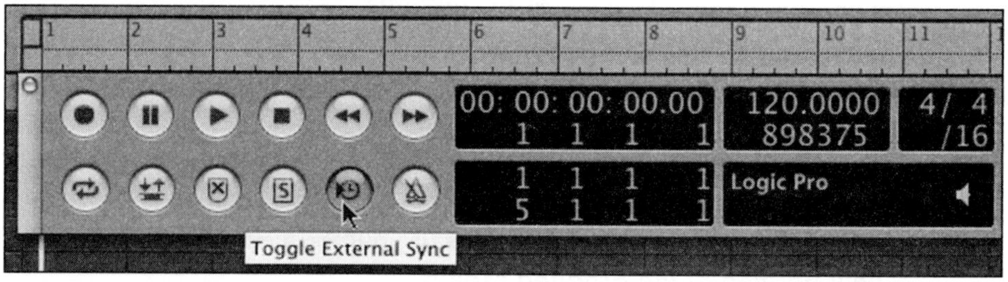

Figure 16.9
To engage external sync in Logic, switch on the Sync button on the Transport; the button will light up when engaged, and the Bar Ruler will turn blue.

When you disengage sync by clicking the Sync button again, the button and Bar Ruler will stop glowing. You can use the Sync button to engage and disengage sync at any time, which is useful if you need to disengage sync for a moment while doing some editing in Logic, then reengage sync.

When Logic is actively receiving sync, a dot will flash in the Sync button in the Transport. This indicates that everything is running smoothly. If you see the dot stop flashing, that indicates there is a sync error. Although Logic has a fairly robust handling of MTC, if you notice the dot stick, you should check your configuration of your external master device to make sure that the MTC or SMPTE signal is sending a high-quality, uncompromised signal. In the case of SMPTE timecode that is being translated to MTC by another hardware device (such as your MIDI interface), be sure to check both hardware devices to make sure they are sending proper sync.

Bar Ruler to Time Ruler

In every graphical window in Logic, you have the option to turn the Bar Ruler into an SMPTE timecode Ruler (or simply Time Ruler). To do this, in the local View menu of the various windows, select **View > Show SMPTE Time Ruler**, and the Bar Ruler for that window will become the Time Ruler you see in Figure 16.10.

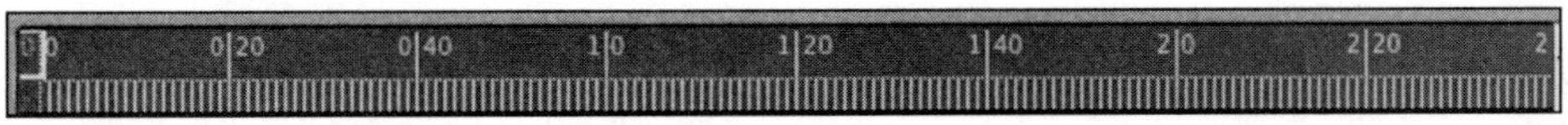

Figure 16.10

You can change the Bar Ruler in the graphical windows in Logic into this Time Ruler.

The Event Lists are exceptions, of course, because they are not graphical windows. You still can choose to switch the positions and lengths to showing SMPTE values instead of bar positions by selecting **View > Position & Length in SMPTE** from their local View menu. Your Event List will change to show all positions in SMPTE timecode as shown in Figure 16.11.

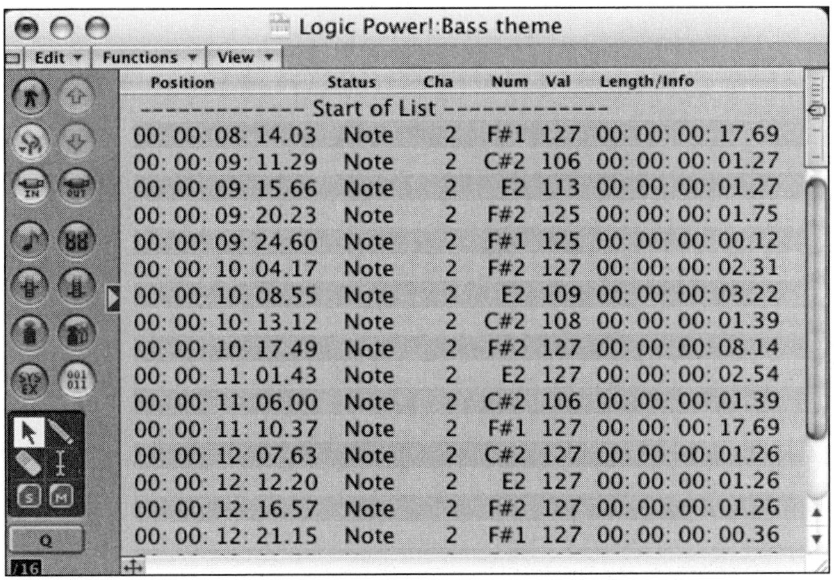

Figure 16.11

You can change the position and length displays in Event Lists to show SMPTE timecode instead of bar positions.

This is particularly valuable when syncing audio to picture because you may want to lock specific regions to specific frames. Holding down the **CONTROL** key will change your rate of movement in the Arrange window to Frames, and holding down **CONTROL + SHIFT** will switch you to subframe movement. You can then use Arrange window commands such as **Regions > Lock SMPTE Position** to lock your region to its SMPTE position, and so on.

EXPERT TIP: POSITIONING A BAR AT A SPECIFIC SMPTE FRAME

If you want a particular bar of your song to fall at a specific SMPTE frame, you'll need to create a Tempo event as discussed in the last chapter so that your song's tempo will change at the exact SMPTE position you want the bar to fall. When you create the Tempo event at the bar you want, open the Tempo List and then set its SMPTE position to the exact frame you want. Logic will ensure that your bar with the tempo change will fall at the SMPTE position you selected. At this point, Logic has adjusted the Bar Ruler itself to match the SMPTE position you chose, so you can go ahead and delete the Tempo event and the bar will still fall where you want it to!

17 Working with Video

For those involved in scoring commercials, industrial videos, motion pictures, or any other visual medium that uses music, Logic provides features to enable you to synchronize your music production with the video. Logic does not enable you to edit your video; for that you need a video production application such as Apple Computer's world class FinalCut Pro—and as you saw in Chapter 13, "Working with Files," you can export your Logic Pro audio to FinalCut Pro via the Export command. Logic Pro will, however, enable you to open your video, view your video alongside your Logic project, and lock your music to particular frames of video.

Logic supports Apple's QuickTime format for digital video. QuickTime is not only the Macintosh standard, but the professional standard of choice. If you want to use video with Logic, make sure it is in the QuickTime format.

Opening Movies

There are two basic ways to open a video in Logic. The first is through **Options > Movie** from the global Options menu (or type **COMMAND + M**). You will be presented with the Open file dialog to choose your video. When you open your video, it will appear in its own window along with your Logic song. Figure 17.1 shows a video opened as part of a Logic song.

Figure 17.1
After selecting **Options > Movie** from the global Options menu, you will be able to view a QuickTime movie along with your Logic project. (All video thumbnails ©Bar Ben-Yossef)

Keep in mind that when you open a video window this way, the window can be hidden behind other windows like any other window. If you want your video always to be visible on top of your Logic project, you can open a video by choosing **Options > Movie as Float** (or type **OPTION + COMMAND + M**). This also will present you with a file dialog to choose a QuickTime movie, but your movie will open in a floating window—meaning that like the Transport, the video window will always remain viewable on top of any other windows you have open.

If you accidentally close your movie, you can assign a key command for Open Movie Again, and if you want to reopen your movie as a floating window, you also can assign a key command for Open Movie Again as Float.

The Video Window

Now that you've opened a video, you'll notice that below the progress bar is a window with three position displays. Figure 17.2 shows the displays.

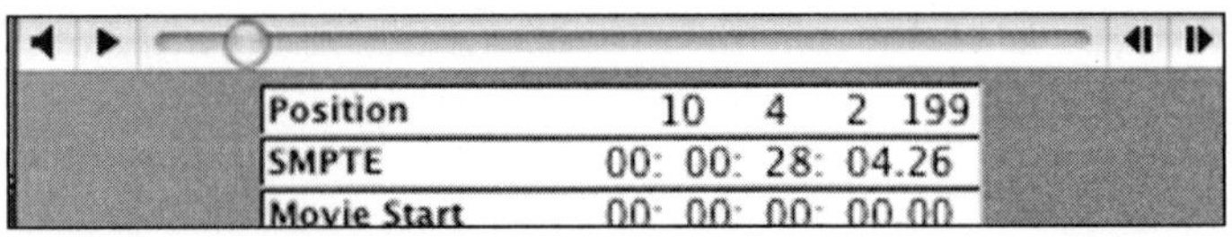

Figure 17.2
The three position displays at the bottom of the movie window.

The top display is a Bar Position display. If you double-click on any of the numbers, you will be presented with a text box where you can enter a specific bar, beat, and measure for the video and Logic song to jump to.

The second display is SMPTE display for the song. You can enter a specific SMPTE position, and your song and video will jump to that position. If you have an SMPTE Offset for your song (see the previous chapter), the SMPTE display will start at a time other than 00:00:00:00.00.

The final display is for Movie Start. You can enter a specific SMPTE position here, and your movie will not start until the song reaches that point. This is independent of the SMPTE Offset, so you can have SMPTE begin at a non-zero point and also set a Movie Start position for your song. You also can use the Movie Start display to set a start time for your movie if you are not using any external SMPTE device at all—the display simply uses SMPTE time because it is the standard time code in the video world, not because you must be synchronizing to external SMPTE hardware to use it.

Image Size

If you want to view your QuickTime movie at full size, clicking the mouse below the movie in the movie window will enlarge the video to its full size. Note that at this size, the video window does not include the position displays described in the previous section. Figure 17.3 shows a QuickTime video at full size in a Logic project.

Figure 17.3

This video has been enlarged to full size. Click anywhere on the video to reduce the video window to normal size.

Clicking anywhere in the enlarged movie will return the video window to normal size.

You also can adjust the image size via the Movie Options menu, which is discussed in the following section.

Movie Options

If you **CLICK+HOLD** anywhere on your QuickTime movie, you will be presented with the Movie Options menu, as shown in Figure 17.4.

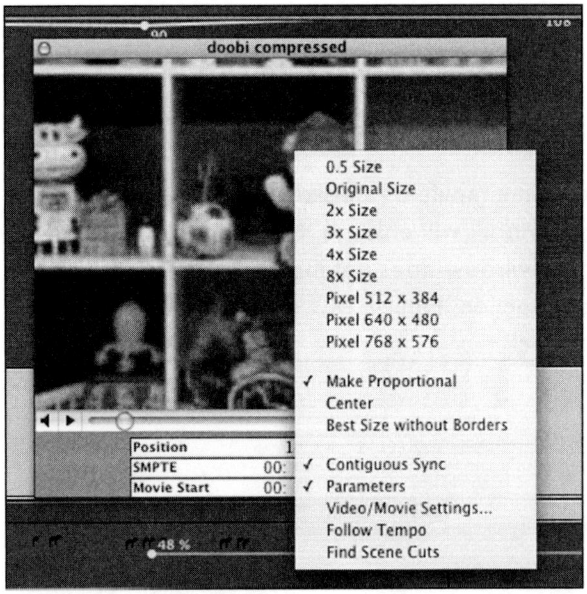

Figure 17.4

You can access the Movie Options menu by click-holding the mouse button anywhere on your QuickTime movie.

This window gives you a number of resizing and synchronization options described below:

- **0.5 Size.** Display your movie at half its original size.
- **Original Size.** Display your movie at its original size.
- **2x Size.** Display your movie at double its original size.
- **3x Size.** Display your movie at triple its original size.
- **4x Size.** Display your movie at quadruple its original size.
- **8x Size.** Display your movie at eight times its original size.
- **Pixel 512 x 384.** Changes the display to NTSC Underscan format, which is 512 × 384 pixels.

- **Pixel 640 x 480.** Changes the display to PAL Underscan (also NTSC Overscan) format, which is 640 × 480 pixels.
- **Pixel 768 x 576.** Changes the display to PAL Overscan format, which is 512 × 384 pixels.
- **Make Proportional.** This will select the next largest proportional setting from the current setting.
- **Center.** This will place your movie window in the middle of your screen (if you have multiple monitors, your video will be placed in the middle of the monitor it is currently on).
- **Best Size without Borders.** This option is the same as clicking in the movie window to make the video full size.
- **Contiguous Sync.** With this option turned on, Logic will control the playback speed of your movie. This ensures that the music and video are in sync at all times. If the movie already has a QuickTime soundtrack, it may be transposed (via sample rate conversion) to fit the Logic tempo if necessary. If you have this option turned off, you will enter Movie Drop Sync, which means that the QuickTime movie will play at its original speed, and if corrections must be made, rather than those corrections being made by Logic adjusting the playback speed of the video, they will be made by adding or dropping frames. If the QuickTime movie has a soundtrack, clicks or pauses may be heard at those points.
- **Parameters.** With this option checked, the Position Displays will show. If this is unchecked, only the video and progress bar will appear in the movie window.
- **Video/Movie Settings.** This opens the Video Settings dialog. This dialog can also be found among the song settings. This dialog is described in the "Video Settings" section, later in this chapter.
- **Follow Tempo.** This will change the SMPTE display to a tempo display, and the song will follow the tempo as opposed to the frame rate. If you are using external sync, any SMPTE Offset will still apply.
- **Find Scene Cuts.** Find Scene Cuts is more or less the same as the Detect Cuts button on the Video track, one of the Global Tracks discussed in Chapter 5. It searches for scene cuts in your QuickTime movie, and creates Movie Markers in the Marker track. Unlike the Video track Detect Cuts button, the Find Scene Cuts command can be restricted to looking for cuts within a Cycle range, Marquee tool selection, or region selection.

Movie Markers

Movie Markers are special Markers locked to a specific SMPTE time. They are discussed in Chapter 5 in the section on the Video track. You can also create them via the Find Scene Cuts command described above, or via the global menu command **Options > Movies > Find Scene Cuts**.

Movie Markers are automatically deleted if you remove the movie from your project. You can also remove them via the global menu command **Options > Movie > Remove Movie Markers**.

> **DON'T FORGET ABOUT GLOBAL TRACKS!**
>
> Remember that in Chapter 5 I discussed the Video track, which is the Global Track that lets you view video thumbnails of your QuickTime movies along with your song. Also, the Movie Markers will show up on the Marker track, another important Global Track. Remember to use these features in tandem with the Video window.

DV Movie Playback over FireWire

If you use a FireWire device for displaying QuickTime video (or a FireWire device connected to monitors for video display), Logic Pro gives you the option to output your previously opened QuickTime video from your Logic song to a FireWire device.

You can activate this option easily by selecting FireWire in the Video Output pull-down menu option in the Video Settings dialog (the Video Settings dialog is detailed below). Your FireWire DV device must be connected for this to work.

For specific details on how your FireWire DV Video device can then use the video being output by Logic, please see the documentation that came with your hardware.

Video Settings

Among the Song Settings dialogs is the Video Settings window. You can access this via the Movie Options menu detailed above or by selecting **File > Song Settings > Video**. Figure 17.5 shows the Video Settings dialog.

Figure 17.5

The Video Settings dialog.

The options of this dialog are described here:

- **Video Output.** If you have a FireWire video device connected, you can choose to output your video either to a window in Logic or to your FireWire digital video hardware. If you do not have any FireWire video device connected to your machine, this has no effect.
- **DV Mode.** This enables you to select one of your FireWire digital video device's video modes. If you don't have a FireWire DV device connected, obviously this parameter does not have any effect.
- **Sound Output.** This determines whether a soundtrack that is already attached to a QuickTime movie you import will be played back through the Macintosh's sound system or will be muted.

Video Preferences

As you can see, there is a button on the bottom-right of the Video Settings window to open the Video Preferences window. You can also access the Video Preferences window via the global menu by selecting **Logic Pro > Preferences > Video**. Figure 17.6 shows the video menu.

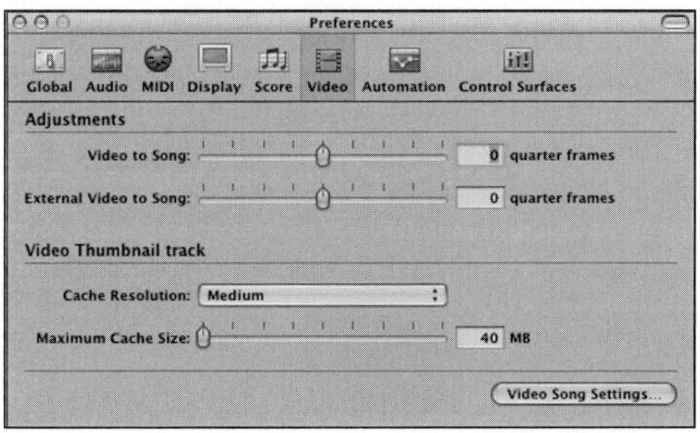

Figure 17.6

The Video Preferences window.

The Video Preferences window includes the following options:

Adjustments

- **Video to Song.** This is a global setting to fine-tune exactly which quarter frame your movie will start on. You can either adjust the slider, or type in a number. The range is –48 to 48 quarter frames.
- **External Video to Song.** This is the same as above, except it fine-tunes the start point for external FireWire video devices in quarter frames. Basically, this lets you compensate for any video hardware latency. The range is the same as above (–48 to 48 quarter frames).

Video Thumbnail Track

- **Cache Resolution.** This determines the resolution of video thumbnails stored in the temporary internal memory cache. Your options are Low, Medium, High, and Best. Obviously, the higher the quality, the more detail in your video thumbnails, but the more memory they take up.
- **Maximum Cache Size.** This determines how large your cache for video thumbnails can be. The memory is only filled when movie data is displayed. You can adjust the cache from 40MB to 32,000MB (32GB).

The Global Movies Submenu

While many of the options to be found in the global Movies submenu at **Options > Movies** have already been covered, some commands are unique to this menu. Figure 17.7 shows the global Movies submenu.

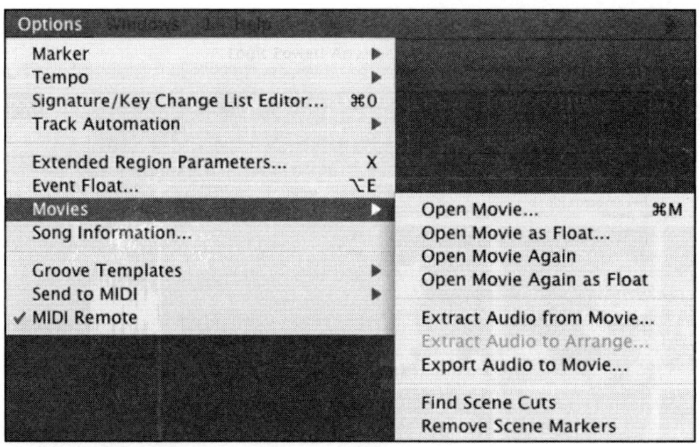

Figure 17.7

The Movies submenu of the global Options menu.

These commands are explained below:

- **Open Movie.** This opens a QuickTime movie, as explained above. **<COMMAND + M>**
- **Open Movie as Float.** This opens a QuickTime movie in a floating window, as explained above.
- **Open Movie Again.** If you close your movie, this will open it again, as explained above.
- **Open Movie Again as Float.** If you close your movie, this will open it again as a floating window, as explained above.
- **Extract Audio from Movie.** This command allows you to extract the soundtrack of a QuickTime movie into audio files, as explained below.
- **Extract Audio to Arrange.** This command is the same as above, except instead of simply adding the extracted audio to your Audio window, it adds it to the selected track in the Arrange window as well.
- **Export Audio to Movie.** This command allows you to export an Audio Track from your Logic project to the QuickTime movie, as explained below.
- **Find Scene Cuts.** This is the same as Find Scene Cuts in the Movie Options menu above.
- **Remove Scene Markers.** This command removes all Movie Markers that were set by the Find Scene Cuts command or Detect Cuts button on the Video track.

Extracting Audio from a QuickTime Movie

If you want to use the soundtrack from a QuickTime movie in your Logic project, you can use the Extract Audio from Movie command to bring the QuickTime audio into your song. Once you select the Extract Audio from Movie command, you will be presented with the Choose Tracks to Export window which lists the Audio Tracks included in the QuickTime movie, as shown in Figure 17.8.

Once you select one or more tracks to export and click OK, Logic will extract the selected track(s) and add them to your Audio window. You can now use them in your song as you would any other audio file.

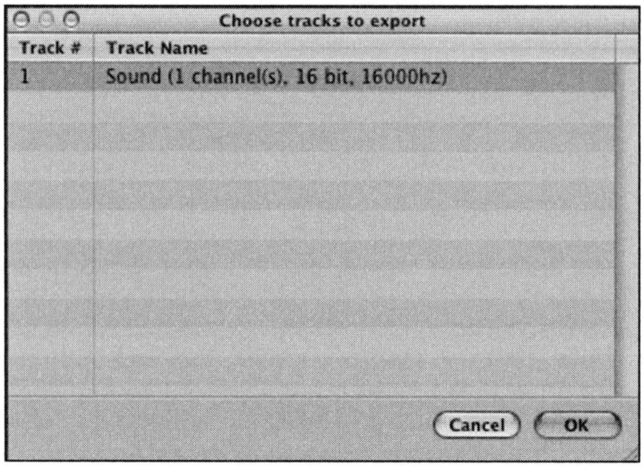

Figure 17.8
The Choose Tracks to Export dialog allows you to select which tracks to Export.

If you want to export the audio from a QuickTime movie directly to a track on your Arrange window, you can use the Extract Audio to Arrange command. To use this command, you need to first select an Audio Track on the Arrange window with the same number of channels as the QuickTime movie audio you wish to extract (in other words, if you are extracting a stereo track from a QuickTime movie, you need to have a stereo track selected in Arrange).

Exporting Audio to a QuickTime Movie

If you wish to add the bounced audio from your song into a QuickTime movie soundtrack, first you will be presented with the QuickTime Sound Settings window to choose your export options, as shown in Figure 17.9.

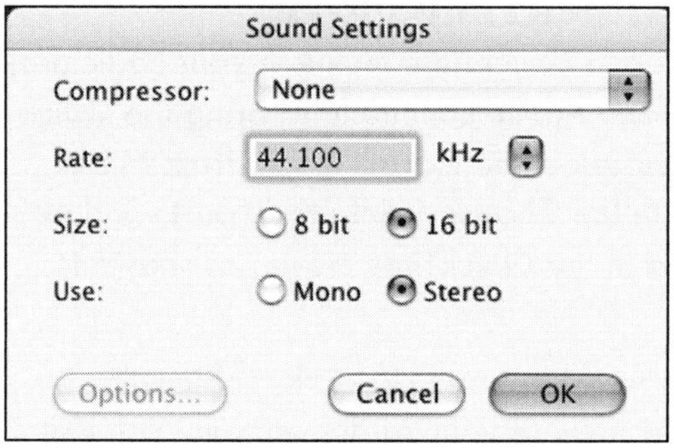

Figure 17.9
The QuickTime Sound Settings dialog is where you set your export preferences.

You are then presented with a Save dialog to save your new movie that includes the exported audio, as shown in Figure 17.10.

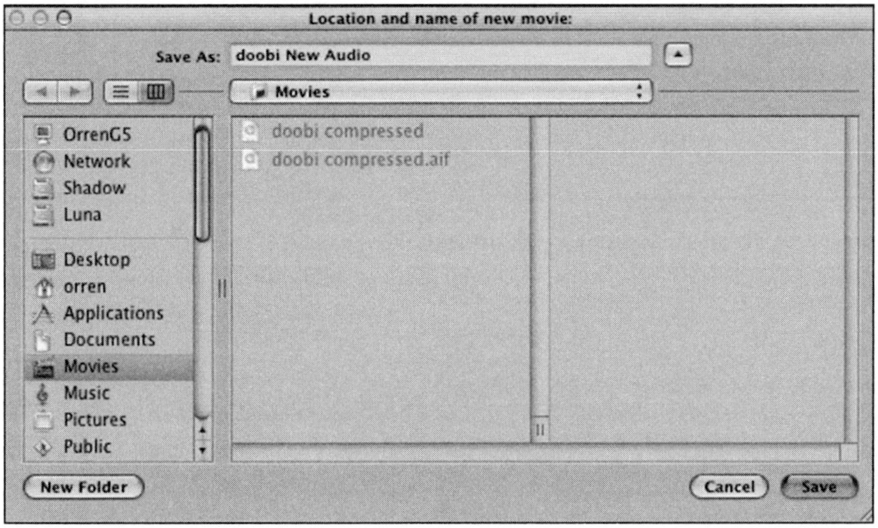

Figure 17.10
You are prompted to save the new movie that includes your exported audio.

After you have chosen a location and name to save your new QuickTime movie, you are prompted to specify which, if any, soundtracks from the original QuickTime movie should be included in the new QuickTime movie file. Figure 17.11 shows this window.

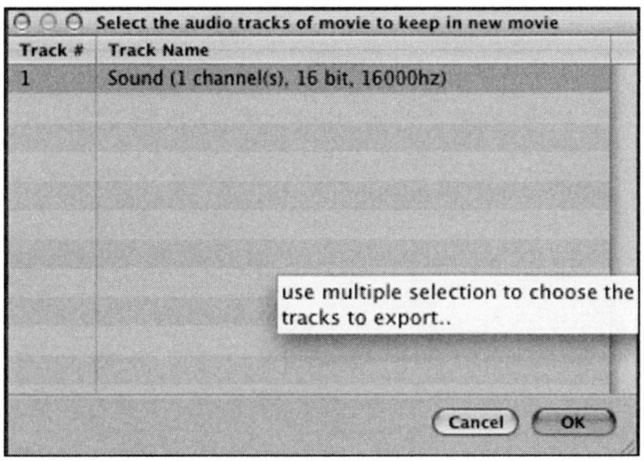

Figure 17.11
You can select which original tracks from the original QuickTime movie to include in the new QuickTime movie.

Finally, Logic will bounce your Logic song (just as if you'd pressed the **BNCE** button on an Output Object channel strip, or selected **File > Bounce**), and then save that bounced audio to your new QuickTime movie.

A Logic Pro 7 Plug-In Reference

Logic has always been famous for including effects that rival those produced by expensive hardware units, and Logic Pro 7 is no exception. Exploring each effect in depth is beyond the scope of this book, but this appendix gives you a list of Logic Pro 7's included effects. The effects are listed in the same order as they are organized in Logic. Each effect is described briefly to give you an idea of when you might want to use it. Remember that each effect has a number of presets—factory programmed settings—that you can try out to get a feel for how to use each effect.

Delay Plug-Ins

Delay effects delay the playback of the audio material in either simple or musically complex ways.

Sample Delay. With this effect, the user can delay playback of audio by 0 to 4,000 samples. This is a no-frills delay, but a very accurate tool for phase correction and realtime sample-accurate adjustments.

Stereo Delay. This is a musical delay that enables users to delay audio using swing patterns, notes, and so on. Stereo Delay offers a full complement of controls to shape the sound and pattern of the effect. It can sync either to Logic's song tempo or to its own internal clock. You can adjust the delay of each stereo channel separately.

Tape Delay. Tape delay is a unique, complex effect that not only offers a musical delay with many user adjustable parameters but also attempts to capture the sound and vibe of analog-style tape-based delay units. It even has a Freeze button for Echoplex-style effects!

Distortion Plug-Ins

Technically, distortion plug-ins increase the level of audio material until they "clip," or break up and distort. Musically, distortion plug-ins can be one of the most dynamic tools for adding color and energy to audio material. All distortion effects include a drive parameter for how hard to drive your audio into clipping, and an output parameter to enable you to adjust the signal so you don't overload your audio interface.

Bitcrusher. This effect distorts your audio by reducing the bit-depth and sampling rate of your audio. It includes a number of different clip level shapes. This plug-in can do anything from adding subtle energy to total sonic destruction.

Clip Distortion. This plug-in offers a plethora of parameters for you to adjust the sound and shape of how the distortion will clip your audio. It includes filter and tone adjustments in addition to the standard distortion parameters.

Distortion. This is a basic distortion, with drive and output parameters as well as a parameter to shape the tone of the distortion. This is similar to the old guitar distortion pedals in operation and sound.

Distortion II. This distortion is based on the distortion section of the EVB3, and has a vintage character.

Guitar Amp Pro. Far more than a simple distortion effect, Guitar Amp Pro is a guitar amplifier simulator that picks up where GarageBand's Guitar Amp leaves off. It offers many different amplifier models, EQ models, speaker simulations, and tremolo and reverb effects.

Overdrive. A slightly more subtle and "vintage" sounding version of the Distortion plug-in.

Phase Distortion. A distortion effect that adds modulation, enabling some very unique coloring of the distorted material.

Dynamics Plug-Ins

These plug-ins affect the dynamics, or amplitude, of the audio material. These effects are useful in controlling audio that has wild variations in volume and in mastering when you are trying to get a consistent level for your material.

Adaptive Limiter. The Adaptive Limiter is an excellent, world-class "lookahead" limiter that delays your audio by a number of milliseconds so that it can determine where the upcoming peaks are. It then reduces those peaks in realtime. Keep in mind that this effect introduces a significant, obvious delay, unlike most of Logic's other plug-ins.

Compressor. This is a basic compressor. It reduces the level of peaks and brings up the level of passages under a threshold so as to compress your audio material into a desired frequency range.

DeEsser. A very specialized form of dynamics processor, a DeEsser focuses on specific frequencies that may have loud sibilant or plosive syllables (loud "s" or "k" sounds, for example) and removes the extra noise.

Enveloper. The Enveloper places a dynamic envelope, like that of a synthesizer envelope, over your audio. This not only can affect the dynamics of your audio, it also can be used to create numerous special effects!

Expander. An expander does the opposite of what a compressor does—it's a compressor that increases the dynamic range of the material above a user-defined threshold.

Limiter. This is a basic limiter that attempts to find peaks in your audio and bring them down to a predetermined level, enabling you to turn up your audio material without the signal overloading the Audio Mixer.

Multipressor. The Multipressor is a multiband compressor, meaning that you can compress different frequency ranges by different amounts or compress only a certain frequency range and not others. This is useful for tightening up one frequency range with compression and leaving others untouched.

Noise Gate. A noise gate closes down the audio playback at a certain threshold to avoid unwanted quiet material on the track from playing. Logic's Noise Gate offers a number of unique parameters to enable it to be used not only as a standard noise gate, but also as a real musical tool—check it out!

Silver Compressor. A very basic compressor plug-in with no GUI and extremely low CPU requirements. This plug-in is the compressor included with Logic Audio (was Logic Silver) and up.

Silver Gate. A very basic noise gate plug-in with no GUI and extremely low CPU requirements. This plug-in is the noise gate included with Logic Audio (was Logic Silver) and up.

EQ Plug-Ins

Equalizer (EQ) plug-ins are the bread and butter of signal processing. These plug-ins enable you to adjust various frequencies in your audio material specifically. Logic includes a number of EQ plug-ins.

Channel EQ. The Channel EQ is the EQ most integrated into the channel strips of Logic Pro 7, as explained in Chapter 12, "Mixing in Logic." It offers eight bands of EQ with various types of cutoff, shelving, and parametric filters. The Channel EQ is perhaps the highest quality, most professional native EQ available on the market today—and Emagic includes it for free!

DJ EQ. A simple, single-band parametric EQ plug-in with the addition of a low shelf filter.

Fat EQ. The Fat EQ is not as advanced or high quality as the Channel EQ, but this EQ still offers five EQ filters with very good sound quality and a low CPU requirement.

High Shelving EQ. A basic high frequency shelving EQ. This enables you to boost or cut a single high frequency you select.

Linear Phase EQ. The Linear Phase EQ looks and functions like the Channel EQ, but it is a far more CPU-intensive effect that insures that the phase of the EQ'd audio never changes.

Low Shelving EQ. A basic low frequency shelving EQ. This enables you to boost or cut a single low frequency you select.

Match EQ. The Match EQ allows you to learn the EQ curve of one audio file, and apply it to another target audio file.

Parametric EQ. A basic single parametric EQ filter.

Silver EQ. A very basic multiband EQ with several filters. This effect is the EQ included with Logic Audio (was Logic Silver) and up.

Filter Plug-Ins

Filter plug-ins filter out frequencies of the audio signal in order to either equalize the audio or to create special effects.

AutoFilter. This effect is somewhat like the resonant filter and modulation section of a synthesizer—you can create unique moving and modulating filters with this effect. If you want to create one-of-a-kind moving sweeps and rhythms with audio, this effect can help!

EVOC 20 Filterbank. This is the filter bank from the EVOC 20 vocoder. It offers up to 20 filters along with modulation, allowing for some very creative special effects.

EVOC 20 TrackOscillator. This is the oscillator from the EVOC 20. Far more than a simple oscillator, it also offers complex modulations and filters for some creative special effects.

Fuzz-Wah. The fuzz-wah from the EVD6. This allows for some vintage sounding wah-wah effects.

High Cut. A very basic high cut filter. This cuts off frequencies above the cutoff frequency.

High Pass Filter. A basic high pass filter. This filters out frequencies below the high pass filter.

Low Cut. A very basic low cut filter. This cuts off frequencies below the cutoff frequency.

Low Pass Filter. A basic low pass filter. This filters out frequencies above the low pass filter.

Helper Plug-Ins

These are handy utility effects when mixing your song. They aren't as sexy as some of the more creative plug-ins, but they come in handy when you need them!

Correlation Meter. This plug-in shows you the correlation of both channels in a stereo pair to each other.

Direction Mixer. This stereo plug-in enables you to vary the pan positioning and adjust the centerpoint of a stereo recording. It also enables you to decode MS (middle side) stereo channels. MS mic positioning is a subject for a book on recording techniques, not Logic, but if you need an MS decoder, this plug-in will do it.

Gain. This simple plug-in enables you to add or subtract gain from a track that is too loud or too soft. It also enables you to invert the phase of a track. The stereo version includes a balance control and can swap the left and right channels or convert to mono.

I/O Plug-In. This is basically an insert for external hardware. You can set which audio input and output to use, and whatever audio device you have connected to your audio interface will then be able to process the audio from your track and return it to Logic's mixer. If you have a studio filled with expensive high-end hardware, this plug-in will quickly become your best friend!

Level Meter. This plug-in offers a simple level meter with double the range of Logic's channel strip level meters, and a few more options.

MultiMeter. For users with more advanced metering requirements, this plug-in includes a spectrum analyzer, a Goniometer and more detailed analysis of stereo signals.

Test Oscillator. This plug-in can generate noise or a steady waveform. You can use this for audio calibration, or any creative use for which you want an oscillator to generate a signal.

Tuner. This is a standard instrument tuner.

Modulation Plug-Ins

Modulation effects modulate the signal in order to create the effect of a wider stereo image, different phase effects, or motion.

Chorus. This is a very basic chorus effect that modulates an audio signal to create anything from a slight lushness to a pulsating detuned effect.

Ensemble. This stereo effect consists of eight separate pitch shifters and three low-frequency oscillators designed to help you create the effect of a huge ensemble of voices or instruments from your source audio.

Flanger. This is a very basic flanger effect that modulates an audio signal to create anything from a slight "sweeping" effect to a wildly detuned "jet engine through a tunnel" metallic sound.

Modulation Delay. This effect combines the Stereo Delay effect with a chorus/flanger modulation section to create a delay effect that moves and modulates.

Phaser. This plug-in modulates the phase of the audio material to create anything from mild to wild sweeping pitch and phase effects.

Ringshifter. Ringshifter is a unique and excellent plug-in that features a ring modulator, frequency shifter, delay, envelope, and LFO. Trust me, you must experience it for yourself!

Rotor Cabinet. This is the rotor cabinet from the EVB3 virtual organ.

Scanner Vibrato. This is the vibrato effect from the EVB3 virtual organ.

Tremolo. This effect enables you to modulate the volume of your track to create tremolo effects with your audio. The plug-in offers many unique parameters and can be synchronized to Logic's tempo if you want.

Spreader. This stereo effect can be used to make the stereo field of your audio seem wider or narrower.

Reverb Plug-Ins

Reverbs effects create the sensation of ambiance and space by adding artificial "reverberations" to your audio material. These plug-ins are useful for creating the sensation of the recording being in a place where it actually wasn't recorded or to create a lush ambiance.

AVerb. The AVerb is a very simple reverb with no GUI and a very low CPU requirement.

EnVerb. EnVerb is a unique reverb that gives you total control over the shape of the reverb envelope, enabling gated and reverse reverb effects. It has a large CPU requirement, but the sound quality is excellent!

GoldVerb. GoldVerb is the stereo reverb that comes with Logic Gold and up. GoldVerb is a very good sounding reverb with a modest CPU requirement.

PlatinumVerb. PlatinumVerb is the reverb that ships with Logic Platinum and up. It is of world-class quality, sounding more lush and including more parameters for fine-tuning than any of the other Logic reverbs. It also has a larger CPU requirement.

SilverVerb. SilverVerb ships with Logic Audio (was Logic Silver) and up. It does not have the breadth of controls or lushness of GoldVerb or PlatinumVerb, but what it does it does very well. It has a lower CPU requirement than either GoldVerb or PlatinumVerb.

Space Designer. This is a "convolution" reverb that allows you to record an impulse response (IR) from a real space and then use that recorded space to generate a synthetic reverb you can use to process audio. It's an amazingly powerful and complex process that can create everything from realistic cathedral spaces to simulations of guitar amplifier speaker cabinets and garages! Space Designer is one of the best convolution reverbs available, so have fun!

Special Plug-Ins

The Special subcategory is sort of a catchall for effects that don't fit in any of the other subcategories.

Denoiser. This plug-in attempts to remove noise from audio material. It is basically a noise gate that can be focused on a very narrow and specific frequency band.

Exciter. An exciter attempts to "excite" the audio by adding high frequency harmonics.

Grooveshifter. Grooveshifter allows you to alter the rhythmic pattern of an audio file.

Pitch Correction. Pitch Correction lets you correct the pitch of off-pitch audio. This is often used to fix a quality vocal that has only a few sour notes, and the like.

Pitch Shifter II. This effect enables you to shift the pitch of your audio.

Spectral Gate. This is one of the most unique effects included with Logic Pro, and the hardest to explain. Basically, it modulates frequencies above and below a threshold, enabling some amazing filtering effects. This is one of those effects you really need to play with to get a feel for what it can do.

SubBass. This plug-in adds a synthesized bass sound at a lower register than your original signal.

Stereo Spread. This stereo effect enables you to manipulate the stereo base far more than the Spreader plug-in.

Vocal Transformer. As its name implies, this plug-in is designed to transform audio by separately adjusting the pitch and formats of the initial audio.

Logic Audio Instruments

Logic includes not only high-quality plug-in effects, but some of the most spectacular Audio Instruments available as well. In fact, many users chose Logic as their platform on the basis of how spectacular the instruments are! Most of these instruments come with a selection of factory presets; give them a listen to get a feel for what each synthesizer can do!

EFM1. The EFM1 (Emagic FM 1) is a simple but completely professional quality FM synthesizer. This synth can create rich, crystalline "digital" sounding basslines, pads, melodies, and special effects.

ES1. Emagic's first audio instrument, the ES1 (Emagic Synthesizer 1) is still known for generating very punchy bass and melody sounds.

ES2. Emagic's far more fully featured ES2 (Emagic Synthesizer 2) offers far more complex wavetable and oscillations than the ES1. It's more complex to program, but can generate spectacular electronic leads, melodies, pads, and basslines.

ES M. The ES M (Emagic Synthesizer Monophonic) is a monophonic instrument designed to be used as a bass synthesizer. Far from a throwaway freebee instrument, this synthesizer can create impressively rich and "phat" bass sounds, as well as other resonant mono synth timbres.

ES P. The ES P (Emagic Synthesizer Polyphonic) can play up to eight voices at a time and is far more flexible than the ES M, although not quite as "phat" when it comes to bass sounds. It is geared toward reproducing many of the synth timbres of classic 1980s mass-produced digital synthesizers.

ES E. The ES E (Emagic Synthesizer Ensemble) was designed to create lush ambient pad and ensemble sounds, but it also can be used for more traditional sounds. This software instrument is excellent for creating glassy and textured ambiences.

EVB3. Emagic's virtual organ, the EVB3 (Emagic Virtual B3), is a physical modeling synthesizer designed to recreate the classic sounds of the Hammond B3 organ.

EVD6. Emagic's virtual clavinet, the EVD6 (Emagic Virtual D6), is a physical modeling synthesizer designed to recreate the classic sounds of the electric clavinet.

EVP88. The EVP88 (Emagic Virtual Piano 88) models the sounds of classic electric pianos such as the Rhodes, Wurlitzer, Electra, and other great '70s instruments.

EXS24mkII. This is Emagic's venerable sampler. The EXS24mkII is not as fully featured as many software samplers out there, but it offers amazing CPU efficiency and integration into Logic Pro.

External. As discussed earlier in the book, this plug-in allows you to use external MIDI instruments on an Audio Instrument track.

GarageBand Instruments. Your GarageBand instruments will all appear here, insuring that any GarageBand songs you open in Logic will play correctly.

Sculpture. Sculpture is perhaps the most advanced physical modeling synthesizer available! It allows you to take physically modeled elements of real sounds (glass, bows, wind, and so on) and create absolutely unique sounds and instruments. You need to try it out to believe it!

UltraBeat. UltraBeat is simply the most advanced software drum synthesizer available. It takes a while to get the hang of its interface, but its sound quality is unmatched. Check out the presets to see for yourself!

B Default Key Command Reference

The following tables compose a comprehensive list of nearly all the key commands available in Logic Pro 7. Keep in mind that other versions of Logic have fewer key commands available and perhaps a few other key commands, so use these tables as a resource, but remember that the ultimate reference for your specific version of Logic is the Key Commands window itself.

Table B.1 Global Key Commands

Assigned Key	Key Command
*	Record
	Record Repeat
	Record Toggle
	Capture Last Take as Recording
	Capture Last Take as Recording & Play
RETURN	Play
.	Pause
0	Stop
SPACE	Play or Stop
[	Rewind
]	Forward
	Fast Rewind
	Fast Forward
	Rewind 1 Frame
	Forward 1 Frame
	Rewind by Format Value
	Forward by Format Value
	Shuttle Rewind
	Shuttle Forward
	Scrub Rewind
	Scrub Forward

Table B.1 Global Key Commands *(continued)*

Assigned Key	Key Command
	Scrub by MIDI Value (-2-)
	Play from Beginning
	Play from Previous Bar
	Play from Left Locator
	Play from Right Locator
	Play from Left Window Corner
	Goto Left Locator
	Goto Right Locator
	Goto Last Play Position
	Stop Goto Last Play Position
	Stop Goto Left Locator
	Goto Position
	Set Left Locator
	Set Right Locator
	Set Left Locator by Song Position
	Set Left Locator by Rounded Song Position
	Set Left Autodrop Point by Song Position
	Set Left Autodrop Point by Rounded Song Position
	Set Right Locator by Song Position
	Set Right Locator by Rounded Song Position
	Set Right Autodrop Point by Song Position
	Set Right Autodrop Point by Rounded Song Position
	Set Locators by Objects
=	Set Rounded Locators by Objects
	Set Locators & Play
	Set Rounded Locators & Play
	Set Rounded Locators & Cycle Play
	Set Rounded Locators & Record
	Set Rounded Locators & Cycle Record
\	Swap Left and Right Locator
	Move Locators Forward by Cycle Length
	Move Locators Backwards by Cycle Length
SHIFT + RETURN	Play from Selection
SHIFT + SPACE	Goto Selection
	Create Marker
	Create Marker Without Rounding
	Delete Marker
	Open Marker List
	Open Marker List as Float
	Open Marker Text
	Open Marker Text as Float
	Set Locators by Marker & Enable Cycle
	Set Locators by Previous Marker & Enable Cycle
	Set Locators by Next Marker & Enable Cycle
	Goto Previous Marker
	Goto Next Marker
	Goto Marker Number

Table B.1 Global Key Commands *(continued)*

Assigned Key	Key Command
OPTION + COMMAND + F1	Goto Marker Number 1
OPTION + COMMAND + F2	Goto Marker Number 2
OPTION + COMMAND + F3	Goto Marker Number 3
OPTION + COMMAND + F4	Goto Marker Number 4
OPTION + COMMAND + F5	Goto Marker Number 5
OPTION + COMMAND + F6	Goto Marker Number 6
OPTION + COMMAND + F7	Goto Marker Number 7
OPTION + COMMAND + F8	Goto Marker Number 8
OPTION + COMMAND + F9	Goto Marker Number 9
OPTION + COMMAND + F10	Goto Marker Number 10
OPTION + COMMAND + F11	Goto Marker Number 11
OPTION + COMMAND + F12	Goto Marker Number 12
OPTION + COMMAND + F13	Goto Marker Number 13
OPTION + COMMAND + F14	Goto Marker Number 14
OPTION + COMMAND + F15	Goto Marker Number 15
	Goto Marker Number 16
	Goto Marker Number 17
	Goto Marker Number 18
	Goto Marker Number 19
	Goto Marker Number 20
	Select Previous Song
	Select Next Song
	Select Song 1
	Select Song 2
	Select Song 3
	Select Song 4
	Select Song 5
	Select Song 6
	Select Song 7
	Select Song 8
	Select Song 9
	Select Song 10
	Select Song 11
	Select Song 12
	Select Song 13
	Select Song 14
	Select Song 15
	Select Song 16
	Select Song 17
	Select Song 18
	Select Song 19
	Select Song 20
/	Cycle
	Drop
	Replace
S	Solo

Table B.1 Global Key Commands *(continued)*

Assigned Key	Key Command
OPTION + S	Set Solo Lock Mode
	Reselect Solo-Locked Regions
	Solo Off for All
	Mute Off for All
	Record Off for All
	Sync Intern/Extern
	Tap Tempo
	Set Tempo Alternative
	MIDI Machine Control
	Toggle MIDI Remote (Always MIDI Remote Controllable)
	Disable MIDI Remote
	Set Next Higher Format
	Set Next Lower Format
C	MIDI/Monitor Metronome Click
	Send Reset Controllers
	Send Discrete Note Offs (Panic)
	Send Maximum Volume
	Send Used Instruments MIDI Settings
	Send All Current Fader Values Except SysEx
	Send All Current Fader Values
	Revert to Current Screenset
SHIFT + CONTROL + 2	Copy Screenset
	Paste Screenset
SHIFT + L	Lock/Unlock Current Screenset
	Next Screenset
	Previous Screenset
	Recall Screenset 1
	Recall Screenset 2
	Recall Screenset 3
	Recall Screenset 4
	Recall Screenset 5
	Recall Screenset 6
	Recall Screenset 7
	Recall Screenset 8
	Recall Screenset 9
	Reclock Song
R	Copy MIDI Events
X	Extended Region Parameters
	Import Settings
OPTION + R	Recording Options
OPTION + M	MIDI Options
	Chase Events
OPTION + P	Preferences
COMMAND + I	Import File
	Open Event Editor
COMMAND + 1	Open Arrange Window
COMMAND + 2	Open Track Mixer

Table B.1 Global Key Commands *(continued)*

Assigned Key	Key Command
COMMAND + 3	Open Score Editor
COMMAND + 4	Open Transform
COMMAND + 5	Open Hyper Editor
COMMAND + 6	Open Matrix Editor
COMMAND + 7	Open Transport
COMMAND + 8	Open Environment
COMMAND + 9	Open Audio Window
	Open Sample Editor
	Open Project Manager
COMMAND + 0	Signature/Key Change List Editor
OPTION + E	Toggle Event Float
E	Toggle Event Editor
	Toggle Arrange Window
	Toggle Track Mixer
	Toggle Score Editor
	Toggle Transform
	Toggle Hyper Editor
	Toggle Matrix Editor
	Toggle Transport
	Toggle Environment
	Toggle Audio Window
W	Toggle Sample Editor
	Toggle Signature Changes List
	Start External Sample Editor
OPTION + Y	Open System Performance
OPTION + X	Open Synchronization Window
OPTION + T	Open Tempo List
	Open Tempo Operations
	Open Tempo Interpreter
OPTION + K	Open Key Commands
OPTION + C	Open Object Colors
COMMAND + M	Open Movie
	Open Movie Again
	Open Movie Again as Float
	Open Audio Record Window
	Toggle (Mute) Audio Inputs
	Toggle (Mute) Audio Tracks
	Toggle (Mute) Audio Aux
	Toggle (Mute) Audio Bus
	Toggle (Mute) Audio Outputs
	Toggle Current Track Automation Off/Read
	Set Current Track to Automation Read
	Toggle Current Track Automation Touch/Read
	Toggle Current Track Automation Latch/Read
	Toggle Current Track Automation Write/Read
	Toggle Current Track Automation MIDI/Read
	Set All Tracks to Automation Off

Table B.1 Global Key Commands *(continued)*

Assigned Key	Key Command
	Set All Tracks to Automation Read
	Set All Tracks to Automation Touch
	Set All Tracks to Automation Latch
	Set All Tracks to Automation Write
	Set All Tracks to Automation MIDI
	Automation Event Edit
	Track Automation Settings
	Toggle Automation Controlling Volume
	Toggle Automation Controlling Pan
	Toggle Automation Controlling Mute
	Toggle Automation Controlling Send Levels
	Toggle Automation Controlling Plug-In Parameters
	Toggle Automation Controlling Solo
	Toggle Automation Quick Access
	Toggle Group Clutch
	Open Group Settings
	Write to End
	Write to Right Locator
	Delete Currently Visible Automation Data of Current Track
	Delete All Automation Data of Current Track
	Delete All Automation Data of All Tracks
	Move Current Object Data to Track Automation
	Move Current Track Automation Data to Object
	Move All Object Control Data to Track Automation
	Move All Track Automation Data to Object
	Refresh Freeze Files
	Refresh Audio Configuration
	Audio Hardware Setup
	Audio Configuration
A	Set Audio Record Path
	Toggle Auto Input Monitoring
	Clear Overload Flag in Audio Channel Display
	Toggle Velocity Engine Support
	Close Window
OPTION + W	Close Floating Window
COMMAND + W	Close Window or Song
	Close Song Without Save
SHIFT + W	Select Next Window
	Redraw Current Window
COMMAND + N	New
	Initialize Song
COMMAND + O	Open
OPTION + COMMAND + W	Close
COMMAND + S	Save
OPTION + COMMAND + S	Save Song As
	Revert to Saved
	Page Setup

Table B.1 Global Key Commands *(continued)*

Assigned Key	Key Command
COMMAND + P	Print
	Import
	Export Selection as MIDI File
COMMAND + Q	Quit
COMMAND + Z	Undo
SHIFT + COMMAND + Z	Redo
OPTION + Z	Undo History
	Delete Undo History
COMMAND + X	Cut
COMMAND + Y	Copy
COMMAND + V	Paste
	Clear
COMMAND + A	Select All
	Zoom Window
	Tile Windows
	Tile Windows Horizontally
	Stack Windows
	Next Plug-In Setting
	Previous Plug-In Setting
	Next EXS Instrument
	Previous EXS Instrument
	Next Plug-In Setting or EXS Instrument
	Previous Plug-In Setting or EXS Instrument

Table B.2 Miscellaneous Key Commands

Assigned Key	Key Command
ESCAPE	Show Tools
	Set Next Tool
	Set Previous Tool
	Set Arrow Tool
	Set Scissors Tool
	Set Glue Tool
	Set Eraser Tool
	Set MIDI Thru Tool
	Set Text Tool
	Set Solo Tool
	Set Pencil Tool
	Set Crosshair Tool
	Set Mute Tool
	Set Finger Tool
	Set Layout Tool
	Set Magnifying Glass Tool
	Set Size Tool
	Set Voice Separation Tool

Table B.2 Miscellaneous Key Commands *(continued)*

Assigned Key	Key Command
	Set Camera Tool
	Set Velocity Tool
	Set Quantize Tool
	Set Audio Crossfade Tool
	Set Automation Tool
	Set Marquee Tool
	Toggle Global Tracks
	Toggle Signature Track
	Toggle Tempo Track
	Toggle Chord Track
	Toggle Beat Mapping Track
	Toggle Marker Track
	Toggle Video Track
	Toggle Transposition Track
	Hide All Global Tracks
	Show All Global Tracks
CONTROL + L. ARROW	Zoom Horizontal Out
CONTROL + R. ARROW	Zoom Horizontal In
CONTROL + U. ARROW	Zoom Vertical Out
CONTROL + D. ARROW	Zoom Vertical In
	Recall Zoom 1
	Recall Zoom 2
	Recall Zoom 3
	Save as Zoom 1
	Save as Zoom 2
	Save as Zoom 3
Z	Zoom to Fit Selection Vertically & Horizontally, Store Navigation Snapshot
	Zoom to Fit Selection Horizontally, Store Navigation Snapshot
	Zoom to Fit Locators, Store Navigation Snapshot
	Store Navigation Snapshot
SHIFT Z	Navigation: Back
	Navigation: Forward
PageUp	Page Up
PageDown	Page Down
Home	Page Left
End	Page Right
	1/3 Page Left
	1/3 Page Right
	1/8 Page Left
	1/8 Page Right
	Page Top
	Page Bottom
	Page Leftmost
	Page Rightmost
P	Hide/Show Parameters

Table B.2 Miscellaneous Key Commands *(continued)*

Assigned Key	Key Command
CONTROL + G	Grid
	Plain Background
V	Catch Clock Position
	Link Window (Same Level)
O	MIDI Out Toggle
I	MIDI In Toggle
M	Mute Objects
	Hyper Draw: Disable
	Hyper Draw: Volume
	Hyper Draw: Pan
	Hyper Draw: Modulation
	Hyper Draw: Pitch Bend
	Hyper Draw: Note Velocity
	Hyper Draw: Other
	Hyper Draw: Autodefine

Table B.3 Arrange and MIDI Region Editor Key Commands

Assigned Key	Key Command
	Go Into Folder or Sequence
	Go Out of Folder or Sequence
SHIFT + COMMAND + A	Deselect All
SHIFT + T	Toggle Selection
SHIFT + F	Select All Following
	Select All Following of Track
SHIFT + I	Select Inside Locators
	Deselect Outside Locators
	Deselect Global Tracks
SHIFT + U	Select Empty Objects
SHIFT + O	Select Overlapped Objects
SHIFT + E	Select Equal Objects
SHIFT + S	Select Similar Objects
SHIFT + H	Select Equal Channels
SHIFT + P	Select Equal Subpositions
SHIFT + M	Select Muted Regions/Events
	Select First
	Select Last
L. ARROW	Select Previous Event
R. ARROW	Select Next Event
SHIFT + L. ARROW	Toggle Previous Region/Event
SHIFT + R. ARROW	Toggle Next Region/Event
SHIFT + V	Scroll to Selection
	Quantize Again
	Quantize: Next Value
	Quantize: Previous Value
	De-Quantize

Table B.3 Arrange and MIDI Region Editor Key Commands *(continued)*

Assigned Key	Key Command
TAB	Note Overlap Correction
SHIFT + TAB	Note Force Legato
SHIFT + U. ARROW	Select Top Line
SHIFT + D. ARROW	Select Bottom Line
	Lines to Channels
	Sustain Pedal to Note Length
	Note Overlap Correction (Selected/Selected)
	Note Force Legato (Selected/Selected)
	Note Overlap Correction for Repeated Notes
	Delete Similar Objects
	Delete but Keep Similar Objects
	Delete and Select Next Region/Event
	Paste at Original Position
	Paste Replace
	Erase Unselected Within Selection
	Repeat Objects
J	Merge Objects/Digital Mixdown
COMMAND + Y	Split Regions/Events by Locators
Y	Split Regions/Events by Rounded Song Position
CONTROL + Y	Split Regions/Events by Song Position
CONTROL + P	Pickup Clock (Move Event to SPL Position)
	Pickup Clock & Select Next Event
	Set Region/Event Start to SPL Position
	Set Region/Event End to SPL Position
	Nudge Event Position by SMPTE Frame +1
	Nudge Event Position by SMPTE Frame -1
	Nudge Event Position by SMPTE Bits +1
	Nudge Event Position by SMPTE Bits -1
	Nudge Event Position by SMPTE Frame + 0.5
	Nudge Event Position by SMPTE Frame - 0.5
	Nudge Event Position by SMPTE Frame + 5
	Nudge Event Position by SMPTE Frame - 5
	Nudge Event Position by Tick +1
	Nudge Event Position by Tick -1
	Nudge Event Position by Format +1
	Nudge Event Position by Format -1
	Nudge Event Position by Beat +1
	Nudge Event Position by Beat -1
	Nudge Event Position by Bar +1
	Nudge Event Position by Bar -1
OPTION + R. ARROW	Nudge Event Position by + Nudge Value
OPTION + L. ARROW	Nudge Event Position by - Nudge Value
CONTROL + OPTION + T	Set Nudge Value to Tick
CONTROL + OPTION + F	Set Nudge Value to Format
CONTROL + OPTION + B	Set Nudge Value to Beat
	Set Nudge Value to Bar

Table B.3 Arrange and MIDI Region Editor Key Commands *(continued)*

Assigned Key	Key Command
CONTROL + OPTION + S	Set Nudge Value to SMPTE Frame
	Set Nudge Value to 0.5 SMPTE Frame
	Nudge Event Length by Tick +1
	Nudge Event Length by Tick -1
	Nudge Event Length by Format +1
	Nudge Event Length by Format -1
	Nudge Event Length by Beat +1
	Nudge Event Length by Beat -1
	Nudge Event Length by Bar +1
	Nudge Event Length by Bar -1
	Nudge Event Length by SMPTE Frame +1
	Nudge Event Length by SMPTE Frame -1
OPTION + U. ARROW	Event Transpose +1
OPTION + D. ARROW	Event Transpose -1
	Event Channel +1
	Event Channel -1
U	Positions/Time Ruler in SMPTE units
	Unlock SMPTE Position
	Lock SMPTE Position

Table B.4 Arrange Window Key Commands

Assigned Key	Key Command
U. ARROW	Select Previous Track
D. ARROW	Select Next Track
L. ARROW	Select Previous Region
R. ARROW	Select Next Region
	Deselect All Regions Except Recording Track
	Set Track & MIDI Thru Parameters by Region/Folder
SHIFT + C	Select Equal Colored Regions
COMMAND + F	Pack Folder
SHIFT + COMMAND + F	Unpack Folder
	Append Track to Track List
	Append Track to Track List with Next Instrument
SHIFT + RETURN	Create Track
SHIFT + CONTROL + RETURN	Create Track with Next Instrument
	Delete Track
	Delete Unused Tracks
	Tracks for Overlapped Objects
	Tracks for Selected Objects
	Toggle Hide View
CONTROL + H	Hide Current Track and Select Next Track
CONTROL + OPTION + H	Unhide All Tracks
CONTROL + M	Toggle Track Mute
	Mute All Tracks of Folder
	Mute All Tracks with Same Instrument of Song

Table B.4 Arrange Window Key Commands *(continued)*

Assigned Key	Key Command
CONTROL + *	Record Enable Track
	Toggle Track Solo
	Individual Track Zoom In
	Individual Track Zoom Out
	Toggle Individual Track Zoom
	Auto Track Zoom
	Individual Track Zoom Reset
	Individual Track Zoom Reset for All Tracks
	Make Alias
	Make Alias but Copy Folder
	Turn Alias to Real Copy
	Reassign Alias
COMMAND + R	Find Original of Alias
SHIFT + A	Select All Aliases of Region
OPTION + J	Audio Crossfade Options for Merge
SHIFT + J	Merge Objects per Tracks
	Snip: Cut Time and Move by Locators
	Insert Time and Move by Locators
	Splice: Insert Snipped Part at Song Position
COMMAND + D	Demix by Event Channel
	Empty Trash
	Open Trash
	Create New Instrument
SHIFT + CONTROL + A	Create Trackname
	Delete Trackname
	Move Selected Regions to Track
T	Adjust Tempo Using Region Length and Locators
	Set Region(s) to Recording Position
CONTROL + R	Convert Regions to Individual Regions
CONTROL + F	Convert Regions to Individual Audio Files
	Adjust Region Length to Locators
	Adjust Region Length to Nearest Bar
CONTROL + S	Strip Silence
N	Normalize
	Normalize w/o Channel
	Normalize w/o Channel & Delay
Q	Fix Quantize
L	Toggle Loop
K	Turn Loops to Real Copies
	Turn Loops to Aliases
D	Erase Duplicated Events
B	Set Optimal Region Sizes Rounded by Bar
CONTROL + B	Set Optimal Region Sizes Rounded by Denominator
	Snap Region Start to Bar
CONTROL + TAB	Remove Overlaps

Table B.4 Arrange Window Key Commands *(continued)*

Assigned Key	Key Command
CONTROL + OPTION + TAB	Tie Regions by Length Change
SHIFT + CONTROL + TAB	Tie Regions by Position Change
	Replace Overlapped Regions
COMMAND + J	Tie Regions Within Locators
	Insert Instrument MIDI Settings as Events
	Erase Inside Locators
	Erase Outside Locators
CONTROL + E	Erase Outside Region Borders
	Crop Regions Outside Marquee Selection
	Remove Groove Template from List
	Make Groove Template
	Import DNA Groove Templates
	Show Channel Strip Only
	View Track Automation
CONTROL + D	Delay in ms
CONTROL + O	Region Content
SHIFT + OPTION + C	Instrument Colors to Regions
SHIFT + OPTION + N	Tracknames to Regions
	Waveform Vertical Zoom × 1 (Normal)
	Waveform Vertical Zoom × 2
	Waveform Vertical Zoom × 4
	Waveform Vertical Zoom × 8
	Waveform Vertical Zoom Out
	Waveform Vertical Zoom In

Table B.5 Environment Window Key Commands

Assigned Key	Key Command
	New Standard Instrument
	New Multi-Instrument
	New Mapped Instrument
	New Fader/Knobs
	New Keyboard
	New Monitor
	New Arpeggiator
	New Transformer
	New Delay Line
	New Voice Limiter
	New Channel Splitter
	New Chord Memorizer
	New Sample Cell
	New Modem Port
	New Printer Port
	New Audio Object

Table B.5 Environment Window Key Commands *(continued)*

Assigned Key	Key Command
CONTROL + DELETE	Clear Cables Only
	Clean Up Positions
	Reset Sizes
	Align Objects
SHIFT + CONTROL + L. ARROW	Object Move Left
SHIFT + CONTROL + R. ARROW	Object Move Right
SHIFT + CONTROL + U. ARROW	Object Move Up
SHIFT + CONTROL + D. ARROW	Object Move Down
CONTROL + OPTION + L. ARROW	Object Width -1 Pixel
CONTROL + OPTION + R. ARROW	Object Width +1 Pixel
CONTROL + OPTION + U. ARROW	Object Height -1 Pixel
CONTROL + OPTION + D. ARROW	Object Height +1 Pixel
CONTROL + C	Hide/Show Cables
CONTROL + P	Protect Cabling/Positions
	Toggle Channel Display Default of Multi Instrument
SHIFT + T	Toggle Selection
	Select Used Instruments
	Select Unused Instruments
SHIFT + D	Select Cable Destination
SHIFT + O	Select Cable Origin
	Goto Layer of Object
TAB	Goto Previous Layer
	Send Selected Fader Values
	Send All Fader Values Except SysEx
	Delete Layer
	Insert Layer
CONTROL + S	Cable Serially
	Apply Buffer Template to Position and Size
	Apply Buffer Template to Position
	Apply Buffer Template to Size
	Apply Buffer Template to Definition
	Apply Buffer Template to Definition, Channel Increment
	Apply Buffer Template to Definition, Number Increment
	Apply Buffer Template to Cable(s)

Table B.6 Score Editor Key Commands

Assigned Key	Key Commands
	Page Edit
	Explode Folders
CONTROL + P	Explode Polyphony
	Hide/Show Instrument Names
	Hide/Show Page Rulers
	Color View: Individual
	Color View: Show Pitch

Table B.6 Score Editor Key Commands *(continued)*

Assigned Key	Key Commands
	Color View: Show Velocity
	Color View: Show Polyphony
	Color View: Force Black & White
	Go to Page #
OPTION + COMMAND + V	Paste Multiple
	Paste Multiple at Original Position
R. ARROW	Next Event
L. ARROW	Previous Event
D. ARROW	Next Staff
U. ARROW	Previous Staff
	Default Syncopation
	Force Syncopation
	Defeat Syncopation
	Default Interpretation
	Force Interpretation
	Defeat Interpretation
CONTROL + S	Stems: Default
CONTROL + Home	Stems: Up
CONTROL + End	Stems: Down
CONTROL + DELETE	Stems: Hide
	Stem End: Default Length
	Stem End: Move Up
	Stem End: Move Down
	Voice/Staff Assignment: Default
	Voice/Staff Assignment: Staff Above Voice
	Voice/Staff Assignment: Staff Below Voice
CONTROL + T	Ties: Default
CONTROL + PageUp	Ties: Up
CONTROL + PageDown	Ties: Down
CONTROL + B	Beam Selected Notes
CONTROL + U	Unbeam Selected Notes
CONTROL + D	Default Beams
	Not Independent
	Independent
	Independent Grace
CONTROL + A	Default Accidentals
SHIFT + #	Enharmonic Shift: #
SHIFT + B	Enharmonic Shift: b
	Flats to Sharps
	Sharps to Flats
	Force Accidental
	Hide Accidental
	Guide Accidental
	Reset Note Attributes
	Reset Line Layout

Table B.6 Score Editor Key Commands *(continued)*

Assigned Key	Key Commands
OPTION + COMMAND + A	Align Object Positions Vertically
	Align Object Positions Horizontally
	Align Object Positions
	Split to Channels
	Nudge Position Up
	Nudge Position Down
	Nudge Position Left
	Nudge Position Right
CONTROL + COMMAND + S	Open Score Style Window
CONTROL + COMMAND + I	Open Instrument Set Window
CONTROL + COMMAND + F	Settings: Global Format
	Settings: Numbers Names
	Settings: Guitar Tablature
	Settings: Clefs & Signatures
	Settings: Score Colors
CONTROL + COMMAND + P	Score Preferences
	Selection to New Instrument Set
	Partbox: 1/1 Note
	Partbox: 1/2 Note
	Partbox: 1/4 Note
	Partbox: 1/8 Note
	Partbox: 1/16 Note
	Partbox: 1/32 Note
	Next Partbox Symbol
	Previous Partbox Symbol
	Next Partbox Group
	Previous Partbox Group
	Attach Symbol: Fermata Up
	Attach Symbol: Fermata Down
	Attach Symbol: Staccato
	Attach Symbol: Staccatissimo
	Attach Symbol: Accent
	Attach Symbol: Strong Accent
	Attach Symbol: Long Accent
	Attach Symbol: Tenuto
	Attach Symbol: Up-Bow
	Attach Symbol: Down-Bow
	Attach Symbol: Flageolet
	Attach Symbol: Pizzicato
	Attach Symbol: Left Hand
	Attach Symbol: Right Hand
	Attach Symbol: Soft
	Attach Symbol: Heavy
	Attach Symbol: Jazz 1
	Attach Symbol: Jazz 2

Table B.6 Score Editor Key Commands *(continued)*

Assigned Key	Key Commands
	Attach Symbol: Jazz 3
	Attach Symbol: Jazz 4
	Attach Symbol: Jazz 5
	Attach Symbol: Jazz 6
SHIFT + CONTROL + Home	Insert: Slur Up
SHIFT + CONTROL + End	Insert: Slur Down
SHIFT + CONTROL + C	Insert: Crescendo
SHIFT + CONTROL + D	Insert: Decrescendo

Table B.7 Event Editor Key Commands

Assigned Key	Key Command
U. ARROW	Scroll to Previous Event
D. ARROW	Scroll to Next Event
	Length as Absolute Position
	Local Position
	Numerical Edit of Event Position
	Duplicate Event and Numerical Edit
CONTROL + V	Copy Value to All Following Events

Table B.8 Hyper Editor Key Commands

Assigned Key	Key Command
CONTROL + RETURN	Create Event Definition
CONTROL + DELETE	Delete Event Definition
	Multi Create Event Definition
CONTROL + T	Convert Event Definition
CONTROL + C	Copy Event Definition
CONTROL + V	Paste Event Definition
	Select All Event Definitions
	Protect Values Toggle
CONTROL + A	Auto Define Toggle

Table B.9 Audio Window Key Commands

Assigned Key	Key Command
U. ARROW	Select Previous Audio File
D. ARROW	Select Next Audio File
	Show Audio File Details
	Hide Audio File Details
SPACE	Play/Stop Region
CONTROL + F	Add Audio File
CONTROL + R	Add Region
CONTROL + DELETE	Delete File(s)
CONTROL + O	Optimize File(s)
CONTROL + B	Backup File(s)
CONTROL + C	Copy/Convert File(s)
CONTROL + M	Move File(s)
	Select Used
SHIFT + U	Select Unused
	Show All Regions
	Hide All Regions
CONTROL + S	Strip Silence
CONTROL + I	Import SDII Regions
CONTROL + E	Export SDII Regions

Table B.10 Sample Editor Key Commands

Assigned Key	Key Command
SPACE	Play/Stop Selection
	Play/Stop All
	Play/Stop Region
	Play/Stop Region to Anchor
	Play/Stop Region from Anchor
COMMAND + B	Create Backup
SHIFT + COMMAND + B	Revert to Backup
	Save a Copy As
SHIFT + COMMAND + S	Save Selection As
SHIFT + R	Region > Selection
SHIFT + COMMAND + R	Selection > Region
L. ARROW	Goto Selection Start
R. ARROW	Goto Selection End
	Goto Region Start
	Goto Region End
D. ARROW	Goto Region Anchor
COMMAND + R	Create New Region
CONTROL + N	Normalize
SHIFT + CONTROL + G	Change Gain
CONTROL + I	Fade In
CONTROL + O	Fade Out

Table B.10 Sample Editor Key Commands *(continued)*

Assigned Key	Key Command
CONTROL + DELETE	Silence
	Invert
CONTROL + R	Reverse
T	Trim
CONTROL + T	Time and Pitch Machine
CONTROL + G	Groove Machine
CONTROL + E	Audio Energizer
	Sample Rate Convert
	Silencer
CONTROL + M	Audio to MIDI Groove Template
	Audio to Score
	Quantize Engine
	Search Peak
	Search Silence

Table B.11 Keyboard Input Key Commands

Assigned Key	Key Command
	Note C
	Note C#
	Note D
	Note D#
	Note E
	Note F
	Note F#
	Note G
	Note G#
	Note A
	Note A#
	Note B
	Rest
	Next Note Will Be Sharp
	Next Note Will Be Flat
	Chord Mode
	Erase
	Step Backwards
	Step Forward
	Octave 0
	Octave 1
	Octave 2
	Octave 3
	Octave 4
	Octave 5
	Octave 6

Table B.11 Keyboard Input Key Commands *(continued)*

Assigned Key	Key Command
	Octave - 2
	Octave - 1
	Octave + 1
	Octave + 2
	1/1 Note
	1/2 Note
	1/4 Note
	1/8 Note
	1/16 Note
	1/32 Note
	1/64 Note
	1/128 Note
	Next Three Notes Are Triplets
	Next Two Notes Are a Dotted Group
	Velocity 16 (ppp)
	Velocity 32 (pp)
	Velocity 48 (p)
	Velocity 64 (mp)
	Velocity 80 (mf)
	Velocity 96 (f)
	Velocity 112 (ff)
	Velocity 127 (fff)
	Sustain Inserted Note(s)
	Quantize Note Starts On/Off

Table B.12 Project Manager Key Commands

Assigned Key	Key Command
	Up
	Down
	Left
	Right
	Scan
	Expanded Scan
	Scan Folder
	Abort Scan Process
	Check for Modified or Deleted Files
	Clear Scanned Data
	Save Project Manager Data
	Install Files From
	Toggle Find Mode
	Toggle Scan Paths Mode
	Toggle Log File Mode
	Set Selected Folder as Display Root

Table B.12 Project Manager Key Commands *(continued)*

Assigned Key	Key Command
	Move Display Root One Level Up
	Move Display Root to Top
	Consolidate Files of Selected Songs
	Add Selected Files to Audio Window
	Find Used Files for Selected Items
	Find Unresolved file References for Selected Items
	Move Used Files for Selected EXS Instruments
	Set Comment 1 for Selected
	Set Comment 2 for Selected
	Show Details for Selected
	Hide Details for Selected
	Move Selected Items
	Copy Selected Items
	Start/Stop Preview
	Back
	Update File List in Find Mode

Table B.13 EXS 24 Editor Key Commands

Assigned Key	Key Command
Select Zones Pointing to Selected Group(s)	
SHIFT + T	Toggle Selection
U. ARROW	Previous Zone/Group
D. ARROW	Next Zone/Group
CONTROL + F	Open File Selector for Selected Zone
CONTROL + Z	New Zone
CONTROL + G	New Group
	View: All/Toggle Mode
	View: Next Zone Parameter
	View: Next Group Parameter
	Move Audio Files
	Copy Audio Files
	Move Audio Files of All Instruments
	Backup/Copy Audio Files of All Instruments
	Move Audio Files of All USED and ACTIVE Instruments of Current Song
	Backup Audio Files of All USED and ACTIVE Instruments of Current Song
	Shift Selected Zone(s) Left
	Shift Selected Zone(s) Right
	Shift Selected Zone(s) Left (Inc. Root Key)
	Shift Selected Zone(s) Right (Inc. Root Key)

Table B.14 Global Control Surfaces Key Commands

Assigned Key	Key Command
	Open Setup
	Open Setup as Float
	Open Controller Assignments
	Open Install
	Open MIDI Monitor
	Open MIDI Monitor as Float
	Scan All Models
	Rebuild Defaults
	Learn New Controller Assignment

Table B.15 Control Surfaces Setup Window Key Commands

Assigned Key	Key Command
	As Icons
	As List

Table B.16 Control Surfaces Install Window Key Commands

Assigned Key	Key Command
	Scan for Selected Models
	Scan All Models
	Add Selected Models

Table B.17 Windows Showing Audio Files Key Commands

Assigned Key	Key Command
	Show File(s) in Finder

C Logic Pro 7 Local Menu Cross-Index

Almost every window in Logic has its own local menus. Many of those local menus share commands. This appendix contains every command in each local menu from the various Logic windows and, for easy reference, is designed to direct you to the page on which each menu command is discussed.

Arrange Window

Edit Menu

Track Menu

Region Menu

MIDI Menu

Audio Menu

View Menu

Audio Window

Audio File Menu

Edit Menu

View Menu

Options Menu

Sample Editor

Audio File Menu

Edit Menu

Functions Menu

Factory Menu

View Menu

The View menu is discussed on page 257.

Audiosuite Menu

The Audiosuite menu is discussed on page 258.

Matrix Editor

Edit Menu

Hyper Editor

Hyper Menu

Edit Menu

This menu is exactly the same as the Edit menu in the Matrix Editor, which is discussed on page 286.

Functions Menu

This menu is similar to the Matrix Editor's Functions menu, which is discussed on page 288.

View Menu

Score Editor

Layout Menu

Edit Menu

This menu is exactly the same as the Edit menu in the Matrix Editor, which is discussed on page 286.

Functions Menu

This menu is similar to the Matrix Editor's Functions menu, which is discussed on page 288.

Attributes Menu

The Attributes menu is discussed on page 326.

Text Menu

The Text menu is discussed on page 327.

View Menu

Options Menu

Track Mixer

Options Menu

View Menu

Project Manager

Edit Menu

Functions Menu

View Menu

Navigate Menu

The Navigate menu is discussed on page 446.

Environment Window

New Menu

The New menu is discussed on page 453.

Edit Menu

View Menu

Options Menu

Layer Submenu

The Layer submenu of the Options local menu is discussed on page 457.

Apply Buffer Template To Submenu

The Apply Buffer Template To submenu is discussed on page 457.

Clean Up Submenu

Import Environment Submenu

D Logic Resources on the Internet

Because Web sites and mailing lists are created and abandoned daily, this is not an attempt to delineate every single Web site with some information on Logic that exists. Rather, this is an attempt to give you some helpful resources and places from which to begin your own searches. Who knows, you might create a Logic Web site or community of your own!

Official Web Sites

Apple Computer's Logic Pro page:
http://www.apple.com/logic/

Apple Computer's Logic Support page:
http://www.apple.com/support/logic/

Emagic's Support page (previous Logic Versions):
http://www.emagic.de/support/support/index.php?lang=EN

Emagic InfoWeb:
http://www.emagic.de/support/infoweb/index.php?lang=EN

International Logic Communities

Logic Users Group (LUG):
http://www.logic-users.org/

Logic-TDM Users Group:
http://groups.yahoo.com/group/logic-tdm/

Sonikmatter Logic Forums:
http://community.sonikmatter.com/cgi-bin/emagic/ultimatebb.cgi

Logic Audio Users Forum:
http://f23.parsimony.net/forum49865/

Logic-Related Web Sites

Swiftkick.com Logic site:
http://www.swiftkick.com

Logic Audio Web ring:
http://m.webring.com/webring?ring=emagiclogic;list

Logic Notation Guide:
http://members.aon.at/prischl/LNG

Omega Art Logic site:
http://www.omega-art.com/logic/index.html

Logic Audio Users Showcase:
http://www.artofthegroove.com/logic/

Index

A

B

F

Q

THOMSON

COURSE TECHNOLOGY

Professional ■ Trade ■ Reference

Get Interactive with Logic®!

Logic CSi Starter
ISBN: 1-59200-478-4 ■ $29.99

Logic Pro CSi Master
ISBN: 1-59200-565-9 ■ $49.99

Your FREE *Logic 7 CSi LE* CD includes one hour of movie tutorials that can be found in *Logic CSi Starter* and *Logic Pro CSi Master*. Fire up *Logic 7 CSi LE* and watch as a DAW pro takes you through key features and techniques for getting the most out of Logic 7.

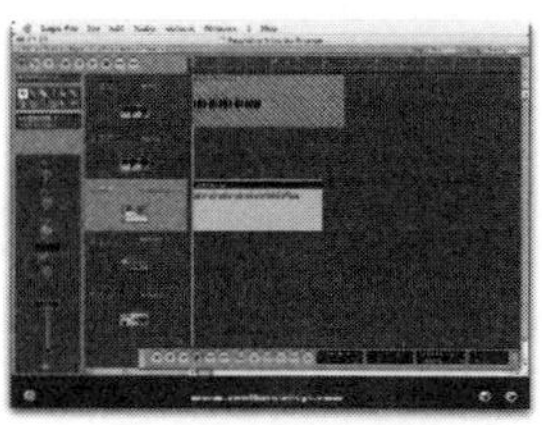

The AutoPlay interface offers a simple way to view each movie tutorial. Launch *Logic 7 CSi LE* and then sit back and soak in the knowledge as movie tutorials play, one after another. The scroll arrows in the interface provide a convenient way to jump to specific movie tutorials. Select the Web link at the bottom for more product information or to view additional CoolTip streaming movie tutorials.

THOMSON

COURSE TECHNOLOGY

Professional ■ Trade ■ Reference

coolbreeze systems

To check out the complete CSi Starter and Master products, go to

www.courseptr.com/musictech

GETTING STARTED:

To check out the *Logic 7 CSi LE* tutorials, double-click the Logic 7 CSi LE-WIN.exe, Logic 7 CSi LE-OSX, or Logic 7 CSi LE-OS9 icon. You will need QuickTime 6 (www.Apple.com) to view the movie tutorials. To run *Logic 7 CSi LE* off your hard drive, copy the Logic 7 CSi LE folder to your hard drive, and double-click the appropriate Logic 7 CSi LE icon found in this folder.

CREDITS:

CSi Tutorials:

Logic Pro CSi Master—
Lars von Sneidern

- Record Overview
- Key Commands
- Loops
- Groups
- Markers

Logic CSi Starter—
George Leger III

- Bussing
- Backing up

Music Loops:

Jeff Ciampa

MINIMUM SYSTEM REQUIREMENTS:

32 MB RAM
50 MB free disk space
16X CD-ROM drive or faster
800x600 display, 1000s of colors
QuickTime 6.0 or greater (supplied)

MACINTOSH®

PPG 300 MHz or faster
System 9.0, OS X 10.2, or higher

WINDOWS®

Pentium III 400 MHz or faster
Windows 98, ME, or XP
16-bit sound card

Please read the READ ME file included on your CD-ROM for the latest specific installation and configuration procedures. If you experience difficulties beyond the information provided, you can request help by sending an e-mail to CT.techsupport@thomson.com or by calling 800.648.7450.

License Agreement/Notice of Limited Warranty

By opening the sealed disc container in this book, you agree to the following terms and conditions. If, upon reading the following license agreement and notice of limited warranty, you cannot agree to the terms and conditions set forth, return the unused book with unopened disc to the place where you purchased it for a refund.

License:
The enclosed software is copyrighted by the copyright holder(s) indicated on the software disc. You are licensed to copy the software onto a single computer for use by a single user and to a backup disc. You may not reproduce, make copies, or distribute copies or rent or lease the software in whole or in part, except with written permission of the copyright holder(s). You may transfer the enclosed disc only together with this license, and only if you destroy all other copies of the software and the transferee agrees to the terms of the license. You may not decompile, reverse assemble, or reverse engineer the software.

Notice of Limited Warranty:
The enclosed disc is warranted by Thomson Course Technology PTR to be free of physical defects in materials and workmanship for a period of sixty (60) days from end user's purchase of the book/disc combination. During the sixty-day term of the limited warranty, Thomson Course Technology PTR will provide a replacement disc upon the return of a defective disc.

Limited Liability:
THE SOLE REMEDY FOR BREACH OF THIS LIMITED WARRANTY SHALL CONSIST ENTIRELY OF REPLACEMENT OF THE DEFECTIVE DISC. IN NO EVENT SHALL THOMSON COURSE TECHNOLOGY PTR OR THE AUTHOR BE LIABLE FOR ANY OTHER DAMAGES, INCLUDING LOSS OR CORRUPTION OF DATA, CHANGES IN THE FUNCTIONAL CHARACTERISTICS OF THE HARDWARE OR OPERATING SYSTEM, DELETERIOUS INTERACTION WITH OTHER SOFTWARE, OR ANY OTHER SPECIAL, INCIDENTAL, OR CONSEQUENTIAL DAMAGES THAT MAY ARISE, EVEN IF THOMSON COURSE TECHNOLOGY PTR AND/OR THE AUTHOR HAS PREVIOUSLY BEEN NOTIFIED THAT THE POSSIBILITY OF SUCH DAMAGES EXISTS.

Disclaimer of Warranties:
THOMSON COURSE TECHNOLOGY PTR AND THE AUTHOR SPECIFICALLY DISCLAIM ANY AND ALL OTHER WARRANTIES, EITHER EXPRESS OR IMPLIED, INCLUDING WARRANTIES OF MERCHANTABILITY, SUITABILITY TO A PARTICULAR TASK OR PURPOSE, OR FREEDOM FROM ERRORS. SOME STATES DO NOT ALLOW FOR EXCLUSION OF IMPLIED WARRANTIES OR LIMITATION OF INCIDENTAL OR CONSEQUENTIAL DAMAGES, SO THESE LIMITATIONS MIGHT NOT APPLY TO YOU.

Other:
This Agreement is governed by the laws of the State of Massachusetts without regard to choice of law principles. The United Convention of Contracts for the International Sale of Goods is specifically disclaimed. This Agreement constitutes the entire agreement between you and Thomson Course Technology PTR regarding use of the software.